LANDMARK CASES IN THE LAW OF

*Landmark Cases in the Law of Contract* offers 12 origin
tract scholars. As with the essays in the companion volume, *Landmark Cases in the Law of Restitution* (Hart Publishing, 2006) each essay takes as its focus a particular leading case, and analyses that case in its historical or theoretical context. The cases range from the early 18th- to the late 20th-centuries, and deal with an array of contractual doctrines. Some of the essays call for their case to be stripped of its landmark status, whilst others argue that it has more to offer than we have previously appreciated. The particular historical context of these landmark cases, as revealed by the authors, often shows that our current assumptions about the case and what it stands for are either mistaken, or require radical modification. The book also explores several common themes which are fundamental to the development of the law of contract: for instance, the influence of commercial expectations, appeals to 'reason' and the significance of particular judicial ideologies and techniques.

CW00797200

# Landmark Cases in the Law of Contract

Edited by

## Charles Mitchell and Paul Mitchell

·HART·
PUBLISHING

OXFORD AND PORTLAND, OREGON
2016

Published in North America (US and Canada) by
Hart Publishing
c/o International Specialized Book Services
920 NE 58th Avenue, Suite 300
Portland, OR 97213-3786
USA
Tel: +1 503 287 3093 or toll-free: (1) 800 944 6190
Fax: +1 503 280 8832
E-mail: orders@isbs.com
Website: http://www.isbs.com

Hart Publishing, 16C Worcester Place, OX1 2JW
Telephone: +44 (0)1865 517530 Fax: +44 (0)1865 510710
E-mail: mail@hartpub.co.uk
Website: http://www.hartpub.co.uk

British Library Cataloguing in Publication Data
Data Available

ISBN: 978-1-50990-504-1

Typeset by Hope Services Ltd, Abingdon
Printed and bound in Great Britain by
TJ International Ltd, Padstow, Cornwall

# Preface to Paperback Edition

The appearance of a paperback edition gives us the opportunity to express our gratitude to Richard Hart, who encouraged the development of the *Landmark Cases* books, and to his successors at Bloomsbury Publishing; their continuing support for the series has led to its expansion beyond anything that we could have imagined when we first suggested the restitution volume in 2004. The success of these collections demonstrates how simultaneously fundamental and problematic landmark cases are: they have a provocative combination of qualities, which seems destined to make them objects of perennial interest and controversy. We hope that the continuation of the series, under the general editorship of Paul Mitchell, will encourage scholars across the whole range of legal disciplines to undertake further investigations of these fascinating phenomena.

# Preface

The essays in this collection, like the essays in the companion volume, *Landmark Cases in the Law of Restitution* (2006), grew out of papers presented at a symposium held at the School of Law, King's College London. We gratefully acknowledge the School's financial assistance.

As with the earlier collection, we gave authors a free choice of case, and complete freedom of method in how to approach their material. The results are predictably diverse: the cases range from the early 18th- to the late 20th-centuries, and deal with an array of contractual doctrines. Some of them call for their case to be stripped of its landmark status (*Smith v Hughes*), whilst others argue that it has more to offer than we have previously appreciated (*Suisse Atlantique*, among others).

But the essays also, perhaps surprisingly, share several common themes. Thus, mundane factual situations have frequently triggered elaborate legal responses (as, for instance, in *Coggs v Barnard*, *Pillans v Van Meirop* and *Johnson v Agnew*). Similarly, otherwise unremarkable transactions such as taking out an insurance policy (*Carter v Boehm*), hiring a theatre (*Taylor v Caldwell*), or a boat (*The Diana Prosperity*) can be thrust into the legal spotlight by external events. There is no need for the parties to be trying to achieve something novel for their contract to become the start of a landmark case.

Another striking theme is the influence of judicial personality and technique. In several cases, what made the decision a landmark was that individual judges had chosen to go beyond the arguments of counsel and develop the law as they felt appropriate. They might carry their brethren along with them (as in *Hochster v De La Tour*) or they might not (*Coggs v Barnard*). There was also a similarity about the kind of arguments used as catalysts for change. Appeals to 'reason' have flourished, perhaps inspired by Lord Mansfield's example, as have invocations of the Civil law (*Taylor v Caldwell*), even if they did not make it to the final draft of the judgment (*Coggs v Barnard*).

A further recurrent and fundamental argument, which has not been universally successful, concerns the role of contract law in facilitating commercial transactions. Some of our cases expressly acknowledge that contract law should fit commercial expectations: Lord Mansfield was probably the most famous exponent of this view (*Pillans v Van Mierop, Carter v Boehm, Da Costa v Jones*), but Lord Campbell, inspired by Mansfield, took the same line (*Hochster v De La Tour*). On the other hand, Lord Mansfield's innovative approach in *Pillans v Van Mierop* was short-lived, and the House of Lords in *Foakes v Beer* acknowledged that its decision was at odds with commercial expectations. The Court of Appeal's decision in *The Hongkong Fir* prioritised justice over certainty, despite the commercial preference for the latter. On this fundamental question of policy the judges have been, and, we expect, shall continue to be, fundamentally divided. There can be little doubt that, as the courts continue to wrestle with this problem, the contract landscape will continue to change, and new landmarks will appear.

CHARLES MITCHELL
PAUL MITCHELL

# Contents

# Contributors

**Michael Bridge** is Cassel Professor of Commercial Law at the London School of Economics and Political Science.

**Roger Brownsword** is a Professor of Law at King's College London.

**David Ibbetson** is Regius Professor of Civil Law at the University of Cambridge.

**Michael Lobban** is Professor of Legal History at the London School of Economics and Political Science.

**Catharine MacMillan** is Professor of Law and Legal History at the University of Reading.

**Gerard McMeel** is Professor of Commercial Law at the University of Manchester.

**Charles Mitchell** is Professor of Law at UCL.

**Paul Mitchell** is Professor of Laws at UCL.

**Donal Nolan** is Professor of Private Law in the University of Oxford and Francis Reynolds and Clarendon Fellow and Tutor in Law at Worcester College Oxford.

**John Phillips** is Professor of English Law at King's College London.

**Warren Swain** is Professor of Law at the University of Auckland.

**Stephen Watterson** is University Lecturer in Law in the University of Cambridge and a Fellow of Trinity Hall Cambridge.

# 1

# Coggs v Barnard (1703)

## DAVID IBBETSON

N O APOLOGY IS needed for the inclusion of *Coggs v Barnard*[1] in a
volume of leading cases in the law of contract. The judgment of Holt
CJ was described by Francis Hargrave as 'a most masterly view of the
whole subject of bailment'[2]; Sir William Jones was happy to treat his *Essay on
the Law of Bailments* 'merely as a commentary' on the decision[3]; and its canon-
ical status as the *fons et origo* of the rules relating to the standard of care
demanded of a bailee was thoroughly established by 1837, when John William
Smith published the first edition of his *Leading Cases in the Common Law*:

> The case of *Coggs v Bernard* is one of the most celebrated ever decided in Westminster
> Hall, and justly so, since the elaborate judgment of Lord *Holt* contains the first well
> ordered exposition of the English law of bailments.[4]

But lurking behind Smith's description of it is the suspicion, uncomfortable to
the Common lawyer, that Holt CJ's exposition of the law involved something
more radical than the articulation of principles which were already in some way
immanent in the earlier case-law. Its status as a leading case depends not only
on its formulation of rules which have now survived for three centuries, but also
on its scouring away of a mass of confusing material which had built up over the
previous 400 years or more.

The present paper is an attempt to understand how this occurred. It will first
examine and contextualise the arguments of counsel and the three puisne
judges, Gould, Powys and Powell JJ, showing how all of these were framed in
terms of the case-law as it had developed over the previous two or three
centuries. That case-law was very messy, and substantially incoherent; so too,

---

[1] *Coggs v Barnard* (1703) 2 Lord Raym 909, 92 ER 107; 3 Lord Raym 163, 92 ER 622; 1 Salk 26,
91 ER 25; 2 Salk 735, 91 ER 613; 3 Salk 11, 91 ER 660; 3 Salk 268, 91 ER 817; 1 Com 133, 92 ER 999;
Holt 13, 90 ER 905; Holt 131, 90 ER 971; Holt 528, 90 ER 1190; B[ritish] L[ibrary] MS Add 34125
111, L[incoln's] I[nn] MS Coxe 64 39, 56, LI MS Hill 52 10*v*
[2] F Hargrave (ed), Coke on Littleton (London, 1775) 89b fn.3.
[3] Sir W Jones, *An Essay on the Law of Bailments*, D Ibbetson (ed), (Bangor, Welsh Legal History
Society, 2007) 59.
[4] JW Smith, *A Selection of Leading Cases on Various Branches of the Law* (London, A Maxwell,
1837) 96.

therefore, were the arguments of counsel and the puisnes. Holt CJ approached the question very differently, giving less weight to the earlier authority and instead choosing to bring a measure of coherence to the law by sub-dividing the types of bailment and fitting them into a principled framework. The paper will focus not so much on what he did as on how he did it. Surviving in the British Library is Holt's own draft of his judgment as it was worked and reworked,[5] and this will be compared with the report of the judgment as it appears in print in Lord Raymond's Reports.[6]

The facts of the case, deducible from the pleadings,[7] are more or less unproblematic. The defendant, William Barnard, undertook to carry several barrels of brandy for the plaintiff, John Coggs, from a cellar in Brooks Market, Holborn, to another in Water Street, some half a mile away just south of the Strand. In the course of unloading into the Water Street cellar one barrel was staved, and brandy spilled out of it onto the roadway. According to the pleadings the amount lost was 150 gallons, though the version reproduced by Salkeld refers to 150 bottles. It seems likely that the latter is a more accurate reflection of the actual amount lost: the market price of brandy at this time was in the region of 10 shillings per gallon,[8] but the damages were ultimately assessed at only £10, rather closer to the value of 150 bottles. Faced with this loss, Coggs brought an action on the case against Barnard, alleging that he had undertaken to carry the barrels but, through his negligence, had caused one of them to be damaged and the contents spilled.

It is possible to penetrate a little further into the circumstances surrounding the case by trying to identify the dramatis personae, though, since the accident behind the litigation was so utterly commonplace that it has left no trace on the historical record, any conclusion must be very tentative. We might plausibly guess that the plaintiff was the goldsmith banker John Coggs, whose business was run from the King's Head on the Strand, just on the south-west corner of Chancery Lane.[9] He would have been sufficiently wealthy to have been pos-

---

[5] BL MS Add 34125 111. There is a neat copy of this text in BL MS Add 35981 122v (with a note that the volume had been lent to Buller J). The latter copy is of assistance in the decipherment of the former, which is not always easy to read, but the former—with its erasures, insertions and interlineations—is indispensable in the reconstruction of Holt's reasoning processes.

[6] *Coggs v Barnard* (n 1 above) 2 Lord Raym 909, 92 ER 107, almost certainly the work of the Inner Templar Herbert Jacob (see BL MS Harg 66 44 (attribution at 1v), Harvard Law School MS 2136 81 (attribution of volume)). Jacob and Raymond lived 'in great intimacy' as student lawyers and shared reports: JH Baker, *English Legal Manuscripts in the United States of America. Part II: 1558–1902* (London, Selden Society, 1990) 315, on Philadelphia Free Library MS LC 14.66.

[7] PRO KB 122/5 m435 (in JH Baker and SFC Milsom, *Sources of English Legal History* (London, Butterworths, 1986) 370); *Coggs v Barnard* (n 1 above) 3 Lord Raym 163, 92 ER 622; 2 Salk 735, 91 ER 613 (with slight variations).

[8] JE Thorold Rogers, *A History of Agriculture and Prices in England* (Oxford, Clarendon Press, 1866–1902) 5.450, 6.421, 7(1).353.

[9] A Heal, *The London Goldsmiths* (Cambridge, Cambridge University Press, 1935) 127; FGH Price, *Handbook of London Bankers* (London, Simpkin, Marshall, Hamilton, Kent & Co, 1890) 39–40; HC Shelley, *Inns and Taverns of Old London* (London, 1909) 92–3.

sessed of several casks of brandy,[10] and Water Street, where the accident occurred, would have been only a couple of minutes walk from his place of work. The defendant, William Barnard, is less easy to identify, but he may well have been the fishmonger's porter of that name, of the parish of St Dunstan's in the East, who died in February 1706.[11] If so, he was literate enough to be able to sign his own will. He was hardly rich, but was by no means a pauper: he left legacies of 20 shillings to each of four siblings and a niece, with a further one shilling to another niece. The rest of his estate went to his widow. We are not told what its value was, but it was clearly sufficient for him to enjoin her in due time to pay out £10 to provide an apprenticeship for one William Turner, a child for whom he seems to have assumed guardianship obligations. There are hints in the reports of *Coggs v Barnard* that he had servants who might have been responsible for the accident, so it may be that he was in business in a small way. It is easy to see *Coggs v Barnard* as a case in which a substantially wealthy man was suing a relatively poor one, but Coggs himself may have been beginning to fall into financial difficulties. Within a few years his goldsmith's business had failed and he and his partner had been adjudged bankrupt.[12] Moreover, in Hilary Term 1703 process was served on him by the former manager of a brass wire works, of which he was the principal partner and treasurer. After several years of litigation this resulted in an award in the sum of over £5000.[13]

The accident was unremarkable, the parties unremarkable. When the case came up before Holt CJ at the London Guildhall early in 1703, there is nothing to suggest that it was seen as anything other than the most routine piece of litigation. The trial duly took place, the jury found a verdict for the plaintiff, and damages were assessed at £10. The defendant, hoping no doubt to be able to avoid having to pay this sum, raised a motion in arrest of judgment, presumably on the technical ground that the plaintiff's claim had been improperly pleaded. Thus it was that the leading case was conceived.

We have only a very scrappy note of the arguments of counsel,[14] but we can deduce from it that there were three relevant issues. First was whether the plaintiff's count should have alleged either that the defendant had received some consideration, or alternatively that he was a common porter—ie a person who made his living as a porter—in which case consideration would be presumed. If it were held that such an allegation was necessary, the second question would

[10] More likely, since the quantity of brandy would have been prodigious even for most heroic of dypsomaniacs, he might have been buying it other than in a personal capacity. He was a former Warden of the Goldsmiths' Company and a member of its Court: WT Prideaux, *A List of the Wardens, Members of the Court of Assistants and Liverymen of the Worshipful Company of Goldsmiths since 1688* (London, Arden Press, 1936) 2.

[11] Lambeth Palace Library, VH/95/104 (original will), VH/94/4/924 (will admitted to probate), VH/98/3 f.76v (note of probate).

[12] Stat 8 Anne c 28 (1709).

[13] *Ball v Coggs* (1710) 1 Brown PC 140, 1 ER 471; *Ball v Lord Lanesborough* (1713) 5 Brown PC 480, 2 ER 809.

[14] LI MS Coxe 64 39.

then arise: whether, properly analysed, the count did in fact contain sufficient indication of consideration or something equivalent to it. The third issue was distinct: whether the defendant was strictly liable for damage or liable only for his negligence. Although formally unrelated to the earlier points, there was a measure of overlap in substance, since on some lines of argument the appropriate test for liability might have depended on whether or not the defendant had received consideration. The issues were not easy to resolve but, importantly, the assumption behind the arguments of counsel was that they should be resolved by reference to authority and principle. There is nothing to suggest that any attempt was made to engineer a break with the past and to put the law of bailments on a new footing.

To understand the first argument it is necessary to sketch in a bit of history. The action on the case had emerged in the middle of the 14th century as the appropriate action to frame a claim based (inter alia) on the misperformance of a contract; until about 1500 it was not appropriate for cases of contractual non-performance.[15] In the early years of the 16th century this restriction was removed, and, taking on the name of *assumpsit*, the action on the case became the normal form of action to complain of any breach of a contract not under seal.[16] Although the form of pleading was the same for misperformance and for non-performance—an allegation that the defendant had assumed and promised to do something but had then either done it badly or not done it at all—by the end of the 16th century it was coming to be recognised that the two types of claim were analytically distinct. This was very clear from *Powtney v Walton* in 1597,[17] where it was held that in an action of *assumpsit* for non-performance it was essential to allege that there had been good consideration for the promise, but in an action for misperformance there was no such requirement. In effect, the former was a claim in contract and the latter a claim in tort.[18]

By the time of *Coggs v Barnard*, it might have been thought, the suggestion that there was a requirement of consideration in a claim for contractual misperformance should have been unarguable. *Powtney v Walton* stood as authority against it; Year Book cases pointed to the acceptability of the action without any consideration where there had been some misfeasance rather than pure nonfeasance[19]; and precedents without any allegation of consideration could be found in the printed Register of Writs.[20] Holt CJ, though, claimed that 'by long and antient practise' these cases had not been followed[21]; and in the leading case of misper-

---

[15] DJ Ibbetson, *A Historical Introduction to the Law of Obligations* (Oxford, Oxford University Press, 1999) 126–30.

[16] *Ibid* 130–51.

[17] *Powtney v Walton* (1597) 1 Ro Abr 10 (Baker and Milsom, *Sources of English Legal History* (n 7 above) 370).

[18] *Carter v Fossett* (1623) Palmer 329, 81 ER 1107 (Jones J): when the claim was in contract it would lie against executors, when in tort it would not.

[19] Baker and Milsom, *Sources of English Legal History* (n 7 above) 358–69.

[20] *Registrum Omnium Brevium* (1687) 110.

[21] BL MS Add 34125 111v.

formance by a carrier, *Mors v Slue*—whose pleadings were said to have been drafted by the leading pleader of the time—it was noted that reference had been made explicitly to the payment which was to be received for the carriage.[22]

Counsel for the plaintiff probably thought that he was on solid ground on this point, all the more so since the defendant's plea of not guilty (rather than *non assumpsit*) might have suggested that he too had accepted that the claim was tortious rather than contractual. Drawing the apparently orthodox distinction of *Powtney v Walton*, he argued, 'If it [the claim] had been founded upon the contract it might have been an objection, but is upon the neglect'.[23] Holt CJ, intervening in the argument, was less convinced: there was no reason why the count should not have followed the normal course and alleged that there had been some payment made by way of consideration. One possible response to this was that the consideration did not have to be mentioned expressly since it was implied: where the defendant was a professional it would be supposed that he was not acting gratuitously, and he could bring a quantum meruit claim even if no consideration had been agreed. This had been held to be so in the case of common (ie professional) carriers,[24] and by parity of reason it would have been a good argument if the defendant was a common porter. There is some suggestion (by Holt CJ, once again intervening in the argument) that it had been found at the trial that he was, but in the argument in arrest of judgment this could only have been relevant if it appeared as a matter of record or could be deduced from the jury's verdict. Holt seems to have hinted that the verdict in the plaintiff's favour must indicate that the defendant was a common porter,[25] but it is not easy to see how such an inference could have been drawn, and it may be that we misunderstand (or the reporter misunderstood) the point that was being made. In any event, no more is heard of it.

Counsel's second response to the objection proved to be more fertile. He argued that the pleadings did in fact show that there had been a good consideration:

> [B]e it upon the contract or neglect it is a good [count] for whenever is a trust reposed to do an act the law joins [?] a consideration for he shall be payd according to a quantum meruit.[26]

This appears to have been intended as an extension of his previous argument: just as a common porter would have had a quantum meruit for his labour if no consideration had been agreed, so would any person who had been entrusted with a task. On the face of it this was unsustainable, since it assumed that nobody would ever agree to do something for another out of simple generosity[27]; but the use of

---

[22] *Coggs v Barnard* (n 1 above) 2 Lord Raym 909, 920; 92 ER 107, 114.
[23] LI MS Coxe 64 39.
[24] The case cited was *Nicholls v More* (1661) 1 Sid 36, 82 ER 954.
[25] LI MS Coxe 64 39, 39v.
[26] LI MS Coxe 64 39.
[27] The point was perhaps made by Holt CJ (LI MS Coxe 64 39, 39v), seemingly distinguishing between carriage by a common porter and carriage by a non-professional out of kindness; but the brief note in the manuscript is very difficult to follow.

the language of trust in formulating it provided the judges with the opportunity to use their imaginations in manipulating the law in the plaintiff's favour.

Leaving to one side the judgment of Holt CJ, it is possible to see the three puisne judges responding in different ways to these arguments. Powys J appears to have followed the primary argument of the plaintiff's counsel that the claim was not based on the contract but on the neglect. The rather lapidary note of his judgment reported by Lord Raymond—'Powys agreed upon the neglect'[28]—is not especially helpful, but it points in this direction; and according to a manuscript report, he referred to the precedents cited from the Register of Writs as focusing on the defendant's default and drew the orthodox distinction found in the Year Books between cases of non-performance which were not actionable and cases of misperformance which were.[29] Only a little elaboration of the latter point is needed to focus it sharply onto *Coggs v Barnard*: cases of non-performance were not actionable in the absence of consideration, while in cases of misperformance there was no such requirement. Since this was a case of misperformance, it followed that the lack of an allegation of consideration was not fatal.

Gould J was more hesitant, but the thrust of his judgment was on rather the same lines, drawing the distinction between misperformance and non-performance. Whether or not the defendant was a common tradesman, where the goods were lost or damaged through his gross neglect[30] he was liable even if he had not received any consideration. Unlike Powys J, though, he provided a reason for this liability—the fact that a 'particular trust' had been reposed in him.[31] The language of trust is the same as that in the plaintiff's counsel's argument, but its function is now completely different. In argument, trust had been used to ground the defendant's right to payment, and hence the conclusion that there had been good consideration, whereas for Gould J it was a self-standing justification for the imposition of what we would regard as tortious liability.

The third puisne, Powell J, rejected the argument that the claim was based on the neglect. There were indeed cases in which the neglect rather than the undertaking was stressed,[32] but in others the weight was put on the undertaking.[33] Faced with this indeterminacy in the case-law he turned to principle. Here he could be more dogmatic: the gist of the actions lay in the undertaking.[34] Still, though, the distinction could be drawn between cases of non-performance and cases where the defendant had taken goods into his custody; only in the former would consideration be required. Like Gould J, he justified liability in the absence of consideration by picking up the language of trust, but he used it in

[28] *Coggs v Barnard* (n 1 above) 2 Lord Raym 909, 910; 92 ER 107, 108.
[29] LI MS Hill 52 10v.
[30] For the significance of the difference between neglect and gross neglect, see below 14–16.
[31] *Coggs v Barnard* (n 1 above) 2 Lord Raym 909, 92 ER 107.
[32] Citing *Waldon v Marshall* YB M 43 Edw III 33 pl.38.
[33] YB H 48 Edw III 6 pl.11; YB H 19 Hen VI 49 pl.5; YB H 2 Hen VII 11 pl.9; YB P 7 Hen IV 14 pl.19.
[34] *Coggs v Barnard* (n 1 above) 2 Lord Raym 909, 910; 92 ER 107, 108.

yet another way. Drawing the analogy with warranties, which were actionable without any consideration,[35] he argued that it was only because the plaintiff had relied on the defendant's warranty—presumably that he would take care—that he had trusted the defendant with his property:

> [W]hen I have reposed a trust in you, upon your undertaking, if I suffer, when I have so relied upon you, I shall have my action.[36]

For all their differences in nuance, it is not difficult to see that the three judgments on this point are built upon the arguments addressed to them by counsel as well as being well grounded in Common-law authority.

The other point raised in the argument in arrest of judgment was specific to the law relating to bailments—the standard of care to be demanded of the bailee. The law in this area was in an extraordinary mess, but perhaps excusably so since the problem was exceedingly intractable.[37] Fundamentally, the problem arose because of the clash of two different approaches to liability. From the middle of the 14th century, it was clearly established that liability in trespass on the case—which we may safely treat as unequivocally tortious at this time—depended on there having been some fault on the part of the defendant,[38] though in cases involving bailments fault was commonly linked not to any objective standard of behaviour but to the failure of the bailee to take the same care of the bailed property as he did of his own goods.[39] From the middle of the 14th century, by contrast, contractual liability was seen as strict, in the sense that the defendant was liable if he had failed to achieve the result contracted for unless he was excused by one of a relatively limited set of recognised circumstances (roughly speaking, act of God, act of the plaintiff, and act of a third party against whom the defendant could not himself have had any action).[40] In actions against bailees these rules clashed. So long as the forms of action could be mapped onto the divide it perhaps did not matter: in an action on the case the defendant would be liable only if he had been at fault; in detinue or account or some other action which could be seen as contractual, the strict liability rule would be applied unless the parties had agreed on something else.[41]

In the 16th century, things had got more complicated. The primary cause of this was the extension of the action on the case to contractual non-performance. As has been seen above, this caused claims for misperformance and non-performance to flow together[42]; and as *assumpsit* adopted the strict liability of

---

[35] R Aston, *Placita Latine Rediviva* (London, 1661) 35–7.
[36] *Coggs v Barnard* (n 1 above) 2 Lord Raym 909, 911, 92 ER 107, 108.
[37] I have attempted to analyse it in my edition of Sir W Jones's *Essay on the Law of Bailments* (n 3 above) 74–95.
[38] Ibbetson, *A Historical Introduction to the Law of Obligations* (n 15 above) 62–3.
[39] *Bowdon v Pelleter* (1315) YB P 8 Edw II (41 SS) 136; *Veel v Wygryme* (1388) YB H 11 Ric II (AF) 163. Ibbetson (ed), *An Essay on the Law of Bailments* (n 3 above) 85.
[40] Ibbetson, *A Historical Introduction to the Law of Obligations* (n 15 above) 91–4.
[41] *Veel v Wygryme* YB H 11 Ric II (AF) 163; YB M 9 Edw IV 40 pl. 22; YB T 3 Hen VII 4 pl.16.
[42] Above, 4.

mediaeval law there was a tendency for the bailee's liability to be seen as strict.[43] Pulling in the opposite direction, around 1530 Christopher St German had attempted to give more shape to the bailee's liability in his text, *Doctor and Student*. This had involved his borrowing heavily from Roman law, directly or indirectly, and framing the default rule of liability in terms of the bailee's fault; if the parties wanted a different rule they should agree it expressly.[44] Cutting across these two competing rules was the question whether it made any difference that the bailee was being paid. There were several distinct reasons why this might be relevant: because bailees who were getting paid should adhere to a higher standard of care, as Roman law had demanded; because it was only if there was consideration that the contractual default rule of strict liability could be applied; or because the law could give effect to a special term imposing liability without fault only if it had been agreed to by contract, and therefore only if some consideration had been given for it. In addition, there arose the evidentiary question of what exactly constituted an agreement on a special term in cases where there was no written contract. The matter was discussed in two inconclusive cases in the late 16th century, *Woodlife v Curtis*[45] and *Mosley v Fosset*,[46] but it was only in *Southcote v Bennet* in 1601 that it received a full airing.[47] Here it was argued that the distinction should be drawn between cases where the defendant had simply undertaken to look after a thing and cases where he had undertaken to keep it secure, to look after it *salvo et secure*. This might have made good sense as a matter of logic, the undertaking to keep the thing secure being interpreted as a contract to achieve a result; but it was practical nonsense. In the absence of a written agreement, how could a jury sensibly decide whether the bailee had agreed to keep the thing or had agreed to keep it *securely*? The King's Bench therefore rejected the distinction, imposing the default rule of strict liability on all bailees.[48] *Southcote v Bennet* was reported in Coke's *Reports*, and hence gained authoritative status, and this rule of strict liability was incorporated in his *Commentary on Littleton* with approval.[49]

*Southcote's case* was cited in argument in *Coggs v Barnard*, and although the note is too brief at this point to be certain what was said about it, it is not too

[43] Nearly all of the evidence for this comes from actions about the carriage of goods by sea, and it may be that the marine insurance market favoured clear liability rules against the background of which the parties could allocate the risks for themselves.

[44] C St German, *Doctor and Student*, Book 2 chap 38, TFT Plucknett and JL Barton (eds), (Seldon Society vol 91, London, 1974) para 2.38, 259–61.

[45] *Woodlife v Curtis* (1597) Moo 462, 72 ER 696; Owen 57, 74 ER 897; Ro Abr *Action sur le Case* C (4).

[46] *Mosley v Fosset* (1598) Moo 543, 72 ER 746, Harvard Law School MS 1004c 3; Cambridge University Library MS Dd 8.48 19; PRO KB 27/1347 m.83.

[47] *Southcote v Bennet* (1601) 4 Co Rep 83b, 76 ER 1061 (from BL MS Harl 6686 f.445v); Cro El 815, 78 ER 1104; JH Beale, 'Southcott *v* Bennett' (1899) 13 *Harvard Law Review* 43 (from Thomas Coventry's report); PRO KB 27/1362 m.500d.

[48] Strictly speaking, perhaps, the rule was imposed on all *contractual* bailees, but the distinction between contract and tort did not arise on the facts of the case.

[49] Co Litt 89b (n 2 above).

difficult to guess. Plaintiff's counsel would have wanted to follow the decision, thereby imposing a rule of strict liability on the defendant; defendant's counsel would have urged the court to depart from it. Each of the puisne judges dealt with the point by distancing himself from *Southcote's case*. For Gould J it was 'a hard case indeed', and 'no man that was not a lawyer' would think to insist on a special term[50]; for Powys J it was unreasonable and not warranted by the authorities[51]; and for Powell J the decision was 'hard' and not justified by the previous authorities, and it was unreasonable to expect the ordinary bailee to know that he had to insist on a special term if he was not to be strictly liable for loss or damage.[52] If *Southcote's case* was not to be followed, and hence strict liability rejected, what, then, was the rule? Powys J, so far as we can judge from the brief report, was silent on the point. Gould J argued that the bailee should normally be liable only for gross neglect, but if there was a special term it would not be unreasonable to make him liable for any loss flowing from his 'miscarriage' or his ordinary neglect.[53] Whether, by the latter, he meant strict liability or liability for some lesser degree of fault is unclear. Powell J simply adopted the rule which had been argued for but rejected in *Southcote v Bennet*, that where a bailee agreed to keep goods safely he would be liable for any loss or damage unless he could bring himself within one of the excusatory circumstances[54]; but in the absence of any special undertaking he would not be so liable.[55] We are not told what the liability would be in the normal case.

The reports at this point are clearly unsatisfactory. We know little more than that *Southcote's case* was disapproved, and the evidentiary implications of this are not worked out. As to the rule applicable in the absence of a special term, only Gould J's view is known. And none of the three tells us how their reasoning should apply on the facts of *Coggs v Barnard* itself, though we might safely guess that the effect of each of their judgments was that the plaintiff should win.[56]

If all that remained to us were the notes of the judgments of the three puisnes, we might guess that *Coggs v Barnard* would have sunk with hardly a trace. The determination that the claim lay without any allegation either that the defendant had received consideration or that the defendant was a common tradesman—though perhaps important in its time—simply reaffirmed the rule which had been laid down clearly in *Powtney v Walton*; and the disapproval of *Southcote v Bennet* would have done no more than clear the way for a later court to define more precisely in what circumstances the bailee would be liable.

---

[50] *Coggs v Barnard* (n 1 above) 2 Lord Raym 909, 92 ER 107.
[51] LI MS Hill 52 10v; cf *Coggs v Barnard* (n 1 above) 2 Lord Raym 909, 914; 92 ER 107, 110.
[52] *Coggs v Barnard* (n 1 above) 2 Lord Raym 909, 911–12; 92 ER 107, 109.
[53] *Coggs v Barnard* (n 1 above) 2 Lord Raym 909, 909–10; 92 ER 107, 107–8.
[54] Above, 10.
[55] *Coggs v Barnard* 2 Lord Raym 909, 911–12; 92 ER 107, 108–9.
[56] A brief note in Holt CJ's draft judgment refers to Gould J being on the side of the plaintiff: BL MS Add 34125 111, 112v.

To put it another way, the status of *Coggs v Barnard* as a leading case depends exclusively on the judgment of Holt CJ. To this we must now turn, looking both at the judgment as reported at length in Lord Raymond's reports and at Holt's own manuscript draft.[57]

Three things are immediately visible from even a cursory examination of Holt's judgment, whether in draft or in the version in Lord Raymond's reports. First, it is very different from what we see of the judgments of the three puisnes, in that it divides bailments into six distinct species and analyses each in turn. Secondly, it bears far less relation to the arguments of counsel than the judgments of the puisnes. And thirdly, it puts far greater weight on legal treatises and on Roman law than do the other three, citing Justinian's *Institutes*, together with the commentary of Vinnius as well as Bracton's *De Legibus et Consuetudinibus Angliae* and St German's *Doctor and Student*. Comparison between the two versions of the judgment brings out a fourth feature: while the draft judgment repeatedly reveals Holt's hesitancy or uncertainty, Lord Raymond's report smooths away these doubts and carries an aura of self-assurance about it. This is visible right at the start. Repeating the point he had made during counsel's argument,[58] he dismissed the precedents in the Register of Writs in which an action had been allowed without laying any consideration. Logically, we might suppose that the inference from this was that the plaintiff's action was not well-founded. None the less—in stark opposition to this—after serious thought, he had resolved that judgment should be given for the plaintiff: though the books were obscure and contradictory, both their authority and their reason supported the action.[59] The report of the final judgment plays down this tension, saying merely that he had 'made a great question' whether the declaration was good and decided that it was.[60]

Holt continued by saying that in order to see when liability should be imposed on the bailee it was necessary to distinguish six different species of bailment: (i) a gratuitous bailment for the benefit of the bailor; (ii) a gratuitous loan for the use of the bailee; (iii) a hiring of goods; (iv) a pledge; (v) a delivery of goods to be carried for reward; (vi) a delivery of goods to be carried or for something else to be done to them, without any reward.[61] The draft judgment makes clear the extent to which this is rooted in Roman law: the first form, 'I call as the Law does a deposit or *depositum*'; the third 'is called in the Law *Locatio et Conductio*'; the fourth is '*vadium* or *pignus* in the Law, in English a pledge or pawn'; the sixth is 'called in the Law *mandatum*, which I call in our law a commission'. Lord Raymond's report scoured out these repeated references to 'the

---

[57] *Coggs v Barnard* (n 1 above) 2 Lord Raym 909, 912–20; 92 ER 107, 113–14 (with LI MS Hill 52 10v, 11–12v, LI MS Coxe 64 56, 56v–58); BL MS Add 34125 111 (with BL MS Add 35981 122v).

[58] Above, 5.

[59] BL MS Add 34125 111, 111v.

[60] *Coggs v Barnard* (n 1 above) 2 Lord Raym 909, 912; 92 ER 107, 109.

[61] BL MS Add 34125 111, 112; *Coggs v Barnard* (n 1 above) 2 Lord Raym 909, 912–13: 92 ER 107, 109–10.

Law', simply listing the six forms.[62] In doing so it domesticated the division of bailments into different species. Although there was no warrant for doing so in any of the earlier case-law, the impression was given that this was the way in which English law had hitherto analysed the bailee's liability.

Having set out his framework, Holt proceeded to analyse each of the six forms in turn.

First was deposit, where goods were bailed to be looked after gratuitously. The starting point for Holt's analysis here, in both the draft judgment and Lord Raymond's report, was that the depositee was liable neither if the goods were stolen nor for their loss by ordinary or common neglect. In the latter version he added that there must be gross neglect.[63] No authority for this is given in either version, though we might suspect that the original basis for it was to be found in Justinian's *Institutes*, where the depositee was liable only for fraud or gross negligence, *dolus* or *culpa lata*.[64] The two-part argument of the draft judgment, in its original form, straightforwardly follows from this: first Holt shows that no liability attaches to the bailee when the goods are stolen; secondly he shows that liability depends on deceit, gross negligence being treated as evidence of this.

The first part of the argument is carefully reasoned. If the bailee were to be liable if the goods were stolen, this must either be because he had undertaken responsibility for theft; because there was a legal rule to this effect—a 'usage and custom'; or because this was required by the rules of natural reason or justice.[65] The first of these possibilities was easily dismissed: the simple acceptance of goods to look after them did not of itself show that the depositee was agreeing to hold himself responsible for the acts of strangers.[66] The second possibility, that there was a 'usage or custom', depended on an analysis of the authorities, and Holt next turned to these.[67] Two Year Book cases of the 14th century suggested that the bailee was not liable in case of theft,[68] the position which Holt favoured. Problematic, though, was a case of 1469, where Danby CJ was reported as saying that the appropriate standard of care was that which the bailee was accustomed to take about his own affairs.[69] This was dealt with by a *ben trovato* interpolation to the effect that at this time Danby was only counsel, having been earlier removed as Chief Justice and not yet restored, so that it was

---

[62] The fact that none of the manuscript reports of his judgment refers to 'the Law' suggests that the change was the work of Holt himself and not simply of the reporter(s), but we cannot be certain of this.

[63] BL MS Add 34125 f.111, 113; *Coggs v Barnard* (n 1 above) 2 Lord Raym 909, 913; 92 ER 107, 110.

[64] Justinian, Inst 3.14.3.

[65] BL MS Add 34125 111, 113v.

[66] BL MS Add 34125 111, 114: 'For it must be agreed acceptance to keep is no expresse undertaking to keep against wrongdoers'.

[67] BL MS Add 34125 111, 114–15.

[68] YB 29 Lib Ass 163 pl.28; YB 8 Edw II 275; Fitz Abr *Detinue* 59 (=*Bowdon v Pelleter* YB P 8 Edw II (41 SS) 136).

[69] YB M 9 Edw IV 40 pl.22.

only the ex parte statement of an advocate.[70] Similar difficulties were caused by a case of 1487, where Brian CJ was reported as having said that where the bailed goods were stolen the bailee was responsible to the bailor[71]; but this, it was said, was only obiter and could therefore safely be ignored. This left only *Southcote's case*,[72] potentially a major stumbling block; but the authority of the case was weakened by the fact that it had been decided by only two of the judges, Gawdy and Clench JJ, *ceteris absentibus*. Moreover, it was inconsistent with a series of cases in which it was held that there would be no liability on a covenant for quiet enjoyment of property where the lessee or bailee was harassed by a third party without right.[73] It followed from this that, apart from *Southcote's case*, there was a strong current of authority—which, it was said, accorded with reason—to the effect that the bailee would not be liable if the goods were stolen.

The second limb of the argument, as it appears in its first form in the draft judgment, was no less clear. The true rule was that to be found in Bracton, quoted at length, that in the absence of any special agreement the depositee would be liable only for fraud; he would not be liable for negligence, for the person who trusted goods to a negligent friend had only himself to blame.[74] The rule was expressed in exactly the same words in Justinian's *Institutes*,[75] which Bracton had simply borrowed, 'and in truth it is the Law of the world, common and naturall justice'.[76] The conclusion followed[77]:

> Hereby it appears that the bailee is bound to keep the goods honestly and faithfully; but not with that care and diligence that the very least neglect shall make him lyable for the losse thereof. But such a negligence must be a light or a small one for if it be grosse, then it will be an Evidence of fraud in the Bailee.

Two observations may be made on the argument as it was first drafted. Most obviously, it was logically coherent. Secondly, it embodied a tension between English law and Roman law, visible at several levels. The first part of the argument was substantially English, raising an issue that had come to predominate in the English cases: whether the bailee was liable if the property was stolen. The second part of the argument, by contrast, was substantially Roman, or at least romanised, with its focus on Bracton and the *Institutes of Justinian* and not a

---

[70] BL MS Add 34125 111, 114*v*. The point was wholly without merit, based on a misunderstanding of a text of W Dugdale: *Origines Juridiciales, Chronica Series* (London, 1666) 66, 70 (cited explicitly at 2 Lord Raym 909, 914; 92 ER 107, 110). Cp Sir J Sainty, *The Judges of England, 1272–1990*, Supp Series, vol 10 (London, Selden Society, 1993) 47.

[71] YB T 3 Hen VII 4 pl.16.

[72] *Southcote v Bennet* (n 47 above).

[73] *Tisdale v Essex* (1613) Hob 34, 80 ER 185; *Broking v Cham* (1617) Cro Jac 425, 79 ER 363; *Chantflower v Priestly* (1603) Cro El 914, 78 ER 11; Noy 50, 74 ER 1019. This section originally preceded the discussion of the Year Book cases: BL MS Add 34125 111, 114 (struck out).

[74] Bracton, *De Legibus et Consuetudinibus Angliae* (London, 1569) 99b. (Thorne (trans), *On the Laws and Customs of England* (Cambridge, MA, Belknap Press, 1968)).

[75] Justinian, Inst 3.14.3.

[76] BL MS Add 34125 111, 118 ('common and naturall justice' interlined).

[77] *Ibid*.

single reference to any English case-law. Holt's division of bailments was thoroughly Roman and thoroughly un-English, so there was a degree of artificiality in treating the cases discussed in the first part of the argument as if they necessarily involved contracts of deposit. One of the Year Book cases, in fact, involved a pledge,[78] in the others no distinction at all was drawn between gratuitous and remunerated bailments; and the cases involving covenants for quiet possession[79] only really fitted into the argument on the assumption that all cases of bailment were fundamentally alike. In so far as the opposition between English and Roman law could be reduced to the distinction between argument from precedent and argument from principle, it was principle which won out, nowhere more clearly in the preference for reason over authority in the treatment of *Southcote's case*. Throughout, Holt was cavalier in his dealings with the English cases, in effect strait-jacketing them into the romanised framework which he was assuming.

The argument as originally drafted may have been logically robust, but the manuscript points to Holt's having had second thoughts which were introducing a degree of instability into his position. These are visible in two ways. First, having shown that even an express undertaking to keep the property safe and secure would not have obliged the promisor to save the promisee harmless against wrongdoers, based on the cases of covenants for quiet possession, there is an interpolated passage from *Doctor and Student* which substantially undermines this conclusion[80]:

> If a man hath goods delivered to him, and hath nothing for the keeping tho he make a promise to deliver them, he is not bound to answer for casualtys, because as to these it is but nudum pactum; but if he hath a consideration *and undertakes to keep them safely* he is bound to keep them against all Events except the Act of God or Tempests inundations or Enemys of the Queen.

Returning to the question at the end of the draft judgment, he repeated this position with a variation: where there was a special acceptance to look after the goods safely the bailee would be liable for any slight negligence, but he would only be liable without more for theft or other acts by third parties if he had received consideration for his promise.[81] It is not clear that this argument worked, for it begged the question why the special acceptance was relevant at all if there was no consideration for it. Secondly, although in his main treatment of deposit he had limited the bailee's liability to cases of fraud and gross negligence, by the time he reached the end of the draft judgment his opinion had clearly changed: the 'mere bailee' was required only to take the same care as he did of his own goods.[82] This involved a significant departure from the Roman

[78] YB 29 Lib Ass 163 pl.28

[79] See n 73 above.

[80] BL MS Add 34125 111, 116v, citing *Doctor and Student* (n 44 above) 128; taken into the text in BL MS Add 35981 122v, 126. Italicised words interlined in BL MS Add 34125.

[81] BL MS Add 24125 111, 130–31.

[82] BL MS Add 24125 111, 129 and 130.

rule which was found in Justinian's *Institutes* and in Bracton, reflecting instead a strand which could be found in the earlier English cases.[83]

The final version of the judgment[84] reflects this instability in Holt's thinking. By comparison with the original form of the draft, the argument is not easy to follow: its framework is not made explicit, and the points are dealt with in a different order. It is perhaps easiest to show this diagrammatically:

| Draft | Final |
| --- | --- |
| D liable for theft of goods only if so agreed, unless some legal authority compels opposite conclusion | D not liable if goods stolen without his fault |
| Simple acceptance does not imply agreement to be responsible for theft | D liable only for gross neglect |
| | *Southcote's case* inconsistent with this, but wrong |
| Authorities do not compel opposite conclusion: Year Books; *Southcote's case*; cases relating to quiet possession of land; [*Doctor and Student*] | Year Book authorities and recent practice agree with principle that liable only for gross neglect |
| In absence of agreement, liability only for fraud, and gross neglect evidence of fraud | Liability only for fraud, and gross neglect evidence of fraud |
| | Cases of quiet possession of land |
| | *Doctor and Student* |

What had started out as an analytical argument directed at the elucidation of the rules of liability has been restructured as a commentary on *Southcote's case*. Its opening sally—'There is I confess a great argument against me'—brings it to the fore; and its final sentence—'So that there is neither sufficient authority nor reason to support the opinion in *Southcote's* case'—brings closure to it. The positive point in the argument, that liability arises only for fraud or its equivalent, is now buried in the middle of the reasoning rather than standing in its own right at the end.

Internally, too, the argument is weakened by the incorporation of the two points identified as afterthoughts to the original draft. The first of these, the

[83] Above, n 39.
[84] *Coggs v Barnard* (n 1 above) 2 Lord Raym 909, 913–15; 92 ER 107, 110–11.

argument from *Doctor and Student*,[85] is relatively trivial, and the final form represents an apparent improvement on Holt's earlier thoughts. Whereas in the earlier version there was an unresolved tension between the cases involving covenants for quiet possession and the passage from *Doctor and Student*, in the final text the transparent inconsistency has disappeared by turning the *Doctor and Student* point into the negative. Instead of saying that a person who has received consideration is liable for all casualties except those flowing from Act of God etc, it says simply that a person who has not received consideration is not liable for all casualties.[86] But it is only an apparent improvement: there is an implication that those who had received consideration would be so liable, and no explanation is given why this should be; and, worse, the quiet possession cases did not in fact involve gratuitous undertakings at all, so that the conflict between them and *Doctor and Student* was as problematic as ever.

The second afterthought was yet more awkward. The draft had originally simply followed Bracton and Justinian in imposing liability for fraud, treating gross negligence of evidence of this, though by the end it was suggesting that the mere bailee, or depositee, was required to take the same care as he did in his own affairs.[87] The final version attempts to hold both positions simultaneously. Gross negligence is stated to be the appropriate standard at the beginning and end of the argument,[88] but in the middle he requires that the depositee look after the property as his own. An attempt is made to reconcile the different lines by turning the latter into a rule of evidence[89]:

> For if he keeps the goods bailed to him, but as he keeps his own, though he keeps his own but negligently, yet he is not chargeable for them, for the keeping them as he keeps his own, is an argument of his honesty.

Hence, it could be said, he was 'bound to no other care of the bailed goods, than he takes of his own',[90] thereby turning it into a rule of substance in obvious conflict with the gross negligence standard. The foundations of this rule were very shaky. In the draft the rule of liability for fraud—with gross negligence as evidence of this—was based on Bracton and Justinian. In the final version the subjective negligence standard is said to be based on Bracton, this time *contrasted* with Justinian's law, where liability was imposed only for fraud and its equivalent gross negligence. It is impossible to make sense of this argument as it stands, since—as was stated in the draft judgment—Bracton's words and Justinian's were to all intents and purposes identical. It is tempting to suspect that Lord Raymond's report is a mangled version of what Holt actually said, but the temptation must be resisted since the same point is found independently in

---

[85] Above, 16.
[86] *Coggs v Barnard* (n 1 above) 2 Lord Raym 909, 915; 92 ER 107, 111.
[87] Above, 15–16.
[88] *Coggs v Barnard* (n 1 above) 2 Lord Raym 909, 913 and 915; 92 ER 107, 110 and 111.
[89] *Coggs v Barnard* (n 1 above) 2 Lord Raym 909, 914; 92 ER 107, 110.
[90] *Coggs v Barnard* (n 1 above) 2 Lord Raym 909, 915; 92 ER 107, 111.

two other reports.[91] It is more likely that Holt had shifted his ground after dealing with the point in the draft, twisting his reasoning in the final judgment to justify the new conclusion without taking note of the fact that the argument in its final form did not hold water.

We might usefully take stock of the treatment of deposit. First, it is clear from the physical text of the draft judgment that Holt was grappling with the issues raised by *Southcote v Bennet*. The interpolated passages reveal the way in which his argument developed, with second thoughts sometimes pulling against earlier ones. Putting the report of the final judgment alongside the draft, it is possible to see the way in which some of the tensions in the draft have been resolved (usually in favour of the second thoughts), but it also has to be recognised that the final version sometimes contains a degenerate form of the argument as found in the draft. That the printed text carries an aura of authority and certainty is no warranty of the quality of its reasoning. Secondly, it is noticeable that when case-law is used, its function is essentially negative, to show that the decision in *Southcote v Bennet* did not follow from the prior authorities. For positive rules, Holt had recourse primarily to Bracton and Justinian. Although the citation of cases produces the appearance of following English authority and of reasoning from case to case, in truth the core of his analysis completely ignored the current of authority. Thirdly, there are clear traces of the universalism which was to be associated with the use of arguments from Natural law: that a rule accorded with 'natural reason' or 'common justice' was good grounds for seeing it as a rule of the Common law.

The second species of bailment dealt with by Holt CJ was the gratuitous loan for use, the Romans' *commodatum*. Here he was content simply to adopt Bracton's text,[92] saying that the borrower was required to take the utmost care and diligence of the property, with the corollary that he should be liable for any slight negligence. Exactly the same standard was demanded in the third contract, hire or *locatio conductio*, and again it was justified solely by reference to Bracton.[93] The only difference between the draft judgment and that reported by Lord Raymond is that the draft is explicit in justifying the adoption of Bracton's rule on the grounds that it accorded with the 'general practice in the world both ancient and modern'[94]—a further example of the universalism noted in the context of deposit. Although there is passing reference to a Year Book case and *Southcote v Bennet*, Bracton is again the source of the liability rule applicable to the fourth species of bailment, pledge, that the pledgee should be required to take 'true diligence' or 'ordinary care'.[95] As in the treatment of deposit, though

---

[91] *Coggs v Barnard* (n 1 above) 1 Com 133, 134; 92 ER 999, 1000; LI MS Hill 52 10v, 11v.

[92] Bracton, *De Legibus et Consuetudinibus Angliae* (n 74 above) 99b: *Coggs v Barnard* (n 1 above) 2 Lord Raym 909, 915; 92 ER 107, 111, cited without being quoted at BL MS Add 34125 111, 119. Holt CJ in fact silently emended the text, which is on the face of it corrupt.

[93] Bracton, *De Legibus et Consuetudinibus Angliae* (n 74 above) 62b; quoted in *Coggs v Barnard* (n 1 above) 2 Lord Raym 909, 916; 92 ER 107, 111; BL MS Add 34125 f.111, 120.

[94] BL MS Add 34125 111, 122.

[95] *Coggs v Barnard* (n 1 above) 2 Lord Raym 909, 917; 92 ER 107, 112; BL MS Add 34125 f.111, 123, quoting Bracton, *De Legibus et Consuetudinibus Angliae* (n 74 above) 99b.

even more obviously so, in these three contracts discussion of English case-law is almost completely absent. Whatever the rules before *Coggs v Barnard* were, they were being supplanted by rules of Roman law mediated through Bracton.

The fifth type of bailment, where goods were delivered by one man to another to be carried, or for other work to be done on them, for reward was treated very differently.[96] Here it was impossible simply to adopt the Roman rule—that the bailee should be required to take care—for there was a host of cases which made carriers strictly liable unless the goods were lost or damaged by the lender, by act of God, or by act of the Queen's enemies (or, perhaps, of any third party against whom no remedy could be had). The 17th-century cases had seemingly treated all such bailees for reward equally, the only distinction drawn being that where the defendant was a professional (or common) tradesman—typically a carrier—it was not necessary explicitly to allege that consideration had been received.[97] In the first version of the draft judgment, Holt CJ adopted the same line, imposing strict liability on all workers for reward, but he subsequently reshaped this by sandwiching his argument between two interpolated passages. In the first of these,[98] right at the beginning of the argument, he introduced a distinction between those who had 'public employments and whose care and business [was] to take charge of other peoples goods', and those who had no such public employment but who were specially retained to do some particular work. The former category consisted of professionals—common carriers, common inn-keepers, common ship-masters and the like—and it was to them alone that the strict liability rule, originally operating generally, was now applied, justified on the grounds of public policy that it would be all too easy for such persons to enter into confederacies with thieves and robbers. The latter category—those who were not professionals—was dealt with in the second interpolated passage,[99] coming towards the end of the original argument. According to this, they were obliged only to their 'own personal care and diligence'. It is not clear whether this was meant to signify reasonable care or the care that the individual took about his own affairs: the former would have been more consonant with Roman law, but since neither Bracton nor Justinian is cited at this point, it may be that Holt was pointing in the direction of the non-Roman subjective test. There were difficulties in the drawing of this distinction, since there were cases in which the strict liability rule had clearly been applied to non-professionals; and in the draft judgment Holt went on to try to explain them away, albeit none too successfully.

The final form of the judgment as reported betrays none of this history. The division between 'public' and 'private' employments was locked in place at the start, with strict liability and its public-policy justification clearly applicable

---

[96] *Coggs v Barnard* (n 1 above) 2 Lord Raym 909, 917–18, 92 ER 107, 112–13; BL MS Add 34125 111, 124–5.
[97] Text to n 24 above.
[98] BL MS Add 34125 111, 123v.
[99] BL MS Add 34125 111, 124v–125v.

only to the former. Private people were obliged only to 'do the best they can', perhaps something slightly different from the 'personal care and diligence' of the draft; but again there was no authority cited for such a standard, and—unlike in the draft—there was now no attempt to explain away the cases of non-professionals, which were simply allowed to pass unmentioned.

This fifth section is perhaps the most important part of the judgment. In introducing the distinction between professionals and non-professionals, Holt was able to admit that there were cases in which strict liability had been imposed and then to marginalise them: they belonged properly not to the law of bailment generally, but only to the law of common carriers, common inn-keepers and the like. In doing this he broke with more than three centuries of history;[100] but he also made it possible to set the law on a footing where the 'tortious' and 'contractual' approaches to liability did not inevitably conflict and hence to introduce into English law a substantially coherent law of bailment.

At this point, finally, Holt reached his sixth type of bailment, where one man agreed gratuitously to do some act for another. He called this commission, but recognised that it was equivalent to the Romans' *mandatum*, citing Bracton, Justinian's *Institutes*, and Vinnius's commentary on the *Institutes* to this effect.[101] This, it had to be assumed, was the form of contract in issue in *Coggs v Barnard*, for in the absence of any allegation that the defendant was to receive anything for his pains it had to be assumed that he was acting for nothing. Counsel for the plaintiff had originally argued that these cases were tortious, based on the defendant's neglect rather than the contract, with the result that liability would be imposed straightforwardly for fault,[102] but Holt rejected this analysis, preferring to follow Roman law and Bracton in treating them as contractual. This inevitably raised the problem that there was apparently no consideration. Following the same tack as Gould and Powell JJ,[103] Holt manipulated the language of trust to generate a consideration. The draft and final judgments[104] are not significantly different, but the draft exposes his reasoning more clearly. It had been held in *Megod's case*[105] in 1586 that the beneficiary of a trust would have an action of *assumpsit* against the trustee to enforce the trust; the existence of the trust was itself consideration for the promise. The same line of reasoning could explain the cases from the late 16th and early 17th centuries where it had been held that a promise by a gratuitous bailee to return the bailed goods would be enforceable in *assumpsit*.[106] Equally it could explain

---

[100] Above, 16.

[101] BL MS Add 24125 111, 126, *Coggs v Barnard* (n 1 above) 2 Lord Raym 909, 918–19; 92 ER 107, 113.

[102] Above, 5.

[103] See text to nn 30–31 above.

[104] BL MS Add 24125 111, 127–9, *Coggs v Barnard* 2 Lord Raym 909, 919–20; 92 ER 107, 113–14.

[105] *Megod's case* (1586) Godb 64, 78 ER 40; BL MS Add 34125 111, 127. See NG Jones, 'Uses, Trusts, and a Path to Privity' [1997] *Cambridge Law Journal* 175, 192–8.

[106] *Riches v Brigges* (1602) Yelv 4, 80 ER 4; *Preston v Tooly* (1587) Cro El 74, 78 ER 334; *Game v Harvie* (1604) Yelv 50, 80 ER 36; *Pickas v Guile* (1608) Yelv 128, 80 ER 86; *Wheatley v Low* (1623) Cro Jac 668, 79 ER 578; *Howlet v Osbourn* (1595) Cro El 380, 78 ER 627.

the common form of *indebitatus assumpsit* for money had and received to the use of the plaintiff. All of these were situations in which the promise was to do something that there was an existing legal obligation to do, be it in Equity or at Common law, but Holt extended the reasoning beyond this. Whenever a person trusted another to do something, he said, that constituted sufficient consideration to support a promise to do it carefully. Hence the precedents from the Register of Writs which had been cited were explicable in purely contractual terms even though there was no allegation of consideration. The point was underlined in an interpolated sentence:

> [F]or tho' they are not in the now most usual and formal way in setting forth in consideration, yet they do in themselves import a sufficient consideration to oblige the defendant.[107]

The second issue raised on the facts of *Coggs v Barnard*, and in analogous cases of gratuitous commissions, was the standard of care which was to be required of the bailee. The language of trust was pressed into play here too.[108] There was a clear difficulty that Roman law had imposed liability only for fraud (and with it, following the orthodox Roman rule, gross neglect), whereas the cases at Common law had been based on the defendant's fault. Holt reconciled these two conflicting rules by arguing that where a person undertook to manage another's affairs and did it negligently, this in itself constituted a deceit.

> He that undertakes carefully and diligently to manage another mans affairs and doth it negligently, is guilty of a deceit, and hath thereby defrauded that person that hath trusted to him. Now to negotiate a man's affairs doth necessary imply a carefull management thereof, for nothing, of that nature can be performed, without care and diligence.[109] In such a case, a neglect is a deceipt to the bailor. For when he intrusts the bailee upon his undertaking to be careful, he has put a fraud upon the plaintiff by being negligent, his pretence of care being the persuasion that induced the plaintiff to trust him. And a breach of a trust undertaken voluntarily will be a good ground for an action.[110]

It is not at all clear why the person undertaking to do some act should be taken to have been trusted to do it carefully and hence be liable for negligence, whereas a person undertaking simply to look after goods should not be treated as having been so trusted; but Holt did not deal with the point. The draft judgment, though, suggests that he was well aware of it. Turning at the end to the facts of *Coggs v Barnard* itself, he noted that the pleadings had stated not simply that the defendant had undertaken to carry the brandy from one cellar to another, but that he had undertaken to do so *salvo et secure*[111]; and a depositee

---

[107] BL MS Add 24125 111, 128v.
[108] BL MS Add 24125 111, 126–7, *Coggs v Barnard* (n 1 above) 2 Lord Raym 909, 919; 92 ER 107, 113.
[109] BL MS Add 24125 111, 127.
[110] *Coggs v Barnard* (n 1 above) 2 Lord Raym 909, 919; 92 ER 107, 113.
[111] BL MS Add 24125 111, 129v.

who undertook to look after property *salvo et secure*, he had argued, would be liable for ordinary negligence.[112] It may be that his mind had been moving this way all along, for at the beginning of the draft judgment, in his summary of the pleadings, the words *salvo et secure* are repeatedly underlined.[113] None the less, as the argument appears in the draft judgment, we are left in considerable doubt whether the ordinary rule in cases of commissions was one of liability for ordinary negligence, as had been argued, or whether liability would be imposed for negligence only where there had been a special undertaking. These doubts are dispelled in the report of the final judgment.[114] The latter point was ignored, leaving intact the rule that liability for negligence was the general rule, since in this context any negligence amounted to a deceit.

Clearly, it was only the judgment of Holt CJ that transformed a relatively insignificant accident in the streets of central London into a leading case of the Common law of contract. The most important reason for this was that it imposed a degree of order onto an area of law that had been notoriously unclear for centuries. JW Smith's judgement that it was 'the first well-ordered exposition of the English law of bailments' is right on the mark. That said, it might have been seen as problematic had his reliance on Roman law been completely transparent. Holt avoided this, though, mediating his Roman law through the writing of the English Bracton, apologising repeatedly for its antiquity but then reinforcing it by repeatedly stressing that it was in accordance with natural reason. With his argument thus framed, the fact that Bracton's text accorded with Justinian's could be turned into a virtue: it showed that Bracton's rational views were consistent with the other legal system worthy of respect. The removal of the references to 'the Law'—meaning the Roman law—in the description of the various types of bailment[115] is not without its significance. Moreover, the apparent Englishness of his analysis is underlined by the repeated reference to English cases: the fact that these were used negatively, or were sometimes interpreted tendentiously so as to support his (romanised) conclusions is only visible on the closest of analysis. Secondly, the references that are found to 'natural reason' and similar ideas tend to seduce the reader into agreement with the judgment, notwithstanding that the words are of rhetorical significance only and have no substantive weight at all. So too, perhaps, with the way in which the language of trust is repeatedly used. Finally, the comparison of the draft judgment and the final form reveals at several points the way in which difficult issues or problematic cases might simply be ignored; where the draft wears its difficulties on its sleeve, the final judgment has much of the character of an *ex cathedra* statement. The Common lawyers of the early 18th century were no doubt grateful to have been given the answers to questions which had taxed them for centuries, and did not examine too closely the reasoning which lay behind those answers. Indeed,

---

[112] See text to n 47 above.
[113] BL MS Add 24125 f.111.
[114] *Coggs v Barnard* (n 1 above) 2 Lord Raym 909, 919; 92 ER 107, 113.
[115] See text to n 62 above.

the fact that the reasoning was sometimes opaque may have played its part in making *Coggs v Barnard* a leading case, turning later lawyers' attention onto the conclusions themselves rather than the way in which they had been reached.

It is, of course, always a matter of chance whether a case becomes a leading one, dependent on the way in which later generations treat it. *Coggs v Barnard*, or at least the judgment of Holt CJ, became the leading case on the law of bailments because lawyers treated it as such. It could easily have been different: the law reports are full of cases which struck out in a new direction but which were not followed subsequently.[116] It is salutary, therefore, to notice in passing an aspect of the case which falls into this latter category—its playing around with the notion of trust within the domain of contractual liability.

Recent work has shown the way in which the trust was analysed in substantially contractual terms by some writers by the early 18th century[117]; the reverse was also the case. Andrew Tooke and William Percivale, the translators of Pufendorf's *De Officio Hominis et Civis* and the fifth book of his *De Juris Naturae et Gentium* respectively, rendered '*depositum*' as 'trust'[118]; and, given the influence of Pufendorf's work on English lawyers at this time, it is likely that this played a part in the bringing together of the two sets of ideas. Perhaps more tellingly, though, a few years earlier Thomas Hobbes' treatment of contracts in his *Elements of Law* is shot through with the language of trust.[119] Whenever there was a contract which was not immediately executed, the party or parties who had not yet performed were said to be trusted to perform their obligations. Neither Pufendorf, as translated, nor Hobbes can necessarily be regarded as linking together contracts with trusts as such, but there are hints of this in the cases of the second half of the 17th century. In *Nicholson v Sherman*,[120] for example, the parallel was drawn between the testamentary executor and the shepherd: an action on the case would lie against the latter for the failure to take proper care of bailed sheep, and so also it should against the former. The great case of privity of contract, *Dutton v Poole*,[121] is underpinned by what appears to be the confusion of equitable and legal thinking.[122] More particularly, from the middle of the 17th century, the liability of the carrier was coming to be seen

---

[116] See, eg *Pillans v van Mierop* (1765) 3 Burr 1663, 97 ER 1035, discussed by Professor McMeel in ch 2 of the present volume.

[117] M Macnair, 'The Conceptual Basis of Trusts in the Later 17th and Early 18th Centuries' in R Helmholz and R Zimmermann (eds), *Itinera Fiduciae* (Berlin, Duncker & Humblot, 1998) 207.

[118] S Pufendorf, *On the Whole Duty of Man according to the Law of Nature* (trans A Tooke) (London 1691) 1.15.7 (178); *Of the Law of Nature and Nations* (trans B Kennett *et al*) (London, 1703) 5.4.7 (21).

[119] T Hobbes, *The Elements of Law*, F Tönnies (ed), (Cambridge, Cambridge University Press, 1928) 1.15.8–10 (77–8).

[120] *Nicholson v Sherman* (1661) 1 Keb 116, 83 ER 846; T Raym 23, 83 ER 13.

[121] *Dutton v Poole* (1679) 3 Keb 786, 84 ER 1011; 3 Keb 814, 84 ER 1028; 3 Keb 830, 84 ER 1038; 3 Keb 836, 84 ER 1041; Jones T 102, 84 ER 1168; 1 Ventr 318, 86 ER 205; 1 Ventr 332, 86 ER 215; 2 Lev 210, 83 ER 523, T Raym 302, 83 ER 156; 1 Freem 471, 89 ER 352.

[122] See D Ibbetson and W Swain, 'Third Party Beneficiaries in English Law: From *Dutton v Poole* to *Tweddle v Atkinson*' in EJH Schrage (ed), *Ius Quaesitum Tertio* (Berlin Duncke & Humblot, 2008) 191.

in trust-based terms. In his *Actions upon the Case for Deeds*, for example, William Sheppard had included carrier's liability under the heading of 'Actions upon the Case for Breach of Trust',[123] and in *Boson v Sandford*[124] Holt CJ had mingled together the ideas of trust and contract in concluding that where goods were 'trusted' jointly to a group of carriers it followed that they were joint contractors so that all had to be joined as co-defendants. 'Every trust', it was said, 'supposes a contract'.[125]

All of these hints of a linkage between ideas of trust and contract were rather allusive, but in *Coggs v Barnard* the argument of Holt CJ had the makings of something a good deal more general. Moving outwards from *Megod's case*, his reasoning suggests that whenever one person trusts another to do something— or, we might put it in more modern terms, whenever one person relies on another to do something—that is sufficient to create a contractual relationship, entitling the party giving the trust to bring a contractual action against the defaulting party. The doctrine of consideration—and hence the underlying sense of the nature of contract—was in a state of fluidity at this time, some lawyers seeing it as the element which created a reciprocal relationship and some as simply a matter of evidence that there was a serious intention to be bound[126]; and if the seed planted by Holt had germinated and taken root we might suppose that this would have foreclosed the questions destined to be raised in 60 or more years later. But it was not to be so. As was to be found in the aftermath of *Pillans v van Mierop*, the reciprocal model of consideration was still well entrenched, and *Coggs v Barnard* was not to become the foundation decision of a new model of contractual liability.

---

[123] W Sheppard, *Actions upon the Case for Deeds* (London, 1675) 292; cf also 314.

[124] *Boson v Sandford* (1690) 3 Mod 321, 323; 87 ER 212, 213; 1 Shower KB 101, 104; 89 ER 477, 479. See too *Buckmyr v Darnall* (1704) 2 Lord Raym 1085, 92 ER 219, treating a relationship of trusting as contractual in the context of the Statute of Frauds.

[125] *Boson v Sandford* (n 124 above) (1690) 3 Mod 321, 323, 87 ER 212,13.

[126] See most clearly J Gilbert's treatise on contract, BL MS Harg 265 40–3. Ibbetson, *A Historical Introduction to the Law of Obligations* (n 15 above) 216–17, 237.

# 2

# *Pillans v Van Mierop* (1765)

## GERARD McMEEL

## A. INTRODUCTION

TWO OF THE most striking topographical features of English contract law are the doctrines of consideration and privity. The former dominates the terrain of ascertaining which promises or agreements attract legal sanction. The latter remains the intellectual starting-point, despite vigorous statutory intervention, of determining the range of enforceability. I have chosen *Pillans v Van Mierop*,[1] a crucial case in the evolution of the doctrine of consideration, as my leading case. To those familiar with the story, my choice may appear startling and contrary (with the necessary Irish inflection). A case which has been repudiated, even (arguably) over-ruled, does not appear to be an ideal candidate even for the controversial appellation of 'leading' case. Nevertheless I intend to suggest that this case is central to the evolution of modern contract law, and, by extension, modern commercial and financial law. One could go further and say it is significant in the evolution of modern commerce and finance, which requires independent courts, eager to facilitate trade, and reasonably stable and ascertainable rules for the conduct of business. The spirit of *Pillans* is the enabling philosophy which has made English law, and Common law more generally, a valuable export commodity in itself, providing the governing regime for much of the world's trade and finance. Almost 250 years later the City of London is recognised as the world's leading financial centre. One is tempted to add the world's leading legal centre, with the services of the City's lawyers a significant export commodity in their own right.[2] The seeds are all there in *Pillans*.

A comparative lawyer cannot but help being drawn to the architectonic structures of consideration and privity, when seeking to orientate himself around

---

[1] *Pillans v Van Mierop* (1765) 3 Burr 1663, 97 ER 1035.

[2] According to a report by International Financial Services London, sponsored by the Commercial Bar Association (COMBAR), it is estimated that legal activity contributed £14.9 billion (1.4%) of the United Kingdom's GDP in 2004: (April 2007) *Counsel* 5.

English contract law.[3] However, I will suggest that—with apologies to Walter Bagehot—these doctrines constitute the 'dignified façade' of our law of contract. The 'efficient secret' lies elsewhere in English law's incredibly flexible and effective doctrines for ascertaining the content and ambit of an agreement. Lord Mansfield, the presiding genius of *Pillans*, was instrumental in promulgating the underlying philosophy and the techniques for implementing that philosophy in *Pillans* and other late 18th century authorities. The case is the *fons et origo* of the modern approach to formation and interpretation disputes.

A note about methodology: this is not an exercise in legal archaeology. I am interested in the broader legal and economic history rather than the particular circumstances of the merchants concerned in the case. This was probably a routine, if not mundane, transaction. I am also interested in the reception of *Pillans* and its ideas. Despite its relatively swift repudiation, it has always awakened the subsequent interest of jurists, probably because of the clarity and economy with which it handles a central debate in our contract law. In contract theory there is a tension between the conception of contract as promise (party intention) and the conception of contract as bargain (consideration). Lord Mansfield famously declared himself for the former.

The particular context was the recurrent problem of a party undertaking to be answerable for the liabilities of another. Where the primary debtor fails, incensed creditors will search around for another party to shoulder the burden. Allegations of such promises are so widespread that we have legislated twice in attempts to ensure that such actions can only proceed if the promise is evidenced by signed writing. We still have extant 17th century and 19th century legislation embodying this policy. However many financial instruments are effectively promises of this sort, and either via compliance with statute or circumvention, they are usually made to work.

## 1. The Rise of Northern European Commerce

The wider context is the rise of the modern economy, which expanded beyond trade in goods, and saw the development of modern financial instruments. The roots of this were diverse, but London was the eventual beneficiary of various political events. John Roberts, in his magisterial survey of world history, noted the shift of 'economic gravity' from Southern to North-Western Europe in the

---

[3] The authors of the leading German comparative text say of English lawyers: 'Some see the doctrine of consideration as an indispensable and characteristic feature of English law, the jewel in the crown. Others, noting that systems on the Continent get by quite well without it, conclude that it could be done away with in England too'. K Zweigert and H Kotz, *An Introduction to Comparative Law*, T Weir (trans), 3rd edn (Oxford, Oxford University Press, 1998) 398. Whilst Lord Wright (and his essay 'Ought the Doctrine of Consideration to be Abolished from the Common Law' (1936) 49 *Harvard Law Review* 1225) is cited as an example of the latter persuasion, no writer is cited from the former camp.

early modern period, during which time the foundations for the Industrial Revolution were laid and the apparatus of modern capitalism emerged[4]:

> One contribution to this was made by political troubles and wars such as ruined Italy in the early sixteenth century; others are comprised in tiny, short-lived but crucial pressures like the Portuguese harassment of the Jews which led to so many of them going, with their commercial skills, to the Low Countries at about the same time. The great commercial success story of the sixteenth century was Antwerp's, though it collapsed in political and economic disaster. In the seventeenth century Amsterdam and London surpassed it. In each case an important trade based on a well-populated hinterland provided profits for diversification into manufacturing industry, services and banking. The old banking supremacy of the medieval Italian cities passed first to Flanders and the German bankers of the sixteenth century, and then, finally, to Holland and London. The Bank of Amsterdam and the Bank of England were already international economic forces in the seventeenth century. About them clustered other banks and merchant houses undertaking operations of credit and finance. Interest rates came down and the bill of exchange, a medieval invention, underwent an enormous extension of use and became the primary financial instrument of international trade.

The Portuguese Jews were also in London, together with Huguenots and a myriad of other nationalities—London and Great Britain taking, as so often, an economic benefit from the intolerance of other regimes. On the accession of George III in 1760 (five years before *Pillans*) some 250 of the 810 merchants who kissed His Majesty's hand had foreign surnames.[5] Neither of the principal party names in our case has an Anglo-Saxon ring. This too has been the experience of the Commercial Court since its inception, with the overwhelming majority of cases featuring one foreign party, and a majority involving entirely overseas entities.[6]

## 2. The Emergence of a Law of Contract

The story of the emergence of modern contract law is the subject of extensive literature.[7] For our purposes it is worth noting that the old action of covenant to some extent embodied a conception of contract as promise. However, access to the King's central courts was soon limited by the insistence that such promises must be evidenced by a sealed deed.[8] This practice still underlies the formal

---

[4] JM Roberts, *The Penguin History of the World* (London, Penguin Books Ltd, 1995) 536.
[5] D Kynaston, *The City of London, Volume I: A World of Its Own 1815–1890* (London, Chatto & Windus, 1994) 11.
[6] Sir R Goff, 'Commercial contracts and the Commercial Court' [1984] *Lloyd's Maritime & Commercial Law Quarterly* 382.
[7] See JH Baker, *An Introduction to English Legal History*, 4th edn (London, Butterworths, 2002) chs 18–20; AWB Simpson, *A History of the Common Law of Contract—The Rise of the Action of Assumpsit* (Oxford, Oxford University Press, 1975).
[8] Baker, *An Introduction to English Legal History* (n 7 above) 318–21.

branch of our law of contract, and is the method generally employed for disposi-
tions of land, but is considered inapt for commerce. The watershed moment was
the eclipsing of the old action of debt by the later action of *assumpsit* ('he undertook'). The former was attended by the ancient mode of proof known as 'wager
of law',[9] whereas the latter entailed the more popular procedure of trial by jury.
*Assumpsit* had gradually taken on the business of contractual misfeasance, then
nonfeasance, and eventually the non-payment of money.[10] The triumph over debt
is associated with *Slade's case*[11] at the beginning of the 17th century.[12]

With respect to the central question of the requirements for a binding contract, English law, with its discrete forms of action, had evolved at least three,
originally clearly distinct, tests.[13] First, in the old action of covenant there developed the jurisdictional pre-condition of a sealed deed. Secondly, in the old form
of action of debt the notion of quid pro quo (which many modern lawyers
assume is synonymous with consideration).[14] Thirdly, *assumpsit*, which is the
source of the doctrine of consideration.[15] This doctrine in its classical sense
requires an element of reciprocity before a promise is legally recognised. There
must be some requested or stipulated counter-promise or counter-performance
for a promise to be enforced. A number of subsidiary propositions are often said
to be derived from the core doctrine. First, consideration must be contemporaneous and not past. Secondly, consideration must move from the promisee (a
vital step in privity reasoning). It is nevertheless said that there is no enquiry into
the adequacy of the exchange stipulated. A penny or a peppercorn is sufficient.

The doctrine incorporates the conception of contract as exchange at the heart
of English law. There are obviously good reasons for such a test. Bargained for
promises are more likely to indicate a serious intention to be bound than a
casual, gratuitous undertaking. But as the sole test for the enforceability of
informal promises in English law, it has always hampered judges who are alive
to the wider question: 'Is this a promise the court should enforce?'

Later in the 17th century, in the wake of *Slade's case*,[16] the legislature
imposed a further requirement for an enforceable contract, namely that certain

---

[9] Baker, *An Introduction to English Legal History* (n 7 above) 321–6. For wager of law see 4–6,
and for the rise of the jury 72–4.

[10] J Oldham, *English Common Law in the Age of Mansfield* (Chapel Hill, University of North
Carolina Press, 2004), 80–82.

[11] *Slade's case* (1603) 4 Co Rep 91a, 92b; 76 ER 1072.

[12] Baker, *An Introduction to English Legal History* (n 7 above) ch 19. For *Slade's case* see 341–5
and also J Oldham, *English Common Law in the Age of Mansfield* (n 10 above) 82–3.

[13] Sir W Holdsworth, *A History of English Law* (London, Methuen & Co, 1903–72) VIII.1-48.

[14] Baker, *An Introduction to English Legal History* (n 7 above) 322–3.

[15] Baker, *An Introduction to English Legal History* (n 7 above) 339–41. Assumpsit was broader
in some respects than the modern law of contract, and obviously contained the roots of much of the
common law of restitution. For another example of a non-contractual deployment of the form of
action (albeit consideration was still an issue) see its use in the collection of port fees in respect of
Great Yarmouth in *Mayor of Yarmouth v Eaton* (1763) 3 Burr 1402, 97 ER 896, where Lord
Mansfield—two years before *Pillans*—found the 'making of a port itself is sufficient consideration'.
(at 1406).

[16] *Slade's case* (see n 11 above) *ibid*.

promises (including to answer for another's debt) had to be evidenced by signed writing: Statute of Frauds 1677, section 4. Both the doctrine of consideration and the 1677 Act feature in *Pillans*, and the latter is put to interesting use.

## 3. The Emergence of Commercial Law

English substantive commercial law basically originated in the 18th century. Whilst some specialist issues of mercantile law—especially in relation to maritime events—may have deeper roots, the principles and rules in respect of insurance, bills of exchange and other commercial transactions only appear with clarity in this era. Revisionist accounts of our legal history have persuasively scotched the myth of a reception of substantive legal rules from a supposedly coherent medieval *lex mercatoria*.[17]

In contrast to subjects such as land law where the source of our concepts and doctrines are largely unknown, the founders of our commercial law are clearly identifiable. Milsom, considering our ability to identify innovation at Common law (as opposed to in Chancery), observed[18]:

> The common law itself is to a surprising degree anonymous, largely because the intellectual initiative has come from the bar rather the bench and has been directed to the single case rather than to the state of the law. In the single case the difficulty has always been to escape from the past, and there has been little opportunity to look to the future. Only where events or a bold hand had produced a clean slate, as with the mercantile work of Holt and Mansfield, could individuals in some sense mould the law.

My chosen case, *Pillans*, is a brilliant example of Lord Mansfield's 'bold hand' cutting free from the past, with his eye firmly on the future.

His predecessor as Chief Justice of the King's Bench, Holt, is perhaps most famous for his taxonomy of bailments in *Coggs v Barnard*.[19] Traditionally Holt CJ has received a bad press for his hostility to promissory notes, principally in *Clerke v Martin*[20] and *Buller v Crips*,[21] albeit his mercantile reputation on this score has recently received a sympathetic rehabilitation from Professor Rogers.[22] Nevertheless, Parliament still reversed the result of these decisions in

---

[17] The two principal accounts are JH Baker, 'The Law Merchant and the Common Law before 1700' (1979) 38 *Cambridge Law Journal* 295 and JS Rogers, *The Early History of the Law of Bills and Notes—A Study of the Origins of Anglo-American Commercial Law* (Cambridge, Cambridge University Press, 1995) 12–31. See also J Baker, 'The Law Merchant as a Source of Law' in G Jones and W Swadling (eds), *The Search for Principle* (Oxford, Oxford University Press, 1999) 79.

[18] SFC Milsom, *Historical Foundations of the Common Law*, 2nd edn (London, Butterworths, 1981) 95.

[19] *Coggs v Barnard* (1703) 2 Lord Raym 909, 92 ER 107. For discussion see G McMeel, 'The redundancy of bailment' [2003] *Lloyd's Maritime & Commercial Law Quarterly* 169, 172–5. See also David Ibbetson's contribution to this volume at ch 1.

[20] *Clerke v Martin* (1702) 2 Lord Raym 757, 92 ER 6.

[21] *Buller v Crips* (1703) 6 Mod 29, 87 ER 793.

[22] Rogers, *The Early History of the Law of Bills and Notes* (n 17 above) 173–86.

the Promissory Notes Act 1704, which permitted promissory notes to be nego-tiated (transferred) and sued upon in the same way as bills of exchange.

In contrast, Lord Mansfield's reputation in commercial law is virtually unblemished.[23] William Murray, that rare but splendid creature, a Scottish Tory, was Solicitor-General from 1742, and from 1754 Attorney-General, until his appointment as Chief Justice of the King's Bench two years later. It is impos-sible to improve on Buller J's fulsome tribute to Lord Mansfield in 1787 in *Lickbarrow v Mason*,[24] a seminal case in establishing that bills of lading were documents of title to the goods shipped. Buller J described the hesitancy of judges before the last 30 years (being the period of Lord Mansfield's tenure from 1756[25]) to determine the general principles applicable to mercantile questions. However, since the mid-18th century: 'the commercial law of this country has taken a very different turn from what it did before'. Buller J continued[26]:

> Before that period we find that in the courts of law all the evidence in mercantile cases was thrown together; they were left generally to a jury, and they produced no estab-lished principle. From that time we all know the great study has been to find some cer-tain general principles which shall be known to all mankind, not only to rule the particular case then under consideration, but to serve as a guide for the future. Most of us have heard these principles stated and reasoned upon, enlarged, and explained, till we have been lost in admiration at the strength and stretch of human understand-ing. I should be very sorry to find myself under a necessity of differing from any case on this subject which has been decided by Lord Mansfield, who may truly be said to be the founder of the commercial law of this country.

Lord Mansfield's tenure was fundamental to the establishment of the govern-ing principles of carriage of goods, (marine) insurance, bills of exchange and promissory notes, (to a lesser extent) sales, and also—as I hope to demon-strate—the basic techniques for handling commercial documents which remain essential in commercial and financial contexts. In *Pillans* he boldly took on the doctrine of consideration, which had the potential to frustrate the recognition of seriously-intended undertakings in a commercial context.

---

[23] The current biographies are CHS Fifoot, *Lord Mansfield* (Oxford, Oxford University Press, 1936) and E Heward, *Lord Mansfield* (Chichester, Barry Rose, 1979). See also Lord Campbell, *The Lives of the Chief Justices of England—From the Norman Conquest till the Death of Lord Mansfield* (London, John Murray, 1849) vol II chs 30 to 40. Professor Atiyah suggests in *The Rise and Fall of Freedom of Contract* (Oxford, Oxford University Press, 1979) 121 that 'an adequate biography is still awaited'.

[24] *Lickbarrow v Mason* (1787) 2 Term Rep 63, 100 ER 35 (KB). There were later proceedings in Exchequer Chamber (1790), House of Lords (1793), and again before the King's Bench (1793).

[25] Mansfield was in post from 1756 to 1788, and the tribute is more moving as the court sat with-out Mansfield, who was too ill to attend. Interestingly, Mansfield was manoeuvring for Buller J to be his successor: Campbell, *The Lives of the Chief Justices of England* (n 23 above) 2.549—2.550.

[26] *Lickbarrow v Mason* (1787) 2 Term Rep 63, 73; 100 ER 35. Lord Campbell was similarly ful-some (in respect of the law of bills) when he wrote: 'Lord Mansfield first promulgated many rules that now appear to us to be as certain as those which guide the planets in their orbits'. Campbell, *The Lives of the Chief Justices of England* (n 23 above) 2.407.

## B. THE CASE

### 1. A Note on Terminology

The bill of exchange was once the principal financial instrument facilitating exports and imports, as well as a widespread payment mechanism in domestic situations. Indeed, it is difficult for us in the modern economy, where paper money has yielded to plastic cards and electronic fund transfers, to recapture a world of limited specie and emerging bank notes, where private bills were a significant—if not principal—mode of settling debts.[27] However in the 21st century the use of such instruments is no longer widespread and the magnificent gothic masterpiece of the Bills of Exchange Act 1882 sits broodingly in the statute-book, only rarely consulted. Even the bill's broken-backed cousin, the cheque, is a comparative rarity. Modern financial instruments and electronic payment methods have largely taken their place.

Accordingly, the terminology of the law of bills is no longer common parlance. It is useful to set out the players and the terminology in outline. The original rationale of bills of exchange was to make use of credit which one party (the drawer) had in the hands of another person (the drawee), especially where the two parties were situated in different countries. However the existence of a credit in the hands of a drawee is not necessary for a valid bill.[28] Accordingly, the 'drawer' is the author of the bill who addresses it to another, the 'drawee', requiring the latter to make payment usually to a named payee, or bearer. If the drawee accepts this order he becomes an 'acceptor'.[29] The 1882 Act also distinguishes between 'inland bills' and 'foreign bills'.[30] *Pillans* concerned the latter and more ancient species.

### 2. The Factual Matrix

The case's full title is *Pillans and Rose v Van Mierop and Hopkins*. The usual abbreviation may be misleading, as it is likely the names of each party reflect a

---

[27] Rogers, *The Early History of the Law of Bills and Notes* (n 17 above) 195, describes the 18th century context: 'Merchants and others would regularly have to take bills and notes as a form of payment, since there frequently was no other available payment medium'.

[28] Rogers, *The Early History of the Law of Bills and Notes* (n 17 above) 198: 'The main point of bills was that they permitted a person in one location to make use of funds in the hands of a correspondent in another location'.' However, in *Pillans v Van Mierop* itself the judges treated as irrelevant the question of whether White & Co had any funds to its credit with Van Mierop and Hopkins, that is whether he had any 'effects' with that firm.

[29] The modern definition is: 'A bill of exchange is an unconditional order in writing, addressed by one person to another, signed by the person giving it, requiring the person to whom it is addressed to pay on demand or at a fixed or determinable future time a sum certain in money to or to the order of a specified person, or to bearer'. Bills of Exchange Act 1882, s 3(1). By s 17(1): 'The acceptance of a bill is the signification by the drawee of his assent to the order of the drawer'.

[30] Bills of Exchange Act 1882, s 4.

partnership or firm name.[31] Both merchant and banking enterprises were described as 'houses', although it would be ahistorical to assume there was a perceived dichotomy between mercantile and financial functions, and certainly no regulatory fissure required.

A course of correspondence took place between three merchant houses in Ireland (presumably Dublin), Rotterdam and London respectively. An Irish merchant, White—apparently trading as 'White & Co' (although it is not clear he had any partners in business)—wished to make a payment to one Clifford, presumably another merchant, of £800. In order to do so he wished to draw on Pillans and Rose, a merchant house in Rotterdam, the plaintiffs. He wrote to Pillans and Rose asking them 'to honour his draught for 800l. payable ten weeks after'. They agreed to this proposal, in the words of Wilmot J, 'on condition that they will be made safe at all events'.[32] Accordingly, White was the proposed drawer, Pillans and Rose the drawees and potential acceptors and principal payers, and Clifford was the payee. The use of Pillans and Rose suggests Clifford was either based in, or required payment in, Rotterdam. There is no reference in the case to the underlying transaction which had generated or was to generate White & Co's indebtedness to Clifford. We can speculate that it was probably an import of some Dutch produce into Ireland. What is striking is that the judges were content to focus on the financing arrangements, unconcerned with the underlying deal.

How were Pillans and Rose to be reimbursed for the credit they were extending to White & Co? He proposed giving them credit at a 'good house' in London, or whatever method of reimbursement they chose.[33] In response Pillans and Rose stipulated for a 'house of rank' in London as a condition of their accepting the bill. White & Co named the defendants, Van Mierop and Hopkins, as a suitable house. Pillans and Rose then honoured the 'draught', that is, they accepted it, and became liable as acceptors in respect of it to Clifford or to any person to whom he negotiated the draft, with payment due some 10 weeks later.

### 3. The Correspondence

Various letters were read in evidence. Indeed, from the report it appears that the evidence in the case was either exclusively or at least principally documentary in nature. There is no mention of witness evidence in the report, and certainly no

---

[31] *Pillans* (n 1 above) 3 Burr 1663, 1669 in his judgment, Lord Mansfield describes the defendants as both 'the house of Van Mierop' and 'Van Mierop and Company'.

[32] *Pillans* (n 1 above) 3 Burr 1663, 1672.

[33] This is based on the account of the letter in the report. In his judgment, Lord Mansfield states, somewhat differently, that '[t]he first proposal from White, was "to reimburse the plaintiffs by a remittance, or by credit on the house of Van Mierop"'. *Pillans* (n 1 above) 3 Burr 1663, 1669. Actual reimbursement by a remittance would obviously be comprehended by any mode of reimbursement they chose.

significance was attached to any oral evidence. It seems to have all turned on the documents. This is a common characteristic of modern commercial litigation, and a reflection of the prominence given to contemporaneous mercantile records. It also indicates English law's characteristic focus on what the documents actually say, as opposed to what their authors may have intended when they wrote or signed them.

There were several key letters. First, a letter dated 16 February 1762 from White & Co to Pillans and Rose post-dated Pillans and Rose's honouring of the bills drawn upon them by White & Co, payable to Clifford, but was used to evidence the arrangement. Secondly, a letter from Pillans and Rose to Van Mierop and Hopkins informing them of the arrangement and enquiring

> whether they would accept such bills as they, the plaintiffs, should in about a month's time draw upon the said Van Mierop's and Hopkins's house here in London, for 800l. upon the credit of White.[34]

Thirdly, and at the same time White & Co to Van Mierop and Hopkins, presumably in similar terms, albeit presumably requesting that the house so accommodated him. Fourthly, and crucially, Van Mierop and Hopkins wrote to Pillans and Rose on 19 March 1762 agreeing to honour the bill drawn on the account of White.[35] In the meantime, White 'failed'—that is, became bankrupt—before either any 'draught' had been drawn or indeed Pillans and Rose had forwarded any 'draught' to Van Mierop and Hopkins. Fifthly, Van Mierop and Hopkins wrote to Pillans and Rose subsequently to say 'that White had stopt payment' and desiring Pillans and Rose not to draw, as they could no longer accept their 'draught'. Finally, Pillans and Rose responded to Van Mierop and Hopkins, uncompromisingly insisting 'that they should draw on them, holding them not to be at liberty to withdraw from their engagement'.

## 4. The Initial Proceedings and Counsels' Arguments

At the trial in 1764 before Lord Mansfield, a verdict was entered for Van Mierop and Hopkins. It appears that the trial below was more focused on an allegation of fraud, than the technical doctrine of consideration.[36]

On 25 January 1765, the plaintiffs, represented by the Attorney-General Norton, together with Mr Walker and Mr Dunning, moved for a new trial on the basis that the verdict was against the evidence. This preliminary hearing took place on 11 February 1765, when the correspondence was read.

---

[34] *Pillans* (n 1 above) 3 Burr 1663, 1664. The quote marks are in the report, but the language is obviously suggestive of a paraphrase of the letter's text rather than a literal transcription.

[35] See *Pillans* (n 1 above) 3 Burr 1663, 1672, where Wilmot J paraphrases a response ' "that they will" '.

[36] Cf Fifoot, *Lord Mansfield* (n 23 above) 130.

### (a)  The Arguments of Van Mierop and Hopkins

At that hearing, counsel for the defendants, Van Mierop and Hopkins, were Mr Serjeant Davy and Mr Wallace. They made much of the fact that Pillans and Rose had already effectively extended credit to White & Co for longer than a month[37] prior to Van Mierop and Hopkins' indicating a willingness to accept the proposed reimbursement bill. Accordingly, this was an undertaking to pay another's debt, which required consideration and the apparent consideration was past.[38]

### (b)  The Arguments of Pillans and Rose

In response Pillans and Rose's counsel identified the consideration as follows:

> the liberty given to the plaintiffs 'to draw upon a confirmed house in London,' (which was prior to the undertaking by the defendants,) was the consideration of the credit given by the plaintiff to White's draughts; and this was good and sufficient consideration for the undertaking made by the defendants.

They continued: 'It relates back to the original transaction'. With respect to the then Attorney-General, this was unconvincing. It failed to identify any consideration moving from Pillans and Rose to Van Mierop and Hopkins. Pillans and Rose were exposed by having already extended credit to White. Counsel was, however, able to point out, that

> [i]f any one promises to pay for goods delivered to a third person; such promise being in writing is a good one.

However, that did not circumvent the timing problem. They could, in any event, submit that the promise being in writing at least satisfied the requirement of the statute, referring to the Statute of Frauds 1677.

### (c)  Referral to the Full Court of King's Bench

Despite the patent weakness of the plaintiffs' arguments, and perhaps because they could hardly refuse the Attorney-General (a post which Mansfield previously held), Lord Mansfield and Mr Justice Wilmot decided that the matter should be argued again the next term before the whole Court of King's Bench. The actual arguments raised by the plaintiffs did not feature in the reasons given for new hearing. Lord Mansfield pointed out that the 'nudum pactum' or past consideration argument had not been raised at trial, where he had been satisfied

---

[37] The period between White's letter of 16 February 1762 and Van Mierop's and Hopkins's letter of 19 March 1762.

[38] Citing authority, including *Hayes v Warren* (1731) 2 Strange 933, 93 ER 950. Fifoot notes that most of the other authorities were concerned with guarantees, and could therefore be distinguished: Fifoot, *Lord Mansfield* (n 23 above) 130.

that in the absence of fraud, the defendants' clear written undertaking should be given effect to:

> for that they had engaged under their hands in a mercantile transaction, 'to give credit for Pillans and Rose's reimbursement'.

Mr Justice Wilmot suggested that 'the least spark of a consideration will be sufficient'.[39] Both judges insisted that as a mercantile transaction it was quite different to a naked promise to answer for the debts of another. Lastly, Lord Mansfield concluded this preliminary hearing by observing:

> A letter of credit may be given as well for money already advanced, as for money to be advanced in the future.

## (d) The Argument before the Court of King's Bench

Submissions took place over 29 and 30 April 1765. The plaintiffs were again represented by the Attorney-General Norton, together with Mr Walker and Mr Dunning, who repeated their argument—namely, that it was sufficient for consideration to have moved from White to Pillans and Rose, and that it was not necessary for it to move from Van Mierop and Hopkins. The undertaking of the latter was sufficient to make their promise irrevocable. They sought to distinguish the cases relied upon by the defendants as 'strange cases', lacking 'solid and sufficient reasons' and 'no meritorious consideration at all'.[40]

Serjeant Davy appeared only on the second day, with Mr Wallace holding the fort for the defendants on the first. Davy tried a different tack to start with, namely a fraudulent concealment of facts. Van Mierop and Hopkins were said to have been misled into believing that their undertaking was for a future credit, rather than to provide security for credit already advanced to White. If they had known, it would have been clear that Pillans and Rose were already nervous about whether White was good for the money. Such concealment vitiated the contract. Davy insisted all letters of credit related to future credit. He then repeated his 'promise to pay the debts of another' and 'past consideration' arguments. Lord Mansfield then interjected, asking whether 'any case could be found, where the undertaking holden to be nudum pactum was in writing'.[41] Serjeant Davy had no ready, or at least precise, riposte:

> It was anciently doubted 'whether a written acceptance of a bill of exchange was binding, for want of consideration,' It is so said, somewhere in Lutwyche'.[42]

That 'somewhere' is striking.[43]

---

[39] *Pillans* (n 1 above) 3 Burr 1663, 1666.
[40] *Pillans* (n 1 above) 3 Burr 1663, 1667.
[41] *Pillans* (n 1 above) 3 Burr 1663, 1667.
[42] *Pillans* (n 1 above) 3 Burr 1663, 1669.
[43] Compare the lack of a ready answer in *Bilbie v Lumley* (1802) 2 East 469, 102 ER 448, which set English law on a restrictive approach to the recovery of payments made under a mistake of law for almost two centuries, until *Kleinwort Benson Ltd v Lincoln City Council* [1999] 2 AC 349 (HL).

## 5. The Judgment of the Court of King's Bench

### (a) Lord Mansfield

It seems from the report that Lord Mansfield commenced his judgment almost immediately after Serjeant Davy's vague final submission. This remarkable judgment occupies just over a page of the law report. His Lordship commenced: 'This is a matter of great consequence to trade and commerce, in every light'.

Lord Mansfield accepted that fraud or mala fides would have vitiated the contract. However the correspondence did not suggest that Pillans and Rose doubted White's ability to pay. Accordingly, the matter was one of law. It is noteworthy that in respect of the law of vitiating factors, both Serjeant Davy and Lord Mansfield were ad idem that fraudulent concealment by the plaintiffs would have vitiated the contract.[44] This is a precursor of, and consistent with, another leading case decided the following year. In 1766 in *Carter v Boehm*[45] Lord Mansfield's philosophical underpinning was a broad principle of good faith in commercial transactions. Whilst *Carter v Boehm* concerned a contract of insurance, Lord Mansfield's judgment insisted that all contracts were subject to a duty of good faith. However, subsequently English contract and commercial law developed differently, with no general principle of good faith in mercantile dealings being recognised either in the formation or performance of contracts.[46]

The characterisation of the matter as one of law entailed that at the new trial the matter could be withdrawn from the jury, who might otherwise reach another inconvenient verdict. Furthermore, this was not a question of ordinary law, but one of the 'law of merchants'. The law of merchants and the Common law were both clear that evidence was not required to prove the law of merchants. Lord Mansfield was able to pronounce it himself: 'A nudum pactum does not exist, in the usage and law of merchants'. Lord Mansfield continued in the famous passage from the case[47]:

> I take it, that the ancient notion of want of consideration was for the sake of evidence only: for when it is reduced to writing, as in covenants, specialties, bonds, &c. there was no objection to the want of consideration. And the Statute of Frauds proceeded on the same principle.

[44] *Pillans* (n 1 above) 3 Burr 1663, 1669. See also 1675 (Aston J). Compare Lord Mansfield a decade later in *Trueman v Fenton* (1777) 2 Cowp 544, 547; 98 ER 1232.
[45] *Carter v Boehm* (1766) 3 Burr 1905, 97 ER 1162. Recently described as 'that *locus classicus* of insurance law from the Age of the Enlightenment'. See *Brotherton v Aseguradora Colseguros* [2003] EWCA Civ 705, [2003] 2 All ER (Comm) 298, [24] (Mance LJ). See further Chapter 3 (below).
[46] According to Lord Hobhouse in *Manifest Shipping Co Ltd v Uni-Polaris Ins Co Ltd, The Star Sea* [2001] UKHL 1; [2003] 1 AC 469, [45], 'Lord Mansfield's universal proposition did not survive. The commercial and mercantile law of England developed in a different direction preferring the benefits of simplicity and certainty which flow from requiring those engaging in commerce to look after their own interests'.
[47] *Pillans* (n 1 above) 3 Burr 1663, 1669.

In commercial cases amongst merchants, the want of consideration is not an objection.

Accordingly, here Lord Mansfield runs together all written instruments, aligning bonds with covenants and specialties (which were enforced through the writ of covenant).

Lord Mansfield said it was irrelevant whether or not Van Mierop and Hopkins had any effects of White's in their hands.[48] Their acceptance of the bill was sufficient to make it a promise they could not thereafter retract. Furthermore, they were bound by the initial indication that they would accept the bill, even without completing the formality of accepting it by endorsing it with their signature. In a principle reminiscent of the maxim that 'equity regards as done that which ought to be done', Lord Mansfield held:

> If a man agrees that he will do the formal part, the law looks upon it (in the case of acceptance of a bill) as if actually done.[49]

Finally, to permit Van Mierop and Hopkins to retract was not to be countenanced: 'It would be very destructive to trade, and to trust in commercial dealing, if they could'.[50]

Lord Mansfield's facilitative philosophy could not be more emphatic. The policy choice is explicit. Commercial transactions are different. All serious promises and utterances, or at least those in writing, are to be given effect in that context. The doctrine of consideration is merely one of a number of methods of identifying a serious promise or utterance. Promises under seal and any unsealed writing were other alternative routes to enforceability.

The Statute of Frauds 1677 was pressed into service to bolster the argument. This 17th century legislation embodied a policy aimed at discouraging frivolous or mischievous law suits. Obviously it promoted certainty at the expense of justice in the individual case.[51] However in *Pillans*, rather than being understood as imposing an additional requirement for a binding contract in respect of the agreements falling under it, it was boldly said to evidence the fact that Parliament thought that writing alone would be sufficient.[52] It is easy to sympathise with this approach: the policy of the 1677 Act laid down a different test for enforceable contracts, based on signed writing rather than necessarily requiring a wax seal. *Pillans* was a conscious attempt to shift the law of formal contracts

---

[48] *Pillans* (n 1 above) 3 Burr 1663, 1669. See also at 1673 (Yates J) and 1675 (Aston J).

[49] *Pillans* (n 1 above) 3 Burr 1663, 1669. See also Yates J at 1674: 'A promise "to accept" is the same as an actual acceptance'.

[50] *Pillans* (n 1 above) 3 Burr 1663, 1670.

[51] For the history of the statute see Simpson, *A History of the Common Law of Contract* (n 7 above) 599–620.

[52] Conversely, Lord Mansfield was reluctant to permit the Statute of Frauds to be used as an instrument of fraud, particularly in the context of executory contracts of sale (governed by s 17): *Clayton the Younger v Andrews* (1767) 4 Burr 210, 98 ER 96. See also *Simon v Motivos* (1766) 3 Burr 1921, 97 ER 1170 (auction sales not within mischief of statute).

to embrace all signed written contracts, rather than drawing the line in the sand between deeds and all other agreements.[53]

It is this part of the case—assimilating written contracts to deeds—which attracted most controversy, and was eventually repudiated as a general principle of contract law. However in the context of finance and financial instruments, such as the modern incarnation of the letter of credit, the principle appears still to have force.

## (b)  Mr Justice Wilmot

Mr Justice Wilmot's judgment is the most substantial, and does not wear its considerable learning lightly. Like Lord Mansfield's, it has little to do with the preceding submissions of counsel. It ranges from the origins of the phrase 'nudum pactum' in Roman law, through the great continental jurists, Grotius and Puffendorff, via the civilian influenced Bracton, to the domestic case law.[54] The civilian jurisprudence suggested a rationale for consideration, which is still trotted out in law schools around the Common law world, that 'it was intended as a guard against rash inconsiderate declarations'.[55] Much of the final category of learning consisted of cases—both old and modern—which are 'strange and absurd'.[56] Mr Justice Wilmot refers to the relaxation of the past consideration rule where a request can be identified, and how the strictness of the rule was relaxed in cases where, for example, a claimant buried the defendant's son.[57] His Lordship observed: 'It has been melting down into common sense, of late times'.[58] This is very suggestive of the importance ultimately attached to rationality over authority by this court.

Curiously at this point Mr Justice Wilmot changes tack, and suddenly claims to be able to identify consideration in any event. The fact that once Van Mierop and Hopkins indicated that they would honour the bill, Pillans and Rose were precluded from calling on White for performance of his promise to give them

---

[53] Professor Simpson is notably sympathetic: Simpson, *A History of the Common Law of Contract* (n 7 above) 617–20.

[54] In delivering the unanimous opinion of the judges before the House of Lords in *Rann v Hughes*, Skynner CB was scathing of Wilmot J's scholarship: 'he contradicted himself and was also contradicted by Vinnius in his comment on Justinian'. (1778) 7 Term Rep 350n, 101 ER 1014.

[55] *Pillans* (n 1 above) 1670. Wilmot J's 'inconsiderate' is clearly intended as the modern 'ill-considered'. Wilmot J also cites Plowden 308b. There in 1565 in *Sharrington v Stotton* it was famously said that 'because words are often spoke or uttered by a man without great advisement or deliberation, the law has provided that a contract by words shall not bind without consideration'. However Plowden continued: 'But where the agreement is by Deed, there is more time for resolution'. This is not authority for a distinction between written contracts and oral contracts, but for the traditional English approach.

[56] *Pillans* (n 1 above) 3 Burr 1663, 1671. Wilmot J singled out *Hayes v Warren* (1731) 2 Strange 933, 93 ER 950 (a case on past consideration) and continued: 'I have a very full note of the case. The reason of the reversal of judgment was, "that it did not appear by the declaration, to be either for the benefit, or at the request of the defendant"'.

[57] *Pillans* (n 1 above) 3 Burr 1663, 1671.

[58] *Pillans* (n 1 above) 3 Burr 1663, 1672.

credit at a good house in London, was good consideration. Wilmot J concedes that this was a trivial suspension, but insists the law does not inquire into the adequacy of consideration. A more difficult objection to overcome (at least in settled modern doctrine) is that Van Mierop and Hopkins did not request any such forbearance. Furthermore, there is an element of circularity here. Perhaps recognising the weakness of this supposed consideration, Mr Justice Wilmot concludes by reverting to the language of internationalism and the imperatives of trade and commerce. In this respect he lent support to Lord Mansfield's bold re-drawing of the boundaries between formal and informal contracts.

### (c)  Mr Justice Yates

Mr Justice Yates agreed there should be a new trial: it was 'a case of great consequence to commerce'. In contrast to his preceding brother, his Lordship started instead with the question of whether there was in fact consideration, and concluded that there was. Any forbearance or loss, without necessarily benefiting the other party, would be sufficient. Mr Justice Yates then began to levitate with the aid of his own bootstraps:

> The credit of the plaintiffs might have been hurt by the refusal of the defendants to accept White's bills. They were or might have been prevented from resorting to him, or getting further security from him. It comes within the cases of promises, where the debtee forbears suing the original debtor.

This reasoning is obviously circular. If followed through, the weakest of reliance would justify the enforcement of any promise, regardless of whether it was in writing or not.

In the alternative Mr Justice Yates considered whether consideration was essential in the law of merchants. He reasoned:

> The acceptance of a bill of exchange is an obligation to pay it: the end of their institution, their currency, requires that it should be so.[59]

Accordingly as a matter of pleading, bills were treated as 'special contracts', that is, like deeds, whilst technically they were simple contracts, acceptance of such a bill was by the custom of merchants, a liability to pay.[60] Indeed, acceptance was not necessary: 'A promise "to accept" is the same thing as an actual acceptance'.[61] This judgment turns on the 'virtual acceptance' point and the custom which treated bills as specialties. However, Mr Justice Yates expressed no

---

[59] *Pillans* (n 1 above) 3 Burr 1663, 1674.
[60] This needs treating with caution. For pleading and the custom of merchants see Rogers, *The Early History of the Law of Bills and Notes* (n 17 above) 125–50 and 179, fn 38, where Rogers rejects the view that any 18th century judge regard a bill as a specialty, save as a metaphor.
[61] *Pillans* (n 1 above) 3 Burr 1663, 1674. An approach eventually rejected in *Johnson v Collings* (1800) 1 East 98, 102 ER 40 and *Bank of Ireland v Archer & Daly* (1843) 11 M & W 383, 152 ER 852. See also *Pierson v Dunlop* (1777) 2 Cowp 571, 98 ER 1246 (Lord Mansfield retreating on acceptance).

opinion on the wider question as to whether written mercantile contracts in general were enforceable even in the absence of consideration.

## (d)  Mr Justice Aston

Mr Justice Aston was the most succinct in his concurring judgment: this was a 'plain case' and that the undertaking to accept was sufficient for the bill to be enforced. 'This cannot be called a nudum pactum'. It was not necessary to show that the defendants had any effects of White's. There was no fraud and the defendants had full notice of the facts.[62] However, he did not explicitly concur with Lord Mansfield's broader proposition.

## (e)  Disposal

The court unanimously resolved to set the verdict aside, ordered a new trial and made the rule absolute.

## 6.  The Backlash

## (a)  The written contract front

*Pillans* is sometimes said to have been overruled by the House of Lords in *Rann v Hughes*,[63] albeit may be safer to say that it is 'generally said to have been overruled' in that case on the point that writing is not an alternative test for enforcement to consideration in commercial cases.[64]

*Rann v Hughes*[65] is a strikingly different type of case. In its original enacted form section 4 of the 1677 statute explicitly extended to actions to sue an executor or administrator of a deceased's estate on a promise to pay 'out of his own estate', unless there was a memorandum in writing. The case concerned such a promise.[66] At a trial before Lord Mansfield in Westminster Hall in 1774 the jury found the promise had been made and awarded £483 damages. That was upheld by the full court of King's Bench, but reversed by the Exchequer Chamber.

---

[62]  *Pillans* (n 1 above) 3 Burr 1663, 1675.

[63]  *Rann v Hughes* (1778) 4 Brown PC 27, 2 ER 18 (submissions of counsel); 7 Term Rep 350n, 101 ER 1014 (opinion of the judges before the House of Lords).

[64]  The more cautious formulation is Rogers's *The Early History of the Law of Bills and Notes* (n 17 above) 200, fn 22.

[65]  *Rann v Hughes* (n 63 above) (HL). See Oldham, *English Common Law in the Age of Mansfield* (n 10 above) 84–7. Oldham also discusses the unreported, non-commercial *Losh's Case*, decided in 1775, between *Pillans v Van Mierop* and *Rann v Hughes*. It is also known as *Williamson v Losh*, and despite being unreported found its way into the late 19th century collection of contract cases by Harvard Law School Dean, CC Langdell, *A Selection of Cases on the Law of Contracts* (Boston, Little Brown & Co, 1871) 180, sandwiched between the better known authorities.

[66]  For such promises generally see Simpson, *A History of the Common Law of Contract* (n 7 above) 439–45.

Before the House of Lords, Buller and Dunning appeared for the plaintiffs and submitted[67]:

> In reason, there is little or no difference between a contract which is deliberately reduced into writing, and signed by the parties, without a seal, and a contract under the same circumstances, to which the party at the time of signing it puts a seal or his finger on cold wax. In the case of a deed, *i.e.* an instrument under seal, it must be admitted that no consideration is necessary; and in the year 1765, it was solemnly adjudged in the court of King's bench (*Pillans v. Van Mierop.* 3 Burr. 1663), that no consideration was necessary when the promise was reduced to writing. That opinion has since been recognized in the same court, and several judgments founded upon it; all which judgments must be subverted, and what was conceived to be settled law, totally overturned, if the plaintiffs in this cause were not entitled to recover.

Such might be expected to be the submissions of counsel, but the reference to *Pillans*, and in particular Lord Mansfield's opinion, as settled law for a decade and regularly followed is striking. If they were wrong about that counsel claimed to be able to identify a consideration in the effects which the defendant had of the deceased. However, the declaration had neither alleged that the promise was in writing nor that the assets in the hands of the defendant covered the liabilities.

The Lord Chief Baron of the Exchequer then delivered the unanimous opinion of the judges of the Exchequer Chamber before the House of Lords, which re-asserted traditional doctrine. Skynner CB pronounced[68]:

> It is undoubtedly true that every man is by the law of nature bound to fulfil his engagements. It is equally true that the law of this country supplies no means, nor affords any remedy, to compel the performance of an agreement made without sufficient consideration . . . All contracts are, by the laws of England, distinguished into agreements by specialty, and agreements by parol; nor is there any such third class as some of the counsel have endeavoured to maintain, as contracts in writing. If they be merely written and not specialties, they are parol, and a consideration must be proved.

The House of Lords concurred and *Pillans* was out of favour, at least as a precedent on the enforceability of written promises.

## (b) The Moral Obligation Front

Lord Mansfield obviously regarded his assault on the citadel of consideration as requiring the opening up of at least two fronts. After *Pillans* he developed in the 1770s his parallel 'moral obligation' account of consideration[69] in the cases of

---

[67] *Rann v Hughes* (n 63 above) 4 Brown PC 27, 31.
[68] *Rann v Hughes* (n 63 above) (HL).
[69] Fifoot, *Lord Mansfield* (n 23 above) 134: 'alternative experiment'. More forthright: M Furmston, *Cheshire, Fifoot & Furmston's Law of Contract*, 15th edn (Oxford, Oxford University Press, 2007) 95, 'more insinuating'.

*Atkins v Hill*[70] and *Trueman v Fenton*.[71] Supposed instances included acknow-
ledgements of debts contracted in infancy, or in respect of which limitation had
expired, or promises by executors to pay legacies. In the 1780s, after the
rejection of *Pillans* in the House of Lords, we find Lord Mansfield happily
distinguishing *Rann v Hughes* in *Hawkes v Saunders*,[72] where it was held that
an action lay against an executrix on her promise to pay a legacy where she
knew she had the benefit of assets. He pronounced[73]:

> Where a man is under a legal or equitable obligation to pay, the law implies a promise,
> though none was ever actually made. A fortiori, a legal or equitable duty is a sufficient
> consideration for an actual promise. Where a man is under a moral obligation, which
> no Court of Law or Equity can inforce, and promises, the honesty and rectitude of the
> thing is a consideration. As if a man promises to pay a just debt, the recovery of which
> is barred by the Statute of Limitations: or if a man, after he comes of age, promises to
> pay a meritorious debt contracted during his minority, but not for necessaries; or if a
> bankrupt, in affluent circumstances after his certificate, promises to pay the whole of
> his debts; or if a man promise to perform a secret trust, or a trust void for want of writ-
> ing, by the Statute of Frauds.

*Rann* was distinguished on the grounds that there were no assets or that it was
not alleged there were any assets.[74] Lord Mansfield now accepted the necessity
for consideration, but was stretching its definition as far as he could. In that case
Buller J concisely stated the applicable principle:

> The true rule is, that whenever a defendant is under a moral obligation, or is liable in
> conscience or in equity to pay, that is a sufficient consideration.[75]

The moral obligation assault had greater longevity, surviving until 1840 and
*Eastwood v Kenyon*.[76]

## (c)  Promises to Answer for Another's Liability

Obviously section 4 of the Statute of Frauds 1677 continued and continues to
delimit the enforceability of guarantees.[77] At the end of the 18th century under
the Chief Justiceship of Lord Mansfield's successor, Lord Kenyon, the King's

---

[70] *Atkins v Hill* (1775) 1 Cowp 284, 288—9; 98 ER 1088. Oldham, *English Common Law in the
Age of Mansfield* (n 10 above) 85 dates the development back to 1772 and the unreported case of
*Bromfield v Wilson*.
[71] *Trueman v Fenton* (1777) 2 Cowp 544, 98 ER 1232.
[72] *Hawkes v Saunders* (1782) 1 Cowp 289, 98 ER 1091.
[73] *Ibid* 290.
[74] *Hawkes v Saunders* (n 72 above) 1 Cowp 289, 291. However as observed above, this had been
an alternative submission before the House of Lords in *Rann*.
[75] *Hawkes v Saunders* (n 72 above) 1 Cowp 289, 294.
[76] *Eastwood v Kenyon* (1840) 11 Ad & El 438, 113 ER 482 (Lord Denman CJ).
[77] Note the refusal of the House of Lords to circumvent the Act in *Actionstrength Ltd v
Intenational Glass Engineering IN.GL.EN SpA* [2003] UKHL 17, [2004] 2 AC 541. Contrast the
recent suggestion that a typed name at the end of an e-mail will suffice for the purposes of the Act:
*J Pereira Fernandes SA v Mehta* [2006] EWHC 813 (Civ), [2006] 1 WLR 1543.

Bench opened up a further front for claimants in respect of promises to answer for another's liability. In *Pasley v Freeman*,[78] the seminal case on the tort of deceit, it was held that an action would lie where the defendant made a false representation as to the creditworthiness of a third person to a plaintiff, who then dealt with that third person. It was sufficient that the plaintiff suffered a loss and was not necessary that the defendant should benefit. Lord Kenyon CJ observed[79]:

> There are many situations in life, and particularly in the commercial world, where a man cannot by any diligence inform himself of the degree of credit which ought to be given to the persons with whom he deals, in which case he must apply to those whose sources of intelligence enable them to give that information. The law of prudence leads him to apply to them, and the law of morality ought to induce them to give the information required.

This must have proved the basis for many actions, as it eventually provoked section 6 of the Statute of Frauds (Amendment) Act 1828 (often known as Lord Tenterden's Act), which required false representations to be in signed writing before they could form the basis of an action. This quirky restriction on the scope of deceit has somehow survived into the 21st century. Of course we now live in the post-*Hedley Byrne & Co Ltd v Heller & Partners Ltd*[80] world. Emphatic appellate authority states that the 1828 Act does not to apply to claims which are not based on fraud.[81] Somewhat asymmetrically, we have a formality pre-condition in the law of fraudulent misrepresentation in respect of representations about the creditworthiness of a third party, but no similar rule for a negligent misrepresentation of the same character.

## C. PERSPECTIVES

### 1. The History of the Law of Bills of Exchange

First, it is worth looking at the case from the relatively narrow perspective of the law on bills. Professor Rogers's brilliant study of the origins of our commercial law,[82] through the prism of the law governing bills of exchange, describes the widespread use of such bills in the 18th century as often the only means of discharging a payment obligation. However, they were not always dependable, being only as valuable as the promises of the persons who became obliged under them[83]:

---

[78] *Pasley v Freeman* (1789) 3 Term Rep 51, 100 ER 450.
[79] *Ibid* 3 Term Rep 51, 64.
[80] *Hedley Byrne & Co Ltd v Heller & Partners Ltd* [1964] AC 465 (HL).
[81] *Banbury v Bank of Montreal* [1918] AC 626 (PC).
[82] Rogers, *The Early History of the Law of Bills and Notes* (n 17 above).
[83] Rogers, *The Early History of the Law of Bills and Notes* (n 17 above) 195.

A bill or note might have been transferred from hand to hand in a long chain of payment transactions on the assumption that it would be paid by the drawee or the maker. In the case of bills, however the drawee was not legally bound until acceptance. Thus bills would have been passed from person to person long before it was known whether the drawee would incur any legal obligation to pay.

Even after acceptance the solvency of the drawee/acceptor was still a risk factor. Rogers describes how in modern texts on bills the discussion of the topic of acceptance is highly attenuated. In the leading modern American text it is accomplished in one page.[84] In stark contrast, in 18th century texts acceptance could account for a quarter of the text.[85] Despite the need for certainty in this field, the law yielded to practical reality and permitted both conditional acceptances and partial acceptances by drawees.[86] Furthermore, whilst it is now orthodox that only a party who appends his signature to a bill of exchange can be liable upon it,[87] earlier case law held a drawee liable in some cases, even in the absence of written acceptance. Rogers cites a pronouncement of Chief Justice Holt that 'a bill of exchange might be accepted by parol, tho' the usual way be to do it by writing'.[88]

For Rogers, *Pillans v Van Mierop* is crucial to the resolution of the debate about 'extrinsic acceptance' and 'virtual acceptance'. The former was a separate written undertaking to accept a bill already in existence. The latter was a promise to accept future bills. *Pillans* is a case of 'virtual acceptance'. It seems that Pillans and Rose never even drew up the anticipated reimbursement bills to send to Van Mierop and Hopkins before White & Co failed.

Acceptance financing permitted one merchant who shipped goods to another, and who drew a bill on the consignee, to discount the bill immediately in order to obtain ready funds in respect of the consignment. Greater credit was afforded in cases where a factor (later an accepting house) was willing to permit a merchant to draw a bill on him even prior to the sale or shipment of goods. If the factor's standing was good, the merchant would be able to discount the bill immediately and therefore finance the underlying transaction. As Rogers points out, much of the work done by such bills in oiling the wheels of commerce had already occurred before it reached the drawee for his acceptance.[89] A right of a merchant to draw upon a substantial house such as Barings would be very

---

[84] Rogers, *The Early History of the Law of Bills and Notes* (n 17 above): citing J White and R Summers, *Uniform Commercial Code*, 3rd edn (St Paul, West Publishing Co, 1988) 558. See White and Summers, 4th edn (St Paul, West Publishing Co, 1995) 471–2.

[85] Rogers, *The Early History of the Law of Bills and Notes* (n 17 above) 195–6: citing J Bayley, *A Short Treatise on the Law of Bills of Exchange, Cash Bills and Promissory Notes*, 1st edn (London, Brooke, 1789).

[86] Rogers, *The Early History of the Law of Bills and Notes* (n 17 above) 196–7.

[87] Bills of Exchange Act 1882, ss 17(2) and 23.

[88] *Anon* (1698) Holt 296, 297; 90 ER 1063; Rogers, *The Early History of the Law of Bills and Notes* (n 17 above) 198.

[89] Rogers, *The Early History of the Law of Bills and Notes* (n 17 above) 199.

valuable.[90] Such willingness to accept bills in the future was communicated by means of a 'letter of credit', the very phrase used in *Pillans* by Lord Mansfield.

Such 'letters of credit' have a lineage. The 17th century treatise by Gerard Malynes, *Consuetudo, vel, Lex Mercatoria: or, The Ancient Law-Merchant*,[91] describes the phenomenon. For Rogers the interest in *Pillans* lies not in the usual dicta on consideration, which attract the contract scholars, but rather in the liberal approach to acceptance. This appears in all the judgments, but most prominently in that of Mr Justice Wilmot. However in the early 19th century it was held that a promise to accept future bills could not bind.[92]

Consideration fundamentalism had re-asserted itself. There followed the sclerotic formalism which would attend the final formulation of (the various satellite maxims of) the doctrine of consideration in the full gothic splendour of its Victorian incarnation. So far as bills in particular were concerned, the matter was settled by statute in 1821 which laid down the modern rule that acceptance should be written on the face of the bill.[93] Fundamentalism about form and reliable evidence prevailed.

## 2. The History of the Law of Contract

More generally, *Pillans* is a central case in any account of the history of the Common law of contract, being the case which established the rationalist assault on the formalism inherent in the hegemony of consideration.[94] Whilst, generally speaking, conservatism prevailed in *Rann v Hughes*, the potential challenge by contract as promise to contract as exchange has been appreciated ever since, and has been adopted in some contexts.

Milsom's analysis of consideration stresses the delictual origins of *assumpsit*, and the presence of justified reliance.[95] His conclusion on Mansfield's judgment in *Pillans* is that he faced the same problems as late 20th century scholars trying to make sense of the doctrine of consideration[96]:

> Like the rational Lord Mansfield, we try to assign it some place as an element in a contract itself seen as an entity. But it has always been just the label on a package

[90] Rogers, *The Early History of the Law of Bills and Notes* (n 17 above) 200: citing RW Hidy, *The House of Baring in American Trade and Finance: English Merchant Bankers at Work 1763–1861* (Harvard Studies in Business History) No 14 (1949).

[91] G Malynes, *Consuetudo, vel, Lex Mercatoria: or, The Ancient Law-Merchant*, 3rd edn (1686; reprint Abingdon, Professional Books, 1981); (1st edn, 1622). *Consuetudo* is Latin for 'custom'.

[92] *Johnson v Collings* (1800) 1 East 98, 102 ER 40; *Bank of Ireland v Archer & Daly* (1843) 11 M & W 383, 152 ER 852. See also *Pierson v Dunlop* (1777) 2 Cowp 571, 152 ER 852 (Lord Mansfield retreating on acceptance).

[93] 1 & 2 George IV c 78, s 2; now superseded by Bills of Exchange Act 1882, s 17.

[94] Holdsworth, *A History of English Law* (n 13 above) vol VIII, 29–30, 34–6, 45–8; Baker, *An Introduction to English Legal History* (n 7 above) 351–2; Simpson, *A History of the Common Law of Contract* (n 7 above) 406–7.

[95] SFC Milsom, *Historical Foundations of the Common Law* (n 18 above) 356–60.

[96] SFC Milsom, *Historical Foundations of the Common Law* (n 18 above) 360.

containing many of the separate rules about the liabilities which may arise in the context of a transaction. Separate questions were answered by assertion, and at first they were asked in terms of reliance. Perhaps some answers were not ideal when the questions came to be asked in contractual terms.

This is suggestive of the view that a number of different tests of enforceability may be appropriate, and Milsom himself suggests the example of the United States, where deeds are not employed, but both consideration and reliance may ground liability.

Similarly, Simpson is sympathetic to Lord Mansfield's categorisation of consideration as a matter of evidence, rather than a true substantive requirement[97]:

> [I]n a sense Lord Mansfield's conception of consideration as 'evidence' is historically correct, if the idea is given a somewhat extended sense along the following lines. They jury, before holding the defendant liable, need something more to go on than merely a parole promise, inadequately perhaps proved, but if they can prove a good reason for the making of the promise which is also a good reason for holding the defendant liable then they can with more confidence award damages for breach, the consideration making it more plausible to say both that there was a promise and that it was seriously intended. But it must be emphasized that no such rationalization is to be found in the cases.

This is reminiscent of more modern doctrines where we see the courts reluctant to commit to firm probanda (matters which must be proved), but instead enumerate a number of factors which may tend to show the wrong complained of, such as in discussions of the comparatively recent vitiating factor of economic duress.[98] Both historians' accounts, and in particular Simpson's 'good reason' analysis, also provide grist for Atiyah's critique of modern English law. In contrast to Simpson's sympathy with the evidential categorisation, Baker is emphatic that Mansfield's suggestion 'was not a sound historical argument, but a deliberate attempt to reject the magic of the seal'.[99] As a result, Baker observes, the repudiation of this strategy in *Rann v Hughes* ensured the survival of this 'Tudor' doctrine into the 21st century.

## 3. Economic History

It is also worth placing the case in the wider context of the rise of modern commerce and finance. David Kynaston's account of the history of the City of London takes as its starting point the end of the Napoleonic wars, charting both the social and economic history of the individuals and institutions responsible for making the City great in the 19th century and beyond.[100] However in his

---

[97] Simpson, *A History of the Common Law of Contract* (n 7 above) 407.
[98] *DSND Subsea Ltd v Petroleum Geo-Services ASA* [2000] BLR 530, [131] (Dyson J).
[99] Baker, *An Introduction to English Legal History* (n 7 above) 352.
[100] Kynaston, *The City of London* (n 5 above).

detailed prologue Kynaston concisely sets the scene, identifying the beginnings of the emergence of the merchant banks of the 19th century from the merchant houses of the 18th century. Barings's strength in the 18th century was founded on both its close connection with the powerful merchant house of Hope & Co, which was based in Amsterdam, and its financing of North American trade.[101] Similarly, in the last two decades of the 18th century Bird, Savage & Strange exported manufactured goods to South Carolina (which was then probably the richest State in the newly formed United States), which in turn financed exotic imports such as rice and indigo. Kynaston then identifies the trade practice which underlies our case[102]:

> Credit was the crux, especially since many merchants, at home and abroad, began business with little or no capital. Systems of credit could be complicated things, but the basic mechanism on which they increasingly revolved was the sterling bill of exchange, a negotiable instrument through which a seller was able to receive payment for goods as soon as he had sent them on their way. Towards the end of the century a few of the leading London merchants, above all Barings, were taking on a 'finance' function and becoming what would eventually be termed merchant banks—or, more narrowly, accepting houses—to service the international trading community. It was a profitable business, done on a commission basis; but since it involved guaranteeing bills of exchange that would eventually be sold on the London bill market centred on the Royal Exchange, it was one that demanded the nicest possible judgement of clients, of trades, and of countries.

A number of important contextual factors require highlighting. First, the interest of exporters in payment or adequate assurance of payment by bill of exchange as soon as goods were shipped, probably in return for the bill of lading, representing the cargo at sea; and secondly, the increasing separation of the underlying physical transaction from the associated, but increasingly autonomous, financing mechanism. We observed this in *Pillans*, with the lack of reference to, or apparent interest in, the underlying cargo or traded goods. Thirdly, and crucially was the existence in the 18th century of a developed secondary market in bills. This was focused on the Royal Exchange, with its various specialist 'walks'—'Norway Walk', 'Virginia Walk' and 'Jews Walk'— together with the coffee shops, Garraway's of Change Alley (which was a centre of commodities trading), the 'Jamaica', the 'Jerusalem' and the 'Baltic', fore-runner of the Baltic Exchange. It is likely that bills such as White's bill initially drawn on Pillans and Rose, and the reimbursement bill which Pillans and Rose proposed to draw on Van Mierop and Hopkins, were to be traded or discounted on this secondary market. It would be vital to its attractiveness that such a bill bore the imprimatur of acceptance by a leading merchant house.

---

[101] Kynaston, *The City of London* (n 5 above) 11. At the end of the 18th century following the French invasion of The Netherlands, Hope & Co diminished to a virtual subsidiary of Barings, representing the eventual eclipse of Amsterdam by London: Kynaston (n 5 above) 23.

[102] Kynaston, *The City of London* (n 5 above) 12.

It seems likely, given Lord Mansfield's familiarity with, and lively curiosity concerning, mercantile practice, that he would have been aware of (or, at least, familiarised himself with) these considerations in deciding *Pillans*. It is clear from his remarks at the preliminary hearing that he was sensitive to this issue, and regarded the timing issue as one which might frustrate the trading of such bills. Furthermore, the marketplace and reputation of such houses depended on the honouring of such clear undertakings, which were likely to be circulated and relied on far beyond the original parties to the transaction.

The facts of *Pillans* took place in 1762. The following year a financial crisis struck. The Bank of England, founded in 1694 to finance war with France, had become a proto-Central Bank during the course of the next century. In 1763 it took an important further step in this process by acting as a lender of last resort for the first time in its history.[103] Lord Mansfield cannot have been unaware of this crisis. Despite this, the Bank of England remained a profit-making commercial entity in its own right. From the 1760s onwards it was a major player in discounting commercial bills, thereby providing short-term finance and increasing the liquidity of the marketplace in bills. Its prominence and power in this field was described by Sir Francis Baring[104]:

> Before the Revolution [in France in 1789] our Bank [referring to the Bank of England] was the centre upon which all credit and circulation depended, and it was at that time in the power of the Bank to affect the credit of individuals in a very great degree by refusing their paper.

We also know that in addition to the Bank of England, there were probably some 50 private banks operating in the City of London and engaged in the trade of discounting commercial bills by the 1770s. *Pillans* helped to facilitate this trade.

*Rann v Hughes* was not a bills case, so it may not have had much direct impact on bills practice. However, as we have seen, statute tightened up the rules on 'virtual acceptance' in England in the early 19th century. A decision by the Bank of England in 1837 to tighten up credit by refusing to support three UK merchant banks caused the three houses to fail, leaving some US$10 million of bills drawn by American merchants on them dishonoured, and leading to a rash of bankruptcies amongst American cotton merchants.[105] Once faith is gone, failure follows.

## 4. Comparative Perspective

Every legal system must grapple with the problem of which promises or agreements, and other voluntary arrangements, are to be attended by legal effects.

[103] Kynaston, *The City of London* (n 5 above) 13.
[104] Kynaston, *The City of London* (n 5 above) 14.
[105] Rogers, *The Early History of the Law of Bills and Notes* (n 17 above) 201.

Which promises should attract remedies backed up—ultimately—by the full coercive power of the state? The recognition of such powers to change one's legal rights and obligations through dealings with other citizens is the hallmark of a mature legal system. The apparent—but not real—paradox of the ability to limit one's freedom of action is the core to freedom of contract. We multiply our freedom by the ability to transact with others, in arrangements which ultimately attract legal sanction, and do not only depend on either moral opprobrium or prudential incentives.[106] Such arrangements provide the framework for the market economy. Mutual reliance, co-operation and planning can take place in a context where faith can be placed in such voluntary arrangements.

However, it is trite—but necessary—to point out that no legal system has ever gone to the extreme of enforcing all promises. The obvious counter-examples are social and domestic arrangements, which courts are reluctant to see attended by the full rigour of the law of contract. Something more than promise or agreement is needed. In the words of Professor Goode:

> Some further element is said to be necessary, such as the promisee's knowledge of the promise, his assent to it, the cause of French law, consideration, benefit, reliance, or solemnity of form.[107]

Most systems use both a form-based requirement and at least one other substantive requirement, such as the doctrine of consideration, for informal undertakings.

In their classic comparative text, Zweigert and Kotz entitle the chapter on this core issue: 'Indicia of Seriousness'.[108] They focus immediately on the distinction between promises with some stipulated return, which most systems readily enforce, and promises of gifts. Whilst most systems give effect to gifts perfected by actual delivery, promises to make gifts in the future are generally required to satisfy some further evidential step, such as notarial form in France[109] or deed in England.[110] In respect of informal promises English and American law generally require a requested counter-performance as a necessary condition for legal enforcement: the core idea of the 'extremely complex and subtle' doctrine of consideration.[111] However it may be misleading to suggest that a consideration must be bargained for, if this suggests that there is an enquiry into the adequacy of the return for the promise. Classically, a peppercorn will suffice.[112] Similarly, at

---

[106] C Fried, *Contract as Promise* (Cambridge MA, Harvard University Press, 1981).

[107] R Goode, 'Abstract Payment Undertakings' in P Cane and J Stapleton (eds), *Essays for Patrick Atiyah* (Oxford, Oxford University Press, 1991) 209, 210.

[108] Zweigert and Kotz, *An Introduction to Comparative Law* (n 3 above) 388–99.

[109] Code Civile, Art 931.

[110] Written instruments which traditionally had to be 'signed, sealed and delivered.' The position is now governed by s 1 of the Law of Property (Miscellaneous Provisions) Act 1989, which dispenses with the need for the customary wax seal.

[111] Zweigert and Kotz, *An Introduction to Comparative Law* (n 3 above) 390.

[112] Zweigert and Kotz, *An Introduction to Comparative Law* (n 3 above) 391. Famously, Lord Somervell: 'A peppercorn does not cease to be good consideration if it established that the promisee does not like pepper and will throw away the corn'. *Chappell & Co Ltd v Nestle Co Ltd* [1960] AC 87.

what may be the loveliest parish church in the Kingdom, at Long Melford in Suffolk, a single red rose laid on a tomb constitutes the annual rent for a market.

From the civil law perspective, Zweigert and Kotz consider some of the consequences of the doctrine of consideration 'surprising or even shocking',[113] given that it extends to all gratuitous promises—even in a business context, such as the gratuitous provision of bad advice, or undertaking to look after the property or affairs of another. Liability here will generally only be delictual in nature if loss occurs, and cannot be based on the breach of promise. Similarly, from that perspective, the pre-existing duty rules throw up strange results, such as in the well-known seamen's wages cases.[114] However they note that recent decisions now focus on the presence or absence of improper pressure.[115] English lawyers can only feel uncomfortable as Zweigert and Kotz brilliantly expose the empty formalism of the hunt for consideration in *Williams v Roffey Bros & Nicholls (Contractors) Ltd*,[116] supposedly resulting in some technical 'practical benefit' being identified. They scathingly conclude:

> The implausibility of the point merely shows how useless the doctrine of consideration is as a test of the validity of modifications of contractual arrangements.[117]

They further observe that difficulties are thrown up if the past consideration rule is applied mechanically and the impact on apparently 'binding offers'. However even in England with respect to the variation context and the inability to create binding offers:

> There is fairly general agreement that these outposts of the doctrine are indefensible and that the time has come to abandon them.[118]

However, the civilian approach outlined by Zweigert and Kotz does not identify with certainty an alternative approach, save that it is clear that the treatment of gratuitous promises differs, with many promises which would clearly fail for want of consideration or want of form in England, brought within the fold of enforceable promises on the Continent. Nevertheless, they note the potential of the doctrine of promissory estoppel in this context, particularly in the way it has developed in the United States. Zweigert and Kotz conclude in their comparison of the two approaches[119]:

> We have seen, too, that judges on the Continent approach the question whether a transaction was really gratuitous in a rather cavalier fashion and often hold a promise binding despite lack of form if the promisor was actuated by creditable motives. One

---

[113] Zweigert and Kotz, *An Introduction to Comparative Law* (n 3 above) 392.
[114] *Stilk v Myrick* (1809) 2 Camp 317, 170 ER 1168.
[115] Zweigert and Kotz, *An Introduction to Comparative Law* (n 3 above) 393.
[116] *Williams v Roffey Bros & Nicholls (Contractors) Ltd* [1991] 1 QB 1 (CA).
[117] Zweigert and Kotz, *An Introduction to Comparative Law* (n 3 above) 394. They point out the doctrine of consideration is rarely insisted on in the United States in the context of modifications: eg under the Uniform Commercial Code, § 2-209 (sales). Similarly, the Vienna Convention on the International Sale of Goods 1980 ('CISG') Art 29(1).
[118] Zweigert and Kotz, *An Introduction to Comparative Law* (n 3 above) 399.
[119] Zweigert and Kotz, *An Introduction to Comparative Law* (n 3 above) 399.

could object that this etiolates the requirement of form and creates legal uncertainty, but this objection hardly lies in the mouth of an English jurist when one considers how astute the English judges are at snuffling out some consideration lurking in the background.

The reproach of inventing consideration is here combined with the memorable image of the truffle-hunting pig. It is clear that all systems could benefit from abandoning the search for a monistic answer to the question of which (informal) promises should be enforced. It remains tragic that Lord Mansfield's suggested alternative route of writing in a commercial context was not embraced whole-heartedly.

## 5. Theoretical Perspective

There has been little writing on the doctrine of consideration in recent decades, save to welcome the barely coherent, but pragmatically attractive, decision of the Court of Appeal in *Williams v Roffey Bros & Nicholls (Contractors) Ltd*.[120] In terms of English theoretical writing, the titanic struggle was the Atiyah-Treitel debate of the 1970s. Atiyah's inaugural lecture at the Australian National University, 'Consideration in Contracts: A Fundamental Restatement', is the *locus classicus* of the pragmatic critique of the formalism of the modern doctrine of consideration.[121] Consideration simply meant a good reason for enforcing a promise, or more properly an obligation.

> From being merely a reason for the enforcement of a promise . . . it has come to be regarded as a technical doctrine which has little to do with the justice or desirability of enforcing a promise, or recognizing obligations.[122]

In fact, courts often enforced non-bargain promises for good reasons of policy. Atiyah then describes the variety of such arrangements, hidden from view by an excessive focus on consideration. In the commercial sphere, agency, bailment undertakings and bankers' commercial credits are obvious examples. It should go without saying that I agree wholeheartedly with Atiyah that consideration obscures the variety of voluntary transactions enforced by English law, albeit I may not go down the routes for reform he favours. Professor Treitel's more orthodox riposte is less convincing.[123] However, we can acquit Treitel of inventing the idea of 'invented consideration',[124] which clearly has a much longer history, as demonstrated in the judgments of Wilmot and Yates JJ in *Pillans*.

---

[120] *Williams v Roffey Bros* (n 116 above).

[121] PS Atiyah, 'Consideration in Contracts: A Fundamental Restatement' (Canberra, Australian National University Press, 1971); reprinted as 'Consideration: A Restatement' in PS Atiyah (ed), *Essays on Contract* (Oxford, Oxford University Press, 1986; paperback 1988) 179.

[122] P Atiyah, 'Consideration: A Restatement' (n 121 above) 186.

[123] GH Treitel, 'Consideration: A Critical Analysis of Professor Atiyah's Fundamental Restatement' (1976) 50 *Australian Law Journal* 439.

[124] Compare Atiyah, 'Consideration: A Restatement' (n 121 above) 182–3.

## D. RECEPTION AND THE MODERN LAW

### 1. Professor Atiyah's Account of the Reception of *Pillans v Van Mierop*

Before briefly surveying the modern law to locate the fruits which have resulted from Lord Mansfield's bold propositions, it is worth citing Atiyah's more historical account of the fate of *Pillans v Van Mierop* at the hands of the House of Lords in *Rann v Hughes*[125]:

> to say that Mansfield's views were 'over-ruled' is too simple an account of what was happening. When Mansfield talked of consideration being evidence only, he was in effect saying, or certainly implying, not one proposition, but three:
>
> [1] first, that the primary basis of contractual liability is the intention of the parties, and not the consideration;
> [2] secondly, that consideration is merely evidence of the parties' intentions;
> [3] thirdly, that other forms of evidence (such as, in a business case, a writing,), may be equally satisfactory . . .
>
> *Rann v Hughes* rejected the third of Mansfield's propositions. But the second has been largely accepted, at any rate at the level of theory, and the first has without doubt, formed the very basis of contractual liability for nearly two hundred years (numbering added).

Overall Lord Mansfield's dictum has 'triumphed beyond measure'. However, Atiyah's main thesis is that Mansfield's theory of contractual liability was obsolescent. I agree with Atiyah's historical assessment, but not with his prognosis for the future. As is well known, since the publication of Atiyah's *magnum opus* in 1979, freedom of contract, and neo-classical contract theory have enjoyed a renaissance. Lord Mansfield's philosophy is reflected in modern case law, and is often still directly cited.

### 2. Modern Contract Law

Atiyah's first proposition about *Pillans*—the role of the intention of the parties—forms the intellectual basis of modern contract law, having achieved hegemony in the 19th century.[126] It was developed by Lord Mansfield and his brethren in the King's Bench in the 18th century. According to Baker,

> Even as late as 1800, the content of the law of contracts was slight by comparison with the bulky textbooks in use by 1900. There were many old cases on consideration, and a great deal on pleading.[127]

---

[125] PS Atiyah, *The Rise and Fall of Freedom of Contract* (Oxford, Oxford University Press, 1979) 216.

[126] See generally AWB Simpson, 'Innovation in Nineteenth Century Contract Law' (1975) 91 *Law Quarterly Review* 247.

[127] Baker, *An Introduction to English Legal History* (n 7 above) 350.

However, if one treats as the workaday business of the courts the ascertainment of the intentions of the parties[128]—either in establishing whether a contract has been formed or in discerning the meaning and effect of its terms—the techniques were established in judgments of the King's Bench before the 19th century. Fifoot, Lord Mansfield's biographer, stated that he

> started with the assumption that an agreement, as such, was worthy of sanction. The intention of the parties, not the accidental influence of the forms of action, was to determine the scope of the contract.[129]

One of the first—albeit peculiar from a comparative perspective—orthodoxies of English contract law is that the construction of written documents is a question of law (and therefore for the judge, and not civil juries whilst they were extant in this context). This was clearly established in Lord Mansfield's court. In *Macbeath v Haldimond* he pronounced:

> the evidence consisting altogether of written documents and letters which were not denied, and the import of them was a matter of law and not of fact.[130]

Similarly, the fundamental need for certainty in commercial transactions, which is constantly invoked in this field, was emphasised by Lord Mansfield in *Vallejo v Wheeler*: 'In all mercantile transactions the great object should be certainty'.[131]

Two of the principal features of modern approaches to the construction of contracts are said to be the rejection of literalism in favour of an approach which gives effect to the commercial purpose of a transaction, and a broadly contextual approach to language. In construing an instrument, Lord Mansfield was willing to have regard to the document as a whole, and not just its operative provisions. For example, in *Moore v Magrath*[132] Lord Mansfield stated:

> The deed begins with the preamble usual in all settlements; that is, by reciting what it is the grantor intends to do; and that, like the preamble to an Act of Parliament, is the key to what comes afterwards.

This demonstrates both regard to wider internal context and to the business purpose of the transaction. Beyond the four corners of the instrument he was

---

[128] See also Oldham, *English Common Law in the Age of Mansfield* (n 10 above) 84–7.

[129] Fifoot, *Lord Mansfield* (n 23 above) 121.

[130] *Macbeath v Haldimond* (1786) 1 Term Rep 172, 180; 99 ER 1036. Still orthodoxy: *Pioneer Shipping Ltd v BTP Tioxide Ltd, The Nema* [1982] AC 724 (HL); *Antaios Compania Naviera SA v Salen Rederierna AB, The Antaios* [1985] AC 191 (HL) 199, albeit Lord Diplock was scathing of: 'that insistence upon meticulous semantic and syntactical analysis of the words in which business men happen to have chosen to express the bargain made between them, the meaning of which is technically, though hardly commonsensically, classified in English jurisprudence as a pure question of law'.

[131] *Vallejo v Wheeler* (1774) 1 Cowp 143, 153; 98 ER 1012. Recently quoted with approval by Lord Bingham in *Hombourg Houtimport BV v Agrosin Private Ltd, The Starsin* [2003] UKHL 12, [2004] 1 AC 715, [12].

[132] *Moore v Magrath* (1774) 1 Cowp 9, 12; 98 ER 939. Contrast the orthodox application by the court of parol the evidence rule to prevent oral evidence contradicting a written contract concerning land (which had been admitted at trial by Lord Mansfield) in *Meres v Ansell* (1771) 3 Wils KB 275, 95 ER 1053.

prepared to have regard to the external context, and in particular the obvious commercial context, and what would have been well known to the parties to the transaction. In *Barclay v Lucas*[133] the plaintiffs' house engaged a banking clerk and the defendant provided them with a guarantee in respect of his fidelity. The clerk proved unworthy of the trust of either party and embezzled funds. The defendant contended its bond was vitiated by the admission of a new partner into the plaintiffs' business. Lord Mansfield responded:

> This question turns upon the meaning of the parties. In endeavouring to discover that meaning, the subject-matter of the contract is to be considered. It is notorious that these banking houses continue for ages with the occasional addition of new partners.[134]

The bond was upheld. Good faith in the interpretation of contracts (even in the absence of express stipulation) also demanded that it was in 'the very nature of a sale by auction . . . that the goods shall go to the highest real bidder', and that hired 'puffers' were a fraud on the public.[135]

Lord Mansfield also was able to handle contradictory instruments, resulting from what is sometimes now called the 'patchwork quilt' nature of standard forms. In *Hotham v East India Company* he proclaimed[136]:

> This charter-party is an old instrument informal and, by the introduction of different clauses at different times, inaccurate, and sometimes contradictory. Like all mercantile contracts, it ought to have a liberal interpretation. In construing agreements, I know of no difference between a Court of Law and a Court of Equity.

That is the English approach to the construction of commercial documents in a nutshell. The rejection of any distinction between Common law and equitable principles of construction was emphatically affirmed by the House of Lords in 2001.[137] Whilst the modern restatement of the principles of contractual construction eschews the language of party intention until the fifth of five fundamental propositions, it seems indisputable that the ascertainment of the intentions of the parties—albeit objectively ascertained against the available background—is the underlying aim of this central technique.[138]

Similarly, the most commonly cited guidance on the question whether negotiations have crystallised into a binding a contract is obviously indebted to Lord

---

[133] *Barclay v Lucas* (1783) 3 Douglas 321, 99 ER 676; 1 Term Rep 291n, 99 ER 1100.

[134] *Ibid* 3 Douglas 321, 325.

[135] *Bexwell v Christie* (1776) 1 Cowp 395, 98 ER 1150.

[136] *Hotham v East India Company* (1779) 1 Dougl 272, 277; 99 ER 178, 181. Compare *Hombourg Houtimport BV v Agrosin Private Ltd, The Starsin* [2003] UKHL 12, [2004] 1 AC 715, [12]. Lord Bingham stated there that 'to seek perfect consistency and economy of draftsmanship in a complex form of contract which has evolved over many years is to pursue a chimera'. See also *Beaufort Developments (NI) Ltd v Gilbert-Ash NI Ltd* [1999] AC 266 (HL) 274 where Lord Hoffmann commented: 'In the case of a contract which has been periodically renegotiated, amended and added to over many years, it is unreasonable to expect that there will be no redundancies or loose ends'.

[137] *Bank of Credit and Commerce International SA v Ali* [2001] UKHL 8; [2002] 1 AC 251.

[138] *Investors Compensation Scheme Ltd v West Bromwich Building Society* [1998] 1 WLR 896 (HL) 912–13 (Lord Hoffmann).

Mansfield's approach. Valuable guidance was given on the rules of contractual formation at first instance and in the Court of Appeal in *Pagnan SpA v Feed Products Ltd*[139] in the judgments of Bingham J and of Lloyd LJ. Whilst rarely cited in academic discussions, in practice these principles are regularly cited and applied. Most strikingly, Bingham J asserted:

> The parties are to be regarded as the masters of their contractual fate. It is their intentions which matter and to which the Court must strive to give effect.[140]

Lastly, whilst we have earlier noted the incoherence of the implausible search for consideration in the leading modern case on consideration—the decision of the Court of Appeal in *Williams v Roffey Bros & Nicholls (Contractors) Ltd*[141]—it is still worth citing the dictum of Russell LJ, just to observe how close it comes to embracing Lord Mansfield's bold approach[142]:

> Consideration there must still be but, in my judgment, the courts nowadays should be more ready to find its existence so as to reflect the intention of the parties to the contract where the bargaining powers are not unequal and where the finding of consideration reflect [*scilicet* reflects] the true intention of the parties.

## 3. Modern Commercial Law

We have already mentioned agency and bailment transactions as examples of commercial arrangements which are upheld irrespective of consideration. One could add the modern recognition of a general principle of tortious liability for the negligent provision of services where a party has assumed responsibility for a particular task—be it the provision of advice or information, or the rendering of other services.[143] Furthermore, many financial instruments to this day involve payment obligations which appear to defy the need for consideration. The need for consideration in bills of exchange is moderated by statutory fiat.[144]

### (a) Professor Goode's Concept of Abstract Payment Undertakings

Our leading academic commercial lawyer, Professor Sir Roy Goode, has articulated the concept of the abstract payment undertaking, which he says violates 'every principle of law governing the formation of contracts'.[145] He describes

---

[139] *Pagnan SpA v Feed Products Ltd* [1987] 2 Lloyd's Rep 601 (QBD (Comm Ct) and CA).

[140] *Ibid* 610–11; citing Lord Denning MR in *Port Sudan Cotton Co v Chettiar* [1977] 2 Lloyd's Rep 5, 10 (CA).

[141] *Williams v Roffey Bros* (n 116 above).

[142] *Williams v Roffey Bros* (n 116 above) 18.

[143] *Henderson v Merrett Syndicates Ltd* [1995] 2 AC 145 (HL).

[144] Bills of Exchange Act 1882, ss 27–30.

[145] Goode, 'Abstract Payment Undertakings' (n 107 above) 209–35. Contrast Atiyah's view that there is consideration, albeit supplied by the buyer (a third party): PS Atiyah, 'Consideration: A Restatement' (n 121 above) 222–3.

the insulation of such obligations or instruments from the underlying supply transaction. He instances: the documentary credit; the documentary guarantee or standby credit (sometimes more colourfully known as the 'suicide bond'); the non-documentary inter-bank payment order; and briefly, both the medieval law of bonds and the negotiable instrument.[146] Two motives are usual. First, to insulate such undertakings from defences raised by the obligor arising from the underlying transaction; and secondly, to facilitate the transferability of the payment undertaking (so insulated). The use of a documentary instrument to embody the promise assists in achieving both objectives. The negotiable instrument as it emerged in its final shape in the 19th century, whilst achieving a high level of abstraction, was never entirely divorced from the underlying realities of the transaction. The theory that it was a mercantile specialty, enforceable without consideration, was repudiated. The modern bill is not exposed to the full rigour of the doctrine of consideration, as consideration is presumed by statute, and it need not move from the promisee.[147] Similarly a good faith purchaser for value of the instrument—or a 'holder in due course' in the jargon of bills law— is to a large degree insulated from defects in the title to the bill and defences arising from the underlying contract. However as the holder in due course ultimately only acquires the rights of the original payee, such an instrument is not wholly 'abstract' in the sense intended by Professor Goode.[148]

## (b) Letters of Credit

Perhaps of more interest for our current concerns are Professor Goode's view on documentary credits. During the 20th century documentary credits or letters of credit emerged internationally as one of the principal methods of facilitating and financing export and import transactions, particularly where the parties dealt at arm's length and had little previous trading history.

The documentary credit is a further refinement of the classic use of the bill of exchange as a means of discharging the payment obligation under international sales, and in particular those documentary sales (such as c.i.f. contracts and some f.o.b. transactions, where the price is paid against shipping documents). The use of so-called 'documentary bills' can be seen in section 19(3) of the Sale of Goods Act 1979 (in the same form as the original 1893 Act), whereby the seller tendering the shipping documents (comprising his invoice and, at least, a bill of lading or other carriage contract) also tenders a bill of exchange as

---

[146] On a personal or anecdotal note, I was one of those in attendance for Professor Goode's first undergraduate lecture as the first Professor of Commercial Law at the University of Oxford in academic year 1989–90. The topic was supposed to be documentary credits, but he announced that we could not properly understand this species of contract without first grappling with bills of exchange (which were off the syllabus, and therefore not to be examined), which he proceeded to do brilliantly (albeit without any citation of authority) for the first of four scheduled lectures. It has taken me many years to grasp why this was necessary!

[147] Bills of Exchange Act 1882, ss 27 and 30.

[148] Goode, 'Abstract Payment Undertakings' (n 107 above) 216–17.

drawer, directed to the buyer as drawee. If the buyer refuses to accept the bill, he must return all the documents and no property in the goods passes to him.

The documentary credit employs the international banking system to handle the documents and mechanics of payment. The mechanics are to a large extent prescribed by an international codification of banking practice, the Uniform Customs and Practice for Documentary Credits.[149] Where the sale contract provides for payment by documentary credit the buyer (as 'applicant') approaches a merchant or commercial bank in his country and requests it to open a credit in the name of the seller. The bank (the 'issuing bank') will utilise the services of a correspondent bank in the seller's country. If the latter bank agrees to add its promise to pay to the promise of the issuing bank it becomes a 'confirming' bank, and the credit is 'confirmed.' In an unconfirmed credit the seller (or 'beneficiary') has the benefit of an undertaking to pay from one bank, and in a confirmed credit, the benefit of two banks' promises. The undertaking of the bank(s) replaces the buyer's usual obligation to pay under the sale contract.

Properly analysed, the transaction has now spawned five autonomous, albeit related, contractual relationships. In the leading case of *The American Accord*[150] Lord Diplock described them as follows[151]:

(1) The underlying contract for the sale of goods, to which the only parties are the buyer and the seller; (2) the contract between the buyer and the issuing bank under which the latter agrees to issue the credit and either itself or through a confirming bank to notify the credit to the seller and to make payments to or to the order of the seller (or to pay, accept or negotiate bills of exchange drawn by the seller) against presentation of stipulated documents; and the buyer agrees to reimburse the issuing bank for payments made under the credit. For such reimbursement the stipulated documents, if they include a document of title such as a bill of lading, constitute a security available to the issuing bank; (3) if payment is to be made through a confirming bank the contract between the issuing bank and the confirming bank authorising and requiring the latter to make such payments and to remit the stipulated documents to the issuing bank when they are received, the issuing bank in turn agreeing to reimburse the confirming bank for payments made under the credit; (4) the contract between the confirming bank and the seller under which the confirming bank undertakes to pay to the seller (or to accept or negotiate without recourse to drawer bills of exchange drawn by him) up to the amount of the credit against presentation of the stipulated documents.

Lord Diplock leaves out a fifth contract: the promise to pay owed directly by issuing bank to the seller/beneficiary. Three of the these contracts—the underlying sale, the banking services rendered by the issuing bank to buyer, and by the

---

[149] The UCP was introduced by the International Chamber of Commerce in 1931, and has been revised in 2007 as 'UCP 600'. For discussion see E Ellinger, 'The Uniform Customs and Practice for Documentary Credits (UCP): their development and the current revisions' [2007] *Lloyd's Maritime & Commercial Law Quarterly* 152. We can be sure Lord Mansfield would have been intrigued by this harmonising measure.

[150] *United City Merchants (Investments) Ltd v Royal Bank of Canada, The American Accord* [1983] 1 AC 168 (HL). The other members of the House of Lords agreed with the single speech.

[151] *Ibid* 183.

confirming bank to issuing bank—are entirely orthodox, bipartite, bilateral contracts, with the banking services being remunerated by fee or commission.

In contrast, the undertakings of the issuing bank and the confirming bank to the seller/beneficiary are traditionally said to be difficult to explain in accordance with orthodox English contract law. The undertaking will usually be contained in a document sent by either bank (more commonly, the confirming bank) which advises the beneficiary that a credit is open in his name, identifying the two banks, the opening and closing dates for exercising the rights, and specifying the documents which the beneficiary must present in order to obtain the funds or other financial accommodation (often the acceptance or negotiation of a 'time' bill of exchange deferred for say 90 or 180 days) in return. Professor Goode summarises the conceptual problems this poses for English lawyers[152]:

> Various ingenious theories have been advanced to reconcile the binding effect of the documentary credit with traditional concepts of contract law, for example, that the credit is a guarantee; that the bank issues the credit as agent of the buyer; that the consideration for the credit is a beneficiary's agreement to present the shipping documents, or alternatively is the actual presentation of the documents; that the credit becomes binding as a result of the [seller's] reliance on it, such reliance either constituting acceptance of the offer giving rise to a unilateral contract or making the bank's undertaking binding by estoppel; that the credit is a form of negotiable instrument.

Goode considers that none of these theories adequately explains or justifies the commercial understanding that the banks' obligations are as principals (not merely ministerially on behalf of the buyer), that they arise from communication of the advice that the credit is open, and are irrevocable from the date of advice to the date of expiry.

It is important not to overstate the difficulties for English law of accommodating letters of credit. Once a beneficiary presents the requested conforming documents stipulated under the credit, it would seem axiomatic that the bank is obliged on ordinary principles of unilateral contract reasoning. However the resources of English law appear not to be able to explain the 'irrevocability' of irrevocable letters of credit. That is, it is only the 'binding offer' aspect of the promise which is problematic. On long-established principles ('If you walk to York I will give you £100') the actual presentation of conforming documents surely equates to arriving at the doors of the Minster. It may even be arguable that steps taken in anticipation of performance of tendering—such as shipping the goods and procuring a bill of lading—could preclude the bank offeror from withdrawing his promise.[153] One could go further. There is modern House of Lords authority—albeit the conservatism of commentators has sidelined this analysis—which supports the view that the unilateral contract device is flexible enough in English law to give effect to 'irrevocable offers', if that reflects the intentions of the parties.

---

[152] Goode, 'Abstract Payment Undertakings' (n 107 above) 218. I have substituted 'seller's' for 'buyer's' where it obviously appears in error.

[153] At least if the approach of Denning LJ in *Errington v Errington* [1952] 1 KB 290 (CA) 295 is followed.

The case of *Harvela Investments Ltd v Royal Trust Company of Canada (CI) Ltd*[154] is usually cited for its rejection of referential bids. Two families were locked in a struggle to win control of a company: the Harvey family and the Outerbridge family. RT (the first defendant) invited the plaintiff, Harvela (the Harvey family), and Sir Leonard Outerbridge to submit offers by sealed bid for the controlling stake in the company. The invitation expressly stated:

> We confirm that if any offer made by you is the highest offer received by us we bind ourselves to accept such offer provided that such offer complies with the terms of this telex.[155]

Harvela's offer was CAN$2,175,000. Sir Leonard's offer was

> Canadian $2,100,000 or Canadian $101,000 in excess of any other offer . . . expressed as a fixed monetary amount, whichever is higher.

RT accepted Sir Leonard's bid. The plaintiff claimed it had a binding contractual entitlement to the shares and sought and obtained specific performance, which was upheld by the House of Lords. All members of the House agreed with both Lord Templeman's principal speech and Lord Diplock's 'footnotes'. The latter approached the bindingness of RT's promise as a matter of construction[156]:

> The construction question turns upon the wording of the telex of 15 September 1981 referred to by Lord Templeman as 'the invitation' and addressed to both Harvela and Sir Leonard. It was not a mere invitation to negotiate for the sale of the shares in Harvey & Co. Ltd. of which the vendors were the registered owners in the capacity of trustees. Its legal nature was that of a unilateral or 'if' contract, or rather of two unilateral contracts in identical terms to one of which the vendors and Harvela were the parties as promisor and promisee respectively, while to the other the vendors were promisor and Sir Leonard was promisee. Such unilateral contracts were made at the time when the invitation was received by the promisee to whom it was addressed by the vendors; under neither of them did the promisee, Harvela and Sir Leonard respectively, assume any legal obligation to anyone to do or refrain from doing anything.
>
> The vendors, on the other hand, did assume a legal obligation to the promisee under each contract. That obligation was conditional upon the happening, after the unilateral contract had been made, of an event which was specified in the invitation; the obligation was to enter into a synallagmatic contract to sell the shares to the promisee, the terms of such synallagmatic contract being also set out in the invitation.

The crucial words are: 'Such unilateral contracts were made at the time when the invitation was received by the promisee to whom it was addressed'. This would equally explain the binding force of irrevocable letters of credit from the

---

[154] *Harvela Investments Ltd v Royal Trust Company of Canada (CI) Ltd* [1986] AC 207 (HL).

[155] Compare *Spencer v Harding* (1870) LR 5 CP 561, 563: 'If the circular had gone on, "and we undertake to sell to the highest bidder," the reward cases would have applied, and there would have been a good contract in respect of the persons'. (Willes J).

[156] *Harvela Investments* (n 154 above) 224.

time of receipt by the seller/beneficiary. It can obviously be objected that such an approach is inconsistent with the orthodoxy that unilateral contract's binding force derives from (at least commencing) the stipulated counter-performance in reliance on the offer. However the House of Lords here was clearly and self-consciously expanding the unilateral contract device. It may be objected that Lord Diplock's account was obiter dicta. This will not wash because the obligatory nature of the vendor's obligation was essential to the holding in the case. He was compelled to perform the sale of shares in accordance with the true construction of his offer. It was not merely optional for him to sell to the plaintiff. He had irrevocably bound himself to do so. RT was not free to renounce its offer before it opened the sealed bids. It is just about possible to say that RT was not bound prior to the plaintiffs submitting the higher bid. However the reasoning is clearly wider than that.

One would have expected that academic commentators would have welcomed the House of Lords clearly providing a vehicle for binding irrevocable offers and similar proposals. Surprisingly the decision has been marginalised as unorthodox and has been largely forgotten. This should not be the fate of such a commercially sensible and rational decision. As I have sought to argue it provides an explanation for the binding force of letters of credit.

Returning to Goode, he concludes[157]:

> The state of English jurisprudence on letters of credit is rather curious. It is well over two hundred years since Lord Mansfield's valiant attempt in *Pillans v Van Mierop* (a case involving what was in essence a letter of credit) to demonstrate that contracts were enforceable without consideration was defeated by the House of Lords in *Rann v Hughes* and to this day there is no reported English case which directly holds that a letter of credit becomes binding on receipt despite the lack of consideration in the ordinary sense. . . . But there are dicta in several cases in which the courts have taken it for granted that letters of credit are enforceable undertakings and any argument to the contrary would be likely to receive short shrift at the hands of the judiciary.

Accordingly consideration fundamentalism is eschewed where commercial necessity demands it. Either as a unilateral contract, a sui generis rule, or on Professor Goode's broader conception of autonomous or abstract payment undertakings, the promises are enforced. The spirit of Lord Mansfield and his bold proposition still hold considerable sway. Whilst his boldest proposition in *Pillans* has not yet been accepted, his underlying philosophy remains crucial in contract law and underpins commerce and finance now as then.

---

[157] Goode, 'Abstract Payment Undertakings' (n 107 above) 218–19.

# 3

# Carter v Boehm (1766)

## STEPHEN WATTERSON*

### A. INTRODUCTION

O N 9 MAY 1760, an insurance policy was effected in London on the instructions of Roger Carter, then Deputy Governor of the East India Company's factory at Fort Marlborough, Bencoolen, Sumatra. These instructions had been dispatched from Bencoolen more than eight months previously, addressed to Roger Carter's brother and agent in London. The policy ultimately effected covered the risk of a European enemy assault on Fort Marlborough for one year running from October 1759. However, events had already taken a fateful course. On 5 February 1760, a French privateering expedition under the command of the Count D'Estaing had arrived off the West Coast of Sumatra. Within 10 days, Natal and Tapanouly, two of the East India Company's subordinate settlements to the north of Bencoolen, had fallen. Another six weeks later, D'Estaing's ships had appeared in the sea off Fort Marlborough. By 3 April 1760, it too had fallen into French hands, and the Company's servants there, including Roger Carter, had surrendered and been taken prisoner. Over the ensuing six weeks, the Company's remaining settlements on the West Coast fell to D'Estaing's men.

Carter's resulting insurance claim was resisted by the underwriters on the ground of non-disclosure. It was finally upheld only after protracted litigation, which culminated in the reported decision of the Court of King's Bench in *Carter v Boehm*.[1] Lord Mansfield's judgment in that case unquestionably ranks as a landmark in the development of the law of non-disclosure between parties to insurance contracts. Unfortunately, more than two centuries on, and as the

* I am very grateful to Charles Mitchell and Francis Rose for their comments on an earlier draft of this chapter, and to the staff of the British Library's Asian and African Studies Reading Room for their patience during my long trawls through the India Office Records. I am also indebted to the Society of Legal Scholars, from whom I received a grant to undertake the archival research on which this chapter is substantially based. Any errors are solely my responsibility.
[1] *Carter v Boehm* (1766) 3 Burr 1905, 97 ER 1162; (1766) 1 Black W 593, 96 ER 342. The reported decision is of the Court of King's Bench, hearing and dismissing the insurer's motion for re-trial, which had been brought after a verdict had been given for the insured by a special jury sitting with Lord Mansfield at Guildhall. Lord Mansfield delivered the opinion of the court.

case is relegated to the footnotes of modern texts, its real significance can be missed. As the leading early authority in an area of the law that has come to be viewed—and often criticised—as dramatically pro-insurer in orientation, it is easy to assume that *Carter v Boehm* shared that bias. Little could be further from the truth. Lord Mansfield began his judgment in *Carter v Boehm* with an unprecedented statement of common law principle, one purpose of which was to explain the many circumstances in which an insurer could *not* avoid liability for material non-disclosure by a prospective insured. The same orientation is also evident in the robust manner in which Lord Mansfield proceeded to apply those principles to the case at hand. Every ground for resisting liability offered by Charles Boehm, the underwriter named as defendant in the 1766 litigation, was rejected.

As this area of the law is currently under the scrutiny of law reformers once more,[2] it seems timely to remind ourselves of this important historical reality. To this end, this chapter proceeds in three stages. It begins by outlining so much general historical background as is required for a proper understanding of the litigation, before looking more closely at the nature of Carter's insurance policy. It concludes by revisiting Lord Mansfield's judgment, focusing first on Lord Mansfield's seminal statement of the law of non-disclosure, and then on the court's resolution of Boehm's arguments for avoiding liability.

## B. THE GENERAL HISTORICAL BACKGROUND

### 1. Fort Marlborough, Sumatra

In the early stages of the English East India Company's life, the spices of South-East Asia were thought to offer some of the richest pickings for European traders. To this end, the Company maintained an important trading presence at Bantam, West Java, for much of the 17th century. This foothold was lost in the early 1680s, when the local sultan awarded the privilege of exclusive trade in his territories to the Company's main regional trading rival, the Dutch East India Company. Forced to look elsewhere to continue its involvement in the region's pepper trade, the Company turned to the neighbouring island of Sumatra. A mission culminated in the establishment of a fortified trading settlement in 1685 at Bencoolen, on the West Coast of Sumatra.[3] The fortified settlement was moved two miles to the south of its initial site over the period 1712–16, where 'Fort Marlborough' was established.[4]

---

[2] See Law Commission, *Insurance Contract Law: Misrepresentation, Non-Disclosure and Breach of Warranty by the Insured* (LCCP No 182, 2007).

[3] See, eg J Bastin, *The British in West Sumatra (1685–1825)* (Kuala Lumpur, University of Malaya Press, 1965) xi–xiii. The introductory chapter to this collection of sources contains a brief historical overview of the factory's history from its foundation until 1824.

[4] Bastin, *The British in West Sumatra* (n 3 above) xvii.

By the mid-18th century, the Company's influence on the West Coast had grown to the point where Fort Marlborough was served by a series of coastal out-settlements—including Tapanouly, Natal, Moco Moco, Ippo, Cattown, and Laye to the north, and Salooma, Manna, Cawoor, and Croce to the south. Nevertheless, as in India, where the European Companies characteristically maintained trading centres in close proximity, the English Company was not alone in this region. The Dutch Company maintained trading settlements on the West Coast. Furthermore, in very close proximity on Java lay Batavia, the Dutch Company's headquarters in the East Indies and the hub of a vast Dutch trade network.[5] The English Company would maintain its presence on the West Coast, and an uneasy relationship with its Dutch neighbours, until 1824, when all of its establishments there were finally ceded to the Dutch.[6]

As its name might imply, the settlement at Fort Marlborough was fortified and garrisoned by a small private army.[7] Nevertheless, this was only for the protection of what was fundamentally a trading community, run by merchants in the Company's civil service. Up to the time of its loss in 1760, Fort Marlborough was a subordinate Company factory, under the close supervision of the Company's Presidency at Fort St George, Madras. As such, it was headed by a 'Deputy Governor' and Council, comprising the most senior members of the 25–50 covenanted civil servants stationed there from time to time. To understand the insurance claim in *Carter v Boehm* it must be appreciated that these civil servants led double lives. On the one hand, they were employed to conduct the Company's commercial affairs on Sumatra. This meant, first and foremost, managing the procurement of pepper from the West Coast's plantations, and its safe consignment on the East Indiamen that arrived from London each year. On the other hand, these same civil servants were also private merchants. By the terms of their employment with the Company, they had the privilege of private trade within the East Indies. It was from this private 'country trade', rather than the Company's salaries, that fortunes might be made.

Roger Carter's early career path seems typical of the young men who sought their fortunes as covenanted civil servants at Bencoolen in the first half of the 18th century. Born in 1723, a younger son of a Lincolnshire landowning family, Roger could have had no expectation of inheriting the family's lands.[8] No doubt for this reason, his father, William, petitioned the Court of Directors of the East

---

[5] See, for a short overview, EM Jacobs, *In Pursuit of Pepper and Tea—The Story of the Dutch East India Company* (Zutphen, Walburg Pers, 1991) 73–8.

[6] Treaty Between His Britannick Majesty and the King of the Netherlands Respecting Territory and Commerce in the East Indies, 17 March 1824, Art IX (extracted in Bastin, *The British in West Sumatra* (n 3 above) 190, document 154).

[7] See generally AJ Harfield, *Bencoolen—A History of the Honourable East India Company's Garrison on the West Coast of Sumatra (1685–1825)* (Barton-on-Sea, A&J Partnership, 1995).

[8] The Redbourne Hall deposit held at the Lincolnshire County Archives contains a substantial deposit of documents relating mainly to the Carter family's Lincolnshire estates. The Lincolnshire Archives' Committee, *Archivists' Report No 8* (1956–57) 45–51, usefully summarises the process by which the family acquired and then lost the estates.

India Company in 1741 to have Roger appointed Writer at Bencoolen.[9] The petition succeeded, and in the 14 years that followed his arrival on the West Coast in August 1742, Carter rose steadily through the Company's ranks at Fort Marlborough. After five years as Writer, he rose to Factor[10]; by 1753, he had joined the Council[11]; and by early 1756, he was fourth in Council, soon to be third.[12] By this time, however, he had already made the decision to resign the Company's service and return to London,[13] apparently in a bid to secure his elevation at Fort Marlborough, or some favourable posting elsewhere. The bid succeeded. Arriving in London in late 1756, Carter tendered his services 'in whatever manner may be conducive to the Service of the Company'.[14] The Court of Directors decided that he was the right man to be the new Deputy Governor at Fort Marlborough, at the head of a re-modelled Council of nine.[15]

## 2. The Emerging Threat of a French Attack on Fort Marlborough

Roger Carter did not finally set foot again at Fort Marlborough, to take up his new position as Deputy Governor, until May 1758.[16] In the two years since his departure, events had taken a momentous change of course. The Seven Years' War had begun in Europe; by May 1756 England and France were at war once again; and within a short space of time, direct Anglo-French conflict had spread to India. Fort Marlborough itself was not to remain untouched for long. In mid-August 1759, reliable intelligence reached Deputy Governor Carter that the French had had definite plans to send a substantial force to surprise Fort Marlborough in the previous year. Within six months, in February 1760, these

[9] India Office Records ('IOR') IOR/B/66, Minutes of Meeting of Court of Directors, 6 January 1741, 489. The records show that he was joined by his youngest brother, Lumley, two years later, but that Lumley died in a smallpox outbreak after just over five years.

[10] IOR/G/35/9, List of Covenanted Servants on the West Coast, 1747–48, folio 176 (recording Roger Carter's arrival as Writer on 27 August 1742).

[11] IOR/G/35/9, List of Covenanted Servants on the West Coast, end 1753, folio 426 (sixth in Council). Cf IOR/G/35/9, List of Covenanted Servants on the West Coast, end 1752, folio 390 (not yet on Council).

[12] IOR/G/35/69, Diary and Public Consultations—Fort Marlborough, folio 74v, Account of salary due to Company's servants, 25 December 1755–25 March 1756.

[13] IOR/G/35/68, Diary and Public Consultations—Fort Marlborough, 4 September 1755, folios 138, 138v, 139, and 139v.

[14] IOR/B/74, Minutes of Meeting of Court of Directors, 1 December 1756, 207.

[15] IOR/B/74, Minutes of Meeting of Court of Directors, 17 December 1756, 224. Carter would probably have reached this position in any event, had he remained. By their general letter of 3 December 1755, which did not arrive at Fort Marlborough until after Carter had departed, the Court of Directors provided for a remodelled Council, effective from the letter's receipt, which would have seen Carter leap to second in Council behind a man who had made a similar decision to return to Europe shortly before Carter's own: see IOR/G/35/31, Rough Drafts of Dispatches to Fort Marlborough, Letter from the Court of Directors to Fort Marlborough, 3 December 1755, folio 20 ff, para 67.

[16] IOR/G/35/70, Diary and Public Consultations—Fort Marlborough, 15 May 1758, folio 63v (diary entry).

rumours became reality, when the Count D'Estaing's privateering expedition arrived on the West Coast. It is to these developments that our attention must now turn.

(a) Anglo-French Commercial Rivalry and War in the East Indies

To explain the reasons for the French assault on the West Coast in 1760, and the extent to which this attack could have been anticipated in the preceding months, something must be said about the wider political and economic context.

The assault ultimately had its origins in the long-standing commercial rivalry between the English and French East India Companies in India, and the global war into which England and France were drawn in 1756. The English and French Companies[17] had both maintained a significant trading presence in India for much of the 18th century. By the mid-century, the English Company's interests centred on the three Presidencies at Bombay, Fort William (Calcutta) in Bengal, and Fort St George (Madras) on the Coromandel Coast. The French Company's East Indies headquarters lay south of Madras, at Pondicherry; but like the English Company, it also had a number of lesser settlements, particularly on the Coromandel Coast and in the rich province of Bengal. Also in French possession were the islands of Mauritius (L'Isle de France) and Réunion (Bourbon), important bases for the provisioning and shelter of French shipping.

The two Companies had intermittently come into direct armed conflict in India during the War of Austrian Succession. Less than a decade later, when England and France were drawn into the Seven Years' War in May 1756, a renewal of such hostilities, supported by the Companies' respective governments, was virtually inevitable.[18] Almost immediately, the French Government and Company began to prepare a massive combined armament at Brest and Port L'orient, destined for the East Indies, under the command of Lally, the new French Governor-General. The three divisions left Europe in December 1756 and May 1757. Observing these preparations, the English Government also dispatched a small squadron to India in March 1757, to reinforce the Company and royal forces already in the region. Further reinforcements followed in subsequent years.[19]

---

[17] A recent readable English language introduction to the history and trade of the French East India Companies is DC Wellington, *French East India Companies—A Historical Account* (Lanham, Hamilton Books, 2006). A classic English language account, dedicated to French interests in India from the earliest times until Pondicherry's fall in 1761, is GB Malleson, *History of the French in India*, 2nd edn (London, WH Allen & Co Ltd, 1893).

[18] This war was a truly global conflict. England was brought into conflict in Europe on the side of Prussia against an alliance of France, Austria, and Russia; and in North America, the West Indies and India, against France. Spain entered the conflict belatedly in 1761.

[19] For these developments, see, eg Malleson, *History of the French in India* (n 17 above) 507 ff; JS Corbett, *England in the Seven Years' War* (London, Longmans, Green & Co, 1907) vol 1, ch 14, 336 ff; JR Dull, *The French Navy and the Seven Years War* (Lincoln, University of Nebraska Press, 2005) 62–3, 83, 116–17.

Direct Anglo-French conflict in India re-ignited first in Bengal, and then on the Coromandel Coast, where the French forces finally arrived from Europe in September 1757 and April 1758.[20] They initially secured important successes in that region. Cuddalore rapidly fell in May 1758, followed by Fort St David in June 1758. A delay of several months then followed before the next great military effort began. On 12 December 1758, Lally's forces laid siege to Fort St George. Nevertheless, Fort St George did not fall, and on 16 February 1759, the siege was raised. Thereafter, the tide of the conflict in India increasingly favoured the English forces to the point where, by the summer/autumn of 1760, the last French stronghold at Pondicherry was encircled by land and blockaded by sea. In January 1761, after several difficult months, Pondicherry capitulated.

One factor in this outcome, important to understanding *Carter v Boehm*, was the disposition of the French fleet under D'Aché's command, at critical moments in the conflict.[21] The spring/summer of 1758, which had brought direct conflict between the English and French land forces on the Coromandel Coast, had also brought two inconclusive engagements between the naval squadrons of D'Aché and Pocock in April and August. Not long after the latter, D'Aché insisted on returning with his ships to Mauritius, where his forces were reinforced by several more ships, and troops, from Europe. These new arrivals exacerbated an already chronic shortage of resources at Mauritius, and D'Aché was thus forced to send 12 of his ships to the Dutch colony at the Cape of Good Hope for the winter of 1758–59. In the absence of D'Aché's fleet on the Coast during those months, English ships were able to relieve the besieged Fort St George, and the besiegers, at the end of their own supplies, were forced to abandon the siege. It was not until some time in August 1759 that D'Aché's fleet finally reappeared off the Coromandel Coast. After another inconclusive engagement on 10 September 1759 with Pocock's squadron, D'Aché's ships were able to land reinforcements and supplies at Pondicherry, but then immediately left for Mauritius once again. That was the end of the fleet's effective involvement in the conflict: it remained there throughout 1760. In early 1760, a terrible storm devastated D'Aché's fleet at Mauritius. Before it could depart again, D'Aché received strict orders from France, ordering the fleet to remain at Mauritius in anticipation of a rumoured English assault on the Mascarene Islands. Lally's forces, besieged at Pondicherry, awaited the fleet's return in vain.

---

[20] For the course of the ensuing conflict, see, eg Malleson, *History of the French in India* (n 17 above) ch 12 and Corbett, *England in the Seven Years' War* (n 19 above) vol 1, ch 14, and vol 2, ch 4.

[21] For these developments, see, eg Malleson, *History of the French in India* (n 17 above) ch 12, esp 516–19, 523–5, 531–2, 553–6, 574–5; Corbett, *England in the Seven Years' War* (n 19 above) vol 1, 346–50 and vol 2, ch 4; and Dull, *The French Navy and the Seven Years War* (n 19 above) 116–17, 141, 172–3.

## (b) Contemplation of a French attack on Fort Marlborough

From as early as 1755, the Court of Directors in London, and the West Coast servants, realised that the renewal of Anglo-French war in Europe meant that the Company's interests on the West Coast of Sumatra might be possible objects of French attack. Beginning in 1755, the Court of Directors' general dispatches to the Council at Fort Marlborough related the developing conflict in Europe and what intelligence the Company had of the strength of the forces anticipated for the East Indies. These same letters repeatedly warned the Council to be on their guard, and ordered them to prepare as best they could.[22] The urgency of those warnings measurably increased as the massive French armament was being prepared and dispatched from Brest and Port L'orient for the East Indies.[23] Nevertheless, at this stage, the risk to Fort Marlborough was apparently perceived to be small. The primary target of the French forces was imagined to be India, where Anglo-French rivalry was long-standing and the commercial stakes were highest. The accuracy of this prediction would have been confirmed when news finally arrived at Fort Marlborough and in London of the arrival of Lally's forces at Pondicherry in April 1758, and the ensuing engagements on the Coromandel Coast.

During this time, Roger Carter and his Council at Fort Marlborough appear to have existed in a low-level state of alert. Intelligence slowly arrived of the turbulent events in India, usually via John Herbert, the Company's agent at Batavia. However, none of this intelligence gave the Council reason to think that Fort Marlborough was directly under threat. The Council's principal concern was different: viz, that the conflict in India might disrupt its usual supply routes with the Company's Presidencies there, and leave it critically short of important supplies.

This low-level state of alert changed dramatically in August 1759. The events that brought this change can be traced through the deliberations and correspondence of the Fort Marlborough Secret Committee. This Committee was first established in June 1758, on the basis that there might be circumstances which it might be desirable to avoid being made public 'in the present state of affairs'.[24]

[22] IOR/G/35/31, Rough Drafts of Dispatches to Fort Marlborough, Letter from the Court of Directors to Fort Marlborough, 3 December 1755, folio 20 ff, para 75; *ibid* 29 December 1756, folio 48 ff, para 5; *ibid* 8 February 1758, folio 79 ff, paras 4–5; 8 November 1758, folio 101 ff, paras 5–7; *ibid* 13 February 1759, folio 111 ff, paras 5–8.

[23] IOR/G/35/31, Rough Drafts of Dispatches to Fort Marlborough, Letter from the Court of Directors to Fort Marlborough, 8 February 1758, folio 79 ff, paras 4–5. Cf subsequently, *ibid* Letter 13 February 1759, paras 5–8, which is more optimistic in tone.

[24] IOR/G/35/70, Diary and Public Consultations—Fort Marlborough, 30 June 1758, folio 83v (decision to create committee); IOR/G/35/12, Letter from Fort Marlborough to the Court of Directors, 10 March 1759, folio 35 ff, para 75 (reporting this decision).

Nevertheless, for almost a year afterwards, nothing of that nature emerged,[25] and the Committee did not meet for the first time until May 1759.[26]

First came a false alarm. On 18 May 1759, the *Anna Catherina* arrived at Fort Marlborough from Batavia.[27] The sloop had been specially hired there by John Herbert, to provide speedy delivery of an important packet of secret correspondence. Two letters conveyed important news about the conflict in India—in particular, the commencement and progress of the siege at Fort St George.[28] A third, dated 5 April 1759, was of more immediate significance. In it, Herbert related third-hand reports of what were said to be nine French ships bound for Bencoolen, and of a French ship and sloop, waiting in the Straits of Sunda[29] to intercept English shipping. Herbert doubted the first report, but had thought the second sufficiently credible to require special precautions for the security of the *Anna Catherina*'s packet of correspondence. By the time Herbert's letter reached the Secret Committee at Fort Marlborough, however, it was apparent that neither sighting was accurate. His letter was read at the Secret Committee's first meeting on 18 May 1759, but no action was taken.[30]

Three months later, in August 1759, the Secret Committee reacted very differently. On 14 August, a new bundle of correspondence arrived from Batavia, again from John Herbert. One letter brought good news: Herbert reported that the siege of Fort St George had been raised on 16 February 1759.[31] The other news was more ominous. Herbert reported a major Dutch armament at Batavia, ostensibly bound for the Coromandel Coast to protect the Dutch settlements there, but believed to be destined for an offensive in Bengal.[32] Even more

[25] IOR/G/35/12, Letter from Fort Marlborough to the Court of Directors, 10 March 1759, folio 35 ff, para 75 (nothing yet under secret heading); IOR/G/35/12, Letter from Roger Carter and Richard Preston, Fort Marlborough, to the Secret Committee of the Court of Directors, 16 September 1759, folio 287 ff, para 1 (reporting that several matters had occurred of a nature not proper to be immediately made public).

[26] IOR/G/35/12, Minutes of the Secret Committee, Fort Marlborough, 18 May 1759, folios 266–7.

[27] IOR/G/35/70, Diary and Public Consultations—Fort Marlborough, 18 May 1759, 148 (diary entry).

[28] IOR/G/35/12, Letter from John Herbert, Batavia, to the Secret Committee, Fort Marlborough, 15 March 1759, folios 258–9v (commencement of siege on 12 December 1758); IOR/G/35/12, Letter from John Herbert, Batavia, to the Secret Committee, Fort Marlborough, 18 March 1759, folios 259v–60 (progress of siege up to 16 January); IOR/G/35/12, Minutes of the Secret Committee, Fort Marlborough, 18 May 1759, folios 266–7. These communications were pre-empted by news brought by the *Welcome* private trader, which arrived from Bengal on 30 April 1759: IOR/G/35/70, Diary and Public Consultations—Fort Marlborough, 30 April 1759, 134 (diary entry); *ibid* 4 May 1759, 137–8 (news reported).

[29] These are the straits separating Sumatra and (to its south) Java.

[30] IOR/G/35/12, Letter from John Herbert, Batavia, to the Secret Committee, Fort Marlborough, 5 April 1759, folios 260–61v; IOR/G/35/12, Minutes of the Secret Committee, Fort Marlborough, 18 May 1759, folios 266–7.

[31] IOR/G/35/70, Diary and Public Consultations—Fort Marlborough, 15 August 1759, 254 (reporting the contents of a letter from John Herbert, Batavia, of 5 July 1759).

[32] The news was conveyed by duplicates of letters sent directly to Fort St George, which John Herbert had dispatched to Fort Marlborough: see IOR/G/35/12, Letter from John Herbert, Batavia, to Fort St George, 16 June 1759, folios 280–81; *ibid* 5 July 1759, folios 281–2.

crucially, Herbert also forwarded a letter to Roger Carter from Alexander Wynch, dated 4 February 1759 at the Cape of Good Hope.[33] This letter is highly significant to an understanding of *Carter v Boehm*.

(c)  Alexander Wynch's Letter

Wynch was a man known to Roger Carter. He had been an East India Company employee in India for over 20 years, and latterly a Council member at Fort St George, the Presidency to which Fort Marlborough was subordinate.[34] In mid-1756, Wynch was appointed acting Deputy Governor at Fort St David, where he remained until 2 June 1758, when the place surrendered to Lally's forces following a short siege.[35] Wynch was released by the French in October 1758, whereupon he resigned from the Company's service on the grounds of failing health and took his passage for Europe,[36] apparently on a Danish ship.[37] It is likely that the vessel on which Wynch departed stopped at the Dutch colony at the Cape of Good Hope for the purposes of provisioning or repair.[38] In any event, there is no doubt that Wynch's stay at the Cape coincided with the substantial gathering of French ships which D'Aché had dispatched there for the winter of 1758–59.[39]

Wynch's purpose in writing was to transmit intelligence of the strength of the French forces gathered at the Cape, so that the Company's servants and the English forces on the Coromandel Coast might know the extent of the French forces that were expected to arrive there in mid-1759. To this end, letters were dispatched to Batavia, for transmission to Fort St George and Admiral Pocock,[40] and to Fort Marlborough[41]; the same news was communicated to the

---

[33]  IOR/G/35/12, Letter from Alexander Wynch, Cape of Good Hope, to Roger Carter, 4 February 1759, folios 262v–4.

[34]  For early biographical information, see H Davison Love, *Vestiges of Old Madras 1640–1800* (London, John Murray Ltd, 1913) vol 2, esp 318–19, 390, 394, 401, 437, 477, 481–2 and vol 3, esp 3–5.

[35]  Davison Love, *Vestiges of Old Madras* (n 34 above) vol 2, 482. Details of the capitulation, including the articles of capitulation signed by Wynch et al, can be found in IOR/H/95, 145–7, 212–13.

[36]  Davison Love, *Vestiges of Old Madras* (n 34 above) vol 2, 482.

[37]  See, eg IOR/H/95, Letter from Capt Martin to Rt Hon William Pitt, undated, folio 171 ff.

[38]  For a description of the Dutch colony, the so-called 'tavern of the two seas', see CR Boxer, *The Dutch Seaborne Empire 1600–1800* (London, Penguin Books, 1965) ch 9. In the 18th century, there were often more foreign sails anchored there than Dutch; there were profits to be made from selling local produce and services to foreign Indiamen: *ibid* 276.

[39]  See 64 above.

[40]  IOR/P/D/41, Military and Secret Consultations—Madras, 26 June 1759, 298–9, recording the receipt of two letters from Wynch of 4 and 23 February 1759, from Batavia via a Dutch ship.

[41]  IOR/G/35/12, Minutes of the Secret Committee, Fort Marlborough, 22 August 1759, folios 267–9, considering Wynch's letter of 4 February 1759, received from Batavia on 14 August 1759, with a request to forward a copy of the same intelligence to Madras. The Fort Marlborough Secret Committee correctly concluded that it was then too late in the season for any purpose to be served by that precaution.

Company in London by letters received via Copenhagen.[42] All of these letters also conveyed the further piece of intelligence which was of critical significance to Carter: viz, the news of French plans to attack Fort Marlborough.

The letter sent to Roger Carter at Fort Marlborough, dated 4 February 1759, related[43]:

> From a Conversation I had with some French Gentlemen I find your Place attracts their Notice, and that there was a scheme last Year of sending a Ship with about 400 Military to surprize your Settlements, this I judged proper to mention to you that you might be upon your Guard, should they hereafter put [it] in practice.

The corresponding letter sent to Fort St George, of the same date, elaborated[44]:

> I learnt from some French Gentlemen, that there was an Intention the last Year *of sending the Ship they took from the Dutch*, with about 400 Military to Bencoolen in order to surprize that Settlement; this then mentioned to Mr Carter, that he may be upon his Guard, should they at any time hereafter put a Scheme of that kind into Execution (emphasis added).

Viewed in context, Wynch's intelligence has an important degree of plausibility. Although Wynch might have learned of the French plans during his imprisonment after the capitulation of Fort St David, the best analysis is that this was new intelligence, subsequently obtained from conversations with Frenchmen who landed at the Cape colony from the French ships whose movements Wynch was witnessing and reporting. The Dutch ship in question was almost certainly the ship captured by D'Aché near Pondicherry in early August 1758, in retaliation for the Dutch action at Negapatam, in allowing a French ship there to be seized by the English squadron.[45] The ship's use in an opportunistic raid on the West Coast's settlements has particular plausibility, in light of the financial difficulties which hindered the progress of Lally's forces from their arrival on the Coromandel Coast in late April 1758, and which left Lally unable to pay or properly provision his troops. These difficulties had led Lally, shortly after Fort St David's capitulation on 2 June 1758, to postpone immedi-

---

[42] IOR/B/75, Minutes of Meeting of Court of Directors, 27 June 1759, 386, recording correspondence from Wynch at the Cape of Good Hope, of February 1759, received by way of Copenhagen. Wynch apparently dispatched this correspondence in advance of his own departure, on two Europebound Danish ships that sailed on 21 February 1759. See IOR/P/D/41, Military and Secret Consultations—Madras, 26 June 1759, 300 ff (entering a copy of a letter of 23 February 1759 from Wynch at the Cape of Good Hope, in which this is reported).

[43] IOR/G/35/12, Letter from Alexander Wynch, Cape of Good Hope, to Roger Carter, 4 February 1759, folios 262v–4.

[44] IOR/P/D/41, Military and Secret Consultations—Madras, 26 June 1759, 299, entering a copy of the letter.

[45] The capture is noted in Malleson, *History of the French in India* (n 17 above) 531–2. For contemporary confirmation, see IOR/P/C/52, Select Committee Consultations—Madras, 10 August 1758, 308–9 (reports of capture by English squadron of French vessel after August engagement); *ibid* 22 August 1758, 349 (reports of retaliatory capture of a 'large Dutch ship'); *ibid* 28 August 1758, 358 (reports of the arming of the ship with 50 guns). See similarly, eg IOR/H/95, Letter from Robert Palk to Rt Hon William Pitt, 3 July 1759, folios 179, 185 (naming the ship as the *Harlem*).

ate plans for a further assault on the English Company's settlements, to enable him to divert a substantial number of his troops on a two-month expedition against Tanjore, in search of money and supplies.[46]

## (d)  The Response at Fort Marlborough to Wynch's Letter

Roger Carter and the Secret Committee at Fort Marlborough knew only what Wynch's letter disclosed on its face. Even so, its brief terms were sufficient to provoke an instant response. Captain Frith, commander of the Fort Marlborough garrison, was immediately ordered to recommend a plan of defence in case of French attack.[47] A week or so later, on 22 August 1759, the Secret Committee convened to consider what should be done. The surviving minutes record its initial reaction[48]:

> It appearing from Mr Wynch's Letter that the French have entertain'd a design of surprizing this place and as it is probable that they may not have entirely dropt their Scheme, the Committee now take into Consideration what are the best measures to be pursued to prevent such a design's proving effectual, shou'd they hereafter attempt it, as well as what is necessary to be done for the security of our expected shipping.

In the ensuing meeting, a paper of instructions was drawn up and approved, containing signals etc for shipping, to be strictly observed by all commanders during their stay on the West Coast; a survey was ordered of the entrance to Bencoolen Bay, to ensure the safety of ships which, in an emergency, might need to approach close to shore; and secret instructions were drafted to the Company's residents at Fort Marlborough's out-settlements. Next, Captain Frith's preliminary plans for defence were scrutinised, and the Committee resolved to write to him, informing him of those parts that were considered necessary and practicable to be implemented. Finally, the Committee ordered the military officers to report on Fort Marlborough's military resources and the state of its fortifications, and to make recommendations for their improvement.

Two weeks later, on 7 September 1759, the Committee reconvened to consider these reports and what further action was required.[49] The officers' recommendations for the construction of batteries were accepted; however, any more ambitious plans for the building of a wall and ditch around Fort Marlborough were rejected on grounds of cost and the absence of the necessary skilled persons to conduct the work.

---

[46] Malleson, *History of the French in India*, (n 17 above) esp 525–31, and generally on these difficulties, ch 12.

[47] IOR/G/35/12, 'A Plan for defending Fort Marlborough if attack'd by the French', 22 August 1759, folios 269v–70v.

[48] IOR/G/35/12, Minutes of the Secret Committee, Fort Marlborough, 22 August 1759, folio 268.

[49] IOR/G/35/12, Minutes of the Secret Committee, Fort Marlborough, 7 September 1759, folios 271–2. The letter from the officers at Fort Marlborough, dated 6 September 1759, follows the minutes: *ibid* folios 274–6v.

These steps having been taken for the security of Fort Marlborough, the Secret Committee's next priority was to communicate these and other recent developments to the Court of Directors and to seek assistance with their plight. In this they were in luck. On 2 September, the *Earl of Holderness* and the *Pitt* had arrived in company at Bencoolen.[50] They were the first Europe-bound ships to arrive, and to offer a direct means of communication with the Company in London, since the departure of the *London* and the *Egmont* six months earlier.[51] The *Earl of Holderness*, one of the annual pepper boats, had to be detained for several months to gather its pepper cargo.[52] However, the *Pitt* was then Europe-bound, on its return from a path-breaking journey to China.[53]

When the *Pitt* left Bencoolen for Europe on 24 September 1759, it had two important packets of correspondence on board. Roger Carter's instructions to the *Pitt's* commander, Captain Wilson, betray their contents.[54] Packet A was to be forwarded by a trusty officer, with all possible dispatch, immediately on the ship's arrival at any port of Great Britain and Ireland. Packet B was meanwhile to remain on board until the arrival of the *Pitt* in the Thames, and be delivered as soon afterwards as convenient.[55] Both packets were always to be kept on hand, and slung with proper weights, so that in case of enemy attack during the voyage, and no probability of an escape, they might in the last extremity be thrown overboard.

The *Pitt* finally arrived safely at Kinsale, Ireland, on 23 February 1760.[56] From there, Packet A seems to have been immediately dispatched by express means to East India House in London, where it appears to have arrived on 1 March 1760.[57] There can be no doubt about its contents. One inclusion was a general letter, dated 21 September 1759, which was read at the Court of Directors' next meeting on 4 March 1760.[58] Arranged under the conventional headings, no one

---

[50] IOR/G/35/70, Diary and Public Consultations—Fort Marlborough, 2 September 1759, 273 (diary entry).

[51] IOR/G/35/70, Diary and Public Consultations—Fort Marlborough, 23 March 1759, 103 (diary entry)

[52] IOR/G/35/70, Diary and Public Consultations—Fort Marlborough, 2 September 1759, 273 (arrival of the *Earl of Holderness*); *ibid* 4 October 1759, 306 (departure for the north); *ibid* 18 December 1759, 471 (arrival from the north); IOR/G/35/12, Letter from Fort Marlborough to the Court of Directors, 5 February 1760, folio 481 ff, para 1 (sailing for Europe on 7 February 1760).

[53] See n 165 below.

[54] IOR/G/35/12, Directions from Roger Carter and Richard Preston to Captain William Wilson, Commander of the *Pitt*, 22 September 1759, folio 334.

[55] Packet B contained standard items of information relating to the commercial activities at Fort Marlborough (eg journals, ledgers, letters sent and received, accounts): see IOR/G/35/12, List of contents of Packet B sent via the *Pitt*, 21 September 1759, folio 332.

[56] IOR/L/MAR/B/525, index to the marine records for the *Pitt*.

[57] See, eg the contemporary press reports that on 1 March 1760, the Company received an account of the *Pitt's* arrival at Kinsale: eg *London Chronicle* (1–4 March 1760) 219, col 1; *London Evening Post* (1–4 March 1760) 1, cols 1–2. The same can be inferred from the minutes, noted in n 58 below.

[58] IOR/B/75, Minutes of Meeting of Court of Directors, 4 March 1760, 637, recording the reading of a general letter from Fort Marlborough of 21 September 1759. There is no record of Carter and Preston's letter to the Secret Committee of the Court of Directors of 16 September 1759 having been read at this or subsequent meetings.

reading it in London would imagine that there was anything seriously awry. However, the same packet also contained a further, substantial body of material not intended to be made public, addressed only to the Secret Committee of the Court of Directors.[59] In the ordinary course, this secret material would not have been disclosed at the general meeting of the Court.[60] And it would have told a very different story.

The secret material sent by the *Pitt* included copies of all correspondence to and from the Secret Committee up to the time of the *Pitt*'s departure, and minutes of the Secret Committee's meetings during the same period. It therefore included a copy of Wynch's letter of 4 February 1759 and records of all of the secret deliberations that had followed its receipt on 14 August 1759. Even more critical, however, was a secret letter from Roger Carter and Richard Preston at Fort Marlborough, dated 16 September 1759. This letter assumed fundamental importance in the litigation in *Carter v Boehm*, and for good reason. No reader could doubt how seriously Wynch's letter was being treated by Roger Carter and the other Secret Committee members in September 1759, and how ill-prepared Fort Marlborough was for a French attack.

Carter and Preston's secret letter of 16 September 1759 related[61]:

It is with much concern We are to acquaint your Honors, that by a Letter from Alexander Wynch Esq, dated at the Cape of Good Hope the 4th February last to the Deputy Governor, We are informed that your Settlements on this Coast have attracted the notice of the French, who last year, had actually a Design on foot, to attempt taking this settlement by surprize, which they purported to do with one Ship, and about Four hundred Troops.

As it is very probable that the Enemy may hereafter revive their intention, though for the present We may suppose they have dropt it, We have taken the necessary precautions, as well for the Security of such Shipping as may be on the Coast at the time, as for the defence of the Settlement.

There followed an exhaustive account of the steps that had been taken, to counter any French threat. Carter and Preston painted a bleak picture. Steps had been taken which would 'at least render it a very difficult matter to surprize [the place]'. Thus, look-out houses and guards had been established at suitable sites on the coast, with instructions for signals to be made on sighting shipping; and entrenchments were being made at the places where there was any likelihood of the enemy's attempting to land.[62] However, should the enemy land, and be too strong in the field, there would be no option but to retreat into the country, which it was hoped would prove too dangerous for any French force

---

[59] The contents of the secret packet dispatched on the *Pitt* are confirmed by the list of contents of the duplicate secret packet subsequently dispatched on the *Earl of Holderness* to the Secret Committee of the Court of Directors, dated 31 December 1759: IOR/G/35/12, folio 409.

[60] See further n 168 below.

[61] IOR/G/35/12, Letter from Roger Carter and Richard Preston, Fort Marlborough, to the Secret Committee of the Court of Directors, 16 September 1759, folio 287 ff, paras 10–11.

[62] *Ibid* para 12.

to follow.[63] To retire to Fort Marlborough and attempt to defend the place would mean the 'absolute loss of everything'.[64] The military stores were too poor, and the Fort itself too weak, to make any such defence practicable. The gunpowder was largely bad, stocks of small arms were low, and there were no large guns to place on the entrenchments raised to defend the approaches to Fort Marlborough.[65] Furthermore, whilst the military officers had recommended ways of making the defences at Fort Marlborough tenable against a European enemy, no steps could sensibly be taken in that direction.[66] There were no skilled persons at Fort Marlborough capable of properly directing and completing the works, and it was thought better to wait for the long-awaited arrival of expert assistance from Fort St George or Bombay than to spend a very considerable sum on works that might be found wanting.[67] Carter and Preston concluded with a final, uncertain plea for assistance[68]:

> We must leave to your Honors consideration, how far the present increase of your Investment, & the favourable prospect which your Settlements on this Coast in general bear, may render it worthy of your attention to increase our Works & Means of Defence; at least, so as to make our Enemies not think us so very easy a Conquest, as by the force they purposed to send against us, We may at present suppose they do.

Other correspondence no doubt remained onboard the *Pitt*, consistently with Captain Wilson's instructions, until the *Pitt*'s arrival in the Thames in mid-April. Amongst that correspondence was one final, crucial letter. This was a private letter from Roger Carter to his brother, dated 22 September 1759, in which he instructed his brother to take out insurance on his behalf in London, against the risk of a European enemy attack on Fort Marlborough. Acting on these instructions, on 9 May 1760, his brother effected the policy that was to trigger the litigation in *Carter v Boehm*.

### 3. The Origins of the Attack on Fort Marlborough: D'Estaing's Expedition

It is clear that in September 1759, when Roger Carter's insurance instructions were dispatched to London, there was a substantially heightened fear of a French attack on Fort Marlborough. The direct cause of this fear, and the reason for Carter's insurance instructions, was the letter which had arrived from Wynch in the middle of the previous month. Just over six months later, the feared attack came. However, it did not come from the source that Wynch's letter had given Carter cause to fear: viz, the French fleet gathered at the Cape over

---

[63] IOR/G/35/12 (n 61 above) para 18.
[64] IOR/G/35/12 (n 61 above) para 18.
[65] IOR/G/35/12 (n 61 above) para 13.
[66] IOR/G/35/12 (n 61 above) para 17.
[67] IOR/G/35/12 (n 61 above) para 17.
[68] IOR/G/35/12 (n 61 above) para 19.

the winter of 1758–59.[69] Rather, it was the product of the opportunism of one man: the Count D'Estaing.[70]

D'Estaing, a career soldier, had arrived in India in April 1758, at the head of the battalion of the Lorraine regiment that had left France with Lally in May 1757.[71] He was immediately involved in all of the major early actions,[72] but that involvement was to be short-lived. On 13 December 1758, one day into the siege of Fort St George, D'Estaing was taken prisoner in Madras's Black Town.[73] Over the ensuing weeks, and particularly once the siege ended, the two sides negotiated for his release by some suitable exchange for English prisoners in India.[74] No mutually acceptable terms were found. By early May 1759, Governor Pigot at Fort St George had determined that the best course was for D'Estaing to proceed to Europe, on his parole of honour, to be exchanged there.[75]

D'Estaing left Pondicherry for Mauritius in May 1759, ostensibly Europe-bound. However, D'Estaing was a man of action, and it seems unlikely that he ever had any real intention of returning to Europe, as his English captors, and his parole, required. Whilst at Pondicherry, he had presented Lally with plans for a sea expedition to Bengal, and for a further expedition against the kingdom of Cochinchine and in the Philippines.[76] The demands of the conflict in India ultimately prevented these being put into effect, but D'Estaing's efforts continued on his arrival at Mauritius. He immediately approached the French Governor there, Monsieur de Magon, with plans for an ambitious privateering expedition to the China Seas.[77] Magon eventually agreed. D'Estaing was given the use of two armed Company vessels, the *Condé* and the *Expedition*.[78]

D'Estaing's expedition left Mauritius on 1 September 1759, before the return of the French fleet from the Coromandel Coast. Their subsequent course appears to have been determined more by opportunism than by careful planning.[79] They spent the autumn months in the Persian Gulf, where they captured two significant prizes, as well as the East India Company's factory at Gambroon.

---

[69] On this, see further 104–6 below.

[70] The most substantial modern biography of D'Estaing is the French language work of J Michel, *La vie aventureuse et mouvementée de Charles-Henri comte d'Estaing* (Verdun, Michel, 1976). The only sustained English language discussion of D'Estaing's privateering expedition appears to be P Crowhurst, *The Defence of British Trade* (Folkestone, Dawson, 1977) 237–40 and 'D'Estaing's Cruise in the Indian Ocean: A Landmark in Privateering Voyages' (1972) 35 *Studia* 53.

[71] Michel, *Charles-Henri comte d'Estaing* (n 70 above) 27–34.

[72] Michel, *Charles-Henri comte d'Estaing* (n 70 above) 35–40.

[73] Michel, *Charles-Henri comte d'Estaing* (n 70 above) 39–40. It is suggested that D'Estaing had approached a group of soldiers in Madras's Black Town, but discovered too late that they were English troops. Turning his horse to flee, he fell and was captured: Malleson, *History of the French in India* (n 17 above) 537–8; Davison Love, *Vestiges of Old Madras* (n 34 above) vol 2, 555–6.

[74] The negotiations emerge from the deliberations of the Madras Military and Secret Committee: IOR/P/D/41, Military and Secret Consultations—Madras, 23 February 1759, 16; *ibid* 29 March 1759, 95–7; *ibid* 16 April 1759, 118–20; *ibid* 3 May 1759, 155–6.

[75] IOR/P/D/41, Military and Secret Consultations—Madras, 3 May 1759, 155.

[76] Michel, *Charles-Henri comte d'Estaing* (n 70 above) 43–4.

[77] Michel, *Charles-Henri comte d'Estaing* (n 70 above) 44.

[78] Michel, *Charles-Henri comte d'Estaing* (n 70 above) 45–6, 48.

[79] Michel, *Charles-Henri comte d'Estaing* (n 70 above) 46–51.

Thereafter, in November, the ships began their journey eastwards for the straits that provided the doors into the China Seas. This journey proved unexpectedly difficult, and on 4 February 1760, when D'Estaing's expedition reached Ayer Bungis, a small Dutch settlement to the north of the West Coast of Sumatra, his men were in no state to undertake an ambitious sea expedition into the China Seas.[80] D'Estaing's attention therefore turned to more immediate targets: the English Company's interests on the West Coast. The Company's northern-most out-settlements of Natal and Tapanouly fell in quick succession. Following a short stay at the Dutch settlement at Padang in March, D'Estaing's expedition then set sail southwards for Fort Marlborough. On 31 March 1760, the French ships were sighted off Bencoolen. By 3 April, the inevitable had happened. Roger Carter and the Company's servants at Fort Marlborough had surrendered. The Company's remaining out-settlements on the West Coast fell into French hands over the ensuing weeks.

At Fort Marlborough, Roger Carter and the rest had had no hint of this impending storm until 20 February 1760, when a letter arrived from Richard Wyatt, the Resident at the northern out-settlement of Natal, reporting the arrival of the two French ships on 6 February 1760.[81]

> I wrote you this morning (by a Boat which sailed immediately) that I had advice by Noquedah Lebbee, that two large French ships were at Ayer Bungy, and had sailed from thence for this Place, and were then in sight from the Hill . . . They are now both come in sight, but show no Colours, and are in cha[s]e of the Sloop Resolution, which was dispatched this morning, and they seem to gain on her, but night coming on may favour her escape . . . I have this morning sent an Express to Tapanooly, to put Mr Nairne on his Guard.

It was a very rude awakening. News of D'Estaing's earlier raids in the Persian Gulf had certainly reached the Company's servants at Bombay in late October 1759,[82] and at Madras by January 1760.[83] However, no one at those places appears to have suspected that D'Estaing's next stop might be Sumatra. Unaware of these developing events further afield, public and private business at Fort Marlborough appears to have resumed its normal pattern after the *Pitt*'s departure in late September 1759. Indeed, by early 1760 at least, Roger Carter might have been forgiven for feeling secure. 12 months after Wynch's letter arrived from the Cape, no French force had appeared; news, such as Carter had, was of English successes in India; and the most recent intelligence of the French

---

[80] Michel, *Charles-Henri comte d'Estaing* (n 70 above) 46–51.

[81] IOR/G/35/12, Letter from Richard Wyatt, Natal, to the Secret Committee, Fort Marlborough, 6 February 1760, 6pm, folio 492.

[82] IOR/P/D/43, Military and Secret Consultations—Madras, 11 February 1760, 155–7, where a letter from Bombay, dated 26 December 1759, is entered, reporting receipt of the first intelligence around the end of October.

[83] IOR/P/D/43, Military and Secret Consultations—Madras, 14 January 1760, 62; *ibid* 11 February 1760, 157–61.

fleet suggested that it was out of harm's way, sheltering at Mauritius for the winter months.[84]

## C. CARTER'S INSURANCE POLICY

Having set *Carter v Boehm* in its wider historical context, we are better placed to understand Boehm's allegations of non-disclosure, and the court's response to them. Before turning to this, however, more must be said about Carter's insurance policy. The origin of Carter's instructions should now be clear. Less easy to perceive clearly today, and relatively easy to misperceive, are the purpose and form of the policy that was effected in London on 9 May 1760.

### 1. The Purpose of Carter's Policy

If Fort Marlborough were to fall to a European enemy, then Deputy Governor Carter might lose his position at Fort Marlborough and his associated salary.[85] However, that consideration cannot explain the policy effected on his instructions in May 1760. The £10,000 sum insured[86] was over 30 times Carter's annual wage as Deputy Governor.[87] The four percent premium[88] alone was equal to more than one year's salary, and there is evidence that he was prepared to pay very substantially more.[89] In September 1759, Carter remitted £600 to his brother Thomas in London, via certificates drawn on the Company, sent on board the *Pitt*.[90] A further £1,750 was remitted in early February 1760, via certificates sent on board the *Earl of Holderness*.[91]

---

[84] IOR/G/35/12, Letter from the Secret Committee, Fort St George to the Secret Committee, Fort Marlborough, 7 November 1759, folio 353; IOR/G/35/12, Minutes of the Secret Committee, Fort Marlborough, 20 December 1759, folio 399 (considering the letter).

[85] In fact, after Fort Marlborough's fall in April 1760, Roger Carter made his way with the other West Coast prisoners to Madras, in accordance with the terms of their paroles of honour. During his stay there, and until he finally resumed his position at Fort Marlborough in September 1762, he and the other West Coast servants were paid their usual salary by the Company's government at the Presidency of Fort St George, Madras: see esp IOR/P/240/19, Public Consultations—Madras, 30 September 1760, 453. In the interim, Fort Marlborough had been elevated to the status of an independent Company Presidency, headed by a 'Governor', rather than a 'Deputy Governor'.

[86] *Carter* (n 1 above) 3 Burr 1905, 1907; 97 ER 1162, 1163.

[87] The annual salary for the Deputy Governor had been £200 for many years, but Carter appears to have been allowed an extra £100: see, eg IOR/G/35/12, Letter from Roger Carter to the Court of Directors, 10 March 1759, folios 65, 70.

[88] *Carter* (n 1 above) 1 Black W 593, 593; 96 ER 342, 343.

[89] See too the further passage from the insurance instructions, noted by Lord Mansfield, indicating that in the event of a Dutch War, Carter would wish to have insurance at any rate: *Carter* (n 1 above) 3 Burr 1905, 1908n; 97 ER 1162, 1168n.

[90] IOR/G/35/12, Letter from Fort Marlborough to the Court of Directors, 21 September 1759, folios 302–31, with certificates listed at folio 331.

[91] IOR/G/35/12, Letter from Fort Marlborough to the Court of Directors, 31 December 1759, folios 411–29, with certificates listed at folio 429. The records show that remittances on this scale were wholly unprecedented for Roger Carter. They were also unusual for Company servants

Carter's policy is ultimately comprehensible only in light of his double life as a Company-covenanted servant. What he principally feared was the loss of the merchandise and/or treasure at Fort Marlborough that formed the subject-matter of his private trading activities within the East Indies.[92] A contemporary later described Carter as a man 'conspicuous for his abilities in trade, & in the management of [the West Coast] Government'[93]; and in the period that immediately followed his return to the West Coast as Deputy Governor in May 1758, Carter's private trading activities seem to have been extensive. Indeed, by late 1759, some junior Company servants were complaining that Carter was monopolising the country-trade at their expense. To quote one: '[o]ur Governour Mr Carter will carry all the trade at Marlbro, and nobody can do anything worthwhile'.[94] Similar accusations embittered Carter's eventual resignation from the Governorship at Fort Marlborough in 1767.[95] Whether or not these accusations were justified, the substantial scale of Carter's trading activities immediately prior to the French assault on Fort Marlborough is indicated by the uncontradicted evidence of a witness in the litigation in *Carter v Boehm* that on 8 February 1760,

> [Carter] bought . . . goods to the value of 4000 l, and had goods to the value of above 20,000 l and then dealt for 50,000 l and upwards.[96]

Against this background, it is reasonable to assume that when Carter sent his insurance instructions to his brother by the *Pitt* in September 1759, the policy he sought was to be a bona fide hedge against the inevitable injury to his private trading interests if the feared French attack on Fort Marlborough should come. This seems to be put beyond doubt by a note to Burrows' report, which records that Carter wrote to his brother that he was

> 'now more afraid than formerly, that the French should attack and take the settlement' . . . And therefore he desire[d] to get an insurance made upon his stock there.[97]

---

generally, except as a way of remitting their fortunes to England in advance of their impending departure from the East Indies.

[92]   On the double lives of East India Company covenanted servants, see 61 above.

[93]   British Library, Private Papers, MS Eur D737/1, Letter from Hew Steuart to his sister, 10 February 1766.

[94]   Nottinghamshire Archives, Private Papers, DD/N/203c/21, Letter from Stokeham Donstan to George Donstan, 12 December 1759; see too DD/N/203c/20, Letter from Stokeham Donstan to George Donstan, 15 March 1759.

[95]   IOR/G/35/75, Diary and Public Consultations—Fort Marlborough, 80 ff (letter from Roger Carter of 31 January 1767 entered); IOR/G/35/75, Diary and Public Consultations—Fort Marlborough, 159 ff (letter from Roger Carter of 25 May 1767 entered, giving an account of his private trading activities from 1762–65, in his defence against such accusations).

[96]   See *Carter* (n 1 above) 3 Burr 1905, 1913; 97 ER 1162, 1164. See too private correspondence between Roger Carter and the Company, in which he claimed to have had a private cargo worth £3,000 on board the *Denham* East Indiaman, which was deliberately sunk in the waters off Bencoolen shortly before D'Estaing's assault on Fort Marlborough: IOR/G/35/12, Letter from Roger Carter, Fort St George, to the Court of Directors, 28 October 1760, folio 559 ff, paras 3–5.

[97]   *Carter* (n 1 above) 3 Burr 1905, 1913n; 97 ER 1162, 1166n.

## 2. The Form of Carter's Policy

As Carter's policy has not been found, its form must be inferred from the incomplete details revealed in the case-reports. These are sufficient to suggest an important disjunction between Carter's purpose and the policy's form, which calls for explanation. As reported, Carter's policy was not an ordinary indemnity insurance policy. It did not entitle Carter to an indemnity only in so far as his stock-in-trade at Fort Marlborough was shown to have been lost in a European enemy assault. It involved a different bargain, whereby the whole insured sum of £10,000[98] would be payable if Fort Marlborough was lost to a European enemy[99] within 12 months of October 1759,[100] without inquiry into whether or to what extent Carter had any interest at stake. Central to this analysis are the policy terms 'interest or no interest'[101] and 'without the benefit of salvage'.[102]

In 1760, a policy in these terms would have been comprehensible as a wagering policy. At that time, wagers were prima facie valid and enforceable at common law. So, too, were wagers in the form of insurance policies.[103] Difficulties nevertheless arose if such instruments were used by wagering parties, because the courts tended to construe insurance policies on property as contracts of indemnity. This brought a series of inconvenient corollaries for wagering parties, who meant to play only for the whole insured sum, irrespective of the existence and extent of any real loss to the party 'insured'. To avoid this construction and its corollaries, various forms of words came to be inserted into policies of this nature, which reaffirmed their character as wagers. Typical in wagering policies insuring property against marine risks were the terms found in Carter's policy: 'interest or no interest', 'free from average', and 'without benefit of salvage'.[104] Marshall explained their role as follows[105]:

[98] *Carter* (n 1 above) 3 Burr 1905, 1907; 97 ER 1162, 1163.

[99] *Carter* (n 1 above) 1 Black W 593, 594; 96 ER 342, 343; (1766) 3 Burr 1905, 1907, 1908, 1911, 1912 and 1915–16; 97 ER 1162, 1163, 1165, and 1167–8. The precise definition of the insured-against event is considered at 90–93 below.

[100] The commencement date is inconsistently reported as either 1 or 16 October: *Carter* (n 1 above) 3 Burr 1905, 1906 and 1911; 97 ER 1162, 1163 and 1165; (1766) 1 Black W 593, 594; 96 ER 342, 343.

[101] *Carter* (n 1 above) 3 Burr 1905, 97 ER 1162; (1766) 1 Black W 593, 96 ER 342, 343 (where these terms are noted).

[102] *Carter* (n 1 above) 3 Burr 1905, 97 ER 1162 (where these terms are noted).

[103] See the early discussions of wagering policies in, eg JA Park, *A System of the Law of Marine Insurance*, 4th edn (London, J Butterworth, 1800) ch 14, esp 259–60; S Marshall, *A Treatise on the Law of Insurance*, 2nd edn (London, J Butterworth, 1808) vol 1, 119–42, esp 122–6; J Arnould, *A Treatise on the Law of Marine Insurance and Average* (London, W Benning & Co, 1848) § 116. A comprehensive legislative attempt to tackle wagers in the form of insurance policies came with the Life Assurance Act 1774; ordinary wagers were tackled by the Gaming Act 1845. For discussion, see Warren Swain's chapter in this volume.

[104] Marshall, *A Treatise on the Law of Insurance* (n 103 above) vol 1, 119–21, 122–3; similarly, Arnould, *A Treatise on the Law of Marine Insurance and Average* (n 103 above) vol 1, §§ 16 and 116.

[105] Marshall, *A Treatise on the Law of Insurance* (n 103 above) vol 1, 121; similarly, Arnould, *A Treatise on the Law of Marine Insurance and Average* (n 103 above) § 116.

[A wagering policy] is usually conceived in the terms, '*interest or no interest*', or '*without further proof of interest than the policy*,' to preclude all enquiry into the interest of the insured. And, as a consequence of the insured's having no interest in the pretended subject of the policy, it follows that the insurer cannot be liable for any partial loss. A partial loss is not an event sufficiently defined and precise to be the criterion of a wager; and nothing but that sort of misfortune which is considered as amounting to a total loss can decide it. The parties mean to play for the whole stake; and when the underwriter pays a loss, he cannot, as in the case of an insurance upon interest, claim any benefit from what may have been saved; and to preclude all claim of that sort, the words, '*free of average, and without benefit of salvage*,'[106] are always introduced into wager policies.

In 1745, Parliament intervened to tackle the mischiefs presented by policies of this nature, in a limited sphere.[107] Policies on British vessels and cargoes, expressed in these terms, were declared void.[108] Beyond this, the common law was left unaffected for another three decades. Thus, in the absence of some specific public policy objection to the particular wager, a wager taking the form of an insurance policy on 'interest or no interest' terms would be valid and enforceable at common law.

Carter was not, of course, a true 'wagering' party. He sought the policy as a bona fide hedge against the risk of the loss of his valuable stock-in-trade at Fort Marlborough in a European enemy assault. If his policy nevertheless took the form of an 'interest or no interest' policy on Fort Marlborough, another explanation must be found. It seems likely to be practical. The best explanation is that Carter would have faced considerable difficulty in proving, to the satisfaction of an underwriter and/or a court in London, that he had owned stock at Fort Marlborough at the time of the enemy's attack, its value, and the extent to which it was lost.[109] Probative difficulties of this type underlay the introduction

---

[106] The phrase 'without benefit of salvage' would now be understood as precluding what modern marine insurance lawyers would understand as two separate rights: the insurer's right, on indemnifying his insured for an actual or constructive total loss, to acquire whatever remains of the insured subject-matter (the 'salvage'), under the doctrine of abandonment; and the insurer's right, on indemnifying his insured, to acquire his insured's subsisting rights of action against third parties, under the doctrine of subrogation. Both rights can be understood as necessary incidents of an indemnity insurance contract, operating to prevent the insured from profiting by obtaining more than a full indemnity for his loss. The latter right originated as an incident of the former during the 18th century, and the two doctrines remained imperfectly distinguished until *Simpson & Co v Thomson* (1877) 3 App Cas 279. See C Mitchell and S Watterson, *Subrogation: Law and Practice* (Oxford, Oxford University Press, 2007) ch 10(B).

[107] 19 Geo II c 37.

[108] 19 Geo II c 37, s 1. For contemporary discussion, see Park, *A System of the Law of Marine Insurance* (n 103 above) ch 14; Marshall, *A Treatise on the Law of Insurance* (n 103 above) 126–9.

[109] A subsidiary factor, supporting the same conclusion, might have been a desire not to publicise the character of Carter's stock-in-trade. Cf the preamble to 19 Geo II c 37, indicating that one concern underlying the legislation was that 'interest or no interest' policies provided a cloak beneath which parties could undertake prohibited trade. A further subsidiary factor might have been uncertainty about the legal position if some of the stock was held by Carter for sale on commission rather than on his own account. For evidence of such activity, see Lincolnshire Archives, Redbourne Hall deposit, Ledger, 2 Red 4/4/10, loose item (f) (counsel's opinion on a claim by a party for whom Roger Carter was commission agent at the time of the French attack).

of 'interest or no interest' terms into what were originally bona fide insurance policies.[110] And Lord Mansfield himself was later to suggest that the difficulty of bringing witnesses from abroad to prove an insured's interest was the reason for the exclusion of foreign ships and cargos from the 1745 Act,[111] which rendered void marine policies on 'interest or no interest' terms.[112]

### D. LORD MANSFIELD'S JUDGMENT

Having clarified the historical background to Carter's insurance claim, we are better placed to re-consider Lord Mansfield's judgment in *Carter v Boehm*.[113] Three aspects of this require examination[114]: Lord Mansfield's seminal statement of the disclosure obligations of parties to insurance contracts, with which he began his judgment; his subsequent findings regarding the context in which the policy was effected, and the policy's true construction; and finally, his treatment of Boehm's defences to liability. The theme that consistently emerges is that *Carter v Boehm* was absolutely not a 'pro-insurer' decision. Every argument advanced by Boehm failed. This might perhaps be explained by the inherent weakness of his case, exacerbated by the court's indisposition to find for a man suspected of misconduct.[115] But this would be to miss the decision's real significance. Lord Mansfield's seminal statement of the law was primarily important for its emphatic recognition that there were limits to an insurer's ability to avoid liability for non-disclosure by his insured. Boehm's case was a weak case only because of those limits, and because of the court's inclination to apply them robustly to the case at hand.

### 1. The Law of Non-disclosure

Whatever might be the case today, *Carter v Boehm*'s landmark status in 1766, and in the decades that immediately followed, stemmed from Lord Mansfield's

---

[110] See eg Marshall, *A Treatise on the Law of Insurance* (n 103 above) vol 1, 122.

[111] 19 Geo II c 37, s 1.

[112] *Thellusson v Fletcher* (1780) 1 Doug 315 316; 99 ER 203.

[113] Burrows' report indicates that Carter's insurance policy came before Lord Mansfield on more than one occasion: see (1766) 3 Burr 1905, 1906–7 and 1911–13; 97 ER 1162, 1163 and 1165–6. Two common law actions on the policy came before Lord Mansfield and a special jury at Guildhall in 1762, concluding in a verdict for the insured. There was then a protracted period of litigation in equity, in which the underwriters sought to obtain further evidence to assist their case: *Carter* (n 1 above) 3 Burr 1905, 1912; 97 ER 1162, 1166. This finally led to a further trial before Lord Mansfield and a special jury at Guildhall, again concluding in a jury verdict for the insured. The reported 1766 decision of the Court of King's Bench was a decision on a motion for a retrial: see n 1 above. There are clear hints that Lord Mansfield was influenced by the fact that the underwriters' protracted inquiries had produced very little in support of their case.

[114] These substantially correspond to the three stages in which Lord Mansfield himself progressed through the issues, as indicated at *Carter* (n 1 above) 3 Burr 1905, 1909; 97 ER 1162, 1164.

[115] See section I below.

preliminary exposition of the Common law principles governing disclosure between insured and insurer. Prior to Lord Mansfield's rise to the King's Bench in 1756, there was a remarkable dearth of reported cases on the law of insurance, and the few reports that existed were of very poor quality. Hence *Carter v Boehm* was significant primarily for Lord Mansfield's unprecedented attempt to set out the Common law rules, more or less comprehensively, and in a manner that provided unequivocal guidance to insureds, insurers, and their counsel.[116]

It is nevertheless important to be clear about what it was about the substance of Lord Mansfield's exposition that was truly noteworthy in 1766. His exposition had three essential elements. The first was his emphatic statement that an insurance policy might be avoided where the insurer was induced to underwrite the policy by the insured's failure to disclose a material fact, even where the insured had no fraudulent intention.[117] However important, it is reasonably clear that *Carter v Boehm* was not the origin of this principle. Both the argument in the case, and the handful of earlier cases found in the reports and contemporary treatises,[118] suggest that it was already an accepted proposition, in Equity[119] and at Common law.[120] Properly understood, it is the other two essential elements of Lord Mansfield's statements that must be regarded as remarkable: viz, his explanation of the law's normative basis, and of the circumstances in which an insurer could not avoid liability for non-disclosure by his insured.

Lord Mansfield's account of the law's normative basis will probably be familiar even to modern insurance lawyers. In simple terms, an insured's obligations were the product of a mutual requirement of pre-contractual good faith, applied to the special character of insurance contracts. The 'governing principle' 'applicable to all contracts and dealings', Lord Mansfield explained, was that

---

[116] See esp the preliminary exposition in J A Park, *A System of the Law of Marine Insurances* (London, J Butterworth, 1787) for a useful account of the development of the law (including the reasons for its underdevelopment prior to Lord Mansfield's rise to the King's Bench). See too the summary account, relying heavily on Park, in J Oldham, *English Common Law in the Age of Mansfield* (Chapel Hill, University of North Carolina Press, 2004) 124–30.

[117] *Carter* (n 1 above) 3 Burr 1905, 1909–10; 97 ER 1162, 1164–5.

[118] A number of otherwise unreported cases are summarised in J Weskett, *A Complete Digest of the Theory, Laws and Practice of Insurance* (London, Frys Couchman & Collier, 1781); and Park, *A System of the Law of Marine Insurances* (n 116 above). A useful overview of the law's sources, and of the sparse 17th and 18th century English literature, is found in S Marshall, *A Treatise on the Law of Insurance* (n 103 above) ch 1.

[119] *De Costa v Scandret* (1723) 2 P Wms 169, 24 ER 686.

[120] *Anonymous* (c 1693) Skin 327, 90 ER 146; *Seaman v Fonnereau* (c 1740) 2 Strange 1183, 93 ER 1115; *Roberts v Fonereau* (1742) (noted in Park, *A System of the Law of Marine Insurances* (n 116 above) 176); *Rookes v Thurmond* (1743) (noted in Weskett, *Theory, Laws and Practice of Insurance* (n 118 above) 114–15); *Green v Bowden* (1759) (noted in Weskett, *Theory, Laws and Practice of Insurance* (n 118 above) 115–8); *Williams v Touchet* (1759) (noted in Weskett, *Theory, Laws and Practice of Insurance* (n 118 above) 118); *Ross v Bradshaw* (1761) 1 Black W 312, 96 ER 175; *Wilson v Ducket* (1762) 3 Burr 1361, 97 ER 874; *Hodgson v Richardson* (1764) 1 Black W 463, 96 ER 268. The brief reports, coupled with the ambiguity of the language of 'fraud' in this context, can make the court's exact conclusions regarding the insured's state of mind difficult to discern with certainty.

[g]ood faith forbids either party by concealing what he privately knows, to draw the other into a bargain, from his ignorance of that fact, and his believing the contrary.[121]

This principle had particular resonance in the field of insurance contracts, 'contract[s] upon speculation', for the responsibilities of insureds. It was characteristic of such transactions that many facts necessary to a proper calculation of the risk being undertaken by the insurer lay peculiarly within the insured's private knowledge.[122] An insurer characteristically relied, and must be entitled to rely, on the insured's having disclosed and fairly represented such matters.[123] If the insured did not disclose them, whether by accident, negligence or fraud, and the insurer was induced by his ignorance to contract under a misapprehension as to the nature of the risk being run, the insurer could deny liability.[124]

The full significance of this explanation will be missed unless it is viewed within the entire framework of principle that Lord Mansfield articulates, and in light of the actual decision in *Carter v Boehm*. It is strongly arguable that Lord Mansfield was concerned to explain why an insurance contract might be avoided for material non-disclosure principally in order to show how, and why, there had to be limits to an insurer's entitlement to avoid liability. What Lord Mansfield had identified was ultimately a limited rationale, turning on the existence of an inequality of accessible information bearing on the contract's subject-matter, the risk undertaken, which rendered the insurer dependent on disclosure by his prospective insured. In the ensuing paragraphs of his judgment, Lord Mansfield proceeded to offer an unprecedented list of the circumstances in which an insurer could not legitimately complain of non-disclosure,[125] almost all of which can be deduced from that limited rationale. It was the emphatic recognition and application of those limits in *Carter v Boehm* that really marked the case out in 1766, and provides the primary reason why the case deserves to be remembered today.

One such limit was explicit in Lord Mansfield's initial formulation of the insured's obligations. In the absence of proof of fraudulent intention, an insurer could only avoid liability if the non-disclosure was shown to be 'material' to the risk undertaken. For many years after *Carter v Boehm*, English law's standard of 'materiality' remained remarkably under-analysed. An objective standard, involving an inquiry into the influence which the concealed matter would have had on a prudent or reasonable underwriter, was not authoritatively confirmed

---

[121] *Carter* (n 1 above) 3 Burr 1905, 1910; 97 ER 1162, 1164. There are earlier traces of this assumption in *Hodgson v Richardson* (1764) 1 Black W 463, 465; 96 ER 268, 269 (Yates J): 'The concealment of material circumstances vitiates all contracts, upon the principles of natural law. A man, if kept ignorant of any material ingredient, may safely say that it is not his contract'.

[122] *Carter* (n 1 above) 3 Burr 1905, 1909; 97 ER 1162, 1164.

[123] *Carter* (n 1 above) 3 Burr 1905, 1909; 97 ER 1162, 1164.

[124] *Carter* (n 1 above) 3 Burr 1905, 1909; 97 ER 1162, 1164.

[125] None of the cases cited in n 120 above provides any hints as to these limits, and subsequent textbook treatments, noted at 82–4 below, indicate that *Carter v Boehm* offered the first reported statements in this regard.

until late in the 19th century[126]; and it was more than another century before the House of Lords authoritatively clarified the required standard of influence.[127] However, a close reading of Lord Mansfield's express words, together with the actual decision in *Carter v Boehm*, suggests that Lord Mansfield may have contemplated a relatively demanding objective 'different risk' standard. Any non-disclosure would have to vary the risk undertaken, in the mind of a reasonable underwriter.[128]

The greater part of Lord Mansfield's statement of principle was concerned to elaborate a number of additional circumstances in which an insurer could make no complaint of non-disclosure by his insured. Reported by Burrows in somewhat tortuous terms,[129] the passages can be distilled into the following major propositions. An insurer could not complain of non-disclosure of any matter he knew, by whatever means, or ought to have known; nor of any matter in relation to which he had waived disclosure, or had assumed the burden of inquiry. He could not complain of non-disclosure of matters of general public notoriety; nor of matters that an underwriter in the ordinary conduct of his business could be expected to know or inform himself of. He was required to make his own independent assessment of the risk undertaken, and so could not expect to be informed of the insured's own apprehensions or speculations. And he could not complain of the insured's failure to disclose matters that would lessen the risk undertaken.

Neither the reports of *Carter v Boehm*, nor contemporary treatises, provide any insights into the origins of these important passages. In particular, it is unclear whether they reflected what would have been matters of general agreement in the mercantile world, in England or elsewhere, or whether they reflected a true creative leap on Lord Mansfield's part.

Whatever the correct explanation may be, Lord Mansfield's statements in *Carter v Boehm* were to have a remarkably enduring status.[130] In the decades that immediately followed, they were to provide the backbone of the accounts

---

[126] See *Ionides v Pender* (1874) LR 9 QB 531; *Rivaz v Gerussi* (1880) 6 QBD 222. There are traces of an objective approach of this character in very much earlier cases: eg *Durrell v Bederley* (1815) Holt 283, 286; 171 ER 244, 245 (Gibb CJ) (direction to jury); *Reid & Co v Harvey* (1816) 4 Dow PC 97, 106; 3 ER 1102, 1105 (counsel's argument).

[127] *Pan Atlantic Insurance Co Ltd v Pine Top Insurance Co Ltd* [1995] 1 AC 501 (HL).

[128] See esp Lord Mansfield's language in *Carter* (n 1 above) 3 Burr 1905, 1909, 1911; 97 ER 1162, 1164 and 1165 (which is most consistent with a 'different risk' analysis) and his treatment of the materiality of Wynch's letter, discussed at 100–4 below (which manifests an objective judgment regarding its significance). Cf too Lord Mansfield's robust rejection of the relevance of the broker's evidence regarding how the actual insurer would have responded to the facts not disclosed (which could not be strong evidence, given the uniqueness of the case, of reasonable *market* practice): *Carter* (n 1 above) 3 Burr 1905, 1918; 97 ER 1162, 1168–9.

[129] See *Carter* (n 1 above) 3 Burr 1905, 1910–11; 97 ER 1162, 1164–5.

[130] For subsequent decisions by Lord Mansfield himself that appear to involve the limits articulated in *Carter v Boehm*, see *Planche v Fletcher* (1779) 1 Doug 251, 99 ER 164 (matters of common notoriety); *Court v Martineau* (1782) 3 Doug 161, 99 ER 591 (waiver of disclosure); *Mayne v Walter* (1782) noted in Park, *A System of the Law of Marine Insurances* (n 116 above) 195–6 (waiver of disclosure). These tend to suggest a general disposition, consistent with the resolution of *Carter v Boehm*, to interpret and apply the limits in a robust manner, in favour of honest insureds.

in leading treatises. When Park's *A System of the Law of Marine Insurance* first appeared in 1787,[131] Lord Mansfield's entire judgment was reproduced, in laudatory terms[132]:

> To have given this very elaborate and learned argument in the state in which it was delivered, certainly requires no apology; because from it may be collected all the general principles, upon which the doctrine of concealments, in matters of insurance, is founded, as well as all the exceptions, which can be made to the generality of those principles. To have abridged such an argument, would have very much lessened the pleasure of the reader, and would have been an injury to the venerable judge, who in that form delivered the opinion of the court.

*Carter v Boehm* subsequently received more critical treatment in Marshall's *Treatise on the Law of Insurance*,[133] which first appeared in 1802. Quoting Lord Mansfield's judgment in full at the end of his chapter on 'Concealment',[134] Marshall expressed strong reservations about the decision.[135] He was nevertheless forced to admit that the principles stated by Lord Mansfield were 'in general, abstract propositions of indisputable truth, and [were] laid down with admirable clearness and precision'.[136] Consistently with this, Marshall's discussion of 'what things need not be disclosed' was substantially a verbatim copy of the exceptions articulated by Lord Mansfield in *Carter v Boehm*, with the addition of a further exception, reflected in other decisions of Lord Mansfield, for matters falling within an express or implied warranty.[137]

When Marshall first wrote, he was able to quote no more than a handful of decisions, apart from *Carter v Boehm*, in exemplification of 'what things need not be disclosed'.[138] Over the 19th century, a growing number of reported cases

---

[131] Park, *A System of the Law of Marine Insurance* (n 116 above) ch 10, esp 183–93.

[132] Park, *A System of the Law of Marine Insurance* (n 116 above) 193. *Carter v Boehm* is the earliest authority cited for the proposition that there may be cases where a policy will not be avoided by non-disclosure. Park continues by citing a handful of later cases, remarking that '[t]he rules, then advanced and illustrated, have since been confirmed by the opinion of the judges upon similar questions': *ibid* 193. This text's manner of presentation continued into the 8th edition: F Hildyard (ed), *Park—A System of the Law of Marine Insurances*, 8th edn (London, Saunders & Benning, 1842) vol 1, ch 10.

[133] Marshall, *A Treatise on the Law of Insurance* (n 103 above).

[134] Marshall, *A Treatise on the Law of Insurance* (n 103 above) ch 11.

[135] Marshall, *A Treatise on the Law of Insurance* (n 103 above) 483–4, considering that the result was not 'warranted even by the principles which his lordship lays down as the basis of it'. Marshall's quotation of Lord Mansfield's judgment is annotated with footnotes, expressing doubts about a number of its factual assumptions/findings, and about Lord Mansfield's application of the principles he had stated. However, Marshall also thought that the policy should have been void on public policy grounds, because it necessarily placed the insured in a position of conflicting duties: *ibid* 484, and see 96–7 below.

[136] Marshall, *A Treatise on the Law of Insurance* (n 103 above) 484 fn.

[137] *Haywood v Rodgers* (1804) 4 East 590, 102 ER 957 (foreshadowed by Lord Mansfield's decision in *Shoolbred v Nutt* (1782), noted in Park, *A System of the Law of Marine Insurance* (n 116 above) 229a). Only two other cases are noted in the 2nd edition's (14 page) section: *ibid* 473–86.

[138] Marshall, *A Treatise on the Law of Insurance* (n 103) ch 11, 473–84. This text's manner of presentation continued into the 5th edition: see W Shee (ed), *Marshall—A Treatise on the Law of Marine Insurance*, 5th edn (London, Shaw & Sons, 1865) ch 11.

developed under this head, but really did little more than explore the implications of the principles stated by Lord Mansfield in *Carter v Boehm*, on particular facts. Unsurprisingly, there are few reported cases in which an insurer failed because he knew the fact allegedly concealed.[139] Equally unsurprisingly, rather more cases clustered around the principles that an insurer cannot complain of non-disclosure of matters of common notoriety, or of what the insurer can reasonably be expected to know or inform himself, in the ordinary course of his business. Many of these were relatively uncontroversial cases involving trade usages or similar matters of general commercial knowledge.[140] However, 19th century courts were also inevitably forced to confront the rather more difficult question of whether an insurer could complain of non-disclosure of facts that might be directly disclosed by, or inferred from, the growing number of information sources developed for the underwriting community at Lloyd's.[141] Beyond these, a number of cases illustrated, without significantly illuminating, the potentially important principle that 'waiver of disclosure' will preclude complaint[142]; whilst very few raised the uncontroversial principles that an insured need not disclose his speculations or apprehensions,[143] or what lessens the risk.[144] Overall, this jurisprudence seems remarkable for the relative absence of sustained doctrinal argument and discussion; the rarity with which *Carter v Boehm* is expressly mentioned; and the absence of critical comment on Lord Mansfield's statements. The inference that might be drawn, of their enduring tacit acceptance, is suggested by Mellor J's observations in *Bates v Hewitt* in 1867[145]:

> So far as I know, the judgment of Lord Mansfield has never been qualified or questioned. The only part of it upon which any doubt has been raised is, as to the

---

[139] Cf *Planche v Fletcher* (1779) 1 Doug 251, 99 ER 164.

[140] Cf *Vallance v Dewar* (1808) 1 Camp 503, 170 ER 1036; *Tennant v Henderson* (1813) 1 Dow PC 324, 3 ER 716; *Tate & Sons v Hyslop* (1885) 15 QBD 368; *The Bedouin* [1894] P 1; *Mercantile Steamship Co Ltd v Tyser* (1880) LR 7 QBD 73; *Asfar & Co v Blundell* [1896] 1 QB 123. And more generally, *Planche v Fletcher* (1779) 1 Doug 251, 99 ER 164; *Thomson v Buchanan* (1782) 4 Brown PC 482, 2 ER 329.

[141] See esp *Friere v Woodhouse* (1815–17) Holt 572, 171 ER 345; *Elton v Larkins* (1831) 5 Car & P 86, 172 ER 888; (1832) 8 Bing 196, 131 ER 376; (1832) 5 Car & P 385, 172 ER 1019; *Mackintosh v Marshall* (1843) 11 M & W 116, 152 ER 739; *Foley v Tabor* (1861) 2 F & F 663, 175 ER 1231; *Gandy v Adelaide Marine Insurance Co* (1871) LR 6 QB 746; *Morrison v Universal Marine Insurance Co* (1872) LR 8 Ex 40, rvd on a different point, (1873) LR 8 ER 197. Cases also raised the more general question, how far an insurer could complain of non-disclosure of facts that could or might be inferred from knowledge that he had or ought to have had: esp *Bates v Hewitt* (1867) LR 2 QB 595; *Gandy v Adelaide Marine Insurance Co* (1871) LR 6 QB 746.

[142] Cf *Beckwith v Sydebotham* (1807) 1 Camp 116, 170 ER 897; *Fort v Lee* (1811) 3 Taunt 381, 128 ER 151; *Hull v Cooper* (1811) 14 East 479, 104 ER 685; *Boyd v Dubois* (1811) 3 Camp 138, 170 ER 1331; *Freeland v Glover* (1806) 7 East 457, 103 ER 177, all of which were cited in later works, not always easily, under this head. See, eg EL de Hart and RI Simey (eds), *Arnould on the Law of Marine Insurance*, 7th edn (London, Stevens & Sons, 1901) §§ 618–622.

[143] Cf *Thomson v Buchanan* (1782) 4 Brown PC 482, 2 ER 329; *Bell v Bell* (1810) 2 Camp 475, 170 ER 1223.

[144] Cf *Westbury v Aberdein* (1837) 2 M & W 267, 150 ER 756.

[145] *Bates v Hewitt* (1867) LR 2 QB 595, 610.

admissibility in evidence of the opinions of brokers . . . as to the materiality of the facts not communicated.[146] That judgment rests on a sound principle, and has always been considered as laying down the true rules which govern the law of insurance (footnotes omitted).

Even clearer evidence of the enduring status of Lord Mansfield's statements came 40 years further on, with the codification of the Common law governing marine insurance in the Marine Insurance Act 1906. That Act's basic structure, in sections 17 and 18, bears an unmistakable resemblance to Lord Mansfield's account. Section 17 states the mutual obligations of good faith of insurer and insured. Section 18 then states basic obligation on an assured to disclose every material circumstance known to him,[147] the applicable standard of materiality,[148] and then, finally, and crucially, the exceptions[149]:

> (3) In the absence of inquiry the following circumstances need not be disclosed, namely:
> (a) Any circumstance which diminishes the risk;
> (b) Any circumstance which is known or presumed to be known to the insurer. The insurer is presumed to know matters of common notoriety or knowledge, and matters which an insurer in the ordinary course of his business, as such, ought to know.
> (c) Any circumstance as to which information is waived by the insurer;
> (d) Any circumstance which it is superfluous to disclose by reason of any express or implied warranty.

In *Chalmers' Marine Insurance Act*,[150] *Carter v Boehm* is the earliest, and in one case, the only authority, cited in the notes to paragraphs (a), (b) and (c). Even paragraph (d) was reflected in other decisions of Lord Mansfield.[151]

It is an important question, beyond the scope of this chapter, whether beneath this coincidence of general principles, the balance of the law in fact altered. It is conceivable that it could and did, without fatally undermining *Carter v Boehm*'s authority. A number of the exceptions formulated by Lord Mansfield are inherently susceptible to very different interpretations, reflecting very

---

[146] For discussion of this early debate, see, eg Arnould, *A Treatise on the Law of Marine Insurance and Average* (n 103 above) § 212; JW Smith, *A Selection of Leading Cases on Various Branches of the Law*, 2nd edn (London, A Maxwell, 1841) vol 1, 283–6, a discussion continued in later editions. In *Carter* (n 1 above) 3 Burr 1905, 1918; 97 ER 1162, 1168–9, Lord Mansfield refused to admit the actual broker's opinion that Boehm would not have underwritten the policy if the matters not disclosed had been revealed. In later cases, Lord Mansfield was assumed, perhaps wrongly, to be laying down a general principle regarding the admissibility of the evidence of brokers and/or underwriters.

[147] Marine Insurance Act 1906, s 18(1).

[148] Marine Insurance Act 1906, s 18(2).

[149] Marine Insurance Act 1906, s 18(3).

[150] ER Hardy Ivamy, *Chalmers' Marine Insurance Act 1906*, 10th revised edn (London, Tottel Publishing, 1993).

[151] See *Shoolbred v Nutt* (1782) noted in Park, *A System of the Law of Marine Insurance* (n 116 above) 229a. See, subsequently, *Haywood v Rodgers* (1804) East 590, 102 ER 957. Cf also *Ross v Bradshaw* (1761) 1 Black W 312, 96 ER 175 (life insurance).

different conceptions of where the line should properly be drawn between what insureds should tell their insurers without inquiry, and what insurers should know or seek to inform themselves of, by inquiry of the insured or otherwise.[152] Advocates of narrowly-defined exceptions could emphasise Lord Mansfield's initial emphatic statement of the insured's obligation, and the importance of preserving the strongest incentives for full disclosure.[153] Conversely, advocates of more widely-defined exceptions could emphasise Lord Mansfield's limited rationalisation of the insured's obligation as a corrective for an inequality of accessible information, the mutuality of the requirement of good faith that arguably Lord Mansfield assumes, and the actual manner in which Lord Mansfield resolved the case at hand.[154]

## 2. The Context and Construction of the Policy

Lord Mansfield's statement of law in *Carter v Boehm* placed important obstacles in the way of Boehm's success, which Boehm's counsel may not have predicted when proceedings first commenced. Two further factors combined to make Boehm's task even more difficult: Lord Mansfield's findings regarding the context in which Carter's insurance policy was effected in London; and his findings regarding the proper construction of the policy, and in particular, the insured-against contingency.

### (a)  The Circumstances in which Carter's Insurance Policy was Effected

Lord Mansfield prefaced his consideration of Boehm's particular allegations of material non-disclosure with the following account of the circumstances in which Carter's policy was effected in London in May 1760[155]:

> The policy was signed in May 1760. The contingency was 'whether Fort Marlborough was or would be taken, by a European enemy, between October 1759, and October 1760'.
> The computation of the risque depended upon the chance, 'whether any European power would attack the place by sea.' If they did, it was incapable of resistance.
> The under-writer at London, in May 1760, could judge much better of the probability of the contingency, than Governor Carter could at Fort Marlborough, in September 1759. He knew the success of the operations of the war in Europe. He knew what naval force the English and French had sent to the East Indies. He knew, from a

---

[152] Cf analogously, the opposing conclusions reached in the *Pan Atlantic* litigation, regarding the standard of materiality assumed in *Carter v Boehm*: see *Pan Atlantic Insurance Co Ltd v Pine Top Insurance Co Ltd* [1995] 1 AC 501. Steyn LJ in the Court of Appeal, and Lord Lloyd (dissenting) in the House of Lords took Lord Mansfield to be articulating a relatively demanding standard of materiality. Lord Mustill (giving the leading judgment for the majority in the House of Lords) reached an opposite conclusion.
[153] See, esp the reasoning of the court in *Bates v Hewitt* (n 145 above).
[154] See, esp the arguments reflected in the 'waiver of disclosure' cases noted at nn 267–269 below.
[155] *Carter* (n 1 above) 3 Burr 1905, 1914–15; 97 ER 1162, 1167.

comparison of that force, whether the sea was open to any such attempt by the French. He knew, or might know, every thing which was known at Fort Marlborough in September 1759, of the general state of affairs in the East Indies, or the particular condition of Fort Marlborough, by the ship which brought the orders for the insurance. He knew that ship must have brought many letters to the East India Company; and, particularly, from the governor. He knew what probability there was of the Dutch committing or having committed hostilities.

Under these circumstances, and with this knowledge, he insures against the general contingency of the place being attacked by a European power.

Set against Lord Mansfield's preceding exposition of the law, the purpose of this account seems clear: viz, to emphasise the prima facie obstacles to Boehm's successfully resisting liability for non-disclosure. Lord Mansfield's premise was that the context in which Carter's policy was underwritten by Boehm lacked the substantial inequality of accessible information, and resulting necessary dependence of the insurer on disclosure by his prospective insured, that provided the normative basis for the law's allowing an insurer to avoid liability for non-disclosure. An understanding of the historical context of *Carter v Boehm* enables us to see quite how robustly adverse to Boehm's interest that analysis was.

Lord Mansfield's principal proposition was that Boehm, in London in May 1760, was substantially better placed accurately to estimate the likelihood of the insured-against contingency's occurring than Carter was in September 1759. This is difficult to dispute. If the contingency was the loss of Fort Marlborough to a European enemy,[156] an insurer would be concerned to estimate the likelihood of a European enemy attempting an assault, and of any assault succeeding. By May 1760, there was no substantial inequality of accessible information as regards either.

The likelihood of a European enemy attempting an assault on Fort Marlborough would principally be a function of events in Europe and the course of the Anglo-French conflict in the East Indies. By nature, these were not events falling peculiarly within Carter's knowledge. Indeed, by May 1760, the state of general intelligence in London regarding them was unquestionably in advance of the state of intelligence in Sumatra in September 1759. This was obviously true of European events, but it was also true of the Anglo-French conflict. Carter's most recent intelligence concerning events in India probably did not extend beyond the early spring of 1759.[157] In contrast, by May 1760, news had

---

[156] This is the assumption most favourable to Boehm, which Lord Mansfield makes in the quoted passage, though it does not reflect the construction of the policy that Lord Mansfield ultimately prefers: see 90–3 below.

[157] This would have been apparent to Lord Mansfield from the secret letter of Carter and Preston which was in evidence before the court. See IOR/G/35/12, Letter from Roger Carter and Richard Preston, Fort Marlborough, to the Secret Committee, Court of Directors, 16 September 1759, folio 287 ff, para 2, in which Carter and Preston related what they knew of events in India, and in particular, related that they had received reports from Batavia in August of the raising of the siege of Fort St George on 16 February 1759, but that their last direct communication from that Presidency was from the autumn of 1758. See further 104–5, nn 235–6 below.

certainly reached London of events from the summer and autumn of that year.[158]

The likelihood of any attempted assault by a European enemy succeeding would principally be a function of the strength of Fort Marlborough's defences, relative to the strength of any enemy force. The effect of Lord Mansfield's findings earlier in his judgment was that there was also no substantial inequality of accessible information in relation to this. It was notorious amongst those in London who interested themselves in East Indies affairs that Fort Marlborough was essentially a trading community, and not a military establishment; that it was only intended and constructed to withstand a native attack; and that if attacked by a European enemy, it would fall.[159] Assuming such knowledge, any calculation of the insured risk would depend only on a calculation of the chances of a European attack.[160]

There is no doubt that this absence of any substantial inequality of accessible information regarding the circumstances likely to influence an insurer's calculation greatly complicated Boehm's task. It inevitably made it difficult for Boehm to satisfy a court that, in view of what he knew or could reasonably have known, any information not disclosed had actually affected his risk assessment, and/or would have affected a reasonable insurer's risk assessment. It also inevitably made it difficult for Boehm to identify any fact not disclosed by Carter, about which he was not precluded from complaining on the basis that it fell within one of the exceptions articulated by Lord Mansfield. Most were readily classifiable as matters of 'general intelligence' or 'common notoriety'.

The absence of any substantial inequality of accessible information did not mean, however, that Carter and Boehm had equal information. There were at least two matters, known to Carter in September 1759, and potentially influencing an insurer's estimate of the risk, that could not be assumed to be matters of general intelligence in London by May 1760. They formed the basis of Boehm's strongest allegations of non-disclosure, examined below. One was the existence and contents of Wynch's letter to Carter.[161] Another was the particular state of Fort Marlborough's fortifications in September 1759.[162]

---

[158] See the London press reports of March–April 1760, noted at n 240 below. Carter probably did not receive intelligence about the same events until late December 1759, as noted in the text to n 236 below.

[159] See *Carter* (n 1 above) 3 Burr 1905, 1912–13; 97 ER 1162, 1166, where Lord Mansfield's findings regarding the general condition of Fort Marlborough are followed by the findings that 'the general state and condition of the said fort, and of the strength thereof, was, in general well known, by most persons conversant or acquainted with Indian affairs, or the state of the Company's factories or settlements; and could not be kept secret or concealed from persons who should endeavour by proper inquiry, to inform themselves'. It is clear that Fort Marlborough's defensive weaknesses were long-standing, and a recurring topic in the general dispatches between Fort Marlborough and the Court of Directors: see generally Harfield, *Bencoolen* (n 7 above).

[160] See *Carter* (n 1 above) 3 Burr 1905, 1914; 97 ER 1162, 1167: 'The computation of the risque depended upon the chance, "whether any European power would attack the place by sea." If they did, it was incapable of resistance'.

[161] See 67–9 above, and 94–9 below.

[162] See 71–2 above, and 99–104 below.

Lord Mansfield's second major proposition in his account of the London context of Carter's policy may have been designed to pre-empt the success of these arguments. His account concluded with the observation that, whatever might otherwise be known in London, Boehm knew or might have known everything known at Fort Marlborough in September 1759 regarding events in the East Indies, and the particular state of Fort Marlborough's fortifications, via the *Pitt*, which brought Carter's insurance instructions to England.[163] On the face of it, this comes dangerously close to the proposition that everything material known to Carter was known to, or knowable by, Boehm by May 1760.

The basis for this remarkable second proposition is an important fact, known to Lord Mansfield but not revealed by the case reports. Every fact that Carter knew in September 1759, and had allegedly concealed, was communicated by Carter via the packet of secret correspondence dispatched on the *Pitt* for the attention of the Secret Committee of the Court of Directors.[164] It obviously followed that on the *Pitt*'s arrival in Europe, none of the facts allegedly concealed were exclusively within Carter's private knowledge, and further, that they were known in London, in some quarters. However, on one reading of Burrows' report, Lord Mansfield went rather further than this. Boehm must have known that the Company would have received correspondence from Carter via the *Pitt*, and might at least have discovered its contents by means of inquiry open to him. This is a very difficult assumption to sustain.

The arrival of an East Indiaman like the *Pitt* would certainly have been keenly awaited in London, as the primary source of news from the East Indies. A snapshot of the contemporary press suggests the *Pitt*'s arrival may have attracted particular attention, because of a path-breaking journey to China.[165] It also suggests that the *Pitt* was a means by which news of recent events in the East Indies became matters of general intelligence in London,[166] and that this included news of some events, known to Carter in September 1759 and potentially bearing on

[163] *Carter* (n 1 above) 3 Burr 1905, 1914–15; 97 ER 1162, 1167.

[164] See 70–2 above, where the contents of this secret packet are discussed. It included Carter and Preston's secret letter of 16 September 1759, which reported (inter alia) the poor state of Fort Marlborough's fortifications (paras 12–19), Wynch's letter (paras 10–11), and the Dutch armament at Batavia (para 7): IOR/G/35/12, Letter from Roger Carter and Richard Preston, Fort Marlborough, to the Secret Committee of the Court of Directors, 16 September 1759, folio 287 ff. It also included a copy of Wynch's letter to Roger Carter. Lord Mansfield had Carter and Preston's letter before him.

[165] London papers noted its arrival, reporting that on 1 March 1760, the Company received an account of the *Pitt*'s arrival at Kinsale (where it had arrived on 23 February 1760: IOR/L/MAR/B/525, index to marine records): eg *London Chronicle* (1–4 March 1760) 219, cols 1; *London Evening Post* (1–4 March 1760) 1, cols 1–2. The *Pitt*'s remarkable China voyage is reported in the same papers, following the *Pitt*'s subsequent arrival in the Thames in mid-April: eg *London Chronicle* (15–17 April 1760) 370, col 2; similarly, *London Evening Post* (15–17 April 1760) 1, col 2. For discussion of the voyage, see P Crowhurst, *The Defence of British Trade* (Folkestone, Dawson, 1977) ch 7, esp 229–33.

[166] See esp *London Chronicle* (1–4 March 1760) 219, cols 1–2 (advices received via the *Pitt* regarding Colonel Clive's exploits); similarly, *London Evening Post* (1–4 March 1760) 1, col 1. The *Pitt* arrived in Company with the *Warren*, which brought more recent intelligence from Fort St George of events on the Coromandel Coast after the raising of the siege of Fort St George.

the risk insured-against: viz, news of the Dutch armament at nearby Batavia, which reports suggest came from the *Pitt*'s crew.[167] Nevertheless, there is no evidence that the contents of Carter's correspondence addressed to the Secret Committee of the Court of Directors similarly became public. Indeed, it is inherently unlikely that it would: such secret correspondence would ordinarily have had a very limited circulation, even within the Company's Directorship.[168] For the same reason, the lesser claim that Boehm might have discovered the contents of the correspondence by inquiry of the Company,[169] seems questionable. It may depend on some bold but unarticulated assumptions about Boehm's personal connections and influence.[170]

(b) The Construction of the Policy: The Insured-against Contingency

The fate of Boehm's allegations in *Carter v Boehm* was not just vitally shaped by the court's findings regarding the context in which the policy was effected. It was also vitally shaped by the court's findings regarding the proper construction of the policy, and in particular, the insured-against contingency. This was a matter fiercely disputed by the parties in argument.[171] At first sight, this may seem surprising: on any analysis, the insured-against contingency had occurred,

---

[167] *London Evening Post* (11–13 March 1760) 1, col 2. See further 109–10 below. The final sentence of Lord Mansfield's description of the context of the policy, in which he refers to Boehm's knowledge of the likelihood of Dutch aggression, suggests that he may have recognised this: *Carter* (n 1 above) 3 Burr 1905, 1915; 97 ER 1162, 1167.

[168] The Secret Committee comprised a small number of the full body of Directors. The Court Books show that letters addressed to the Secret Committee might be read to the full Court of Directors, but that this was not routinely the case. Instead, the minutes and proceedings of the Secret Committee, to the extent that they were no longer sensitive, would periodically be read at the meetings of the full Court of Directors. Unlike the general letter from Fort Marlborough of 21 September 1759, there is no record of Carter and Preston's secret letter of 16 September 1759 having been read to the full Court of Directors (see 70, n 58), but the Court Books do indicate that they subsequently received a summary of the Secret Committee's deliberations during this period. See IOR/B/75, Minutes of Meeting of Court of Directors, 1 April 1760, 672 (reading of minutes and proceedings of the 'Committee of Secrecy' from 5 December 1759 to 31 March 1760).

[169] Cf similarly, Marshall, *A Treatise on the Law of Insurance* (n 103 above) 482n: 'What he wrote to the company was not likely to be made public, and therefore not likely to come to the knowledge of the underwriter!'. Lord Mansfield's assumption is also difficult to square with the Company's resistance to disclosing Carter and Preston's secret letter during the litigation: see 95 below.

[170] Boehm undoubtedly occupied prominent positions in some of the City's key institutions at this time, including a directorship of the Bank of England: see R Roberts and D Kynaston, *The Bank of England—Money, Power & Influence 1694–1994* (Oxford, Oxford University Press 1995) appendix 2. JG Parker, 'The Directors of the East India Company 1754–1790' (PhD thesis, University of Edinburgh, 1977) is a good starting-point for further inquiry into the nature and extent of Boehm's family or other connections to the East India Company's directorship. I am grateful to Professor Huw Bowen, University of Leicester, for directing my attention to this.

[171] See *Carter* (n 1 above) 3 Burr 1905, 1908; 97 ER 1162, 1163–4, where counsel's arguments are summarised. Counsel for the insured: '[T]his insurance, was in reality, no more than a wager; "whether the French would think it their interest to attack this fort; and if they should, whether they would be able to get a ship of war up the river, or not"'. Counsel for the insurer: 'This wager is not only "whether the fort shall be attacked:" but "whether it shall be attacked and taken"'.

and Boehm was prima facie liable to pay the insured sum. On closer examination, however, the reason is obvious. The parties saw that the construction preferred might vitally affect the success of Boehm's defence, that Carter was guilty of material non-disclosure in failing to disclose Fort Marlborough's weak defensive state in September 1759.

Lord Mansfield's firm conclusion was that the contingency in the parties' contemplation was an attack on Fort Marlborough by a European enemy. It was not, as Boehm's counsel had contended, the loss of Fort Marlborough, so as to require Fort Marlborough to be attacked and taken.[172] There are two reasons why this conclusion is striking. First, it was a notably pro-insured construction of the policy: it greatly facilitated the court's rejection of Boehm's allegation that Fort Marlborough's weak defensive state in September 1759 was a 'material' matter which Carter was obliged to disclose.[173] Secondly, that construction probably required an important implication into Carter's policy, varying its express terms. Although this point can be obscured by poor reporting of the case, the best account of the policy's express terms suggests that the insurer's liability in terms depended upon the loss of Fort Marlborough to a European enemy, and not merely an attack on the place. That is, the policy's express terms were more consistent with Boehm's analysis of the insured-against contingency than that which the court eventually preferred. In Lord Mansfield's words,

> [t]he policy is against the loss [of] Fort Marlborough, from being destroyed by, taken by, or surrendered unto, any European enemy, between 1st of October 1759, and 1st of October 1760.[174]

Pointing in the same direction was the 'all or nothing' nature of the insurer's liability. If the insured-against contingency occurred, the insurer was liable to pay the insured sum of £10,000, in full and without further inquiry.[175]

There is obvious room for disagreement about the process by which Lord Mansfield felt able to conclude, in the face of the policy's express terms, that the insured-against contingency was a European enemy attack. It would certainly be consistent with the general orientation of his judgment if his conclusion was simply the result of a strong inclination to find against Boehm. However, a preferable alternative analysis is that it reflected a bona fide attempt to make commercial sense of the policy's unusual terms, in view of the policy's known purpose.[176]

---

[172] *Carter* (n 1 above) 3 Burr 1905, 1916–17; 97 ER 1162, 1167–8.

[173] See 97–9 below.

[174] *Carter* (n 1 above) 3 Burr 1905, 1911; 97 ER 1162, 1165. Different descriptions of the contingency elsewhere in the report are unreliable, in that they do not seem to state the express terms of the policy, but instead, to express the outcome of Lord Mansfield's exercise in construction: viz, his implied reading down of the policy's express words. See too the reported terms of Carter's counsel's argument, quoted in n 171 above, the sense of which is that even if the form of the policy suggested the contrary, its substance was a policy against a European enemy attack only.

[175] See 77 above. Properly understood, this was what Lord Mansfield meant when he said that the policy 'insures against a total loss': *Carter* (n 1 above) 3 Burr 1905, 1916; 97 ER 1162, 1167.

[176] See 75–9 above.

Central to understanding this is the apparent disjunction between the form and purpose of the policy, previously explained.[177] Had Carter been a true wagering party, without any substantial interest in Fort Marlborough's fate, there would have been no pressing reason for the court to take the policy otherwise than at face value. It would not be irrational for the parties to wager 'all or nothing' on whether Fort Marlborough might be lost to a European enemy. The problem confronting the court, however, was that Carter was not a true wagering party.[178] To the knowledge of the insurer and the court, he sought to insure his stock-in-trade at Fort Marlborough against loss in the event of a European enemy assault on the place.[179] The policy's express terms were less obviously well-tuned to that different purpose. On the one hand, the insurer was only liable in the most extreme event of an assault culminating in the fall of Fort Marlborough. On the other hand, if that event occurred, the insurer would be liable for the full insured sum, without further inquiry.

On examination, Lord Mansfield's reconciliation appears to have been as follows.[180] The insured-against contingency was a European enemy attack on Fort Marlborough, and not its loss. Though at first sight inconsistent with the policy's express terms, this analysis could be reconciled with them and with the policy's purpose, via the assumption that the parties knew that Fort Marlborough was only designed to withstand native attack, and so anticipated that it would fall if it were subject to an attack by a European enemy. Assuming such knowledge, it was not commercial nonsense for the parties to bargain that the insured sum should be payable in full, and without further inquiry, in the event of a European enemy attack. The parties would anticipate that any European enemy attack on Fort Marlborough would result in a total loss of Carter's stock-in-trade there, the value of which exceeded the sum insured.[181] This analysis is the best way of making sense of the following passage in Burrows' report, where Lord Mansfield explains his analysis of the insured-against contingency[182]:

> The utmost which can be contended is, that the underwriter trusted to the fort being in the condition in which it ought to be . . . What is that condition? All the witnesses agree 'that it was only to resist the natives, and not an European force.' The policy insures against a total loss; taking for granted 'that if the place was attacked it would be lost.'

[177] See 75–9 above.
[178] See 75–9 above.
[179] See 75–6 above.
[180] See esp *Carter* (n 1 above) 3 Burr 1905, 1915–16; 97 ER 1162, 1167–8. Identical assumptions about the policy's purpose, and what the parties knew about its subject-matter, could have supported a construction which took the policy at face value, taking the insured-against contingency as the *loss* of Fort Marlborough; but even on this basis, Carter's non-disclosure would not have been 'material', for reasons explained at 98–9 below.
[181] See, eg *Carter* (n 1 above) 3 Burr 1905, 1907 and 1913; 97 ER 1162, 1163 and 1166.
[182] *Carter* (n 1 above) 3 Burr 1905, 1915–16; 97 ER 1162, 1167.

The contingency therefore which the under-writer has insured against is, 'whether the place would be attacked by an European force; and not whether it would be able to resist such an attack, if the ships could get up the river.'

Lord Mansfield never made any clear finding whether Boehm actually knew that Fort Marlborough was only designed to withstand native attack.[183] However, he had previously found that this was generally known, amongst those who concerned themselves with East Indies' affairs. On that basis, it seems that Lord Mansfield was adopting an objective interpretative approach, construing the parties' express/implied intentions in light of the knowledge that they could reasonably be expected to have about the policy's subject-matter. Consistently with this approach, Boehm could not have demanded that the policy be construed in accordance with his own, ex hypothesi unreasonable state of ignorance regarding Fort Marlborough's true condition.

### 3. Boehm's Defences to Liability

With Lord Mansfield's statement of law, and his findings regarding the context and construction of Carter's policy in view, we can turn to the court's treatment of Boehm's defences to liability. In the absence of any finding of fraudulent intention on Carter's part, Boehm's case depended on establishing material non-disclosure. This required Boehm to identify some matter, known to Carter or his agent but not disclosed, that varied the risk which Boehm undertook in May 1760 when he underwrote Carter's policy—viz, the risk of a European enemy attack on Fort Marlborough within one year from October 1759.

The strongest allegation, that Carter knew of a subsisting French scheme to attack Fort Marlborough, was not available to Boehm. There was no such scheme, to Carter's knowledge, in September 1759, when the insurance instructions were dispatched. And whilst D'Estaing's expedition certainly did come to Carter's knowledge in Sumatra by late February 1760, it was impossible to convey this knowledge to London before the policy was effected. Counsel quite rightly refrained from arguing that this non-disclosure would vitiate Carter's policy.[184]

In those circumstances, Boehm was left to allege non-disclosure of three other matters, to which Lord Mansfield added a fourth. They were: the poor defensive state of Fort Marlborough in September 1759; Alexander Wynch's letter to Roger Carter of February 1759, in which he reported the unimplemented French plans of 1758; Carter's apprehension that the French were more likely than

---

[183] See 88 above.
[184] See now the Marine Insurance Act 1906, s 19(2), which contains an exception for exactly this sort of case, where policies are effected by agents: the policy will be vitiated by non-disclosure of every material circumstance 'which the assured is bound to disclose, unless it comes to his knowledge too late to communicate it to the agent'.

before to attack, expressed in his letter to his brother of 22 September 1759; and finally, Carter's grounds for fearing the outbreak of a Dutch war. These allegations, and the court's treatment of them, are examined in the sections that follow.

### E.  MATERIAL NON-DISCLOSURE (I): THE DEFENSIVE CONDITION OF FORT MARLBOROUGH

#### 1. Background

Boehm's first objection to liability under the policy relied on Fort Marlborough's weak defensive condition. It was probably the objection most strongly pressed, at least on the motion for re-trial.[185] As formulated by counsel, the argument was that Carter was guilty of material non-disclosure in failing to disclose Fort Marlborough's defensive state in September 1759. An alternative formulation, reflected in some reports of Lord Mansfield's discussion of the allegation, was that there was an implied warranty in Carter's policy that Fort Marlborough was in a good defensive state, which had been breached.[186]

Viewed in its historical context, the force of Boehm's argument is obvious. On 24 September 1759, when the *Pitt* left Sumatra for London with Deputy Governor Carter's insurance instructions on board, Carter unquestionably knew that Fort Marlborough was unlikely to be able to withstand a concerted European attack. Its vulnerability had been a constant cause for concern for the Company's West Coast servants in the preceding years. It was also unequivocally confirmed by the inquiries conducted by the military officers, on the orders of Carter and the Secret Committee in August–September 1759, immediately following the arrival of Wynch's letter.[187]

What made this first allegation particularly attractive for Boehm was that the available evidence incontrovertibly showed that Carter knew of, but had failed to disclose, Fort Marlborough's weak defensive state. By their secret letter of

---

[185] *Carter* (n 1 above) 3 Burr 1905, 1908; 97 ER 1162, 1164: 'It is begging the question to say, "that a fort is not intended for defence against an enemy." The supposition is absurd and ridiculous. It must be presumed that it was intended for that purpose: and the presumption was "that the fort, the powder, the guns, &c were in a good and proper condition." If they were not, (and it is agreed that in fact they were not, and that the governor knew it,) it ought to have been disclosed. But if he had disclosed this, he could not have got the insurance'.

[186] In Burrows's report, the implied condition argument is interwoven with an argument about material non-disclosure: *Carter* (n 1 above) 3 Burr 1905, 1915–16; 97 ER 1162, 1167. In Blackstone's briefer report, the reasoning is arguably in implied conditions terms only: 1 Black W 593, 595; 96 ER 342. The argument was founded on an analogy with the warranty of seaworthiness implied into marine insurance policies. Later cases were to confirm that these arguments were alternatives: an insured was not obliged to disclose matters falling within the scope of an express or implied warranty. See n 137 above.

[187] IOR/G/35/12, Minutes of the Secret Committee, Fort Marlborough, 22 August 1759, folios 267–9 (discussed at 69 above); *ibid* 7 September 1759, folios 271–2 (discussed at 69 above).

16 September 1759, described above, Carter and Preston comprehensively reported Fort Marlborough's dire position to the Secret Committee of the Court of Directors.[188] At the time of the 1762 actions on Carter's policy, the Company had apparently refused to deliver this letter to the parties, 'because it contained some matters which they did not think proper to be made public'.[189] However, Boehm *was* able to obtain possession of the letter for the purposes of the 1766 trial/motion for re-trial.[190]

Lord Mansfield's statement of the law in *Carter v Boehm*, and his subsequent findings of fact, were nevertheless to expose important vulnerabilities in Boehm's case. First, Boehm's allegation that Fort Marlborough's weak defensive state was material to the insured risk depended heavily on a construction of the policy which Lord Mansfield ultimately rejected: viz, that the insured-against contingency was the loss of Fort Marlborough to a European enemy.[191] Secondly, Lord Mansfield's statement of the law in any event made the parties' relative states of knowledge regarding Fort Marlborough's defensive state critical. Lord Mansfield made a number of findings in this regard, which—directly or indirectly—were to prove fatal to Boehm's argument.[192]

These findings have already been considered. Their relationship to Boehm's first allegation needs to be clearly perceived. The allegation is best understood as an allegation that Carter had not disclosed the particulars of Fort Marlborough's defensive state in September 1759, which Carter and Preston related in their secret letter of 16 September 1759. Some passages in Lord Mansfield's judgment suggest an assumption that Boehm could have discovered these particulars, by means of inquiry open to him, in May 1760. This is a very questionable assumption, as previously explained,[193] and it was not necessary for Lord Mansfield's decision. Even if the particulars of Fort Marlborough's defensive state in September 1759 were not known to, or reasonably discoverable by, members of

---

[188] IOR/G/35/12, Letter from Roger Carter and Richard Preston, Fort Marlborough, to the Secret Committee of the Court of Directors, 16 September 1759, folio 287 ff, paras 10–18 (discussed at 71–2 above).

[189] See *Carter* (n 1 above) 3 Burr 1905, 1911; 97 ER 1162, 1165. It can be inferred that Lord Mansfield is referring to Carter and Preston's letter. The request for copies of the Company's 'late Advices' from Bencoolen for the 1762 trial is recorded in IOR/B/77, Minutes of Meeting of Court of Directors, 10 February 1762, 292. Carter and Preston's letter would have revealed the intelligence-gathering activities of John Herbert, the Company's agent at Batavia. But on balance, the Company's sensitivities are most likely to have stemmed from a desire to keep concealed their efforts to obtain Chinese slaves via the supracargoes at Canton: IOR/G/35/12, Letter from Roger Carter and Richard Preston to the Secret Committee of the Court of Directors, 16 September 1759, folio 287 ff, paras 3–6.

[190] See *Carter* (n 1 above) 3 Burr 1905, 1913, 1913n; 97 ER 1162, 1166, 1166n. The Company's records put beyond doubt that the secret letter of 16 September 1759 was the letter brought to court: see the resolutions that the 'Proper Officer' on being subpoenaed should attend, with the letter, the insurance cause being tried between 'William Black and Charles Boehm Esqrs' and Roger Carter: IOR/B/81, Minutes of Meeting of Court of Directors, 4 December 1765, 272; *ibid* 19 February 1766, 363.

[191] See 90–93 above.

[192] See 88 above.

[193] See 89–90 above.

the London underwriting community in May 1760, Boehm knew or could reasonably be expected to know the 'general state' of the place, or could have discovered the 'general state' of the place by reasonable inquiry. Hence he knew or could have known that it was a trading settlement, fortified and garrisoned to resist native attack only, and ex hypothesi unable to withstand an attack by a European enemy.

## 2. The Court's Rejection of the Argument

### (a) 'Waiver of Disclosure'

Lord Mansfield's first response was that Boehm had waived disclosure of Fort Marlborough's defensive state by Carter, and taken the burden of inquiry upon himself. Lying behind this response was a dilemma that Carter necessarily faced as a consequence of his position as Company servant and Deputy Governor. It was quite conceivable that Carter could not disclose the particulars of Fort Marlborough's defensive state in September 1759, except at the cost of breaching his obligations of confidentiality to his employer.[194] Carter's own perception of the sensitivity of this information in September 1759 is certainly suggested by his chosen means of communication via the *Pitt*. The matter was not mentioned in the Fort Marlborough Council's general letter of 21 September 1759, addressed to the Court of Directors[195]; nor in Carter's private letter to his brother of 22 September 1759.[196] It was mentioned only in Carter and Preston's secret letter of 16 September 1759, addressed to the Secret Committee of the Court of Directors.[197] This was a mode of communication that would have ensured that it had a very limited readership even within the Company's Directorship in London.

Against this background, Lord Mansfield might have answered that the dilemma was for the insured to resolve, and that he bore the risk of his failure to disclose.[198] However, Lord Mansfield's actual response offered a very different reconciliation of the competing interests of insurer and insured. He was willing to find that Boehm had accepted the burden of inquiry into Fort

---

[194] For an example of the covenant typically signed by covenanted servants of the Company, which included an express confidentiality clause, see IOR/O/1/1.

[195] IOR/G/35/12, Letter from Fort Marlborough to the Court of Directors, 21 September 1759, folios 302–31. See 70 above.

[196] This is implicit in Boehm's counsel's argument, that 'the plaintiff' (that is, Carter's brother) ought in any event to have inquired about Fort Marlborough's state: see *Carter* (n 1 above) 3 Burr 1905, 1908; 97 ER 1162, 1164.

[197] IOR/G/35/12, Letter from Roger Carter and Richard Preston, Fort Marlborough, to the Secret Committee of the Court of Directors, 16 September 1759, folio 287 ff. See 71–2 above.

[198] Cf Marshall's even more extreme response, writing 50 years later, which was that a policy that placed an insured in such a dilemma should be void on public policy grounds: Marshall, *A Treatise on the Law of Insurance* (n 103 above) 484.

Marlborough's defensive state.[199] This conclusion followed from Boehm's having underwritten the policy, without inquiry, in the following circumstances.

First, Boehm knew that he could not reasonably depend on the insured's having disclosed all circumstances that might bear adversely on his calculations, because he knew that Carter was duty-bound to his employer not to disclose Fort Marlborough's defensive state. In Lord Mansfield's words,

> [t]he underwriter knew the insurance was for the governor. He knew the governor must be acquainted with the state of the place. He knew the governor could not disclose it, consistent with his duty.[200]

Secondly, Boehm was not exclusively dependent on disclosure by Carter in practice, because Fort Marlborough's defensive state was not exclusively within Carter's private knowledge, and could be ascertained by other means. In Lord Mansfield's words,

> [i]t was a matter as to which he might be informed various ways: it was not a matter within the private knowledge of the governor only.[201]

By themselves, these central premises can be regarded as rather unfavourable to Boehm, the insurer. Thus, it seems particularly difficult to sustain the assumption that Boehm might have readily obtained information regarding Fort Marlborough's particular condition in September 1759, rather than merely its general condition, for reasons already explained.[202] However, if read in conjunction with other passages of Lord Mansfield's judgment, his analysis in these passages may not have been as robust as the reports suggest. It is probable that Lord Mansfield's conclusions also depended on a third unstated circumstance: viz, that Boehm had reasons to undertake his own burdensome inquiries, because he had reasons to suspect that Carter was withholding adverse knowledge regarding Fort Marlborough's defensive state.[203] Such reasons, if required, could easily be found.[204]

(b) 'Immateriality' of the Poor State of the Fortifications

Burrows' report indicates that Lord Mansfield ultimately did not seek to rely on the 'waiver of disclosure' argument.[205] An alternative answer was available in any event: viz, the particulars of Fort Marlborough's defensive state in September 1759 were not material to the risk undertaken.

---

[199] See *Carter* (n 1 above) 3 Burr 1905, 1915; 97 ER 1162, 1167.
[200] *Carter* (n 1 above) 3 Burr 1905, 1915; 97 ER 1162, 1167.
[201] *Carter* (n 1 above) 3 Burr 1905, 1915; 97 ER 1162, 1167.
[202] For discussion of this assumption, see 88–90 above.
[203] For discussion of the passages manifesting this assumption, see 110–15 below.
[204] For discussion, see 114–15 below.
[205] *Carter* (n 1 above) 3 Burr 1905, 1915; 97 ER 1162, 1167 ('But, not to rely on that', viz, the waiver of disclosure/assumption of the burden of inquiry argument).

Lord Mansfield's conclusion that Carter's non-disclosure was 'immaterial' emerges only very obliquely from Burrows' report. Its basis should nevertheless be obvious. Lord Mansfield's preferred construction of the insured-against contingency meant that Carter's policy rendered the full insured sum payable, without further inquiry, in the event of an attack on Fort Marlborough by a European enemy.[206] It followed that the existence and extent of Boehm's liability as insurer depended only on whether a European enemy attacked Fort Marlborough, and not upon how far any attack was successful. It further followed that a reasonable insurer's risk assessment would only depend on factors influencing the likelihood of an attack being attempted by a European enemy. Hence, and subject to one caveat, the state of Fort Marlborough's defences was immaterial to the risk undertaken.

The caveat is that the state of Fort Marlborough's defences certainly did affect the likelihood of a European enemy attack, in that its notorious weakness made it a substantially more tempting target for small-scale, opportunistic raids of the type planned by the French in 1758, and ultimately carried into effect by D'Estaing in 1760. Carter and Preston clearly appreciated this in September 1759, when they wrote their secret letter to the Court of Directors.[207] However, whilst Lord Mansfield did not expressly address this point, he could easily have dismissed it. Lord Mansfield unquestionably considered that a London underwriter could reasonably be expected to know that Fort Marlborough was only designed to withstand native attack. Assuming that knowledge, he would know enough to indicate that Fort Marlborough would be a tempting target for a raid by a European enemy. That risk assessment would *not* be adversely affected by additional knowledge of the precise particulars of Fort Marlborough's weak defensive state in September 1759. A distant European enemy, planning a raid on the place, could not reasonably be expected to be aware of such details.

For very similar reasons, Boehm's first allegation would almost certainly have failed even if Lord Mansfield had preferred the construction of the insured-against contingency suggested by Boehm's counsel: viz, the loss of Fort Marlborough to a European enemy, and not merely an attack on the place. A reasonable underwriter, knowing that Fort Marlborough was only designed to withstand native attack, would contemplate that any attack on Fort Marlborough by a European enemy would result in its loss, and thus render him liable for the full insured sum.[208] The understanding of the risk being under-

---

[206] See the discussion of the construction of the insured-against contingency at 90–93 above.

[207] See IOR/G/35/12, Letter from Roger Carter and Richard Preston, Fort Marlborough, to the Secret Committee of the Court of Directors, 16 September 1759, folio 287 ff, para 19, quoted at 72 above.

[208] On examination, it seems that the breach of implied warranty argument was rejected on a similar assumption: viz, it was not necessary or reasonable to imply a warranty that Fort Marlborough was in a good defensive state to withstand a European enemy attack, in the light of the knowledge that the parties had or could reasonably be expected to have that Fort Marlborough was only designed to withstand a native attack. See *Carter* (n 1 above) 1 Black W 593, 595; 96 ER 342, 343: '[T]he fort, it is said, was not in the condition it ought to be. That condition ought only to

taken would not be adversely affected by additional knowledge of the precise particulars of Fort Marlborough's weak defensive state in September 1759. The only factors influencing his assessment of the risk would be those influencing the likelihood of an attack being attempted. This alternative route to the same conclusion is suggested by a preliminary passage in Lord Mansfield's judgment, discussed earlier,[209] in which he sets out the nature of Carter's policy[210]:

> The policy was signed in May 1760. The contingency was 'whether Fort Marlborough was or would be taken, by an European enemy, between October 1759, and October 1760.'
>
> The computation of the risque depended upon the chance, 'whether any European power would attack the place by sea,' If they did, it was incapable of resistance.

## F. MATERIAL NON-DISCLOSURE (II): ALEXANDER WYNCH'S LETTER FROM THE CAPE OF GOOD HOPE

### 1. Background

Boehm's other arguments of non-disclosure focused directly on Carter's failure to disclose matters that might have affected the insurer's assessment of the risk of a European attack on Fort Marlborough. The strongest of these was the allegation that Carter had not disclosed the existence and contents of the letter that he had received from Alexander Wynch, dated 4 February 1759 at the Cape of Good Hope. This was the letter which reported French plans of 1758 to send a ship and 400 men to surprise the Company's West Coast settlements. This allegation required serious consideration by the court. Wynch's intelligence increased the perception of the risk of a French attack of both Carter in Sumatra and the Company in London, to an extent sufficient to prompt special precautions even as late as February 1760.

The heightened state of alert which Wynch's letter produced at Fort Marlborough, and the fundamental impact which it had on Carter's conduct, official and private, has already been considered.[211] Surviving contemporary sources indicate that an equivalent change in perception also occurred at East India House in London. By late June 1759, the Court of Directors had received a similar letter directly from Wynch, via Copenhagen.[212] The Directors' words and acts at the time of their next general dispatches to Fort Marlborough suggest that Wynch's letter had also increased their concerns for their West Coast

be to resist an Indian force: it was notorious that it could not resist an European attack'. Similarly, at 3 Burr 1905, 1915–16; 97 ER 1162, 1167: 'The utmost which can be contended is, that the underwriter trusted to the fort being in the condition in which it ought to be: in like manner as it is taken for granted, that the ship insured is seaworthy. What is that condition? All the witnesses agree "that it was only to resist the natives, and not an European force"'.

[209] See 86–90 above.
[210] *Carter* (n 1 above) 3 Burr 1905, 1914; 97 ER 1162, 1167.
[211] See 67–72 above.
[212] See 67–8, n 42 above.

servants, even though it was by then many months since the French plans were to have taken effect. The letter in question, dated 4 February 1760,[213] expressly referred to Wynch's reports[214]:

> You will long before receipt hereof have been advised of the several French Ships . . . which had been at the Cape of Good Hope in the beginning of last year as also of some others which the Gentlemen who were passengers on the *Grantham* and *Ilchester* had got information of during their stay at that place and whereof Mr Wynch took care to give our Deputy Governour an account by the way of Batavia, this it cannot be doubted had its due effect in your taking every possible precaution to be guarded from a Surprize or Sudden Attack from any part of the Enemy's force which you might have reason to judge would be directed against the West Coast.

The Court of Directors evidently considered that Wynch's letter to Carter would have justifiably provoked a heightened state of alert, and special measures, at Fort Marlborough. The remainder of the letter also shows the Court of Directors itself adopting or recommending a quite unprecedented combination of measures for Fort Marlborough's security.[215] Perhaps the most compelling single measure is the Directors' promise of 200 military recruits.[216] During the Seven Years' War, the general demands for manpower made it extremely difficult for the Company to raise troops[217]; and 200 European recruits represented a substantial addition to the garrison's existing strength.[218] In the Directors' own words,

> [t]he Military Stores now consigned to you together with the Officers and Soldiers upon these ships will show our Care of the West Coast.[219]

## 2. The Court's Rejection of the Argument

In light of the response of Carter and the Company to Wynch's intelligence, Lord Mansfield's response to Boehm's second allegation initially looks surpris-

---

[213] IOR/G/35/31, Rough Drafts of Dispatches to Fort Marlborough, Letter from Court of Directors to Fort Marlborough, 6 February 1760, folio 135 ff.

[214] *Ibid* para 19.

[215] IOR/G/35/31 (n 213 above) para 37 (indent for military stores fully complied with; additional guns not requested to be sent); para 42 (60 barrels of gunpowder sent to make up for those not received by earlier ships); para 71 (Fort Marlborough to be placed in a respectable condition not only to resist the 'Country Powers' but also to make a good defence against a European enemy); para 71 (Company's Presidencies in India to be directed to forward such military stores as they could spare); para 71 (special, secret committee to be established at Fort Marlborough); paras 55, 88 ff (regulations prescribed for the governance of Fort Marlborough in times of military emergency, recently laid down for the Company's Presidencies in India and 'especially absolutely necessary in time of war'); para 92 (200 military recruits to be sent); para 93 (four infantry companies of 100 men to be formed in future).

[216] IOR/G/35/31 (n 213 above) para 92.

[217] See IOR/G/35/31 (n 213 above) para 4, where these difficulties are expressly mentioned.

[218] On the garrison's history, see generally Harfield, *Bencoolen* (n 7 above). Sickness, deaths and desertions would reduce the effective numbers significantly below full strength, and had done so in the preceding period.

[219] IOR/G/35/31 (n 213 above) para 71.

ing. He did not hesitate in endorsing the jury's conclusion that Wynch's intelligence was not material. In simple terms, no underwriter in London in May 1760 could reasonably consider that this intelligence increased the risk being undertaken. Indeed, if anything, the intelligence would have suggested that the risk of French attack on Fort Marlborough was reduced. Lord Mansfield's reasoning emerges from the following passage in Burrows' report[220]:

> It was said—If a man insured a ship, knowing that two privateers were lying in her way, without mentioning that circumstance, it would be a fraud—I agree with it. But if he knew that two privateers had been there the year before, it would be no fraud, not to mention that circumstance: because, it does not follow that they will cruise this year at the same time, in the same place; or that they are in a condition to do it. If the circumstance of 'this design laid aside' had been mentioned, it would have tended rather to lessen the risque than increase it: for, the design of a surprize which has transpired, and been laid aside, is less likely to be taken up again; especially by a vanquished enemy.

The first available explanation for this robust conclusion is simply that the court did not have before it the material required to appreciate fully the significance of Wynch's letter. The credibility of Wynch's intelligence stemmed from its having come from the French forces gathered at the Cape of Good Hope over the winter of 1758–59, which Wynch was witnessing and reporting. Although this would have been apparent from the terms of Wynch's letter, it would not have been apparent from the material actually before the court: Boehm's counsel did not provide any further information regarding the authorship, content and context of Wynch's letter, beyond what was incidentally revealed by Carter and Preston's secret letter of 16 September 1759.[221] This is immediately surprising, because means of further illumination certainly did exist. Thus, copies of Wynch's letter were dispatched from Bencoolen in the same secret packets as Carter and Preston's letter,[222] which Boehm had brought before the court, and survived in the Company's possession.[223] Similarly, at the trial, Carter's counsel had offered to read the letter which the Court of Directors

---

[220] *Carter* (n 1 above) 3 Burr 1905, 1917; 97 ER 1162, 1168. The preceding sentence, 'This is a topic of mere general speculation; which made no part of the fact of the case upon which the insurance was to be made', is difficult to make sense of.

[221] IOR/G/35/12, Letter from Roger Carter and Richard Preston, Fort Marlborough, to the Secret Committee of the Court of Directors, 16 September 1759, folio 287 ff, para 10, quoted at 71 above.

[222] The Company received two copies, one in the original secret packet sent via the *Pitt* in September 1759, and a second in the duplicate of this packet sent via the *Earl of Holderness*, which eventually sailed for London in early February 1760. See IOR/G/35/12, List of contents of a duplicate secret packet, duplicating that sent via the *Pitt*, sent on the *Earl of Holderness*, folio 409.

[223] See today, IOR/G/35/12, Letter from Alexander Wynch, Cape of Good Hope, to Roger Carter, 4 February 1759, folios 262v–264. Annotations to this letter indicate that it is the copy sent in the duplicate secret packet sent on the *Earl of Holderness*: see n 222 above. The first paragraph of Carter and Preston's letter would probably have been sufficient to indicate that a copy of Wynch's letter was being enclosed with it.

had received from Wynch,[224] but this was objected to by Boehm's counsel, and the account was not read.[225] The inference that Lord Mansfield drew from this failure to provide or permit further illumination regarding Wynch's intelligence was that it must have been 'very doubtful'.[226] As Burrows reports,[227]

[w]hat that letter was; how [Wynch] mentioned the design, or upon what authority he mentioned it; or by whom the design was supposed to be imagined, does not appear. The defendant has had every opportunity of discovery; and nothing has come out upon it, as to this letter, which he thinks makes for his purpose.

The plaintiff offered to read the account [Wynch] wrote to the East India Company: which was objected to; and therefore not read. The nature of that intelligence therefore is very doubtful.

Although this first explanation needs careful consideration, it ultimately seems inadequate. The thrust of Lord Mansfield's ensuing reasoning is that, even if Wynch's intelligence was wholly credible, taking it in its 'strongest light', the intelligence was still only a 'report of a design to surprise, the year before; but then dropt'[228]; and that such a report could not be 'material'.

On examination, Lord Mansfield's robust conclusion is much more satisfactorily explained on a second basis. Adopting an objective 'different risk' standard of materiality, Boehm needed to show that Wynch's intelligence would have adversely affected the risk perception of a reasonable London underwriter in May 1760, who was asked to insure Fort Marlborough against the risk of a European enemy attack for one year from October 1759. Lord Mansfield clearly assumed that in May 1760, a London underwriter could reasonably be expected to know of the recent state-supported conflict between the English and French East India Companies in India. He also clearly assumed that that knowledge would be sufficient to suggest to a London underwriter that there was some risk of an attack by French forces on the English Company's interests in Sumatra. If disclosed in May 1760, Wynch's letter would have confirmed the correctness of that risk assessment, to the extent that it would have shown that Fort Marlborough, previously merely a possible target, had definitely been in the enemy's contemplation. However, it would not follow that in May 1760, the knowledge of the definite but unimplemented plans of 1758 would adversely affect a London underwriter's perception of the risk of a French attack during the policy's term. Whether the underwriter's perception would be affected in this way would fundamentally depend on the underwriter's assessment of the likelihood of the 1758 plans being revived during that period. This, in turn,

[224] This was almost certainly the letter which the Court of Directors received directly from Wynch by way of Copenhagen some time in June 1759: see IOR/B/75, Minutes of Meeting of Court of Directors, 27 June 1759, 386, recording the reading of correspondence from Wynch at the Cape of Good Hope of February 1759, received by way of Copenhagen.
[225] *Carter* (n 1 above) 3 Burr 1905, 1917; 97 ER 1162, 1168.
[226] *Ibid.*
[227] *Carter* (n 1 above) 3 Burr 1905, 1916–17; 97 ER 1162, 1168.
[228] *Carter* (n 1 above) 3 Burr 1905, 1917; 97 ER 1162, 1168.

would fundamentally depend on what in May 1760 the underwriter could reasonably be expected to know about the recent course of the Anglo-French conflict in the East Indies.

The key to unlocking Lord Mansfield's reasoning is the fact that the state of Carter's knowledge regarding this conflict in September 1759, and the likely state of a London underwriter's knowledge in May 1760, were materially different. This difference can explain how Lord Mansfield could justifiably reject Wynch's letter as immaterial, despite clear evidence that its receipt had had a fundamental impact on Carter's conduct in August–September 1759. Carter and Preston's secret letter of 16 September 1759 would have incidentally revealed that Carter's reaction rested on incomplete information about the Anglo-French conflict in India, which did not extend substantially beyond the ending of the siege of Madras.[229] An underwriter in May 1760 could reasonably be expected to have substantially more recent and complete information. Even more critically, that information could also reasonably be expected to result in a very different assessment of the likelihood of the French plans of 1758 being revived. Those plans were conceived in the first few months of the conflict on the Coromandel Coast, after the French forces had scored some important successes. Beginning, however, with the raising of the siege of Madras on 16 February 1759, the tide of the Anglo-French conflict had increasingly turned against the French. Armed with knowledge of that altered background, a London underwriter might reasonably conclude that the French plans of 1758 could not be, or would not be, revived during the policy's term: any available sea and land forces would be consumed by the conflict in India.[230] On that basis, Wynch's letter would have no adverse affect on the underwriter's risk assessment.

That this was what Lord Mansfield intended is suggested by the final, crucial clause of Burrows' report of his reasoning:

> the design of a surprize which has transpired, and been laid aside, is less likely to be taken up again; *especially by a vanquished enemy* (emphasis added).[231]

A contemporary of Lord Mansfield would have recognised this as a reference to ailing French fortunes in India. Looking back, one might have niggling concerns

---

[229] IOR/G/35/12, Letter from Roger Carter and Richard Preston, Fort Marlborough, to the Secret Committee of the Court of Directors, 16 September 1759, folio 287 ff, para 2, in which they related to the Court of Directors what they had learned from letters directly from Fort St George, or indirectly via letters from John Herbert. See further n 235 below.

[230] It is of some interest to note that the most recent reports of the Company to its General Court, at which 'all the Directors' and 'a large Appearance of the Generality' (the shareholders) were present, struck a remarkably positive tone at this time, based on accounts from Fort St George up to mid-August 1759, received by the *Warren*, which had arrived at Kinsale in company with the *Pitt*: see IOR/B/75, Minutes of Meeting of General Court of East India Company, 19 March 1760, 658 ff.

[231] *Carter* (n 1 above) 3 Burr 1905, 1917; 97 ER 1162, 1168. This is perhaps even clearer from Blackstone's abbreviated report of Lord Mansfield's reasoning in 1 Black W 593, 595; 96 ER 342, 344: 'It is said, that, if the insured knows of a design by a privateer to attack a ship, the concealment would be fraudulent. I agree it; but not if designed a year before, and dropped. A design, which had transpired and was dropt, was not likely to be renewed by a vanquished enemy'.

that Lord Mansfield was assuming knowledge that only hindsight could afford[232]: whatever the actual state of the conflict in India in May 1760, it is not obvious that what could then have been known in London would have warranted the assumption that the French were a 'vanquished enemy'. Nevertheless, Lord Mansfield's basic point is clear: viz, that what a London underwriter in May 1760 could know about the Anglo-French conflict would have justified the conclusion that the unimplemented plans of 1758 would not be revived during the policy's term.

## G. MATERIAL NON-DISCLOSURE (III): CARTER'S ANTICIPATION OF A FRENCH ATTACK

### 1. Background

Boehm's third allegation of material non-disclosure also bore on the likelihood of a French attack. On its face, it was the substantially weaker argument that Carter had failed to disclose his anticipation of a French attack. Its evidential basis was the letter sent by Carter to his brother of 22 September 1759, in which he gave his brother his instructions to insure. Carter confessed that he was[233]

> now more afraid than formerly, that the French should attack and take the settlement; for, as they cannot muster a force to relieve their friends at the coast, they may, rather than remain idle, pay us a visit. It seems, that they had such an intention, last year.

It was this speculation about a possible French attack which, according to Boehm, should have been disclosed.

The meaning of Carter's words only becomes clear in light of Carter's limited knowledge of the course of the Anglo-French conflict in India in 22 September 1759, when he wrote to his brother. By Wynch's letter received on 14 August 1759 via Batavia, Carter knew about the French ships gathered at the Cape of Good Hope over the winter 1758–59.[234] He also had second-hand reports that the siege of Fort St George had ended on 16 February 1759, by which time the French ships and reinforcements had not reappeared off the Coromandel Coast, to relieve the besieging French forces.[235] However, the Fort Marlborough

---

[232] This problem resurfaces elsewhere in Lord Mansfield's judgment. See esp 3 Burr 1906, 1916; 97 ER 1162, 1168, dealing with the third allegation of non-disclosure: 'It is a bold attempt, for the conquered to attack the conqueror in his own dominions'.

[233] *Carter* (n 1 above) 3 Burr 1905, 1913n; 97 ER 1162, 1166.

[234] See 64, 67–8 above.

[235] See the secret letter sent contemporaneously on the *Pitt*: IOR/G/35/12, Letter from Roger Carter and Richard Preston, Fort Marlborough, to the Secret Committee of the Court of Directors, 16 September 1759, folio 287 ff, para 2. This letter reports that they had no more recent news from Fort St George than that conveyed by the *Duke*, which arrived on 9 February 1759, with letters of 31 October 1758: IOR/G/35/70, Diary and Public Consultations—Fort Marlborough, 9 February 1759, 40 (diary entry). Their intelligence regarding events on the Coromandel Coast came via John Herbert on 14 August 1759: IOR/G/35/70, Diary and Public Consultations—Fort Marlborough,

records suggest that that was all. Intelligence of subsequent events—the delayed return of D'Aché's ships to the Coromandel Coast in August 1759, the sea battle between the French and English squadrons on 10 September, and the departure of D'Aché's ships for Mauritius in early October—did not arrive at Fort Marlborough until late December.[236]

Viewed against that background, it is clear that Carter's observations are speculations about the likely movements of the French fleet. In short, his meaning is that

> as [the French fleet] cannot . . . relieve [the French forces on the Coromandel Coast], they may, rather than remain idle, pay us a visit. It seems, that they had such an intention last year.

Carter had evidently inferred from Wynch's letter of 4 February 1759 that the news of French plans to attack Fort Marlborough had come from the French forces at the Cape over the winter 1758–59, and thus that the threat to Sumatra was likely to come from the forces then gathered there. He knew that those ships could not lend early assistance to the French forces on the Coromandel Coast, because of the distance between the Cape and that region. He may also have been assuming that the presence of the English squadron off the Coast might prevent their landing in subsequent months. Whether or not that is right, Carter certainly knew that the arrival of the monsoon season would make it dangerous for either fleet to remain on the Coast much beyond September 1759. On that basis, he appears to have made the further deduction that the French fleet might choose to occupy itself over the summer or autumn months in some other way.

Thus understood, the weakness of Boehm's third allegation should be obvious. The observations allegedly concealed were simply Carter's own speculations about the likely movements of the French fleet, based on dated and incomplete intelligence about the general state of the Anglo-French conflict in the East Indies. By May 1760, when Carter's policy was underwritten, a London insurer could hope to exercise his judgment on the basis of substantially more up-to-date and complete intelligence regarding the circumstances that would bear on the likelihood of the French fleet diverting itself from the conflict on the Coromandel Coast, to surprise the Company's West Coast settlements. This

---

14 August 1759, 249 (diary entry recording receipt of correspondence from Batavia); *ibid* 15 August 1759, 254 (consultation considering a letter from John Herbert of 5 July 1759, bringing news of raising of siege of Madras).

[236] The next significant intelligence probably came via the *Fort Marlborough*, which arrived on 20 December 1759, with a letter from Fort St George of 7 November 1759: IOR/G/35/70, Diary and Public Consultations—Fort Marlborough, 20 December 1759, 480 (diary entry recording arrival of the *Fort Marlborough*); IOR/G/35/12, Letter from the Secret Committee, Fort St George to the Secret Committee, Fort Marlborough, 7 November 1759, folio 353; IOR/G/35/12, Minutes of the Secret Committee, Fort Marlborough, 20 December 1759, folio 399 (considering the letter). The letter reported an engagement between the English and French ships on 10 September 1759; the disembarkation of land forces by the French at Pondicherry; the departure of the French ships for (it was believed) Mauritius on 2 October 1759; and the departure of the English ships for Bombay on 17 October 1759.

would include: the general course of the Anglo-French conflict; the movements of the French ships that had been at the Cape over the winter of 1758–59 during the summer-autumn of 1759; and the strength of the forces recently dispatched for the East Indies from England and France.

## 2. The Court's Rejection of the Argument

It cannot be a surprise that Boehm's third allegation failed. Burrows records Lord Mansfield's response as follows[237]:

> This is no part of the fact of the case: it is a mere speculation of the governor's from the general state of the war. The conjecture was dictated to him from his fears. It is a bold attempt, for the conquered to attack the conqueror in his own dominions. The practicability of it in this case, depended upon the English naval forces in those seas; which the underwriter could better judge of at London in May, 1760, than the governor could at Fort Marlborough in September, 1759.

According to Blackstone's abbreviated report, Lord Mansfield's answer was that: 'This was a mere speculation of the governor, and not a matter of fact'.[238]

A number of answers can be extracted from these passages, when read in conjunction with the rest of Lord Mansfield's judgment. The first is that Carter's observation was not material to the risk assumed by Boehm. Adopting an objective, 'different risk' standard of materiality, it would be easy to conclude that the risk assessment of a reasonable underwriter, asked to underwrite a policy in London in May 1760, would not be adversely affected by Carter's manifestly unreliable speculations of September 1759. This conclusion would follow a fortiori if what could reasonably be known about the Anglo-French conflict in the London underwriting community by May 1760 would have indicated that there was little or no likelihood of French ships and forces being diverted to surprise the West Coast settlements, as Carter feared.[239] Whether or not this was so, a snapshot of the London papers of the time at least suggests that some of the most recent intelligence would have falsified the premises on which Carter's apprehensions were based. By March 1760, the papers carried reports from French sources of D'Aché's belated return to the Coromandel Coast, the engagement between the English and French squadrons, the landing of troops and supplies at Pondicherry, and the return of D'Aché's damaged ships to Mauritius.[240]

---

[237] *Carter* (n 1 above) 3 Burr 1905, 1916; 97 ER 1162, 1168.

[238] *Carter* (n 1 above) 1 Black W 593, 595; 96 ER 342, 343.

[239] See the similar assumptions, on which Lord Mansfield appears to reject Boehm's allegation regarding Wynch's letter, discussed at 102–4 above.

[240] See eg *London Chronicle* (27–29 March 1760) 309, col 2 (carrying reports of these events from Paris, based on letters of October 1759 brought by a French frigate); see too *London Chronicle* (8–10 April 1760) 349, col 2. Cf *London Chronicle* (13–15 March 1760) 262, cols 2–3 (extracts of letters from English officers in Pocock's fleet, of 12 and 13 August 1759, still then waiting for D'Aché's arrival). Reliable reports from English sources of these events may not have arrived in London

The legal principles stated by Lord Mansfield presented two other insupera-
ble objections to Boehm's third allegation. One was that an insured is not
obliged to disclose his own speculations; an insurer is expected to exercise an
independent judgment.[241] Another was that an insured is not obliged to disclose
matters of 'political speculation' or 'general intelligence', about which an
insurer is expected to inform himself.[242] Here, what Carter had allegedly concealed was unquestionably his own speculation, and with one exception, none
of the facts on which that exercise of judgment depended were facts of which an
underwriter in London in May 1760 could expect to be informed by the insured.
They were all facts relating to the general course of the Anglo-French conflict in
the East Indies: viz, matters that Lord Mansfield describes as matters of 'political speculation' or 'general intelligence'. The one exception was the letter
received by Carter from Wynch on 14 August 1759, reporting the French plans
of 1758. On its face, Carter's speculation relied heavily on this letter.
Nevertheless, this could not render that speculation a matter that ought to have
been disclosed to Boehm. Instead, Carter's failure to disclose the existence and
contents of the letter could and did provide the basis for the independent allegation of non-disclosure, already considered.

## H. MATERIAL NON-DISCLOSURE (IV): CARTER'S GROUNDS
## FOR APPREHENDING A DUTCH WAR

### 1. Background

A fourth allegation of non-disclosure was raised by Lord Mansfield, rather than
by Boehm's counsel.[243] It principally rested upon an inference drawn from
Roger Carter's letter to his brother of 22 September 1759, by which the request
for insurance was made. Carter reportedly commented that 'in case of a Dutch
war, I would have it (the insurance) done at any rate'.[244] This showed, Lord

before the end of May: see *London Chronicle* (27–29 May 1760) 518, col 3 (reporting the arrival of
the *Diligence* Packet from Madras after a passage of seven months); *London Chronicle* (29–31 May
1760) 521, cols 1–2 (letter from Fort St George of 5 November 1759); *London Chronicle* (31 May–
3 June 1760) 529, cols 1–3, 530, cols 1–3 (letter from Vice Admiral Pocock, Madras Road,
12 October 1759); *London Chronicle* (7–10 June 1760) 553, cols 1–2, 554, cols 1–2 (letter from Fort
St George of 2 November 1759).

[241] This is reported in different terms. According to Burrows' report, at 3 Burr 1905, 1910
and 1911; 97 ER 1162, 1165: '[t]he under-writer . . . needs not be told general topics of speculation';
further '[m]en argue differently, from natural phenomena, and political appearances: they have different capacities, different degrees of knowledge, and different intelligence. But the means of
information and judgment are open to both: each professes to act from his own skill and sagacity;
and therefore neither needs to communicate to the other'. According to Blackstone's report, at 1
Black W 593, 594; 96 ER 342, 343, 'as men reason differently from the same facts, he need not be told
another's conclusion from known facts'.

[242] See further 109 below.

[243] *Carter* (n 1 above) 3 Burr 1905, 1917; 97 ER 1162, 1168.

[244] *Carter* (n 1 above) 3 Burr 1905, 1917n; 97 ER 1162, 1168n.

Mansfield concluded, that Roger Carter was then 'principally apprehensive of a Dutch war',[245] and yet he had neither disclosed that apprehension, nor the grounds on which it rested, to the insurer.

Lord Mansfield was unable to identify the specific grounds for Carter's apprehension, in the absence of argument on the point. However, surviving contemporary sources offer important insights into what they might have been. The Dutch Company had long been the English Company's major commercial rival in this region,[246] and the Company's surviving records reveal that relations between the West Coast servants and their Dutch neighbours were often strained. Indeed, they indicate that from the outset of Carter's period as Deputy Governor, the Company's servants at Fort Marlborough were complaining bitterly of local Dutch interference with their shipping and trade.[247] Properly understood, however, Carter's fear of a 'Dutch war' in September 1759 had a different basis. It was not the long-standing local commercial rivalry, but rather, the very recent intelligence of a substantial Dutch armament being prepared at Batavia, the Dutch Company's HQ in the East Indies. This intelligence came via two letters from John Herbert, the Company's agent there, which arrived at Fort Marlborough on 14 August 1759.[248] Their contents were summarised by Carter and Preston, in their secret letter of 16 September 1759.[249]

> [The letters conveyed] intelligence of an Armament the Dutch were sending from Batavia, to consist, when reinforced at Ceylon, of 600 Europeans & 1600 Bugganeese, given out to act as Auxiliaries on the Coast of Coromondel, & protect their Settlements from the injuries of the French; but generally believed, to be real[l]y intended for Bengal, to reestablish their trade there, or possibly to create troubles, which may prove prejudicial to your Honors Concerns in that Kingdom.

The report of the Dutch scheme was broadly accurate. In the wake of Clive's victory at Plassey in 1757, the English Company's influence in the rich province of Bengal had greatly increased. In 1759, the Dutch Company did indeed dispatch a substantial force to Bengal, in an effort to resurrect its commercial fortunes there. The expedition was nevertheless short-lived. It ended in catastrophic failure.[250]

---

[245] *Carter* (n 1 above) 3 Burr 1905, 1917; 92 ER 1162, 1168.

[246] See 60–61 above.

[247] See, eg IOR/G/35/11, Letter from Fort Marlborough to Fort St George, 14 June 1758, folio 345 ff, para 6; *ibid* Letter from Roger Carter to Fort St George, 14 June 1758, folio 362 ff, para 3; *ibid* Letter from Fort Marlborough to the Court of Directors, 31 December 1758, folio 408 ff. See too the continuing complaints evident at the time of the *Pitt's* departure: IOR/G/35/12, Letter from Fort Marlborough to the Court of Directors, 21 September 1759, folio 302 ff.

[248] IOR/G/35/12, Letter from John Herbert to Fort St George, 16 June 1759, folios 280–81; *ibid* 5 July 1759, folios 281–3.

[249] IOR/G/35/12, Letter from Roger Carter and Richard Preston, Fort Marlborough, to the Secret Committee of the Court of Directors, 16 September 1759, folio 287 ff, para 7.

[250] The Dutch scheme is noted in, eg F Gaastra, 'War, Competition and Collaboration: Relations between the English and Dutch East India Companies in the Seventeenth and Eighteenth Centuries' in HV Bowen et al (eds), *The Worlds of the East India Company* (Rochester, The Boydell Press, 2002) 59.

However reliable, John Herbert's letters did not suggest any imminent Dutch threat to Fort Marlborough from the armament. Nor, more importantly, were they taken to imply such a threat, when they came to be considered by the Fort Marlborough Secret Committee at its meeting of 22 August 1759.[251] The direct threat was perceived to be in Bengal, and on the basis that John Herbert had already taken steps to ensure that the Company's servants there were apprised of the armament, the Committee resolved that no further action was necessary.[252] Properly understood, the heightened state of alert at Fort Marlborough first signalled in the August meeting, and the special precautions immediately taken against enemy attack, had the different basis already noted.[253] They were the result of Wynch's letter, and its forewarnings of a French attack, which Roger Carter had received by the same secret packet from Batavia on 14 August 1759.[254] Lord Mansfield's summary of the contents of Carter's letter to his brother in *Carter v Boehm* indicates that Carter's insurance instructions were primarily the result of the same apprehension.[255]

## 2. The Court's Rejection of the Argument

The fourth allegation of material non-disclosure was superficially the strongest, as Lord Mansfield acknowledged. In September 1759, Carter unquestionably had grounds for fearing a Dutch war, which were not disclosed to the insurer, and it would be difficult to dispute their materiality to the risk undertaken. Lord Mansfield nevertheless had no doubts that the allegation should be rejected. Unaware of the source of Carter's fears, he speculated that the grounds must have comprised 'political speculation' and 'general intelligence',[256] which both sides agreed did not have to be disclosed to an insurer.[257]

The surviving contemporary sources indicate that this was an inspired speculation. The Dutch armament at Batavia which provided the undisclosed grounds

[251] IOR/G/35/12, Minutes of the Secret Committee, Fort Marlborough, 22 August 1759, folio 267v (reciting the reading of John Herbert's letters of 16 June and 5 July 1759).

[252] Confirmed by IOR/G/35/12, Letter from Roger Carter and Richard Preston, Fort Marlborough, to the Secret Committee of the Court of Directors, 16 September 1759, folio 287 ff, para 8.

[253] See 65–72 above.

[254] See IOR/G/35/12, Minutes of the Secret Committee, Fort Marlborough, 22 August 1759, folios 267–69; IOR/G/35/12, Letter from Roger Carter and Richard Preston, Fort Marlborough, to the Secret Committee of the Court of Directors, 16 September 1759, folio 287 ff, paras 7–9 (dealing with the news of the Dutch armament), paras 10–19 (reporting the letter from Wynch, and the special measures which had been taken to prepare Fort Marlborough for the possibility of a French attack).

[255] See *Carter* (n 1 above) 3 Burr 1905, 1913n; 97 ER 1162, 1166: 'The latter letter (to his brother) owns that he is "now more afraid than formerly, that the French should attack and take the settlement; for, as they cannot muster a force to relieve their friends at the coast, they may, rather than remain idle, pay us a visit. It seems, that they had such an intention, last year." And therefore he desires his brother to get an insurance made upon his stock there'.

[256] *Carter* (n 1 above) 3 Burr 1905, 1917–18; 97 ER 1162, 1168.

[257] *Carter* (n 1 above) 3 Burr 1905, 1918; 97 ER 1162, 1168.

for Carter's apprehension could not have been public knowledge in London in late September 1759, when the *Pitt* set sail from Fort Marlborough with Carter's insurance instructions. However, it could be and was public knowledge in London when the insurance policy was effected, eight months later, in May 1760. In early March 1760, London papers contained reports of the armament from a source which should not come as a surprise: the *Pitt*, which had arrived at Kinsale in Ireland on 23 February 1760.[258] The reports indicate that the *Pitt*'s crew learned of the armament when she put into Batavia on her return journey from China in late August 1759,[259] shortly before her arrival at Fort Marlborough on 2 September 1759.

## I. FRAUDULENT AVOIDANCE BY THE INSURER

Having rejected the four particular allegations of material non-disclosure, and having acquitted Carter of any fraudulent intention, Lord Mansfield raised one final, overriding objection to Boehm's attempt to resist liability. If he could avoid liability for Carter's material non-disclosure, Lord Mansfield said, a rule designed to encourage good faith and prevent fraud would become an instrument of fraud. Burrows' report records Lord Mansfield's reasoning in the following terms[260]:

> The reason of the rule against concealment is, to prevent fraud and encourage good faith.

> If the defendant's objections were to prevail, in the present case, the rule would be turned into an instrument of fraud.

> The underwriter, here, knowing the governor to be acquainted with the state of the place; knowing that he apprehended danger, and must have some ground for his apprehension; being told nothing of either; signed this policy, without asking a question.

> If the objection 'that he was not told' is sufficient to vacate it, he took the premium, knowing the policy to be void; in order to gain, if the alternative turned out one way; and to make no satisfaction, if it turned out the other: he drew the governor into a false confidence, 'that, if the worst should happen, he had provided against total ruin;' knowing, at the same time, 'that the indemnity to which the governor trusted was void.'

> There was not a word said to him, of the affairs of India, or the state of the war there, or the condition of Fort Marlborough. If he thought that omission an objection at the time, he ought not to have signed the policy with a secret reserve in his own mind to make it void; if he dispensed with the information, and did not think this silence an objection he cannot take it up now, after the event.

---

[258] IOR/L/MAR/B/525, index to the marine records for the *Pitt*.
[259] See, esp *London Evening Post* (11–13 March 1760) 1, col 2.
[260] *Carter* (n 1 above) 3 Burr 1905, 1918–19; 97 ER 1162, 1169.

What has often been said of the Statute of Frauds may, with more propriety, be applied to every rule of law, drawn from principles of natural equity, to prevent fraud—'That it should never be so turned, construed, or used, as to protect, or be a means of fraud.'

These passages are difficult to interpret, yet a great deal potentially turns on them. Lord Mansfield was clearly assuming that an insurer's failure to inquire may debar him from avoiding liability for material non-disclosure vis-à-vis an honest insured. Less clear is when Lord Mansfield envisaged that being the case. Three very different analyses are available, with dramatically different consequences for the balance of the law between insured and insurer. Any conclusion regarding *Carter v Boehm*'s ultimate orientation depends heavily on which is preferred.

The first analysis, lying at one extreme, is that Lord Mansfield meant that an insurer cannot avoid liability where he failed to inquire of his insured, knowing that the insured might have knowledge on a particular subject and yet had disclosed nothing.[261] In practice, if accepted, this analysis would always or almost always compel an insurer to make inquiry of his insured. It thus comes dangerously close to reversing what has consistently been assumed to be the law's starting-point, implicit in Lord Mansfield's statement of the law: viz, that a prospective insured is obliged to disclose material facts known to him, and that this means obliged without inquiry.[262] Marshall, writing 200 years ago, saw this[263]:

> Upon whom does the obligation lie; the insured to disclose what he knows, or the underwriter to fish it out by questioning the broker or agent? The argument goes to prove, that if the underwriter ask no questions, the insured is obliged to disclose nothing; which is true only with respect to matters of public notoriety

For this reason alone, this radical first interpretation seems impossible to accept.

A second analysis, lying at the opposite extreme, is that Lord Mansfield meant only that an insurer cannot avoid liability where his failure to inquire is shown to be fraudulent. No one would dispute that an insured's obligation to disclose material facts should not be a cloak for dishonest conduct by insurers. The difficulty with this second analysis is different: viz, its application in *Carter*

---

[261] This was apparently Marshall's reading: Marshall, *A Treatise on the Law of Insurance* (n 103 above) 483 fnn, where a succession of criticisms of Lord Mansfield's final words are offered in the notes: 'It is here assumed that the underwriter knew that the policy was void.—How could he know that it was void by reason of a concealment, without knowing what was concealed? Upon whom does the obligation lie; the insured to disclose what he knows, or the underwriter to fish it out by questioning the broker or agent? The argument goes to prove, that if the underwriter ask no questions, the insured is obliged to disclose nothing; which is true only with respect to matters of public notoriety—. . . How could he judge of the omission, without knowing what was omitted?—. . . How could he be supposed to dispense with information when the silence of the insured was, according to all practice, a proof that he had none to communicate?'.

[262] See for a clear early statement of an insurer's legitimate position of passivity, see *Bridges v Hunter* (1813) 1 M & S 15, 18; 105 ER 6, 7 (Lord Ellenborough CJ).

[263] Marshall, *A Treatise on the Law of Insurance* (n 103 above) 483 fn.

*v Boehm* required some controversial factual assumptions, remarkably adverse to the insurer. In his judgment, Lord Mansfield unquestionably emphasises circumstances that should have afforded Boehm reason to suspect that the insured had failed to disclose some material matter. However, it is a large leap from there to the conclusion that Boehm fraudulently failed to inquire: viz, that Boehm knew that the insured had not disclosed some material matter, and that that non-disclosure would entitle him to avoid liability, and yet he had deliberately failed to inquire with the dishonest intention of profiting in all events.

A third analysis, lying between these extremes, is that an insurer cannot avoid liability vis-à-vis an honest insured where he consciously failed to inquire of the insured, in circumstances where he had reasons to suspect that a material matter had not been disclosed.[264] Support for this analysis can be found in passages indicating that Boehm's failure to inquire would have the same consequence, whether or not he had any fraudulent intention[265]:

> If he thought [the omission to disclose] an objection at the time, he ought not to have signed the policy with a secret reserve in his own mind to make it void; if he dispensed with the information, and did not think this silence an objection; he cannot take it up now, after the event.

Consistently with Lord Mansfield's express words, this third analysis can be understood as a principle designed to prevent 'fraud' in two senses.

First, a principle depending only on proof of a failure to inquire, despite reasons to suspect non-disclosure, might be appropriate to avoid any risk that the law might be exploited by insurers who were in fact guilty of fraudulent non-inquiry. Arguably, Lord Mansfield's earlier statements, in which he appears to accuse Boehm of dishonesty, were only intended to present a hypothetical: viz, that if insurers in Boehm's position could avoid liability by pleading 'I was not told', the law might become a tool for the dishonest to achieve their ends.

Secondly, the same principle might be warranted to prevent 'fraud' in a broader sense. It is evident that Lord Mansfield was concerned that an honest insured, of whom inquiry might be made but is not, will afterwards conduct his affairs on the assumption that his policy is valid, and that he has effectively hedged his risks. Thus Lord Mansfield observes in the passage quoted that Boehm, by his failure to inquire, 'drew the governor into a false confidence, "that if the worst should happen, he had provided against total ruin"'.[266] It might be inferred from this that Lord Mansfield was at least partly concerned to avoid the injustice arising if an insurer could rely on his insured's honest failure to disclose material facts to avoid liability and compel the insured to bear the

---

[264] This limitation is implicit in Lord Mansfield's earlier statement of principle: see *Carter* (n 1 above) 3 Burr 1905, 1911; 97 ER 1162, 1165. Good faith, he said, prevented an insured holding an insurer to a contract, where he had failed to disclose material facts which he knew, but of which the insurer was ignorant, *and had no reason to suspect*.

[265] *Carter* (n 1 above) 3 Burr 1905, 1911, 1918–19; 97 ER 1162, 1169.

[266] See *Carter* (n 1 above) 3 Burr 1905, 1918; 97 ER 1162, 1169.

risk of loss, where the insurer's failure to inquire (despite reasons to suspect non-disclosure) had denied the insured the opportunity of correcting his omission and ensuring the policy's validity.

The wider interest of this intermediate analysis of Lord Mansfield's words lies in its relationship with the modern law. Today, an insurer's failure to inquire of a prospective insured may certainly prevent the insurer from avoiding liability, via the objection that the insurer has waived disclosure of the relevant matters. Understandably, however, this exception has been carefully policed by the courts: over-hasty findings of 'waiver of disclosure' following an insurer's failure to inquire would threaten fatally to undermine the primacy of the insured's obligation to disclose.[267] Unfortunately, the courts have not found it easy to identify where the dividing line should be drawn. The prevailing approach today appears to involve an inquiry as to whether the insured's presentation of the risk, on its own or in conjunction with such other facts as the insurer knows or is presumed to know, should have raised a suspicion in the mind of a reasonable insurer that some material fact had not been disclosed. Where this is so, and the insurer fails to make such inquiry of the insured as a reasonably careful insurer would make, he will be held to have waived disclosure of any material fact that such inquiry would reveal.[268] Thus formulated, the 'waiver of disclosure' exception can initially appear broad, but in practice, its application is very much restricted by the primacy of the insured's obligation to disclose. Other things being equal, an insurer can assume that the insured has performed his obligation, and fairly represented the risk. And other things being equal, therefore, he can assume that no information has been withheld that would materially affect the risk as represented. Additional circumstances must suggest that that assumption is illegitimate.

In recent litigation, Lord Mansfield's closing remarks in *Carter v Boehm* have been resurrected in support of a very expansive interpretation of the exception for waiver of disclosure.[269] Such arguments failed. One response was that *Carter v Boehm* was a decision turning on its own facts. Another was that the law has moved on since 1766. The apparent assumption is that modern courts, being more inclined to emphasise the primacy of an insured's obligation to disclose, and more sensitive to the insurance practices that have been shaped by it, are now less willing than Lord Mansfield may have been to allow a failure to inquire to defeat an insurer's allegation of non-disclosure. This possibility

---

[267] See, classically, *Greenhill v Federal Insurance Co Ltd* [1927] 1 KB 65 (CA) 72 (Lord Hansworth), 85–7 (Scrutton LJ), 89 (Sargant LJ).

[268] See *Container Transport International Inc v Oceanus Mutual Underwriting Association (Bermuda) Ltd (No 1)* [1984] 1 Lloyd's Rep 476 (CA) (esp Parker and Stephenson LJJ); *Marc Rich & Co AG v Portman* [1996] 1 Lloyd's Rep 430 (Longmore J), [1997] 1 Lloyd's Rep 225 (CA); *WISE Underwriting Agency Ltd v Grupo Nacional Provincial SA* [2004] EWCA Civ 962, [2004] 2 Lloyd's Rep 483.

[269] See esp the treatment of counsel's arguments in *Marc Rich & Co AG v Portman* [1996] 1 Lloyd's Rep 430 (Longmore J), [1997] 1 Lloyd's Rep 225 (CA), and again in *WISE Underwriting Agency Ltd v Grupo Nacional Provincial SA* [2004] EWCA Civ 962, [2004] 2 Lloyd's Rep 483.

certainly cannot be ruled out. However, re-examination of *Carter v Boehm* in its context, and of Lord Mansfield's judgment as a whole, suggests that any gap between now and then is narrower than it might appear.

If the question is asked, whether a reasonably careful insurer would have inquired about the state of Fort Marlborough's fortifications, a combination of several circumstances might strongly suggest an affirmative answer. First, Lord Mansfield assumed that Boehm knew that Carter might be duty-bound not to disclose Fort Marlborough's defensive state in September 1759. No insurer having this knowledge could have safely proceeded on the assumption that if Carter had any adverse knowledge, he would have volunteered it. Secondly, Lord Mansfield also assumed that Boehm knew or might reasonably be expected to know of the character of the Company's establishments in the East Indies, and more particularly, that Fort Marlborough was only designed to withstand native attack. No insurer having this knowledge could reasonably assume that Fort Marlborough was in a state to withstand a European attack, without further inquiry. Thirdly, even without such knowledge, the nature of the insurance request, taken together with the form of the policy underwritten, might be sufficient to raise a similar suspicion. As we have seen, Carter's request was for a policy covering his stock-in-trade at Fort Marlborough against loss in a European enemy assault. It might be inferred from this that the place was thought indefensible. This inference might be reinforced by the circumstance that the policy underwritten rendered the insured sum payable in full and without further inquiry in the event of such an assault.

If the similar question is asked, whether a reasonably careful insurer would have inquired whether Carter knew facts bearing on the likelihood of a European enemy attack, which he had not disclosed, an affirmative answer might also be reached. Once again, the nature and timing of the insurance request seems fundamentally important. The policy was not such as would be effected in the ordinary course of business, against ordinary perils. It appears to have been a policy insuring only against European enemy attack, for a premium that represented a very substantial sum of money. Lord Mansfield certainly regarded the policy as exceptional, even unique.[270] Once this is appreciated, it is easier to accept that the insurer ought to have suspected that circumstances known to Carter, but not disclosed, gave him special cause to fear that such attack might occur. Other circumstances might suggest the same, or would at least suggest that a London underwriter could not reasonably assume, from Carter's silence, that he had no particular reasons for fearing a European enemy attack. Prime amongst these would be the circumstance that the request came

---

[270] See esp *Carter* (n 1 above) 3 Burr 1905, 1912; 97 ER 1162, 1165, where in the context of the dealing with the public policy objection to the policy's validity, Lord Mansfield observes that insurance of this nature 'so seldom happens, (I never saw one before)'. See also 3 Burr 1905, 1918; 97 ER 1162, 1168, where Lord Mansfield rejects the broker's evidence as to how the underwriters would have reacted to disclosure, on the basis that it was an opinion 'without the least foundation from any previous precedent or usage'.

against the background of direct conflict in the East Indies between England and France, a conflict about which the insured, resident in the East Indies, might initially be better placed to know than a London underwriter.

## J. THE PUBLIC POLICY OBJECTION

It is unlikely to be noticed today that Lord Mansfield also raised a preliminary objection to Carter's claim that did not go to non-disclosure at all. This was that the policy might be void on grounds of public policy:

> [a]n objection occurred to me at the trial, 'whether a policy against the loss of Fort Marlborough, for the benefit of the governor, was good;' upon the principle which does not allow a sailor to insure his wages.[271]

At first sight puzzling, Lord Mansfield's meaning here is revealed by the analogy he draws with the law's treatment of sailors' wages. When *Carter v Boehm* was decided, merchant sailors' wages were structured in a manner that incentivised their doing their utmost for the security of the ship and cargo.[272] Governed by the maxim that 'freight is the mother of wages', no wages might follow in the event of loss of the ship by wreck or capture,[273] a harsh conclusion sometimes expressly rationalised on the basis that

> if the mariners shall have their wages in these cases, they will not use their best endeavours to hazard their lives to preserve the ship.[274]

This risk was considered so significant that a statute then in force actually prohibited the payment of more than half of the wages due to seamen on a merchant ship, before the ship's safe return to Great Britain or Ireland.[275] On the same basis, and as Lord Mansfield must have been aware, it was a common feature of maritime laws at this time that a sailor could not insure his wages,[276] on the basis that an insurance 'safety-net' might produce the same undesirable disincentives. Lord Mansfield rightly recognised that this analogy suggested that

---

[271] *Carter* (n 1 above) 3 Burr 1905, 1912; 97 ER 1162, 1165; (1766) 1 Black W 593, 594; 96 ER 342, 343.

[272] See eg P Earle, *Sailors—English Merchant Seamen 1650–1775* (London, Methuen, 2007) ch 3, esp 31–8 (but note the custom in certain trades of paying a proportion of the pay in advance).

[273] In effect, it seems to have been an implied condition of the seaman's contract with the ship-owner that wages were dependent on the earning of freight: eg *Arnould on the Law of Marine Insurance* (n 142 above) § 244.

[274] Earle, *Sailors* (n 272 above) 36–7 (quoting a contemporary source).

[275] 8 Geo I c 24, s 7.

[276] See earlier, esp N Magens, *An Essay on Insurances* (London, Haberkorn, 1755) vol 1, § 19 (where the effect of maritime ordinances of Amsterdam, Rotterdam and Stockholm, collected in vol 2, is summarised). For later accounts of English law, eg Park, *A System of the Law of Marine Insurances* (n 103 above) 11–12; Marshall, *A Treatise on the Law of Insurance* (n 103 above) vol 1, 89–91. Cf also BM Emerigon, (trans) S Meredith, *A Treatise on Insurances* (London, J Butterworth, 1850) 191–2 (describing the effect of French ordinances, and noting their coincidence with rules of Antwerp and Amsterdam).

Deputy Governor Carter should not be permitted to insure against the loss of Fort Marlborough to a European enemy, for his own benefit. The 'safety-net' of insurance might similarly reduce the incentive of persons occupying his position to take resolute steps for the defence of the place.

Lord Mansfield ultimately resisted this analogy, and dismissed the objection.[277] Unpacked, his conclusion rested on the following substantial considerations. First, it was unlikely the safety of Fort Marlborough would be significantly affected by Carter's acts or omissions. By implication, the case was therefore unlike that of a ship, whose safety inevitably depends on its crew's resolute conduct.[278] Secondly, the law did not consistently reflect the policy that dictated that insurance policies insuring sailors' wages should be invalid. A ship's captain could insure his cargo onboard, or if part-owner of the vessel, could insure his share; similarly, the captain of a privateering vessel could insure his share in the profits of the venture. Thirdly, as a policy of this type was extremely rare, it was unlikely that any mischief would follow by example as a result of its being allowed to stand. Finally, it would not be just to allow the insurer, who took the premium knowing of the insured's status, subsequently to overturn the policy on the basis that that status precluded him from insuring.

## K. CONCLUSION

There can be no questioning *Carter v Boehm*'s landmark status in the development of the law of non-disclosure between parties to an insurance contract. The detailed historical re-analysis undertaken in this chapter enables us to see more clearly why it warrants that status, and why, almost 250 years later, it still deserves to be remembered. It was absolutely not a pro-insurer decision, and we are now better placed to see why. Any contemporary law reformer, concerned for the modern law's shape and balance, might usefully reflect on three particular aspects of the judgment.

First, pervading Lord Mansfield's judgment is the overriding necessity for an inequality of accessible information between insurer and insured, which leads the insurer to depend on disclosure by his prospective insured. This necessity is clear from Lord Mansfield's preliminary exposition of the normative basis for requiring a prospective insured to disclose material facts, and for allowing his insurer to avoid liability where he does not. It underpins Lord Mansfield's unprecedented account of the circumstances in which an insurer cannot complain of non-disclosure, most of which can be derived from those normative underpinnings. It underpins Lord Mansfield's general account of the context in

---

[277] *Carter* (n 1 above) 3 Burr 1905, 1912; 97 ER 1162, 1165.
[278] Though Lord Mansfield does not say this in *express* terms, it is the interpretation that may make most sense of the observation that 'this place, though called a fort, was really but a factory or settlement for trade . . . and he, though called a governor, was really but a merchant': *Carter* (n 1 above) 3 Burr 1905, 1912; 97 ER 1162, 1165.

which Carter's policy was effected, the clear purpose of which was to emphasise that there was no significant inequality of accessible information in the case at hand. Finally, and perhaps most importantly, it was the absence of any significant inequality of accessible information that ultimately lay at the heart of the failure of Boehm's particular allegations of material non-disclosure.

Thus, we can now see that one reason why Boehm's allegations failed was that, in light of what the insurer knew or ought to have known when the policy was effected, the facts allegedly concealed would not have adversely affected a reasonable insurer's risk assessment. In another instance, the answer was that the facts allegedly concealed were matters of general public notoriety, no less accessible to the insurer than to the insured. In yet another instance, the answer was that what was allegedly concealed was the insured's own speculation, and that the law's role was properly limited to correcting inequalities of information on which an insurer's judgement is to be exercised; it did not extend to correcting disparities in the parties' skill and judgement. A final, overriding objection was that the insurer had failed to take advantage of means of information available to him, in the form of inquiry of the insured or of some other source, when what he knew or ought to have known should have compelled the conclusion that he had not been fully informed, and that such inquiries were required.

Secondly, pervading Lord Mansfield's judgment is also the premise that standards of good conduct apply, in some form or other, to both parties to an insurance contract. Lord Mansfield expressly recognised that an insurer owed his insured a corresponding obligation to disclose material facts. Even more significantly in practice, the law regulating the insured's obligation and its consequences would not be allowed to become a cover or excuse for fraud, nor even for negligence. Insurers could not expect to be wholly passive recipients of all information necessary to estimate the risk being undertaken. They would be expected to know, or inform themselves of, certain types of information not peculiarly in the insured's knowledge, in the ordinary proper conduct of their business. And even in the case of information not of this type, any insurer who failed to take advantage of means of information available to him, where the circumstances ought to have suggested that he could not assume that he had been fully informed, did so at his peril. In both of these respects, Lord Mansfield's judgment reflects some very robust findings, adverse to Boehm, the insurer. The resulting signals to the underwriting community ought to have been unmistakable.

Finally, also pervading Lord Mansfield's judgment is the premise that courts must be sensitive to the law's impact on honest insureds. It is very clear that Lord Mansfield regarded Carter as an honest man, who did not appreciate that the facts not disclosed were significant and/or considered himself duty-bound not to disclose them. It would be inconsistent with Lord Mansfield's initial statements of the law to claim that he thought that either of these circumstances alone would excuse the insured's failure to disclose material facts: he expressly held that even accidental non-disclosure would entitle the insurer to avoid liability. Nevertheless, Lord Mansfield's judgment does disclose a sensitivity to the unfortunate consequences that would follow, if insurers were allowed too readily to avoid liability vis-à-vis honest insureds, who have arranged their affairs on the assumption that their risks have been hedged. At the most general level, this sensitivity is evident in the close scrutiny to which Lord Mansfield subjected each of the insurer's allegations of non-disclosure, and his apparent readiness to make factual findings or assumptions adverse to the insurer's interest.

At a more specific level, it is also evident in Lord Mansfield's assumption that an insurer could not be permitted to avoid liability vis-à-vis an insured who had honestly failed to disclose, where the insurer could not reasonably assume that he had been fully informed, and where his failure to inquire had deprived the insured of all opportunity of correcting the omission. It is evident in Lord Mansfield's subtle discussion of whether Carter's policy should be void on public policy grounds. And it is no less evident in Lord Mansfield's readiness to conclude that Boehm had assumed the burden of inquiry into Fort Marlborough's condition, in light of his knowledge that Carter might be duty-bound to keep it secret.

# 4

# *Da Costa v Jones* (1778)

WARREN SWAIN

## A. INTRODUCTION

IN TOBIAS SMOLLETT'S novel *The Adventures of Ferdinand Count Fathom*, the Count describes a visit to a London gaming house[1]:

> In one corner of the room might be heard a pair of lordlings running their grand-mothers against each other, that is, betting sums on the longest liver; in another, the success of the wager depended upon the sex of the landlady's next child; and one of the waiter's happening to drop down in apoplectic fit, a certain noble peer exclaimed 'Dead, for a thousand pounds!' The challenge was immediately accepted; and when the master of the house sent for a surgeon to attempt the cure, the nobleman who set the price upon the patient's head, insisted upon his being left to the efforts of nature alone, otherwise the wager should be void.

Wagering was a popular pastime amongst all social classes in 18th century England.[2] The wagers witnessed by Count Fathom were of a common type,[3] but wagers came in many different guises. An anecdote from 1709 recalls how four Members of Parliament raced their hats in a river and

> ran halloing after them; and he that won the prize was in greater rapture than if he carried the most dangerous point in Parliament.[4]

According to one witness, wagers 'very frequently . . . originate over the bottle or porter pot'.[5] Some were certainly bizarre. One reader in *The Spectator* in

---

[1] T Smollett, *The Adventures of Ferdinand Count Fathom* (London, W Johnston, 1753) 126.

[2] Anon, *An Essay on Gaming* (London, 1761) 2; WS Lewis (ed), H Walpole, *Horace Walpoles's Correspondence*, vol 24 (Oxford, Oxford University Press, 1967) 55, 11 November 1774 to Sir Horace Mann. For later accounts, see J Ashton, *The History of Gambling in England* (London, Duckworth, 1898) 150–72; P Langford, *A Polite and Commercial People* (Oxford, Oxford University Press, 1992) 571–4.

[3] G Clark, *Betting on Lives: The Culture of Life Insurance in England 1695–1775* (Manchester, Manchester University Press, 1999) 50–51. Clarke took a sample from the betting book of White's Club in London between 1743–52: 35% of wagers related to death, 17% to birth and 10% to marriage.

[4] J Malcolm, *Anecdotes of the Manners and Customs of London During the Eighteenth Century* (London, 1808) 132.

[5] *Ibid* 161.

1711 described a wager that the Isle of Wight is a peninsula, another that the World is round.[6]

In his defence of the practice, one anonymous author observed that there was a 'clamour against gaming'.[7] Gaming was said to be 'an inlet to drinking and debauchery'.[8] If some writers were to be believed, those who gambled could also expect more unpleasant consequences. The essayist Richard Hey listed more than 50, ranging from financial ruin, to loss of interest in the opposite sex through impaired health, madness and suicide.[9] But his seemingly comprehensive list was incomplete. He omitted to mention the possibility that wagering might lead to legal proceedings.

## B. THE CHEVALIER D'EON: A QUESTION OF GENDER

It would be difficult to disagree with *The Gentleman's Magazine* of 1777, which described *Hayes v Jacques*, a case concerned with a similar wager to the one at issue in *Da Costa v Jones*, as 'the most extraordinary case that perhaps, ever happened in this or any other country'.[10] The wager which caused all the trouble was certainly an extraordinary one. It concerned the gender of the well-known Frenchman then resident in Britain, the Chevalier d'Eon. D'Eon was born in Tonnerre in Burgundy in 1728.[11] A secretary to the French ambassador

---

[6] D Bond (ed), *The Spectator* (Oxford, Oxford University Press, 1965) vol 2, 145 dated 16 August 1711.

[7] Anon, *A Modest Defence of Gaming* (London, R & J Dodsley, 1754) 5; J Rosenberg-Orsini, *Moral and Sentimental Essays* (London, 1785) 43 'much has been said and written against gaming'. For examples of attacks on gaming see: W De Britaine, *Humane Prudence*, 9th edn (London, Richard Sare, 1702) 134; J Woodward, *A Disswasive from Gaming* (London, 1718); J Brown, *On the Pursuit of False Pleasure, and the Mischiefs of Immoderate Gaming* (London, W Bowyer, 1752); A Stretch, *The Beauties of History; or, Pictures of Virtue and Vice, Drawn from Real Life* (London, 1770) vol 1, 294; W Dodd, *Sermons to Young Men* (London, 1771) vol 2, 262; W Penn, *The Selected Works of William Penn*, 3rd edn (London, 1782) vol 4, 32; J Fallowfield, *Miscellaneous Essays Divine and Moral* (Whitehaven, 1788) 35; T Rennell, *The Consequences of the Vice of Gaming* (London, 1794); Anon, *Tales for Youth, or the High Road to Renown, Through the Paths of Pleasure* (London, William Lane, 1797) 104.

[8] J Collier, *Essay Upon Gaming* (London, J Morphew, 1713) 36.

[9] *A Dissertation on the Pernicious Effects of Gaming* (Cambridge, 1783). Richard Hey was a well known essayist of the period and at the time a Fellow of Magdalene College Cambridge, see RA Anderson rev. R Mills, 'Hey, Richard' *Oxford Dictionary of National Biography* (Oxford, Oxford University Press, 2004). The observation that gaming led to suicide was a common one: Addison (pseud.), *Interesting Anecdotes, Memoirs, Allegories, Essays, and Poetical Fragments* (London, 1794) vol 3, 55; Anon, *An Essay on Gaming* (London, 1761) 2.

[10] *The Gentleman's Magazine* (London, 1777) 346.

[11] For more detailed accounts of the life of the Chevalier d'Eon written in English see: C Vizetelly, *The True Story of the Chevalier D'Eon* (London, Tylston, Edwards, Marsden, 1895); M Coryn, *The Chevalier D'Eon* (London, Thornton Butterworth, 1932); E Nixon, *Royal Spy: The Strange Case of the Chevalier D'Eon* (New York, Reynal & Co, 1965); C Cox, *The Enigma of the Age. The Strange Story of the Chevalier D'Eon* (London, Longmans, 1966); G Kates, *Monsieur D'Eon is a Woman* (Baltimore, John Hopkins University Press, 2001); JM Rogister, 'D'Éon de Beaumont, Charles Geneviève Louis Auguste André Timothée' *Oxford Dictionary of National Biography* (n 9 above). There is also an incomplete autobiography: G Kates (ed), Chevalier d'Eon, *The Maiden of*

in Russia in the mid-1750s, he then became a Captain in the Dragoons during the Seven Years' War. As a reward for the important part that he played in negotiating the Treaty of Paris of 1763, d'Eon was appointed as temporary French ambassador in London. His hopes that the appointment would become permanent were dashed when he was passed over in favour of Comte de Guerchy. Relations between the two men quickly soured. A low point was reached when d'Eon made the startling claim that Guerchy had attempted to have him poisoned.[12] The situation was complicated by d'Eon's membership of the so-called 'King's Secret', a spy network set up by Louis XVth. In this capacity he held papers which would be a great embarrassment to the King were they to enter the public domain. Attempts by the French Government to resolve the problem by persuading the English Government to extradite d'Eon came to nothing. Meanwhile d'Eon continued his feud with Guerchy by publishing *Lettres, mémoires & négociations particulières du Chevalier d'Éon*.[13] The book was a best seller and the talk of fashionable London.[14] In a letter to the Earl of Hertford the same year, Horace Walpole wrote:

> He (d'Eon) has great malice, and great parts to put the malice in play. Though there are even many bad puns in his book, a very uncommon fault in a French book, yet there is much wit too.[15]

A libel writ from Guerchy concerning d'Eon's account of the French embassy soon followed. Walpole also reported that the Privy Council discussed the possibility of criminal proceedings. Lord Mansfield was said to be in favour of such a course of action.[16] In April 1764, the Attorney-General began proceedings against d'Eon for seditious libel.[17] In July d'Eon failed to appear and the King's Bench found in Guerchy's favour in his libel action.[18] At this point a surprise announcement shifted matters in d'Eon's favour when a disgruntled former collaborator of Guerchy alleged that there was indeed a plot to kill d'Eon.[19]

---

*Tonnerre: the Vicissitudes of the Chevalier and Chevaliére d'Eon de Beaumont* (Baltimore, John Hopkins University Press, 2001).

[12] A letter to Louis XVth and his patron Comte de Broglie, dated 18 November 1763, making the allegation is reproduced by Kates, *Monsieur D'Eon is a Woman* (n 11 above) 109–11.

[13] *Lettres, mémoires & négociations particulières du Chevalier d'Éon* (The Hague, 1764).

[14] D Le Marchant (ed), H Walpole, *Memoirs of the Reign of King George the Third* (London, Richard Bentley, 1845) vol 1, 392–4.

[15] *Walpole, Horace Walpoles's Correspondence* (n 2 above) vol 38 (Oxford, Oxford University Press, 1974) 354, 356, 27 March 1764 to the Earl of Hertford.

[16] *Walpole, Horace Walpoles's Correspondence* (n 2 above) vol 38, 354, 356, 27 March 1764 to the Earl of Hertford.

[17] *Walpole, Horace Walpoles's Correspondence* (n 2 above) vol 38, 376, 378, 20 April 1764. An attempt to stall the criminal proceedings by d'Eon by arguing that the material witnesses were abroad was unsuccessful: *R v D'Eon* (1764) 3 Burr 1513, 97 ER 955.

[18] *The Annual Register 1764* (London, 1765) 85–6. Where a defendant failed to appear it was standard practice to award a judgment in default against him, see J Sellon, *An Analysis of the Practice of the Court of King's Bench and Common Pleas* (London, T Wheildon, 1789) 48. D'Eon surrendered himself to the King's Bench the following year and was outlawed, see *The Annual Register 1765* (London, 1766) 99.

[19] W Prest (ed), *The Letters of Sir William Blackstone 1744–1780* (London, Selden Society, 2006) 192.

Guerchy returned to France in 1766, where he died the following year.[20] Unfortunately for d'Eon, his troubles were only just beginning.

In the early 1770s, rumours began to circulate that d'Eon was female,[21] generating 'much noise among the knaves and fools of the metropolis'.[22] The source of these rumours has never been definitively identified. D'Eon would later accuse Princess Dashkova, who visited England from Russia in 1770.[23] But given that she was a child of 11 when d'Eon left Russia and did not even mention d'Eon in her memoirs,[24] she is an unlikely suspect.[25] A more credible explanation is that, for reasons of his own, d'Eon began the rumours himself.[26]

By the end of 1770, Horace Walpole was reporting it as a fact that d'Eon was a woman.[27] Predictably d'Eon was mocked by satirists. In a cartoon of 1771, d'Eon appeared before a jury of matrons with a caption 'They pronounce the matter doubtful'.[28] He also was depicted as half-man and half-woman.[29] Others made fun of the fact that d'Eon was a Freemason[30] and a friend of John Wilkes.[31]

A number of cartoons also depict the wagers concerning d'Eon's gender. In one, d'Eon stands in front of a table containing a document on which is written 'A policy of 25 PCt On the Ch'D'Eon Man or Woman'; in another headed 'A Deputation from Jonathan's[32] and the Freemasons', stockbrokers hold up a

[20] According to Walpole, *Memoirs of the Reign of King George the Third* (n 14 above) vol 3, 102–3 his death was 'hastened by mortifications he had received from d'Eon'.

[21] *The London Magazine 1777* (London, 1777) 445 dated the beginning of the rumours as the winter of 1770. For examples of press speculation on the subject see *Public Advertiser* 12 March 1771; *Gazetteer and New Daily Advertiser* 11 March 1771; *London Evening Post* 9–12 March 1771.

[22] *The British Magazine and General Review* (London, 1772) vol 1, 258.

[23] D'Eon, *The Maiden of Tonnerre* (n 11 above) 20.

[24] E Dashkova, *Memoirs of Princess Dashkova* (London, Henry Colburn, 1840).

[25] Kates, *Monsieur D'Eon is a Woman* (n 11 above) 192.

[26] Kates, *Monsieur D'Eon is a Woman* (n 11 above) 192.

[27] Walpole, *Horace Walpoles's Correspondence* (n 2 above) (Oxford, Oxford University Press, 1939) vol 4, 493–4, 14 December 1770 from Madame du Deffand.

[28] D George, *Catalogue of Political and Personal Satires Preserved in the Department of Prints and Drawings at the British Museum* (London, British Museum, 1952) vol 5, no 4862. The matrons depicted were all leading society ladies of the period. A jury of matrons was used when it was, for example, necessary to determine whether a woman was pregnant in a criminal trial or to determine matters of inheritance: see J Oldham, 'The Origins of the Special Jury' (1983) 50 *University of Chicago Law Review* 137, 171–2; J Oldham, *The Varied Life of the Self-Informing Jury* (London, Selden Society 2005) 31–43.

[29] George, *Catalogue of Political and Personal Satires* (n 28 above) vol 5, no 4871; no 5427.

[30] George, *Catalogue of Political and Personal Satires* (n 28 above) vol 5, no 4865; no 4873. The Freemasons were becoming an influential body in England during the mid-18th century: see M Jacob, *Living the Enlightenment: Freemasonry and Politics in Eighteenth Century Europe* (New York, Oxford University Press, 1991) 52–72.

[31] George, *Catalogue of Political and Personal Satires* (n 28 above) vol 5, no 4872, which showed d'Eon being led up to the altar in marriage by John Wilkes. John Wilkes was the famous politician and writer. Like d'Eon he was no stranger to the courts. As publisher of the *North Briton* he was prosecuted for seditious libel, see P Thomas, 'Wilkes, John' *Oxford Dictionary of National Biography* (n 9 above).

[32] Jonathan's Coffee house was a meeting place for brokers, which became the London Stock Exchange: R Michie, *The London Stock Exchange. A History* (Oxford, Oxford University Press, 2001) 20; E Markman, *The Coffee House. A Cultural History* (London, Weidenfeld & Nicholson, 2004) 166–84.

piece of paper containing the words 'Petition from the Bulls and Bears in Change Alley'.[33] An advertisement in the *Westminster Gazette* gives some idea of the sort of wagers that were on offer[34]:

> The gentleman declares d'Eon (alias the Chevalier d'Eon) a woman . . . this declaration he supports with a bet of any sum of money from one to five thousand guineas. Or, he proposes to anyone, who will deposit five hundred guineas in the hands of his banker, to pay ten thousand pounds if d'Eon proves herself either a man, hermaphrodite, or any other animal than a woman.

The *London Magazine* described payments of 10 to 15 guineas in return for 100 guineas should d'Eon prove to be female.[35] According to Walpole, 'very great sums were wagered on the question'.[36] His claim is borne out by contemporary newspaper accounts. In 1771 it was estimated that £60,000 had been wagered on d'Eon's gender.[37] By early 1777 that figure had risen to £120,000.[38] Given the size of individual wagers, the total sums involved may have been even higher.[39] John Wesket would later claim that the wagers led to the bankruptcy of a number of underwriters.[40]

In the early 1770s, some began to suspect that d'Eon had a financial interest in the outcome of the wagers. Above the caption 'Chevalier D-E-n returned or the stockbrokers outwitted', d'Eon, dressed as a man, addresses one of the stockbrokers: 'Well broker how have you manag'd our scheme?', the broker replies: 'Glad to see you return'd Chevalier, we have took the knowing ones in swingingly'.[41] In fact there is no evidence to suggest that d'Eon was complicit in the wagers despite his precarious financial position.[42]

On becoming King, Louis XVIth was anxious to secure the return of his grandfather's secret papers still in d'Eon's possession. Negotiations were conducted on the King's behalf by Pierre-Augustin Caron de Beaumarchais.[43] Later on he was assisted by Charles-Claude Théveneau de Morande, a French journalist, blackmailer and spy living in London.[44] Armed with the knowledge that the King was prepared to allow d'Eon to live as a woman on his return to

---

[33] Change Alley was the location for Jonathan's Coffee House.

[34] *Westminster Gazette*, 7–10 September 1776.

[35] *London Magazine* (n 21 above) 444.

[36] Walpole, *Memoirs of the Reign of King George the Third* (n 14 above) vol 4, 329.

[37] *London Evening Post*, 11–14 May 1771.

[38] *London Chronicle*, 5 May 1777.

[39] According to one report, £75,000 would remain in the country which would otherwise have been transmitted to Monsieur Panchard in Paris, see *Morning Chronicle*, 3 February 1778.

[40] J Wesket, *A Complete Digest of the Theory, Laws, and Practice of Insurance* (London, 1781) 584.

[41] George, *Catalogue of Political and Personal Satires* (n 28 above) vol 5, no 4865.

[42] For a good snap shot of his finances see BL Add MS 11340.

[43] Beaumarchais was perhaps best known as the playwright who wrote *The Barber of Seville* and *The Marriage of Figaro*.

[44] S Burrows, 'Théveneau de Morande, Charles-Claude' *Oxford Dictionary of National Biography* (n 9 above); S Burrows, 'A Literary Low-Life Reassessed: Charles Théveneau de Morande in London, 1769–1791' (1998) 22 *Eighteenth Century Life* 76.

France, both men saw the opportunity for personal profit from the wagers.[45] With this in mind, Morande offered d'Eon large sums of money to co-operate in the wagers.[46] D'Eon refused the offer and their friendship was at an end. D'Eon challenged Morande to a duel with the result that he was bound over to keep the peace. Morande responded by conducting a campaign against d'Eon. The claim that d'Eon was a woman appeared repeatedly in the press.[47] By late 1776, the allegations that d'Eon was involved in the wagers began to resurface. In an article in the *Public Ledger* in September 1776, it was claimed that

> The public can be assured that MISS D'Eon had a capital stake depending on the event of the policies opened on her sex. The whole thing was a bubble, and many of the biters will be bitten.[48]

The same allegation was repeated two days later.[49] The *Public Advertiser* pleaded:

> Come, Madame, be candid, though but for a moment. Answer me this question. Would not the sum you receive for secreting your sex, induce you to discover it?[50]

D'Eon retaliated with a libel action against one of the newspapers, the *Public Ledger*, and Morande. The libel action helped to bring matters to a head over the wager. The *Westminster Gazette* reported that the quarrel 'is the only thing that could have made known for a certainty' the sex of d'Eon.[51] When the libel action came before the King's Bench in November 1776,[52] Morande produced an order from Louis XVIth giving d'Eon permission to return to France. It was alleged that d'Eon, in his own handwriting, had changed references in the document from masculine to feminine. Morande admitted that d'Eon had been offered £10,000 to reveal her gender but had refused because the offer consisted of a share in the policies, whereas d'Eon wanted payment in cash. D'Eon claimed that it was Morande himself who had made the offer.[53] Several affidavits to the effect that d'Eon was offered money to co-operate in the wagers were sworn during the libel action but Morande was not named as a party. Copies appeared in the *Morning Chronicle* the following year.[54] Morande also claimed that d'Eon had accepted a smaller sum to go into hiding. Despite the strong whiff of foul play, Lord Mansfield dismissed the action with an abrupt 'Let the rule be discharged'.

---

[45] Kates, *Monsieur D'Eon is a Woman* (n 11 above) 231 suggests that the two men were involved in bets totalling £100,000 some of which was bet on behalf of Paris financiers.

[46] Kates, *Monsieur D'Eon is a Woman* (n 11 above) 241.

[47] For further examples see Kates, *Monsieur D'Eon is a Woman* (n 11 above) 243.

[48] *Public Ledger*, 2 September 1776.

[49] *Public Ledger*, 4 September 1776.

[50] *Public Advertiser*, 6 September 1776. See also the *Westminster Gazette*, 10–14 September 1776.

[51] *Westminster Gazette*, 6–12 August 1776.

[52] *Public Ledger*, 25 November 1776; *Public Advertiser*, 29 November 1776.

[53] The memorandum written by d'Eon making these allegations is reproduced in Cox, *The Enigma of the Age. The Strange Story of the Chevalier D'Eon* (n 11 above) 108–9.

[54] *Morning Chronicle,* 15 July 1777.

With fortunes to be won and lost, those with policies started to become anxious.[55] Fearing that d'Eon was about to return to France, which would prevent the question of his gender from being settled, some of those with wagering contracts engaged lawyers and prepared to enforce their agreements through the courts. At the same time, some of the brokers attempted to cut their losses by entering into agreements to pay up to 70 percent of the value of the wagers in return for an agreement to have the wagers cancelled.[56]

## C. THE FIRST ACTION: *HAYES v JACQUES*

It was reported that three actions to enforce the wagers were commenced in early 1777 and that 'most first rate counsel are retained on one side or the other'.[57] The first of the trio, the unreported *Hayes v Jacques*, came on before Lord Mansfield in July. Full accounts of the case appeared in the press.[58] The court-room was packed for the occasion with an audience eager to hear the salacious details and, no doubt, some who had entered into wagers.[59] Mr Jacques, a surgeon, had entered into an agreement with Mr Hayes, an under-writer. Like many wagers of the period, the contract resembled an ordinary insurance policy. Jacques had paid Hayes premiums of 15 guineas for a number of years. Hayes agreed to match each premium with 100 guineas should d'Eon prove to be a woman.

Francis Buller, who would later enjoy a distinguished career on the Bench, opened for the plaintiff.[60] He began by claiming that he would prove that d'Eon was a woman, which the *Morning Chronicle* reported 'occasioned a good laugh'. D'Eon's former physician then swore that to his 'certain knowledge', d'Eon was a woman. D'Eon was particularly incensed in what he saw as breach of trust by his doctors.[61] It would be difficult to imagine anyone less impartial than the next witness. It was none other than d'Eon's old enemy, Morande. Although Morande may, at least to begin with, have genuinely believed that

---

[55] For example a letter signed a 'Policy Loser' appeared in the *Morning Post*, 27 August 1776: 'It is but common justice to the public so long imposed upon by this female adventurer that her dupes should give a summary of the most interesting particulars of her infamous transactions, by these means they would essentially serve the world at large, and particularly oblige your humble servant'.

[56] *London Chronicle*, 5 May 1777.

[57] *Ibid.*

[58] *London Magazine* (n 21 above) 378–9; *The Gentleman's Magazine* (n 10 above) 346–7; *Morning Chronicle*, 2 July 1777.

[59] *Morning Chronicle, ibid.* D'Eon himself observed that 'half the world' seemed to be there, see Kates, *Monsieur D'Eon is a Woman* (n 11 above) 248.

[60] Francis Buller was later a Justice of the King's Bench and Common Pleas, see J Oldham, 'Buller, Francis Sir' *Oxford Dictionary of National Biography* (n 9 above). The plaintiff was also represented by James Wallace who later became Attorney-General, see GM Ditchfield, 'Wallace, James' *Oxford Dictionary of National Biography* (n 9 above).

[61] D'Eon, *The Maiden of Tonnerre* (n 11 above) 27. As d'Eon himself conceded, his physicians had kept their own counsel until they were subpoenaed as witnesses.

d'Eon was a woman,[62] he also stood to gain financially from the wagers[63] and therefore it was in his interests to convince the jury that d'Eon was female. What his testimony lacked in truth it made up for in impact:

> That she (d'Eon) had even proceeded so far as to display her bosom on the occasion . . . and had exhibited the contents of her female wardrobe, which consisted of sacques,[64] petticoats, and other habiliments calculated for feminine use . . . and then permitted him to have manual proof of her being in truth a woman.

James Mansfield, counsel for Jacques and later Chief Justice of the Common Pleas,[65] began his argument for the defence by questioning whether this was a proper action to bring before that court on the grounds that it

> was one of those gambling, indecent, and unnecessary cases that ought never to be permitted to come into a court or justice.

Instead of presenting witnesses prepared to deny that d'Eon was female, Mansfield argued that, because the plaintiff had greater knowledge that d'Eon was female, he was at an unfair advantage. This was a bold move given that outside a narrow range of situations even Equity was not prepared to set aside bargained for agreements on the grounds of unfair advantage.[66] Perhaps predictably the argument was not well received by Lord Mansfield, who responded with an anecdote told in a 'facetious and pointed manner' about two men who entered into a wager about the dimensions of a statue of Venus:

> One of the gentlemen said, 'I will not deceive you; I tell you fairly I have been there and measured it myself'. 'Well (says the other) and do you think I would be such a fool as to lay if I had not measured it?'

The Court once more descended into laughter.

When Lord Mansfield came to address the jury, he 'expressed his abhorrence of the transaction' and 'wished it had been in his power in concurrence with the jury, to have made both parties lose'. He was, nevertheless, forced to concede that it was not an illegal contract nor was it indecent. In consequence it was binding. If the plaintiff could discharge the difficult burden of proving that d'Eon was a woman then he could recover. Lord Mansfield seems to have accepted the evidence of plaintiff's witnesses at face value—remarking that any other interpretation would mean that they had committed perjury. Unsurprisingly, given

---

[62] Kates, *Monsieur D'Eon is a Woman* (n 11 above) 215.

[63] For details of these potential gains, see Kates, *Monsieur D'Eon is a Woman* (n 11 above) 230–34.

[64] A sacque is a woman's hip-length jacket.

[65] M Davis, 'Mansfield, James Sir' *Oxford Dictionary of National Biography* (n 9 above).

[66] Mere advantage taking was not enough for Equity to set aside an agreement. The transaction needed to come within the definition of fraud laid down in *The Earl of Chesterfield v Janssen* (1750) 2 Ves Sen 125, 155–7; 28 ER 100–101 (Ch). Hence, for example, an inadequate price alone was insufficient to justify rescission see: *Heathcote v Paignon* (1787) 2 Bro CC 167, 29 ER 96 (Ch). On the limits to Equity jurisdiction in contract see: M Lobban, 'Contractual Fraud in Law and Equity' (1997) 17 *Oxford Journal of Legal Studies* 441.

Lord Mansfield's direction, the jury took just two minutes to reach a verdict in favour of the plaintiff. Hayes recovered £700 by way of damages.

## D. TWO MORE ACTIONS: *DA COSTA v JONES* AND *ROEBUCK v HAMMERTON*

*Da Costa v Jones* came on before Lord Mansfield and a jury in December 1777.[67] The declaration stated that, on 4 October 1771, in consideration that the plaintiff would pay 75 guineas, the defendant promised to pay 300 pounds should d'Eon prove to be female. Morande was the leading witness for the plaintiff once again. But Buller also called three new witnesses.[68] The defence counsel, Bearcroft and Cowper, had not appeared in the earlier trial and they tried a different tactic. For the first time witnesses were called to testify that d'Eon was a man. The first witness, a naval Lieutenant, said that he had lodged with D'Eon who had 'seen him with his waistcoat and stockings off' and had 'always imagined him to be a man'. Two fellow Freemasons also testified that d'Eon would not have been admitted to the Lodge had he been female. But the reports of the case suggest that all three lacked the conviction of the plaintiff's witnesses, who 'positively' asserted that d'Eon was female. Once more the jury found in the plaintiff's favour awarding damages of £225. In *Roebuck v Hamilton*, the third case on wagers, a verdict was again given in the plaintiff's favour.[69] There matters rested until early the following year when both actions were heard before the court sitting *in banc*, giving Lord Mansfield an opportunity to examine the legal status of wagers.

## E. WAGERS AND THE LAW OF CONTRACT IN THE 18TH CENTURY

Several old authorities suggested that wagers constituted valid contracts.[70] As Buller J observed,

[67] The proceedings are reported in the *Daily Advertiser*, 17 December 1777; *Gazetteer*, 18 December 1777. Lord Mansfield's trial notes are reproduced in J Oldham, *The Mansfield Manuscripts and the Growth of English Law in the Eighteenth Century* (Chapel Hill, University of North Carolina Press, 1992) vol 1, 534.

[68] In addition to de Morande and d'Eon's doctors, the court also heard testimony from Elizabeth Lautum who was the wife of d'Eon's landlord, friend and wine merchant. Mary Christie, a former servant of d'Eon also gave evidence. The third witness, Elizabeth Coutans, is described in one report as a lady living in Tavistock Street. Lord Mansfield took the unusual step of striking her evidence out in his trial notes, see Oldham, *The Mansfield Manuscripts* (n 67 above) vol 1, 534.

[69] Oldham, *The Mansfield Manuscripts* (n 67 above) vol 1, 539.

[70] For older authority on the enforcement of a wager see: *Andrews v Herne* (1661) 1 Lev 33, 83 ER 283 (KB), *Walcot v Tappin* (1661) 1 Keb 56, 83 ER 808 (KB). AWB Simpson, *A History of the Common Law of Contract* (Oxford, Oxford University Press, 1987) 534–5; JH Baker, *The Oxford History of the Law of England Volume VI 1483–1558* (Oxford, Oxford University Press, 2003) 820, 859.

Till the case of *Da Costa v Jones* the question was never agitated, or the mischievous consequences of sustaining such actions discussed.[71]

The matter was given greater impetus in the 18th century because many wagers took the form of insurance contracts. By the mid-18th century, insurance was a major industry in Britain, which attracted considerable sums from other jurisdictions.[72] One critic of this type of wagering contract suggested that they were detrimental to the national interest[73]:

> They render insurance suspected, foreigners apprehensive, the security of commerce precarious, contaminate probity, create ill will, as amongst other gamblers, produce lame ducks, and may in time introduce at Lloyds as well as Jonathan's such apposite and polite appellations as Bull and Bear.

Statute intervened to prevent wagering by marine insurance.[74] A desire to prevent the work that he had done to develop the law of insurance from unravelling[75] probably lay behind the distinction drawn by Lord Mansfield between insurance and wagering[76]:

> There are two sorts of policies of insurance; mercantile and gaming policies. The first sort are contracts of indemnity, and indemnity only . . . The second sort may be in the same form; but in them there is no contract of indemnity, because there is no interest on which a loss can accrue.

As Lord Mansfield pointed out when applying the statute, 'the use of it (insurance) was perverted by its being turned into a wager'.[77] The same distinction can be found in another statute prohibiting wagering by insurance, which provided that

> no insurance shall be made . . . on the life or lives of any persons, or any other event or events whatsoever, wherein the person . . . shall have no interest whatsoever.[78]

*Roebuck v Hammerton*[79] showed that some of the wagers on the gender of d'Eon could be caught under the statute.

The position of wagers entered into prior to the statutes or otherwise excluded was more complicated. In *Jones v Randall*,[80] four years before *Da*

---

[71]   *Good v Elliott* (1790) 3 TR 693, 697; 100 ER 808, 810 (KB).

[72]   H Raynes, *A History of British Insurance*, 2nd edn (London, Pitman, 1964) esp 135–83.

[73]   Wesket, *Theory, Laws, and Practice of Insurance* (n 40 above) lvi. For a similar view, see: J Park, *System of the Law of Marine Insurance*, 2nd edn (London, T Wheildon, 1790) 262.

[74]   (1746) 19 Geo 2 c 37. On the application of the statute, see *Kent v Bird* (1777) 2 Cowp 583, 98 ER 1253 (KB); *Grant v Parkinson* (1781) 3 Doug 16, 99 ER 515 (KB).

[75]   On the contribution of Lord Mansfield to the law of insurance see: Park, *System of the Law of Marine Insurance* (n 73 above) iii; CHS Fifoot, *Lord Mansfield* (Oxford, Oxford University, Press, 1936) 82–117; Oldham, *The Mansfield Manuscripts* (n 67 above) vol 1, 450–78.

[76]   *Lowry v Bourdieu* (1780) 2 Doug 468, 470; 99 ER 300 (KB); *Kent* (n 74 above) 2 Cowp 583, 585.

[77]   *Kent* (n 74 above) 2 Cowp 583, 585.

[78]   (1774) 14 Geo III c 48.

[79]   *Roebuck v Hammerton* (1778) 2 Cowp 737, 98 ER 1335 (KB).

[80]   *Jones v Randall* (1774) 1 Cowp 37, 98 ER 954 (KB).

*Costa v Jones*,[81] Lord Mansfield had demonstrated that he was prepared to adopt a flexible view when it came to the validity of wagering contracts[82]:

> But it is argued, and rightly, that notwithstanding it is not prohibited by any positive law, nor adjudged illegal by any precedents, yet it may be decided to be so upon principles; and the law of England would be a strange science indeed if it were decided on precedents only . . . The question then is, whether this wager is against principles? If it be contrary to any, it must be contrary either to principles of morality, for the law of England prohibits every thing which is *contra bonos mores*; or it must be against principles of sound policy; for many contracts which are not against morality, are still void as being against the maxims of sound policy.

The wager in *Jones v Randall* concerned the outcome of litigation in which the current parties were also involved. It was held to be valid. Lord Mansfield's admission during the course of argument in *Da Costa v Jones* that '[n]ever was a question more doubtful how it would be decided till it was actually determined'[83] showed that by resorting to principle rather than precedent, the outcome of litigation could sometimes be hard to predict. Indeed it was sometimes said that in Lord Mansfield's hands the law was rendered uncertain.[84] Given that he stressed the importance of certainty in commercial cases over and over again such criticism are a little unfair.[85] But the fact that Lord Mansfield was so open about the importance of public policy and morality in wagering cases is further evidence that wagering contracts, even in the form of insurance contracts, were seen as a class apart from ordinary commercial contracts and special considerations needed to be applied to their enforcement.

Lord Mansfield had already made clear during the trial of *Da Costa v Jones* that he was unhappy about these wagers coming before the Courts,[86] but he once more reiterated that: 'Indifferent wagers upon indifferent matters, without interest to either of the parties, are certainly allowed by the law of this country, in so far as they have not been restrained by particular Acts of Parliament'.[87] The wager in *Da Costa v Jones* was not covered by statute and the defendant was required to demonstrate that the wager ought not to be enforced on other grounds. Bearcroft and Cowper put forward two main arguments. The first was

---

[81] *Da Costa v Jones* (1778) 2 Cowp 729, 98 ER 1331 (KB).

[82] *Jones* (n 80 above) 1 Cowp 37, 39; 98 ER 954, 955.

[83] *Da Costa* (n 81 above) 2 Cowp 729, 733; 98 ER 1331, 1333.

[84] 'Junius' was a particularly vocal critic, see J Cannon (ed), *The Letters of Junius* (Oxford, Oxford University Press, 1978) Letter XLI 209–10. Lord Campbell, who admired Lord Mansfield, recalled the successful efforts of a few narrow-minded and envious people to disparage him soon after his death', see Lord Campbell, *The Lives of the Chief Justices of England* (London, John Murray, 1849) vol 2, 397.

[85] *Medcalf v Hall* (1782) 3 Doug 113, 115; 99 ER 567 (KB) where Lord Mansfield said: 'Nothing is more mischievous than uncertainty in mercantile law'. See also *Milles v Fletcher* (1779) 1 Doug 231, 232; 99 ER 152 (KB); *Simond v Boydell* (1779) 1 Doug 268, 270–71 (KB); 99 ER 177; *Tindal v Brown* (1786) 1 TR 167, 168; 99 ER 1034 (KB); *Nutt v Hague* (1786) 1 TR 323, 330; 99 ER 1119 (KB).

[86] *Daily Advertiser*, 17 December 1777.

[87] *Da Costa* (n 81 above) 2 Cowp 729, 734; 98 ER 1331, 1334.

that such a wager should be struck down because it tended to introduce indecent evidence. Lord Mansfield seemed to reject this submission:

> For indecency of the evidence is no objection to its being received, where it is necessary to the decision of a civil or criminal right.[88]

A second argument that the wager 'affects the peace and comfort of a third person, and, as such the peace of society' was more favourably received[89]:

> Here is a person who appears to all the world to be a man; is stated upon the record to be 'Monsieur Le Chevalier D'Eon'; has acted in that character in a variety of capacities; and has his reasons and advantages in so appearing. Shall two indifferent people, by a wager between themselves, injure him so, as to try in an action upon that wager, whether . . . he is a cheat and impostor; or, shew that he is a woman, and be allowed to subpoena all his intimate friends, and confidential attendants, to give evidence that will expose him all over Europe? It is monstrous to state. It is a disgrace to judicature.

A wager about a third person could be perfectly valid at Common law. In *Earl of March v Pigott*,[90] two young men entered into a wager about whose father would live longest. Such a wager, being 'no reflection or injury'[91] to the third party, was upheld. *Da Costa v Jones* was different. Because the wager was 'manifestly a gross injury to a third person'[92] it could not be enforced. The wager in *Earl of March v Pigott* brought no discredit on either of the fathers.

*Da Costa v Jones* was not the only wager to be declared invalid. A wager on the outcome of an election between two voters was set aside because:[93]

> One of the principal foundations of this constitution depends on the proper exercise of this franchise, that the election of members of Parliament should be free, and particularly that every voter should be free from pecuniary influence in giving his vote.

One of the ironies of *Da Costa v Jones* was that, despite Lord Mansfield's frequently expressed dislike of wagers, the decision also offered some comfort for those wanting to enforce wagers because Lord Mansfield re-stated the rule that wagers were *prima facie* enforceable. To be invalid a wager needed to be contrary to statute, public policy or morality.

The statutory restrictions on wagering were something of a hotchpotch designed to deal with very specific situations. In addition to insurance cases, an earlier statute had outlawed wagers on the War of Spanish Succession.[94] The impact of the statutes on wagering in practice is difficult to assess. There was certainly a perception that statutory regulation on gaming was widely

---

[88] *Da Costa* (n 81 above) 2 Cowp 729, 734, 98 ER 1331, 1334.
[89] *Da Costa* (n 81 above) 2 Cowp 729, 735–6; 98 ER 1331, 1335.
[90] *Earl of March v Pigott* (1771) 5 Burr 2802, 98 ER 471 (KB).
[91] *Da Costa* (n 81 above) 2 Cowp 729, 736; 98 ER 1331, 1335.
[92] *Da Costa* (n 81 above) 2 Cowp 729, 736; 98 ER 1331, 1335.
[93] *Allen v Hearn* (1785) 1 TR 56, 59; 99 ER 971 (KB).
[94] (1708) 7 Ann c 16.

flouted.[95] As was pointed out in *Roebuck v Hammerton*,[96] the statutes were only designed to stop wagering in the form of insurance.

The Common law was more difficult to predict. In *Atherfold v Beard*,[97] Ashhurst J was candid[98]:

In my opinion the Courts have gone far enough in encouraging impertinent wagers. Perhaps it would have been better for the public, if the Courts had originally determined that no action to enforce the payment of wagers should be permitted.

A wager speculating on the amount to be collected through duties on hops was said to be 'against sound policy'.[99] Buller J went even further: 'I do not find that it has ever been established as a position of law, that a wager between two persons, not interested in the subject-matter, is legal'.[100]

*Good v Elliot*[101] saw a wager on whether a third party had bought a wagon. Grose J pointed out that were it the case that all wagers were void, there would have been no need for 'the elaborate opinion delivered by Lord Mansfield'[102] in *Da Costa v. Jones*. In his opinion:

We may take the rule to be that those wagers are bad, which by injuring a third person disturb the peace of society, or which militate against the morality or sound policy of the kingdom.[103]

The way in which Grose J justified *Da Costa v Jones* was perhaps narrower than Lord Mansfield intended. The wager was bad not merely because it injured a third person but also because the injury to d'Eon disturbed the peace of society.[104] He also stressed that the recent statute was not designed to invalidate all wagers but only those in the form of insurance.[105] Ashhurst J and Lord Kenyon delivered broadly similar opinions. It is implicit in both judgments that 'an injury to a third party' was designed to catch those wagers which damaged the reputation of the third party.[106] Buller J favoured a more radical solution. He argued that the wager fell within the third party exception, which he took to

---

[95] Country Justice of the Peace, *Serious thoughts in regard to the publick disorders, with several proposals for remedying the same* (London, 1750) 10; T Erskine, *Reflections on Gaming, Annuities and Usurious Contracts* (London, 1776) 10–11.

[96] *Roebuck* (n 79 above) 2 Cowp 737, 98 ER 1335–6.

[97] *Atherfold v Beard* (1788) 2 TR 610, 100 ER 328 (KB).

[98] *Ibid*, 2 TR 610, 615; 100 ER 331.

[99] *Atherfold* (n 97 above) 2 TR 610, 615.

[100] *Atherfold* (n 97 above) 2 TR 610, 616.

[101] *Good* (n 71 above) 3 TR 693, 100 ER 808.

[102] *Ibid* 3 TR 693, 694.

[103] *Good* (n 71 above) 3 TR 693, 695; 100 ER 808, 809.

[104] *Good* (n 71 above) 3 TR 693, 695; 100 ER 808, 809. There is some ambiguity on this point in *Da Costa* (n 81 above) 2 Cowp 729, 735; 98 ER 1331.

[105] *Good* (n 71 above) 3 TR 693, 696; 100 ER 808, 809.

[106] *Good* (n 71 above) 3 TR 693, 703; 100 ER 808, 813 (Ashhurst J), at 704; 814 (Lord Kenyon). Lord Kenyon's relatively liberal line is slightly surprising given his well known dislike of gaming, see GT Kenyon, *The Life of Lloyd, First Lord Kenyon: Lord Chief Justice of England* (London, 1873) 356–7.

mean that a wager about a third party or his property was void.[107] He also suggested that all wagers should be outlawed.[108] The statute was also said to prohibit all wagers in which the parties had no interest.[109]

## F. WAGERS AND THE LAW OF CONTRACT IN THE 19TH CENTURY

Buller J was not the only late 18th century judge to take a harsh line against wagering contracts.[110]

Writing in the early 19th century, Joseph Chitty detected judicial hostility towards wagers[111]:

> And some judges at Nisi Prius have exercised a very extended discretion, in refusing to try actions on wagers, which, although not strictly illegal, have raised questions in which the parties have no interest, and have been of trifling, ridiculous, or contemptible nature.

Chitty provided a list of authorities to back up his claim that, more often than not, judges were striking down wagers.[112] Oliphant disagreed. In his opinion, 19th century judges 'began to look more favourably on sporting transactions'.[113] The decision closest to *Da Costa v Jones* concerns another remarkable figure, the prophetess Joanna Southcott.[114] A wager that she would shortly give birth to a boy was held invalid.[115] The 19th century is caricatured by some writers as a period dominated by the notion of freedom of contract, but freedom of contract certainly had its limits.[116] Lord Ellenborough pointed out that

> [w]herever the tolerating of any species of contract has a tendency to produce a public mischief or inconvenience, such a contract has been held to be void.[117]

Judges had a considerable amount of discretion when it came to striking down wagers, but it was still necessary to bring the wager within one of the

---

[107] *Good* (n 71 above) 3 TR 693, 699–700; 100 ER 808, 811.

[108] *Good* (n 71 above) 3 TR 693, 697; 100 ER 808, 810.

[109] *Good* (n 71 above) 3 TR 693, 702; 100 ER 808, 812.

[110] *Brown v Leeson* (1792) 2 H Bla 43, 46; 126 ER 421 (Lord Loughborough) (CP). Park, *System of the Law of Marine Insurance* (n 73 above) 260 also thought that the courts were hostile to wagers.

[111] J Chitty, *A Practical Treatise on the Law of Contracts Not Under Seal* (London, S Sweet, 1826) 155–6.

[112] *Shirley v Sankey* (1800) 2 B & P 130, 126 ER 1196 (CP); *Hartley v Rice* (1808) 10 East 22, 103 ER 683 (KB); *Henkin v Guerss* (1810) 12 East 247, 104 ER 97 (KB).

[113] G Oliphant, *The Law Concerning Horses, Racing, Wager and Gaming* (London, 1847) 188.

[114] S Bowerbank, 'Southcott, Joanna' *Oxford Dictionary of National Biography* (n 9 above). In 1814 a number of her followers believed that she was pregnant with the new Messiah. She was nearly 65 at the time.

[115] *Ditchburn v Goldsmith* (1815) 4 Camp 152, 171 ER 49 (KB).

[116] Most famously by PS Atiyah, *The Rise and Fall of Freedom of Contract* (Oxford, Oxford University Press, 1979). Contracts in restraint of trade were another example on which see: JD Heydon, *The Restraint of Trade Doctrine*, 2nd edn (Sydney, Butterworths, 1999) ch 1; *Mitchell v Reynolds* (1711) 1 P Wms 181, 24 ER 347; Fort 295, 92 ER 859; 10 Mod 130, 88 ER 660.

[117] *Gilbert v Sykes* (1812) 16 East 150, 156–7; 104 ER 1048 (KB).

exceptions. The rule that a wager was valid unless it fell under a statute or one of the Common law exceptions still stood.[118] But the demise of wagering contracts was not far off. In 1845, statute intervened once more but, unlike earlier provisions, it provided an almost total prohibition on wagering contracts[119]:

> All contracts or agreements whether by parole or in writing by way of gaming or wagering shall be null and void; and that no suit shall be brought or maintained in any court of Law or Equity for recovering any sum of money or valuable thing alleged to be won upon any wager.

After *Da Costa v Jones*, the Chevalier d'Eon was summoned back to France. He was ordered to dress as a woman by Louis XVIth. But his stay there was cut short by the French Revolution and he returned to London. Virtually destitute because he was no longer in receipt of a pension, he was forced to sell his library and other trinkets.[120] He was reduced to appearing in public entertainments[121] and fencing tournaments.[122] His last years were lived in poverty.

The reasons why d'Eon was content to live as a woman were complicated. Kates has argued that

> d'Eon's switch was not a compulsion but an intellectual decision . . . D'Eon did not become a woman to trick others; rather, he chose to become a woman because he deeply admired the moral character of women and wanted to live as one of them.[123]

To begin with d'Eon may also have seen his transformation as a way of securing his safe passage back to France. For the rest of his life, d'Eon remained ambiguous about his gender. In his autobiography he explained,

> What distinguishes my birth was that I was born with a caul and that my sex was hidden in nibibus.[124]

Some who met him had no such doubts. James Boswell confided to his journal in 1786, 'She appeared a man in woman's clothes'.[125]

The truth of d'Eon's gender was only revealed in 1810 when, on his death, his longstanding companion Mrs Cole came to prepare his body for burial. An autopsy carried out by the famous surgeon Thomas Copeland and attended by such worthies as the Earl of Yarmouth and Sir Sidney Smith pronounced him a

---

[118] *Hussey v Crickitt* (1811) 3 Camp 168, 173; 170 ER 1345 (Heath J) (KB).

[119] (1845) 8 & 9 Vic c 109. For the application of the statute, see F Pollock, *Principles of Contract at Law and in Equity* (London, Stevens & Sons, 1876) 241–2. For a useful summary of the modern law, see GH Treitel, *The Law of Contract*, 11th edn (London, Sweet & Maxwell, 2003) 520–21; *Hill v William Hill (Park Lane) Ltd* [1949] AC 530 (HL).

[120] *The Times*, 4 May 1791.

[121] *The Times*, 20 June 1791.

[122] Kates, *Monsieur D'Eon is a Woman* (n 11 above) 275, which reproduces a poster announcing a fencing match featuring d'Eon.

[123] Kates, *Monsieur D'Eon is a Woman* (n 11 above) xxiii.

[124] D'Eon, *The Maiden of Tonnerre* (n 11 above) 3.

[125] I Lustig and F Pottle (eds), J Boswell, *The English Experiment 1785–1789* (London, Heinemann, 1986) 48.

man.[126] Even then there was no end of the controversy. A letter to *The Times* four months later alleged that they 'were deceived, and certified in error'.[127] D'Eon was buried in St Pancras Old Church. In a sad coda to the story his grave was destroyed when some of the churchyard was lost to an expansion of the nearby Midland Railway.[128] As for *Da Costa v Jones*, the decision is a monument to the difficulties that judges encounter when the law of contract runs up against public policy.

---

[126] *The Times*, 25 May 1810.

[127] *The Times*, 5 Sept 1810.

[128] An account of the work around St Pancras in 1865, records that the main excavation came to be supervised by the novelist, then architect, Thomas Hardy, whose job it was to prevent a repeat of the year before, when in a smaller excavation, bones had been carried off by navvies and sold to the bone-mills. See: T Coleman, *The Railway Navvies* (Harmondsworth, Penguin, 1968) 167–8. I am grateful to my father Mr CM Swain for drawing this passage to my attention.

# 5

# Hochster v De La Tour (1853)

## PAUL MITCHELL

### A. INTRODUCTION

*H*OCHSTER v DE LA TOUR[1] is one of the most important, and controversial, cases in 19th century contract law. Sir Guenter Treitel would even place it in the top three.[2] The legal proposition it established was both simple and radical: where one of the parties to a contract told the other party that he was not going to perform it, the other party could be excused from performance and sue immediately for breach of contract, in spite of the fact that no performance was yet due. By recognising this doctrine of 'anticipatory breach', the Court of Queen's Bench developed the common law in a way that, despite its intuitive attraction, has proved difficult to explain theoretically.[3] Most obviously, it is difficult to see how a party could be in breach of contract when the terms of the contract did not yet require anything of him.

The first part of this essay explores the common law position immediately before *Hochster*, revealing that the ideas underpinning the decision had been previously articulated, although they had not quite been drawn together in the way that the Queen's Bench was to do. The second part focuses on the case itself, explaining what was most likely to have influenced the court to decide as it did. The final part of the essay examines the influence and legacy of the decision.

---

[1] *Hochster v De La Tour* (1853) 2 E & B 678, 118 ER 922 (QB).

[2] GH Treitel, *Landmarks of Twentieth Century Contract Law* (Oxford, Oxford University Press, 2002) 2.

[3] See, eg J Dawson, 'Metaphors and Anticipatory Breach of Contract' (1981) 40 *Cambridge Law Journal* 83; Q Liu, 'Claiming damages upon an anticipatory breach: why should an acceptance be necessary?' (2005) 25 *Legal Studies* 559; M Mustill, 'Anticipatory Breach of Contract: The Common Law at Work' in *Butterworths Lectures 1989–90* (London, Butterworths, 1990) 1; JC Smith, 'Anticipatory Breach of Contract' in E Lomnicka and C Morse (eds), *Contemporary Issues in Commercial Law* (London, Sweet & Maxwell, 1997) 175. For a comparative perspective see D Carey Miller, 'Judicia Bonae Fidei: A New Development in Contract?' (1980) 97 *South African Law Journal* 531; J Gulotta, 'Anticipatory Breach—A Comparative Analysis' (1975–76) 50 *Tulane Law Review* 927.

## B. THE COMMON LAW IN 1853

*Hochster*'s case was not the first in which the courts had had to consider the legal consequences of parties jeopardising the future successful performance of a contract. Indeed, since at least the 17th century, the courts had been developing rules and principles to identify when an innocent party could bring an action despite the contract remaining unperformed on his part. As John William Smith was to write, in the year before *Hochster* was decided,

> Few questions are of so frequent occurrence, or of so much practical importance, and at the same time so difficult to solve.[4]

The following two sections focus on situations where the defendant was liable despite performance apparently not yet being due.

### 1. The Defendant Disables Himself From Performance

One situation in which questions arose about an action for breach before performance was due was where the parties had become engaged to be married. Each was seen as making an enforceable contractual promise,[5] the breach of which gave rise to damages.[6] Clearly there was a breach if, on the agreed wedding day, one of the parties refused to go through with it. But what if, before the agreed wedding day, the defendant married someone else? In *Harrison v Cage*[7] the Court of King's Bench held that there was an immediate breach, the defendant having disabled herself from performance by the 'pre-contract'.[8]

This idea of disabling oneself by marrying another person was expanded and developed in two important 19th century cases—*Short v Stone*[9] and *Caines v Smith*.[10] The issue in both cases was that the defendants had promised to marry the respective claimants within a reasonable time of a request by the claimant. In both cases the defendants had married other people; and their former fiancé(e)s had, understandably, not requested that they carry out their prior engagement. This absence of a request gave rise to two distinct legal arguments. First, it was said that the claimant's request was a condition precedent to the defendant's liability. Secondly, it was argued that, because no request had yet been made, it could not be assumed that the contract would be broken when it was made: by that time, for instance, the defendant's current spouse might have died, leaving the defendant free to marry again.

---

[4] JW Smith, *A Selection of Leading Cases on Various Branches of the Law*, 2nd edn (London, A Maxwell, 1852) vol 2, 8.

[5] This is no longer the case: see the Law Reform (Miscellaneous Provisions) Act 1970 s 1.

[6] *Holcroft v Dickenson* (1672) Carter 233, 124 ER 933 (CP) (breach by fiancé); *Harrison v Cage* (1698) 1 Lord Raym 386, 91 ER 1156 (KB) (breach by fiancée).

[7] *Harrison v Cage* (1698) 1 Lord Raym 386, 91 ER 1156 (KB).

[8] *Ibid* 387, 1156.

[9] *Short v Stone* (1846) 8 QB 358, 115 ER 911.

[10] *Caines v Smith* (1847) 15 M & W 189, 153 ER 816 (Ex).

Both arguments failed. In *Short v Stone* the answer to both of them was held to lie in focusing on the feelings and intentions of the parties at the time of entering into the contract.[11] That intention was 'to marry in the state in which the parties respectively are at that time'.[12] It was, therefore, irrelevant that the defendant might become available again: by marrying someone else, the defendant had breached a promise to stay single. And, by committing that breach, the defendant also

> must be taken to dispense with the contract so far that the other may have an action against him without a request to marry.[13]

The real force of the analysis on this second point lay not so much in its giving effect to the intentions of the parties—we may doubt that the parties had given any thought to it—but rather in the way that it excused the claimant from going through with a pointless (and, in the circumstances, tasteless) performance. Thus, as Coleridge J commented,[14]

> The promise to marry within a reasonable time after request must mean after request within a time when it might reasonably be made. If the defendant disables himself from fulfilling such a request, then, in the first place, he dispenses with the request, because it has become impossible to make the request effectually, and, secondly, he has broken his own contract, because he is no longer able to fulfil that.

A concern to avoid wasteful, pointless performance was also to be found in other cases, including, later, *Hochster v De La Tour*.

Whilst the reasoning in *Caines v Smith*[15] echoed *Short v Stone* on the issue of dispensing with the request, the analysis of the breach point was different. Alderson B said:

> Why should we presume that the wife will die before the lapse of a reasonable time, or in the lifetime of her husband? We ought rather to presume the continuance of the present state of things; and while that continues, it is clear that the defendant is disabled from performing his contract.[16]

Although the reasoning of Alderson B led, on the facts, to the same conclusion as the Court of Queen's Bench in *Short v Stone*, the difference was potentially highly significant. It would seem that if the defendant's spouse had died, the court could not 'presume the continuance of the present state of things'. If that presumption could not be made it would be difficult, on the analysis of Alderson B, to identify a breach. For the Court of Queen's Bench, by contrast, the breach consisted not in remaining married to someone else, but in having changed status after the contract was made.

---

[11] *Short* (n 9 above) 8 QB 358, 369; 115 ER 911, 915.
[12] *Short* (n 9 above) 8 QB 358, 369; 115 ER 911, 915.
[13] *Short* (n 9 above) 8 QB 358, 369; 115 ER 911, 915
[14] *Short* (n 9 above) 8 QB 358, 370; 115 ER 911, 915.
[15] *Caines v Smith* (1847) 15 M & W 189, 153 ER 816 (Ex).
[16] *Ibid* 15 M & W 189, 190; 153 ER 816, 817 (Ex).

Behind this difference in analytical approach lay a deeper, as yet unarticulated question: Was the defendant in these cases to be seen as breaching a present obligation (such as the obligation to remain single), or as breaching in advance an obligation not yet strictly due? The obvious difficulty with the latter approach was that it brought forward the time of performance, to a point in time earlier than that to which the defendant had agreed. As one later commentator pointed out, this was 'to enlarge the scope' of the defendant's obligation.[17] So the better option seemed to be to analyse the position in terms of breaching a present obligation. But this option was not free from difficulty. In *Short v Stone* the court had drawn on the parties' presumed intentions in order to find a present, ongoing obligation to remain single. It was, in effect, an implied term. But in other factual situations it might be problematic to imply such a term; and even if it could be implied, there might be difficulties over its precise content.

These uncertainties about the scope and basis of the doctrine, however, tended to remain beneath the surface, and the rule was applied outside the marriage context. For instance, in *Bowdell v Parsons*[18] Lord Ellenborough CJ held that a breach of contract was sufficiently alleged against a seller of hay who, it was stated, had delivered the hay to other buyers: 'by the defendant's selling and disposing of the rest of the hay to other persons, he disqualified himself from delivering it to the plaintiff'.[19] Similarly, in *Amory v Brodrick*[20] it was held that the assignor of a bond breached his contract with the assignee to avow, ratify and confirm any actions brought by the assignee, when he released the debtor under the bond from his obligations. The Court of King's Bench held that, by executing the release, he had 'wholly disabled himself from avowing, &c'.[21]

One particularly emphatic illustration was provided by *Ford v Tiley*,[22] in which the defendant had promised to grant a lease of a public house to the claimant 'with all possible speed after he should become possessed of or in possession of'[23] it. At the time of the agreement the premises were tenanted under a lease which expired at midsummer 1827; but in June 1825 the defendant granted a further lease to the same tenants for 23 years. The claimant sued immediately, only to be met with the objection that the action was premature. Bayley J made it clear that this objection was incorrect[24]:

---

[17] S Williston, *The Law of Contracts* (New York, Baker, Voorhis & Co, 1921) vol 3, §1319 (at 2371).

[18] *Bowdell v Parsons* (1808) 10 East 359, 103 ER 811 (KB).

[19] *Ibid* 10 East 359, 361; 103 ER 811, 812 (KB).

[20] *Amory v Brodrick* (1822) 5 B & Ald 712, 106 ER 1351 (KB).

[21] *Ibid* 5 B & Ald 712, 716; 106 ER 1351, 1353 (Holroyd J) (KB).

[22] *Ford v Tiley* (1827) 6 B & C 325, 108 ER 472; (1827) 5 LJ (OS) KB 169 (reporting the retrial) (KB).

[23] *Ibid*.

[24] *Ford v Tiley* (n 22 above) 6 B & C 325, 327 (KB). A different view of *Ford v Tiley* is given in Mustill, 'Anticipatory Breach of Contract: The Common Law at Work', *Butterworths Lectures 1989–90* (London, Butterworths, 1990) 1, 20–22. It is submitted, however, that this view is unconvincing. In particular, it is difficult to understand the criticism of Bayley J's judgment as 'not even mentioning' the timing point (at 21), when Bayley J did expressly deal with it in the passage quoted below.

by the lease of June 1825, the defendant has given up his right to have the possession, and has put it out of his power, so long as the lease of June 1825 subsists, to grant the lease he stipulated to grant. It is very true, the defendant may obtain surrender of that lease before midsummer 1827, and then he will be in a condition to grant the lease he stipulated to grant; but the obtaining such a surrender is not to be expected, and the authorities are, that where a party has disabled himself from making an estate he has stipulated to make at a future day, by making an inconsistent conveyance of that estate, he is considered as guilty of a breach of his stipulation, and is liable to be sued before such day arrives.

Although the theoretical problems hinted at in the marriage cases caused little difficulty in practice, they did not completely go away. Thus, in *Lovelock v Franklyn*,[25] where the agreement was for the transfer of the defendant's interest in a house if the claimant paid him 140*l* within seven years, it was held that the defendant's transferring his entire interest to a third party was an immediate breach. That was clearly correct, since the defendant had promised to perform at any point in the seven-year period, and he had now incapacitated himself from doing so. But Lord Denman CJ was at pains to distinguish the case from a situation where the defendant's obligation was to sell or lease a property on a fixed date in the future. There, he suggested, there would be no breach if the defendant disposed of the property before the date fixed for performance, because 'the party had the means of rehabilitating himself before the time of performance arrived'.[26] These dicta could not be reconciled with the ratio of *Ford v Tiley*.[27] Nor did they sit easily alongside Denman CJ's analysis in *Short v Stone*,[28] delivered three days earlier. Perhaps the point was that, whilst an obligation to remain single could be implied on the facts of *Short*, no obligation to remain owner could be implied in an agreement to transfer property at a future date. But that explanation does not get us very far: why is no implication to be made in the latter case? Possibly it is because property—particularly land—might be legitimately alienated by way of mortgage, or other security, and the parties must be presumed to have accepted that possibility. At any rate, it seems unrealistic to assume that a purchaser promising a fixed price for property will be indifferent to its being passed around before delivery; apart from anything else, such intervening ownership might affect its value. Whatever the true reason that Lord Denman had in mind, these cases illustrated that, although its precise basis could have been clearer, the self-disablement principle provided a powerful tool for releasing innocent parties from pointless performance and allowing them to sue immediately, both within and beyond the marriage context.

---

[25] *Lovelock v Franklyn* (1846) 8 QB 371, 115 ER 916.
[26] *Ibid* 8 QB 371, 378; 115 ER 916, 918–19.
[27] *Ford v Tiley* (n 22 above).
[28] *Short v Stone* (n 9 above).

## 2. The Defendant Prevents the Claimant from Performing

A second situation where the courts allowed an action before the claimant appeared to be strictly entitled to it, was where the defendant had prevented the claimant from performing. In other words, if the defendant had stopped the claimant from fulfilling the condition precedent to the defendant's liability, the courts did not insist on that condition being satisfied.

The early cases took a strict approach to prevention. For instance, in *Blandford v Andrews*[29] the claimant sought to enforce an agreement under which the defendant had undertaken to procure a marriage between the claimant and Bridget Palmer before the Feast of St Bartholomew. The defendant claimed that he was excused from performance by reason of the claimant's actions in going to Bridget and telling her that she was a whore, and that if she married him he would tie her to a post. The Court of Queen's Bench, however, held that the claimant had not prevented performance, since

> these words, spoken before the day, at one time only, are not such an impediment but that the marriage might have taken effect.[30]

A similarly strict idea of prevention could be seen in *Fraunces's Case*,[31] which concerned the construction of a will under which John Fraunces was to lose his estate if he 'prevented' the executors from removing certain movables. The court unanimously held that denial by words was not enough,

> but there ought to be some act done; as after request made by the executor to shut the door against them, or lay his hands upon them.[32]

Coke CJ referred to a case concerning the master of St Catharine's, who had let three houses on condition that the leases were forfeited if the lessee harboured a lewd woman there for more than six months. In an action by the master for forfeiture, the tenant had replied that the master commanded the woman to stay there. This reply was held bad in law, since the

> master had no colour to put the lewd woman into possession; for which cause the lessee might well put her out.[33]

A further plea, that the master had turned the lessee out and installed the woman by force was, however, held to be good in law.

Clearly, merely being unco-operative was not to be confused with preventing fulfilment of a condition. But even this strict doctrine had some potential application to less unusual contractual circumstances. For instance, where a

---

[29] *Blandford v Andrews* (1599) Cro Eliz 694, 78 ER 930 (QB).
[30] *Ibid.*
[31] *Fraunces's Case* (1609) 8 Co Rep 89b, 77 ER 609 (CP).
[32] *Ibid* 8 Co Rep 89b, 91a; 77 ER 609, 613 (CP).
[33] *Fraunces's Case* (n 31 above) 8 Co Rep 89b, 92a; 77 ER 609, 614 (CP).

contractual payment was to be made on receipt of property, and the defendant refused to accept the property, it was held that 'a tender and refusal would amount to performance'.[34] But even here, the courts proceeded cautiously, subjecting the pleading of the tender to highly critical scrutiny.[35]

Ultimately it was to take a characteristically untechnical analysis from Lord Mansfield CJ to give the doctrine real commercial effectiveness. In *Jones v Barkley*[36] there was an agreement for the defendant to pay £611 to the claimants if the claimants would assign their interest in certain stock to a third party and also execute a release of all claims that they might have against that third party. The claimants prepared a draft of the release for the defendant's approval, but he refused to read it, saying that he did not intend to pay. The claimants then brought what the report describes as 'a special action on the case, for non-performance of an agreement',[37] to which the defendant pleaded that the claimants had never assigned the interest or executed the release. The claimants demurred and their demurrer was upheld by the Court of King's Bench.

As can be seen from the facts described above, *Jones v Barkley* did not fit easily into the existing doctrine of prevention. There was clearly no question of physical force. Moreover, both the assignment and the release could have been executed by the claimants had they so wished, since there was nothing to suggest that the third party beneficiary of the arrangement would have refused to accept them. Counsel for the claimants met this difficulty by arguing that the claimants' actions were 'equivalent to . . . performance of their part of the agreement'.[38] He went on to elaborate, saying that[39]

> [w]herever a man, by doing a previous act, would acquire a right to any debt or duty, by a tender to do the previous act, if the other party refuses to permit him to do it, he acquires the right as completely as if it had been actually done; and, if the tender is defective, owing to the conduct of the other party, such incomplete tender will be sufficient; because it is a general principle, that he who prevents a thing from being done, shall not avail himself of the non-performance, which he has occasioned.

No authority was cited in support of this general principle.

Lord Mansfield CJ, however, was not to be deterred by a lack of authority. 'If ever there was a clear case', he said, 'I think the present is'.[40] 'Take it on the reason of the thing' he continued:

> The party must shew he was ready; but, if the other stops him on the ground of an intention not to perform his part, it is not necessary for the first to go farther, and do a nugatory act. Here, the draft was shown to the defendant for his approbation of the

---

[34] *Blackwell v Nash* (1721) 1 Str 535, 93 ER 684 (KB).
[35] *Lancashire v Killingworth* (1701) 1 Lord Raym 686, 91 ER 1357(KB).
[36] *Jones v Barkley* (1781) 2 Dougl 684, 99 ER 434 (KB).
[37] Ibid.
[38] *Jones v Barkley* (n 36 above) 2 Dougl 684, 685–6; 99 ER 434 (KB).
[39] *Jones v Barkley* (n 36 above) 2 Dougl 684, 686; 99 ER 434, 435 (KB).
[40] *Jones v Barkley* (n 36 above) 2 Dougl 684, 694; 99 ER 434, 439 (KB).

form, but he would not read it, and, upon a different ground, namely, that he means not to pay the money, discharges the plaintiffs from executing it.[41]

Willes and Ashhurst JJ concurred, as did Buller J, who added that *Blandford v Andrews* was distinguishable, since there

> the defendant had agreed to use his endeavours, and, notwithstanding what had been done by the plaintiff, he might have prevailed on the woman, before the time elapsed, to marry him.[42]

The most obvious innovation in *Jones v Barkley* was the looser approach to prevention. Although the defendant's co-operation was unnecessary for the fulfilment of the condition, the defendant was to be regarded as having stopped the claimant 'on the ground of an intention not to perform on his part'. This was not really prevention; rather, it was a good reason for the claimant to be excused from further performance. As Lord Mansfield had suggested, such a rule was sensible, because otherwise the claimant would be forced to persevere with a performance that he knew was not wanted. But as well as this consideration of economic efficiency, there was the mysterious 'general principle' referred to by counsel. This was almost certainly a borrowing from Roman law, in particular Justinian's *Digest* 50.17.1.161, which stated that

> [i]n iure civile receptum est, quotiens per eum, cuius interest condicionem non impleri, fiat quo minus impleatur, perinde haberi, ac si impleta condicio fuisset. quod ad libertatem et legata et ad heredum institutiones perducitur. quibus exemplis stipulationes committuntur, cum per promissorem factum esset, quo minus stipulator condicioni pareret.[43]

Lord Mansfield, whose expertise in Roman law was well known, may well have recognised the allusion. At any rate, the combination of civilian-inspired principle and commercial pragmatism had prompted an important advance in the common law.

The looser approach to prevention which *Jones v Barkley* authorised was still good law at the time of the decision in *Hochster v De La Tour*. For instance, it was relied upon in *Laird v Pim*,[44] where purchasers of land had gone into possession before conveyance, but then refused to complete. It was held that there was no need for the vendors to prove title and execute a conveyance before bringing their action for damages. Similarly, in *Cort v The Ambergate*,

---

[41] *Jones v Barkley* (n 36 above) 2 Dougl 684, 694; 99 ER 434, 440 (KB).

[42] *Jones v Barkley* (n 36 above) 2 Dougl 684, 694–5; 99 ER 434, 440 (KB).

[43] 'It is established in the civil law that whenever anyone in whose interest it is for a condition to be fulfilled arranged for it not to be fulfilled, the position is regarded as being the same as if the condition had been fulfilled. This is applied to liberty and legacies and institutions of heirs. And stipulations are also entered into on this basis when the promisor prevented the stipulator from obeying the condition'. A Watson (ed), *The Digest of Justinian* (Philadelphia, PA, University of Pennsylvania Press, 1985) II, 50.17.1.161.

[44] *Laird v Pim* (1841) 7 M & W 474, 151 ER 852 (Ex).

*Nottingham and Boston and Eastern Junction Railway Company*[45] the contract was for the supply of 3900 tons of cast-iron railway chairs, but after delivery of about half of that quantity the defendant indicated that it would not be prepared to take any more. The defendant argued that the claimants had failed to perform the condition of manufacturing and offering the remaining 2000 tons of chairs, and that the defendant had done nothing to prevent them from fulfilling that condition. The court was quick to point out that prevention did not require physical restraint, making the following interventions in argument[46]:

> Coleridge J. Suppose a man said, 'If you come for such a purpose, I will blow your brains out'. That would be no physical prevention.

> Lord Campbell C.J. Such a threat might be used ten days before the act was to be done.

The theme was continued in the court's judgment:

> It is contended that 'prevent' here must mean an obstruction by physical force; and, in answer to a question from the Court, we were told it would not be a preventing of the delivery of goods if the purchaser were to write, in a letter to the person who ought to supply them, 'Should you come to my house to deliver them, I will blow your brains out'. But may I not reasonably say that I was prevented from completing a contract by being desired not to complete it?[47]

However, although the principle laid down in *Jones v Barkley* was firmly established by the 1850s, it was not entirely unproblematic. One difficulty concerned its scope: How much missing performance would the principle presume in the claimant's favour? In *Smith v Wilson*[48] the contract was for the shipment of goods from London to Montevideo and a return voyage with another cargo. The ship began its voyage, but was seized and returned to London; once it had been restored to its owner (the claimant) he approached the freighter (the defendant) for instructions, but the defendant refused and renounced the charterparty. The claimant sued for the freight due on both voyages, relying on *Jones v Barkley* to show that he had been prevented from performance of a condition. Lord Ellenborough CJ, however, held that *Jones* did not apply[49]:

> [T]he difference between the two cases is this; in the one, by doing an act in the power of the party to have done, he would have acquired a full and instant right to the duty demanded; in the other, by doing the act tendered to the full extent to which the party tendering was able to perform it, he would still have only taken certain steps of remote and uncertain effect towards the attainment of the object and completion of the event necessary to be obtained and completed, in order to vest a right to the duty demanded in the party demanding it.

---

[45] *Cort v The Ambergate, Nottingham and Boston and Eastern Junction Railway Company* (1851) 17 QB 127, 117 ER 1229.
[46] *Ibid* 17 QB 127, 139; 117 ER 1229, 1234.
[47] *Cort v The Ambergate* (n 45 above) 17 QB 127, 145; 117 ER 1229, 1236.
[48] *Smith v Wilson* (1807) 8 East 437, 103 ER 410 (KB).
[49] *Ibid* 8 East 437, 444; 103 ER 410, 413–14 (KB).

This was not a completely convincing analysis. Assuming that the contract was not discharged by the delay,[50] the freighter was surely in breach of contract in refusing to give the necessary instructions about delivery. In these circumstances it would be wasteful to require further performance before bringing an action, just as it would have been in *Jones v Barkley*. The problem with *Smith v Wilson* was, it is submitted, a different one. It related not to the scope of the decision in *Jones v Barkley*, but to its effect.

What the claim in *Smith v Wilson* highlighted was a potential ambiguity in *Jones*. *Jones* had made it clear that where a defendant renounced his contract, the claimant was not required to fulfil unperformed conditions before suing. The claimant was excused, or, to put it as counsel had done in that case, 'the [claimant] acquires the right as completely as if it had been actually done'.[51] The potential ambiguity about *Jones* was whether it permitted the claimant merely to sue for damages, or whether it went further, and allowed the claimant to sue on the fiction that he had actually performed. If the latter were the correct interpretation, the claimant would be able to recover the contract price despite not having incurred the expenses of performance. This, essentially, is what the claimant in *Smith v Wilson* was trying to do.

There are several reasons why the Court of King's Bench in *Jones* was unlikely to be endorsing the idea that the claimant would sue on the fictional basis that he had performed the condition. Perhaps the strongest reason is that the claimant was not claiming the contract price: the claim was for damages.[52] Furthermore, the general principle about an innocent party acquiring a right 'as completely as if it had actually been done' was only articulated by counsel. The fact that none of the judges adopted it may indicate that they wished to be more cautious. Finally, one powerful theme in the judgments concerned the avoidance of waste; it is hardly likely that the judges intended their decision to give rise to the equally wasteful result that a defendant must pay for a performance that he has never received.

There was, therefore, no general principle that a claimant who was prevented from performing a condition precedent had all the rights available to a claimant who had fulfilled such conditions. There was, however, some support for a special rule, applicable mainly to employment, and known as the doctrine of constructive service. Under this doctrine, where an employee was wrongfully dismissed part way through the period by reference to which his salary was paid, and he offered to work the remainder of the period, he was to be treated, as a matter of law, as if he had served the whole period. Thus, in *Gandell v Pontigny*[53] a clerk who was paid quarterly was dismissed part way through a quarter; he offered to continue, but his employer refused. The clerk brought an

---

[50] Eg *Jackson v Union Marine Insurance Co* (1874) LR 10 CP 125.

[51] *Jones v Barkley* (n 36 above) 2 Dougl 684, 686; 99 ER 434, 435 (KB).

[52] This may have been lost sight of at the retrial: F Dawson, 'Metaphors and Anticipatory Breach of Contract' (1981) 40 *Cambridge Law Journal* 83, 91–5.

[53] *Gandell v Pontigny* (1816) 4 Camp 375, 171 ER 119 (NP).

action in *indebitatus assumpsit*, to which it was objected that no action for work and labour could lie for work and labour that had not been done. Lord Ellenborough, however, disagreed:

> If the plaintiff was discharged without a sufficient cause, I think this action is maintainable. Having served a part of the quarter and being willing to serve the residue, in contemplation of law he may be considered to have served the whole.

Although the doctrine was not confined to employment cases,[54] its precise scope was not clear, nor were its origins. Smith, arguing for its limitation to employment, attributed it to (unspecified) 'decisions on the law of settlement'.[55] Addison, on the other hand, pointed to the Roman law support for a wider doctrine in the general wording of Justinian's *Digest* (D.50.17.1.161),[56] which had probably been influential in *Jones v Barkley*.

This uncertainty about the doctrine's scope and basis may well have contributed to judicial doubts about it as the 19th century wore on. In *Archard v Hornor*[57] Lord Tenterden CJ held that a claimant bringing an *indebitatus assumpsit* claim could recover only for the time actually served. *Gandell v Pontigny* was not referred to and, indeed, would have been distinguishable since there was no offer to continue work in *Archard*. Later cases, however, regarded Lord Tenterden's one sentence analysis as unavoidably conflicting with *Gandell v Pontigny*, and expressed a strong preference for Lord Tenterden's view. They did not, however, go quite so far as to abolish the doctrine of constructive service. In *Smith v Hayward*,[58] for example, it was said to be unnecessary to decide the point because the action had been brought before the end of the period during which the employee was claiming to have constructively served. In *Fewings v Tisdal*,[59] similarly, the claimant formulated his claim so as to avoid the question.

As a result of this judicial caution, constructive service could not be deleted from the books. For instance, in the first edition of his *Leading Cases* Smith included a tentative account of the doctrine in his note on *Cutter v Powell*.[60] The hesitancy was judicially noted, and approved,[61] but the doctrine lingered on. Smith continued to deal with it in his second edition,[62] published in the year before *Hochster v De La Tour*.

The continuation of the doctrine of constructive service was, it is submitted, unfortunate. Viewed purely on its own terms it was unconvincing: here was a

---

[54] Eg *Collins v Price* (1828) 5 Bing 132, 130 ER 1011 (CP) (school fees).

[55] Smith, *A Selection of Leading Cases on Various Branches of the Law* (n 4 above) vol 2, 20.

[56] See n 43 above. Cave (ed), *Addison on the Law of Contracts*, 6th edn (London, Stevens and Sons, 1869) 372.

[57] *Archard v Hornor* (1828) 3 C & P 349, 172 ER 451 (NP).

[58] *Smith v Hayward* (1837) 7 Ad & E 544, 112 ER 575 (QB).

[59] *Fewings v Tisdal* (1847) 1 Ex 295, 154 ER 125.

[60] JW Smith, *A Selection of Leading Cases on Various Branches of the Law* (London, A Maxwell, 1837).

[61] *Goodman v Pocock* (1850) 15 QB 576, 582; 117 ER 577, 579 (Patteson J).

[62] Smith, *A Selection of Leading Cases on Various Branches of the Law* (n 4 above) vol 2, 20–21.

claimant recovering on a count for work and labour that he had not done. Such a fictitious basis of recovery might have been justifiable if it was the only way to do justice between the parties, but the doctrine had the potential to cause injustice. As the courts had acknowledged, to avail himself of the doctrine, the employee had to remain ready to resume work until the end of the stipulated period.[63] In other words, he had to remain idle; and if he took other work he lost his claim. An employee who could easily obtain alternative employment had no legal obligation, and no incentive, to do so: the fact that he could have avoided losing wages was legally irrelevant.

The position where the employee sued for damages for breach of contract was very different. There subsequent offers of employment by either a third party or the defendant himself were relevant to mitigation of damage: if the claimant had increased his loss through 'his own misconduct and folly',[64] that increase was not recoverable. Furthermore, evidence of actual offers was not necessary. As Erle J explained in *Beckham v Drake*,[65]

> [t]he measure of damages . . . is obtained by considering what is the usual rate of wages for the employment here contracted for, and what time would be lost before a similar employment could be obtained. The law considers that employment in any ordinary branch of industry can be obtained by a person competent for the place, and that the usual rate of wages for such employment can be proved, and that when a promise for continuing employment is broken by the master, it is the duty of the servant to use diligence to find another employment.

A year later, in *Goodman v Pocock*,[66] the same judge drew on the contrast between the doctrine of constructive service and the rules on mitigation of damages in contract to explain his dissatisfaction with the former[67]:

> I think the true measure of damages is the loss sustained at the time of dismissal. The servant, after dismissal, may and ought to make the best of his time; and he may have an opportunity of turning it to advantage.

In short, the contractual rules were seen as being both an accurate method of assessing compensation ('the true measure') and as appropriately reflecting how the innocent party should respond to the breach ('may and ought to make the best of his time'). The constructive service doctrine, he felt, did neither.

## 3. The Overall Position

The law relating to contractual liabilities arising before performance was apparently due was, therefore, well developed by the time that *Hochster v De La Tour*

---

[63] *Smith v Hayward* (n 58 above).
[64] *Speck v Phillips* (1839) 5 M & W 279, 283; 151 ER 119, 120 (Alderson B) (Ex).
[65] *Beckham v Drake* (1849) 2 HLC 579, 606–7; 9 ER 1213, 1223.
[66] *Goodman* (n 61 above).
[67] *Goodman* (n 61 above) 15 QB 576, 583–4; 117 ER 577, 580 (QB).

came to be decided. But that is not to say that the decision in *Hochster* was inevitable. Whilst it was recognised that liability could arise in particular situations, none of those situations obviously fitted the factual matrix in *Hochster*. As we shall see, the defendant merely told the claimant that his contractually promised services would not be required. The defendant had not disabled himself from performance, nor had he obviously prevented the claimant from fulfilling a condition precedent to the defendant's liability. Certainly he had indicated that he would not perform the contract, but in the prevention cases the time for performance had always elapsed before the action was brought. If *Hochster* was to be fitted into the prevention category, some concept of anticipatory prevention would have to be recognised. On the other hand, allowing a claimant to terminate as soon as the defendant indicated that he would not perform would give considerable scope for the principle of mitigation: the claimant could—and, as a matter of law would be presumed to—take all reasonable steps to find employment elsewhere. So far as the interplay of broad principles was concerned, the outcome in *Hochster* was finely balanced.

There was also a question about authority. In *Phillpotts v Evans*,[68] which concerned a sale of wheat, the buyer had told the seller that he no longer wanted the goods and would not accept them if tendered. The wheat was, at that point, already on its way to the buyer and, when it arrived, the buyer did as he had intimated, and rejected it. The sole question was whether damages should be assessed by reference to the market price at the date of the defendant's notice, or the market price at the date of the seller's tender of the goods. The Court of Exchequer held that the correct date was the date of tender, with Parke B offering a trenchant analysis of why the date of notice was irrelevant:

> If [counsel for the defendant] could have established that the plaintiffs, after the notice given to them, could have maintained the action without waiting for the time when the wheat was to be delivered, then perhaps the proper measure of damages would be according to the price at the time of the notice. But I think no action would then have lain for the breach of contract, but that the plaintiffs were bound to wait until the time arrived for delivery of the wheat, to see whether the defendant would then receive it. The defendant might then have chosen to take it, and would have been guilty of no breach of contract; for all that he stipulates for is, that he will be ready and willing to receive the goods, and pay for them, at the time when by the contract he ought to do so. His contract was not broken by his previous declaration that he would not accept them; it was a mere nullity, and it was perfectly in his power to accept them nevertheless; and, vice versa, the plaintiffs could not sue him before.[69]

Parke B reasserted this view in *Ripley v M'Clure*,[70] a case in which the defendant had expressed the intention not to receive a cargo as he was contractually bound to do.

---

[68] *Phillpotts v Evans* (1839) 5 M & W 475, 151 ER 200 (Ex).
[69] *Ibid* 5 M & W 475, 477; 151 ER 200202 (Ex).
[70] *Ripley v M'Clure* (1849) 4 Ex 345, 154 ER 1245; (1850) 5 Ex 140, 155 ER 60.

[I]f the jury had been told that a refusal before the arrival of the cargo was a breach [said Parke B], that would have been incorrect. We think that point rightly decided in *Phillpotts v Evans*[71].

The task facing counsel for the claimant in *Hochster v De La Tour* was, therefore, somewhat daunting. Not only was there the obvious obstacle of contrary authority to be overcome; there was also the problem that the facts did not quite fit into any of the recognised categories for liability. A court finding for the claimant would have to be persuaded to be both independent-minded and creative.

## C. *HOCHSTER v DE LA TOUR*

### 1. The Facts

Albert Hochster and Edgar de la Tour first met in April 1852, in Egypt.[72] Hochster was acting as courier for a man named Maskill; de la Tour was a 'private gentleman' on his travels. De la Tour made arrangements with Maskill to join his party and, for the rest of the trip, Hochster acted as de la Tour's valet. De la Tour was evidently in financial difficulties at this time, because he borrowed various sums of money from Hochster, which were repaid on the parties' return to England.

In May 1852 de la Tour wrote to Hochster, stating that he intended to make another journey, this time to Switzerland, and wished Hochster to act as his courier. He called on Hochster and the parties agreed terms of 10*l* per month, commencing on 1 June 1852. Although the defendant later sought to deny that any contract had been made, arguing that 'what the plaintiff had construed into a contract was merely what had occurred in conversation',[73] the jury held that there was a binding contract at this point. At the same meeting de la Tour asked Hochster to obtain a passport for him. To this end the parties went together to Coutts, the bankers, to obtain the necessary letter, and Hochster then went on to the Foreign Office, where he paid for the passport with his own money.

'Some time after', according to Hochster's version of events,

the defendant wrote again to the plaintiff, stating that his friends had told him that it would be very foolish to spend 300*l* in three months, and that the plaintiff's charge of 10*l* per month was preposterous, and that he should not require his services[74].

---

[71] *Ibid* 4 Ex 345, 359; 154 ER 1245, 1251.
[72] *Hockster v De Latour*, *The Times* (25 April 1853) 7 (report of trial before Erle J). The detailed facts given here are taken from the report's summary of the claimant's evidence.
[73] *Ibid*.
[74] *Hockster v De Latour* (n 72 above).

The defendant, Hochster added, had refused to pay any compensation. Other accounts give a less abrupt version of de la Tour's final letter. The summary in *The Times* when the case was being argued in the Queen's Bench states that[75]

> After communicating with his friends the defendant thought it prudent to break his contract, and wrote a letter to the plaintiff, in which he said, his friends were amazed that he, with an income of only 500*l* a year, should have entered upon an enterprise which would entail an expense of 300*l* in three months, and concluded by telling the plaintiff that he should not require his services, but, that he would endeavour to recommend him to another party.

The *Weekly Reporter*'s version also indicates that, in his letter, de la Tour said that

> he wished to know what sum there was due to the plaintiff in obtaining a passport for himself, which the plaintiff had done at the defendant's request[76].

We may never know exactly what the letter said. The claimant may have been over-sensitive to it, reading de la Tour's friends' criticisms as directed at him, when they were in effect being directed at de la Tour himself. Certainly de la Tour seems to have been financially inept—the money problems he experienced in Egypt were proof of that, let alone his failure to budget for his trip to Switzerland—and it may be unfair to regard him as arrogant. Perhaps what really provoked Hochster's sense of being badly treated was that he was dealt with as if he were a mere servant or tradesman, whose services could be dispensed with at will. He may have felt that his professional status as a courier called for different treatment.[77]

At any rate, one thing was clear: the engagement was off. Hochster brought his action for breach of contract on 22 May, and was not long out of work. He secured an appointment to accompany Lord Ashburton on a tour of the Continent commencing on 4 July 1852 at the same basic rate of 10*l* per month.

## 2. Counsel's Arguments

The trial of *Hochster v De La Tour* took place before Erle J and a jury on 22 April 1853. As soon as the claimant had finished giving evidence, counsel for the defendant took the point that there was no cause of action since 'one side alone could not make a breach of contract before the time arrived for its fulfilment'.[78] What was required, he argued, was a continuing refusal to perform

---

[75] *Hochster v De Latour, The Times* (11 June 1853) 7 (QB).
[76] *Hochster v De Latour* (1853) 1 WR 469 (QB).
[77] Such distinguished men as Adam Smith, Thomas Hobbes and John Locke had acted as guides for wealthy aristocrats making grand tours. Hibbert, *The Grand Tour* (London, Thames Methuen, 1987) 20–23.
[78] *Hochster v De Latour* (n 72 above).

extending to the time that performance was actually due. Erle J recognised the force of this submission, saying

> he should decide against him, but would give him leave to move on account of the strong authority which [counsel] had produced[79].

Judgment for the claimant was entered, with damages being assessed by the jury at 20*l*. A rule arresting this judgment was later granted and, on 10 June 1853, Hannen appeared for the claimant, to show cause against that rule.

Hannen began by anticipating his opponents' reliance on *Phillpotts v Evans*[80] and *Ripley v M'Clure*.[81] The analysis in those cases, he argued, should not be read as applying to all situations of a refusal to perform; rather, it should be read as applying only to those refusals which were capable of being retracted before performance was due. What made a refusal incapable of being retracted was, essentially, that it had been acted upon[82]:

> If one party to an executory contract gave the other notice that he refused to go on with the bargain, in order that the other side might act upon that refusal in such a manner as to incapacitate himself from fulfilling it, and he did so act, the refusal could never be retracted.

He cited *Cort v The Ambergate, Nottingham and Boston and Eastern Junction Railway Company*[83] in support of that proposition.

Hannen then went on to address the point about the timing of the action. Again, he argued that the apparently universal language used by Parke B in *Phillpotts v Evans* and *Ripley v M'Clure* could not be supported in its widest sense, for it was clear that when a party disabled himself from performance—as, for instance, in the cases concerning marriage—the claimant was not required to wait until the time when performance was due. At this point Lord Campbell CJ interrupted, to ask[84]:

> It probably will not be disputed that an act on the part of the defendant incapacitating himself from going on with the contract would be a breach. But how does the defendant's refusal in May incapacitate him from travelling in June? It was possible that he might do so.

Hannen's reply, as reported by Ellis and Blackburn was as follows[85]:

> It was; but the plaintiff, who, as long as the engagement subsisted, was bound to keep himself disengaged and make preparations so as to be ready and willing to travel with the defendant on the 1st June, was informed by the defendant that he would not go on with the contract, in order that the plaintiff might act upon that information; and the plaintiff then was entitled to engage himself to another, as he did.

[79] *Hockster v De Latour* (n 72 above).
[80] *Phillpotts v Evans* (n 68 above).
[81] *Ripley v M'Clure* (n 70 above).
[82] *Hochster v De La Tour* (1853) 2 E & B 678, 683; 118 ER 922, 924 (QB).
[83] *Cort v The Ambergate* (n 45 above).
[84] *Hochster* (n 82 above) 2 E & B 678, 684 (QB).
[85] *Hochster* (n 82 above) 2 E & B 678, 684 (QB).

The Law Journal reporters summarised it slightly differently[86]:

> Where the contract is such as to require preparation for its performance, and the conduct of one party before the day is such as reasonably to lead the other party to think there is no use in making such preparation, such conduct must be considered the same in effect as if the party had disabled himself from performance. There should be readiness and willingness to perform down to the time of actual performance; and if before that there is such retraction as to warrant the other party in acting upon it, that is sufficient to support an action.

As reported by Ellis and Blackburn, that was pretty much the end of counsel's substantive argument. However, the report in *The Jurist* indicates that Hannen made a further point about the existing remedies available. Referring to Smith's discussion of the doctrine of constructive service in his note to *Cutter v Powell*, Hannen observed[87]:

> [I]t is said, that a servant who is wrongfully dismissed may recover the whole of his wages in an action of indebitatus assumpsit, if the action is brought after the expiration of the term for which he was hired. But in many cases that count would not include the special damage arising from the expenditure of money which the party had incurred in preparing to complete the contract

Hannen's argument was a sophisticated and original exposition of the law. He circumvented the difficulty of Parke B's remarks in *Phillpotts v Evans* and *Ripley v M'Clure* by reading them narrowly—in a way that was not obvious from the judgments themselves—and limiting them to situations where the refusal could not be retracted. The central idea in his submissions was that if the defendant induced the claimant to rely on his statement about non-performance, the statement could not subsequently be disowned. The language Hannen was using—particularly as reported in the Law Journal reports—was very close to an assertion of estoppel.

Having articulated the central principle of justifiable reliance, Hannen then skilfully rearranged the case law to illuminate it. *Cort*'s case, which had appeared to be an authority against the claimant, could now be presented as supporting the claimant, since there the claimant had indeed relied on the defendant's representation. The requirement of prevention—which was the true basis of the decision in *Cort*, and which would not have favoured the claimant if applied strictly in *Hochster*—was pushed into the background. Similarly, the cases on the defendant disabling himself from performance, which seemed not to help the claimant in *Hochster* (because the defendant had not disabled himself), could be repositioned to support the claimant. Here the claimant had been induced by the defendant's representation to disable himself from performing, so the situation was analogous to the defendant's disability cases; and the 'defendant's disability' cases showed that actions would lie before performance was due.

---

86 *Hochster* (1853) 22 LJ(QB) 455, 456–7.
87 *Hochster* (1853) 17 Jur 972, 973 (QB).

The discussion of constructive service was also important, despite its neglect by Ellis and Blackburn. What Hannen had to say about the precise application of the doctrine was perhaps not very compelling on the facts of *Hochster*: expenditure incurred at the defendant's request, for his benefit, surely would be recoverable in *indebitatus assumpsit*. More importantly, Hannen was reminding the court of the alternative remedy that was still available to claimants who did not take steps to mitigate their loss. Offering full payment to those who remained idle whilst denying any remedy to those who promptly took steps to improve their position was not obviously attractive. In effect, Hannen was reminding the judges of the claimant's meritorious conduct whilst avoiding a crude plea for sympathy.

Hannen's submissions, so far as we can judge from printed summaries, were an effective and impressive performance. Crompton J was quick to pick up Hannen's hint about mitigation, commenting that he was[88]

> inclined to think that the [claimant] may . . . say: 'Since you have announced that you will not go on with the contract, I will consent that it shall be at an end from this time; but I will hold you liable for the damage I have sustained; and I will proceed to make that damage as little as possible by making the best use I can of my liberty'.

Lord Campbell CJ also made clear his approval, saying that Hannen's opponents 'have to answer a very able argument'.[89] As it turned out, Hannen's submissions were a turning point in his career: Lord Campbell's praise secured him a part in the *Shrewsbury Peerage Case* (1857–58), after which 'his rise was rapid both in London and on circuit'.[90]

Hugh Hill QC and Deighton, for the defendant, began their argument by reasserting the more orthodox interpretations of *Cort*, *Phillpotts* and *Ripley*. *Cort*, they argued, was distinguishable, since there the action had been brought after performance was due. *Phillpotts* and *Ripley* showed that the declaration of an intention not to perform was not in itself a breach of contract. But they were quickly diverted from this exposition of the authorities by interventions from the Bench. Crompton J asked whether the claimant could not

> on notice that the defendant will not employ him, look out for other employment, so as to diminish the loss?[91]

Lord Campbell CJ expressed a similar concern: 'So that you say the plaintiff, to preserve any remedy at all, was bound to remain idle'.[92] Erle J identified a further undesirable consequence of upholding the defendant's submissions[93]:

[88] *Hochster* (n 82 above) 2 E & B 678, 685 (QB).
[89] *Hochster* (n 82 above) 2 E & B 678, 685.
[90] Polden, 'Hannen, James Baron Hannen (1821–1894)' *Oxford Dictionary of National Biography* (2004–06).
[91] *Hochster* (n 82 above) 2 E & B 678, 686.
[92] *Hochster* (n 82 above) 2 E & B 678, 686.
[93] *Hochster* (n 82 above) 2 E & B 678, 686.

Suppose the defendant, after the plaintiff's engagement with Lord Ashburton, had retracted his refusal and required the plaintiff to travel with him on 1st June, and the plaintiff had refused to do so, and gone with Lord Ashburton instead? Do you say that the now defendant could in that case have sued the now plaintiff for a breach of contract?

Counsel did their best, replying that a declaration of intention not to perform should be seen as an offer to rescind the agreement, which the claimant could choose either to accept or reject. But it was clear that, by this point in the hearing, the court was more concerned with the practical consequences of the defendant's position than with the technical legal analysis.

## 3. The Judgment

The unanimous judgment of the Court of Queen's Bench was delivered a fortnight later by Lord Campbell CJ. Lord Campbell began by setting out what he described as the defendant's 'very powerful'[94] contention that the claimant could not bring an action until his employment was due to begin. However, Lord Campbell continued, this proposition could not be universally true: in cases of promises to marry in the future, the action lay as soon as one of the parties married someone else. The explanation for the marriage cases could not be that performance was impossible—it was not impossible, since the defendant's spouse might die before the defendant was due to marry the claimant.[95] Rather, there was a breach of an immediate obligation[96]:

[W]here there is a contract to do an act on a future day, there is a relation constituted between the parties in the meantime by the contract, and that they impliedly promise that in the meantime neither will do any thing to the prejudice of the other inconsistent with that relation. As an example, a man and woman engaged to marry are affianced to one another during the period between the time of the engagement and the celebration of the marriage. In this very case, of traveller and courier, from the day of the hiring till the day when the employment was to begin, they were engaged to each other; and it seems to be a breach of an implied contract if either of them renounces the engagement.

The judgment then proceeded to consider whether, as a matter of principle, the claimant should have to remain bound to perform after the defendant's declaration. 'It is surely much more rational' said Lord Campbell,[97]

and more for the benefit of both parties, that, after the renunciation of the agreement by the defendant, the plaintiff should be at liberty to consider himself absolved from any future performance of it, retaining his right to sue for any damage he has suffered

---

[94] *Hochster* (n 82 above) 2 E & B 678, 688.
[95] *Hochster* (n 82 above) 2 E & B 678, 688.
[96] *Hochster* (n 82 above) 2 E & B 678, 689.
[97] *Hochster* (n 82 above) 2 E & B 678, 690.

from the breach of it. Thus, instead of remaining idle and laying out money in preparations which must be useless, he is at liberty to seek service under another employer, which would go in mitigation of the damages to which he would otherwise be entitled for a breach of the contract.

Broader considerations of justice were also seen as supporting the claimant's case[98]:

> The man who wrongfully renounces a contract into which he has deliberately entered cannot justly complain if he is immediately sued for a compensation in damages by the man whom he has injured: and it seems reasonable to allow an option to the injured party, either to sue immediately, or to wait till the time when the act was to be done, still holding it as prospectively binding for the exercise of this option, which may be advantageous to the innocent party, and cannot be prejudicial to the wrongdoer.

Finally, the judgment addressed the potential difficulties relating to the assessment of damages. These difficulties, it suggested, should not be exaggerated. Damages were to be assessed by the jury, who could take all contingencies into account in arriving at an appropriate sum. It followed that the verdict for the claimant given at the trial was correct.

The most remarkable thing about this judgment was how little it had in common with the argument of counsel for the successful claimant. Thus, whilst counsel had attempted to re-interpret the language used by Parke B in *Phillpotts v Evans* and *Ripley v M'Clure* so as to distinguish those remarks, the court was impatient of such subtleties. If Parke B had meant to say that a refusal in advance of performance being due could never be a breach, he was wrong; it was as simple as that.[99] More fundamentally, the court did not adopt counsel's argument about the importance of the claimant's detrimental reliance on the defendant's statement. For the court, it was not a question of the declaration becoming unretractable; rather, the declaration was itself a breach of the implied term not to do anything to the prejudice of the other party pending performance. In the judges' view, the claimant's decision to act on the statement merely made it 'reasonable' to give him the 'option' to sue immediately. If the claimant decided to wait and see if the defendant would perform, and the defendant failed to do so, the claimant would not lose his remedy.

Such boldness was particularly surprising from a court where the judges often disagreed with each other. Indeed, the frequency of disagreement started to demoralise Lord Campbell CJ, who wrote in his diary later the same year that he found his work so 'irksome' that he

> would as soon be beaten well all the time with a cudgel as preside in Queen's Bench with . . . on one side and . . . on the other.[100]

---

[98] *Hochster* (n 82 above) 2 E & B 678, 691.

[99] *Hochster* (n 82 above) 2 E & B 678, 692–3. See also the same criticisms of those two cases, made by a similarly constituted Court of Queen's Bench, in *Cort v The Ambergate, Nottingham and Boston and Eastern Junction Railway Company* (1851) 17 QB 127, 147.

[100] Hardcastle (ed), J Campbell, *Life of John, Lord Campbell* (London, John Murray, 1881) 2.317–2.318 (Diary entry from 24 December 1853).

He later said of Erle J, that '[w]ith him I had differed oftener than with any other judge'.[101] No one reading the judgment in *Hochster v de la Tour* could have suspected these conflicts. What, then, could have prompted a unanimous Court of Queen's Bench to go so much further, and on such a broader basis, than counsel had been prepared to argue? The answer, it is submitted, is to be found in an examination of the individual judges involved, and the fundamental political questions raised by the facts of the case.

Lord Campbell CJ, who presided in the Court of Queen's Bench, had been Chief Justice since 1850. Before his appointment to that position he had a long and distinguished career as a barrister, politician and author. His literary work—particularly his *Lives of the Chief Justices* (1849)[102]—offers us revealing insights into how he believed the Chief Justice should best fulfil his duties. As one contemporary reviewer recognised, 'the hero, and deservedly the hero of Lord Campbell's biographies'[103] was Lord Mansfield. Commenting on Mansfield's appointment in 1756, Campbell wrote:

> Although he did not then delineate in the abstract the beau ideal of a perfect judge, he afterwards proved to the world by his own practice that it had been long familiar to his mind.[104]

Campbell had a particularly high regard for Lord Mansfield's development of commercial law, which he described as follows[105]:

> As respected commerce, there were no vicious rules to be overturned,—he had only to consider what was just, expedient and sanctioned by the experience of nations further advanced in the science of jurisprudence. His plan seems to have been to avail himself, as often as opportunity admitted, of his ample stores of knowledge, acquired from his study of the Roman civil law, and of the juridical writers produced in modern times by France, Germany, Holland and Italy,—not only in doing justice to the parties litigating before him, but in settling with precision and upon sound principles a general rule, afterwards to be quoted and recognised as governing similar cases.

The importance of 'settling with precision and upon sound principles a general rule' could be seen equally in Campbell's own articulation of the implied term in *Hochster v De La Tour*.[106] However, the facts of *Hochster* did not give any scope to draw on Continental jurisprudence—for which Lord Campbell was to express his admiration elsewhere[107]—since Pothier followed the approach of Justinian's *Digest* (D50.17.1.161) in stating that a contracting party prevented

---

[101] *Ibid* 2.383.

[102] John Lord Campbell, *Lives of the Chief Justices of England* (London, John Murray, 1849).

[103] N Senior, 'Lord Campbell's *Chief Justices*' 93:189 *Edinburgh Review* (Jan 1851) 97, 129. For the attribution of this anonymous review to Senior see Levy, *Nassau W Senior* (Newton Abbott, David & Charles, 1970) 313–14.

[104] Campbell, *Lives of the Chief Justices of England* (n 102) II.393.

[105] Campbell, *Lives of the Chief Justices of England* (n 102) II.404.

[106] See quotation at n 96 above.

[107] Swain, 'The Will Theory of Contract in the Nineteenth Century: Its Influence and Limitations' in Lewis, Brand and Mitchell (eds), *Law in the City* (Dublin, Four Courts Press, 2007) 163, 165.

from fulfilling a condition was to be placed in the same position as if he had ful-filled it.[108] There was no civil law doctrine equivalent to anticipatory breach.[109]

Campbell's assessment of Mansfield's attitude to precedent also casts light on his approach to *Hochster v De La Tour*[110]:

> PRECEDENT and PRINCIPLE often had a hard struggle which should lay hold of Lord Mansfield; and he used to say that he ought to be drawn placed between them, like Garrick between TRAGEDY and COMEDY. Though he might err, like all other mortals, where there was no fixed rule of law which could not be shaken without danger, he was guided by a manly sense of what was proper, and he showed that he considered 'law a rational science, founded upon the basis of moral rectitude, but modified by habit and authority'.

The central role of rationality here is mirrored in the court's analysis in *Hochster*, as is the readiness not to be constrained by authority. For Campbell, it was clear that what made Mansfield a great judge was that, whilst others were content to follow authority as 'a matter of faith',[111] Mansfield's decisions were dictated by his acute perception of what 'reason' required.

What 'reason' required on the facts of *Hochster v De La Tour* was not imme-diately obvious. Legal logic (which might not be the same as 'reason') seemed to suggest that one could not be in breach of a contract before one was due to per-form it. But the facts of *Hochster* engaged with wider issues of rationality. Fundamentally, they raised the question about what the law should do where one contracting party was told in advance that his services would not be required. Did the law require him to wait around in case the other party changed his mind? If the law did require the claimant to wait, it was positively discouraging him from exercising his right to work elsewhere. And at the time of the decision in *Hochster*, a person's right to work was seen as absolutely fundamental.

The centrality of freedom of labour had been famously established by Adam Smith in *The Wealth of Nations*.[112] Indeed, 'the propensity to truck, barter, and exchange one thing for another'[113] was seen by Smith as the foundation of the entire economic system. In his view, it was essential to the success of the system that the freedom to contract should be uninhibited: a free and competitive market was the only way to maximize efficiency.[114] Smith's ideas were tremen-dously influential and formed the basis of the school of classical economics, which flourished throughout the early 19th century.[115]

---

[108] J Pothier, *Treatise on the Law of Obligations*, D Evans (trans) (Philadelphia, PA, Robert Small, 1826) vol 1, 107–9 [212].

[109] Zimmermann, *The Law of Obligations* (Oxford, Oxford University Press, 1996) 815–16 fn 228.

[110] Campbell, *Lives of the Chief Justices of England* (n 102) II.417.

[111] Campbell, *Lives of the Chief Justices of England* (n 102) II.439.

[112] A Smith, *An Inquiry Into the Nature and Causes of The Wealth of Nations* (Edinburgh, 1776); subsequent references are to the Dent edition (London, 1910).

[113] *Ibid* Book I, ch II, 12.

[114] A helpful summary of Smith's thought is given in PS Atiyah, *The Rise and Fall of Freedom of Contract* (Oxford, Oxford University Press, 1979) 294–303.

[115] *Ibid* 304–5.

It is hardly possible that the judges who decided *Hochster* could have been unaware of this economic thinking.[116] Indeed, there is evidence to show that they were aware. Erle J, for instance, had developed and articulated the doctrine of mitigation in a series of judgments which emphasised and incentivised the optimal use of labour.[117] Later, in his capacity as Chairman of the Trades Union Commissioners, he was to claim that the law gave the fullest protection to freedom of labour and capital[118]:

> *Every person has a right under the law, as between him and his fellow subjects, to full freedom in disposing of his own labour or his own capital according to his own will. It follows that every other person is subject to the correlative duty arising therefrom, and is prohibited from any obstruction to the fullest exercise of this right which can be made compatible with the exercise of similar rights by others.*

Even if the interference were not in itself unlawful, it would, in Erle's view, still give rise to liability if it interfered with the claimant's right.[119]

Lord Campbell's familiarity with classical economic ideas would have come directly from his political experience, and from his involvement in law reform. He had been a Member of the House of Commons throughout the 1830s, when the influence of economists had been at its height.[120] Furthermore, Campbell was a committed Whig,[121] as were many of the economist MPs,[122] so he may well have shared, as well as heard, their views. One particularly striking parallel with *Hochster v De La Tour* was the reform of the poor laws, which was debated in Parliament throughout the 1830s and 1840s. The problem with the existing poor laws was perceived as being that they were not administered in a way that encouraged self-reliance.[123] As Nassau Senior, the moving spirit of the reforms, put it, the prevailing system 'must diminish industry by making subsistence independent of exertion'.[124] He described the aim of the 1834 Poor Law Amendment Act as being

> [t]o raise the labouring classes, that is to say, the bulk of the community, from the idleness, improvidence, and degradation, into which the ill-administration of the laws for their relief has thrust them.[125]

[116] 'It is scarcely possible that any educated man growing to maturity between (say) 1800 and 1850 could not have read a good deal of the new political economy and radical political utilitarianism': Atiyah, *The Rise and Fall of Freedom of Contract* (n 114 above) 293.
[117] *Beckham v Drake* (1849) 2 HLC 579, 606–7; 9 ER 1213, 1223; *Goodman v Pocock* (n 61 above) 15 QB 576, 583–4; 117 ER 577, 580; *Emmens v Elderton* (1853) 4 HLC 624, 656; 10 ER 606, 618. He was also a party to the decision in the lower court in *Elderton v Emmens* (1848) 6 CB 160, 136 ER 1213, see especially at 178, 1219–20.
[118] W Erle, *The Law Relating to Trade Unions* (London, Macmillan 1869) 12.
[119] *Ibid.*
[120] F Fetter, 'The Influence of Economists in Parliament on British Legislation from Ricardo to John Stuart Mill' (1975) 83 *Journal of Political Economy* 1051.
[121] He was, for instance, a member of Brooks's Club, which he described, in a letter to his father, as 'the stronghold of the Whigs': Hardcastle (ed), *Life of John, Lord Campbell* (n 100 above) 1.409.
[122] Fetter, 'The Influence of Economists in Parliament (n 120) 1053.
[123] For a more detailed account, see Levy, *Nassau W Senior* (n 103 above) 80–90.
[124] Levy, *Nassau W Senior* (n 103 above) 80.
[125] Levy, *Nassau W Senior* (n 103 above) 90.

The reform of the poor laws powerfully illustrated how a system of self-consistent legal rules, designed with the best of motives, could be exposed by economic analysis as unfit for its purpose. Senior took a similar approach, though with less immediate success, to his critique of property law. In his evidence to the Real Property Commission (1828), chaired by Lord (then Mr) Campbell, he advocated radical simplification of the conveyancing system, so as to facilitate the transfer of land. He returned to the point in his review of Campbell's *Lives of the Chief Justices*, where he described the English system of conveyancing as 'a disgrace to a civilised nation',[126] and Coke's exposition of it as

> a memorial of his utter unfitness to discover or even to understand the real purposes for which laws ought to be made.[127]

Campbell could not have been unaware of what Senior, 'one of the most influential of the classical economists',[128] thought that those real purposes were.

The judgment in *Hochster v De La Tour* should, therefore, be seen not as merely an important innovation in the law of contract. Clearly it was innovative, but it also reflected a very distinctive attitude to the role of the appellate judge (as personified by Lord Mansfield), and a readiness to shape common law rules by reference to extra-legal notions of rationality and efficiency. It deserves its landmark status for all three reasons.

## D.  THE EFFECTS OF *HOCHSTER v DE LA TOUR*

The doctrine of anticipatory breach, as created by *Hochster v De La Tour*, remains good law today, and has been approved by the House of Lords several times.[129] But that is not to say that it has been seamlessly incorporated into the fabric of the common law. On the contrary, challenges to the scope, basis, and even the existence of the doctrine have emerged in the case law. In this Part those challenges are outlined, and the responses to them evaluated.

### 1.  The Nature of Repudiation

In *Hochster v De La Tour* itself there could be no dispute that the defendant had renounced the contract. But other factual situations were less clear, and the courts showed a consistent reluctance to recognise less explicit conduct as a

---

[126] Senior, 'Lord Campbell's *Chief Justices*' (n 103 above) 105.
[127] Senior, 'Lord Campbell's *Chief Justices*' (n 103 above) 104.
[128] Atiyah, *The Rise and Fall of Freedom of Contract* (n 114 above) 317.
[129] *Martin v Stout* [1925] AC 359 (HL); *Moschi v LEP Air Services Ltd* [1973] AC 331 (HL); *Woodar Investment Development Ltd v Wimpey Construction UK Ltd* [1980] 1 WLR 277 (HL).

renunciation. For instance, in *In re Agra Bank*[130] it was held that a bank did not renounce its contractual obligation to pay under a letter of credit by stopping payment generally. Page Wood VC said that he found it

> quite impossible to bring this case within the principle of the cases . . . especially the courier's case, *Hochster v De La Tour*, which went as far as any.[131]

Similarly, inviting one's creditors to a meeting, showing them a bleak financial statement of one's situation and asking for more time to pay did not show an intention to abandon the contract.[132] Even a letter setting out in detail all the party's failed attempts to obtain the funding necessary to complete the contract was not enough, because it went on to say that the party would continue trying.[133] As Megaw LJ put it, 'the expression of this "hope, however forlorn" is quite inconsistent with a final refusal'.[134] It was also essential to place the defendant's statement in its factual and legal context: a refusal to provide a cargo for a ship, for example, might appear to be a renunciation of the charterer's obligations, but if the refusal was made on the first of several days provided by the contract for loading, that appearance was deceptive.[135] In essence, there was a fine line between pessimism and renunciation; and if the party receiving a gloomy communication read too much into it, and terminated the contract, he himself would be liable for breach. Only the clearest renunciation could be acted on with confidence.[136]

Where a party made an assertion about his legal position, the courts were confronted with a further difficulty. On the one hand, a genuine attempt to ascertain one's own rights or duties seemed to be the opposite of a refusal to perform legal obligations. But, on the other hand, if one party asserted that he was not required to perform because some condition was not satisfied, and, as a matter of law, that assertion was incorrect, the party was effectively refusing to perform his contract. The courts' resolution of the problem has not been consistent.[137] Support for the view that the party's mistaken assessment of his legal rights was irrelevant could be found in *Danube and Black Sea Railway and Kustendjie Harbour Company (Limited) v Xenos*,[138] where the defendant's erroneous belief that his agent had exceeded his authority in making the contract was given no weight. In *Woodar Investment Development Ltd v Wimpey*

---

[130] *In re Agra Bank* (1867) LR 5 Eq 160.

[131] *Ibid* 164.

[132] *In re Phoenix Bessemer Steel Company* (1876) 4 Ch D 108 (Ch & CA).

[133] *Anchor Line Ltd v Keith Rowell Ltd, The Hazelmoor* [1980] 2 Lloyd's Rep 351 (CA).

[134] *Ibid* 354.

[135] *Avery v Bowden* (1855) 5 E & B 714, 119 ER 647 (QB); (1856) 6 E & B 953, 119 ER 1119 (Ex Ch).

[136] *Spettabile Consorzio Veneziano di Armamento e Navigazione v Northumberland Shipbuilding Company Limited* (1919) 121 LT 628 (CA).

[137] JC Smith, 'Anticipatory Breach of Contract' in E Lomnicka and C Morse (eds), *Contemporary Issues in Commercial Law: Essays in Honour of AG Guest* (London, Sweet & Maxwell, 1997) 175, 176.

[138] *Danube and Black Sea Railway and Kustendjie Harbour Company (Limited) v Xenos* (1861) 11 CB(NS) 152, 142 ER 753 (CP); (1863) 13 CB(NS) 825, 143 ER 325 (Exch Ch).

*Construction UK Ltd*,[139] however, the House of Lords favoured the opposite view, holding that there was no renunciation where the defendant insisted on his own erroneous interpretation of a crucial contractual term.

To some extent the uncertainties illustrated by the cases on repudiation are inherent in any rule that allows proof of intention by conduct. However, it is submitted that the approach to renunciation adopted by the House of Lords in *Woodar*'s case makes that uncertainty unnecessarily larger, and complicates what should be a simple rule. It is also difficult to reconcile with broader contractual principles, in particular the principle that liability for breach of contract is strict.

## 2. The Requirement of Acceptance

In *Hochster v De La Tour* the claimant had decided to act immediately on the defendant's renunciation, and to put an end to the contract. Shortly afterwards, in *Avery v Bowden*,[140] Lord Campbell CJ took the opportunity to confirm the decision in *Hochster*, and to make it clear that for liability to arise under the *Hochster* doctrine, it was essential for the claimant to have ended the contract. Thus, where, under a charterparty, the charterer refused to supply a cargo in conformity with the contract and told the captain that 'there was no use in his remaining there any longer',[141] no liability arose if the captain continued to insist upon having a cargo. In other words, there was no right to damages under *Hochster* if the innocent party affirmed the contract.

One question prompted by this rule concerned what the innocent party had to do to show that he was exercising his option to terminate. In *Hochster* itself, the claimant could be said to have acted to his own detriment—in the sense that he disabled himself from performance by making alternative, conflicting, arrangements with Lord Ashburton—and there was some support for the view that detrimental reliance was necessary. Thus, in *Danube and Black Sea Railway and Kustendjie Harbour Company (Limited) v Xenos*,[142] a charterer who had been told that the ship-owner would not perform his obligation made another contract with a different ship-owner. The Court of Common Pleas held that the claimant had exercised his option to terminate, but seemed unsure whether the alternative contract was crucial. Erle CJ, the only member of the court who had been involved in *Hochster v De La Tour*, seemed to think not.[143] Williams J, however, gave a rather different exposition of the law[144]:

---

[139] *Woodar Investment Development Ltd v Wimpey Construction UK Ltd* [1980] 1 WLR 277 (HL).

[140] *Avery v Bowden* (1855) 5 E & B 714, 119 ER 647 (QB); (1856) 6 E & B 953, 119 ER 1119 (Ex Ch).

[141] *Avery v Bowden* (1855) 5 E & B 714, 728; 119 ER 647, 652–3; (1856) 6 E & B 953, 975; 119 ER 1119, 1127 (Cresswell J).

[142] *Danube and Black Sea Railway* (n 138 above) (CP).

[143] *Danube and Black Sea Railway* (n 138 above) 11 CB(NS) 152, 176; 142 ER 753, 763 (CP).

[144] *Danube and Black Sea Railway* (n 138 above) 11 CB(NS) 152, 178; 142 ER 753, 763–4 (CP).

the cases . . . have fully established, that, if before the time for the performance of the contract arrives, one of the parties thereto not merely asserts that he cannot or will not perform it, but expressly repudiates and renounces it, the party to whom the promise is made may treat that as a breach of contract, at his option; at all events, where he has in consequence thereof acted so as to interfere with the performance of the contract on his part according to its original terms.

Byles J held a similar view. It was 'plain', he said[145]

that if, in consequence of that renunciation of the contract by Xenos, the company were induced to incur liability and expense, and, still more, to make another contract for the transport of their goods by another vessel, the defendant must be held bound by it . . . indeed, the law does require that there shall be some act done by the other party to intimate his assent to the renunciation of the contract, beyond his saying so.

Keating J referred back to *Phillpotts v Evans*,[146] in which Parke B had said that a refusal to perform before the date for performance was not a breach.

What distinguishes this case from *Phillpotts* [he explained,] is, that here there is the strongest evidence of the company having acted upon the refusal of Xenos to perform his contract.[147]

The case went on to the Exchequer Chamber,[148] but the judgment was, unfortunately, very short, and did not deal expressly with the question of detrimental reliance. The judges may, however, have been hinting at a preference for the view of Erle CJ when they said that

[u]pon receiving notice from Xenos that he would not receive the cargo upon the terms agreed upon, the company had a right at once to treat that as a breach.[149]

'At once' might suggest that there was no need for detrimental reliance.

It is submitted that the view of Erle CJ was the more convincing. The need for detrimental reliance had indeed been emphasised in *Hochster v De La Tour*, but only in the claimant's arguments; the judgment, as we have seen, proceeded on a different, wider basis. A vital part of that basis was that the claimant should take all reasonable steps to mitigate his loss. But it was not necessary, in order to have a claim under the principle in *Hochster*, to show that those steps had been successful. On the contrary, if the steps had been unproductive, the award of damages would be larger. In other words, detrimental reliance clearly was relevant to the *Hochster* principle, but it was relevant only to mitigation of loss, not to whether liability arose at all.

The fact that liability under *Hochster* could only arise where the claimant exercised his right to end the contract also gave rise to two further questions. The first concerned a matter of substance: Was *Hochster* confined to situations where

---

[145] *Danube and Black Sea Railway* (n 138 above) 11 CB(NS) 152, 180–81; 142 ER 753, 764 (CP).
[146] *Phillpotts v Evans* (n 68 above).
[147] *Danube and Black Sea Railway* (n 138 above) 181, 765 (CP).
[148] *Danube and Black Sea Railway* (n 138 above) (Exch Ch).
[149] *Danube and Black Sea Railway* (n 138 above) 13 CB(NS) 825, 827; 143 ER 325, 326 (Exch Ch).

what the defendant expressed the intention to do would, if carried out, have given the claimant a right to terminate? The answer, given in *Johnstone v Milling*,[150] was 'Yes'. There it was said that the renunciation of the landlord's covenant to rebuild demised premises could not give rise to liability under *Hochster*, since an actual breach of that covenant would not entitle the tenant to terminate the lease. In *Afovos Shipping Co SA v Romano Pagnan and Pietro Pagnan, The Afovos*[151] Lord Diplock went further, holding that the doctrine of anticipatory breach required a threatened 'fundamental' breach,[152] as distinct from the threat to breach a term which the parties had merely agreed should give rise to a right to terminate. There has been no challenge to this rule, and it is submitted that the basic position, as set out in *Johnstone v Milling*, has considerable logical force: it would make little sense to allow a claimant to terminate the contract for a threatened breach if the actual breach itself would not have entitled him to terminate. But it is not clear that Lord Diplock's extension of the doctrine is equally convincing: if the parties choose to raise a term to the status of a condition, it seems sensible to attach to that term all of the consequences that attach to conditions arising by force of law.[153] If the parties were prepared to agree that a failure to satisfy the term should give the innocent party the right to terminate, it is difficult to see why a renunciation of that term should not give rise to the same rights.

The second question concerning termination was, on the face of it, merely about terminology. It arose because, whilst the courts accepted that there could be no liability under *Hochster* unless there was termination, it was not clear how this position should be encapsulated. One possibility was to say that the breach was not 'complete'[154] until acceptance by the other party. Another possibility, advanced by Bowen LJ in *Johnstone v Milling*,[155] was to say that the declaration of intention was not a breach at all[156]:

> It would seem on principle that the declaration of such intention by the promisor is not in itself and unless acted on by the promisee a breach of the contract; and that it only becomes a breach when it is converted by force of what follows it into a wrongful renunciation of the contract. Its real operation appears to be to give the promisee the right of electing either to treat the declaration as brutum fulmen, and holding fast to the contract to wait till the time for its performance has arrived, or to act upon it, and treat it as a final assertion by the promisor that he is no longer bound by the contract, and a wrongful renunciation of the contractual relation into which he has entered. But such declaration only becomes a wrongful act if the promisee elects to treat it as such.

---

[150] *Johnstone v Milling* (1886) 16 QBD 460 (CA).
[151] *Afovos Shipping Co SA v Romano Pagnan and Pietro Pagnan, The Afovos* [1983] 1 WLR 195 (HL).
[152] *Ibid* 203.
[153] *Bettini v Gye* (1876) 1 QBD 183.
[154] *Avery v Bowden* (1855) 5 E & B 714, 722; 119 ER 647, 650 (Watson, Atherton and Mellish, counsel for the defendant).
[155] *Johnstone v Milling* (n 150 above).
[156] *Johnstone v Milling* (n 150 above) 472–3.

In the same case Lord Esher MR went further, being driven to explain the requirement for acceptance in terms of rescission. After referring to *Hochster*, he said[157]:

> the doctrine relied upon has been expressed in various terms more or less accurately; but I think that in all of them the effect of the language used with regard to the doctrine of anticipatory breach of contract is that a renunciation of the contract, or, in other words, a total refusal to perform it by one party before the time for performance arrives does not, by itself, amount to a breach of contract but may be so acted upon and adopted by the other party as a rescission of the contract so as to give an immediate right of action. When one party assumes to renounce the contract, that is, by anticipation refuses to perform it, he thereby, so far as he is concerned, declares his intention then and there to rescind the contract. Such a renunciation does not of course amount to a rescission of the contract, because one party to a contract cannot by himself rescind it, but by wrongfully making such a renunciation of the contract he entitles the other party, if he pleases, to agree to the contract being put an end to, subject to the retention by him of his right to bring an action in respect of such wrongful rescission.

This had gone beyond a mere search for appropriate terminology; it had become an exercise in reclassification.

Of course, it might not often matter exactly what terminology was used to get to the result. But sometimes it could matter. For instance, if an issue arose about jurisdiction, it could be crucial to know where the breach occurred: was it when a letter expressing the intention not to perform the contract was posted abroad, or when it was received in England? In *Cherry v Thompson*,[158] which predated *Johnstone v Milling*, it was held that the breach occurred on posting. And, although that analysis was difficult to reconcile with Bowen LJ's approach (unless one gave the acceptance some retroactive effect) and inconsistent with Lord Esher MR's (which denied a breach), it was followed in later cases.[159]

The root of the problem over terminology could be traced back to *Hochster v De La Tour*. There the court had made clear how important it was that the remedy depended on termination, but the reason given was not one of legal analysis. Rather, reason (or rationality) called for a rule which would liberate the claimant from the restrictions of his now useless contract, and allow him to make the best of his opportunities elsewhere. This reason had no obvious legal equivalent. Its closest legal counterpart was the doctrine of mitigation; but mitigation had no role unless there had already been a breach. Perhaps it would have been better if later courts had expressly recognised that *Hochster v De La Tour* created a new species of breach of contract, for which no action would lie unless the innocent party terminated. Certainly that would have been preferable

---

[157] *Johnstone v Milling* (n 150 above) 467.
[158] *Cherry v Thompson* (1872) LR 7 QB 573.
[159] *Holland v Bennett* [1902] 1 KB 867 (CA); *Mutzenbecher v La Aseguradora Espanola* [1906] 1 KB 254 (CA); *Martin v Stout* [1925] AC 359 (HL).

to the awkward attempts to force the doctrine into some existing category: such an approach was at best inelegant, and at worst potentially misleading.

## 3. The Basis of the Rule

The cases dealt with so far in this Part all acknowledged *Hochster v De La Tour* as good law, whilst trying to expound and develop its principles. But judicial approval of the decision was not universal, and in *Frost v Knight*[160] the Court of Exchequer advanced a series of criticisms of the decision which, in its view, showed that the case had been wrongly decided.

*Frost v Knight* involved facts which were obviously suited to the application of anticipatory breach: the parties had agreed to marry on the death of the defendant's father (who disapproved of the match); but, before that unhappy event, the defendant renounced the engagement. Kelly CB, who gave the leading judgment, was not unsympathetic to the claimant's situation,[161] but he was unconvinced that she could have a remedy for breach of contract. The fundamental difficulty, in his view, was that no contractual obligation had been breached[162]:

> to say that the contract is broken, is simply to utter an untruth. One contracts in 1870 to pay another 1000l on the 1st of January 1871. To say that the contract is broken before the year 1870 is at an end is undeniably and self-evidently untrue.

That, he continued, was as true of the facts of *Hochster v De La Tour* as it was of the case before him. Lord Campbell's judgment 'will be found', he said[163]

> when carefully considered, to amount to no more than an argument upon the reasonableness of affording some remedy to the plaintiff, where, by reason of the declaration of the defendant that he would not take him into his service when the 1st of June should arrive, he was obliged either to remain unemployed until the 1st of June, and lose the opportunity of obtaining another employment, or to accept any other engagement that might be offered to him and so disentitle himself to maintain an action, on the ground that he could not aver that he was ready and willing to perform his part of the agreement.

In short, the courts had introduced a 'fiction'[164] in order to create a remedy. Channell B expressed his agreement.[165]

When the case was heard by the Exchequer Chamber,[166] however, *Hochster v De La Tour* was restored. Cockburn CJ made it clear that

---

[160] *Frost v Knight* (1870) LR 5 Exch 322 (Ex).
[161] *Ibid* 336: 'the painful and embarrassing situation in which she has been placed by the declaration made to her by the defendant'.
[162] *Frost v Knight* (n 160 above) 327.
[163] *Frost v Knight* (n 160 above) 329.
[164] *Frost v Knight* (n 160 above) 331.
[165] *Frost v Knight* (n 160 above) 337.
[166] *Frost v Knight* (1872) LR 7 Exch 111 (Ex Ch).

the promisee may, if he thinks proper, treat the repudiation of the other party as a wrongful putting an end to the contract, and may at once bring his action as on a breach of it.[167]

He also explained that this was not a mere matter of authority: the rule in *Hochster* operated 'for the common benefit of both parties'.[168]

But, although the Exchequer Chamber had disapproved the decision of the court below, the criticism that the *Hochster* principle rested on a 'fiction' did not disappear. Since the doctrine was now too well-established to be abandoned, the concern about fiction prompted judges to identify some other basis for the rule. The explanation that established itself was that the defendant's declaration allowed the claimant to treat his future breach as inevitable, and sue him for it in advance.[169] Thus, in *Maredelanto Compania Naviera SA v Bergbau-Handel GmbH, The Mihalis Angelos*[170] Mocatta J said that[171]

the doctrine of anticipatory breach is an artificial one. It may be said to be one of the legal fictions which remains very much alive. At the date of a renunciation and its acceptance there is in truth no actual breach of contract, since the time for its performance has not yet arrived.

He went on to explain that this artificiality caused difficulties[172]:

Once there is a renunciation and an acceptance of it, there is in the eyes of the law a breach and the contract is at an end, but the assumed and in law inevitable failure to perform is one at the date in the future when performance would have been required had there been no anticipatory breach. It is in relation to that assumed future breach of contract, which by law is anticipated, that damages have to be assessed.

When the case reached the Court of Appeal Lord Denning MR was quick to point out that Mocatta J had misunderstood the doctrine. 'The renunciation itself is the breach',[173] he said, and Megaw LJ agreed.[174] Edmund Davies LJ, on the other hand, seemed to accept the inevitable future breach argument when he said that the claimant's argument was mistaken because it required the court to 'anticipate not only a breach, but the *worst* breach'.[175] In *Afovos Shipping Co SA v Romano Pagnan and Pietro Pagnan, The Afovos*[176] Lord Diplock also seemed to support the inevitable future breach analysis, when he said that the effect of renunciation was that

---

[167] *Ibid* 113.
[168] *Frost v Knight* (n 166 above) 113.
[169] *Universal Cargo Carriers Corp v Citati* [1957] 2 QB 401 (QB).
[170] *Maredelanto Compania Naviera SA v Bergbau-Handel GmbH, The Mihalis Angelos* [1971] 1 QB 164 (QB & CA).
[171] *Ibid* 182.
[172] *The Mihalis Angelos* (n 170 above) 182.
[173] *The Mihalis Angelos* (n 170 above) 196.
[174] *The Mihalis Angelos* (n 170 above) 209–10.
[175] *The Mihalis Angelos* (n 170 above) 201.
[176] *Afovos Shipping Co SA v Romano Pagnan and Pietro Pagnan, The Afovos* [1983] 1 WLR 195 (HL).

the party not in default need not wait until the actual breach; he may elect to treat the secondary obligations of the other party as arising forthwith.[177]

It is submitted that this recourse to ideas of inevitable future breach was both unnecessary and unconvincing. It was unnecessary because the principle in *Hochster v De La Tour* did not rest on a fiction. It rested, as the court in *Hochster* had made clear, on an implied term that the parties would not act to each other's prejudice pending performance. Of course, one might disagree with the court's readiness to imply such a term,[178] but that is a different question. The inevitable future breach explanation was also unconvincing. Not only was it highly artificial, it also missed the point. In situations such as *Hochster v De La Tour*, for instance, the future breach was not inevitable: the defendant might change his mind after all. The point was that the claimant should not be obliged to wait around to see; he should be allowed (and encouraged) to seek alternative employment.

## E.  CONCLUSION

Albert Hochster went on to become an art dealer and importer, trading at 26 Gerrard Street in London[179]; the theft of two Dresden china ornaments from those premises prompted his only other recorded activity as a litigant.[180] Of Edgar de la Tour there is no trace. But the litigation that brought these two men to the Court of Queen's Bench has done anything but fade into obscurity, and it fully deserves its continuing landmark status. If anything, its importance has tended to be underestimated as a result of misplaced criticism and the pursuit of terminological orthodoxy. In particular, the criticisms and terminological obscurity introduced by later courts may have inhibited its use as a general principle. The ideas behind it could, for instance, cast light on the proposition that a party can foist unwanted contractual performance on another.[181] The principle of not acting to the other party's prejudice pending performance might suggest a broader general idea about good faith. In short, once the full significance of *Hochster v De La Tour* is appreciated, it can be seen not only as *the* landmark case in anticipatory breach, but also as having the potential to be a landmark for other areas of contract law as well.

---

[177] *Ibid*, 203.
[178] Contrast the view of Mustill, 'Anticipatory Breach of Contract: The Common Law at Work' (n 24 above), who (at 42) describes the implied term as 'fanciful' with Smith, 'Anticipatory Breach of Contract' (n 137 above) at 178: 'well within the modern doctrine of implied terms'.
[179] Exhibition Culture in London 1878–1908 website: www.exhibitionculture.arts.gla.ac.uk. The building is now Gerrards Corner restaurant.
[180] *R v Dixon*, The Times (6 August 1878) 10.
[181] *White & Carter (Councils) Ltd v McGregor* [1962] AC 413 (HL).

# 6

# Taylor v Caldwell (1863)

## CATHARINE MACMILLAN

### A. INTRODUCTION

A LANDMARK CASE IS one which stands out from other less remarkable cases. Landmark status is generally accorded because the case marks the beginning or the end of a course of legal development. *Taylor v Caldwell*[1] is regarded as a landmark case because it marks the beginning of a legal development: the introduction of the doctrine of frustration into English contract law. This chapter explores the legal and historical background to the case to ascertain if it is a genuine landmark. A closer scrutiny reveals that while the legal significance of the case is exaggerated, the historical significance of the cases reveals an unknown irony: the case is a suitable landmark to the frustration of human endeavours. While the existence of the Surrey Music Hall was brief, it brought insanity, imprisonment, bankruptcy and death to its creators.

### B. VICTORIAN PLEASURES

#### 1. The Pleasure Gardens

The tale of the Surrey Music Hall reflects the development of entertainments and pleasures in Victorian London. There was a 'leisure revolution' in Victorian England,[2] brought about by decreased working hours and the increased free time spent in new, more pleasurable, fashions. It has been noted that 'the market constituted the chief generator of cultural activity in Victorian Britain'.[3] Cultural pursuits were dependent upon private finance and this dependency underpins the history of the Surrey Music Hall. The Music Hall arose from the

---

[1] *Taylor v Caldwell* (1863) 3 B & S 826, 122 ER 309; SC 32 LJQB 164; 8 LT 356; 11 WR 726 (Court of Queen's Bench). All further references are to the report at 3 B & S.
[2] See, eg, J Lowerson and J Myerscough, *Time to Spare in Victorian England* (Trowbridge/Esher, The Harvester Press, 1977); KT Hoppen, *The Mid-Victorian Generation 1846–1886* (Oxford, Clarendon Press, 1998) chs 10 and 11.
[3] Hoppen, *The Mid-Victorian Generation 1846–1886* (n 2 above) 374.

Surrey Zoological Gardens in Newington, Surrey, an area then just outside the metropolis of London. The Zoological Gardens began under the auspices of Edward Cross. In 1831 Cross brought his menagerie of animals from the Strand to the grounds of Walworth Manor House. These he converted into zoological gardens which contemporaries considered more impressive than those of Regent's Park. The principal attractions were the animals, the gardens, paintings of famous scenes and portrayals of dramatic events such as the eruption of Mount Vesuvius.[4] Dickens described the pleasures of a similar garden[5]:

> We love to wander among the illuminated groves, thinking of the patient and laborious researches which had been carried on there during the day, and witnessing their results in the suppers which were served up beneath the light of the lamps, and to the sound of music, at night. The temples and saloons and cosmoramas and fountains glittered and sparkled before our eyes; the beauty of the lady singers and the elegant deportment of the gentlemen, captivated our ears; a few hundred thousand of additional lamps dazzled our senses.

In 1847, after Cross's retirement, the lease for the property was acquired by Cross's assistant, William Tyler. Tyler purchased the lease with the aid of a mortgage and continued to operate the business in a largely profitable fashion until the mid-1850s, at which point the business of running the Zoological Gardens ran into difficulty. The takings were not so great as they had been and Tyler's mortgagee became concerned. A plan was devised to transform the gardens into a new endeavour. The Royal Surrey Gardens Company (Limited) was created to realise the plan to create a new series of extravagant amusements centred around a series of musical concerts. While the mid-Victorian Londoner's taste for pleasure gardens was waning, his taste for music in the form of promenade concerts was increasing.

## 2. Promenade Concerts

Promenade concerts originated as a form of entertainment popular in European capitals, notably Paris, Vienna and London, during the 1830s. The promenade concert was entertainment designed not for a limited number of cultured concert-goers but for ordinary people who wanted pleasant entertainment in attractive surroundings at a comparatively low price. The audience was not seated, but standing and able, if they chose, to move about. Partly as a result of the introduction of promenades, the number of concerts increased dramatically in European capitals. Although the London promenades were never to involve

---

[4] Similar events followed. Mount Vesuvius was replaced in 1839 with 'Iceland and Mount Hecla', followed by the 'City of Rome' (which occupied five acres of the gardens), the Temple of Ellora', 'London during the Great Fire', the 'City of Edinburgh', and 'Napoleon's passage over the Alps'.

[5] C Dickens, 'Vauxhall-Gardens by Day' in *Sketches by Boz* (London, Penguin Books, 1995) 153–5.

ballroom dancing, as the Viennese promenades did, the link with dance was clear as the conductors provided a programme filled with waltzes, polkas and quadrilles. Key to the success of the promenade was the persona of the musical conductor, who was also generally a composer. Promenades appeared in London towards the end of the 1830s as imitations of the immensely popular promenades of the Parisian Phillipe Musard.

The man who gave his name to the early London promenades was Louis Jullien.[6] Born in Sisteron, France in 1812, Jullien received extensive musical tutelage from his father, a military bandmaster. In his teens, Jullien served successively in the French navy and army. Following his departure, or possibly desertion, from the army, Jullien made his way to Paris in the early 1830s. There he studied music at the Conservatoire, leaving with an undistinguished record. He began to compose quadrilles and to conduct promenade concerts in Paris. Jullien was a dandy: above all, he was a showman and a crowd pleaser. He was able to entertain his audience in a way unmatched by his competitors and enjoyed great success in Paris in the final years of the 1830s. He arrived in London in 1840 to provide promenade concerts. Londoners loved him, for Jullien[7]

> not only conducted but acted. He was ceremonious, grandly emotional. He would appear in a demonstrative shirt-front, conduct with a demonstrative beat, would be warmed by the excitement of a quadrille into standing up on his gilt chair, wherein at the conclusion of a symphony, he would sink back with demonstrative exhaustion ('charming languor'). He was melodramatic, transpontine.

Jullien's technique was to present his show on a massive scale, with a huge orchestra, numbering in the hundreds and sometimes accompanied by an enormous choir. He was keen to present the leading singers of the day. His programme would consist of light music, principally dance music, interspersed with more serious pieces by composers such as Beethoven, Mozart and Mendelssohn. He sought to entertain people who would never attend a more serious concert and advertised his concerts in a manner unmatched by his competitors. Jullien struggled in London to find a venue large enough to house all of his performers and his ever-growing audiences. In the summer of 1845 Jullien began his long association with the Surrey Gardens when he held his first *Concert Monstre* to commemorate the accession of Queen Victoria, similar in scale and grandeur to those given in Paris at the *Jardin turc* and the *Champs Elysées*. Jullien conducted 300 instrumentalists on an outside platform to entertain an audience of 12,000 people. Jullien's concerts had an important cultural significance and became 'a feature of London life . . . in a way that could not be claimed by any other musical institution'.[8]

---

[6] A Carse, *The Life of Jullien* (Cambridge, W Heffer & Sons, 1951).
[7] H Davison, *From Mendelssohn to Wagner, being the memoirs of JW Davison* (London, WM Reeves, 1912) 109.
[8] Carse, *The Life of Jullien* (n 6 above) 65.

The 1850s were a critical time for the development of music in England. It has been described as a time during which there was a movement of 'musical idealism'.[9] This idealism was a part of the political context of its time; a kind of musical politics which 'attacked both aristocratic and bourgeois values'.[10] There was a shift from benefit concerts, high culture and virtuosi towards a varied classical repertory and music defined by popular taste. The promenade concerts played an important role in this process. They attracted a different audience than earlier concerts, an audience composed of some artisans and occasionally working men, but mainly people from the lower and middle levels of the middle class. The personalities who led these concerts—Johann Strauss in Vienna, Philippe Musard in Paris and Louis Jullien in London—showed the enormous commercial potential for classical music that lay in the middle class.[11]

## 3. The Surrey Music Hall

It was to tap into this enormous commercial potential that the concert hall at the Surrey Gardens was constructed. Because of a lack of concert halls, Jullien generally held his promenades in theatres, a device which was not considered satisfactory by either performers or audiences. By 1855, however, plans were afoot to change that. A group of promoters under the direction of James Coppock, a solicitor and Parliamentary election agent, resolved to take advantage of the new Joint Stock Company Acts to develop the Surrey Zoological Gardens. Jullien appears to have been involved with the promoters from the outset, although he was never involved in the management of the business.[12] The prospectus outlined the venture[13]:

> it is clear, from the great success of last season that much larger results may be achieved, and that the public require accommodation beyond that which any single proprietor would venture to give. The application of capital, with liberal but judicious outlay, is imperatively called for; and now, by the Limited Liability Act, no danger can accrue to the parties supplying it.

In November 1855 the animals in the menagerie were sold by auction to ready the site for further development,[14] and by January 1856 the Royal Surrey Gardens Company (Limited) was formed. In March it put out its prospectus and of the 4,000 shares offered (at £10 each) 3,740 were applied for and 3,256 were taken up. The prospectus outlined the development plans:

---

[9] W Weber, *Music and the Middle Class: the Social Structure of Concert Life in London, Paris and Vienna between 1830 and 1848*, 2nd edn (Aldershot, Ashgate, 2004) 152.

[10] *Ibid* xxii.

[11] Weber, *Music and the Middle Class* (n 9 above) 128.

[12] It is not clear why Jullien was not involved in the management of the concern, nor why he was never a director of the resulting company. It may have been because of his earlier bankruptcy in 1848, which arose from a failed attempt to create an English national opera.

[13] *The Times* (24 August 1857) 9.

[14] By auction on 27 November 1855: *The Times* (14 November 1855) 2.

it is proposed to erect buildings of a character and magnitude to command the attention of the public, comprising a music-hall capable of accommodating 10,000
people.[15]

The entertainments would extend beyond the Music Hall to encompass con-
servatories, aviaries, aquaria, paintings, 'exhibitions of various kinds' and fireworks, all 'affording amusement to promenaders'.[16] Music was, however,
central to the venture from its very outset and Jullien was to provide it. By the
end of April the company was organised with limited liability and the building
works were reported as making rapid progress.[17]

The Music Hall was the central feature of the redevelopment of the Surrey
Gardens. In the words of one contemporary,

a scheme was hatched for the transformation of the Zoological Gardens into a sort of
Crystal Palace with a gigantic music hall.[18]

The construction of an enormous concert hall was necessary to accommodate
Jullien's massive orchestral ensembles and to provide sufficient space for the
thousands who came to hear the promenade concerts. The promoters chose
Horace Jones as the architect. Victorian architecture is noted by the enormous
proliferation of architectural styles; Jones favoured Gothic styles and what he
described as 'Italian'.[19] Victorian architecture was marked by new choices of
building materials. Railways had made possible the delivery of different forms
of stone and brick, and technological and engineering advancements made it
possible for architects to construct buildings with the use of iron. Victorian
architects of the mid-century were challenged to meet the new demands of use
for buildings and to balance these demands with advancing technology and the
proliferation of different styles.[20] Jones's work was revolutionary in employing
structural, and sometimes decorative, ironwork in constructing his buildings.[21]
The Surrey Gardens Music Hall was one of the great ironwork constructions of
London. It was constructed just at the very end of the time-period in which these
constructions began to go into decline because of changing building regulations
in London. These building regulations actively discouraged the use of exposed-
iron construction; the regulations were premised on concerns about oxidisation
and fragmentation. There was also great concern about fire hazards in the

---

[15] *The Times* (24 August 1857) 9.
[16] *Ibid.*
[17] *The Times* (21 April 1856) 7. The directors of the new company were Messrs Bain, Beale,
Chappell, Coppock, Holmes and Wyld.
[18] Davison, *From Mendelssohn to Wagner* (n 7 above) 216–17.
[19] Pevsner had his doubts about this designation in some instances: S Bradley and N Pevsner,
*London 1: the City of London* (London, Penguin Books, 1999) 339.
[20] For a discussion of these challenges, see J Mordaunt Crook, *The Dilemma of Style,
Architectural Ideas from the Picturesque to the Post-Modern* (London, John Murray, 1987) ch 4.
[21] Something of his style can still be observed in London from his construction of Smithfield
Market (completed in stages between 1866–83) and his reconstructions of Billingsgate Market
(1874–78) and Leadenhall Market (1880–81). The Music Hall was his first major commission.

ironwork buildings; in addition to the increasingly stringent building regulations, it was also difficult to obtain adequate fire insurance for the buildings. In architectural terms, the destruction of the Surrey Gardens Music Hall by fire went some way to discrediting iron architecture, particularly in London.[22] Jones himself never gave up on the use of ironwork as a building material or on Gothic as a style: his last construction was the design of the London landmark, Tower Bridge.[23]

The construction of Jones's gigantic music hall proceeded very quickly and it was complete by the spring of 1856; the cost was immense—some £25,000.[24] The Surrey Gardens Music Hall was suitably enormous: at 170 feet long, 60 feet wide and 72 feet high,[25] it was larger and more suitably constructed than any of its rivals. It was considerably better than its nearest rival in size, Exeter Hall on the Strand, which 'possessed every fault that a building for public gatherings could possibly have'.[26] The Music Hall held 10,000 people and a further 2,000 could hear music from balconies and verandahs: its construction greatly facilitated the ambulatory nature of promenade concerts. The building was judged a great success by observers, both in its construction and in its suitability for music. The *Athenaeum* described the building as one which defied all 'architectural proprieties' but conceded that 'no one could have expected that a building so floridly decorated should have turned out so capital a music-room'.[27] *The Times*'s music critic gushed over its acoustic properties:

the adaptation of the Surrey Music-hall for sound was placed beyond a doubt. In this essential no other building in Great Britain can be compared with it.[28]

The Music Hall opened on 5 July 1856 with an inaugural concert organised and conducted by Jullien. Jullien did not disappoint the thousands who turned up for a day of music, and chose that Victorian favourite, Handel's *Messiah*, as the work to be performed. Appropriately enough, amongst the singers was Mr Sims Reeves, the man who figured at the end of the Music Hall. *The Times* declared Jullien's efforts to be 'one of the best performances of Handel's masterpiece ever heard in London'.[29] Jullien conducted an enormous orchestra composed of musicians from most of London's orchestras; the chorus was similarly immense, comprised of men and women from not only London choirs but from all the major cities of the north, brought to the metropolis by the new railways. '[R]arely, indeed, has there been a more imposing choral

[22] Crook, *The Dilemma of Style* (n 20 above) 124.
[23] Tower Bridge conceals its ironwork structure within its Gothic masonry. The design was not without its contemporary critics; see Crook, *The Dilemma of Style* (n 20 above) 123.
[24] *The Times* (24 August 1857) 9. The cost included the refurbishment of the gardens.
[25] Davison, *From Mendelssohn to Wagner* (n 7 above) 217.
[26] CE Pearce, *Sims Reeves, Fifty Years of Music in England* (London, Stanley Paul & Co, 1924) 111.
[27] Quoted in Pearce, *Sims Reeves, Fifty Years of Music in England* (n 26 above) 191.
[28] *The Times* (16 July 1856) 9
[29] *Ibid*.

assemblage'.[30] Following the afternoon's *Messiah* was an evening concert comprised of vocal and instrumental music conducted by Jullien,

> who according to his established and respected custom, mingled with the lighter and more ephemeral pieces certain compositions of the great masters.[31]

The crowds loved it and *The Times* pronounced it a most 'auspicious beginning to a new and important undertaking'.[32] It is only with hindsight that the massive thunderstorm which ended the evening appears foreboding.

The Music Hall enjoyed a good beginning and was used to host events requiring accommodation for large numbers of people. The directors of the Royal Surrey Gardens Company donated the use of the Music Hall and Gardens for a dinner to honour the Guards upon their return from the Crimea. An estimated 20,000 spectators attended and the Company's directors turned admission receipts of £1,100 over to the Guards.[33] The Music Hall received use of a spiritual nature as it was also hired out on Sunday nights to Charles Spurgeon. Spurgeon was one of the great Victorian Baptist ministers, who 'has by a style of oratory peculiar to himself become the object of great popularity'.[34] Spurgeon had attracted numbers so great that he soon outgrew his chapel and moved to the 5,000-seat Exeter Hall. He rapidly filled this hall and only the Music Hall could provide appropriate accommodation. It was during a sermon in October 1856 that the inherent dangers of such a large building became apparent. With upwards of 14,000 people in the building, concerted and false cries of 'fire' were made. The result was a mass panic as people were unable to exit the building: seven people died and many others were seriously injured. The 'dreadful accident' indicates how fortunate it was that the building was empty when it did later burn down.[35]

While the Hall was regularly let for these mass events, the principal entertainments were Jullien's enormous promenade concerts and the diverse amusements linked to them. It is uncertain whether Jullien had persuaded the directors to establish the Royal Surrey Gardens or whether the directors persuaded Jullien to enter into a financial and contractual relationship with the Company. At the outset of the relationship, each claimed to have persuaded the other and at the end of the relationship each side blamed the other for the problems that arose. Jullien was appointed as the Director of Music and Conductor, and he undertook to organise promenade concerts in July, August and September of

---

[30] *The Times* (n 28 above).

[31] *The Times* (n 28 above).

[32] *The Times* (n 28 above).

[33] *The Times* (26 August 1856) 7.

[34] *The Times* (20 October 1856) 8.

[35] Fire was a constant danger and concern in such large halls. The Report of the Select Committee on Theatrical Licenses and Regulations (1866) (no 373) stated that it was the opinion of the Committee that it was desirable that any Act of Parliament regulating the licensing of theatres, music halls and places of entertainment should render compulsory the inspection of such places as to their stability of structure, due security against fire and the means of ingress and egress: iii, para 5.

each year. He was to be paid for these concerts by the Company. Jullien, in turn, purchased large numbers of shares in the Company. Each side depended upon the other for the venture to be successful: Jullien had to have a large concert hall and the Music Hall was the largest concert hall in the metropolis. The Company, in turn, needed someone who could draw large crowds on a nightly basis. It was this dependency upon a single man that was to cause problems in the functioning of the Surrey Gardens, as Jullien proved to be the only promoter remarkable enough to make the Music Hall function profitably. His concerts were grand affairs for a modest price. His extravagant musical fêtes lasted most of the day and, for a shilling,[36] customers could enter the grounds at three in the afternoon and partake of all the pleasures of the gardens and their amusements.[37] Following a firework display beside the lake, the fêtes ended at 10 pm. Jullien combined the rare ability of bringing in masses of people at low prices whilst simultaneously pleasing music critics. Respectable people attended promenade concerts; continual concern was voiced about the possible attendance of thieves[38] or prostitutes.[39] *The Times* carefully pointed out how well-behaved Jullien's audiences were. The Victorians supported leisure as a source of moral and personal improvement to those who partook of it. On this account, the promenades were regularly applauded:

> [T]he Royal Surrey Gardens, with their new hall and their musical director, may be the means eventually of doing a great deal for the moral culture and improvement, as well as for the mere healthy relaxation of the masses.[40]

Jullien engaged the leading singers of the day and foremost amongst these was Sims Reeves. Jullien was the first to provide Sims Reeves with a leading operatic character before a London audience at Drury Lane in 1847. This appearance was praised by Hector Berlioz who wrote that

> Reeves has a beautiful natural voice, and sings as well as it is possible to sing in this frightful English language.[41]

---

[36] Or the purchase of a £10 share in the Company entitled the bearer to a season's admission.

[37] The amusements were an eclectic mix, indicative of the Victorians's concern to educate combined with their fascination with the bizarre. An indication of the sort of amusements available can be seen in the following extract: 'The exhibitions outside, too numerous to particularize in detail, comprised, among other things, the performances of a military band, an old English morris dance, Ethopian serenaders. The brothers Elliott, with their remarkable "classical delineations" on the "double trapeze"; a complete Spanish ballet . . . the "poses gymnastiques" of Herr Connor, who threw no less than 54 back somersaults in succession; 10 balloons of fair dimensions, "semaphorie and telegraphic", various entertainments, musical and otherwise on the lake; and . . . a "*café chantant*," . . . in which Miss Rose Braham and other vocalists took part, much to the pleasure of those who preferred the open air in the gardens to the heated atmosphere of the Music-hall. The whole concluded with a grand display of fireworks, with the extra attraction of Mademoiselle Pauline Violanti . . . upon the tight rope across the lake': *The Times* (25 August 1857) 12.

[38] See, eg, *The Times* (4 September 1856) 10.

[39] See, eg, the application for a licence renewal for the Surrey Gardens in *The Times* (21 October 1858) 9.

[40] *The Times* (19 July 1856) 9.

[41] Quoted in Sims Reeves, *His Life and Recollections written by Himself* (London, Simpkin Marshall and London Music Publishing Co, 1888).

Sims Reeves became the leading tenor of his day, one for whom Sullivan wrote parts, a favourite of Queen Victoria's,[42] and, while popular for his operatic parts in his early years, he increasingly turned to oratorio and concert work which was performed before mass concerts. Sims Reeves also acquired notoriety for being absent from performances. Sir Frederick Pollock, himself a Wagnerian enthusiast but whose parents were keen fans of Sims Reeves, wrote that as to Sims Reeves's appearing at any given performance 'there was a constant element of doubt until the last moment'.[43] While Pollock attributed these absences to a great concern on the part of Sims Reeves to preserve his voice[44] and Sims Reeves himself vociferously defended his absences on the grounds of illness,[45] the likely reason for the uncertainty of his appearances was his nerves.[46] As we shall see, the uncertainty of Sims Reeves' appearances and the state of his health was to have a bearing on the arguments in *Taylor v Caldwell*.

The first season of the Surrey Gardens Music Hall was an excellent one. Jullien's concerts met with financial success and critical acclaim[47]:

> [T]hus ended the inaugurative season of a new enterprise which has achieved, notwithstanding the frequent prevalence of unfavourable weather, a success with few precedents, the origin of which, it may be recorded with satisfaction, is principally traceable to the new music-hall and the varied and attractive performance of vocal and instrumental music designed by the experience and directed by the skill and judgment of M. Jullien, whose great distinction is to have been able to show that the public generally may be gratified and amused by the more refined no less than by the commoner manifestations of the musical art. The cheers with which he was greeted, on being recalled at the end of the concert last night, were the expression of a genuine sentiment.

The season was so successful that the Company had stated in their first half-yearly report that they were able to pay a dividend on the paid up capital of five per cent. The actual dividend declared was 10 per cent, the maximum

---

[42] He sang for her on her birthday in May 1857: Pearce, *Sims Reeves, Fifty Years of Music in England* (n 26 above) 196.

[43] Sir F Pollock, *For My Grandson, Remembrances of an Ancient Victorian* (London, John Murray, 1933) 113.

[44] A point upon which Pollock decided that 'Sims Reeves was justified. Occasional disappointment of an audience was for the gain of a younger generation who would otherwise never have heard him': *ibid*.

[45] See, eg, his letter to the editor in *The Times* (25 February 1869) 12, following a non-appearance which resulted in a lawsuit. More commonly, announcements were made publicly by promoters, eg *The Times* (30 January 1852) 1. Sims Reeves also detested giving encore performances and his indispositions apparently encouraged audiences to demand them. At one of the Surrey Gardens concerts, he refused the audience's repeated calls for an encore and for half an hour the concert would not proceed. Sims Reeves apparently stared the crowd down, stating: 'I'm too much of an Englishman to be beaten when I have right on my side', and waited for the audience to calm down: Pearce, *Sims Reeves, Fifty Years of Music in England* (n 26 above) 212.

[46] The *New Oxford Dictionary of National Biography*, entry for Reeves, (John) Sims.

[47] *The Times* (1 October 1856) 6.

permissible.[48] *The Times* reported that a 'considerable revenue is expected' in the next season.[49]

## 4. The Music Hall Faces Troubles

To all outward appearances, the next season began well with a 16-day musical festival conducted by Jullien that 'surpassed expectation'.[50] A grand military festival was held for Mrs Seacole, the Creole nurse who had tended the Crimean wounded.[51] Jullien conducted 'a gigantic combination of military music' composed of nine military bands in all,[52] together with his own orchestra and the chorus of the Royal Surrey Choral Society, 'constituting a vocal and instrumental force of little short of 1,000 performers'.[53] Sims Reeves sang ('magnificently') Purcell's 'Come if you dare'. The Company was perceived by the public as a solid endeavour and shares were sought for purchase.[54]

Behind the scenes, however, all was not well with the Company.[55] It was not on as secure a footing as had been thought and it faced stiff competition for audiences when the Crystal Palace began its first Handel Festival.[56] The takings were down and the Company needed money badly. A second ordinary general meeting was held at the beginning of April. It had been announced that ordinary business would be conducted and many shareholders stayed away. Those who attended were kept waiting in the Music Hall until the appointed time for the meeting had expired and were then shown into a room provisioned plentifully with sandwiches and wine. The accounts were simply set out on a table,[57] and before many shareholders had had time to look at them, it was moved that the accounts be received, approved and adopted. By a majority of two votes, the accounts passed. Immediately after the meeting, some shareholders began to examine matters more closely. It transpired that the accounts were in a perilous state. The previous dividend had been provided from the capital. The Company had paid £14,000 for the lease of the Surrey Gardens, a gross overvalue given

---

[48]  *The Times* (16 October 1856) 5.

[49]  *Ibid.*

[50]  *The Times* (2 July 1857) 5.

[51]  Mary Seacole had been 'ruined by the peace which others welcomed with such enthusiasm' (*The Times* (28 July 1857) 10) because she had laid in large stores of supplies and provisions which could not be moved or sold at the end of the Crimean War. She came to England and was rapturously received by the Guards at their dinner the previous year.

[52]  *Ibid.* The bands were those of the 1st and 2nd Life Guards, the Royal Horse Guards Blue, the Grenadier Guards, the Coldstreams, Scots Fusileers, Royal Engineers, Royal Artillery, and Marines.

[53]  *The Times* (n 51 above).

[54]  *The Times* (12 August 1857) 4.

[55]  The account is derived from *The Times* (24 August 1857) 8.

[56]  Carse, *The Life of Jullien* (n 6 above) 91.

[57]  It was later alleged by one of shareholders' leaders that the accounts had, in any event, omitted the mortgage and the unsecured debts: WA Coombe, letter to the editor, *The Times* (1 September 1857) 10.

that the lease had less than 12 years to run.[58] The lease had been purchased from Tyler who had then been able to pay his mortgagee, Mr Coppock, who had been paid in shares and seems to have retained a lien over the property. Prior to this purchase, the lease had been offered for sale for 18 months without any prospective purchasers. Coppock, it will be recalled, was the principal director in the Company. He had assured shareholders, when asked about the lease, that it had a long time to run, some 50 years. What the shareholders also discovered was that any improvements erected on the property, including their grand Music Hall, would become the property of the owner upon the expiration of the short lease. The Company had unsecured creditors to the extent of £11,500. As if this was not sufficiently grave, the property was subject to pay a septennial fine to the Dean and Chapter of Canterbury: £2,000 would have to be paid in five years' time. The directors had declared dividends when there was no money to pay them and, even worse, had carried on with another £4,000 worth of new buildings by Jones when they knew there was no money to pay for them. The second issue of shares, which increased the capital account against the original shareholders, had been made in an attempt to pay for these buildings.

All summer the discontented shareholders, led by a Mr WA Coombe, sought answers from the directors to difficult questions. The entire affair became public in August when the architect, Horace Jones, also a shareholder, sought an order for the winding up of the Company[59] on the ground that £11,500 was owed to creditors and without a shilling of assets. The event came as a 'thunderbolt' to some of the shareholders.[60] The shareholders, led by Coombe, sought an adjournment. The shareholders complained that a great fraud had been worked upon them—principally by Coppock—and that Jones was acting on behalf of the directors in seeking the winding up order. The shareholders' concern was a very real one: if the Company were wound up, it would benefit the directors by removing queries about, and responsibility for, their behaviour: the greatest cost would be to the shareholders who lost their money. The shareholders were angry enough about matters to suggest that certain directors ought to be indicted. The Commissioner adjourned the proceedings to allow the shareholders' committee to meet with the directors in an attempt to restructure the Company.

Jullien announced at the shareholders' meeting that he was the principal unsecured creditor, owed some £6,000. Jullien's position was particularly unpleasant, as he had to pay his musicians and vocalists. The cheques he had received for his salary from the Company had been dishonoured. Whatever the arrangement entered into between the shareholders and the directors, the latter left the running of the Company in the hands of Jullien.[61] Jullien was concluding the season

[58] It was stated in later proceedings that the true value of the lease was probably about £2,000: *The Times* (28 August 1857) 9.
[59] *The Times* (24 August 1857) 9.
[60] *Ibid.*
[61] *The Times* (25 August 1857) 12.

with a grand festival of promenade concerts, complemented by diverse amusements in the gardens. The legal troubles continued. The adjourned hearing before the Commissioner came before him again on 27 August and was, again at the shareholders' request, re-adjourned. The shareholders sought a way to force Coppock and Tyler to disgorge most of their £14,000 and to bring the Company's capital down to a manageable amount.[62] An angry exchange of correspondence between the directors, shareholders and creditors ensued in *The Times*. The creditors met in September to try to protect their interests and those of the shareholders. It was then appreciated that the deed of settlement did not give the directors the power to give bills of exchange in the name of the Company. This was an important discovery because the unsecured creditors were owed £10,000 on bills of exchange, for which the directors were personally liable[63]: a matter subsequently established in court.[64]

Throughout the autumn and early winter of 1857, the shareholders and creditors continued to battle with the directors. It was a protracted and somewhat meaningless affair: it

> might almost as well have been a discussion among a number of the most talkative birds ever contained in the Surrey-gardens.[65]

In November, the first bankruptcy arose out of the affair when a certificate of bankruptcy was granted to the previous owner, Tyler. The Commissioner was very concerned as to the possibility of running the Company on a profitable basis, and urged the parties to put aside feeling and to treat this as business. By mid-December, the two sides reached some agreement. The shareholders' representative stated that they could find no reason for charging the directors with misappropriating money, for the failure was caused by bad management. The hearing was again adjourned to allow settlement with the creditors. The following day, Coppock died of heart failure, apparently brought on by the stress of the affair.[66] Jullien did not conduct his promenade concerts in 1858. It may well be that he had had a falling out with the shareholders who now controlled the Company through Coombe. Coombe's season was not a successful one; the advertisements were small, the entertainments nowhere near as grand as they had been, and by the end of the year, the police alleged that prostitutes were entering the gardens.[67] Ominously, a benefit concert was held for Coombe in September 1858.[68]

---

[62] The situation is outlined in Coombe's letter to the editor (n 57 above), *The Times* (1 September 1857) 10.

[63] *The Times* (16 September 1857) 10.

[64] The Court of Exchequer found three of the directors so liable in *Eastwood v Bain, Holmes and Coppock*, *The Times* (29 June 1858) 11.

[65] *The Times* (19 October 1857) 9.

[66] *The Times* (21 December 1857) 10.

[67] *The Times* (21 October 1858) 9.

[68] *The Times* (15 September 1858) 1.

In October of 1858 the Company ceased functioning, when Coombe was arrested for debt and imprisoned. He was released in March 1859; the Commissioner thought there was no reason to prolong the imprisonment as there was nothing in his conduct which called for the court's reprehension.[69] The Company was wound up in bankruptcy. Once the Court of Chancery made its decree, the property was advertised for sale by auction.[70] It appears that Caldwell and Bishop purchased the lease of the Surrey Gardens at the auction and were determined to carry on with the promenade concerts.

The difficulty that they faced was that without Jullien it was impossible to sell sufficient tickets to make the venture profitable. A tragic fate befell Jullien as a result of the Company's failures. He was deeply in debt and fled to Paris in May 1859 as a result. Once there, he was arrested and imprisoned for debt until the end of July. Upon his release he disappeared from view. By the beginning of 1860 he was beginning to plan concerts in Paris. He wrote a pitiful letter to his friend Davison, stating that 'if only I can get on my horse again, I shall fall off no more'.[71] He pleaded with Davison to try and get his orchestral manuscripts from the Surrey Gardens' creditors, for without his papers he was like a workman without his tools.[72] Shortly thereafter, Jullien was reported to be indigent to the point of destitution and signs of complete mental breakdown were evident. A Jullien Festival was planned for London in July to assist the conductor; by March, Jullien had been admitted to a lunatic asylum in Paris. He died a few days later, possibly by suicide. The Jullien Festival went ahead to raise money for his destitute widow. Jullien's leading singers and musicians performed without fee; amongst them was Sims Reeves. Had the Surrey Music Hall venture succeeded, contemporary London's promenades would be traced not to Sir Henry Wood but to Jullien.

## 5. The Demise and Destruction of the Music Hall

Sims Reeves does not seem to have sung again at the Music Hall. He was frequently engaged at Crystal Palace, with its large and successful shows. The Surrey Music Hall, in contrast, struggled greatly. Caldwell and Bishop worked to restore its reputation and the arrangement with the theatrical speculators, Taylor and Lewis, was a part of this endeavour. Caldwell and Bishop were in the final stages of the Hall's refurbishment when disaster struck. Plumbers repairing the roof left for their dinner. The fire they thought had been left in a place of safety set a part of the roof ablaze. A strong wind fanned the flames down the roof. By the time the fire brigades made their way to the site to pump the lake water onto the roof, it was too late. The entire structure burnt down

---

[69] *The Times* (12 March 1859) 11.
[70] *The Times* (29 April 1859) 16.
[71] Davison, *From Mendelssohn to Wagner* (n 7 above) 242.
[72] Davison, *From Mendelssohn to Wagner* (n 7 above) 242.

within three hours. So determined were Caldwell and Bishop to make a profit that scarcely were the fire engines out of sight

> when the band of the Gardens commenced playing, and an announcement was posted informing the public that the price of admission was one shilling.[73]

The building was so damaged as to be irreparable, although it was fully insured. Given the financial difficulties of running the enormous Hall in Jullien's absence, it is no surprise that it was not rebuilt. It had stood for less than five years. A year later, St. Thomas's Hospital was reconstructed on the site. It is now covered by a small park and a large local authority housing estate.[74]

## C. ENGLISH CONTRACT LAW AND IMPOSSIBILITY

When Taylor and Lewis brought their action, the state of English contract law concerned with impossibility was tolerably certain, although not without difficulties. Impossibility arises in two ways: existing impossibility and subsequent impossibility.

### 1. Initial Impossibility

English law recognised that a contract to perform something physically impossible resulted in a void contract in cases of a patent absurdity, eg

> to overturn Westminster Hall with his finger; or to make the Thames overflow Westminster Hall; or to drink up the sea; or touch the sky with his hand.[75]

This rule only applied when the initial impossibility was evident to all of the parties at the time of contracting. If the impossibility was not evident at the time of contracting, then the party who had undertaken to perform the impossible was liable in damages for the non-performance of this impossibility. In *Thornborow v Whitacre*,[76] Holt CJ stated that

> where a man will for a valuable consideration undertake to do an impossible thing, though it cannot be performed, yet he shall answer damages.[77]

The court was of this view because the impossibility was only as to the promisor's ability to perform that which he had undertaken to perform, and 'the defendant ought to pay something for his folly'.[78] The contract had to be lawful to be valid; a contract to perform an illegal act was void

---

[73] *The Times* (12 June 1861) 5.
[74] It is not far from the Oval Cricket Ground.
[75] JJ Powell, *Essay upon the Law of Contracts and Agreements* (London, J Johnson and T Whieldon, 1790) 161.
[76] *Thornborow v Whitacre* (1705) 2 Lord Raym 1164, 92 ER 270.
[77] *Ibid* 2 Lord Raym 1164, 1165; 92 ER 270, 271 (Holt CJ).
[78] *Ibid.*

for it would be absurd that an obligation, which derives its sanction from the law, should put us under a necessity of doing something which the law prohibits.[79]

In short, if the initial impossibility arose from a patent absurdity or a prohibition of law, the contract was not good; if the impossibility arose from an undertaking provided by the promisor, he was liable.

## 2. Subsequent Impossibility

In cases where the impossibility of performance was subsequent to the contract's formation the rule was harsh. Subsequent impossibilities were governed by *Paradine v Jane*.[80] The case concerned the action of a landlord for rent due from his tenant pursuant to his lease. The tenant defended this action on the ground that he had been dispossessed from his land by an alien enemy of the king. The plaintiff demurred.[81] Rolle J decided that the tenant was liable for his rent, for he had contractually assumed this obligation. A distinction was drawn between obligations imposed by the law and obligations accepted by the promisor under his own contract[82]:

> where the law creates a duty or charge, and the party is disabled to perform it without any default in him, and hath no remedy over, there the law will excuse him . . . but when the party by his own contract creates a duty or charge upon himself, he is bound to make it good, if he may, notwithstanding any accident by inevitable necessity, because he might have provided against it by his contract.

This distinction came to stand[83] for the rule that a subsequent impossibility would excuse a party from obligations imposed by the law, but not obligations assumed by his own contract. Professor Ibbetson stated that

> it seems likely that the formulation of Rolle J. in *Paradine v Jayne* was intended to go further than was demanded by the arguments of counsel, and to state the law in terms of absolute liability in contract.[84]

In *Paradine v Jane* absolute liability in contract worked a hardship upon the tenant: his liability for rent was not excused despite his inability to occupy the land. He was also unlikely to succeed in a cross-action against the landlord for damages arising from his loss of possession, because there is no indication that

---

[79] Powell, *Essay upon the Law of Contracts and Agreements* (n 75 above) 164.

[80] *Paradine v Jane* (1647) Aleyn 26, 82 ER 897; Style 47, 82 ER 519.

[81] The case has received a detailed consideration from D Ibbetson in 'Fault and Absolute Liability in Pre-Modern Contract Law' (1997) 18 *Journal of Legal History* 1 and 'Absolute Liability in Contract: the Antecedents of *Paradine v Jayne*' in FD Rose (ed), *Consensus ad Idem* (London, Sweet and Maxwell, 1996) ch 1.

[82] *Paradine v Jane* (n 80 above) Aleyn 26, 27; 82 ER 897, 897.

[83] It took a period of time for the 'law to settle down with this rule': Ibbetson, 'Fault and Absolute Liability in Pre-Modern Contract Law' (n 81 above) 23.

[84] Ibbetson, 'Fault and Absolute Liability in Pre-Modern Contract Law' (n 81 above) 23.

the landlord had covenanted to make himself liable for dispossession arising from the actions of a hostile stranger.[85] The harshness of absolute liability was recognised in the 19th century. As one critic wrote[86]:

> The law of England differs from the law of all other countries by the peculiar strictness with which it construes and enforces contracts. The act of God and the King's enemies, to which may be added those of the national government having a commanding or prohibitory force, are the only accidents that can excuse an obligor from performing his engagement.

The merit of absolute liability lies in the simplicity of its application. The initial question is how was the duty imposed: by law[87] or by express contractual term? If it were the latter the promisor was liable for performance unless the contract provided for the non-performance, or the impossibility of performance could be attributed to the other party. The liability probably appears harsher to modern eyes than to those who were subject to it because, as one case reports, 'the parties know what they are about'[88] when they formed these contracts. The parties knew what liabilities they were assuming when they contracted and could attempt to provide against them; failing this, they were aware of the risks that they had assumed and would have been able to insure against these risks, if they chose. The harshness of absolute liability was dealt with in ways that prevented what modern eyes view as subsequent impossibilities from arising. Those subsequent impossibilities that could not be prevented from arising often formed legal exceptions to this absolute standard, for to do otherwise would be to create an absurdity. We turn now to consider how the structure of contractual arrangements and the rules governing them worked to reduce the number of cases of subsequent impossibility that might arise.

## 3. Contractual Arrangements

Contracts then, as now, could be either entire or severable. In the case of an entire contract the entire fulfilment of the promise by either was a condition precedent to the fulfilment of the promise by the other. It was

---

[85] Sir GH Treitel, *Frustration and Force Majeure*, 2nd edn (London, Thomson, Sweet & Maxwell, 2004) 22–3.

[86] Anon. 'Art III. Execution of a Contract Impossible' (1833) 10 *American Jurist & Law Magazine* 250, 251.

[87] The phrase 'where the law creates a duty' encompassed not only the modern distinction between contractual and non-contractual duties, but also terms which were implied by law within a contract: Treitel (n 85 above) 20.

[88] *Beale v Thompson* (1803) 3 B & P 405, 433; 127 ER 221, 235 (Lord Alvanley CJ); reversed: (1804) 4 East 546, 102 ER 940 (Court of King's Bench).

wholly immaterial whether the exact and complete performance of the whole contract be rendered impossible by overwhelming necessity or be occasioned by the negligence of the other party.[89]

If the party could not, for whatever reason, provide complete performance, no action would lie for the recovery of the consideration.[90] Contracts were also divided into absolute contracts and conditional contracts; the latter was not simply an executory contract 'but it is a contract, whose very existence and performance depend on a contingency and condition'.[91] The condition upon which the contract depended could be either precedent or subsequent. By creating a contract dependent upon a condition precedent, parties could ensure that the risk of a particular thing happening or not happening clearly fell upon one party. Since one party alone had assumed the risk of this event, the event could not generally be said to be one that rendered the contract impossible of performance. The event was, instead, a risk assumed by that party.

(a) Contractual Arrangements and Inevitable Accidents: Shipping

The use of these devices can be seen in the context of shipping. A condition precedent was frequently employed in the carriage of goods by sea to overcome the manifold problems that could arise in these ventures. The parties would provide as a condition precedent that the goods would arrive at the port stipulated; should the goods not arrive, the contract was at an end.[92] If, for example, a ship was wrecked and the cargo not delivered at the place and by the date stipulated, the vendors would not be answerable for the non-delivery of the cargo.[93] Where one of the parties assumed an absolute undertaking, for example to load and unload a ship within a certain period of time, the prevention of this by natural events such as the Thames freezing would not absolve the party of this responsibility.[94] The shipping merchant might also make the arrival of a ship by a certain time, or the arrival of another ship, the condition precedent of receiving a homeward cargo.[95] While a charter party was generally a reciprocal contract, it was also possible to contract in such a way as to make the performance of the contract mandatory upon one party and optional upon the other. In this instance, if the party subject to the mandatory obligation was unable to perform

---

[89] William W Story, *A Treatise on the Law of Contracts Not Under Seal* (Boston, Little, Brown & Co, 1847) §22.

[90] See, eg, *Cutter v Powell* (1795) 6 TR 320, 101 ER 573.

[91] Story, *A Treatise on the Law of Contracts Not Under Seal* (n 89 above) §26.

[92] *Hawes v Humble* (1809), referred to in the footnotes to *Boyd v Siffkin* (1809) 2 Camp 326, 170 ER 1172. See also *Hayward v Scougal* (1812) 2 Camp 56, 170 ER 1080; *Storer v Gordon* (1814) 3 M & S 308, 105 ER 627 (where the cargo was seized by a foreign government).

[93] *Idle v Thornton* (1812) 3 Camp 274, 179 ER 1380.

[94] *Barret v Dutton* (1815) 4 Camp 333, 171 ER 106. In the same case the freighter was not held to be liable for delay occasioned by difficulty in obtaining customs clearances because the customs house had burnt down.

[95] *Shadforth v Higgins* (1813) 3 Camp 385, 170 ER 1419.

this obligation for reasons beyond his control, he was still bound by it and liable in damages unless it came with an excepted risk.[96]

In contracts concerned with the carriage of goods by sea express contractual provisions were made to exclude liability in certain instances: the perils of the sea, eg

> the act of God, the king's enemies, fire, and all and every other dangers and accidents of the seas, rivers, and navigation, of whatever nature and kind soever excepted.[97]

Such exceptions could also be provided in other kinds of contracts. Courts viewed the determination of whether or not a risk fell within the exception clause as a question of fact and evidence rather than of law. In this determination the judge would have recourse to the usage of trade and practice among merchants.[98] The exceptions were strictly construed.[99] It remained to be determined whether the loss arose without negligence on the part of the master.[100]

While parties structured their contracts in such a way as to provide for the allocation of risk or the exception of risk arising from future events, the law itself operated to provide an excuse for non-performance in two instances. A carrier was excused from performance where he was prevented from it by an act of God or by the King's enemies.[101] The act of God had to be a natural accident (eg, lightning, earthquake or tempest) and it could not be an accident arising from the negligence of man.[102] The act of God had to be an immediate one.[103] If there was any possibility that the parties could have provided against the occurrence of the event in their contract, the event was not one which excused performance. Thus, an outbreak of an infectious disease within the port for which the ship was destined did not excuse the non-performance.[104] In addition, the contract for the carriage of goods could be dissolved by law upon the occurrence of certain extrinsic events arising out of hostilities. If, before the commencement of the carriage, war or hostilities broke out between the state in

---

[96] *Shubrick v Salmond* (1765) 3 Burr 1637, 97 ER 1022. The court seems to have followed the authority urged upon it by the merchant, namely, *Paradine v Jane*. Courts seem, however, to have allowed the master of the vessel some leeway for reasonable actions where he had been prevented from complying with the contractual provisions: *Puller v Stainforth* (1809) 11 East 232, 103 ER 993.

[97] *Colvin v Newberry* (1832) 6 Bligh NS 167, 170; 5 ER 562, 563–4. Similar exception clauses can be found in *Storer v Gordon* (n 92 above) and in *Deffell v Brocklebank* (1821) 3 Bligh PC 561, 564; 4 ER 706, 708.

[98] *Pickering v Berkeley* (1648) Style 132, 82 ER 587.

[99] Eg, in the case of a restraint by princes and rulers, the exception only covered actual rather than expected restraint, even if the expectation was reasonable: *Atkinson v Ritchie* (1809) 10 East 530, 103 ER 877.

[100] JH Abbott, *A Treatise of the Law relative to Merchant Ships and Seaman*, 5th edn (London, Joseph Butterworth & Son, 1827) 256.

[101] Abbott, *A Treatise of the Law relative to Merchant Ships and Seaman* (n 100 above) 251.

[102] *Company, Trent & Mersey Navigation v Wood* (n 110 below), referred to in *Forward v Pittard* (1785) 1 TR 27, 99 ER 953.

[103] *Smith v Shepherd*, cited in Abbott, *A Treatise of the Law relative to Merchant Ships and Seaman* (n 100 above) 251.

[104] *Barker v Hodgson* (1814) 3 M & S 267, 105 ER 612.

which the ships or cargo belonged and that for which they were destined, or commerce between them was prohibited, then the contract for the carriage was at an end. If the war, hostilities, or prohibition occurred after the commencement of the carriage but before delivery, the same rule probably applied. If the war or hostilities occurred between the place to which the ship or cargo belonged and any other nation for which they were not destined, the contract was not at an end, even though the carriage might be more difficult or hazardous as a result of the hostilities.[105] While contracts were dissolved by the outbreak of war, they were not dissolved where there was an embargo or a temporary restraint by governments[106] because the parties could have provided for such an event in their contract.

## 4. Exceptions and Qualifications to Contractual Liability

In certain instances the law qualified the absolute liability of a contracting party and excused him from performance without liability to pay damages. These exceptions were narrowly construed and applied by courts.

### (a) Common Carriers and Bailees

Bailment arose when there was a delivery of a thing for some object or purpose and upon a contract to conform to the object or purpose of the trust.[107] Where the bailment arose to carry or deliver goods, the bailee was excused from liability where he could establish[108] that the loss arose as a result of the acts of God or of the King's enemies.[109] An act of God was an inevitable accident which arose from natural causes, without human intervention.[110] It encompassed

---

[105] Abbott, *A Treatise of the Law relative to Merchant Ships and Seaman* (n 100 above) 427.

[106] *Hadley v Clarke* (1799) 8 TR 259, 101 ER 1377. Where, however, the embargo was imposed by another country which worked against a British merchant, the contract was at an end: *Touteng v Hubbard* (1802) 3 B & P 291, 127 ER 161. In this case, Lord Alvanley CJ thought that *Paradine v Jane* made good sense but that it would be wrong for a British merchant to effectively act against his country's own interests.

[107] The definition is paraphrased from J Story, *Commentaries on the Law of Bailments*, 8th edn (Boston, Little, Brown and Co, 1870) §110.

[108] *Forward v Pittard* (n 102 above).

[109] *Coggs v Bernard* (1703) (sub nom *Coggs v Barnard*) 2 Lord Raym 912, 918; 92 ER 109, 112 (Holt CJ). See further Chapter 1 (above). It became the case that in contracts for the carriage of goods by sea the express exceptions for the acts of God or of the King's enemies would be placed in the bill of lading or the charter party. A problem that could arise when foreign contracts of affreightment were entered into, in which most countries the civil law exceptions of overwhelming force (*vis major*) or accident without fault (*casus fortuitus*) were implied, because in such an instance, the English exceptions would be omitted. The resulting problem that could arise was that if the foreign law did not govern the contract, the ship owner or master would not have the protection that an English owner or master would have expressly sought: *Chartered Mercantile Bank of India v Netherlands India Steam Navigation Company* (1883) 6 B & S 101, 132; 122 ER 1135, 1146 (Willes J).

[110] *Company, Trent and Mersey Navigation v Wood* (1785) 4 Douglas 286, 290; 99 ER 884, 886 (Lord Mansfield).

loss by lightning or storms, by the perils of the seas, by an inundation or earthquake, or by a sudden death or illness.[111]

Fire was not an act of God unless caused by lightning.[112] Acts of the King's enemies were those of a public enemy.[113] It was immaterial whether the carriage of goods was by sea or by land.[114] The duties of a bailee, and the exceptions, arose by operation of the general law. This was significant for two reasons. First, parties could stipulate otherwise in their contracts; a bailee could expressly covenant to assume a liability excepted by the general law.[115] Secondly, because these exceptions arose by operation of the general law, they were within the first proposition of *Paradine v Jane*: where a duty was imposed by law and the party was unable to perform it without fault upon him, the law excused him. As Professor Treitel states, *Coggs v Bernard* stands outside the strict contractual liability imposed by *Paradine v Jane* rather than constituting an exception to it.[116] It is significant, however, that Blackburn J referred to 'the great case of *Coggs v Bernard*' in deciding *Taylor v Caldwell*. The significance apparent to contemporaries was that in a common form of contract the law would excuse cases of non-performance because of impossibility.[117] While this did not in principle form an exception to strict contractual liability, in practice, it operated to alleviate its harshness and to prevent absurdities.

## (b) Supervening Illegality

Where parties entered into a contract the performance of which was subsequently rendered illegal by British law, the contract was discharged without liability on the part of either party. Where the parties covenanted that a man would not do something that was lawful and an act of Parliament compelled him to do it, the contract was discharged: 'the statute repeals the covenant'.[118] Likewise, where the parties covenanted to do something lawful, and Parliament subsequently made this unlawful, the contract was discharged.[119] A complication, notably apparent in shipping, was the distinction drawn between supervening illegality brought

---

[111] Story, *Commentaries on the Law of Bailments* (n 107 above) §25.

[112] *Forward v Pittard* (n 102 above).

[113] *Forward v Pittard* (n 102 above).

[114] *Company, Trent and Mersey Navigation v Wood* (n 110 above) *ibid* (Buller J).

[115] Story, *Commentaries on the Law of Bailments* (n 107 above) §§10, 31. Story expressed some doubt as to whether or not there was a power to vary by contract the ability to accept loss which arose by inevitable accident: §36.

[116] Treitel, *Frustration and Force Majeure* (n 85 above) 31.

[117] Although the verdict of the jury was such as to indicate that they did not find that an act of God prevented the contractual performance of the defendant, the address of Cockburn CJ to the jury in *Cohen v Gaudet* (1863) 3 F & F 455, 176 ER 204 gives an indication of how the overall matrix of contractual and legal duties would operate in such instances.

[118] *Brewster v Kitchel* (1679) Holt KB 175, 90 ER 995 (Holt CJ). The principle was approved by Hannen J in *Baily v De Crespigny* (1869) LR 4 QB 180, 186.

[119] *Ibid*. Although, if the parties had covenanted to do something then unlawful, and the act of Parliament made it lawful, this did not repeal the covenant.

about by British law and supervening illegality brought about by foreign law. In the latter case, this was viewed as an impossibility in fact, for which the parties ought to have made contractual provision. Where the parties were prevented from contractual performance by reason of a supervening change in foreign law, the contract was therefore not discharged.[120] Where the supervening illegality arose under British law, the contract was dissolved at once, so absolutely and inevitably that not even the consent of the parties could revive it.[121] The proposition was at one point stated more broadly to encompass situations in which hostility between Britain and another state involved one or both of the parties in a breach of his moral duty to his Sovereign.[122] This did not develop into a broader ground of contractual discharge.

## (c) Contracts for Personal Services

In some instances a contract to provide personal services was discharged by the provider's death because his executors were not liable to tender the performance. The common law construed this exception, if it was one, narrowly.[123] As early as 1597 it had been held that

> a covenant lies against an executor in every case,—although he is not named; unless it be such a covenant as is to be performed by the person, of the testator, which they cannot perform.[124]

In the curious case of *Hall v Wright*,[125] it was said that where there was a contract for personal services which could only be performed by the contractor, his executors would not be liable for the performance. It was also stated that no liability attached to the person who contracted to perform a personal service but who became permanently disabled from so performing it.[126] The case law was inconsistent, however, and did not entirely support these statements. The

---

[120] *Blight v Page* (1801) 3 B & P 295, 127 ER 163; *Barker v Hodgson* (1814) 3 M & S 267, 270; 105 ER 612, 613: 'Is not the freighter the adventurer, who chalks out the voyage, and is to furnish at all events the subject matter out of which freight is to accrue?' (Lord Ellenborough CJ); *Spence v Chodwick* (1847) 10 QB 517, 116 ER 197.

[121] *Esposito v Bowden* (1855) 4 E & B 963, 979; 119 ER 359, 365 (Lord Campbell CJ). See also *Touteng v Hubbard* (1802) 3 B & P 291, 299; 127 ER 161, 166; *Esposito v Bowden* (1855) 4 E & B 963, 976; 119 ER 359, 364; and *Barker v Hodgson* (n 120 above) *ibid*.

[122] *Atkinson v Ritchie* (n 99 above) 534–5, 878 (Lord Ellenborough CJ).

[123] It is striking that such an excuse is not mentioned in either CG Addison, *A Treatise on the Law of Contracts*, 4th edn (London, Stevens and Norton, 1856) nor J Chitty, *A Practical Treatise on the Law of Contracts*, 5th edn JA Russell (ed) (London, S Sweet, 1853).

[124] *Hyde v Dean and Canons of Windsor* (1597) Cro Eliz 552, 78 ER 798. In addition, later cases such as *Boast v Firth* (n 204 below), *Poussard v Spiers* (n 215 below) and *Robinson v Davison* (n 204 below) were to rely directly upon *Taylor v Caldwell* rather than any earlier base.

[125] *Hall v Wright* (1859) El Bl & El 765, 120 ER 695.

[126] *Ibid* El Bl & El 765, 794–5; 120 ER 695, 706 (Pollock CB). Although Pollock wrote in dissent, this point seems to have been accepted by later judges. In the Queen's Bench, Crompton J made much the same point, *Hall v Wright* (1858) El & Bl El 746, 749; 120 ER 688, 690, and his reasons were accepted in the Exchequer at 788, 704 (Martin B).

contract had to be for services which could only be provided by the contracting party. A payment of money was not excused by death,[127] nor was a contract to take delivery of goods, unless the quantity of goods had to be selected or ordered by the now deceased contractor.[128] Where, however, the executors performed the deceased's services, they could recover for this performance.[129] It was also held in cases where the employee was unable to perform his services for several months that he was able to recover his wages,[130] even where he was permanently unable to perform.[131] In one instance the executors of a master's apprentice had to instruct the apprentice themselves or arrange for him to be instructed by someone skilled in the trade.[132] In short, the obiter dicta in *Hall v Wright* only applied where to attempt to enforce the contract would have resulted in an absurdity, or where the contract could only be performed personally.[133]

(d) The Sale of Goods

In *Taylor v Caldwell*, Blackburn J also relied upon the qualification of absolute liability which arose in a contract for the sale of goods. It was possible to transfer property in the goods from the vendor to the purchaser before delivery. If the property had passed and the goods perished before delivery, the vendor was excused from delivery.[134] He relied upon *Rugg v Minett*[135] and stated that it seemed to be based upon the ground that the destruction of the thing excused the vendor from fulfilling his contract to deliver. Although this has been criticised as an inadequate authority for his proposition,[136] other, uncited, authorities do exist to the same effect.[137] Blackburn J had discussed the matter extensively in his treatise on sale and provided an analysis of the law which was supported by other authorities: he therefore employed *Rugg v Minett* only to indicate where changes had first been introduced into the law.[138] Where

---

[127] *Sanders v Esterby* (1617) Croke Jac 417, 79 ER 356.

[128] *Wentworth v Cock* (1839) 10 Ad & El 42, 113 ER 17.

[129] *Marshall v Broadhurst* (1831) 1 Cr & Jervis 403, 148 ER 1480.

[130] *Beale v Thompson* (1804) 4 East 546, 102 ER 940; *Cuckson v Stones* (1858) 1 El & El 248, 120 ER 902.

[131] *Chandler v Grieves* (1792) 2 H Bl 606, 126 ER 730.

[132] *Walker v Hull* (1665) 1 Levinz 177, 83 ER 357.

[133] The point, and the concern about the consistency of the case law, is made in 'Contracts Impossible of Peformance', the *Irish Law Times*, reproduced in (1883) 16 *Central Law Journal* 105, 106–7.

[134] *Taylor v Caldwell* (n 1 above) 122 ER 309, 314.

[135] *Rugg v Minett* (1809) 11 East 210, 103 ER 985. Although he did not rely on this, he made the same statement in his treatise on the sale of goods: C Blackburn, *A Treatise on the Effect of The Contract of Sale* (London, William Benning & Co, 1845) 152

[136] Treitel, *Frustration and Force Majeure* (n 85 above) 2-017.

[137] See, eg, *Rohde v Thwaites* (1827) 6 B & C 388, 108 ER 495 and *Alexander v Gardner* (1835) 1 Bing NC 671, 131 ER 1276. See also S Comyn, *The Law of Contracts and Promises*, 2nd edn (London, Joseph Butterworth, 1824) 143.

[138] Blackburn, *A Treatise on the Effect of The Contract of Sale* (n 135 above) 151–61. It seems likely that he had *Rugg v Minett* in mind as the most significant of these cases rather than the one most applicable to his situation.

undelivered goods had not yet been ascertained, property remained in the vendor; if the goods were destroyed they were at the vendor's risk.[139]

## D. THE DECISION IN *TAYLOR v CALDWELL*

It was within this legal context that Taylor and Lewis sought damages from Caldwell and Bishop for their breach of contract in not supplying the Surrey Music Hall and Gardens for four Monday nights in the summer of 1861. They sought £58 to cover their wasted expenditures, for 'divers sums expended and expenses incurred by them in preparing for the concerts'.[140] It is interesting that the parties sought to recover the cost of their reliance rather than the profit they would have expected to receive for the concerts. Not only would the anticipated profit have been difficult to prove, but it may also have been slight: the advertisements for their fêtes[141] were small, not only in comparison with Jullien's extravaganzas but also with the competing attractions at Crystal Palace. While Taylor and Lewis offered only Sims Reeves as their main attraction,[142] Crystal Palace advertised attractions at length, of which Blondin, the conqueror of Niagara, was the principal one.[143] Two of the defendants' pleas were important. They pled not only that they were wholly exonerated and discharged from their agreement and the performance thereof but also that[144]

> there was a general custom of the trade and business of the plaintiffs and the defendants, with respect to which the agreement was made . . . and which was part of the agreement, that in the event of the Gardens and Music Hall being destroyed or so far damaged by accidental fire as to prevent the entertainments being given according to the intent of the agreement, between the time of making the agreement and the time appointed for the performance of the same, the agreement should be rescinded and at an end; and that the Gardens and Music Hall were destroyed and so far damaged by accidental fire as to prevent the entertainments, or any of them, being given . . . between the time of making the agreement and the first of the times appointed for the performance . . . and continued so destroyed and damaged until after the times appointed for the performance of the agreement had elapsed, without the default of the defendants or either of them.

[139] *Logan v Mesurier* (1847) 6 Moore 116, 13 ER 628.
[140] *Taylor v Caldwell* (n 1 above) 122 ER 309, 310. It has been impossible to ascertain whether or not one of these expenditures was a retainer paid to Sims Reeves for his planned appearance.
[141] *The Times* (11 June 1861) 1 and (10 June 1861) 1.
[142] Other artistes had been engaged by Taylor and Lewis in accordance with their contract with Caldwell and Bishop. The advertisements also announce the performances of Mesdames Poole, Palmer, Rebecca Isaacs, J Wells, M Wells, Emma Heywood, Mina Poole, Nina Vincent, and Annie Fowler; Messrs Sims Reeves, Montem Smith, JL Hatton, Fowler, Chaplin, Hneyr: *The Times* (11 June 1861) 1.
[143] *Ibid.*
[144] *Taylor v Caldwell* (n 1 above) 3 B & S 826, 827–8. It is interesting to see the argument arise in the context of theatrical and musical productions, an area in which one of the few exceptions to the absolute liability in contract existed, namely the rendering of personal services by performing artists.

At the trial[145] before Blackburn J and a common jury, the defendants appear to have argued that they were not bound to restore the Music Hall and that they had been prepared to provide the gardens, orchestra and the ruined Hall to the plaintiffs on the provision of the stipulated sum. The defendants failed to prove that it was the custom of the trade to rescind the contract in the event of fire or other accidental cause preventing the concerts from proceeding. A verdict was given for the plaintiffs, with liberty to the defendants to move to the court above to enter the verdict for them if that court was of the opinion that they were not liable.

It was on this basis that the matter was argued in January 1863 before Cockburn CJ, Wightman, Crompton and Blackburn JJ. The plaintiffs showed cause with two arguments. First, the contract was not a 'letting' of the Hall. This was important because had this been a lease, the plaintiffs would have been bound to pay the rent regardless of the condition of the land and buildings. Secondly, liability was absolute following *Paradine v Jane* and fire did not excuse the defendants from the performance that they had contractually assumed. This was a compelling argument, for the defendants had not contractually excused their performance in the event of the subject-matter's destruction and the jury had refused to find that it was trade custom that such destruction rescinded the contract. The defendants raised two weak arguments. First, the contract amounted to a demise and the plaintiffs were bound to pay the £100 for each of the four nights.[146] The argument was a weak one because the terms of the contract make clear that what the parties intended was a Jullien-like promenade concert in which the two parties co-operated to provide the concert. The defendants had undertaken to supply the Gardens and Music Hall *and* the necessary bands *and* a diversity of amusements and al fresco entertainments of various descriptions nightly.[147] The second argument raised by the defendants hinted at what they had failed to establish as a trade custom, namely that in the event that a supervening impossibility in the nature of an act of God arose, the contract was rescinded without liability on their part. The argument is recorded as 'the words "God's will permitting" override the whole agreement'.[148] It is unlikely that Blackburn J's decision is based on this argument because the words in the contract were not intended to subject the entire agreement to God's will, which had never been accepted as encompassing fires caused by man.[149] The most likely explanation for the words was that they qualified the attendance of the principal attraction, Sims Reeves. His attendance was always an uncertain matter and Pollock, in his memoirs, leaves little doubt that the words had been

---

[145] Court of Queen's Bench, 18 December 1861, *The Times* (19 December 1861) 10.

[146] Although not cited, *Izon v Gorton* (1839) 5 Bing NC 501 supports this argument.

[147] The other amusements listed were coloured minstrels, fireworks and illuminations, a ballet (but only if permitted), a wizard, Grecian statutes, tight-rope performances, rifle galleries, air-gun shooting, Chinese and Parisian games, boats on the lake and, if the weather permitted, other aquatic entertainments: *Taylor v Caldwell* (n 1 above) 3 B & S 826, 828–9; 122 ER 309, 311.

[148] *Taylor v Caldwell* (n 1 above) 3 B & S 826, 832; 122 ER 309, 312.

[149] *Forward v Pittard* (n 102 above).

inserted to cover the possibility that Sims Reeves would not attend.[150] The contract was thus drafted in such a way as to excuse the plaintiffs from the absolute obligation of providing the fickle star.

The plaintiffs should have succeeded.[151] It might have been hard upon the defendants to bear the risk of this loss, although there are hints that they received insurance for their losses.[152] Even if it were a hardship, the law was quite clear in its position that the defendants had, by their contract, taken upon themselves the burden of providing the Music Hall and, by not excepting its loss, assumed the risk of not providing it. The fire was caused by human actions initiated by the defendants.[153] Blackburn J used the case to introduce an incremental change to absolute liability in contract. That this incremental change was apparently of his initiative, rather than counsel's, is strikingly similar to his later decision in *Kennedy v Panama, New Zealand and Australian Royal Mail Co Ltd*,[154] a case which was to provide an explicit introduction of the doctrine of mistake into English contract law.[155] In these initiatives, Blackburn J was responsible for introducing both frustration and mistake into English contract law; his actions mark him as one of the 'creative minds in a creative age'.[156]

Blackburn J introduced this change into the law using a method similar to that which he was later to employ in *Kennedy's case*.[157] He began by describing the situation. The contract did not amount to a letting because possession had never passed; nothing, however, turned on the letting point.[158] In the giving of these concerts, the contract made clear that the existence of the Music Hall was essential to fulfill the contract because the contemplated entertainments could not be given without it. The destruction of the Music Hall was a supervening event, which occurred without the fault of either of the parties and was so

---

[150] Pollock, *For My Grandson, Remembrances of an Ancient Victorian* (n 43 above) 113.

[151] In this sense it might be said that a landmark case is one where the party expected to succeed does not.

[152] *The Times* (19 December 1861) 10. It is not clear whether or not the insurance would have covered such incidental losses as the plaintiffs'. It is also possible that the insurance was held by the defendant's landlord.

[153] For these reasons, fire was not regarded as an act of God because measures could be taken to prevent it or to put it out.

[154] *Kennedy v Panama, New Zealand and Australian Royal Mail Co Ltd* (1867) LR 2 QB 580, 8 B & S 571.

[155] The case was accepted by Lord Atkin in *Bell v Lever Bros* [1932] AC 161 as support for the doctrine, and although Lord Phillips was to criticise this in *The Great Peace* [2002] EWCA Civ 1407, [2002] 3 WLR 1617, it remains as one of the significant early mistake cases. Interestingly, counsel in *Kennedy's* case (n 154 above) raised *Taylor v Caldwell* in argument; Blackburn J did not rely upon it in giving judgment and it is likely that he drew a clear distinction between existing impossibility (which might be a mistake) and subsequent impossibility (which was to become frustration).

[156] CHS Fifoot, *Judge and Jurist in the Reign of Victoria* (London, Stevens & Sons, 1959) 135.

[157] Treitel, *Frustration and Force Majeure* is critical of the substance of Blackburn J's decision: (n 85 above) 42–4.

[158] In making this statement, Blackburn J can be interpreted as stating that these implied conditions could, in appropriate circumstances, be read into a lease. The matter was to be of considerable concern in the future development of the law until it was laid to rest in *National Carriers v Panalpina* (n 229 below).

complete a destruction that the contemplated concerts could not be given. The examination of promenade concerts indicates that Blackburn J was right: without the splendid and enormous Music Hall, there was no venue suitable for staging the concerts. The issue was whether the defendants were liable in the circumstances to make good the loss of the plaintiffs. The contract itself had made no provision for this event and so 'the answer to the question must depend upon the general rules of law applicable to such a contract'.[159]

Blackburn J set and affirmed the general rule: where there was a positive contract to do a thing not in itself unlawful, the contractor was obliged to perform or to pay damages. He then stated the incremental change:

> this rule is only applicable when the contract is positive and absolute, and not subject to any condition either express or implied.[160]

The condition was one which related to something essential for the performance of the contract. Where the parties clearly contemplated that the contract could not be fulfilled unless something existed—such that at the outset the continued existence of the thing formed the foundation of the contract—and neither party had warranted that such a thing would exist, if it ceased to exist without the fault of the contractor (and before any breach) such that performance became impossible, the parties were excused from their performance. As has been noted above, such an implication had been argued in previous cases[161] and had been rejected on the ground that such implications would tend to disturb commercial certainty and were not conditions that had been within the parties' contemplation. Blackburn J was at pains to point out that the implication was one made in furtherance of 'the great object' of construing the contract in such a way as to fulfill the intention of the contractors.[162] His assertion is an unlikely one. It seems entirely accurate that the parties had not considered the question of what would occur if the Music Hall had burnt down. It also seems entirely accurate on the basis of the existing law that they would have expected one or the other of them to have been entirely responsible: if it was a lease, the risk lay with the plaintiffs; if it was not, the risk lay with the defendants. While Blackburn J's assertion goes some way in meeting possible criticisms of the decision,[163] it does

---

[159] *Taylor v Caldwell* (n 1 above) 833, 312.

[160] *Ibid.*

[161] See, eg, *Atkinson v Ritchie* (n 99 above) in which counsel had argued that 'other necessary exceptions might be implied' and that a paramount duty was imposed by law to act for the benefit and safety of the crew, ship, cargo and state to which the master belonged; 10 East 531, 103 ER 877. The majority of the court had also been adamant in refusing to extend the exceptions and implied conditions in *Hall v Wright* (n 125 above).

[162] *Taylor v Caldwell* (n 1 above) 834, 312. It is on this basis that it has been argued that the case was one in which rules of law were devised behind the façade of the will theory of contract; DJ Ibbetson, *A Historical Introduction to the Law of Obligations* (Oxford, Oxford University Press, 1999) 224.

[163] Primarily that the decision was inconsistent with the slightly earlier case of *Hall v Wright* (n 125 above).

not reflect the underlying assumptions of the parties. If it did, it seems likely that the jury would have found such a trade usage.[164]

To demonstrate that this principle already existed in English law, Blackburn J argued both by comparison and by analogy. For comparison, he chose the civil law of Justinian's *Digest* and Pothier's *Treatise of Obligations*. In doing so he recognised that while the civil law was not authority in an English court 'it affords great assistance in investigating the principles on which the law is grounded'.[165] The comparison bolstered the conclusion that Blackburn J had reached on the matter.[166] Blackburn J stated that in Roman law an exception was implied in the obligation such that if the foundation of the contract ceased to exist through no fault of either party, then the parties were excused from further performance. Blackburn J relied upon portions of the *Digest*[167] which dealt with continued life of a slave, and he probably used it because it tied together nicely with the analogy he was about to make with common law contracts for personal services. His use has been criticised by Buckland,[168] who pointed out that the Romans identified common law supervening impossibility as *casus*. Its effect in different transactions was not always the same. Roman law recognised two forms of contractual obligations; the remedies under the older system were *stricti iuris* and under the later system, the remedies were *bonae fidei iudicia*. The obligations in the former system were unilateral, in the latter system they were bilateral.[169] A contract of hire fits within the second system. In the situation where unilateral obligations co-existed, such as a *stipulatio* met with a counter stipulation, *casus* had the effect of releasing one party but if this occurred before the other party had performed his obligation, the other party would still be bound: 'the release was of the party, no less and no more'.[170] Blackburn J's use of Roman law was inapposite in reaching the conclusion that *casus* excused both the parties because he relied upon texts that were on *stricti iuris* unilateral relations. *Casus* would only release both parties where *casus* made both performances impossible. Blackburn J apparently failed to realise that the texts upon which he relied had nothing to do with a bilateral bonae fidei contract of hire. In a bonae fidei contract, the release of the other party is not made by a release by *casus*

---

[164] It may be that the entire basis for Blackburn J's decision was that the jury, being a common jury and not a special jury, simply came to the wrong conclusion as to trade custom. Judges were often critical of the abilities of juries but in this case such an argument is too speculative to be asserted strongly.

[165] *Taylor v Caldwell* (n 1 above) 3 B & S 826, 835; 122 ER 309, 313.

[166] The comparative use of the civil law was not that different from the use contemporary judges have made of French and German law.

[167] *Digest*, 45.I. 23, 33.

[168] WW Buckland, 'Casus and Frustration in Roman and Common Law' (1932–33) 46 *Harvard Law Review* 1281, 1287–8.

[169] *Ibid* 1281.

[170] Buckland, 'Casus and Frustration in Roman and Common Law' (n 168 above).

but on the very different principle that, *ex fide bona*, a party ought not to be called upon to pay for a service he has not had.[171]

Buckland concluded that 'the Roman law cannot be made responsible for the rules laid down'.[172] Blackburn J's use of Pothier's *Treatise of Obligations* is accurate in applying what Pothier stated: that a debtor is freed from his obligation when the thing which forms the matter and object of the obligation is destroyed:

> the debtor of a specific thing is discharged from his obligation, when the thing is lost, without any act, default or delay on his part.[173]

This was

> subject to an exception, when he has, by a particular clause in the contract, expressly assumed the risk of such loss upon himself.[174]

While it is questionable whether or not the principle was applicable in the common law,[175] Blackburn J clearly sought to base his incremental change upon a broader principle.[176] Pothier was regarded by lawyers of the era as a source of rational and scientific jurisprudence and he was a writer with whom Blackburn J had a great deal of familiarity.[177] Neither the Digest nor Pothier supported the implied term solution that Blackburn J devised, and Buckland was right when he wrote that the decision in *Taylor v Caldwell* 'is a little surprising'.[178] The use of comparative materials was likely undertaken to indicate that other legal systems were able to excuse performance in cases of impossibility.

[171] Buckland, 'Casus and Frustration in Roman and Common Law' (n 168 above) 1287.

[172] Buckland, 'Casus and Frustration in Roman and Common Law' (n 168 above) 1300.

[173] RJ Pothier, *Treatise of Obligations*, WD Evans (trans) (London, Strahan, 1806) P III. c VI, A III §633. Some confusion exists as to the exact passage due to the reporter's inaccurate citation. Pothier had started from the general proposition that 'there cannot be any debt without something being due, which forms the matter and object of the obligation whence it follows, that if that thing is destroyed, as there is no longer any thing to form the matter and object of the obligation, there can be no longer any obligation. The extinction of the thing due, therefore, necessarily induces the extinction of the obligation': *ibid* P III. c VI, A I §613. 19th century civilian lawyers in France and Germany faced their own difficulties with regard to the impossibility they had inherited as a part of their Roman legacy: see J Gordley, *Foundations of Private Law* (Oxford, Oxford University Press, 2005) ch 15 'Impossibility and Unexpected Circumstances'.

[174] Pothier, *Treatise of Obligations* (n 173 above) P III. c VI, A III §633.

[175] Buckland and McNair argued that until this decision and the cases that followed it the common law position was almost exactly opposite that of Roman law: *Roman Law and Common Law* (London, Cambridge University Press, 1965) 242.

[176] It was a technique that Blackburn J employed again in *Kennedy's case* (n 154 above) when he stated that the decision in *Street v Blay* (1831) 2 B & Ad 456 was the same as the Civil law: *Digest* 18.1.9, 10 and 11. In that case, Blackburn J likely sought to rationalise the existing English cases around a Roman principle.

[177] Blackburn J was the author of the then leading treatise on the sale of goods, *A Treatise on the Effect of The Contract of Sale* (n 135 above) and he employed Pothier's writings within the treatise as an analytical tool. He was, however, careful to warn his readers that Pothier's positions were not necessarily universally true of the civil law and 'far less to be taken as authorities for English Law': 172. He was cognisant of the substantially different results that arose in the civilian and common law legal systems: 188–9.

[178] Buckland, 'Casus and Frustration in Roman and Common Law' (n 168 above) 1288.

Having set out what he understood to be the principle in the civil law for comparative purposes, Blackburn J proceeded to reason by analogy with the existing qualifications to the principle of absolute liability in English law. He sought to ascertain the underlying rationale to these qualifications in order to apply this rationale.[179] Happily for Blackburn J, he discovered that the underlying rationale in the common law was entirely in accordance with the principles upon which the civil law proceeded. The three qualifications that he chose were: contracts for personal services; contracts for the sale of goods; and contracts which involved the loan of chattels or bailment. There is a common weakness shared between all three of these instances and this weakness undermines Blackburn J's attempt to ascertain the underlying rationale. The weakness is that it is arguable that in none of the instances did the contract cover the impossibility that arose. It is likely, however, that Blackburn J considered these applications to make readily apparent that the rule in *Paradine v Jane* was one to which the law admitted certain practical exceptions, and that another exception would not, by itself, remove the rule. It was also important to indicate that this was an area in which his development would have limited scope. He may also have felt it necessary to clearly justify what he was doing because the course of action he took does not appear to have received the benefit of counsel's arguments.

Blackburn J examined the authorities[180] in which the obligation to perform a personal service had not been found to be binding upon the executors following the provider's death. This appeared as a genuine qualification to absolute liability, although it was very narrowly construed. It was also the case that where one sought the personal services of an individual, it was not contemplated by the recipient that the services would be performed by another.[181] In these cases, Blackburn J found the underlying rationale that excused the parties from their non-performance was that the nature of the contract implied a condition of the continued existence of the contractor, or his essential abilities, to perform the personal services. This is an interesting conclusion to reach and one contrary to *Hall v Wright*. Blackburn J had no hesitation in reaching the conclusion rejected in the earlier case. The possibility that the law refused to make the executors liable because in these instances it would create an absurdity was not considered.

Blackburn J then noted that this implied condition of the continued existence of 'the life', or 'the abilities of the life', could also be discerned in instances where the contract depended upon the continued existence of a 'thing'. He began with the contract of sale, and in those instances where the property, and thus the risk, had passed to the purchaser who awaited delivery. If the chattel perished without fault of the vendor, the vendor was excused from the obligation of the

---

[179] Treitel has pointed out that Blackburn J employed the same technique in *Rylands v Fletcher*, deducing a general principle from a series of specific examples, in order to create a strict liability in tort. Treitel, *Frustration and Force Majeure* (n 85 above) 42.

[180] *Hyde v The Dean and Canons of Windsor* (n 124 above), *Marshall v Broadhurst* (n 129 above), *Wentworth v Cock* (n 128 above), *Hall v Wright* (n 125 above).

[181] Although, as we have seen, authority did exist that where suitable arrangements could be made, this would be acceptable: *Walker v Hull* (n 132 above).

delivery of the chattel although the purchaser was required to pay the purchase price. Blackburn J supported this rule with *Rugg v Minett*[182] and Pothier's *Treatise on the Contract of Sale*, as translated by Blackburn in his own treatise.[183] Pothier stated that when the thing due ceased to exist, so too did the obligation. Thus, in a contract for sale, as soon as the sale was perfected, the thing sold is at the risk of the purchaser although it has not yet been delivered. If it should perish without the fault of the vendor, the purchaser was still bound to pay for it. The underlying rationale was that English law recognised that the continued existence of the thing was an implied condition of the contract; if the thing ceased to exist without the fault of the contracting party, the contracting party was excused performance. There are two weaknesses to this. First, it would be an absurdity to require the vendor to deliver that which no longer existed. Secondly, because the parties contracted on the basis that the sale of specific, or ascertained, goods acted to pass property and thus risk to the purchaser, the vendor had never assumed an obligation to deliver the goods in the event of destruction.

The third qualification Blackburn J examined was the loan of chattels and bailments.[184] Where the chattel perished without fault of the bailee or carrier the impossibility of performance excused the borrower or bailee of his obligation. This use is subject to two criticisms. First, Blackburn J's characterisation of the exception[185] was over broad. The law recognised different divisions of bailments dependent upon whom the bailment sought to benefit.[186] Attendant upon these different divisions were different standards of care[187]. Secondly, in all of these cases, it was understood from the outset that the bailee or carrier did not undertake an absolute liability for the care of the thing given over to him.

The utility of Blackburn's use of these three instances is that they were all instances in which the law allowed parties to structure their affairs to allow them to predict with whom the risk of destruction lay. They were also instances in which the law operated to remove the prospect of a subsequent impossibility from arising. The use of these instances would remind lawyers that absolute liability did not arise in all instances and that the creation of another instance would not necessarily be objectionable. It would have been impossible for the

---

[182] *Rugg v Minett* (1809) 11 East 210, 103 ER 985. Treitel, *Frustration and Force Majeure* has criticised this as an inappropriate choice as it was not truly a case involving specific goods (n 85 above).

[183] Blackburn refers to *Blackburn on the Contract of Sale*, but he does so because he has translated the relevant portion of Pothier's *Contract of Sale* into English; an English version of Pothier's work existed in America but seemingly not in England at this time. It is interesting that Blackburn felt the need to direct readers to a translation from French into English but not from the Latin of the *Digest* into English. The portion of *Blackburn on the Contract of Sale* referred to contains no opinion of Blackburn's.

[184] He cites *Sparrow v Sowgate* (1623) Jones W 29, 82 ER 16; *Williams v Lloyd* (1628) Jones W 179, 82 ER 95; and *Coggs v Bernard* (n 109 above).

[185] '[I]n all contracts of loan of chattels or bailments if the performance of the promise of the borrower or bailee to return the things lent or bailed, becomes impossible because it has perished, this impossibility . . . excuses the borrower or bailee from the performance', *Taylor v Caldwell* (n 1 above) 3 B & S 826, 838–9.

[186] Story, *Commentaries on the Law of Bailments* (n 107 above) §3.

[187] Story, *Commentaries on the Law of Bailments* (n 107 above) §9.

concerts to be held without the Music Hall; to award damages would have been an absurdity. Blackburn J drew the underlying principle that[188]

> in contracts in which the performance depends on the continued existence of a given person or thing, a condition is implied that the impossibility of performance arising from the perishing of the person or thing shall excuse the performance. In none of these cases is the promise in words other than positive, nor is there any express stipulation that the destruction of the person or thing shall excuse the performance; but that excuse is by law implied, because from the nature of the contract it is apparent that the parties contracted on the basis of the continued existence of the particular person or chattel.

Blackburn J found that the parties had contracted on the basis of the continued existence of the Music Hall and this existence was essential to performance: when it ceased to exist without fault of either party both were excused from their further obligations. The court found for the defendants. The effect of the decision was to ensure that the entire loss arising from the venture did not fall upon one party alone but was shared between both contracting parties.[189]

Blackburn J's decision did not seek to challenge the rule in *Paradine v Jane*; indeed, it reaffirms this rule. The judgment hints that the situation before the court was distinguishable from *Paradine v Jane* where the tenant's performance was still possible. Rather than distinguish the earlier case, Blackburn J sought a different route around the problem of absolute liability: one of an implied condition. There was nothing new in the device of an implied term. What was new was that the device was employed by the court where counsel had not argued it. The essential question that arises from the judgment in *Taylor v Caldwell* is why the court chose to imply these conditions at all. Unfortunately, the answer to this question is by no means clear. A number of possible answers present themselves. First, there had been criticisms of this rule of absolute liability in the 19th century:

> the doctrine that it [*Paradine v Jane*] lays down is in direct opposition to common sense and common justice. For the accidents of life are so various, that it is impossible to foresee them all, and to require of a contracting party that he should foresee and provide for them, is to require an impossibility.[190]

It seems probable that this difficulty was one which Blackburn J had considered. A second possible answer is that the reluctance of courts to reallocate liability in cases of subsequent impossibility had been rationalised on the basis that to do so was to re-write the parties' contract: that the courts would create a contract for the parties by their decision.[191] The use of an implied condition sought to

---

[188] *Taylor v Caldwell* (n 1 above) 3 B & S 826, 839; 122 ER 309314.

[189] Whether this was a just allocation of the losses arising cannot be ascertained: we know that the plaintiffs suffered certain reliance losses, it seems equally possible—given the known facts—that the defendants had suffered losses in engaging the diverse amusements and readying the hall for the concerts.

[190] Anon, 'Art III. Execution of a Contract Impossible' (n 86 above) 251.

[191] Anon, 'Art III. Execution of a Contract Impossible' (n 86 above) 252.

prevent judicial remaking on the basis of the fulfillment of the parties' intention. A third possibility lies in the fact that the decision as to whether or not something came within an existing qualification was one made with reference to previous case law on the effects of fires, lightning, embargoes and so forth. It may have appeared easier to devise a form of exception, which, although a disguised rule of law, operated in accordance with the actual facts of each given case. A fourth possibility is that the use of an implied condition to excuse performance had the effect of discharging the performance owed by both parties. The effect of such a discharge has the appearance of equality in the allocation of loss, or at least, appears in principle more attractive than making one of the parties bear all of the loss. A fifth possibility lies in the intellect of Blackburn J himself. He was a learned lawyer who sought to order and to explain the structure of the common law in such a way as to facilitate future development. His efforts in *Taylor v Caldwell* were not unique; they were early indications of a great common law judge. He may well have found this an unsatisfactory area of law; it is striking that he appeared as counsel or was the reporter in a number of supervening impossibility cases. As one familiar with the civil law, he was aware that other legal systems dealt with supervening impossibility by excusing further performance. To implement such excuses directly was not a route open to him and he chose an accepted common law route: the incremental change. That it was based upon an implied condition—implied from the parties' intent—fitted neatly within the common law of contract as it was then developing. In this sense, it may be that the decision in *Taylor v Caldwell* is a manifestation of an increasingly sophisticated legal system.

That all of these possible answers, either in isolation or in conjunction with each other, existed can be seen within a sixth possible answer. *Taylor v Caldwell* is, in many ways, best seen as a continuation of the debate that arose in *Hall v Wright*.[192] The case was odd: the plaintiff sued her fiancé for a breach of promise of marriage. The defendant alleged, inter alia, that he was excused from performing the agreement because after the promise had been made he became, and remained, afflicted with a serious bodily disease.[193] He was incapable of marriage due to the great danger to his life and was unfit for the married state. Blackburn J described the case as 'much discussed'[194] and *The Law Times* wrote of an 'astounding decision . . . at variance with the dictates of reason, justice and morality'.[195] It caused great divisions of opinion amongst the judges who heard it. The Queen's Bench judges were equally divided[196] and when the junior judge

---

[192] The decision was criticised on many grounds. See, eg 'Contracts Impossible of Performance', originally published in *The Irish Law Times* and republished in (1883) 16 *Central Law Journal* 105.

[193] From the descriptions given in the case, it appears that he was afflicted with tuberculosis. Sadly, his predictions proved true for he died before the Exchequer Chamber gave judgment: (1860) 6 *The Jurist (NS)* 193, 198.

[194] *Taylor v Caldwell* (n 1 above) 3 B & S 826, 833; 122 ER 309, 310.

[195] *The Law Times* (3 December 1859) 121. The author was considerably aggrieved that the woman had received the money without having to take the man with it.

[196] *Hall v Wright* (1858) El & Bl El 746, 120 ER 688.

withdrew his opinion, the defendant succeeded. On the plaintiff's appeal to the Exchequer Chamber,[197] the judges were as divided: four found for the plaintiff and three for the defendant. The division turned on whether the rule of absolute liability established in *Paradine v Jane* applied to all contracts or whether it was limited to certain kinds of contracts. Another fundamental difference was whether or not it was reasonable or necessary to imply conditions into the performance of a contract such that if these conditions were not met, the parties were discharged from performance. The majority applied the rule in *Paradine v Jane* because it was thought that contractual certainty required it and that it was better to adhere to this rule than to create an exception which destroyed legal certainty and could be generally inconvenient.[198]

The real division between the judges in the Exchequer Chamber lay in whether or not to imply a condition in these circumstances. It was also expressed that to imply a condition would allow a party to set up their own infirmity as a ground for discharge[199] and that to imply a condition into the contract would be to guess at the parties' contract rather than to construe it.[200] The dissenting judges viewed the contract as subject to implied conditions, including the fitness of the parties: once these failed, performance was discharged. The authority of *Paradine v Jane* was misapplied because it begged the question of whether or not the contract was one made subject to implied conditions.[201] In reaching this conclusion, the dissenting judgments referred to the personal services contracts in which death excused performance, or at least, meant that the executors were not obliged to perform the services. The dissenting judgments recognised that the conditions are implied out of necessity or in the interests of reasonability.[202] Pollock CB acknowledged that to imply a condition in these cases was really to create a legal exception.[203] It is plausible that what Blackburn J did in *Taylor v Caldwell* was to revisit the decision in *Hall v Wright* and place the law upon a more secure footing.[204]

## 1. Contemporary Reactions to the Decision

Whatever the reasons behind Blackburn J's extraordinary decision, it is clear that *Taylor v Caldwell* did not establish the doctrine of frustration whereby the

[197] *Hall v Wright* (1859) El & Bl El 765, 120 ER 695.
[198] This view is best expressed in the reasons of Martin B, *Hall v Wright* (n 197 above) El & Bl El 765, 789.
[199] *Hall v Wright* (n 197 above) 792 (Williams J).
[200] *Hall v Wright* (n 197 above) 785 (Willes J).
[201] *Hall v Wright* (n 197 above) 777 (Bramwell B), 775 (Watson B).
[202] *Hall v Wright* (n 197 above) 784 (Bramwell B).
[203] *Hall v Wright* (n 197 above) 794.
[204] In *Boast v Firth* (1868) LR 4 CP 1, the judge distinguished *Hall v Wright* in preference to the decision in *Taylor v Caldwell* (at 8). The relationship between the two cases is also explained in the decision in *Robinson v Davison* (1871) LR 6 Exch 269.

parties were excused from contractual performance when a supervening impossibility arose. This can be seen from the reaction of contemporary observers. The small and incremental nature of the change provided by Blackburn J attracted almost no immediate reaction in legal journals. There was no recognition that this decision worked against the absolute liability imposed by *Paradine v Jane*, let alone an acknowledgement that a new doctrine of contract law had begun. *The Jurist* did not report the case and briefly summarised it.[205] *The Solicitor's Journal* gave a brief summary and explained that this was a case of implied conditions in contract.[206] *The Law Times* reported the original hearing of the case at the end of Hilary Term[207] and noted that judgment was pending[208] but never did manage to report the decision itself. In fairness, the paper was, at the time, rather concerned about the merits of pending legislation prohibiting poisonous birdseed. The *American Law Register* noted briefly that the parties had been discharged from performance because of impossibility but went no further.[209] After the decision in *Appleby v Myers*[210] it was recognised in the *Jurist* that *Taylor v Caldwell* seems to have worked a change upon the law, but neither the nature nor the desirability of the change were commented upon.[211]

## 2. Later Decisions

Decisions shortly after *Taylor v Caldwell* indicate that the judiciary did not regard the case as establishing a new doctrine. *Appleby v Myers* is regarded as a case which approved *Taylor v Caldwell*, and yet a careful reading does not support this interpretation. The court found the application of implied terms useful in reaching its conclusion but did not accept the argument of counsel that the decision in *Taylor v Caldwell* meant that the entire contract was subject to the implied term that the factory would continue to exist and that performance on both sides was discharged when it no longer did. In addressing this argument, Montague Smith J was sceptical of *Taylor v Caldwell*:

> the Court of Queen's Bench *may have properly adopted and applied this principle* in the case of the contract before them: but we think it cannot be correctly applied to the present case (emphasis added).[212]

---

[205] (1863) IX(1) *The Jurist (NS)* 48 and 163. It was summarised under two headings: one being contract and implied terms and conditions, and the other being landlord and tenant, implied conditions
[206] (1862–63) VII *The Solicitor's Journal & Reporter* (13 June 1863) 602.
[207] *The Law Times* (28 January 1863) 184.
[208] *The Law Times* (11 April 1863) 313.
[209] (1863–64) 12 *American Law Register* 442.
[210] *Appleby v Myers* (1866) LR 1 CP 615.
[211] Anon, 'Inevitable Accident', reprinted in (1866) 2 *Upper Canada Law Journal (NS)* 236.
[212] *Appleby v Myers* (n 210 above) 622. When stating the implied condition in *Taylor v Caldwell*, the judge refers to it as one stated 'no doubt in general terms'.

Courts declined to imply conditions in cases where they could usefully have been employed.[213] Absolute liability co-existed with the new implied conditions of *Taylor v Caldwell* for some time.[214] There are indications that Blackburn J himself did not see his incremental change as one which was intended to over-turn the doctrine of absolute liability and that the use of an implied condition was to be used sparingly, only in the cases of supervening impossibilities which could work an absurdity.[215] The early judicial treatment of the decision sup-ports the view that it was intended to introduce an incremental change based on sanctity of contract, rather than a new doctrine which undermined this sanctity.

## 3. Commentators

The 19th century commentators regarded *Taylor v Caldwell* as adding a limited exception to the existing qualifications to *Paradine v Jane*. In their second report on contract,[216] the Indian Law Commissioners noted that a person who fails to do an act he has undertaken to do by contract shall pay damages to the person to whom the obligation was owed. An express 'Exception' was set out to this general rule that[217]

> [a] man incurs no liability through the non-performance of an act which he has engaged by contract to do, where, since the date of the contract, the performance of the act has been rendered unlawful, or has been made impossible by some event of which he did not, expressly or by implication, take upon himself the risk.

The illustration of this exception was *Taylor v Caldwell*, suitably modified to give a hire price in rupees. The resulting Indian Contract Act extended the prin-ciple of *Taylor v Caldwell* to make it an implied condition in all contracts that the performance should remain possible.[218]

Addison's treatise explained *Taylor v Caldwell* as an exception to the rule of absolute liability on the grounds that a supervening act of God had made

---

[213] See, eg, *Baily v De Crespigny* (1869) LR 4 QB 180; *Carstairs v Taylor* (1871) LR 6 Exch 217, *The Teutonia* (1872) LR 4 PC 171; *Jacobs v Crédit Lyonnais* (1884) 12 QBD 589.

[214] See, eg, *Re Arthur* (1880) 14 Ch D 603; *Chartered Mercantile Bank of India v Netherlands India Steam Navigation Company* (1883) 6 B & S 101, 122 ER 1135; 10 QBD 540; *Lloyd v Guibert* (1865) LR 1 QB 115. In some cases, the co-existence was for some time: Treitel, *Frustration and Force Majeure* (n 85 above) 53–5.

[215] In *Ford v Cotesworth* (1868) LR 4 QB 127; affirmed (1870) LR 5 QB 544, Blackburn J gave a decision in which he relied upon *Barker v Hodgson* (n 104 above), a case based upon *Paradine v Jane*. He also appears to approve of counsel's argument based upon absolute liability in *Geipel v Smith* (1872) LR 7 QB 404, 407. In a contract for personal services in which the artiste was unable to perform due to illness, *Poussard v Spiers* (1876) 1 QBD 410, 24 WR 870, Blackburn J did not con-sider the application of *Taylor v Caldwell* despite counsel's argument on this point.

[216] *Copies of Papers showing the present position of the Question of a Contract Law for India* (1868), No 239.

[217] *Ibid* para 28, 12.

[218] F Pollock, *Principles of Contract At Law and In Equity* (London, Stevens and Sons, 1876) 353 explained that this was a departure from English law.

the performance impossible unless the terms of the contract make clear that the obligor was bound in any event.[219] Addison's treatise was an old one and the addition is made without substantive change to the topic. More recently composed treatises were written by Anson and Pollock. Anson dealt briefly with the subject of subsequent impossibility.[220] The general rule was set out in *Paradine v Jane*. To this rule, the law admitted three limited exceptions. The second of these was based upon *Taylor v Caldwell*: where the continued existence of a specific thing was essential to the performance of the contract and it was destroyed without the fault of the parties, a discharge operated. As was his fashion, Pollock gave a somewhat more convoluted account which set out the general rule in *Paradine v Jane* and then explained *Taylor v Caldwell* as an exception 'where the performance of the contract depends upon the existence of a specific thing'.[221]

## E. HOW THE EXCEPTION BECAME THE RULE

Blackburn J's incremental change might have disappeared if it had not received desirable attention. Nothing in the immediate treatment of the case indicated that it would be considered the foundation of a new contractual doctrine. Within two decades, however, the flexibility of the approach offered by an implied condition became apparent and the case was frequently raised in arguments. As this occurred, the link between *Taylor v Caldwell* and discharge for impossibility was built up.[222] From a judicial perspective, this fictitious device allowed courts to impose a rule of law while appearing to do so on the grounds of the parties' intentions. The device had the advantage of allowing a contract to be discharged not only in the face of a subsequent impossibility, but also in the face of radically changed circumstances which left performance possible, but without the purpose the parties had intended.[223] It also included situations in which the adventure was frustrated; primarily shipping cases where the event so disrupted the schedule of the contract that its purpose was lost. The broadness of this device allowed many different events to be swept up under the new rubric of 'impossibility' or 'frustration'. In this process, Blackburn J's implied condition device became a doctrine. As McElroy noted, it was the application of the case to the 'Coronation Cases' and to the numerous cases that arose from the

---

[219] CG Addison, *A Treatise on the Law of Contracts*, 9th edn (London, Horace Smith, Stevens and Sons, 1892) 133–4.

[220] Sir WR Anson, *Principles of the English Law of Contract* (Oxford, Clarendon Press, 1879) 314–17. The other two exceptions were legal impossibility and a contract for personal services.

[221] Pollock (n 218 above) 415.

[222] In addition to the treatises cited above, the treatment by CG Tiedeman, 'Impossibility of Performance as a Defense to Actions Ex Contractu' (1881) 12 *Central Law Journal* 4, 8–10 illustrates the process underway from an American perspective.

[223] The 'Coronation Cases'—in which a room or a seat was still capable of occupation, but not of allowing the viewing of the cancelled coronation—are a good example.

massive disruption of commercial activities brought about by the First World War that extended the doctrine enormously.[224] By 1920, Scrutton LJ remarked that the numerous cases decided on this new exception had made a 'serious breach in the ancient proposition' of *Paradine v Jane*.[225] The exception had come to dominate the rule. Glanville Williams noted, with some despair, that in the half-century following the decision, three separate concepts were swept together under the *Taylor v Caldwell* ruling: first, the discharge of contracts for physical impossibility (those actually covered by the ruling); secondly, the frustration of the adventure, or commercial impossibility; and thirdly, the discharge of contracts for a failure of consideration.[226] It is in this sense that *Taylor v Caldwell* marked a starting point for the development of a new doctrine that was not fully developed until the House of Lords' decisions in *Davis Contractors Ltd v Fareham UDC*,[227] in which Lord Radcliffe recognised that the doctrine of frustration did not depend upon a condition implied by the parties but upon the operation of a rule of law[228] and *National Carriers Ltd v Panalpina (Northern) Ltd*,[229] in which it was recognised that the doctrine of frustration extended to leases.[230] In the intervening period, the ruling in *Taylor v Caldwell* was to cause an enormous number of problems.[231]

It is correct to view *Taylor v Caldwell* as a landmark case in the law of contract. We can trace the development of a new contractual doctrine of frustration to this case because it was the case which initiated questions about the absolute liability of contractual obligations and instigated the change which developed into a new doctrine. And while frustration is not entirely the right legal term for the situation that arose between Taylor and Caldwell, it is an entirely suitable term to describe the Surrey Music Hall and those involved with it during its short existence.

[224] RG McElroy, *Impossibility of Performance* (Cambridge, Cambridge University Press, 1941) 133.

[225] *Ralli Brothers v Compañia Naviera* [1920] 2 KB 287, 300.

[226] McElroy, *Impossibility of Performance* (n 224 above) 'Introduction', xxvii–xl.

[227] *Davis Contractors Ltd v Fareham UDC* [1956] 1 AC 696 (HL).

[228] Lord Radcliffe stated, after considering the fiction of implied terms: 'perhaps it would be simpler to say at the outset that frustration occurs whenever the law recognizes that without default of either party a contractual obligation has become incapable of being performed because the circumstances in which performance is called for would render it a thing radically different from that which was undertaken by the contract. *Non haec in foedera veni*. It was not this that I promised to do': *ibid* 728–9.

[229] *National Carriers Ltd v Panalpina (Northern) Ltd* [1981] 1 AC 675 (HL).

[230] And by doing so, arguably finished Blackburn's original statement that it did not matter if the contract between Taylor and Caldwell was a lease or not.

[231] These problems are beyond the scope of this paper, but they revolve around the difficulty of utilising the fiction of implied terms, loss allocation following the discharge of the contract, and the restitution of unjust enrichments. The underlying problem of when something is the foundation of a contract remains in English law.

# 7

# Smith v Hughes (1871)

## JOHN PHILLIPS

### A. INTRODUCTION

T HE PURPOSE OF this paper is to demonstrate that *Smith v Hughes*[1] has been wrongly interpreted in the context of the authority on which it is based and has been given an exaggerated importance in the law of contract. It has led us on a false trail, where (at least in some contexts) mistakes or misapprehensions by those entering contractual obligations are treated as negativing consensus. Outside those cases which can be properly explained on the basis of misrepresentation or uncertainty, in this author's view a more appropriate mechanism for determining whether mistake should have an exculpatory effort is unconscionability. This reflects an underlying philosophy that the entry into a contract involves an assumption of risk (with a corollary duty imposed on each party to protect its position). Any effect on the validity of the assumed obligation should not arise from a mistake per se. Rather the focus of the inquiry should be directed to any conduct of the contracting party which may have exploited the disadvantaged position of the mistaken party.

The view that there is a link between mistake and an absence of consensus does not have a long pedigree. Prior to *Smith v Hughes* there was little discussion of the relationship in the standard contract texts.[2] Indeed, in these texts mistake is not recognisable as the separate doctrine it has become today.[3] The terminology of mistake only came into our legal vocabulary in the early 20th century. So far as precedent allows, this author argues it should be jettisoned.

---

[1] *Smith v Hughes* (1871) LR 6 QB 597.

[2] See, generally, AWB Simpson, 'Innovation in Nineteenth Century Contract Law' (1975) 91 *Law Quarterly Review* 247, 267.

[3] For example, J Chitty, *Law of Contracts not under Seal*, 5th edn, J Russell (ed) (London, S Sweet, 1853) refers to mistake only in the context of the following: rectification (at 112); the recovery of money paid (at 96); errors in the particulars of a contract for the sale of land (at 267); errors in items set out in an account stated (at 572); the principle that the parol evidence rule cannot be applied to explain a written contract in the absence of an ambiguity in its terms (at 96).

## B. THE FACTS

The facts of *Smith v Hughes* are well known, but they are re-stated here to put the case and arguments in proper context.

Smith, the plaintiff, a farmer, offered to sell oats at 35 shillings a quarter to Hughes, the defendant, a trainer of racehorses. The plaintiff showed a sample of oats to the defendant's manager (the defendant's brother), who said he would like to show the sample to the defendant. The next day the defendant wrote to offer to buy the oats at 34 shillings per quarter, this price being agreed. Some of the oats which the defendant had ordered were delivered, but the defendant afterwards returned them on the ground that the oats delivered were new oats and he thought he was buying old oats. The plaintiff subsequently brought an action for the price in respect of the oats which had been delivered and, additionally, an action for damages for the loss he had made on the re-sale of the oats that the defendant had agreed to buy, but refused to take. The trial judge left two questions to the jury (as stated by Cockburn CJ)[4]:

> first, whether the word 'old' had been used with reference to the oats in the conversation between the plaintiff and the defendant's manager; secondly, whether the plaintiff had believed that the defendant believed, or was under the impression, that he was contracting for old oats.

If, in either case, the answer was in the affirmative then the jury was directed to enter a verdict for the defendant. The jury found for the defendant, but did not specifically answer each question separately (because it was not asked to do so).

The Court of Queen's Bench was concerned solely with the correctness or otherwise of the trial judge's direction, which in the event all three appellate judges held to be inadequate, albeit for different reasons. A re-trial was ordered.

Our central focus in this paper is the Court's opinion on what is now commonly termed 'unilateral mistake as to the terms of a contract' (although the Court itself never adopts this terminology). But, by way of diversion, we can begin our discussion by isolating two other issues raised by the case—caveat emptor and sale by sample.

## C. CAVEAT EMPTOR

*Smith v Hughes* is often cited as a decision enunciating a clear statement of the rule of caveat emptor. Undeniably, it was clearly held on the facts by all three judges that a mistake as to quality will not affect the validity of the contact and that 'a mere abstinence from disabusing the purchaser of that impression is not fraud or deceit'.[5] This was so 'whatever may be the case in a court of morals'.[6]

---

[4] *Smith v Hughes* (n 1 above) 602.
[5] *Smith v Hughes* (n 1 above) 607 (Blackburn J).
[6] *Smith v Hughes* (n 1 above) 607 (Blackburn J).

*Smith v Hughes*, however, is not an unambiguous authority for the principle of caveat emptor. Only Blackburn J sets out the rule in general terms.[7] Both Cockburn CJ and Hannen J specifically link the application of the principle of caveat emptor to the facts before the court, which involved a sale by sample.[8]

The Court of Appeal decision in *Smith v Hughes* escaped the attention of the national press, but not the *Surrey County Chronicle* of 15 June 1871, whose editorial described the result of the case as 'very interesting to both farmers and consumers'. The importance was seen, however, not in any aspect of the reasoning (mostly in Hannen J's judgment) relating to unilateral mistake, but in the consideration of the rule of caveat emptor. The editorial (selectively) para-phrased passages from the judgments which related to this issue and concluded:

> In offering for sale goods improving by time, is the vendor bound to declare their age? Such seems to be the affirmative by the judge of the Surrey County Court and in the negative by the judges of the Court of Queen's Bench sitting in Banco.

So the popular debate about the Court of Appeal decision in *Smith v Hughes* at the time was directed towards its perceived unequivocal endorsement of the rule of caveat emptor (which it did not in fact do), rather than any complexities of the law relating to mistake as to the terms of a contract. More surprisingly, this view of the significance of *Smith v Hughes* was reflected in the legal texts of the late 19th century, most of which cited the decision only as authority for this rule,[9] or simply in the context of a sale by sample.[10] The 14th edition of Chitty, published in 1904[11] still did not refer to the potential impact of *Smith v Hughes* when there was a unilateral mistake as to the terms of the contract.

In parenthesis, it should be said that it is probable that the plaintiff would have been judged harshly in 'a court of morals'. The clear advice at the time—some contained in voluminous treatises—was that new oats should never be given to horses 'until the March winds have dried the last year's crop'.[12] Even year-old oats were described as too young for racehorses.[13] The consequences of not adopting the advice appear to have been severe. New oats were described as acting 'prejudicially to the bowels and kidneys',[14] so that 'the horse eating

---

[7] *Smith v Hughes* (n 1 above) 607 (Blackburn J).

[8] *Smith v Hughes* (n 1 above) 603 (Cockburn CJ); 608 (Hannen J).

[9] Eg GG Addison, *Treatise on the Law of Contracts*, 9th edn, H Smith (ed) (London, Stevens & Sons, 1892) 112.

[10] Eg J Chitty, *Law of Contracts not Under Seal*, 14th edn, J Lely (ed) (London, Sweet & Maxwell, 1904) 345: 'As to the buyer's mistaken view of the character of samples, and the non-obligation of the seller to undeceive him, see *Smith v Hughes*'. Cf, however, F Pollock, *Principles of Contract at Law and Equity* (London, Stevens & Sons, 1876) 373, who refers to the crucial passage by Hannen J and appears to appreciate its significance.

[11] J Chitty, *Law of Contracts not Under Seal* (n 10 above).

[12] JH Walsh, *The Horse; in the Stable and the Field*, 4th edn (London, 1862) 223. See also G Armatage, *The Horse; its Varieties and Management in Health and Disease* (London, 1893) 62.

[13] Walsh, *The Horse; in the Stable and the Field* (n 12 above) 224. It was also emphasised that although oats were regarded as the most desirable fodder for racehourses only oats of the highest quality should be fed to them. See R Fitzwygram, *Horses and Stables* (London, 1869) 47–8.

[14] Walsh, *The Horse* (n 12 above) 224.

them becomes flabby, sweats profusely and often throws out an eruption known as "surfeit" '.[15] It would be surprising, almost inconceivable, that this would not have been known to a farmer who customarily sold oats to trainers of racehorses.

## D. SALE BY SAMPLE

*Smith v Hughes* involved a sale by sample, but it is an issue largely ignored by counsel and by the Court of Appeal. One might suppose that if the goods supplied had not complied with the sample it would have been the central pivot of the defence. Even prior to the Sale of Goods Act 1893 there would have been an implied term that the sale should conform with the sample, so the defendant could have successfully defended the claim on that basis, even in the absence of an express warranty that the goods were old. Conversely, if the goods did conform, at first blush it is difficult to have much sympathy for the defendant, since he had nearly two days to examine the sample of oats and, presumably therefore, did not make a proper inspection.

There is some reference to sale by sample in the judgments. As we have seen,[16] for both Cockburn C J and Hannen J the fact the defendant was given a sample reinforces the application of caveat emptor on the facts. Additionally, Hannen J states (without explanation) that his conclusion that there should be a new trial is re-inforced '[h]aving regard to the admitted fact that the defendant bought the oats after two days detention of the sample'.[17]

Yet, it appears to have been no part of the defendant's case that the oats which were delivered did not conform with the sample. There is, it is suggested, a simple explanation. The defendant and the defendant's brother did examine the sample, but (erroneously) thought it consisted of old oats. The task of distinguishing old oats and new oats was notoriously difficult, as evidenced by publications of the time giving advice to racehorse owners. Buyers were told that the 'glazed' appearance of new oats was absent in old oats, but warned that 'badly saved new oats may in this respect resemble old oats'.[18]

The difference between the 'fresh and milky taste' of new oats compared with the 'slightly bitter taste of old oats' may also be less apparent in 'very dry seasons'.[19] Similarly, in 'fine seasons' (such as 1871) new oats, which are generally softer in texture, may 'come to the market almost as dry and hard as old'.[20]

[15] Walsh, *The Horse* (n 12 above) 224.

[16] *Smith v Hughes* (n 1 above) 603 (Cockburn CJ); 608 (Hannen J).

[17] *Smith v Hughes* (n 1 above) 611. The only case cited in respect of this issue is *Scott v Littledale* (1858) 27 LJQB 201 but it concerned a different issue, namely, whether or not the seller could himself take advantage of the fact that the proper sample had not been delivered. It was held that he could not. The case is not pertinent to this discussion.

[18] Fitzwygram, *Horses and Stables* (n 13 above) 54.

[19] Fitzwygram, *Horses and Stables* (n 13 above) 54–5.

[20] Fitzwygram, *Horses and Stables* (n 13 above) 55.

Farmers were also known for adopting deceptive practices, especially kiln drying, to make new oats resemble the higher-value old oats.[21]

More is revealed by the evidence of the defendant at the second trial (as reported in *Surrey Gazette* of 21 July 1871). The defendant testified that the sample which the plaintiff exhibited was not large and that it had been 'produced out of his pocket where it has been loose', in his view, for two or three days. The defendant appears to have viewed the act of keeping the oats in this way as an act of deception, and, indeed, it seems to have been another device adopted by farmers with the object of giving such 'badly saved' new oats the appearance of being old.

## E. AND NOW TO MISTAKE

The principle of unilateral mistake as set out by *Smith v Hughes* is generally regarded as encapsulated by this passage in the judgment of Hannen J (as applied to the facts of that case)[22]:

> If, therefore in the present case, the plaintiff knew that the defendant, in dealing with him for oats, did so on the assumption that the plaintiff was contracting to sell him old oats, he was aware that the defendant apprehended the contract in a different sense to that in which he meant it, and he is thereby deprived of the right to insist that the defendant shall be bound by that which was only the apparent and not the real bargain.

Expressed in general terms, the proposition is that a party cannot insist that the defendant is bound by the contract if he knows that the defendant is mistaken as to the terms of the contract.

Most subsequent judicial decisions and commentators[23] have treated the application of this rule as resulting in a failure of offer and acceptance. Thus, in *Hartog v Colin and Shields*[24] the offeror intended to offer to sell hare skins at a price per piece, but by mistake he made an offer at a price per pound. This meant that the total price was excessively low since there were three pieces (or thereabouts) in each pound. It was held that the buyer 'could not reasonably have supposed that the offer contained the plaintiff's real intention',[25] apparently accepting the offeror's argument that there was 'no contract'[26] between the parties. And, more recently, Lord Phillips, citing *Smith v Hughes* and *Hartog v Colin and Shields*, considered the rule to be that

[21] Fitzwygram, *Horses and Stables* (n 13 above) 53.
[22] *Smith v Hughes* (n 1 above) 610.
[23] Eg J O'Sullivan and J Hilliard, *The Law of Contract*, 2nd edn (Oxford, Oxford University Press, 2006) paras 3.37–3.43; GH Treitel, *The Law of Contract*, 11th edn (London, Sweet & Maxwell, 2003) 304; J Beatson, *Anson's Law of Contract*, 28th edn (Oxford, Oxford University Press, 2002) 324.
[24] *Hartog v Colin and Shields* [1939] 2 All ER 566 (KB).
[25] Ibid 568.
[26] *Hartog v Colin and Shields* (n 24 above) 567.

if the offeree knows that the offeror does not intend the terms of the offer to be those that the natural meaning of the words would suggest, he cannot, by purporting to accept the offer, bind the offeror to a contract.[27]

Again, this consequence is described in terms of an absence of consensus.

Whilst there is a general acceptance that the application of the principle of *Smith v Hughes* negates the existence of a contract, there is also a sense that this legal position has been accepted without question as the basis for the relevant decisions. Take *Hartog v Colin and Shields* itself. One commentator asserts that the court concluded that there was 'no contract'[28] between the parties. Yet Singleton J did not expressly state whether or not the contract was void or voidable, simply concluding that 'the plaintiff could not reasonably have supposed that the offer contained the offeror's real intention',[29] without any analysis of the precise effect of this principle. The reference to the negation of a contract appears only in the argument of counsel (referred to in parenthesis by Singleton J). It is not suggested here that the accepted view of *Hartog v Colin and Shields* is wrong (since the court apparently accepted counsel's argument) but the case is illustrative of how a non-appellate decision with little analytical depth can be regarded as enshrining important principle.

More critically, the principle set out in Hannen J's judgment in *Smith v Hughes* (above) may be one interpretation of the decision in *Smith v Hughes*, but in the author's view the judgments of Cockburn CJ and Blackburn J do not clearly support this conclusion. And, importantly, the judgment of Hannen J itself fails to put the authority upon which it is based in proper context.

First, the judgments: Cockburn CJ devotes most of his reasoning to a (rather long-winded) explanation of caveat emptor. Eventually he turns, almost as an afterthought,

to deal with the argument which was *pressed upon* us, that the defendant intended to buy old oats and the plaintiff to sell new so the two minds were not ad idem (emphasis added).

In rebutting this proposition, Cockburn CJ takes 'the exactly parallel'[30] example of a person buying a horse without a warranty, believing it to be sound when it is not. This, he states, would not render the contract void simply because the seller must have known from the price agreed or from the 'general habits as a buyer of horses'[31] that the buyer thought the horse was sound. Cockburn CJ then concludes that the trial judge was wrong in leaving the second question to the jury. It will be observed that there is no reference in this example to any belief by the buyer that the seller warranted the horse was sound. It is not, therefore, 'an exactly parallel case' to the second jury question because in its terms

[27] In *Shogun Finance Ltd v Hudson* [2004] 1 AC 919 (HL) [123].
[28] Treitel, *The Law of Contract* (n 23 above) 309.
[29] *Hartog v Colin and Shields* (n 24 above) 568.
[30] *Smith v Hughes* (n 1 above) 606.
[31] *Smith v Hughes* (n 1 above) 606.

that question encompasses a very different case, namely 'where the plaintiff had believed that the defendant believed . . . that he was *contracting* for old oats'.[32] Cockburn CJ's example is just another illustration of caveat emptor. So in analysing the second question left to the jury, either Cockburn CJ does not understand it or he is implicitly rejecting Hannen J's legal proposition. In any event, there is nothing of principle here.

As for Blackburn J, he concludes that the second question put to the jury would not make the distinction between buying a horse believed to be sound and one believed to be warranted to be sound 'obvious to the jury'.[33] But nowhere does he enunciate any principle equivalent to that set out by Hannen J.

Thus we are left with the direction of future contract law moulded by the judgment of Hannen J, who relies as authority only upon William Paley's work, *The Principles of Moral and Political Philosophy*.[34] So who is this figure who has so influenced our law of contract? It is interesting—perhaps instructive—to explore in some detail his views, in particular, those on the nature of a promise.

Born in 1743 and educated at Christ's College Cambridge, William Paley was not a lawyer, but a moral philosopher, who advanced the idea that one should contribute to the wellbeing of society for the purpose of achieving the pleasures of Heaven. He thus defined moral virtue as

> the doing of good to mankind, in obedience to the will of God, and for the sake of ever-lasting happiness.[35]

Paley has been described as a 'theological utilitarian',[36] who contributed to the ideological climate that made Bentham a more acceptable figure to a society that was then largely governed by religious values.[37]

In reality it is not unfair to say that his view on aspects of the law reflected some strange contradictions. He ranted against the inequality that resulted from the exploitation of private property, but at the same time supported landed wealth as promoting social order. He saw the function of sentencing as a deterrent to crime rather than simply punishment, yet defended the death penalty for stealing horses and sheep. And he supported equality in tax matters (proposing a graduated income tax), yet rejected the view that Parliament should be based on a popular vote.[38]

---

[32] *Smith v Hughes* (n 1 above) 602.

[33] *Smith v Hughes* (n 1 above) 608.

[34] W Paley, *The Principles of Moral and Political Philosophy*. The earliest edition that this author could obtain was published in London by R Faulder in 1785.

[35] See the foreword by DL Le Mahieu to W Paley, *The Principles of Moral and Political Philosophy* (Indianapolis, Liberty Fund, 2002) xvi.

[36] *Ibid*.

[37] Paley, *The Principles of Moral and Political Philosophy* (n 36 above) foreword, xxv.

[38] See, generally, DL Le Mahieu (n 36 above); MM Garland, *Cambridge Before Darwin: The Ideal of a Liberal Education 1800–1860* (Cambridge, Cambridge University Press, 1980) 52–69; P Searby, *A History of the University of Cambridge, Vol 3, 1750–1870* (Cambridge, Cambridge University Press, 1997) 295–313.

Relevantly in this context, his views on the nature of a promise may be regarded as idiosyncratic. He regarded a promise as equivalent to a vow made to God, and, in terms of either 18th century or modern contract law, had an exaggerated notion of how expectations could be created by 'tacit promises' (as he termed them). He gave this example[39]:

> Taking, for imitance, a relation's child, and educating him for a liberal profeffion, or in a manner fuitable only for the heir of a large fortune, as much obliges us, to place him in that profeffion, or leave him fuch a fortune, as if we had given him a promife to do fo, under our hands and feals.

More specifically, in relation to the interpretation of promises, he rejected the notion that an equivocal promise should be interpreted in the sense that the promisor intended it, on the basis 'you might excite expectations, which you never meant, nor would be obliged to satisfy'.[40] Likewise, the promisee's view of the promise should be rejected because the promisor would then be drawn into engagements which he never intended to make.[41] This is, perhaps, uncontroversial. He then formulated a rule, which is quoted in *Smith v Hughes*[42] (not quite in full) by Pollock in argument, and by Hannen J. In Paley's view, promises should be interpreted according to how the promisor believed that the promisee accepted the promise:

> It muft therefore by the fenfe (for there is no other remaining) in which the promifer believed that the promifee accepted his promife.[43]

Two comments may be made here. The first is that it is not true, as Paley asserts, that there is 'no other remaining' sense in which promises can be interpreted. There is another approach, which is to interpret the contract as it would appear to a reasonable person in the position of the parties. Blackburn J in *Smith v Hughes* (sensibly not referring to Paley) articulated an approach of this nature[44]:

> whatever a man's real intention may be, he so conducts himself that a reasonable man would believe that he was assenting to the terms proposed by the other party, and that other party upon that belief enters into the contract with him, the man thus conducting himself would be equally bound as if he had intended to agree to the other party's terms.

This formulation is not without its complexity,[45] since it also regards the subjective understandings of the parties as relevant. Yet the approach is not

---

[39] Paley, *The Principles of Moral and Political Philosophy* (n 35 above) Book III, ch 5, 108. On this view, present Law Schools would be under a duty to find placements for all their students!!!
[40] Paley, *The Principles of Moral and Political Philosophy* (n 35 above) 107.
[41] Paley, *The Principles of Moral and Political Philosophy* (n 35 above).
[42] *Smith v Hughes* (n 1 above) 610 (Hannen J) (and 600 in argument).
[43] Paley, *The Principles of Moral and Political Philosophy* (n 35 above) 107.
[44] *Smith v Hughes* (n 1 above) 607.
[45] See, generally, R Brownsword, 'New Note on the Old Oats' (1987) 131 *Solicitors' Journal* 384. The note also argues that the case supports the view that a party will not easily be relieved of a bad bargain.

dissimilar from that which (with some embellishment) was adopted by Lord Hoffmann in *Investors Compensation Scheme v West Bromwich Building Society*.[46]

Once such an objective approach is taken to the interpretation of contracts, cases that are sometimes linked to theories of mistake can be explained on the basis of uncertainty. For example, *Raffles v Wichelhaus*,[47] where the seller intended to sell cotton 'ex *Peerless*' (the ship leaving Bombay in December) and the buyer intended to buy cotton 'ex *Peerless*' on another boat by the same name (leaving Bombay in October), can be explained on the basis of uncertainty. Both were reasonable interpretations of the contract, so that its subject-matter could not be properly identified. There are examples elsewhere of this analysis. Thus, in *Mercantile Credits v Harry*[48] the defendant guaranteed the performance by two named persons of their obligations under a lease with the plaintiff. There were in fact two leases between these persons and the plaintiff. Each of these leases could reasonably be interpreted as referring to the lease mentioned in the guarantee. As the terms of the guarantee made it clear that the guarantee related only to a single lease, the guarantee was held to be void for uncertainty, as failing to properly identify the subject-matter encompassed by it.[49]

The second comment that arises from Paley's approach to interpretation of promises is that it was adopted by Hannen J in *Smith v Hughes* without regard to the context in which it was made. Paley explains that he has formulated the principle in order to 'exclude *evasion* where the promisor attempts to make his *escape* through some ambiguity in the expressions used' (emphasis added).[50] He gave this example[51]:

> Temures promifed the garrifon of Sebaftia, that, if they would furrender, *no blood fhould be fhed*. The garrifon furrendered; and *Temures buried them all alive*. Now Temures fulfilled the promife, in one fenfe, and in the fenfe too in which he intended it at the time; but not in the fenfe in which the garrifon of Sebaftia actually received it, nor in the fenfe in which Temures himfelf knew that the garifon received it; which laft fenfe, according to our rule, was the fenfe he was in confcience bound to have performed it in (emphasis added).

This is illuminating because it shows that Paley, as a moral philosopher, was concerned not so much with defining a general approach to the interpretation of contracts, but with preventing behaviour which was calculated to deceive—in modern parlance, to prevent unconscientious behaviour. And this equates precisely to the author's view as to how we should approach the law of mistake.

---

[46] *Investors Compensation Scheme v West Bromwich Building Society* [1998] 1 WLR 896 (HL).

[47] *Raffles v Wichelhaus* (1864) 2 H & C 906, 159 ER 375. It is not easy, however, to discern much of principle from the short judgment, which mainly consists of counsel's argument.

[48] *Mercantile Credits v Harry* [1969] 2 NSWR 248

[49] *Ibid* 250 (McFarlan J).

[50] Paley, *The Principles of Moral and Political Philosophy* (n 35 above) 108.

[51] Paley, *The Principles of Moral and Political Philosophy* (n 35 above) 108.

A related aspect of *Smith v Hughes* that merits analysis is the commonly accepted view that the effect of the principle enunciated by Hannen J is to negate consent. This view has led to a seemingly endless debate as to whether contract formation should be determined by a subjective or objective approach.[52] *Smith v Hughes* also probably influenced *Cundy v Lindsay*,[53] which squarely placed the law of unilateral mistake as to identity on the absence of consensus and has created an illogical difference of approach (recently enshrined by the House of Lords) between 'face to face' situations and written contracts.

Yet, the judgments in *Smith v Hughes* do not unequivocally support the generally accepted view that there is no contract in cases of a unilateral mistake of a fundamental term. It is true that counsel's argument is put on this basis. Yet the language of Hannen J (who, it should be remembered, is the only member of the Court to endorse fully the principle of unilateral mistake) is more equivocal. He speaks in terms of the plaintiff 'being deprived of the right to insist'[54] that the defendant be bound by the apparent bargain, and subsequently emphasises that the result of the rule is to 'relieve'[55] the defendant of the obligation. This is more the terminology of a contract rendered voidable than the language of absence of consensus. It is true Hannen J, relying on *Raffles v Wichelhaus*,[56] does emphasise that it is essential to the creation of a valid contract that both parties should agree to the *same thing* in the same sense, but (as we have seen) this can be interpreted as simply re-stating the rule that a contract must have certainty of subject-matter.

Cockburn CJ has nothing to say at all on the consequence of the rule. So it is only Blackburn J who clearly

> apprehend[s] that if one of the parties intends to make a contract on one set of terms, and the other intends to make a contract on another set of terms . . . there is no contract.[57]

But Blackburn J himself qualifies this, stating that this rule is subject to how the circumstances would be construed by a reasonable person, so he is not directly dealing with Hannen J's principle of unilateral mistake.

There is a postscript to the Court of Appeal's decision to order a new trial, which took place at Epsom County Court. The trial is not officially reported,

---

[52] See, generally: T Endicott, 'Objectivity, Subjectivity and Incomplete Agreements' in J Horder (ed), *Oxford Essays in Jurisprudence*, 4th Series (Oxford, Oxford University Press, 2000) 151; W Howarth, 'The Meaning of Objectivity in Contract' (1984) 100 *Law Quarterly Review* 265; JP Vorster, 'A Comment on the Meaning of Objectivity in Contract' (1987) 104 *Law Quarterly Review* 274.

[53] *Cundy v Lindsay* (1878) 2 App Cas 459. As to the difficulties of interpretation of *Smith v Hughes* see C MacMillan, 'Mistaken Arguments: The Role of Argument in the Development of a Doctrine of Contractual Mistake in Nineteenth-Century England' (2003) 6 *Current Legal Issues* 285, 302–5.

[54] *Smith v Hughes* (n 1 above) 610.

[55] *Smith v Hughes* (n 1 above) 610.

[56] *Raffles v Wichelhaus* (n 48 above).

[57] *Smith v Hughes* (n 1 above) 607.

but an account does appear in the *Surrey Advertiser and County Times* of 22 July 1871. It seems that the reasoning of Hannen J escaped the attention of the second trial judge, who left 'the following points' to the jury:

> First, whether the word 'old' was used in the conversation between the plaintiff and the defendant. Secondly, whether the defendant believed the plaintiff contracted to sell old oats and, if so, whether he [the defendant] had reasonable grounds for that belief

So far as the second question is concerned, this direction does not encapsulate the principle of unilateral mistake set out by Hannen J, which is so often cited in academic works. In relation to the second point it omits the vital requirement that the plaintiff must be shown to have knowledge of the defendant's mistake. The direction to the jury in the second trial appears less adequate than in the first, which was the subject of the appeal. Unsurprisingly the jury could not agree, 'three being of one opinion and two of another'. The jury were discharged and the plaintiff's claim failed. All in all it was a good day at the races for Mr Hughes.

## F. UNCONSCIONABILITY

As we have seen, some cases of mistake can be regarded as illustrations of uncertain contracts, because the subject-matter cannot be properly identified. Others, often classified as mistake cases, are really no more than voidable contracts induced by misrepresentation. An example is *Denny v Hancock*,[58] where an error made by a buyer in respect of the boundary of certain land, which he bought at an auction, was induced by a sketch plan prepared by the vendor's agent. The court uses the language of mistake, but the decision not to specifically enforce the contract is easily justifiable on the basis of misrepresentation.

Outside these categories, it is argued in this paper that mistake as a concept in the law of contract can be subsumed within the general principles of unconscionability. Indeed (despite *Smith v Hughes*) in the context of unilateral mistake as to the terms of the contract when a claim for rectification is being made, there is much support for this approach. Such a claim has been upheld where one party is mistaken as to the terms of the contract and the other party knows of or (possibly) suspects the existence of the mistake. Whilst the doctrine is not perhaps fully developed, its essence is said to be based on the fact that the defendant has 'acted unconscionably and unfairly'[59] in taking advantage of the error. An illustration is *Commission for New Towns v Cooper (Great Britain) Ltd*.[60]

On the facts the Commission (the successor to the Milton Keynes Development Authority) entered into an agreement with a lessee, which provided that the

---

[58] *Denny v Hancock* (1870) LR 6 Ch App 138.
[59] An expression used in *Templiss Properties Ltd v Hyams* [1999] All ER (D) 404 (Ch).
[60] *Commission for New Towns v Cooper (Great Britain) Ltd* [1995] Ch 259 (CA)

Commission was to undertake building works so as to adapt the premises to the lessee's specifications. As part of the agreement the lessee was granted various options. These included a 'larger premises' option which required the Commission to take an assignment of the lease if the lessee gave notice it wished to take a new lease of larger premises from the Commission; a 'sideland' option which gave the lessee an opportunity to acquire a lease of a site adjacent to leased premises; and, significantly, a 'put option' which obliged the Commission to take an assignment of the lease from the lessee upon the lessee giving notice. The 'put option' effectively gave the lessee an opportunity to terminate the lease and was expressed as being 'personal' to the lessee.

The Commission did not carry out the agreed works according to the specifications. A dispute arose and the lessee withheld rent pending its resolution. Cooper subsequently acquired the lessee's business and took an assignment of the lease. At a meeting between the Commission and Cooper to resolve the dispute Cooper conducted its negotiations so as to give the impression that it would expand its business (perhaps exercising the 'larger premises' or 'sideland' option) when this was not the case. In fact Cooper wished to acquire the 'put option' (which would enable it effectively to terminate the lease), but without alerting the Commission, who would have refused to grant it. No mention was therefore made of the 'put option' and the defendant ensured that the discussions centred only upon the dispute regarding the building works and the rent. In the final documentation agreeing a settlement a general provision was included which treated Cooper 'in all respects as having the same rights and benefits under the original documentation as [the original lessee].'

In the result it was held, as a matter of construction, that the 'put option' did not come within the ambit of the generally worded clause since the context of the negotiations had nothing to do with the put option. But, alternatively, Stuart Smith LJ would have been prepared to decide the case on the basis of the following principle[61]:

> Were it necessary to do so in this case I would hold that where A intends B to be to be mistaken as to the construction of the agreement, so conducts himself that he diverts B's attention from discovering the mistake by making false and misleading statements, and B in fact makes the very mistake that A intends, then notwithstanding that A does not actually know, but merely suspects that B is mistaken, and it cannot be shown that the mistake was induced by any misrepresentation, rectification may be granted. A's conduct is unconscionable and he cannot insist on performance in accordance to the strict letter of the contract: that is sufficient for rescission.

*Smith v Hughes* is not relied upon, or apparently cited, in *Commission for New Towns v Cooper (Great Britain) Ltd*. This is despite its obvious potential application to the facts since it is reasonably clear on the evidence that Cooper knew of the Commission's mistaken belief that the 'put option' was not included within the negotiated settlement. After all this was the very objective

---

[61] *Ibid*, 280.

of Cooper's approach to the negotiations. Nor is *Smith v Hughes* relied upon in other rectification cases of the same genre.[62]

There is, of course, good reason for this. *Smith v Hughes* is inconvenient for the claimant in such cases since he wishes to enforce the contract as rectified. But it is odd indeed that the courts are upholding the validity of contracts as rectified, whilst the application of the principle in *Smith v Hughes* (commonly interpreted as negativing consent) would deny their validity at all.

The rectification cases do not, of course, mean that *Smith v Hughes* is now to be discarded, but they do provide some support for the view that in the cases of unilateral mistake as to terms of the contract the essential focus of the inquiry should be on the conduct of the non-mistaken party. It is true that there is no direct support for this approach in *Smith v Hughes* itself which did not articulate the law in terms of unconscionability in this way. This, however, is hardly surprising since it was a pre-Judicative Act case, decided in the Queen's Bench division two years before the emergence of the doctrine of unconscionable bargains in the context of expectant heirs in *Earl of Aylesford v Morris*.[63] Yet, as explained, Paley's *Principles of Moral and Political Philosophy*, relied on by Hannen J, is in reality directed at unconscionable behaviour by one contracting party. Indeed, in *Hartog v Colin and Shields*, which has been treated as the most direct application of *Smith v Hughes*, counsel's argument that there was 'no contract' between the parties was underpinned by notions of unconscionable behaviour[64]:

> There really was no contract, because you know that the document which went forward to you, in the form of an offer, contained a material mistake. You realised that, and *you sought to take advantage of it* (emphasis added).

Similarly, in other successful defences based upon mistake the fault of the non-mistaken party (albeit conduct falling short of an actionable misrepresentation) in contributing to the mistake has been decisive. Thus in *Scriven Bros & Co v Hindley & Co*[65] the defence succeeded since the party seeking to enforce the contract 'had by his own negligence . . . caused, or contributed to, the mistake'.[66]

The application of unconscionability to situations where one party has made a fundamental mistake as to the terms of a contract has the conceptual

---

[62] See *Well Barn Shoot Ltd v Shackleton* [2003] EWCA Civ 02, [2003] All ER (D) 182; *Templiss Properties Ltd v Hyams* [1999] All ER (D) 404 (Ch). Note that in *OT Africa Line v Vickers Plc* [1996] 1 Lloyd's Rep 700 (QB) 703, there is reference to how knowledge of the mistake as to terms may lead to an absence of consensus (referring to *Raffles v Wichelhaus* (n 48 above) but remarkably *Smith v Hughes* is still not cited.

[63] *Earl of Aylesford v Morris* (1873) 8 Ch App 484.

[64] *Hartog v Colin and Shields* (n 24 above) 567.

[65] *Scriven Bros & Co v Hindley & Co* [1913] 2 KB 564 (KB). Fault here is not being used in the sense of unconscionable or unfair conduct by the non-mistaken party, but rather as indicating negligence in the failure to avoid ambiguity in the catalogue of sale. But the case does illustrate the relevance of conduct in mistake cases.

[66] *Ibid* 569.

advantage that it directly focuses upon the central issue that arises, namely, conduct by the non-mistaken party which can be characterized as unconscionable and unfair (this being exactly the terminology adopted in the rectification cases concerning unilateral mistake). Indeed, this is the raison d'etre of the doctrine of unconscionability. Additionally, since the contract is voidable it has advantages of a more pragmatic nature, allowing for flexible relief taking into account the interests of the parties and whether or not there has been any material alteration of position by the non-mistaken party.

If, as argued, the focus of any exculpatory effect of a mistake as to the terms of contract is to be based on unconscionability, more precise parameters of the relevant principle need to be established. In *Commission for New Towns v Cooper (Great Britain) Ltd* Stuart Smith LJ imposed a requirement that the defendant must have engaged in conduct that 'diverts attention' from the mistake. Another formulation (in the Australian High Court case of *Taylor v Johnson*[67]) is that the non-mistaken party must have 'deliberately set out to ensure'[68] that the mistaken party does not 'become aware of the existence of the mistake or misapprehension'.[69]

It is arguable, however, that greater conceptual uniformity and clarity would be achieved by the application of the general doctrine of unconscionable bargains, at least in the form developed in other common law jurisdictions. The elements of the doctrine of unconscionable bargains are first, that the party seeking relief must be at a 'serious disadvantage' because of some weakness or disability; and, second, that the disadvantage has been exploited by the other party in a 'morally culpable' manner; and finally the terms of the contract must be unfair or oppressive.[70]

The law of unconscionable bargains is less developed in the United Kingdom compared with other common law jurisdictions, most notably Australia. There the 'serious disadvantage' may arise not only from 'constitutional disadvantages' (which can include lack of business knowledge or acumen), but also 'situational' disadvantages. These embrace a whole range of factors which, depending on the context, can include the circumstance of the negotiations, the selective bargaining position of the parties, the length and complexity of the negotiations, and any excessive pressure applied during these negotiations.[71] The doctrine has also been said to be applicable to companies, which may involve looking behind the corporate structure at the special disadvantages of the directors and imputing them to the company.[72]

---

[67] *Taylor v Johnson* (1983) 151 CLR 422 (Aus HC).

[68] *Ibid* 432.

[69] *Taylor v Johnson* (n 68 above).

[70] See, generally, *Alec Lobb (Garages) Ltd v Total Oil (Great Britain) Ltd* [1983] 1 WLR 87 (Ch) 94–5; *Hart v O'Connor* [1985] AC 1000 (HL); *Boustany v Pigott* (1993) 69 P & CR 298 (PC).

[71] See, generally, J O'Donovan and J Phillips, *The Modern Contract of Guarantee*, 4th edn (looseleaf version, 2006) para 4.1910. See also, especially, *Commercial Bank of Australia v Amadio* (1983) 151 CLR 447.

[72] *Commonwealth Bank of Australia v Ridout Nominees Pty Ltd* [2000] WASC 37.

The facts of *Commission for the New Towns v Cooper (Great Britain) Ltd* itself are such that they would be encompassed by the general doctrine of unconscionable bargains. The Commission was in a position of serious disadvantage in the negotiations since Cooper's conduct had been to create the false impression that there would be an expansion of its business and that the 'put option' was irrelevant to it. Furthermore, Cooper sought to include a provision which purported to assign to it the 'put option' when it knew that the Commission would not have agreed to it and did not realise that it was doing so. In sum, Cooper took advantage of the 'situational' disadvantageous position of the Commission in the negotiations.

But the general doctrine of unconscionability does not mandate the specific requirements that the non-mistaken party has either 'divert[ed] attention' from the mistake or has 'deliberately' taken steps to ensure that the mistaken party 'does not become aware of the mistake'. These requirements are no longer essential elements but become merely part of a broad factual matrix, embracing all relevant 'constitutional and situational' disadvantages (as set out earlier in this section). This enables a wider—perhaps more subtle—inquiry to be made.

There is one especially difficult case. Sometimes the only evidence is that the non-mistaken party has taken advantage of an error by the mistaken party in the latter's understanding of the terms of the contract.[73] The parties otherwise have equivalent commercial status (being either legally aware and/or legally represented) and there is no evidence that the non-mistaken party has engaged in conduct that either induced or concealed the mistake. The application of some Australian jurisprudence[74] on unconscionability suggests that such a case may within come its rubric on the basis that the mistaken party is in a position of 'situational disadvantage' since he has made a mistake as to the terms of the contract, and the other party (knowing of that mistake) has acted unconscionably in entering into the contract.

Yet this seems not only artificial but also to expand the concept of unconscionable bargains too far. At a fundamental level it also raises the issue of whether the law should differentiate so sharply between a unilateral mistake as to terms and a unilateral mistake as to quality, the latter having no effect on the validity of the contract. There is no better illustration than *Smith v Hughes* itself where Hannen J stated on the facts[75]:

> in order to relieve the defendant it was necessary that the jury should find not merely that the plaintiff believed the defendant to believe that he was buying old oats, but that he believed the defendant to believe that he, the plaintiff, was contracting to sell old oats.

[73] In the absence of knowledge of the mistake the contract will take effect according to its term: *Centrovincial Estates v Merchant Investors Assurance Co Ltd* [1983] Com LR 158 (CA).

[74] It is sufficient to be in a position of special disadvantage if a party does not understand the complexities or risks of the underlying transaction. See, eg *Budget Stationery Supplies Pty Ltd v National Australia Bank* [1996] 7 BPR 14,891; *State Bank of New South Wales v Hibbert* (2000) 9 BPR 17,543 [70]. And see O'Donovan & Phillips, *The Modern Contract of Guarantee* (n 72 above) para 4.1910.

[75] *Smith v Hughes* (n 1 above) 610.

It was held that the direction of the trial judge would not have made the distinction clear to the jury. Indeed, this is not surprising since it is very much a lawyer's distinction. Those in the commercial world can see very little difference between these mistakes. In both cases the mistaken party takes the view (rightly or wrongly) that he should have been told the true facts. Yet the law has taken the position that if a party knows the other is mistaken as to a term of the contract he must correct it. Otherwise, (if we follow the accepted view of *Smith v Hughes*) no contractual obligation ever arises. There is, however, no similar duty to correct a mistake as to quality. We argue, or assume, in this case that the mistaken party should protect its position by making relevant inquiries (even if he cannot reasonably do so). In any event, he assumes a contractual risk—caveat emptor applies.

It does not seem so radical to impose a similar obligation upon a negotiating party (assuming he is not in a real sense in a position of 'serious disadvantage') to protect his position by seeking a clarification of the terms of the contract or to carefully read the written contract. Indeed many potential mistakes as to terms will be easier to identify and resolve than mistakes as to quality.

The precise parameters of behaviour that may be regarded as unconscionable is no doubt open to debate, and, in particular, a choice needs to be made as whether conduct is to be measured against a whole range of factors (as in the general doctrine of unconscionability) or by a more specific test (as set out, for example, by Stuart Smith LJ in *Commission for New Towns v Cooper (Great Britain) Ltd*. But the central thrust of this paper is that the focus of the inquiry should be the conduct of a contracting party who may have exploited the disadvantaged position of the mistaken party.

So far our discussion has centred upon unilateral mistake as to terms. If (as argued) unconscionability is to be the determining principle for any exculpatory effect of mistake in contract, there are clear implications for other situations where mistake has been held to have an effect. Common mistake (as set out in *Bell v Lever Bros*[76]) should have no effect on the validity of the contract, absent any unconscionable behaviour by the defendant. *Great Peace Shipping Ltd v Tsavliris Salvage (International) Ltd*[77] now precludes equitable relief for common mistake. This equates with the author's view since in the majority of situations where relief was granted there was either a failure of the claimant to protect its position or the claimant was assuming a normal and acceptable contractual risk. Thus in *Grist v Bailey*[78] (when the parties wrongly assumed a house was subject to a statutory tenancy) the solicitor who both managed the property and acted for the vendor from the inception of the negotiations only made proper inquiries to determine whether a tenancy existed after the exchange of contracts Similarly, in *Magee v Pennine Insurance*[79] (where a com-

[76] *Bell v Lever Bros* [1932] AC 161 (HL).
[77] *Great Peace Shipping Ltd v Tsavliris Salvage (International) Ltd* [2003] QB 679 (CA).
[78] *Grist v Bailey* [1967] Ch 532 (Ch).
[79] *Magee v Pennine Insurance* [1969] 2 QB 507 (CA).

promise agreement was based on the false assumption that the insured had a valid contract of insurance), the insurance company could have made proper inquiries as to the validity of the policy prior to entering into the compromise agreement, but did not do so. And, finally and most dramatically, in *Solle v Butcher*[80] (where the parties wrongly believed the rent of a flat was no longer controlled by the Rent Restriction Act) the tenant, who sought to reduce his rent to the controlled level, had himself taken that view after taking counsel's advice and had so informed the landlord. Indeed, it is arguable here that the tenant was simply relying on his own unconscionable conduct to avoid the contract.

As to cases of unilateral mistake as to identity, we must leave these aside since the die is cast. The House of Lords has gone its own way in *Shogun Finance Ltd v Hudson*.[81] But this author shares the view of many others that in such cases the contracts should be treated as voidable on the basis of misrepresentation, itself a form of unconscionable conduct. In other so-called mistake cases the message from this paper is clear. The unifying feature should be unconscionability.

---

[80] *Solle v Butcher* [1950] 1 KB 671 (CA).
[81] *Shogun Finance Ltd v Hudson* [2004] 1 AC 919 (HL). For an excellent analysis of the law, see C MacMillan, 'Rogues, Swindlers and Cheats: The Development of Mistake of Identity in English Contract Law' (2005) 64 *Cambridge Law Journal* 711.

# 8

# Foakes v Beer (1884)

## MICHAEL LOBBAN*

### A. THE CASE AND THE PROBLEM

O N 11 AUGUST 1875, Mrs Julia Beer recovered a judgment for £2090
19s in the Court of Exchequer against Dr John Weston Foakes. Unable
to pay this sum, he entered into an agreement in December 1876, that
'in consideration' of an initial payment of £500 and 'on condition' of six-
monthly payments of £150 to Mrs Beer or her nominee 'until the whole of the
said sum of £2090 shall have been fully paid and satisfied', she would not take
proceedings to enforce the judgment. Foakes made the regular payments
according to the agreement. In June 1882, the final instalment of the original
debt was paid off. However, Foakes had not paid any of the interest on the judgment debt to which Mrs Beer was by statute entitled,[1] and proceedings were
therefore begun on her behalf to allow execution on judgment, to recover £302
19s 6d of interest.[2] In July 1882 the master directed that there should be a trial
to determine what, if anything, was due on the agreement. A trial took place
before Cave J, where argument turned on whether interest was to be paid under
their agreement, and a common jury found for Dr Foakes.

The parties to the suit were strangers to each other. Foakes was a physician,
a licentiate of the Society of Apothecaries. Born at Mitcham in 1824, he had
studied at the University of Giessen, before returning to establish a practice in
Grosvenor Square. He had attracted some attention 'for his untiring energy and
successful treatment of Cholera during the fearful outbreak in 1866,' but
became better known in the public press after 1870 for developing a new method
of treating gout.[3] Foakes was seeking to make his fortune at a time when many

* Research for this paper was done during my tenure in a British Academy Research Readership,
as part of work on the law of obligations in the nineteenth century for the Victorian volumes of the
New Oxford History of the Laws of England. The support of the British Academy is gratefully
acknowledged.

[1] 1 & 2 Vic c 110, s 17.

[2] At the time of the agreement, she had already been entitled to £113 16s 2d interest.

[3] Quotation from the *Victoria Magazine* cited in John W Foakes, *Gout and Rheumatic Gout:
A New Method of Cure*, 10th edn (London, Simkin, Marshall & Co, 1886) flyleaf.

novel kinds of medical remedies were being sold to the public.[4] Keen to attract patients, he published a book aimed at the public, rather than the medical profession, which was regularly reissued down to 1886. Nothing is known of Mrs Beer, save that she was a client of Henry Williams Mackreth, a solicitor who also acted for Foakes. The subject-matter of the original litigation was bills of exchange drawn by Mackreth and accepted by Foakes, as payment for a loan of £2400 from the solicitor. Mackreth had indorsed £2000 worth of bills to Beer, 'the money being hers to the extent of £1500 or thereabouts'.[5]

Foakes and Mackreth had both experienced financial difficulties in the past. In 1865 Mackreth's partner, WOJ Tucker, had started to engage in fraudulent transactions for his own purposes, misappropriating money and drawing unauthorised cheques and bills in the name of the firm, Gibbs, Tucker & Mackreth. He then absconded, leaving Mackreth embroiled in a series of lawsuits.[6] In 1866 the firm had also acted for Foakes in placing newspaper advertisements for his book. These advertisements were to be paid for by bills of exchange accepted by Foakes, with the debt being guaranteed by the firm. After a bill had been dishonoured by Foakes, Mackreth found himself in court again, disputing his liability on the guarantee.[7] To add to his difficulties, he had also engaged in speculative investments in an era of company booms, which generated further losses. In October 1867 Mackreth duly entered a composition agreement with his creditors, agreeing to pay them a shilling in the pound, in two instalments, in March and September 1868.[8]

Mackreth later resumed his career as a solicitor, becoming a partner in Mackreth, Bramall & White of 47 Lime Street. His relationship with Foakes broke down and in 1875, the year of Mrs Beer's lawsuit, he also sued the doctor in respect of other bills. Foakes offered a lump sum to settle all the debts, but Mackreth refused. Instead, he proceeded to judgment and sought execution for it. Only when it was apparent that no money would be forthcoming—over a year after the judgment—was the agreement made with Foakes. It may be assumed, therefore, that the real parties to the dispute were Foakes and Mackreth, for Mrs Beer herself had nothing to do with any of these arrangements. They were negotiated between Mackreth and Foakes's new solicitor, Smith, who drew up the agreement, which was approved by Mackreth on behalf of Mrs Beer.[9] The question of interest payments was not mentioned during the

---

[4] See AWB Simpson, 'Quackery and Contract Law: *Carlill v Carbolic Smoke Ball Company* (1893)' in his *Leading Cases in the Common Law* (Oxford, Clarendon Press, 1995) 258.
[5] Evidence of HW Mackreth, as reported in House of Lords Record Office, HL/PO/JU/4/3/363 (cited below as 'HLRO Foakes') 9.
[6] Mackreth successfully resisted liability in a number of suits: see *Forster v Macreth* (1867) LR 2 Exch 163 and *Atkinson v Mackreth* (1866) LR 2 Eq 570.
[7] *Clarke v Mackreth* (1866) *The Times* (2 July 1866) 11 col b. Mackreth had by now left the partnership.
[8] For this information, and further litigation involving Mackreth, see *In re Universal Banking Corporation, ex parte Strang* (1870) 5 Ch App 492.
[9] HLRO Foakes (n 5 above) 9.

discussions, but given Mackreth's experience in these matters, it is very unlikely that he was duped by the sly penmanship of another solicitor into forgoing what was due to his client.[10] In any event, Mackreth continued to receive the biannual payments. But when asked in May 1882 how much remained to be paid, Mackreth did factor in the interest, and told Foakes's new solicitor that over £444 remained to be paid. When only £90 was paid, the action was commenced.

The case went to the Queen's Bench Division in May 1883. The court agreed with the trial court's decision that there had been no provision for the payment of interest in the contract between Foakes and Beer. At this hearing, counsel for the plaintiff, APB Gaskell, raised the point for which the case became known: that a promise to take a lesser sum in discharge of a greater debt was not binding. Authority for this proposition was found in a case of 1719, *Cumber v Wane*.[11] However, the argument was rejected. 'Judges have long tried to escape from the doctrine, which is a reproach to English law', Watkin Williams J said,

> that a creditor may not make a valid agreement to take a smaller sum than the amount of his debt.[12]

Mrs Beer 'ought not, in equity and conscience, be permitted to repudiate' her agreement. In any case, he felt that the fact that Foakes agreed to pay instalments to any of Mrs Beer's nominees constituted consideration.[13] The plaintiff thereupon took the case to the Court of Appeal, and succeeded there. As Brett LJ saw it, no consideration had been given for the plaintiff's agreement to give Foakes time, and so the promise not to seek to recover the interest was not binding.[14] As to the argument that the plaintiff might have recovered nothing at all if she had insisted on being paid all at once—and that she might therefore have received some form of practical benefit from the arrangement—Brett dismissed it as being 'a matter of prudence and not of law'.[15]

Foakes appealed to the House of Lords, which confirmed the decision of the Court of Appeal. Lord Selborne LC pointed out that, since the agreement was not under seal, it could only be enforced either if it operated by way of accord and satisfaction, so as to extinguish the claim for interest, or if it was supported by consideration. He did not feel there had been accord and satisfaction here. At common law, a party could only waive a debt after it had become due by deed, or through an 'accord and satisfaction' by which the innocent party accepted

---

[10] Sir GH Treitel writes, 'What seems to have happened was that Dr Foakes's solicitor dug a technical trap for Mrs Beer and the House of Lords arranged an equally technical rescue', *Some Landmarks of Twentieth Century Contract Law* (Oxford, Clarendon Press, 2002) 25.

[11] *Cumber v Wane* (1719) 1 Stra 426, 93 ER 613; sub nom *Cumber v Wade* 11 Mod 342, 88 ER 1077.

[12] *Beer v Foakes* (1883) 11 QBD 221 (QB) 223.

[13] HLRO Foakes (n 5 above) 11. See also *Beer v Foakes* (1883) 52 LJ QB 427 (CA) 428.

[14] *Beer v Foakes* (1883) 11 QBD 221 (CA) 224. Contrast the wording in another report (52 LJ QB 712): 'the mere fact that the plaintiff gave time to the person who owed the money will not make the agreement binding, for she might have changed her mind, and then there would be no consideration for it'.

[15] *Beer v Foakes* (1883) 52 LJ QB 712 (CA).

something from the debtor in satisfaction of the debt.[16] It was not enough to have a mere agreement to discharge. There also had to be a 'satisfaction',[17] which was in effect equivalent to consideration. It had to be something of value given to the innocent party for his 'accord'. Although courts were unconcerned with the value of what was done or given in satisfaction of the right to sue on the debt, since this was a matter to be determined by the parties' accord, it had to be something of value in the eyes of the law. In any event, Selborne did not feel that Foakes could argue that there had been an accord and satisfaction when he made the agreement with Mrs Beer, since no complete satisfaction was possible as long as any instalments were outstanding, while nothing was done at the time of the final payment which amounted to an acquittance.

The case therefore turned on whether the promise to pay the debt without the interest was backed by consideration. The only consideration given for this promise, in Selborne's view, was the down payment of £500 (since Foakes had not bound himself to pay any more). This raised the question whether a court could 'treat a prospective agreement, not under seal, for satisfaction of a debt, by a series of payments on account to a total amount less than the whole debt, as binding in law.'[18] To answer this question in the affirmative, he said, would squarely contradict the rule set out by Coke in *Pinnel's Case* in 1602[19]:

> that payment of a lesser sum on the day in satisfaction of a greater, cannot be any satisfaction for the whole, because it appears to the Judges that by no possibility, a lesser sum can be a satisfaction to the plaintiff for a greater sum: but the gift of a horse, hawk, or robe, &c. in satisfaction is good. For it shall be intended that a horse, hawk, or robe, &c might be more beneficial to the plaintiff than the money, in respect of some circumstance, or otherwise the plaintiff would not have accepted of it in satisfaction.

*Pinnel's Case* was concerned not with consideration, but with satisfaction.[20] However, the judges in the Lords treated it as a rule which applied to consideration, regarding the two doctrines as interchangable. Drawing on this case,

---

[16] The same rules applied to all waivers of breaches of contractual obligation: an innocent party's right to damages was only waived by an accord and satisfaction.

[17] However, a contract on which the party in breach could be sued came to be considered to be satisfaction, since it created a new right in place of the old: *James v David* (1793) 5 TR 141, 101 ER 81. But the court had to be shown that the promise or agreement was taken in satisfaction: *Flockton v Hall* (1849) 14 QB 380, 117 ER 150.

[18] *Foakes v Beer* (1884) 9 App Cas 605 (HL) 612.

[19] *Pinnel's Case* (1602) 5 Co Rep 117a, 77 ER 237. Cf Edward Coke, *The First Part of the Institutes of the Laws of England*, F Hargrave and C Butler (eds), 13th edn (London, E Brooke, 1788) 212b, where Coke noted that 'where the condition is for payment of £20, the obligor or feoffor cannot at the time appointed pay a lesser sum in satisfaction of the whole, because it is apparent that a lesser sum of money cannot be a satisfaction of a greater . . . If the obligor or feoffor pay a lesser sum either before the day, or at another place than is limited by the condition, and the obligee of feofee receives it, this is good satisfaction'.

[20] See the restatement of the rule and its logic in J Chitty, *A Treatise on the Law of Contracts*, JA Russell (ed), 6th edn (London, S Sweet, 1857) 668. Cf SM Leake, *The Elements of the Law of Contracts* (London, Stevens and Sons, 1867) 468.

Selborne, who admitted that it might be an improvement to allow the release without deed of part of a debt on payment of any sum accepted by the creditor, held it 'impossible, without refinements which practically alter the sense of the word, to treat such a release or acquittance as supported by any new consideration proceeding from the debtor.'[21] He dismissed the idea that the assurance of payment of a smaller sum could be such a benefit to a creditor who might be kept at arm's length as would constitute sufficient consideration. There had to be, he said, 'some independent benefit, actual or contingent, of a kind which might in law be a good and valuable consideration for any other sort of agreement not under seal'.[22]

Lord Blackburn concurred with Selborne's judgment, but only after spending much time outlining reasons for overruling *Pinnel's Case*. He observed that there were two points made in Coke's dictum. The first point was that, 'where a matter paid and accepted in satisfaction of a debt certain might by any possibility be more beneficial to the creditor than his debt, the Court will not inquire into the adequacy of the consideration'. So, a payment the day before a debt was due would count as consideration, however little was actually paid. This point, Blackburn felt, was relevant to *Pinnel's Case*. In that case, he noted, the defendant had in fact paid a smaller sum on a day before payment was due, but had failed to plead payment in full satisfaction of the debt. The case was thus determined on a point of pleading. The second point in Coke's dictum— that a lesser sum paid on the day could not discharge a larger debt—was therefore obiter. Although, Blackburn noted, numerous courts had endorsed Coke's proposition,[23] the doctrine itself was based on error and was open for the Lords to revisit. Blackburn argued that in Coke's era, those who had paid lesser sums in satisfaction of larger debts merely pleaded the general issue, leaving it to the jury to decide whether the smaller sum had been accepted in satisfaction. Where a defendant made the special plea that he had paid a 'beaver hat' or a 'pipe of wine',[24] it was a sham plea made with a view to delay the case, and not to raise a substantive issue. Moreover, he observed that there had been no case which decided that a smaller sum could not discharge a larger debt between *Pinnel* in 1602 and *Cumber v Wane* in 1721, which suggested to Blackburn that juries were happy enough to allow this kind of discharge of a debt.

Furthermore, in his view, the rule as reported in *Pinnel's Case* was based on the incorrect notion that it could never be of benefit to a party to accept a smaller sum in settlement of a larger debt. Blackburn explained[25]:

---

[21] *Foakes v Beer* (n 18 above) (HL) 613.

[22] *Foakes v Beer* (n 18 above) (HL) 614.

[23] *Fitch v Sutton* (1804) 5 East 230, 102 ER 1058; *Down v Hatcher* (1839) 10 Ad & El 121, 113 ER 47; *Thomas v Heathorn* (1824) 2 B & C 477, 481; 107 ER 461, 463.

[24] These examples were taken from *Young v Rudd* (1695) 5 Mod 86, 87 ER 535, and Joseph Chitty (the elder), *A Treatise on the Parties to Actions*, 7th edn (London, S Sweet, 1844) vol III, 92.

[25] *Foakes v Beer* (n 18 above) (HL) 622.

What principally weighs with me in thinking that Lord Coke made a mistake of fact is my conviction that all men of business, whether merchants or tradesmen, do every day recognise and act on the ground that prompt payment of a part of their demand may be more beneficial to them than it would be to insist on their rights and enforce payment of the whole. Even where the debtor is perfectly solvent, and sure to pay at last, this often is so. Where the credit of the debtor is doubtful it must be more so.

Despite these doubts, having failed to persuade the other judges of this view, Blackburn concurred with the rest of the court. Lord FitzGerald countered Blackburn's arguments with the observation that the rule had been settled since *Pinnel's Case*, and had been repeated in the textbooks. In his view,

it is not the rule which is absurd, but some of those distinctions, emanating from the anxiety of judges to limit the operation of a rule which they considered often worked injustice.[26]

Dr Foakes had to pay.

At the heart of the dispute in *Foakes v Beer* was the question whether an apparently strict rule as to consideration should give way in the face of commercial reality. As the *Solicitor's Journal* pointed out after the case, it was hard to see in logic how the payment of a smaller sum could be consideration for a large debt. But 'practically speaking' it was more comprehensible,

because, if a man is put to sue for his debt, he will be delayed for a long time, and, perhaps, never recover it at all.[27]

Nevertheless, the business community did not seem to notice the decision in *Foakes v Beer*. Businessmen had their own ways of avoiding the pitfalls of commercially inconvenient common law rules. The rule it settled was therefore one which generated much heated debate among lawyers through the 19th century more for doctrinal reasons than practical ones.

The doctrine defended by the Lords had long come in for criticism, most famously from the editors of J W Smith's *Leading Cases*, JS Willes and HS Keating. This work included a chapter on *Cumber v Wane*, which (rather than *Pinnel*) was regarded in the mid-19th century as the root of the rule. The textbook stated the rule thus[28]:

a creditor cannot bind himself by a simple agreement to accept a smaller sum in lieu of an ascertained debt of larger amount, such an agreement being nudum pactum. But if there be any benefit, or even any legal possibility of benefit, to the creditor thrown in, that additional weight will then turn the scale, and render the consideration sufficient to support the agreement.

Like *Pinnel's Case*, *Cumber v Wane* was a case about accord and satisfaction. However, since the defendant had given a promissory note for £5 in satisfaction

---

[26] *Foakes v Beer* (n 18 above) (HL) 628–9.
[27] 'The Doctrine of *Cumber v Wane*' (1884) 29 *Solicitor's Journal* 94.
[28] JW Smith, *A Selection of Leading Cases on Various Branches of the Law*, JS Willes and HS Keating (eds), 4th edn (London, William Maxwell, 1856) vol I, 252.

of a claim in an action of *indebitatus assumpsit* for £15, it also raised questions about consideration, since a promissory note was a promise to pay in future. When *Smith's Leading Cases* discussed the case, it was therefore as interested in what the case said about consideration as what it said about satisfaction. In *Cumber v Wane*, counsel for the plaintiff, Wearge, argued that since an actual payment of a smaller sum could only amount to satisfaction of a larger debt if paid before the due day, a promise to pay a smaller sum in future—which was the effect of a promissory note—could not constitute satisfaction. He added that a promissory note could not constitute satisfaction of a contract debt, since 'it is the same security'.[29] Fazakerly, for the defendant, answered that the sum due here was not an ascertained one—since it would be for a jury to award damages for breach—and that the giving of a note reduced it to a certainty. Although Fortescue J found this a compelling argument, after consideration, Pratt J gave the judgment for the whole court, which found the plea bad. He ruled that[30]:

> as the plaintiff had a good cause of action, it can only be extinguished by a satisfaction he agrees to accept; and it is not his agreement alone that is sufficient, but it must appear to the Court to be a reasonable satisfaction; or at least the contrary must not appear, as it does in this case. If £5 be (as is admitted) no satisfaction for £15 why is a simple contract to pay £5 a satisfaction for another simple contract of three times the value?

This was a dictum which troubled later commentators in two respects. First, they had little difficulty in finding consideration for the agreement to accept the £5 note, since the note was not simply a promise to pay but a valuable security which could be negotiated, and since the debt claimed was unliquidated and therefore uncertain. Secondly, Pratt's comment about the need to convince the court that there was 'reasonable satisfaction' appeared to raise a question of the adequacy of consideration, which it was accepted courts should not look into. The editors of *Smith's Leading Cases* therefore argued that *Cumber v Wane* was

> founded upon vicious reasoning and false views of the office of a court of law, which should rather strive to give effect to the engagements which persons have thought proper to enter into, than cast about for subtle reasons to defeat them upon the ground of being unreasonable.[31]

---

[29] *Cumber v Wade* (1719) 11 Mod 342, 342; 88 ER 1077, 1078. He cited the case law which showed that a bond could not be given in satisfaction for a bond: *Lovelace v Cocket* (1609) Hob 68, 80 ER 218; *Norwood v Grype* (1599) Cro El 727, 78 ER 960. Bacon's *Abridgment* later argued that such cases were to be explained by the fact that by the time the new bond was given, the sum due would have been the penal sum, and not the sum for which the bond was given. Giving a new bond would therefore amount to giving a smaller sum for what was now a larger debt. M Bacon, *A New Abridgment of the Law,* H Gwillim and CE Dodd (eds), 7th edn (London, J & WT Clarke et al, 1832) vol I, 48.

[30] *Cumber v Wane* (1719) 1 Stra 426, 426–7; 93 ER 613, 614. See also the report in 11 Mod 342, 88 ER 1077 *sub nom Cumber v Wade.*

[31] Smith, *A Selection of Leading Cases* (n 28 above) vol I, 253. The idea that judges could weigh the adequacy of consideration was widely criticised. See, eg *Sibree v Tripp* (1846) 15 M & W 23, 36; 153 ER 745, 751.

By the time *Foakes v Beer* came to the Lords, the doctrine it upheld had come in for strong criticism. Frederick Pollock wrote in 1876 that the common law was 'committed to the absurd paradox' that a £100 debt could be discharged by the payment of a peppercorn on the due day, or ten shillings on any earlier day,

> but that nothing less than a release under seal will make his acceptance of £99 in money at the same time and place a good discharge.

Fortunately, 'modern decisions have confined this absurdity within the narrowest possible limits'.[32] In 1881, Sir George Jessel MR noted the 'extraordinary peculiarity' of the rule, calling it 'one of the mysteries of English Common Law'.[33] In 1867 the Indian Law Commissioners proposed abrogating the rule in its entirety. In their draft bill for India,

> [a] person who is entitled to claim performance of an engagement may dispense with or remit such performance, wholly or in part, or may accept instead of it any satisfaction which he thinks fit.[34]

The illustration they added, which was incorporated in the Indian Contract Act of 1872, made it manifest that one could accept a smaller sum in discharge of a larger debt.[35]

## B. EROSION OF THE DOCTRINE OF CONSIDERATION BEFORE *FOAKES v BEER*

*Foakes v Beer* came at a crossroads for consideration, and raised questions as to its very purpose. Those who favoured reform of the law were only too well aware that the strict rule found in *Pinnel's* case had been modified significantly in a number of areas to benefit commerce. For instance, early 19th century courts had begun to recognise that a debtor could make a valid composition of his debts with his creditors without drawing up a deed. Composition agreements effected by a deed of trust, assigning the assets of the bankrupt to trustees for the benefit of creditors, clearly passed the *Pinnel* test, since they were embodied in a deed.[36] They had long been upheld in law and equity, and any attempts by individual creditors to pressure the debtors into giving additional securities for the payment of the full debt were frowned on.[37] But where no deed had been drawn up, late 18th century courts were less happy with compositions. Edward

---

[32] F Pollock, *Principles of Contract at Law and in Equity* (London, Stevens & Sons, 1876) 160.

[33] *Couldery v Bartrum* (1881) 19 Ch D 394, 400.

[34] PP 1867–8 (239) XLIX 601, 13.

[35] Indian Contracts Act 1872, s 63 illustration (b). It may be noted that James Shaw Willes, one of the editors of *Smith's Leading Cases*, was one of the members of the Commission which proposed this alteration.

[36] Eg, *Mawson v Stock* (1801) 6 Ves 300, 31 ER 1062.

[37] See *Spurret v Spiller* (1740) 1 Atk 105, 26 ER 69; *Cockshott v Bennett* (1788) 2 TR 763, 766; 100 ER 411, 413, where Ashhurst said 'the debt was annihilated by the deed of composition; and the plaintiffs had consented to take a smaller sum than their original debt'.

Law discovered this in 1787 in *Heathcote v Crookshanks*, when he argued that a creditor should not be permitted to sue his debtor after agreeing to (and benefiting from) a composition. His argument that *Cumber v Wane* had 'repeatedly' been 'denied by this Court to be law',[38] was rejected by the King's Bench.[39] The status of compositions entered into without deeds remained unsettled for some time.[40] In *Fitch v Sutton* in 1804, Law, now Lord Ellenborough, abandoned the view he had articulated in *Heathcote*, holding (on the authority of *Cumber v Wane*) that a composition of £17 10s could not extinguish a £50 debt. Although the case was one of accord and satisfaction, Ellenborough saw it as raising a question of consideration:

[t]here must be some consideration for the relinquishment of the residue; something collateral, to shew a possibility of benefit to the party relinquishing his further claim, otherwise the agreement is nudum pactum.[41]

In 1809 Ellenborough changed his mind once more. In *Steinman v Magnus*, there was no deed, but half of the composition was secured by acceptances given by one creditor, Garland. The Chief Justice distinguished this case from *Fitch*, by holding that it would be a fraud on Garland for the plaintiff to recover the 80 percent residue of his debt after the composition had been agreed.[42] In taking this position, he was influenced by a number of cases which sought to protect other creditors of an insolvent trader from being defrauded.[43] For instance, although the late 18th century King's Bench held that a trader could, after his bankruptcy, promise to pay a debt extinguished by the bankrupt's certificate,[44] Lord Kenyon held that a subsequent promise to pay could not be enforced where there had been a composition deed, since such a contract

affected all the other creditors, by rendering abortive all that they had intended to do for the bankrupt, in compounding their debts.[45]

---

[38] *Heathcote v Crookshanks* (1787) 2 TR 24, 26; 100 ER 14, 15. The benefit was that the defendant would not give a preference to other creditors, and that the actions of all creditors were suspended by the agreement.

[39] Buller J ruled that '[i]f the debtor had assigned over . . . all his effects to a trustee, in order to make an equal distribution among all his creditors, that would have been a good consideration in law for the promise': *Heathcote v Crookshanks* (1787) 2 TR 24, 28; 100 ER 14, 16.

[40] In *Cooling v Noyes* (1795) 6 TR 263, 101 ER 544, Lord Kenyon wondered whether such an agreement would be binding if a specific fund had been appropriated for the creditors, but found in the case before him that as the agreement was procured by a misrepresentation, it could not in any event be sustained.

[41] *Fitch v Sutton* (1804) 5 East 230, 232; 102 ER 1058.

[42] *Steinman v Magnus* (1809) 11 East 390, 393–4; 103 ER 1055, 1056.

[43] Ellenborough was particularly influenced by the 1788 case of *Cockshott v Bennett* (1788) 2 TR 763, 100 ER 411 (in which he had been counsel) where the King's Bench held void a promissory note given by a debtor to a creditor, who had refused to execute a composition deed until he was given such a security for the remainder of his debt.

[44] The consideration for the promise was the moral obligation to pay: *Trueman v Fenton* (1777) 2 Cowp 544, 98 ER 1232.

[45] *Cockshott v Bennett* (1788) 2 TR 763, 765; 100 ER 411, 413.

In *Steinman v Magnus* the King's Bench refused to allow the creditor who had agreed a composition to sue for his full debt. This opened the way for composition contracts to be regarded as having a consideration. In the aftermath of bankruptcy reforms of 1825, which sought to encourage composition deeds,[46] courts were especially keen to give them full effect. In *Good v Cheesman* in 1831, the plaintiff was held bound by a composition agreement.[47] The doctrinal basis for avoiding the rule in *Pinnel's* case was explained by Parke J thus[48]:

> [h]ere each creditor entered into a new agreement with the defendant, the considera-
> tion of which, to the creditor, was a forbearance by all the other creditors who were
> parties, to insist upon their claims. Assumpsit would have lain on either side to enforce
> performance of this agreement, if it had been shewn that the party suing had, as far as
> lay in him, fulfilled his own share of the contract.

This analysis suggested that the consideration for the debtor promising to pay a smaller sum than was due to each creditor was his entering into a contract with all his other creditors, binding them to forbear from suing him for what was owed. This was beneficial to the creditors, since it avoided the chance that one of them might, by litigating first, obtain all the available assets.[49] But in fact, the doctrine was often supported on the principle of a consideration given by each creditor to the others, rather than on the consideration of the debtor entering into contract with others. Thus, in *Reay v White* in 1833, Bayley B ruled,

> [t]he question is not between the plaintiffs [ie, the creditors] and the defendants [ie, the
> debtors], but between the plaintiffs and the other creditors . . . There is a distinct
> undertaking by the plaintiffs, that they will do as the other creditors have done.[50]

It was accepted in the mid century that if, when modifying their contract to allow the debtor to pay a smaller sum, the creditor and debtor introduced a new party to the contract, then the new contract would supplant the original one, leaving the smaller sum to be paid.[51] By the time of *Foakes v Beer*, Lord FitzGerald could therefore say that compositions were supported 'on the rather

---

[46] Section 4 of 6 Geo IV c 16 enacted that entering into a trust deed would henceforth not itself constitute an act of bankruptcy. The earlier law, which treated composition deeds as such acts, clearly made them risky unless all creditors joined.

[47] For the facts of the case, see *Good v Cheesman* (1830) 4 C & P 513, 172 ER 805.

[48] *Good v Cheesman* (1831) 2 B & Ad 328, 335; 109 ER 1165, 1167–8.

[49] In *Alchin v Hopkins* (1834) 1 Bing (NC) 99, 102; 31 ER 1055, 1056, Tindal CJ endorsed the view of *Good v Cheesman* that 'there has been a substitution of a new agreement, by mutual con-sent, and on good consideration, in the stead or place of the old contract'.

[50] *Reay v White* (1833) 1 C & M 748, 751; 149 ER 600, 602. Equally, in 1857 Williams J, in the Exchequer Chamber, explained that 'no such agreement can operate as a defence, if made merely between the debtor and a single creditor[. T]he other creditors, or some of them, must also join in the agreement with the debtor and with each other, for otherwise it would be a bare contract to accept a less sum in satisfaction of a greater': *Boyd v Hind* (1857) 1 H & N 938, 947; 156 ER 1481, 1485.

[51] *Henderson v Stobart* (1850) 5 Exch 99, 155 ER 43. It was long settled that the payment of a lesser sum by a third party constituted consideration to discharge a larger debt: *Welby v Drake* (1825) 1 C & P 557, 171 ER 1315.

artificial consideration of the mutual consent of other creditors.'[52] Whatever the doctrinal basis, it was accepted as a matter of commercial practice that compositions between debtors and their creditors was a desirable part of everyday commercial practice.

A second area where early 19th century courts qualified the rule in *Pinnel's* case concerned the debts of partners. They allowed retiring partners to be freed of their share of the partnership debts. As a number of cases showed, when the surviving partners fell on hard times, a creditor might well wish to seek a remedy against a solvent retired partner. As with composition deeds, it took some time for the courts to allow the retired partner to be absolved of the debts. While it was settled that if a creditor took a fresh security from the continuing partner, this replaced the earlier one,[53] it was held in *Lodge v Dicas* in 1820 that a mere agreement only to look to the remaining partner would not suffice. The agreement by the plaintiff to abandon a claim against the retiring partner was, Bayley J said, a mere *nudum pactum*, unless there was some new consideration.[54]

This position was softened in 1834, in *Thompson v Percival*, where one of two brothers retired from a partnership. Although unaware of the dissolution, the plaintiffs were told to look only to the continuing partner, on whom alone they later drew a bill. When the bill was dishonoured, and the partner failed, the question was raised whether the retired partner could be sued. The King's Bench held that it was a matter for the jury to decide whether the plaintiffs had agreed to take the surviving partner as their sole debtor. Despite the earlier cases, the judges held that such an agreement would not be a *nudum pactum*.[55] Denman CJ ruled that taking a bill of exchange from one of the debtors provided sufficient consideration. But he went further, suggesting that the mere fact of looking to one partner might constitute consideration[56]:

> many cases may be conceived in which the sole liability of one of two debtors may be more beneficial than the joint liability of two, either in respect of the solvency of the parties, or the convenience of the remedy, as in cases of bankruptcy, or survivorship, or in various other ways: and whether it was actually more beneficial in each particular case, cannot be made the subject of enquiry.

This suggestion was acted on in 1853 in *Lyth v Ault*. 'It may at first appear paradoxical,' Parke B observed here, 'but the sole responsibility of one of many

---

[52] *Foakes v Beer* (n 18 above) (HL) 630.

[53] See *Evans v Drummond* (1801) 4 Esp 89, 170 ER 652; *Reed v White* (1803) 5 Esp 122, 170 ER 759. See also the comments of Bayley J in *Bedford v Deakin* (1818) 2 B & Ald 210, 216; 106 ER 344, 346, that while a creditor could not be prejudiced by the mere agreement of partners, his right to sue 'may be destroyed by the creditor consenting to accept of the separate security of one partner in discharge of the joint debt'.

[54] *Lodge v Dicas* (1820) 3 B & Ald 611, 614; 106 ER 784, 785. See also *David v Ellice* (1826) 5 B & C 196, 108 ER 73.

[55] During argument, Parke J observed that *David v Ellice* 'was not satisfactory to the profession': *Thompson v Percival* (1834) 5 B & Ad 925, 927; 110 ER 1033, 1034–5.

[56] *Thompson v Percival* (1834) 5 B & Ad 925, 933; 110 ER 1033, 1036. See also Parke B's comments in *Kirwan v Kirwan* (1834) 2 Cr & M 617, 624; 149 ER 907, 910.

partners may be of greater value than that of all'.[57] In his view, a sole liability was a different kind of security than a joint one, which made it consideration. Yet Parke's view of consideration seemed to embrace the possibility of a practical benefit.[58]

The rule in *Pinnel's* case was also not applied to bills of exchange. This was rooted in the custom of merchants, according to which a holder of a bill of exchange could renounce his claim, and waive the liability of the acceptor.[59] As Littledale J put it in 1826, the acceptor of a bill of exchange could

> be discharged by an express agreement among the parties that he shall be so, by an express renunciation by the holder of his liability, by payment, or by neglect on the part of the holder to get paid when he had proper means of payment in his power.[60]

According to Joseph Story, where the renunciation was clear, the acceptor would be discharged

> if there be a sufficient consideration, or an act done on the part of the Acceptor, which might not otherwise have been done, which affects his interests.[61]

This element of reliance was not stressed by other writers, though one writer justified the existence of the rule allowing waiver here on the grounds that parties to bills who were told that recourse would not be had to them 'are almost sure, in consequence, to alter their conduct and position'.[62] Such a discharge could be verbal, but it had to be express and clear,[63] and had to be a renunciation of the whole bill, and not just a part of it.[64] This rule was clearly an anomaly since in other cases, the release of a debt had to be by deed or with consideration. Its justification was explained by the editor of *Byles on Bills* on the grounds that foreign legal systems did not recognise the distinction between

---

[57] *Lyth v Ault* (1852) 7 Exch 669, 671 and 673; 155 ER 1117, 1118 and 1119. For instance, he pointed out, if one was owed money jointly by a rich old man and a poor young one, it was more advantageous to have the sole liability of the old man than the joint of both, since if the old man died, the creditor would at once have the security of his real and personal estate, which would not be the case if the liability was joint.

[58] It became settled in the mid nineteenth century that in these cases of novation, all that had to be shown was the agreement of the creditor to accept the liability of the new partnership: see *Hart v Alexander* (1837) 2 M & W 484, 150 ER 848.

[59] JB Byles, *A Practical Treatise of the Law of Bills of Exchange*, 4th edn (London, S Sweet, 1843) 147; J Story, *Commentaries on the Law of Bills of Exchange*, 2nd edn (London, V & R Stevens and GS Norton, 1847) § 266. See also *Whatley v Tricker* (1807) 1 Camp 35, 170 ER 867.

[60] *Farquhar v Southey* (1826) M & M 14, 16. The liability of a drawer, who was in effect only a surety, was more easily discharged. See also the comments of Mansfield CJ in *Fentum v Pocock* (1813) 5 Taunt 192, 128 ER 660.

[61] Story, *Commentaries on the Law of Bills of Exchange* (n 59 above) § 266, citing *Whatley v Tricker* (1807) 1 Camp 35, 170 ER 867, whereby the acceptor entered into an arrangement with his creditors after the renunciation.

[62] JB Byles, *A Treatise of the Law of Bills of Exchange*, MB Byles (ed), 11th edn (London, H Sweet, 1874) 197. See JA Russell (ed), *Chitty on Bills of Exchange*, 11th edn (London, H Sweet, 1878) 212 for a statement of the rule without qualification.

[63] *Dingwall v Dunster* (1779) 1 Doug 247, 99 ER 161.

[64] *Parker v Leigh* (1817) 2 Stark 228, 171 ER 629. For a mid-century example, see *Foster v Dawber* (1851) 6 Exch 839, 155 ER 785.

releases under seal and those not under seal. Since it would be inconvenient to introduce such distinctions when dealing with instruments used internationally, the same law merchant was agreed to be used for all bills.[65]

## C. SEEKING CONSIDERATION IN *FOAKES v BEER*

When it came to accommodating business needs, courts had clearly taken great strides to attempt to qualify the rule in *Pinnel's* case, often by stretching the doctrine of consideration. The mid 19th century also saw two further doctrinal developments, examining what could amount to a benefit to the promisor, which might have been drawn on by the judges in *Foakes v Beer*, had they wanted to find consideration. But as will be seen, the nature of the case was such as not to give the court much scope to apply them.

Firstly, it had been settled by the mid century that the manner of payment might make a difference. Overruling the authority of *Cumber v Wane* on this issue, the Court of Exchequer ruled in *Sibree v Tripp* in 1846 that giving a negotiable security could satisfy a liquidated debt of a larger amount.[66] For Pollock CB, giving a negotiable instrument was equivalent to giving a chattel in satisfaction of a debt, the value of which courts had never looked into.[67] Parke B agreed that 'the satisfaction is by giving a different thing, not part of the sum itself, having different properties.'[68] The notion that a negotiable instrument could discharge a larger debt was confirmed in 1882 by the Queen's Bench Division in *Goddard v O'Brien*, where the defendant settled a debt for over £125 with a £100 cheque.[69] Although the cheque was treated by the parties merely as a means to pay money owed—it had simply been cashed by the plaintiff, and not negotiated—the fact that it was by its nature negotiable counted for the court.

Foakes's counsel sought to argue that the manner in which the debt was to be paid in his case constituted consideration. Foakes, it was contended, agreed to

---

[65] Byles, *A Treatise of the Law of Bills of Exchange* (n 62 above) 197. The rule was confirmed in 1882 in the Bills of Exchange Act, although this legislation specified that the discharge had to be written.

[66] Earlier courts still followed the view of *Cumber v Wane* that a negotiable instrument given for a lesser sum could not discharge a larger debt: see *Thomas v Heathorn* (1824) 2 B & C 477, 481, 107 ER 461, 462.

[67] *Sibree v Tripp* (1846) 15 M & W 23, 32; 153 ER 745, 749.

[68] *Sibree v Tripp* (1846) 15 M & W 23, 34; 153 ER 745, 750. Alderson B added at 15 M & W 38, 153 ER 752: 'If for money you give a negotiable security, you pay it in a different way'. At 15 M & W 36, 153 ER 751, Parke B explained away *Thomas v Heathorn* by saying that 'although the bill accepted by the defendant was a negotiable security, it does not appear that it was given by way of accord and satisfaction'. But at the same time as they noted that the rule from *Cumber* did not apply where negotiable instruments were given, they accepted the general proposition that a larger debt could not be discharged by a smaller sum.

[69] Grove J noted that the doctrine in *Cumber v Wane* had been much qualified; indeed 'I am not sure that it has not been overruled'. He also found the rule odd: 'To say that you may receive something which is not money,—a chattel for instance, of inferior value,—but that you cannot receive money, is to my mind a very singular state of the law' (*Goddard v O'Brien* (1882) 9 QBD 37, 39).

pay the debt in a manner which was advantageous to the plaintiff, by paying it in instalments to her nominee, Mackreth. The Queen's Bench Division accepted the argument. But it was based on an error. As was observed by the judges in the Court of Appeal and in the Lords, Foakes had not in fact bound himself to pay in instalments. The agreement was only that he would not be sued, as long as he paid regularly. As Selborne pointed out, Foakes gave no 'new security, in the shape of negotiable paper, or in any other form'.[70] The payment of the rest of the money at deferred dates, by the creditor's indulgence, could not be consideration. Similarly, in the Court of Appeal, Brett LJ held that the stipulation to pay the nominee could not be taken into account as it had 'no legal or practical meaning'.[71] For the payment of the instalments to constitute consideration, the argument would have had to be raised that this was in effect a unilateral contract, which Foakes had completed by paying on time. But counsel did not make this kind of argument, nor was it considered by the court.[72]

The rule in *Goddard v O'Brien* still found favour for a time.[73] But the tide soon turned. In 1911, in *Hiramchand Punamchand v Temple*, Fletcher Moulton LJ doubted whether it was correctly decided, since (in his view), the cheque was given as a conditional payment of the sum, and not in substitution of the debt.[74] His reasoning was doctrinally sound. Later 19th century courts, seeking to explain why bills and cheques could be given for past debts without violating the past consideration rule, held that they were only conditional payments, with the debt reviving if they were not paid.[75] The problem of explaining this doctrinal conundrum for bills and cheques was made irrelevant by the Bills of Exchange Act of 1882, which simply enacted that past consideration was valid for such instruments. Until *Hiramchand Punamchand*, courts that were keen to allow parties to settle debts in a way suitable to commerce ignored the problem of the nature of the bill or cheque, but by the early 20th century courts were clearly less happy to glide over doctrinal difficulties to encourage business. *Goddard v O'Brien*'s standing as an authority was further undermined in 1966, in *D & C Builders v Rees*, where the Court of Appeal held that a cheque was to be regarded only as a conditional payment, unless the creditor had specifically requested the payment to be made by cheque rather than in cash.[76]

---

[70] *Foakes v Beer* (n 18 above) (HL) 611.

[71] *Beer v Foakes* (1883) 11 QBD 221 (CA) 224.

[72] This leading case on unilateral contracts was of course *Carlill v Carbolic Smoke Ball Company* [1893] 1 QB 256, nearly a decade later.

[73] See, eg *Bidder v Bridges* (1887) 37 Ch D 406, where a litigant lost his right to interest, having accepted a cheque in settlement of a judgment debt.

[74] *Hiramchand Punamchand v Temple* [1911] 2 KB 330.

[75] *Currie v Misa* (1875) LR 10 Ex 153, 163. This view was endorsed by the House of Lords in *M'Lean v the Clydesdale Banking Company* (1883) 9 App Cas 95.

[76] *D & C Builders v Rees* [1966] 2 QB 617, 632–3. In this case, the court was looking for ways to assist the creditor against a debtor who had acted unconscionably. Cf Parke J's observation in *Robinson v Read* (1829) 9 B & C 449, 455; 109 ER 167, 170: '[U]nless a bill is taken by choice instead of cash, it is not equivalent to payment'.

There was a second route through which consideration might have been found in *Foakes v Beer*. It had long been established that a forbearance to sue could constitute a consideration, provided that there was at least a prima facie claim between the parties and that the claim was not wholly without foundation.[77] The promisor did not have to have a valid claim in fact, but there had to be some 'reasonable doubt' as to the matter in dispute between the parties.[78] Merely desisting from suing 'any stranger [one] may happen to meet in the street' did not count.[79] But as the century went on, the degree of doubt required diminished towards a vanishing point. In 1849, the Common Pleas held it unnecessary to allege that the party forbearing to sue had any well-founded claim. 'Although there were no claim', Wilde CJ ruled, 'the defendant might stipulate for the renunciation of the possibility of claim', which would provide consideration for money paid over.[80] Four years later, the same court held that the withdrawal by a defendant of a plea of infancy in litigation could constitute consideration, regardless of whether the plea were true or false.[81] Equally, courts seemed untroubled by the question of how long the forbearance to sue was to ensue. Thus, a promise to give a bank added security for an existing debt, in consideration of its forbearing to enforce payment of the existing debt, was upheld, even though the bank might bring an action at any time after the giving of the new security.[82] Provided the courts were persuaded that there was a valid forbearance, it could provide consideration either for the payment of a smaller sum for a larger debt, or indeed a larger sum for a smaller debt.[83]

This doctrine opened the way for agreements to be upheld which settled unliquidated claims for money owed by an agreed, but smaller, sum. In *Wilkinson v Byers* in 1834, the King's Bench held that the payment by a defendant of a lesser sum than the amount *claimed* in a lawsuit was consideration for a promise by the plaintiff to stay proceedings and pay his costs, since in such a case it was far from certain what the jury might award. As Parke J put it,

> [p]ayment of a less sum than the demand has been held to be no satisfaction in the case of a liquidated debt; but where the debt is unliquidated, it is sufficient.

In such a case, the claim would be reduced to certainty without the plaintiff having to proceed with the litigation.[84] Littledale J based his decision in this case on an Elizabethan case, *Reynolds v Pinhowe*, whose facts were not unlike *Foakes v*

---

[77] Thus, before forbearance could count as consideration, it had to be evident that the party forbearing to sue would have had a right to sue someone: *Jones v Ashburnham* (1804) 4 East 555, 102 ER 905. See also *Tooley v Windham* (1590) Cro El 206, 78 ER 463; *Fabian v Plant* (1691) 1 Show KB 183, 89 ER 525.

[78] *Longridge v Dorville* (1821) 5 B & Ald 117, 106 ER 1136.

[79] *Edwards v Baugh* (1843) 11 M & W 641, 646; 152 ER 962, 964.

[80] *Tempson v Knowles* (1849) 7 CB 651, 653; 137 ER 258, 259.

[81] *Cooper v Parker* (1853) 14 CB 118, 139 ER 49.

[82] *Alliance Bank v Broom* (1864) 2 Dr & Sm 289, 62 ER 631.

[83] *Smith v Algar* (1830) 1 B & Ad 603, 109 ER 911.

[84] *Wilkinson v Byers* (1834) 1 Ad & El 106, 113; 110 ER 1148, 1050. See also *Sibree v Tripp* (1846) 15 M & W 23, 153 ER 745.

*Beer.*[85] Pinhowe had recovered £5 in an action from Reynolds, and promised to acknowledge satisfaction of the judgment, in consideration of £4 paid. Reynolds later sued in assumpsit for breach of this agreement, and Pinhowe demurred, alleging there was no consideration in paying £4 in lieu of a £5 debt. But the court found for the plaintiff, considering it a benefit to the defendant to have had his money

> without suit or charge: and it may be there was error in the record, so as the party might have avoided it.[86]

The conclusion Littledale J drew from this case—that an agreement to accept a smaller sum to settle a suit applied to liquidated as well as unliquidated claims—was applied in 1855 in *Cooper v Parker.*[87] This case made clear the fact that mid-century judges were unhappy with the rule against allowing smaller sums to discharge larger debts.[88] For these mid-century judges, the consideration provided by the debtor paying the smaller sum was the benefit to the plaintiff of not having to continue the litigation.

If it was well settled by 1884 that a forbearance to sue could constitute consideration, it was a doctrine which was not of much help to Dr Foakes, for it was not an argument considered by the court.[89] The Lords might have found consideration in the avoidance of further litigation, of the kind which did ensue. But it was hard to read the contract in these terms, for it spoke of Mrs Beer forbearing to sue in consideration of Dr Foakes's payments of a debt due by an existing judgment of a court. The contract, in other words, was not drawn in such a way as to offer loopholes to judges seeking them.

## D. *FOAKES v BEER* AND THE DEFENCE OF CONSIDERATION

The House of Lords in *Foakes v Beer* was thus squarely faced with the question whether performing an existing duty owed to the other party could constitute consideration. This went to the very heart of what constituted consideration. It was a question which had already been debated by the jurists who were seeking to write new, principled treatises of contract law, and one which would continue to be discussed in the decades after the Lords made its decision. In its decision to enforce the rule in *Pinnel's* case, the Lords made a clear determination

[85] This case was cited by Littledale J in *Wilkinson v Byers* (1834) 1 Ad & El 106, 110 ER 1148.

[86] *Reynolds v Pinhowe* (1595) Cro El 429, 78 ER 669.

[87] *Cooper v Parker* (1855) 15 CB 822, 139 ER 650. Here, the Exchequer Chamber upheld a settlement whereby a plaintiff in a County Court case agreed to receive a £30 in settlement of a £50 claim, after the defendant withdrew his (possibly untenable) infancy plea. Parke B criticised the position taken in *Down v Hatcher* (1839) 10 Ad & El 121, 113 ER 47.

[88] *Cooper v Parker* (1855) 15 CB 822, 828; 139 ER 650, 652 (Martin B): 'I shall always be ready to concur in such a judgment as tends to allow parties to contract for themselves what engagements they please'.

[89] It was however raised by counsel: *Foakes v Beer* (n 18 above) (HL) 607.

that the doctrine of consideration was not to be watered down any further, since it was seen as a vital element of English contract law, which could not be eroded.

Jurists agreed that the doctrine of consideration was a cornerstone of the common law of contract. Not even the most devoted will theorist argued that it could be simply abolished in favour of a doctrine of intention to create legal relations.[90] But there was some uncertainty among them as to its meaning. Traditional definitions of consideration spoke of it in terms of a benefit to the promisor or a detriment to the promisee.[91] As has been seen, mid century judges, seeking to relax the rules of consideration, often focused on the question of whether the promisee received a benefit from the promise. But by the time of *Foakes v Beer*, greater stress was laid on the element of detriment. The key influence here was Christopher Columbus Langdell, who in his *Summary of the Law of Contracts* declared that 'detriment to the promisee is a universal test of the sufficiency of consideration', and that 'benefit to the promisor is irrelevant' to the issue of consideration.[92] A similar view was adopted by Frederick Pollock in later editions of his treatise on contract.[93] Anson's definition did not lay so much stress on detriment, but did note that the consideration consisted of something done by the promisee.[94]

This raised the question of what constituted a detriment to the promisee. Late 19th century academics spilled much ink on debating whether the performance of existing duties could constitute a consideration. Although it had been settled in a series of mid 19th century cases that the performance of a duty already owed to a third party could constitute consideration for a promise to another,[95] jurists were troubled by it. Langdell was especially bothered by Martin B's comment in *Scotson v Pegg* that 'any act done whereby the contracting party receives a benefit is a good consideration'.[96] In his view, there could be no consideration in *performing* what one was already bound to do for a third party, since it could involve no new detriment. But he felt that there could be consideration in *promising* to perform what one was already so bound to perform, since the promisee incurred 'a detriment by giving another person the right to compel him

[90] For the tension between this doctrine and consideration, see S Williston, 'Consideration in Bilateral Contracts' (1914) 27 *Harvard Law Review* 506, fn 13.
[91] See J Comyns, *A Digest of the Laws of England*, (London, W Strahan, 1780) vol I, 138 (Action on the Case, Assumpsit); *Currie v Misa* (1875) LR 10 Ex 153, 162.
[92] CC Langdell, *Summary of the Law of Contracts*, 2nd edn (Boston, Little, Brown & Co, 1880) 81–2.
[93] 'Consideration means not so much that one party is profited as that the other abandons some legal right in the present, or limits his legal freedom of action in the future': F Pollock, *Principles of Contract*, 4th edn (London, Stevens & Sons, 1885) 167.
[94] 'Consideration therefore is something done, forborne, or suffered, or promised to be done, forborne, or suffered by the promisee in respect of the promise. It must necessarily be *in respect of the promise*, since consideration gives to the promise a binding force': WR Anson, *Principles of the English Law of Contract*, 6th edn (Oxford, Clarendon Press, 1891) 72.
[95] *Shadwell v Shadwell* (1860) 9 CB NS 159, 142 ER 62; *Scotson v Pegg* (1861) 6 H & N 295, 158 ER 121.
[96] *Scotson v Pegg* (1861) 6 H & N 295, 299; 158 ER 121, 123; Langdell, *Summary of the Law of Contracts* (n 92 above) 81–2.

to do it'.[97] Consideration was thus present only where a party promised to perform what he was already under an obligation to do for a third party. Pollock—always ready to let convenience overrule logic—was less precise than Langdell, but accepted Langdell's reasoning on this matter.[98] Anson felt more uncomfortable with the notion. He was unconvinced by Langdell's solution, since it assumed that the promise to the new party to perform would be upheld by a court as a valid promise, backed by consideration. This, he argued, was merely begging the question. In Anson's view, a better explanation was that once the promisor promised a new party to perform his existing duty, he was no longer in a position to agree with the third party to terminate their agreement, but now needed the assent of the new party as well. This could, for Anson, be seen as a detriment.[99]

If a promise to perform an existing duty to a third party could be seen as consideration, almost all late 19th century jurists agreed—both before and after *Foakes v Beer*—that a promise to perform an existing duty owed to the promisee could not be. The most common manifestation of this issue was (as in *Foakes v Beer*) that of a promise to pay part of an existing debt. Anson, who felt that *Foakes v Beer* had been rightly decided, felt it was neither unreasonable nor inconvenient to 'require particular solemnities to give to a gratuitous contract the force of a binding obligation'.[100] Theorists also considered the situation where the promisor promised to perform an act for the promisee which he was already bound to do for him. The few English authorities that existed held that promises to perform the same thing twice could not count as consideration,[101] a doctrine which English treatise writers found little fault with. In a number of American jurisdictions, courts had, by contrast, upheld contracts in which one party performed the same thing agreed under an earlier contract, but for a different price or on different terms.[102] But many American jurists were uneasy with these cases. Samuel Williston, for example, argued that they could not be sustained, either on a theory that the original contract had been rescinded and another substituted, or on a consideration that actual performance of the work was worth more to the defendant than the damages or penalty he would receive

---

[97] Langdell, *Summary of the Law of Contracts* (n 92 above) 105. Langdell hence felt that *Shadwell v Shadwell* and *Scotson v Pegg*—where there was no *promise* to perform an existing duty, but merely its performance—were wrongly decided.

[98] See F Pollock, *Principles of Contract*, 7th edn (London, Stevens & Sons, 1902) 178, and the note in 9th edn (London, Stevens & Sons, 1921) 202.

[99] WR Anson, *Principles of the English Law of Contract* (Oxford, Clarendon Press, 1879) 81. This view was accepted by Pollock, *Principles of Contract* (n 98 above) 179, as well as by later writers (eg CJ Hamson, 'The Reform of Consideration' (1938) 54 *Law Quarterly Review* 238).

[100] Anson, *Principles of the English Law of Contract* (n 94 above) 86.

[101] *Harris v Watson* (1791) Peake 102, 170 ER 94; *Stilk v Myrick* (1809) 2 Camp 317, 170 ER 1168.

[102] *Lattimore v Harsen* 14 Johns 330 (NY Supp 1817); *Munroe v Perkins* 26 Mass (9 Pick) 298 (Mass 1830); *Goebel v Linn* 47 Mich 489, 11 NW 284 (Mich 1882). See also *Hackley v Headley* 45 Mich 569, 8 NW 511 (Mich 1881).

for breach of the first contract. In his view, these decisions were contrary 'to general principles universally admitted'.[103]

The one writer who was happy with the idea that the performance of existing duties—whether the payment of debts or the performance of acts—could constitute consideration, was James Barr Ames. In his view, the decision in *Foakes v Beer*—'repugnant alike to judges and men of business'—was wrongly decided, being based on a misunderstanding by the judges of earlier case law.[104] *Pinnel's* case, he pointed out, was not about consideration at all. The rule it applied—that a smaller sum could not satisfy a larger debt—was 'simply the survival of a bit of formal logic of the mediaeval lawyers,'[105] which predated the doctrine of consideration. The logic was obvious enough: £10 could not satisfy a £20 debt, simply because £10 could never be £20. But the Lords (he felt) had overlooked early modern cases which showed that while part payment could not, as a matter of logic, be a *satisfaction* of a larger debt, it could be *consideration* for a promise to cancel a debt.[106] In Ames's view, the two doctrines had become confused thanks to Lord Ellenborough's confusing consideration and satisfaction in *Fitch v Sutton*. For Ames, the medieval rule that there could be no accord and satisfaction of a debt by part payment should have ceased to have any practical operation when it was supplanted by the rule of *Bagge v Slade* that payment of part of a debt was good consideration for the creditor's promise to relinquish the rest.

Ames also believed that a promise to perform an act that one was already bound to the promisee to perform[107] could constitute consideration. For while Ames accepted Langdell's contention that consideration had to be a detriment to the promisee, he argued that *any* act or forbearance could constitute consideration, provided that it was not against public policy. This definition, he argued, 'unquestionably makes for individual freedom of contract and for logical simplicity in the law'.[108] Ames felt that a *promise* to perform a pre-existing contractual duty to the counter-promisor could constitute consideration, since the promise itself was a sufficient 'act' to fit his definition.[109] This would mean that a promise to pay money could constitute consideration for a promise by the creditor to accept less than the full debt.[110] Ames disputed Pollock's contention that

---

[103] S Williston, 'Successive Promises of the Same Performance' (1894–5) 8 *Harvard Law Review* 30, 32.
[104] JB Ames, 'Two Theories of Consideration—I. Unilateral Contracts' (1899) 12 *Harvard Law Review* 515, 531.
[105] *Ibid* 521.
[106] He gave as authority *Bagge v Slade* (1616) 3 Bulst 162, 81 ER 137; 1 Roll Rep 354, 81 ER 530; and *Rawlins v Lockey* (1639) 1 Vin Abt 308, pl 24.
[107] Eg *Peck v Requa* 13 Grey 407 (Mass 1859).
[108] Ames, 'Two Theories of Consideration—I. Unilateral Contracts' (n 104 above) 531.
[109] JB Ames, 'Two Theories of Consideration—II. Bilateral Contracts' (1899) 13 *Harvard Law Review* 27.
[110] English case law denied this: *Lynn v Bruce* (1794) 2 H Bl 317, 126 ER 571.

an express promise by A to B to do something which B can already call on him to do can in contemplation of law produce no fresh advantage to B or detriment to A.[111]

For as Ames pointed out, the law did not measure the adequacy of consideration, provided it existed. It was indeed a truism for 19th century writers that courts had no means to measure the adequacy of consideration, and that parties were to be left free to put their own value on bargains.[112] In Ames's view, the making of a new promise was an act by A, which he was not obliged to give:

> [i]f B thought it sufficiently for his interest to give a counter promise in exchange for A's promise, and the mutual agreement is open to no objection on grounds of policy, why should not the court give effect to this bargain as fully as to any other?

Since mutual promises were consideration for each other, there was no reason not to uphold such a contract.[113]

While Ames did not argue for the abolition of the doctrine of consideration, his interpretation of the doctrine appeared to render it superfluous. Provided that there was a bargain between the parties which was not against public policy, it was to be upheld. For Ames, an accepted promise to make a gift would bind the promisor with no further formalities. These views were not accepted by his English contemporaries. Pollock felt that since a promise to accept would in Ames's terms also be an act, the American's analysis would open the way

> to the modern civilian conception that the giving and acceptance of any serious promise whatever suffice to create an obligation.[114]

But this was not, he felt, English law. *Foakes v Beer* thus did not merely represent a defence of the *Pinnel's* case: it was a reaffirmation of the centrality of consideration in contract law.

Ames's view may not have convinced Pollock, but it did influence the Law Revision Committee, which in 1937 recommended abolishing the rule in *Pinnel's* case and accepting as valid consideration a promise to do what one was already bound to do. By the 1930s it was widely agreed that the rule in *Pinnel's* case was commercially inconvenient, and should be abolished; though some commentators felt that safeguards needed to be introduced to protect promisors from duress.[115] The committee clearly felt that there were major problems with the entire doctrine of consideration. It failed to distinguish clearly between

---

[111] Pollock, *Principles of Contract* (n 98 above) 177.

[112] This was the same kind of argument that Willes and Keating made in their note to *Cumber v Wane* in Smith, *A Selection of Leading Cases* (n 28 above) vol I, 253: 'Carried to its full extent, the doctrine of *Cumber v Wane* embraces the exploded notion, that in order to render valid a contract not under seal, the adequacy as well as the existence of the consideration must be established'.

[113] For Ames, it made no sense for courts to uphold the agreement in cases such as *Lyth v Ault* but not in *Foakes v Beer*. These cases showed little more than that at common law a 'bird in the hand is worth less than a bird in the bush!': Ames, 'Two Theories of Consideration—II. Bilateral Contracts' (n 109 above) 39–40.

[114] F Pollock, *Principles of Contract*, 9th edn (London, Stevens & Sons, 1921) xi.

[115] Hamson, 'The Reform of Consideration' (n 99 above) 238–9. See also (1937) 1 *Modern Law Review* 103.

onerous and gratuitous contracts, but had become a technical doctrine which could be evaded by the courts finding a nominal consideration, which risked frustrating the intention of the parties. Although many people wanted 'to see the doctrine abolished root and branch', the committee felt that it was too embedded in the system to be removed, and had to be reformed.[116] In the end, the committee's recommendations were not implemented by legislation and consideration remained unreformed.

In retrospect—and in light of the hostility to the rule in *Pinnel's* case which had developed by 1937—the decision of the Lords in *Foakes v Beer* may seem puzzling. After a century in which the doctrine of consideration was watered down in commercial contexts, the Lords declined the opportunity to take a further radical step forward. The reason for this was that neither the judges, nor most academics, were convinced in the era after 1880 that consideration could be dispensed with. Consideration remained an essential component of contracts not under seal. Even those who subscribed fully to the will theory of contract, such as Anson, felt that consideration was needed to make an informal contract actionable. The doctrine made for 'logical completeness' in English contract law, though the development of the doctrine had been 'silent' and its necessity challenged by Mansfield.[117] This author did not spend much time discussing the purpose of consideration, further than to say that it was to give evidence of the parties' intention.[118] Nonetheless, Anson did not flinch from seeking to defend the integrity of the rules of consideration, and did not suggest that they could be replaced by a test focusing on the intention to create legal relations.[119] His contemporary Pollock—despite an enthusiasm for Savigny shared with Anson—also inclined more towards a bargain theory of contract than towards the will theory. Even in his early editions, he spoke of the 'act or forbearance of the one party, or the promise thereof' as 'the price for which the promise of the other is bought.'[120] The doctrine of consideration was an essential component of a bargain theory,[121] which may explain why Pollock remained keen on it.[122] Moreover, even though Pollock

---

[116] Law Revision Committee, Sixth Interim Report, Cmd 5449 (1937) 17.

[117] Anson, *Principles of the English Law of Contract* (n 94 above) 46.

[118] WR Anson, *Principles of the English Law of Contract* 8th edn (Oxford, Clarendon Press, 1895) 43 spoke of it giving 'further evidence' of their intention, while at 105 he stated that '[c]onsideration is not one of several tests, it is the only test of intention'.

[119] He did, however, discuss the need for such intentions: Anson, *Principles of the English Law of Contract* (n 118 above) 40–1.

[120] Pollock, *Principles of Contract* (n 93 above) 167. In his early editions, Pollock noted that the requirement of consideration was a condition imposed by a positive rule of English law, rather than being an elementary constituent of an agreement (*ibid* 8). In later editions, he continued to note the English peculiarity of the doctrine, but put greater emphasis on the need for informal contracts to be bargains: *Principles of Contracts*, 8th edn (London, Stevens & Sons, 1911) 10.

[121] Hamson, 'The Reform of Consideration' (n 99 above) 234.

[122] However, Pollock's own description of consideration (like Anson's) rooted it in historical developments rather than in analytical necessity. But unlike Anson, he did not root the need for consideration in evidence: 'The main end and use of the doctrine of Consideration in our modern law . . . is to furnish us with a reasonable and comprehensive set of rules which can be applied to all informal contracts without distinction of their character or subject-matter' (Pollock, *Principles of Contract* (n 93 above) 183).

was noted for bringing Savigny's views on the intention to create legal relations to an English public, his own treatment of the matter in his textbook was almost as cursory as Anson's.[123] Academics like Pollock, who had read their Savigny,[124] knew that an offer and acceptance were not enough to make a contract. The agreement had to be invested 'with the character of an obligation'.[125] In the absence of a developed doctrine identifying an intention to create legal relations, English jurists continued to believe that it was only the presence of consideration which invested informal agreements with obligatory force. Little wonder, then, that the Lords in *Foakes v Beer* were not prepared to abandon consideration.

## E. *FOAKES v BEER* AND THE PROBLEM OF PROMISSORY ESTOPPEL

Jurists who were prepared to defend consideration remained uneasy with the rule of *Foakes v Beer*. Ten years after the Law Revision Committee's report, Denning J seemed to discover a way to draw its sting. In *Central London Property Trust Ltd v High Trees House Ltd*, he declared that

> a promise to accept a smaller sum in discharge of a larger sum, if acted upon, is binding notwithstanding the absence of consideration.

This was, Denning held, 'the natural result of the fusion of law and equity', and one which had not been 'considered in *Foakes v Beer*'. For Denning, the principle derived from

> cases in which a promise was made which was intended to create legal relations and which, to the knowledge of the person making the promise, was going to be acted on.[126]

He sought in effect to apply a reliance theory of contract in English law, removing the need for consideration altogether. The doctrine of *High Trees* was later described as a kind of 'promissory estoppel'.[127] This new doctrine provided an exception to the rule that the common law did not enforce gratuitous promises. According to the doctrine, where one party made a promise or 'representation in the nature of a promise'[128] which was acted or relied on by the other party,

---

[123] Pollock, *Principles of Contract* (n 93 above) 13.

[124] FC von Savigny, *Das Obligationenrecht*, (Berlin, Deit & Co, 1851–3) vol I, §§ 2–4.

[125] WR Anson, *Principles of the English Law of Contract*, 3rd edn (Oxford, Clarendon Press, 1884) 4–5.

[126] *Central London Property Trust Ltd v High Trees House Ltd* [1947] KB 130, 135 and 134.

[127] In *High Trees*, he had taken care to point out that it was not an estoppel: *High Trees* (n 126 above) 134.

[128] Sir GH Treitel, *The Law of Contract*, 11th edn (London, Thomson, Sweet & Maxwell, 2003) 107. In *Combe v Combe* [1951] 2 KB 215, 220, Denning used the formula, 'where one party has, by his words or conduct, made to the other a promise or assurance which was intended to affect the legal relations between them'.

then the promisor would not be permitted to 'revert to the previous legal relations',[129] where it would be inequitable for him to do so.[130]

Although the doctrine of promissory estoppel was new to mid-20th century English law, it was an idea which had gained currency in early 20th century American law.[131] It was first championed by Samuel Williston. Why, he asked in 1913,

> should not a promise be enforced, if the promisor might reasonably suppose the promisee would act in reliance on the promise, and if the promisee has in fact done so?[132]

He included and named the doctrine in his textbook on *Contracts* in 1920.[133] The doctrine emerged in America out of a series of cases involving promises to make charitable gifts. Where such a promise was made, and the charity incurred liabilities on the faith of the promise, courts held that it was not a gratuitous, but an enforceable promise. Although such cases could be explained in traditional terms of consideration—with the charity being seen to incur liabilities at the request of the promisor—by the late 19th century, American courts used the term estoppel in their judgments.[134] Thanks to Williston's analysis of promissory estoppel, and its generalisation in the Restatement of Contracts, the doctrine came to be applied more broadly.[135] As Williston perceived, liability in such cases depended on injurious reliance on promises. Where there had been such reliance, American courts allowed plaintiffs to sue on the gratuitous promise, using the doctrine as a 'sword'.[136] These were 'informal contracts created without a manifested mutual assent'.[137]

Given the evolution of this doctrine in late 19th and early 20th century America, and given that *Foakes v Beer* was decided after the very fusion of law and equity which Denning invoked in *High Trees*, it is worth asking why the doctrine articulated in the latter case was not considered in the former. Denning

---

[129] *Combe v Combe* [1951] 2 KB 215, 220.

[130] This qualification was added by Lord Denning MR in *D & C Builders v Rees* [1965] 3 All ER 837 (CA) 841.

[131] Contracts Restatement (1932) § 90.

[132] HW Ballantine, 'Is the Doctrine of Consideration Senseless and Illogical?' (1912–13) 11 *Michigan Law Review* 425. Ballantine went on to endorse this view in the article at 426.

[133] S Williston and GJ Thompson, *Selections from Williston's Treatise on the Law of Contracts* (New York, Baker Voorhis & Co, 1938) § 139.

[134] Eg *School Dist of City of Kansas v Stocking* 138 Mo 672, 40 SW 656 (Mo 1897) (where Macfarlane J held that if 'expense was incurred and the liability created in furtherance of the enterprise the donor intended to promote, and in reliance upon the promises, they will be taken to have been incurred and created at his instance and request, and his executors will be estopped to plead want of consideration'. See also *University of Vermont v Buell* 2 Vt 48 (Vt 1829); *University of Des Moines v Livingston* 57 Iowa 307, 10 NW 738, 739–40 (Iowa 1881); *Young Men's Christian Association v Estill* 140 Ga 291, 78 SE 1075 (Ga 1913); *Allegheny College v National Chautauqua County Bank of Jamestown* 159 NE 173 (NY 1927).

[135] See Learned Hand J's comments in *James Baird Co v Gimbel Bros* 64 F 2d 344 (2nd Cir 1933).

[136] *Ricketts v Scorhorn* 57 Neb 51, 77 NW 365 (Neb 1898).

[137] Williston and Thompson, *Selections from Williston's Treatise on the Law of Contracts* (n 133 above) § 139.

lay the blame at the door of *Jorden v Money*,[138] the mid-19th century case which had held that 'a representation as to the future must be embodied in a contract or be nothing',[139] and justified his departure from it by noting that the law had not stood still since that case was decided. Others agreed that *Jorden v Money* had curtailed a natural development of estoppel, which would have enabled it to be used as a cause of action.[140] But as shall now be seen, English judges and jurists at the end of the 19th century simply did not see any room for the development of the kind of doctrine articulated by Williston and Denning. For judges throughout the 19th century were very reluctant to develop a view of law which would permit liability to be rooted in reliance on a mere representation, unpaid for by any consideration.

## 1. Estoppel by Representation in Early 19th Century Law and Equity

The common law doctrine of estoppel by representation and the equitable doctrine of holding parties to make good their representations have often been seen as the roots of Denning's doctrine, whose growth was impeded by *Jorden v Money*. The doctrine of estoppel by representation developed in the early 19th century trover cases,[141] drawing on the evidentiary doctrine that a party who had admitted the truth of certain facts was prevented from denying it.[142] In 1831, Parke J ruled

> that a party having made admissions by which another has been led to alter his condition, is estopped from disputing their truth with respect to that person and that transaction.[143]

The establishment of the doctrine of estoppel by representation was generally associated with *Pickard v Sears*, another action of trover. In this case, Lord Denman CJ ruled that[144]:

---

[138] *Jorden v Money* (1854) 5 HLC 185, 10 ER 868. Denning himself in *High Trees* (n 126 above) felt the need to distinguish the case.

[139] *High Trees* (n 126 above) [1947] KB 130, 134 and 135.

[140] David Jackson, 'Estoppel as a Sword' (1965) 81 *Law Quarterly Review* 84 and 223. It may be noted that in *High Trees*, Denning J did not limit the doctrine to a defence.

[141] *Clarke v Clarke* (1806) 6 Esp 61, 170 ER 830; *Like v Howe* (1806) 6 Esp 20, 170 ER 817; *Heane v Rogers* (1829) 9 B & C 577, 586—7, 109 ER 215, 218.

[142] According to MM Bigelow, *A Treatise on the Law of Estoppel*, 2nd edn (Boston, Little, Brown & Co, 1876) ch 18, the common law notion that a party would not be permitted to deny the truth of representations acted on by another came from the equitable doctrine of holding parties to make good their representations (for which see *Evans v Bicknell* (1801) 6 Ves 174, 183, 31 ER 998, 1002). For the early 19th century developments, see M Lobban, 'Contractual Fraud in Law and Equity, c 1750–c 1850' (1997) 17 *Oxford Journal of Legal Studies* 453–6.

[143] *Stratford and Moreton Railway Company v Stratton* (1831) 2 B & Ad 518, 526, 109 ER 1235, 1238.

[144] *Pickard v Sears* (1837) 6 A & E 469, 473; 112 ER 179, 181. In this case, goods which belonged to the plaintiff had been in the possession of a third party, against whom a *fieri facias* had issued. After the goods were seized, the plaintiff discussed with the party who had sought the *fieri facias* how the debt of the third party—for which the execution was sought—could be settled, but

where one by his words or conduct wilfully causes another to believe the existence of a certain state of things, and induces him to act on that belief, so as to alter his own previous position, the former is concluded from averring against the latter a different state of things existing at the same time.

In 1848, Parke B held that for the doctrine to apply, it had to be evident to the person addressed that the one making the statement intended his representation to be acted on.[145] The representation courts looked for was 'such as to amount to the contract or licence of the party making it'. By this, Parke B meant that to be operative, the representation had to be as unambiguous and as intentional as a contractual offer.[146] Where such a clear statement was made implying the abandonment or non-existence of a right, it was considered that it would be a fraud on the party who relied on it to go back on it.

Although estoppel was rooted in the idea that it would be a fraud on the representee to go back on one's statement, it was not necessary for the party making the representation to have any fraudulent intent. It only required a 'wilful' act. By this, Parke B explained,[147]

> we must understand, if not that the party represents that to be true which he knows to be untrue, at least, that he means his representation to be acted upon, and that it is acted upon accordingly; and if whatever a man's real intention may be, he so conducts himself that a reasonable man would take the representation to be true, and believe that it was meant that he should act upon it, and did act upon it as true, the party making the representation would be equally precluded from contesting its truth.

This comment was of course much drawn on by late 19th century contract lawyers in explaining the 'objective' nature of contractual intent. But the mid-century courts which developed this doctrine as a defence in trover cases did not apply it to contractual situations. They did not enforce promises intended to be contractually binding, which had been relied on, but which had not been paid for by consideration.[148] No one doubted that consideration, as well as contractual intent, was essential for the formation of a contract.

Moreover, the approach of the common law to representations left little room for a doctrine of estoppel within contract law itself. Where a representation had

without ever mentioning that the goods in fact belonged to him. When they were subsequently sold to the defendant, he was held estopped from claiming them. Although no representation had been made to the defendant, the plaintiff was estopped from denying the passing of property in the goods.

[145] *Freeman v Cooke* (1848) 2 Exch 654, 663; 154 ER 652, 656. In *Howard v Hudson* (1852) 2 E & B 1, 10; 118 ER 669, 673, Lord Campbell CJ held that it had to be shown by the party seeking to take the benefit of the estoppel 'both that there was a wilful intent to make him act on the faith of the representation, and that he did so act'. Parke's ruling sought to clarify an ambiguity created by Denman's judgment in *Gregg v Wells* (1839) 10 A & E 90, 98, 113 ER 35, 38.

[146] *Freeman v Cooke* (1848) 2 Exch 654, 664; 154 ER 652, 657. This view was endorsed more strongly by Pollock CB in *Cornish v Abingdon* (1859) 4 H & N 549, 555–6; 157 ER 956, 959.

[147] *Freeman v Cooke* (1848) 2 Exch 654, 663; 154 ER 652, 656.

[148] Estoppel by representation was only used in the rarest of contract cases. In the rare case in which the doctrine was applied, a party who had acted in such a way as to lead another to believe that he was in a contractual relationship with him was held bound to the contract. See, eg *Cornish v Abingdon* (1859) 4 H & N 549, 157 ER 956.

been made prior to a contract, courts looked at whether it had become a term of the contract, or whether it had been made deceitfully. Despite some doubts in the 1840s over whether an action of deceit could be brought when there was no 'moral fraud', but where a false statement had been made which had been relied on,[149] it was settled by the mid century that a representation not made fraudulently which was not incorporated as a term could not be the subject of an action, however much it had been relied on.[150] Nor could a misstatement of one's intent be seen as amounting to deceit. Common law courts were not attempting to supplant contractual rules by introducing a new form of liability incurred as a result of reliance on statements that were not contractually binding. There was thus little room in the common law for a notion of promissory estoppel, where the promisor would be estopped from going back on a relied-on statement of intent.[151] Where the representation was one of existing fact, made with sufficient clarity and intention to amount to a licence, it was in effect equivalent to a transfer or abandonment of one's rights. But where it was a statement of future intent, to reach the same level of certainty as a 'licence', it had to fulfil the requirements of a contract.

Courts of equity had a longer history of requiring parties to make good their representations than common law courts did. But—as can be seen from marriage cases—equity also looked for either a contract or fraud. 18th and 19th century aristocratic and middle-class marriages were routinely preceded by promises by various parties to settle money on the couple, in consideration of their marriage. Promises to settle money upon a marriage raised no problems of consideration for Chancery judges, for they (unlike some common law ones)[152] had no difficulty in holding that '[m]arriage is the most valuable of all considerations'.[153] Since the Chancery did not regard such arrangements as bargains, the consideration of the marriage did not have to be in response to a request from the promisor. Courts dealing with disputes over marriage settlements therefore did not spend much time in looking to see whether there was consideration for the contract. They did, by contrast, spend much more time looking to see whether the parties had come to a contractual agreement.

Under the Statute of Frauds, marriage settlements would only be enforced if they had been memorialised in a written document which had been signed. The statute ensured that a seriously intended, binding contract had been entered into. It was settled in the 18th century that the Chancery would uphold a marriage settlement which had not been memorialised in a single document, as long

---

[149] M Lobban, 'Nineteenth Century Frauds in Company Formation: *Derry v Peek* in Context' (1996) 107 *Law Quarterly Review* 308. See also *Polhill v Walter* (1832) 3 B & Ad 114, 110 ER 43.

[150] Eg *Baglehole v Walters* (1811) 3 Camp 154, 170 ER 1338; *Pickering v Dowson* (1813) 4 Taunt 779, 128 ER 537; *Dobell v Stevens* (1825) 3 B & C 623, 107 ER 864; *Freeman v Baker* (1833) 5 B & Ad 797, 110 ER 985.

[151] For the American view, see esp *Langdon v Doud* (1865) 10 Allen 433, 92 Mass 433; *White v Ashton* (1873) 6 Sickels 280, 51 NY 280.

[152] *Shadwell v Shadwell* (1860) 9 CB NS 159, 174; 142 ER 62, 68.

[153] *Fraser v Thompson* (1859) 4 De G & J 659, 661; 45 ER 256, 257.

as the court could piece together a written agreement from various documents. However, this written evidence had to show a firm agreement, with an unequivocal promise communicated to the promisee, who married 'in confidence' of the promise.[154] This meant that if a person promising to settle money on the marriage had in any way reserved the right to change his mind—such as writing a letter saying 'I may bind myself' to pay money on a marriage—this was not considered as sufficient evidence to satisfy the statute, since there had to be a clear contractual intent[155] to show on the written evidence that an agreement had been reached.

In cases where no written agreement could be made out, but an unfulfilled parol promise had been made prior to the marriage, equity forced parties to make the representation good if there had been fraud. But it did not regard it as a fraud simply to go back on one's promises.[156] As Lord Parker LC put it,

> where there is no fraud, only relying upon the honour, word or promise of the defendant, the statute making those promises void, equity will not interfere.[157]

By contrast, it was regarded as a fraud for a father to refuse to pay the daughter's portion according to articles drawn up and given to him to sign, after he had allowed the groom to court his daughter and permitted the marriage to take place and the couple to live with him.[158] 18th century courts of equity were thus not overly generous when it came to enforcing promises made prior to marriage. To be enforced, they had either to be embodied in a pre-nuptial written contract, or be found by part performance after marriage which confirmed a contract, or there had to be fraud.

But in 1841 a dictum of Lord Cottenham's seemed to widen the rule considerably. In *De Biel v Thomson,* he stated that[159]

> [a] representation made by one party for the purpose of influencing the conduct of the other party, and acted on by him, will in general be sufficient to entitle him to the assistance of this Court for the purpose of realizing such representation.

The dictum was made in another marriage case, where the bride's father had stated during the pre-nuptial negotiations that he 'intended to leave' his daughter £10,000 in his will. This promise was omitted from the executed settlement,

---

[154] *Ayliffe v Tracy* (1722) 2 P Wms 65, 66; 24 ER 642, 642. See also *Wain v Warlters* (1804) 5 East 10, 102 ER 972.

[155] *Randall v Morgan* (1805) 12 Ves Jun 67, 33 ER 26.

[156] For the distinction between cases of fraud, and those where a party giving a verbal promise to pay was permitted to change his mind, see *Montacute v Maxwell* (1720) 1 P Wms 618, 620; 24 ER 541, 542; *Halfpenny v Ballet* (1699) 2 Vern 373, 23 ER 836; *Wanchford v Fotherley* (1694) 2 Freeman 201, 22 ER 1159. See also JJ Powell, *Essay on the Law of Contracts and Agreements* (Dublin, P Byrne et al, 1796) 298.

[157] *Montacute v Maxwell* (1720) 1 P Wms 618, 620; 24 ER 541, 542.

[158] *Halfpenny v Ballet* (1699) 2 Vern 373, 23 ER 836.

[159] *Hammersley v De Biel* (1845) 12 Cl & F 45, 62n; 8 ER 1312, 1320n. In a later case, Lord Cottenham seemed to root his decision more specifically in the fact of part performance by the baron, in settling the jointure: *Lassence v Tierney* (1849) 1 M & G 551, 572; 41 ER 1379, 1387.

however, and the father later changed his will. Although in fact the case could be determined on 'traditional' lines,[160] Cottenham insisted that it was not necessary to find a 'formal contract'. His broader point, unnecessary for the decision, was that equity would hold a man to his relied-on representations even in the absence of a formal contract or the kind of fraud equity had in the past looked for.[161]

In the context of this case, Cottenham's dictum may have been aimed at softening the rigours of the Statute of Frauds, by upholding pre-nuptial parol agreements to settle property, even in the absence of the taint of fraud which 18th century courts had looked for.[162] But it was soon evident that the dictum could be used to support a claim, where—leaving aside Statute of Frauds formalities—the statement could not be seen to have been made with a clear contractual intent, so that no contract could have resulted. The question whether a mere statement of future intent might be sufficient to support a claim was raised in 1854, in *Maunsell v Hedges*. Here, a man contracted a marriage after being told that his uncle would leave him property in his will. The uncle had refused to settle the property on his nephew, saying 'I shall never settle part of my property out of my power while I exist', but added that 'I am confident that I shall never alter it to your disadvantage'. It was clear here that the correspondence did not amount to a contractual promise to leave the property to the nephew. Nonetheless, Sir Richard Bethell argued that if a statement contained a representation either of past fact, or present intention, this created 'an engagement which cannot be revoked'.[163] Invoking Cottenham's dictum, he argued that a declaration of intent which was acted on was binding.[164]

But Lord Cranworth LC felt that Cottenham's dictum was much too broad. He noted that the uncle had neither made a contractually binding promise, nor a statement of existing fact 'so made as to constitute the ground of a contract' which it would be a fraud to go back on. Since the uncle had explicitly left it in his own power to alter the will, his reassurances could not be seen to have contractual effect. If they were not uttered with the intent to be binding, Cranworth could not see how they could become so.

---

[160] *De Beil v Thomson* (1841) 3 Beav 469, 476; 49 ER 184, 187. In *Maunsell v Hedges*, Lord Cranworth also noted that in *Hammersley* 'it was successfully contended that there was a contract to leave a sum of money': (1854) 4 HLC 1039, 1055; 10 ER 769, 775.

[161] Cottenham's approach appeared to be endorsed in the Lords, though the judges here took greater care to link their dicta to the context of marriages. See eg *Hammersley v De Biel* (1845) 12 Cl & F 45, 78–9; 8 ER 1312, 1327 (Lord Lyndhurst): '[I]f a party holds out inducements to another to celebrate a marriage, and holds them out deliberately and plainly, and the other party consents, and celebrates the marriage in consequence of them, if he had good reason to expect that it was intended that he should have the benefit of the proposal which was so held out, a Court of Equity will take care that he is not disappointed, and will give effect to the proposal'.

[162] That is, when Cottenham stated that it was not necessary to find a 'formal contract', he meant one that would satisfy the statute.

[163] *Maunsell v Hedges* (1854) 4 HLC 1039, 1049; 10 ER 769, 773.

[164] Although Bethell conceded that Eyre had reserved the power of altering the will, he argued that he could not do so 'merely from caprice, or from a change of sentiment': *Maunsell v Hedges* (1854) 4 HLC 1039, 1051; 10 ER 769, 774.

[b]y what words [he asked] are you to define whether a party has entered into an engagement as distinct from a contract, but which becomes a contract by another person acting upon it?

For Cranworth,

[a] contract cannot be at large: it cannot be unilateral; it cannot be performed on one side, and left unperformed on the other.[165]

Only if the promise had been made with contractual intent could it be binding.[166] Lord St Leonards concurred in the decision, also holding that the uncle had not intended to make an irrevocable engagement. But he had clear sympathy for Cottenham's attempt to soften the rigours of the Statute of Frauds. For he said that in general[167]

what is called a representation, which is made as an inducement for another to act upon it, and is followed by his acting upon it, will, especially in such a case as marriage, be deemed to be a contract. If a party will hold out a representation as a condition on which a marriage may take place, and the marriage does take place upon it, he must give effect to that representation.

## 2. The Impact of *Jordan v Money*

It was in the context of debate over the application of Cottenham's doctrine that *Jorden v Money* was litigated. Like *Foakes v Beer*, it involved a dispute over a debt which appeared to have been waived. In the case, William Money, sought to restrain Louisa Jorden (née Marnell) and her husband from executing a common law judgment for a debt. William Money, a young soldier, had borrowed money from Charles Marnell, Louisa's brother, in 1841, to invest in Spanish bonds. Charles had himself joined in the speculation, but when it turned sour, took warrants of attorney from the young man to secure his debt, in the hope of extracting payment from William's father. In 1843, however, he died, leaving his estate to his sister. Louisa, who was very fond of the young man, and felt her brother had acted shamefully, made it clear to the Money family that she considered the debt abandoned. But she retained the documents, and consistently refused to give them up. In 1845, when William was contemplating marriage, his father, George, paid her a visit. During the time when the two families resided in India, he had been very generous to the Marnells. In 1832, he had made over to Louisa a property at Midnapore, to provide her with an income. He now told her that if he were to settle this property on his son in consideration of marriage, the conveyance to her could be set aside as a voluntary one. He proposed that if

---

[165] *Maunsell v Hedges* (1854) 4 HLC 1039, 1057; 10 ER 769, 776.
[166] In this case, had that been the case, the nephew's marriage would have constituted the acceptance, and the marriage would have been consideration.
[167] *Maunsell v Hedges* (1854) 4 HLC 1039, 1059–60; 10 ER 769, 777.

she agreed to abandon the debt, he would agree not to convey away the house. The parties later disagreed over whether Louisa agreed then to abandon the debt. She continued to retain the bonds, but still told family member that she would never use them against William. In August 1845 William married, without any settlement of the Midnapore property being made on him. His wife's family made a settlement on the marriage, on the understanding that Louisa's debt would not be enforced. Two years later Louisa married William Jorden, bringing the debt with her as a marriage portion. By 1850, relations between the families had soured, and in 1850 William Money sought Chancery's help to prevent Louisa and her husband taking action on the security to recover £1856 claimed for debt and interest.

As these facts show, the case involved a statement by Louisa Marnell that she would never enforce a debt on the faith of which a marriage was contracted. William's case rested on two arguments. First, it was claimed that there was a binding agreement between George and Louisa, and that his forbearance to settle the Midnapore property on William was consideration for her discharging the debt. Secondly, it was claimed that since William's marriage took place as a result of Louisa's assurances that she would not enforce the bond, it would be a fraud on her part now to seek to do so. William lost the first argument, since Louisa positively denied George Money's evidence that he had come to an agreement with her. As Lord Cranworth pointed out, it was a settled rule of equity that where a defendant positively denied the assertion of a single witness, the court would not act on that witness's testimony. Even if it existed, the contract could not be proved.[168] But it was the second question which proved more contentious, for it went to the heart of whether a party who had by his representations induced another to change his position was bound to make those representations good. Things had initially looked good for William, when Sir John Romilly MR ruled that in equity[169]

> [i]f a deliberate statement be made by one person to another, who, believing that statement to be true and upon the faith of it, enters into engagements, the person who made the statement shall not be permitted, by any act of his, to falsify it—nay, more, he shall be compelled, as far as lies within his power, to make good the statement he asserted to be true.

But in the Chancery Court of Appeal, Cranworth (rehearsing arguments he would later use in *Maunsell*) pointed out that all the cases where equity held a party liable to make representations good involved misrepresentations of fact. In such cases, the court acted 'on the principle of fraud, not at all on contract'.[170] If Louisa had ever stated that she had released the debt or that the bond was

---

[168] *Money v Jordan* (1852) 2 De G M & G 318, 336–7; 42 ER 895, 902, citing *Evans v Bicknell* (1801) 6 Ves 174, 184; 31 ER 998, 1003.
[169] *Money v Jorden* (1852) 15 Beav 372, 378; 51 ER 581, 584.
[170] *Money v Jordan* (1852) 2 De G M & G 318, 332; 42 ER 895, 900.

invalid, it would be a fraud for her subsequently to attempt to enforce it. But she had not said this. Although William was therefore not entitled on the ground of fraud for relief, Cranworth conceded that he might have got relief had Louisa bound herself before the marriage not to enforce the bond, in consideration of the marriage.[171] But William also lost on this point. For she had made it clear that she only bound herself in honour. However disreputable it might have been to violate one's word of honour, it was not a breach of contract.

In the House of Lords, the Statute of Frauds objection was raised for the first time.[172] Roundell Palmer, for the respondents, could have tried to argue that, while it was no answer to the Statute of Frauds to say that the parties had come to an oral agreement, its effects could be avoided by holding that it was a fraud in equity to go back on an oral contractual promise. This may have been the approach Cottenham had had in mind in *Maunsell*. But he did not choose to do so, given that Mrs Jorden's promise was too ambiguous to count as a contractual one. Instead, he argued that the statute did not apply since this was not a promise made in consideration of marriage at all. This was, he said, an assurance that the debt would not be enforced, on the faith of which a marriage had taken place. He did not claim that this amounted to fraud, but merely said that it was 'a moral equity' that the Chancery would not 'allow one party to mislead another'.[173] A mere representation about future intent which had been acted on would bind. This was an argument rejected by Lord Cranworth. He admitted that both in equity and law, it was settled that a person making a false representation to another, who acted on it, would not be permitted to assert the real truth in place of the falsehood. Moreover (alluding to *Freeman v Cooke*), he admitted that

> it is not necessary that the party making the representation should know that it was false; no fraud need have been intended at the time.[174]

But for the doctrine to apply, there had to be a misrepresentation of a matter of fact, and not one of intention. In his view, for Mrs Jorden to change her mind about her intentions was 'no more a fraud' on William than it would be to promise before his marriage to settle a sum on him, and then fail to do so. For the Lord Chancellor, only a *contractual* representation about her intentions would bind her.

---

[171] '[I]f Mrs Jordan did, before and in consideration of the marriage, bind herself not to enforce the bond or judgment, the Plaintiff might be entitled to relief on the head of contract': *Money v Jordan* (1852) 2 De G M & G 318, 334; 42 ER 895, 900 and 901. Cranworth pointed out that the Statute of Frauds point had not been raised (on which William would have lost), and so he was prepared to see if there was an oral contract. This may indicate that he was willing to accept Cottenham's dictum insofar as it sought to soften the impact of the Statute of Frauds.

[172] Cf the discussion in PS Atiyah, 'Consideration: a Restatement' in PS Atiyah, *Essays on Contract* (Oxford, Clarendon Press, 1990) 233–8.

[173] *Jorden v Money* (1854) 5 HLC 185, 207; 10 ER 868, 879.

[174] *Jorden v Money* (1854) 5 HLC 185, 212; 10 ER 868, 881 (Lord Cranworth LC).

Despite this decision, doubts remained whether a statement of intention which was not contractually valid could still bind.[175] A number of judges after *Jorden v Money* continued to take Cottenham's view that a pre-nuptial oral agreement which did not satisfy the Statute of Frauds could be enforced. In one such case, *Prole v Soady*, Stuart VC said the

> doctrine, which gives all the force of a binding contract to the mere expression of an intention to do something by an instrument revocable in its nature, is too firmly established to be shaken.[176]

In this case, unlike *Jorden v Money*, it was clear that a promise had been made which was intended to be binding. This judge was also prepared to uphold promises that did not satisfy the requirements of the Statute of Frauds to leave property by will. In *Loffus v Maw* (where the testator made an oral promise to his niece to leave him property in his will, to persuade her to continue to be his housekeeper) an objection based on the statute was dismissed as having no application to cases which involved representations. Nevertheless, the transaction upheld was again one which (like the pre-nuptial agreements) could (but for the statute) be seen as contractual.[177]

Judges who continued to invoke Cottenham's dictum were also prepared to stretch it beyond cases where there would have been a contract, but for the statute. In *Coles v Pilkington*, a testator, wishing to dissuade her cousin from moving away to start a new career elsewhere, promised her that she would always be able to live rent free in her house. Although no document was drawn up to satisfy the Statute of Frauds, Malins VC held the cousin was entitled to the benefit of the promise. He admitted that nothing was given in return for the promise, but said that

> there may be other kinds of consideration, and if the conduct of one person induces another to alter his or her conduct, that will make a binding contract.[178]

Quoting Cottenham's ruling in *Hammersley*, he held that this was a case

> in which the representations made . . . must be held to be sufficient to raise a consideration in favour of the Plaintiff.

---

[175] In 1859, Lord Campbell expressed uncertainty over whether *Jorden v Money* had fully settled the 'difference between a misrepresentation of a fact as it actually existed, and a misrepresentation of an intention to do, or to abstain from doing, an act which would lead to the damage of the party thereby induced to do an act on the faith of the representation': *Piggott v Stratton* (1859) 1 De G F & J 33, 52; 45 ER 271, 278. In this case, an injunction was issued to prevent a party from going back on a (true) representation that he had no power under a lease to build on certain land, when he later surrendered the lease and obtained a new one, which did allow him to build. The court rejected counsel's argument that this was at most a representation that he did not intend to exercise his legal right to surrender the lease, which could not be enforced.

[176] *Prole v Soady* (1859) 2 Giff 1, 30; 66 ER 1, 13.

[177] As Stuart VC ruled, if the plaintiff here could 'prove by sufficient evidence that the testator induced her to continue her valuable services on the faith of his representation that he would leave her the property in question at his death, she is entitled to the assistance of the Court': *Loffus v Maw* (1862) 3 Giff 592, 602; 66 ER 544, 548.

[178] *Coles v Pilkington* (1874) LR 19 Eq 174, 177.

Here, the promise of a gift became binding because it influenced the promisee's conduct. In this case, the testator's intention was clear enough. Unlike the marriage cases, however, there was no consideration given. Nonetheless, Malins held that since the promise had been deliberately made and acted on, it could bind notwithstanding the absence of consideration.[179] This was a radical approach, since it in effect sought to enforce a promissory representation which could not (Statute of Frauds issues aside) fall into a traditional understanding of contract.

Stuart VC was also prepared to enforce promises which had been relied on, where no parol contract of any kind could be made out.[180] In *Skidmore v Bradford* in 1869, where a testator had arranged for the purchase of a warehouse in his nephew's name, but had only paid for part of it, he held the estate liable to pay the full outstanding sum, even though no provision to this effect was made in the uncle's will.

> [I]f [Stuart ruled] on the faith of the testator's representation [the plaintiff] has involved himself in any liability, or has incurred any obligation, he cannot be regarded as a volunteer, and if so, the testator's assets are liable to make good the representation on the faith of which the nephew has entered into this contract.[181]

Stuart and Malins were thus prepared to give an extensive application to Cottenham's doctrine.

But they were soon reined in by the Chancery Court of Appeal and House of Lords. In *Caton v Caton*, the Lords overturned a decision by Stuart VC upholding a parol pre-nuptial agreement, since they felt that the decision undermined the Statute of Frauds.[182] The Lords were clearly not prepared to go along with Cottenham's erosion of the statute, which would leave it spineless. Stuart's attempt to apply his doctrine in a commercial context was also frowned on by the higher courts, which reiterated the view of *Jorden v Money* that to be actionable a representation had to be one of existing fact or embodied in a contract.[183] *Jorden v Money* was endorsed once more by the Lords in 1883 in *Maddison v Alderson*, where *Loffus v Maw* was finally overruled. Here, as in *Loffus v Maw*,

---

[179] He also held that there had been sufficient part performance to take it out of the Statute of Frauds. The case was not appealed, but Malins's judgments were frequently overturned. His obituary (*The Times* (17 Jan 1882) 4 col b) noted that '[r]eversals [of his decisions] were so common that his decision was seldom regarded as conclusive, and often became merely an expensive gate to the Court of Appeal'.

[180] *Skidmore v Bradford* (1869) LR 8 Eq 134.

[181] *Ibid* 136. Stuart VC found authority in *Crosbie v M'Doual* (1806) 13 Ves 148, 158; 33 ER 251, 254.

[182] *Caton v Caton* (1867) LR 2 HL 127. Stuart had invoked equity's jurisdiction over fraud, noting that '[t]here is an abundance of decision that, in order to prevent fraud, although the agreement has been made in parol, if anything has been done upon the faith of it, much more if there be anything in writing and signed in part performance of it, the statute will not apply': *Caton v Caton* (1865) 1 Ch App 137, 144.

[183] *Thomson v Simpson* (1870) LR 9 Eq 497; *Thomson v Simpson* (1870) 5 Ch App 659; *Citizen's Bank of Louisiana and New Orleans Canal and Banking Company v First National Bank of New Orleans* (1873) LR 6 HL 352, 360.

an intestate man had promised to leave a life interest in a farm to the appellant, his housekeeper, in order to persuade her to continue to work for him without wages. In the Exchequer Division, Stephen J found for the plaintiff, not on the grounds of her reliance on a representation—for he fully endorsed Cranworth's view that a representation, to be actionable, had to be one of fact—but on the grounds that she had provided consideration for a contract.[184] But the decision was overturned. As the House of Lords held, she could only succeed if the representation of future intent had been a contractual one, and it could only be a contractual one, in a case such as this, if it satisfied the Statute of Frauds.[185] This was a particularly hard case, for the deceased had drawn up the intended will but had failed to have it properly attested.[186] But the Lords felt that even though it was hard on the housekeeper, the need to maintain the Statute of Frauds was too important. Thus, on the eve of *Foakes v Beer*, the two highest courts in England had set their faces against a doctrine which would allow a non-contractual promise which had been relied on to be made good.

*Jorden v Money* confirmed that, in order to be binding, a representation of future intent had to amount to a contractual promise. It was not enough that the person making the representation could foresee, or intended that it should be acted on. Contractual liability could not be rooted in mere reliance on a representation. For the judges in *Jorden*, the crucial point was that the promise had to be made with an intention that it would be irrevocable and binding. The central question was thus whether a contractual offer had been made. As has been seen, *Jorden* did not raise any issues about consideration or reliance or acceptance, for marriage settlements were not regarded as bargains. The marriage itself was seen as consideration. The Chancery did not require the marriage to have taken place in any way at the request of the promisor, or in response to the promise. This meant that, had Mrs Jorden made a clear, unequivocal promise, it would have been a contractual promise—although (had the Lords taken the approach taken in *Caton v Caton*, rather than the one Cottenham wanted) it would have been struck down for failing to comply with the Statute of Frauds.

Since the case defended the notion that a party could only incur contractual liabilities if he had a contractual intent, it might have provided fodder for will theorists who wished to root contractual liability in the will of the parties, without requiring the added ingredient of consideration. Equity's ability to uncover the intentions of the parties gave them much more scope than the mid century common law courts had to probe contractual intent. This might have paved the way for a richer doctrine of the intention to create legal relations. Given equity's aaproach of not requiring the consideration of marriage to be done at the

---

[184] *Alderson v Maddison* (1880) 5 Ex D 293.

[185] In Lord Selborne's view, there was no part performance here which could evade the statute, as the housekeeper's work could be explained without inferring the existence of a contract: *Maddison v Alderson* (1883) 8 App Cas 467, 479–80, drawing on *Dale v Hamilton* (1846) 5 Hare 381, 67 ER 955.

[186] *Alderson v Maddison* (1880) 5 Ex D 293, 295.

request of or for the benefit of the promisor, it might also have paved the way for a smaller doctrine of consideration, such as that striven for by Malins in *Coles v Pilkington*, where there had been a clear promise which had been accepted, by the promisee changing their position. *Jorden v Money* thus did not restrict the House of Lords's freedom of manoeuvre in *Foakes v Beer* to qualify the rule of consideration. For in *Foakes* there was a clear promise and a clear acceptance, embodied in contract which provided that the interest did not have to be paid. What was lacking was consideration. For the Lords in *Foakes v Beer*, there could not be a contractual offer without consideration. *Jorden v Money*, in effect, raised a doctrine which had yet to find its English voice—the doctrine of the intention to create legal relations. Had they chosen to do so, the judges in *Foakes v Beer* might have developed this doctrine in such a way as to remove the need for consideration. For the decision was made at a time when Pollock had already brought to British notice the doctrines of Savigny, for whom the intention to create legal relations was a central element of contract law. The fact that they did not do may be explained by the fact that they were still wedded to a bargain theory where consideration was essential.

## F.  *FOAKES v BEER* AND WAIVER

If Denning J may have thought, in *High Trees*, of allowing his new doctrine to be used as a cause of action, he soon changed his mind. In 1951, he qualified his principle, stating that it could only act as a 'shield'. Consideration, he now said, was 'too firmly fixed to be overthrown by a side-wind', and it remained an essential part of a cause of action.[187] In articulating his original doctrine, Denning had not in fact referred to the American authorities on promissory estoppel, but to old English authorities. As shall now be seen, they did not suggest that estoppel could be used as a cause of action. But neither did they suggest that it could be used in cases such as *Foakes v Beer*. What the late 19th century cases did suggest was that in some situations, a party could suspend the enforcement of his contractual rights for a period, without losing those rights.

The central question behind *Foakes v Beer* and *High Trees* was why a party could not simply waive contractual entitlements. Those who were critical of *Foakes v Beer*, and who sought to argue that debts could be waived, such as Pollock, contended that the function of consideration was 'to govern the formulation of contracts,' rather than 'to regulate and restrain the[ir] discharge'.[188] As the *Solicitor's Journal* put it,

---

[187]  *Combe v Combe* [1951] 2 KB 215, 220.

[188]  Pollock, *Principles of Contract at Law and in Equity* (n 32 above) 160. Pollock's attitude towards the decision in *Foakes v Beer* was a mixture of criticism and deference to authority. In a note on the case, he wrote that it had 'absolutely determined' a doubtful question, and was 'as striking a proof as can be found of the weight wisely given by English courts to authority': (1885) 1 *Law Quarterly Review* 134. A subsequent note critical of *Bidder v Bridges* (n 73 above) in (1888) 4 *Law Quarterly Review* 368 added that the rule was 'intelligible, and if it be held unreasonable should be

though the enforcement by the law of *nuda pacta* might be mischievous and unendurable, there was no hardship involved in making a voluntary forgiveness of an obligation binding.[189]

But the argument that debts could simply be waived was very hard to reconcile with settled common law rules. Parties to a simple contract could vary it or discharge it, before breach, by mere words.[190] Thus an engagement to marry could be terminated simply by one party releasing the other. Where contracts were discharged (as in marriage cases), it was not necessary to claim there had been a new agreement.[191] Where there was a new agreement, it was taken to extinguish a previous one which covered the same ground in an inconsistent way.[192] Where the terms of the contract were varied it was held to substitute a new contract for the old, which would require agreement and consideration.

This rule created problems where variations were made to contracts which needed to be evidenced in writing to comply with the Statute of Frauds, since any alteration of the contract—or any waiver of a term—effectively made a new contract which would require writing.[193] This rule seemed harsh in cases where relatively minor terms had been altered before breach, such as dates for delivery of goods sold. One solution to this problem was suggested in 1813, when Lord Ellenborough ruled that where the vendor of a consignment of bacon (covered by the statute) agreed verbally to a delayed delivery (because the market was slack), the original contract was still in place, and that the parties had only modified its performance. The 'modified' contract was therefore not void for being a new unwritten one.[194] But by 1840, common lawyers had turned away from this position. As Parke B saw it,

> [e]very thing for which the parties stipulate as forming part of the contract must be deemed to be material.

This meant that an agreed time for performance constituted a term of the contract.[195] In his view, the waiver of such any term was in effect a variation of an original agreement, which would need to be in writing to comply with the

set aside by the legislature'. Nonetheless, the tone of his notes showed that he disapproved of the rule in *Pinnel's case* (n 19 above) and he restated his criticisms of it (discussed above at note 32) and his views regarding the functions of consideration in editions of his treatise subsequent to the Lords' decision: eg *Principles of Contract* (n 98 above) 190.

[189] 'The Doctrine of *Cumber v Wane*' (1884) 29 *Solicitor's Journal* 94, 95.

[190] See Chitty, *A Treatise on the Law of Contracts* (n 20 above) 680. See also *Taylor v Hilary* (1835) 1 C M & R 741.

[191] It did not therefore have to be pleaded as a mutual agreement to rescind the original contract: see *King v Gillet* (1840) 7 M & W 55, 151 ER 676.

[192] *Patmore v Colburn* (1834) 1 C M & R 65, 49 ER 996; *French v Patton* (1808) 9 East 351, 103 ER 606.

[193] See, eg *Goss v Lord Nugent* (1833) 5 B & Ad 58, 110 ER 713 and *Marshall v Lynn* (1840) 6 M & W 109, 151 ER 342. But cf *Taylor v Hilary* (1835) 1 C M & R 741, where it was held that the new agreement did not fall within the statute's provisions.

[194] *Cuff v Penn* (1813) 1 M & S 21, 105 ER 8.

[195] *Marshall v Lynn* (1840) 6 M & W 109, 117; 151 ER 342, 345. See also *Stead v Dawber* (1839) 10 Ad & El 57, 113 ER 22.

Statute of Frauds. It followed that contractual variations also required consideration.[196] This approach was commercially inconvenient, as it allowed buyers of goods to request sellers to delay delivery for their own convenience, and then to refuse subsequently to accept delivery of the goods, on the grounds of non-compliance with the Statute of Frauds. But judges nevertheless embraced it.

What of waiver after breach? Innocent parties could waive breaches that would justify termination. In doing so, they did not alter the contractual obligations in question, but merely abandoned their right to treat the contract as discharged. Such waivers—waivers in the sense of electing to affirm rather than to rescind a contract—were familiar enough from property law, where the Chancery would order specific performance where a vendor had waived objections which would entitle him to cancel the contract of sale.[197] They were also to be found in cases where parties failed to appoint arbitrators in time, but continued to act according to the arbitration agreement.[198] Similarly, it was settled in land law that breaches of covenant which justified forfeitures could be waived,[199] albeit without the obligations under the covenant being extinguished.[200] The notion of 'waiver', derived from covenants concerning land, thus involved the idea that the right to elect to terminate a contract would be lost by an affirmation. Judges explaining this settled doctrine sometimes used language which made it look like an estoppel. Thus, in 1827 Lord Tenterden CJ held that a landlord could not enforce a forfeiture after having (with knowledge) received rent, since doing so

> would be an admission that the lease was subsisting at the time when that rent became due, [so] that he could not afterwards insist upon a forfeiture previously committed.

To hold otherwise would be 'productive of great injustice,' since the tenant might have spent money on the property in the interim.[201]

This approach could be applied easily enough to cases not involving land. Thus, in *Alexander v Gardner* in 1835, the plaintiffs contracted to sell a consignment of butter to the defendants which was due for delivery in October. The shipment was delayed, and the defendants agreed to waive the breach. By doing so, the court held, they lost their right to treat the contract as discharged and had to pay for the goods which were delivered late.

> If the Defendants had in the first instance repudiated the bargain on that ground, it is true no action would have lain against them, [Tindal CJ ruled] [b]ut it is found by the

---

[196] Although in *Stead v Dawber* (1839) 10 Ad & El 57, 65; 113 ER 22, 25, Lord Denman declared: '[t]here is nothing to prevent the total waiver, or the partial alteration, of a written contract not under seal by parol agreement,' he only meant that it could be varied by *parol*, rather than that it could be varied without consideration.

[197] Eg *Cutts v Thodey* (1842) 13 Sim 206, 60 ER 80; *Tanner v Smith* (1840) 10 Sim 410, 59 ER 673.

[198] *Hawksworth v Brammall* (1839) 5 Myl & Cr 281, 295; 41 ER 377, 383.

[199] *Doe d Morecroft v Meux* (1825) 4 B & C 606, 107 ER 1185.

[200] See, eg *Doe d Boscawen v Bliss* (1813) 4 Taunt 735, 128 ER 519; *Doe d Flower v Peck* (1830) 1 B & Ad 428, 109 ER 847; *Doe d Baker v Jones* (1850) 5 Exch 498, 155 ER 218.

[201] *Arnsby v Woodward* (1827) 6 B & C 519, 524; 108 ER 542, 544.

jury that they waived the objection; and this being only a parol contract, if the party waives the condition he is in the same situation *as if it had never existed* (emphasis added).[202]

In articulating the law in this way, he was seeking to get around the rule that conditions precedent had to be performed before any liability was incurred. A different means he suggested in another case was to say that a term was 'not a condition, but a stipulation, for non-observance of which the Defendant may be entitled to recover damages'.[203] This was to reclassify the term into something modern lawyers call a warranty. But in neither case did he imply that a right to damages resulting from the breach was, or could be, waived without consideration. The problem for *Foakes v Beer* was that those who owed debts were in the same position as those who owed damages as a consequence of a breach. As has been seen, it was settled doctrine that such debts could not simply be waived. Where an innocent party wanted legally to forgive a breach—removing his right to damages—there had either to be a deed or an 'accord and satisfaction.' If Pollock had doubts about this doctrine, he failed to discuss how to overcome the problem that there had to be satisfaction for a waiver to be valid.[204]

In 1884, it seemed there was no way out of the rule, and hence it was simply reaffirmed in *Foakes v Beer*. But where Pollock was stumped, Denning thought he had found a solution to the problem in a principle preventing

> a party from insisting upon his strict legal rights, when it would be unjust to allow him to enforce them, having regard to the dealings which have taken place between the parties.[205]

The 19th century roots of principle are to be traced, not in estoppel by representation in law or equity, but in two other late 19th century decisions. The first was *Ogle v Earl Vane* in 1867. Here, a seller of iron failed to deliver it on time to the buyer, after an accident occurred at his blast furnaces. In the face of this breach of contract, negotiations were entered into with the purchaser to supply the iron at a later date. None was forthcoming, and so the buyers went to market, and sued for the difference in value between the contract price and the market price when they bought the goods. The defendants however claimed that the damages should be measured from the time (eight months earlier) that they breached the contract, when the price was lower.[206] They argued that the

---

[202] *Alexander v Gardner* (1835) 1 Bing NC 671, 677; 131 ER 1276, 1278.

[203] See also his comments in *Lucas v Godwin* (1837) 3 Bing NC 737, 744; 132 ER 595, 597. In any case, he noted, 'in accepting the work done, the Defendant admits that it is of some benefit to him, and that the Plaintiff is entitled to some remuneration'.

[204] Langdell offered a better solution, arguing that there would be an accord and satisfaction if a debtor promised to pay a smaller sum, in exchange for a promise by the creditor never to sue. The accord would be the agreement, the satisfaction the fact that a contract had been made which could be sued on. See Langdell, *Summary of the Law of Contracts* (n 92 above) 108 (§ 88).

[205] *Combe v Combe* [1951] 2 KB 215, 219.

[206] As counsel put it, '[t]he plaintiff is seeking to enforce the original contracts which were broken at the end of July; the measure of damages was then fixed': *Ogle v Earl Vane* (1867) LR 2 QB 275 (QB) 279.

plaintiffs could only claim the higher sum on the basis of an agreement to delay delivery. Such an agreement, they went on, would constitute a new contract, which would be void for not complying with the Statute of Frauds.

This argument failed, and the plaintiff recovered the full sum. But the court had some difficulty in finding a doctrinal basis for the just solution. The plaintiff could not be said to have waived the defendant's breach (in the way permitted in *Alexander v Gardner*), for had he done so, he would have lost the right to terminate the contract and would have had to wait indefinitely for the seller to deliver, without ever being able to go to market. Suggesting an implied term for a delivery within a reasonable time would not overcome this, since such a term would be a new one, implying a new contract which would have to be written. In the Queen's Bench Division, Lush J ignored the doctrinal niceties. In his view, there was no reason why, after breach by the defendant, the plaintiff should not wait at his request, with an understanding between the parties that the buyer should be able to go into market and buy at the then price, if the seller failed to deliver. But the other judges in the Queen's Bench Division and the Exchequer Chamber used different—and inconsistent—reasoning, perhaps troubled by having to explain how a right which had been waived could be resumed.

Blackburn J's solution was to hold that this was 'clearly a case of voluntary waiting, and not of alteration in the contract', which would require writing. He suggested that the distinction between these two positions depended on the parties' intentions. There was, he said, a clear distinction between merely waiting (as was done here), and binding oneself to wait[207] (as was done in *Stead v Dawber*[208] and *Marshall v Lynn*[209]). This analysis treated as interchangeable cases where there had been a variation before breach, and those where there was waiver after breach. In the Exchequer Chamber, the judges took different approaches. Willes J's solution was that there had been 'a contract to purchase forbearance' and that the defendant had to pay for the forbearance he had bought.[210] By contrast, Kelly CB rejected the idea that there had been a new contract. But neither did he view what had occurred as involving a waiver of breach. Rather he focused on the fact that the defendant had proposed a delay, to see if a compromise could be reached[211]:

> [i]t would be contrary to common sense and justice, when there has been a series of proposals by the defendant involving delay for his own benefit, and acquiescence on the part of the plaintiff, that, because there may be no binding contract, varying the terms of the former contract, the plaintiff is to be tied down to the strict letter of the rule as to the measure of damages.

---

[207] *Ibid* 283.
[208] *Stead v Dawber* (1839) 10 Ad & El 57, 113 ER 22.
[209] *Marshall v Lynn* (1840) 6 M & W 109, 151 ER 342.
[210] *Ogle v Earl Vane* (1868) LR 3 QB 272 (Exch Ch) 279–80. Such a contract 'to buy forbearance' would not be covered by the Statute of Frauds.
[211] *Ibid* 279.

Where the plaintiff had been induced by the defendant not to enforce his right to recover damages, these rights were not extinguished but suspended, thanks to the representation of the one party and the reliance by the other.

If Kelly's formulation hinted at an estoppel, Blackburn's articulation was perhaps more influential in paving the way for a rule that

> where one party at the request of and for the convenience of the other forbears to perform the contract in some particular respect according to its letter . . . the contract is not varied at all, but the mode and manner of its performance is altered.[212]

The rule remained problematic insofar as a failure 'to perform the contract in some particular respect strictly according to its letter' could only involve some breach of a term.[213] This was in effect a way of reviving the distinction set out by Lord Ellenborough in *Cuff v Penn*[214] which had so worried Parke B. Nonetheless, by the twentieth century, courts were stressing a distinction between waiver in the nature of 'forbearance' in the performance of a contract (which required no consideration and did not need to comply with the requirements of the Statute of Frauds) and 'waiver amounting to a variation of the contract' (which did), which allowed parties who extended the time for performing a contract to evade the Statute of Frauds.[215] As in Blackburn's formulation, drawing the line between the two was a matter of considering the intentions of the parties.

This case was not recognised by Denning as a root of his notion of promissory estoppel. But it was a root for a doctrine which developed in the twentieth century of waiver in the sense of estoppel, which contrasted with the (traditional) waiver in the sense of election.[216] For Denning, a more important root was the 1877 House of Lords decision in *Hughes v Metropolitan Railway Company*. This case turned on the equitable doctrine of granting relief to lessees against their landlord's right to forfeiture. The respondents in the case held the lease on houses in Euston Road, which they were obliged to repair within six months of notice given to them. After notice had been given by the appellants (the lessors), the parties entered into negotiations for the sale of the property back to the lessors. Repair work was interrupted during these negotiations, and the lessees did not commence them until the time for their completion had nearly expired. When it did, the lessors sought to enforce the forfeiture.

The equitable doctrine raised by this case was an old one. While covenants had strictly to be performed according to common law, equity traditionally gave relief against forfeiture to the party in breach, where the breach was occasioned by unavoidable accident, fraud, or surprise, provided compensation was made

---

[212] *Morris v Baron* [1918] AC 1 (HL) 31 (Lord Atkinson). See also Lindley J's ruling in *Hickman v Haynes* (1875) LR 10 QB 598, 606.

[213] *Morris v Baron* [1918] AC 1 (HL) 31 (Lord Atkinson).

[214] *Cuff v Penn* (1813) 1 M & S 21, 105 ER 8.

[215] *Levey and Company v Goldberg* [1922] 1 KB 688, 690.

[216] See eg JW Carter, *Breach of Contract*, 2nd edn (London, Sweet & Maxwell, 1991) para 1042.

to the party entitled to performance.[217] Lord Erskine LC in 1806 went so far as to suggest that this doctrine could be extended to give relief against forfeiture in cases of simple non-repair. In his view, where the rigid exercise by the lessor of his full legal rights would produce hardship to the lessee, relief should be given in a situation, provided the lessor could still have the full benefit of the contract, and 'a clear mode of compensation can be discovered'.[218] But Erskine's position was doubted by Lord Eldon,[219] and by the mid century it seemed clear that equity would not grant relief against forfeiture for failure to repair. However, there were indications given by some judges that if other 'equitable circumstances' were present, equity might assist the party in breach.[220] It was in this doctrinal context that *Hughes* was heard.

The House of Lords, upholding the decision of the Court of Appeal, held that the lessees would be relieved against the forfeiture, since the communications from the lessors concerning the negotiations had the effect of suspending the notice. The equitable circumstance in this case which was relevant was the conduct of the lessor. As Lord Cairns put it,[221]

> if parties who have entered into definite and distinct terms involving certain legal results—certain penalties or legal forfeiture—afterwards by their own act or with their own consent enter upon a course of negotiation which has the effect of leading one of the parties to suppose that the strict rights arising under the contract will not be enforced, or will be kept in suspense, or held in abeyance, the person who otherwise might have enforced those rights will not be allowed to enforce them where it would be inequitable having regard to the dealings which have thus taken place between the parties.

Although Cairns spoke of the time which elapsed during negotiations being 'waived' by the defendant,[222] it was evident that the decision of the court did not rest on any concept of waiver which would be recognised at common law. As Mellish LJ pointed out in the Court of Appeal, this was not a waiver of the six months' notice. For a waiver to apply, it would have to be seen that the lessors intended to abandon the notice to repair. At common law, he noted, if the notice was waived, it would be 'gone'. By contrast,

> a Court of Equity, though they relieve against the forfeiture, will still compel the lessee to put the house into substantial repair.

[217] *Eaton v Lyon* (1798) 3 Ves 690, 692–3; 30 ER 1223, 1224.

[218] *Sanders v Pope* (1806) 12 Ves 283, 289; 33 ER 108, 110 (Lord Erskine LC). See also *Hack v Leonard* (1724) 9 Mod 90, 88 ER 335.

[219] *Hill v Barclay* (1810) 16 Ves 402, 33 ER 1037. See also J Story, *Commentaries on Equity Jurisprudence*, MM Bigelow (ed), 13th edn (Boston, Little, Brown & Co, 1886) s 1321, saying that equity should not relieve in cases of forfeiture for breaches of covenants for failure to repair. See also *Gregory v Wilson* (1852) 9 Hare 683, 68 ER 687.

[220] *Bargent v Thomson* (1864) 4 Giff 473, 66 ER 792.

[221] *Hughes v Metropolitan Railway Company* (1877) LR 2 App Cas 439, 448.

[222] Ibid 447.

It would only prevent an inequitable forfeiture.[223] The courts which heard *Hughes* did not mention the notion of waiver in the sense of forbearance, which had been raised in *Ogle v Vane*, and reiterated in 1875 in *Hickman v Haynes*.[224] Nor did they mention estoppel. Rather, the decision was rooted in equity's approach to forfeitures.

By 1888, however, the Court of Appeal was prepared to use broader language. In *Birmingham and District Land Company v London and North Western Railway Company*, the court gave relief to a plaintiff who occupied land under a building agreement, which was determinable if buildings were not completed by a certain date. Although building work had been suspended at the request of the landlord, it was declared that the building agreement was subsisting, since an equity was raised to prevent the ejectment of the plaintiff until he had a reasonable time after notice to complete the building. Lindley LJ rested his judgment on *Hughes*, but Bowen LJ—seeking to answer the point that the latter case only related to forfeitures—stated the principle much more broadly[225]:

> [i]f persons who have contractual rights against others induce by their conduct those against whom they have such rights to believe that such rights will either not be enforced or will be kept in suspense or abeyance for some particular time, those persons will not be allowed by a Court of Equity to enforce the rights until such time has elapsed, without at all events placing the parties in the same position as they were before.

This—the broadest statement yet of the principle—was made several years after the Lords decided *Foakes v Beer*.

These late 19th century developments would not have assisted Dr Foakes. For in the cases we have discussed, the court sought to protect a party who had been induced to act on a representation from losing his rights as a result of doing so. They were not intended to generate new unpaid-for rights in the party to whom a representation had been made, as would be the case where a debt was waived. When Denning J drew on cases such as *Hughes v Metropolitan Railway Company* and *Birmingham & District Land Company v London & North Western Railway Company* in *High Trees* to permit a debt to be waived, while merely observing that this 'aspect was not considered in *Foakes v Beer*', he was in fact extending the doctrine much further than it had gone before, as one which could generate new rights.

## G. CONCLUSION

In *High Trees*, *Combe v Combe*, and *D & C Builders v Rees*, Denning established a new doctrine by which a promise that was intended to be binding could

---

[223] *Hughes v Metropolitan Railway Company* (1876) LR 1 CPD 120, 135.

[224] *Hickman v Haynes* (1875) LR 10 CP 598.

[225] *Birmingham & Distict Land Company v London & North Western Railway Company* (1888) 40 Ch D 268, 286.

be enforced, notwithstanding the absence of consideration. But the doctrine was in many ways problematic. For Denning was not simply removing the need for consideration, replacing it with a doctrine where a seriously intended promise which had been accepted by the conduct of reliance would bind, notwithstanding the absence of consideration. The new doctrine did not aim to apply a form of will theory to English law, for it did not rest on a meeting of minds. The requirement of reliance was not regarded as equivalent to a contractual acceptance. Lord Denning MR himself confirmed that the reliance need not be detrimental.[226] Since the doctrine did not give any guidance on how to identify when reliance had occurred, it could not identify when a meeting of minds had occurred, or when the contractual obligation began. Nor could this problem be solved by asserting that this was, in fact, based on a promise theory—according to which a seriously intended promise would be binding as soon as it was made—for the promise was only binding if the court regarded it as one which it would be inequitable to go back on. The fact that the doctrine was a defence only also meant that it should properly be seen not as a doctrine of contract formation, but as one of waiver; but this raised the difficulty of how a waiver could generate new rights.

By 1989 the existence of the doctrine of estoppel helped alter the way consideration was perceived. In *Williams v Roffey Brothers*, the Court of Appeal held that where one party to a contract promised to pay the other party more money to complete the same job, the contract could be upheld as having been made on a good consideration, provided there had been no economic duress exerted by the promisee. The consideration was the 'practical benefit' which the promisor received from the work being done, which in this case was the avoidance of penalties which would otherwise have been incurred.[227] This was to apply to English law an approach to consideration taken by some 19th century American courts,[228] but which had been decisively rejected in England at the time of *Foakes v Beer*.[229] *Williams v Roffey* was a case where the promisee could have raised promissory estoppel, had he been the defendant in an action to recover money already paid. The Court of Appeal's decision therefore sought to give the promisee an equivalent remedy where he was suing for the money promised. This was done by taking an innovative view of consideration, and one which might itself render the doctrine of promissory estoppel unnecessary.

The case was controversial. A number of commentators pointed out the problems raised by the approach of the Court of Appeal to consideration in *Williams v Roffey*. Criticisms were made of the concept of a 'practical' benefit. It was noted that in their theoretical discussions, late 19th century thinkers stressed

[226] *WJ Alan & Co v El Nasr Export* [1972] 2 QB 189 (CA) 213, where Denning MR discussed the doctrine in terms of waiver. Treitel articulates the doctrine thus: 'where the promisee has, after the promise, conducted himself in the way intended by the promisor, it will be up to the promisor to establish that the conduct was not induced by the promise'. *The Law of Contract* (n 128 above) 110.
[227] *Williams v Roffey Bros* [1991] 1 QB 1 (CA) 11 (Glidewell LJ).
[228] Eg *Goebel v Linn* 47 Mich 489, 11 NW 284 (Mich 1882); *Bishop v Busse* 69 Ill 403 (Ill 1873).
[229] *Foakes v Beer* was not mentioned in *Williams v Roffey Bros*.

that a coherent conception of consideration had to be based on a notion of benefit in law, rather than factual benefit.[230] Criticisms also turned on the difficulty of identifying the nature and effect of a practical benefit.[231] *Williams v Roffey* can also be criticised both for ignoring the traditional requirement that consideration must 'move from the promisee'[232] and for linking the presence of consideration with the absence of economic duress.[233] For the critics, *Williams v Roffey* could not be reconciled to a coherent theory of consideration. Nonetheless the decision was welcomed by others as 'squarely facing up to the doctrine of consideration and its place in the modern world'. For them, it was a welcome chance to move away from an exchange model of contract to one where a court would consider fairness and commercial utility more. It also was seen to provide an opportunity 'to declare that *Foakes v Beer* was simply wrong'.[234] Yet the Court of Appeal, in *Re Selectmove Ltd*,[235] declined to take that opportunity, but applied the rule in *Foakes v Beer*, holding that a practical benefit could not constitute consideration for a promise to waive part of a debt. Moreover, *Foakes v Beer* has had some other defenders.[236]

As a result of these developments, English law remains confusingly inconsistent, with the doctrine of consideration highly qualified for promises to perform existing duties, but not so qualified when it comes to waivers of debts. The authority of *Foakes v Beer* has been opposed to that of *Williams v Roffey*, which may itself be seen as an extension of the principle of *High Trees*, which in turn sought to qualify *Foakes v Beer*. Consideration remains in place as a core element of English contract law, but uncomfortably so. In *High Trees* and *Williams v Roffey*, the courts wanted to uphold seriously intended promises, as long as there was no unconscionable, vitiating conduct. The courts were perhaps aiming to develop a promise theory of contract, in place of the bargain theory that underpinned consideration. But, even if some judges may have regarded consideration as

> like the 'clavicle in the cat', the useless remnant of an earlier creature and whose reason has long been forgotten,[237]

so rooted is the doctrine in English law, that they have not had the courage to attempt its direct abolition.[238] As a consequence, they have been unable to

---

[230]   B Coote, 'Consideration and Benefit in Fact and Law' (1990) 3 *Journal of Contract Law* 23.

[231]   See J O'Sullivan, 'In Defence of *Foakes v Beer*' (1996) 55 *Cambridge Law Journal* 225–6.

[232]   See *South Caribbean Trading Ltd v Trafigura Beheer BV* [2004] EWHC 2676 (Comm), [2005] 1 Lloyds Rep 128 [108].

[233]   Under the 'traditional' view of consideration, the absence of a consideration rendered the contract void, while the presence of duress could render an otherwise valid contract voidable.

[234]   J Adams and R Brownsword, 'Contract, Consideration and the Critical Path' (1990) 53 *Modern Law Review* 541, 540n.

[235]   *Re Selectmove Ltd* [1995] 1 WLR 474 (CA).

[236]   Sullivan, 'In Defence of *Foakes v Beer*' (n 231 above) 219.

[237]   OW Holmes, *The Common Law* (Boston, Little, Brown & Co, 1881) 35.

[238]   In any event, no case has come to the Lords which might have the power to overrule such a settled doctrine, as it did in *R v R (rape: marital exemption)* [1992] 1 AC 599.

develop an alternative vision of contract law. The doctrines of *High Trees* and *Williams v Roffey* remain exceptions within a broader contract law which owes more to bargain theory than promise theory, and which looks for agreements rather than promises. While that persists, however, the rule of *Foakes v Beer* must be taken seriously and the doctrines of *High Trees* and *Williams v Roffey* must be seen as problematic.

# 9

# Hongkong Fir Shipping Co Ltd v Kawasaki Kisen Kaisha Ltd, The Hongkong Fir (1961)

DONAL NOLAN

## A. INTRODUCTION

THE DECISION OF the Court of Appeal in *Hongkong Fir Shipping Co Ltd v Kawasaki Kisen Kaisha Ltd, The Hongkong Fir*[1] is generally considered to be one of the most important contract cases of the 20th century. In *Bunge Corp v Tradax Export SA*, for example, Lord Wilberforce said that the judgment of Diplock LJ was 'seminal', and that his analysis had 'since become classical',[2] while Lord Roskill described it as 'a landmark in the development of one part of our law of contract in the latter part of this century'.[3]

Similarly, Sir Guenter Treitel has written that the judgment of Diplock LJ has had an 'enormous' influence, and 'has a fair claim to being the most important judicial contribution to English contract law in the past century'.[4] It is certainly not my intention in this analysis of the *Hongkong Fir* case to take issue with these pronouncements, but I do hope to show that close consideration of the judgments, coupled with an appreciation of the historical background, reveals certain flaws in the current general understanding of the decision. In particular

---

[1] *Hongkong Fir Shipping Co Ltd v Kawasaki Kisen Kaisha Ltd, The Hongkong Fir* [1962] 2 QB 26. This report includes the decision of Salmon J at first instance. However, the most comprehensive report of the first instance proceedings is to be found in [1961] 1 Lloyd's Rep 159, since, unlike in the official reports (and the report at [1961] 2 All ER 257), the judge's analysis of the factual issues is here rendered in full, and not summarised by the reporter. The Court of Appeal's decision is also reported at [1962] 1 All ER 474 and [1961] 2 Lloyd's Rep 478.

[2] *Bunge Corp v Tradax Export SA* [1981] 1 WLR 711 (HL) 714.

[3] *Ibid* 725.

[4] Sir GH Treitel, *Some Landmarks of Twentieth Century Contract Law*, Clarendon Law Lectures (Oxford, Oxford University Press, 2002) 113. See also JW Carter, GJ Tolhurst and E Peden, 'Developing the Intermediate Term Concept' (2006) 22 *Journal of Contract Law* 268, 268 ('few modern decisions have captured the imaginations of contract lawyers' as much as the *Hongkong Fir* case).

I will argue, first, that the reasoning in the case was not as novel as has some-times been suggested; secondly, that the most novel aspect of that reasoning—and the proposition with which the case has now become synonymous—was not as central to the analysis as it is generally assumed to have been; and, thirdly, that another, very important, aspect of the reasoning in the case tends now to be overlooked. I will begin my analysis with an exploration of the historical background to the decision.

### B. THE HISTORICAL BACKGROUND

Although Tony Weir once described the reasoning in the *Hongkong Fir* case as 'wholly novel, indeed revolutionary',[5] in this paper I hope to demonstrate that it was nothing of the sort, reflecting as it did a strong line of authority which had been somewhat obscured by the late 19th-century and early 20th-century emphasis on a rigid binary classification of contract terms into conditions (breach of which entitled the innocent party to treat the contract as discharged) and warranties (breach of which sounded in damages alone). The argument, I should make clear, is not a new one; indeed my thesis is neatly encapsulated in Lord Lowry's statement that in his judgment in the case, Diplock LJ 'shed a new light on old principles; he did not purport to establish new ones'.[6]

The historical development of the doctrine of discharge for breach is a com-plex topic,[7] but for present purposes, an appropriate starting point is *Kingston v Preston*,[8] where Lord Mansfield first gave legal recognition to the idea of mutually dependent promises, whereby a party who was ready and willing to

---

[5] A Weir, 'Contract—The Buyer's Right to Reject Defective Goods' [1976] *Cambridge Law Journal* 33, 35.

[6] *Bunge Corp v Tradax Export SA* (n 2 above) 719. See also *ibid* 717 (Lord Scarman) (in *Hongkong Fir* the Court of Appeal 'rediscovered and reaffirmed' that English law recognises inter-mediate terms); *The Mihalis Angelos* [1971] 1 QB 164 (CA) 193 (Lord Denning) (*Hongkong Fir* a 'useful reminder' of the existence of a category of terms which did not fit into the binary classifica-tion); *Schuler AG v Wickman Machine Tool Sales Ltd* [1974] AC 235 (HL) 262 (Lord Wilberforce) (expressing the opinion that the case did not decide anything new); Lord Devlin, 'The Treatment of Breach of Contract' [1966] *Cambridge Law Journal* 192, 203 ('There is nothing new about [the *Hongkong Fir*] doctrine'); MC Bridge, 'Discharge for Breach of the Contract of Sale of Goods' (1983) 28 *McGill Law Journal* 867, 894n (rejecting 'the view that the *Hongkong Fir* decision intro-duced a novel principle'); Treitel, *Some Landmarks of Twentieth Century Contract Law* (n 4 above) 113 (referring to 'the invention, or perhaps more accurately the rediscovery' of a third type of con-tract term); JC Smith, *Smith and Thomas: A Casebook on Contract*, 11th edn (London, Sweet & Maxwell, 2000) 434 (the courts utilised the concept of an innominate term for many years before it was expressly recognised in the *Hongkong Fir* case); J Beatson, *Anson's Law of Contract*, 28th edn (Oxford, Oxford University Press, 2002) 140 (*Hongkong Fir* gave a new emphasis to a more flexible test which had its roots in older authorities).

[7] For more comprehensive accounts, see JW Carter and C Hodgekiss, 'Conditions and Warranties: Forebears and Descendants' (1976) 8 *Sydney Law Review* 31; Bridge, 'Discharge for Breach of the Contract of Sale of Goods' (n 6 above) 872–912; DW Grieg and JLR Davis, *The Law of Contract* (Sydney, The Law Book Company, 1987) 1199–1213.

[8] *Kingston v Preston* (1773) 2 Doug 689n, 99 ER 437n (KB).

perform his part could maintain an action if the other party neglected or refused to perform his. Five years later, in *Boone v Eyre*,[9] the same judge had to decide the precise extent of this mutual dependency. The plaintiff had conveyed to the defendant a plantation in the West Indies, along with the slaves who worked on it, in return for £500 plus an annuity of £160. The defendant subsequently ceased to make the annuity payments on the basis that at the time the contract was made the plaintiff had not had legal possession of the slaves. Lord Mansfield gave judgment for the plaintiff, and the entirety of his reasoning, as reported, was as follows[10]:

> The distinction is very clear, where mutual covenants go to the whole of the consideration on both sides, they are mutual conditions, the one precedent to the other. But where they go only to a part, where a breach may be paid for in damages, there the defendant has a remedy on his covenant, and shall not plead it as a condition precedent. If this plea were to be allowed, any one negro not being the property of the plaintiff would bar the action.

Lord Mansfield might be taken as suggesting here that only a complete failure of one party's performance would discharge the other's obligations, but the cases that followed indicated that what was in fact required was proof that the failure of performance had substantially deprived the other of the whole benefit which he had expected to obtain from the contract.[11] In *Davidson v Gwynne*,[12] for example—where it was held that the breach of a term requiring a chartered ship to sail 'with the first convoy' did not relieve the charterer from his obligation to pay freight—Lord Ellenborough CJ began his judgment by saying[13]:

> It is useless to go over the same subject again, which has been so often discussed of late. The sailing with the first convoy is not a condition precedent: the object of the contract was the performance of the voyage, and here it has been performed. The principle laid down in Boone v Eyre has been recognised in all the subsequent cases, that unless the non-performance alleged in breach of the contract goes to the whole root and consideration of it, the covenant broken is not to be considered as a condition precedent, but as a distinct covenant, for the breach of which the party injured may be compensated in damages.

During the 19th century, this principle was applied in a series of other charterparty cases, many of which involved delays caused by the breach of a shipowner's obligation to proceed with reasonable dispatch. An early example is *Freeman v Taylor*,[14] where a ship had been chartered to take a cargo to the Cape of Good Hope, and then to make its way to Bombay to pick up a cargo of cotton. Instead of proceeding directly to Bombay from the Cape, the ship went

---

[9] *Boone v Eyre* (1777) 1 H Bl 273n, 126 ER 160n (KB).
[10] *Ibid* 1 H Bl 273, 126 ER 160.
[11] See eg *Duke of St Albans v Shore* (1789) 1 H Bl 270, 126 ER 158 (CP).
[12] *Davidson v Gwynne* (1810) 12 East 381, 104 ER 149 (KB).
[13] *Ibid* 12 East 381, 389; 104 ER 149, 152.
[14] *Freeman v Taylor* (1831) 8 Bing 124, 131 ER 348 (CP).

via Mauritius, where it delivered a cargo of cattle on the owner's account. This delayed its arrival in Bombay by six weeks, and the charterer refused to load. In an action by the owner on the charter, the jury were directed to consider whether the delay had deprived the charterer of the benefit of the contract, and they found that it had. It was held that this had been a proper direction, and a new trial was refused. A case which went the other way is *MacAndrew v Chapple*,[15] where a ship was chartered 'with all convenient speed . . . having liberty to take an outward cargo for owner's benefit direct or on the way, to proceed to Alexandria and there load a full cargo of cotton.' The ship deviated, and arrived at Alexandria a few days late. It was held that the delay afforded no justification for the charterer's refusal to load, but that he was limited to a cross-action for damages. According to Willes J,[16]

> it is . . . settled . . . that a delay or deviation which, as it has been said, goes to the whole root of the matter, deprives the charterer of the whole benefit of the contract, or entirely frustrates the object of the charterer in chartering the ship, is an answer to an action for not loading a cargo; but that loss, delay or deviation short of that gives an action for damages, but does not defeat the charter.

The same principle was also applied in cases where there had been a breach of the obligation of seaworthiness. In *Havelock v Geddes*,[17] for example, it was held that it was no answer to an action for freight that the chartered ship was unseaworthy if the charterers had nonetheless had some use of the vessel, since (applying the test in *Boone v Eyre*) the consideration for the freight had not wholly failed. And in the later case of *Stanton v Richardson*,[18] the test of 'frustration' referred to in *MacAndrew v Chapple* was applied to a case of delay caused by initial unseaworthiness. When the pumps on a chartered vessel had proven incapable of dealing with the moisture that drained from a cargo of wet sugar, the charterer had unloaded the cargo and refused to reload it or to provide another cargo. Cross-actions were brought and at the trial the jury found that the cargo offered was a reasonable one, that since the ship was not reasonably fit to carry it, she was unseaworthy, and that she could not have been made fit to carry the cargo, and so seaworthy, within such a time as would not have frustrated the charter.[19] The Court of Common Pleas held that on these findings, the charterer had been entitled to throw up the charter. Note that here

[15] *MacAndrew v Chapple* (1866) LR 1 CP 643 (CP).
[16] *Ibid* 648. See also *Clipsham v Vertue* (1843) 5 QB 265, 114 ER 1249 (QB) (voyage charter not frustrated by deviation to Newcastle on the approach voyage from London to Nantes).
[17] *Havelock v Geddes* (1809) 10 East 555, 103 ER 886 (KB). See also *Tarrabochia v Hickie* (1856) 1 H & N 183, 156 ER 1168 (ExCh). In *Tully v Howling* (1877) LR 2 QB 182 (CA), by contrast, it was held that a charterer was entitled to throw up a 12-month consecutive voyage charter after initial unseaworthiness had caused a delay of over two months, but this was because (in the words of Mellish LJ at 188) the delay was so prolonged that the charterer was being offered 'something substantially different from that which was contracted to be given'.
[18] *Stanton v Richardson* (1872) LR 7 CP 421 (CP), aff'd (1874) LR 9 CP 390 (ExCh).
[19] The evidence was that it would probably have taken seven or eight months for new pumps to have been procured: *ibid* 424.

the analysis is slightly different from that in the cases involving failure to proceed with reasonable dispatch, since in those cases the delay was caused directly by the breach, whereas here the breach entitled the charterer not to reload until it was cured, and the charterer's right to repudiate then depended on whether or not it looked as though the resultant delay would frustrate the contract. Nonetheless, the essence of the reasoning is the same: only if the consequences of the breach go to the root of the contract is the charterer discharged.

In the 1870s, the principle that a substantial failure of consideration discharged a party from further performance was extended to cases where the failure of consideration was not the result of the other party's breach. The breakthrough came in *Jackson v The Union Marine Insurance Co*,[20] where a ship chartered to carry a cargo from Newport in South Wales to San Francisco had run aground on the approach voyage. It took six weeks to get her off, and the necessary repairs were expected to take six months. Although the delays were the result of an excepted peril, the Court of Common Pleas held that the charterers had been entitled to throw up the charter; *Freeman v Taylor*[21] and *MacAndrew v Chapple*[22] were relied upon. Two years later, the same reasoning was used in *Poussard v Spiers*,[23] where the plaintiff was a singer who had fallen ill in the run up to the opening night of a new opera in which she was to play the leading female role. As a result, she had missed five days of rehearsals and the first four performances, the defendant theatre owners having employed a temporary substitute to perform in her place. On the day of the fifth performance, the plaintiff had recovered sufficiently to tender her services, which the defendants had rejected. On appeal from a decision allowing the plaintiff's action for wrongful dismissal, the Court of Queen's Bench held that her inability to perform on the opening night and in the later performances had gone to the root of the consideration, and that the defendants had therefore been entitled to rescind the contract.

At around the same time, however, we also see the emergence of a rival approach to the question of discharge for breach, in which the focus is on the nature of the term which has been broken, rather than the consequences of its breach. *Bettini v Gye*,[24] a case decided three months before *Poussard v Spiers*,[25] is an important milestone in the development of this alternative approach. As in *Poussard*, the plaintiff in *Bettini* was a performer whose services had been dispensed with, this time because he had missed four days of the six days of rehearsals he was required to attend under the terms of his contract. In this case, however, it was held that the defendant opera director had not been entitled to rescind the contract, since the stipulation as to rehearsals had not gone to the root

---

[20] *Jackson v The Union Marine Insurance Co* (1874) LR 10 CP 125 (ExCh).
[21] *Freeman v Taylor* (n 14 above).
[22] *MacAndrew v Chapple* (n 15 above).
[23] *Poussard v Spiers* (1876) 1 QBD 410 (DC).
[24] *Bettini v Gye* (1876) 1 QBD 183 (DC).
[25] *Poussard v Spiers* (n 23 above).

of the consideration, and was therefore not a condition precedent. The outcome in *Bettini v Gye* was perfectly consistent with the 'failure of consideration' or 'frustration' approach to discharge, but the language used by Blackburn J in his judgment was indicative of an important shift of emphasis. Whether the defendant had been entitled to refuse to accept the plaintiff's services, he said, depended on whether 'this part of the contract' (ie the stipulation as to rehearsals) was

> a condition precedent to the defendant's liability, or only an independent agreement, a breach of which will not justify a repudiation of the contract, but will only be a cause of action for a compensation in damages,

and this in turn depended 'on the true construction of the contract as a whole'.[26]

The idea that the remedies available for a breach of contract depended on the correct construction of the agreement must have had considerable ideological appeal,[27] and it is not therefore surprising to find that by 1893 it had crystallised into the dogma that all the terms of a contract could be classified in advance as either conditions or warranties.[28] The *locus classicus* of this approach is the judgment of Bowen LJ in that year in *Bentsen v Taylor, Sons & Co*,[29] where he said that the classification of a term depended[30]

> as a matter of construction, whether it is such a promise as amounts to a warranty, the breach of which would sound only in damages, or whether it is that kind of promise the performance of which is made a condition precedent to all further demands under the contract by the person who made the promise against the other party—a promise the failure to perform which gives to the opposite party the right to say that he will no longer be bound by the contract.

By its very nature, of course, this approach left no scope for reference to the actual effect of the breach that had taken place; rather the focus was 'on the effect likely to be produced on the foundation of the adventure by any such breach of that portion of the contract',[31] as judged (presumably) from the point of view of the parties at the time the contract was formed. An ex post facto inquiry had therefore been replaced by an a priori one.[32] 1893 was of course also the year in which the Sale of Goods Act was enacted, and the statute fully reflected the spirit of the times by laying down a rigid binary classification of the

---

[26] *Bettini v Gye* (n 24 above) 187.

[27] Additional attractions of this approach would have been (1) that, since the construction of a contract was a question of law, it took the issue of discharge for breach away from juries and placed it 'firmly in judicial hands' (Bridge, 'Discharge for Breach of the Contract of Sale of Goods' (n 6 above) 880); and (2) that it was more congenial to 'the search for certainty and predictability that pervaded 19th century and early 20th century contractual thought' (SM Waddams, *The Law of Contracts*, 4th edn (Toronto, Canada Law Book Inc, 1999) para 588).

[28] For speculation as to why these particular terms came to be used, see Grieg and Davis (n 7 above) 1204. For a history of the words 'condition' and 'warranty', see M Mark (ed), *Chalmers' Sale of Goods Act 1893*, 17th edn (London, Butterworths, 1975) Appendix II, Note A.

[29] *Bentsen v Taylor, Sons & Co* [1893] 2 QB 274 (CA).

[30] *Ibid* 280–81.

[31] *Bentsen v Taylor, Sons & Co* (n 29 above) 281.

[32] See Bridge, 'Discharge for Breach of the Contract of Sale of Goods' (n 6 above) 880.

seller's obligations under a contract of sale. Section 11(1)(b) of the Act referred to a 'condition' as a stipulation 'the breach of which may give rise to a right to treat the contract as repudiated', and a 'warranty' as a stipulation 'the breach of which may give rise to a claim for damages but not to a right to . . . treat the contract as repudiated.' The consequences of this setting of the condition/warranty dichotomy in statutory stone were not limited to sale of goods cases, but spilt over into other areas of contract law,[33] and thereafter the words 'condition' and 'warranty' became legal terms of art of general application.[34]

The result of these developments was that although in the first half of the 20th century the 'failure of consideration' approach flourished in cases involving discharge by frustration,[35] in the context of discharge for breach it was overshadowed by what Karl Llewellyn described as the 'warranty-condition setup'.[36] It did not, however, disappear altogether, as is shown by an interesting case from the 1930s, *Aerial Advertising Co v Batchelor's Peas Ltd*.[37] The plaintiffs had contracted to advertise the defendants' product by flying a plane trailing a banner reading 'Eat Batchelor's Peas' over various urban areas. Unfortunately, the pilot flew over the main square of Salford on Armistice Day at precisely the moment when a large crowd had gathered to observe the two-minute silence. Amidst the outrage that followed the defendants sought to rescind the contract, and Atkinson J held that they were entitled to do so, on the basis that the pilot had breached a term of the contract under which he was required to tell the defendants what he proposed to do and to obtain their approval. There was, however, no suggestion that this term was a condition; rather it seems to have been the very serious consequences of this particular breach which released the defendants from further performance of the contract.[38] In addition, cases concerning termination in instalment sales appear still to have turned on the question of whether the effect of the seller's failure to deliver an instalment was substantially to deprive the buyer of what he was entitled to expect under the contract, although—following the lead given by section 31(2) of the Sale of Goods Act 1893—consistency with the condition/warranty dichotomy was

[33] See Lord Diplock, 'The Law of Contract in the Eighties' (1981) 15 *University of British Columbia Law Review* 372, 375 (s 11(b) 'was responsible for the real damage to the English law of contract').

[34] See *Cehave NV v Bremer Handelsgesellschaft mbH, The Hansa Nord* [1976] QB 44 (CA) 59 (Lord Denning MR).

[35] See, eg *Herne Bay Steamboat Co v Hutton* [1903] 2 KB 683 (CA); *Krell v Henry* [1903] 2 KB 740 (CA).

[36] KN Llewellyn, 'On Warranty of Quality and Society' (1936) 36 *Columbia Law Review* 699, 731. For explicit judicial endorsement of the condition/warranty dichotomy, see *Wallis, Son & Wells v Pratt & Haynes* [1911] AC 394 (HL), where Lord Shaw expressed 'repugnance' at the idea of construing a contract '*ex post facto*'.

[37] *Aerial Advertising Co v Batchelor's Peas Ltd* [1938] 2 All ER 788 (KBD).

[38] In Australia, Isaacs J and Rich J also rejected the a priori classification approach, insisting instead that in the final analysis the focus must be on the effect of the breach: see their dissenting judgment in *Bowes v Chaleyer* (1923) 32 CLR 159 (HCA) 170, and also their judgment in *Fullers' Theatres Ltd v Musgrove* (1923) 31 CLR 524 (HCA) 537–38.

achieved by the characterisation of a sufficiently serious breach as a 'repudiation' by the seller.[39]

Furthermore, in charterparty cases the focus would appear to have remained firmly on the consequences of the breach. In *Inverkip Steamship Co Ltd v Bunge & Co*, for example, Scrutton LJ said that a shipowner would be entitled to abandon a charter because of a charterer's failure to load only if the failure amounted to a repudiation of or final refusal to perform the charter, or 'such a commercial frustration of the adventure by delay . . . as puts an end to the contract',[40] and in *Cargo Ships 'El Yam' Ltd v 'Invotra' NV*,[41] Devlin J held that a variation from the ship's tonnage as stated in a time charter did not entitle the charterer to treat the contract as discharged unless the breach made 'a fundamental difference to that which the [charterer] had contracted to take'.[42] Another decision of Devlin J from the 1950s, *Universal Cargo Carriers Corp v Citati*,[43] is an even more explicit endorsement of the consequences of the breach approach to discharge. The issue was whether a shipowner had been entitled to abandon a voyage charter in the light of the charterer's failure to nominate a berth and provide a cargo. Devlin J paid lip-service to the condition/warranty dichotomy by saying that if time was not of the essence then these obligations were warranties, but he nonetheless said that the owner would have been relieved from his obligations if the delay had become 'so long as to go to the root of the contract',[44] and that the yardstick by which this length of delay was to be measured was 'such delay as would frustrate the charterparty'.[45] This was simply an application, he went on to say, of the well-established doctrine that 'a commercial contract is dissolved on the happening of a supervening event which frustrates the object of the venture'.[46] Thus was the stage set for the decision in the *Hongkong Fir* case, to which I will now turn.

[39] See eg *Maple Flock Co Ltd v Universal Furniture Products (Wembley) Ltd* [1934] 1 KB 148 (CA). Failure of consideration reasoning had been explicitly relied upon in the House of Lords decision which laid the foundation for s 31(2): see *Mersey Steel and Iron Co v Naylor, Benzon & Co* (1884) 9 App Cas 434 (HL) 443–44 (Lord Blackburn). On the relationship between the *Hongkong Fir* doctrine and repudiation, see further FMB Reynolds, 'Discharge by Breach as a Remedy' in PD Finn (ed), *Essays on Contract* (Sydney, Law Book Co, 1987) 190–92; Carter, Tolhurst and Peden, 'Developing the Intermediate Term Concept' (n 4 above) 272.
[40] *Inverkip Steamship Co Ltd v Bunge & Co* [1917] 2 KB 198 (CA).
[41] *Cargo Ships 'El Yam' Ltd v 'Invotra' NV* [1958] 1 Lloyds' Rep 39 (QBD).
[42] *Ibid* 52. Contrast the strict approach taken in sales cases where the goods departed slightly from the contract description: see, eg *Re Moore & Co and Landauer & Co* [1921] 2 KB 519 (CA); *Arcos Ltd v Ronaasen (EA) & Son* [1933] AC 470 (HL).
[43] *Universal Cargo Carriers Corp v Citati* [1957] 2 QB 401 (QBD), aff'd [1957] 1 WLR 979 (CA).
[44] *Ibid* [1957] 2 QB 401, 426.
[45] *Universal Cargo Carriers Corp v Citati* (n 43 above) 430.
[46] *Universal Cargo Carriers Corp v Citati* (n 43 above) 430. For a more thorough exposition of Lord Devlin's thinking on the subject of discharge for breach, see 'The Treatment of Breach of Contract' [1966] *Cambridge Law Journal* 192.

## C. THE FACTS OF *HONGKONG FIR*

On Boxing Day 1956 (a couple of months before Devlin J handed down judgment in *Universal Cargo Carriers*) a time charterparty was signed in Tokyo between the Hongkong Fir Shipping Company Ltd ('the owners') and Kawasaki Kisen Kaisha Ltd ('the charterers'). The ship that was the subject of the charter had been built in Dumbarton in Scotland in 1931, and launched on 14 July 1932 as 'The Ardenvohr'.[47] In 1937 her name had been changed to 'The Kaimata', and in 1954 she had become 'The Antrim'. The owners had agreed to buy 'The Antrim' for £397,500 from a subsidiary of the New Zealand Shipping Company Ltd at around the time they entered into the charter,[48] which refers to them as 'Owners of the vessel called "Antrim" to be renamed "Hongkong Fir"'; indeed, clause 44 of the charter made it expressly subject to the vessel being taken over by the owners 'according to purchase agreement'.[49] The Hongkong Fir Shipping Co itself was apparently not incorporated until after the charter had been signed on its behalf by agents.[50] Presumably, it was merely a vehicle for the ownership of this particular ship, and it seems almost certainly to have been a subsidiary of a Hong Kong-based shipping company called 'Fir Line'.[51] The charterers, Kawasaki Kisen Kaisha Ltd, or 'K' Line, were a Japanese shipping company founded in Kobe in 1919. By 1926, their fleet was the 13th largest in the world, and although they lost all but twelve of their ships in the Second World War, by the time of the charter they had made a remarkable recovery, and were operating over 60 vessels.[52]

The charterparty in question was a Baltime 1939 'Uniform Time Charter', to which had been added nineteen typewritten terms (clauses 26 to 44) agreed by the parties. The period of hire was 24 months—one month more or less at

---

[47] Most of the information in the text concerning the ship is derived from the Miramar Ship Index: www. miramarshipindex.org.nz.

[48] See *Hongkong Fir Shipping* [1961] Lloyd's Rep 159 (QBD) 164 (Salmon J).

[49] Although the ship was therefore well over 20 years old at the time of the charterparty, it seems that she still had considerable life left in her. In 1962, she was sold by the owners to the Indonesian Army, and after a further seven years of operation, under a number of different names, she was finally scrapped in Hong Kong on 10 May 1969, nearly 37 years after her launch: see www. miramarshipindex.org.nz.

[50] See *Hongkong Fir Shipping* [1962] 2 QB 39 (CA) 62, where Upjohn LJ says that it was therefore common ground that the charter could not have been executed until some weeks after it was signed. The charterparty was signed on behalf of the owners by a representative of Dodwell & Co, a British firm of merchants and shipping agents with offices in Hong Kong and Tokyo. Dodwell & Co later became Dodwell P&I, which was taken over by Inchcape P&I in the 1980s.

[51] 'Fir Line' are listed as a founder member of the Hong Kong Shipowners' Association, an organisation formed in 1957 (see www.hksoa.org/about/history.html), and there is a reference in the Lloyd's Law Report of the first instance decision to a letter which 'Fir Line Ltd' wrote to the charterers as agents for the owners: [1961] 1 Lloyd's Rep 159 (QBD) 160.

[52] 'K' Line is still one of Japan's largest shipping companies, as can be seen from their website (www.kline.co.jp), which is the source of the information on their history in the text. They recently featured in another important decision of an English court, this time the House of Lords: see *Whistler International Ltd v Kawasaki Kisen Kaisha Ltd, The Hill Harmony* [2001] 1 AC 638.

charterer's option—with delivery of the vessel to be made in Liverpool in February or March 1957, and hire was fixed at 47 s per deadweight ton per 30 days, on the ship's deadweight of 9,131 tons, with the result that the overall hire payable under the charter would, all things being equal, have been just over £500,000 (around £7–8 million in today's money).[53] Clause 1 of the charter referred to the vessel 'being in every way fitted for cargo service', and clause 3 obliged the owners 'to maintain [the vessel] in a thoroughly efficient state in hull and machinery during service', although the owners were to be held responsible for delays during the currency of the charter only if these were attributable to want of due diligence on the part of them or their manager 'in making the vessel seaworthy and fitted for the voyage' (clause 13). The charter contained an 'off-hire' clause (clause 11), under which hire was not payable if the ship was laid up for repair, and the charterer also had the option of adding any such 'off-hire' time to the charter period (clause 32).

The vessel was delivered to the charterers in Liverpool on 13 February 1957, and immediately set out in ballast to Newport, Virginia, where it was intended that she would pick up a cargo of coal for carriage to Osaka via Cristobal in the Panama Canal Zone. The crossing was stormy, but not exceptionally so, and the ship arrived at Newport a fortnight later, where she loaded her cargo and was off hire for a couple of days for repairs. She left Newport on 6 March and after arriving at Cristobal on 15 March, she was off hire for about eleven days, having 'met with two serious accidents on the way'.[54] The ship left Cristobal on 26 March bound for Osaka, but about a week later she had a major breakdown on her scavenge pump, which made it unsafe for her to cross the Pacific. She therefore put in to San Pedro in California for repair, and was out of action for another three weeks or so. She finally made it to Osaka on 25 May, but by that time her main engine and auxiliaries had suffered serious corrosion, and the necessary repairs lasted for fifteen weeks, with the result that she was not ready to put to sea again until mid-September. In early June and again on 27 July, the charterers had written to the owners repudiating the charter, and in mid-August the owners had responded that they would treat the contract as cancelled by the charterer's wrongful repudiation and claim damages. On 11 September, the charterers once again wrote repudiating the charter and the owners formally accepted that repudiation two days later. On 8 November, the owners issued a writ claiming damages for wrongful repudiation of the charter, the parties having apparently agreed to have their dispute tried in the Commercial Court in London in substitution for the arbitration provided for in the charterparty.[55]

[53] Treitel (in *Some Landmarks of Twentieth Century Contract Law* (n 4 above) 113) claims that the overall hire payable would have been 'just under £15.5 million', but the basis on which he arrived at this figure, which equates to over £200 million in today's money, is not clear. Estimates of sums in 'today's money' are based on the Retail Price Index, and the calculations have been carried out by www.measuringworth.com.
[54] *Hongkong Fir Shipping* [1962] 2 QB 26 (QBD) 29.
[55] See the beginning of the judgment of Sellers LJ in the Court of Appeal, as reported in the Lloyd's Law Reports: *Hongkong Fir Shipping* [1961] 2 Lloyd's Rep 478 (CA) 485.

It is worth noting at this point that freight rates had fallen dramatically during the course of 1957. The huge movements in freight rates that took place at the time were the result of the crisis triggered by the nationalisation of the Suez Canal Company by the Egyptian leader Abdul Nasser in July 1956. This had led to an Israeli invasion of the Sinai peninsula in October that year, which was coupled with an attempt by British and French forces to take over the canal itself. In response, the Egyptians had blocked the canal, and shipping was therefore forced to take the much longer route round the Cape of Good Hope. The result was a severe shortage of shipping space, and by December 1956, when the charterparty in *Hongkong Fir* was signed, freight rates had shot up to an historic high. It seems to have been assumed at the time that the canal would not re-open for a number of years, and the combination of heightened demand and huge profits caused shipowners to place orders for many more vessels. However, the canal was re-opened much earlier than expected, in March 1957, with the result that the demand for shipping space fell back just as the new ships were beginning to come on stream. Freight rates then plunged, and shipping fell into a deep recession. The extent of the drop in freight rates is starkly illustrated by the Interscale Tanker Freight Index, which fell from a high of 456 in December 1956 to just 60 by the autumn of 1957. If the figures given by Salmon J at first instance in *Hongkong Fir* were accurate, then the effect on general freight rates was less spectacular, but nonetheless marked: by mid-June 1957 they had fallen to 24 s per ton, half the charter rate, and by mid-August they stood at 13 s 6 d per ton, less than a third of the charter rate.[56] Presumably these developments played a part in the decision of the charterers to repudiate the charter. Whether they also affected the outcome of the litigation is less clear,[57] but the fact that the purported termination was almost certainly an opportunistic one ought at least to be borne in mind in an assessment of the decision.


## D. THE DECISION OF SALMON J

The case came before Salmon J (later Lord Salmon) at the end of January 1961. The question which he had to answer was whether or not the charterers had been entitled to throw up the charter. They claimed that they had been so entitled by virtue of any one of three alleged breaches by the owners: a breach of the obligation in clause 1 of the charter to deliver a seaworthy vessel; a breach of the obligation in clause 3 to maintain the vessel in an efficient state; and a breach of the obligation to deliver a vessel capable of making about 12½ knots in good conditions. Alternatively, the charterers argued that they were entitled to

---

[56] See *Hongkong Fir Shipping* [1961] 1 Lloyd's Rep 159 (QBD) 166.

[57] Salmon J said that the 'catastrophic fall in the freight market' was not material when considering whether or not the delays had frustrated the charter ([1962] 2 QB 26 (QBD) 39), and although Sellers LJ noted the fall in freight rates at the beginning of his judgment in the Court of Appeal ([1962] 2 QB 39, 54), no further mention of the point was made in the judgments in that court.

repudiate the charter because of the failure of the owners to remedy these breaches within a reasonable time, or within such time as would have avoided frustration of the commercial purpose of the charter. The fact that each side instructed three counsel, and that the hearing lasted 15 days, would suggest that the case was a complex one, though this was probably more to do with the issues of fact involved than the issues of law.[58]

Those issues of fact revolved around both the state of the ship and the efficiency of her crew. As to the former, Salmon J concluded that the ship had been in reasonably good condition when delivered to the charterers, but that because of its age it needed to be maintained by 'an experienced, competent, careful and adequate engine room staff'.[59] And that was where the problem had lain. The learned judge had no doubt that the vessel had been unseaworthy on delivery by reason of the incompetence and insufficiency in numbers of its engine room staff. Of particular importance in this respect was the evidence concerning the chief engineer, a Mr Mack. His predecessor, a Mr Ramsay ('apparently a very difficult man'[60]), had been dismissed on 12 February, the day before the ship set out from Liverpool. There was at the time a severe shortage of good engineers, and after a meeting in a London railway station in the early hours of the same day between Mr Mack and the manager of the owners' London agents, the former had been offered the job. This was despite the fact that he admitted to having been sacked by Shell in 1951 for drunkenness, and that there was no time to take up his references. Salmon J noted that the owners' agents had expressed themselves satisfied with Mr Mack's assurance that he was no longer a drunkard, and that 'they thought that he did not look like one', but commented that in such cases 'appearances are notoriously deceptive, and assurances vain'.[61] So indeed it turned out, since at every port at which the *Hongkong Fir* called, Mr Mack was 'hopelessly drunk' and unable to supervise repairs, and although the judge accepted that he was never observed to be under the influence while at sea, he did so 'without much conviction' since some of the decisions which Mr Mack took seemed explicable only on the basis 'either that he was fuddled with drink or quite extraordinarily incompetent'.[62] The ineptitude of the chief engineer was compounded by the fact that the engine-room was severely undermanned, and the resultant failure properly to maintain the ship was, the judge found, the cause of the delays. It followed that the owners were in breach both of their obligation to deliver a seaworthy ship and of their obligation to maintain the ship in an efficient state. Furthermore, they were not saved by clause 13, since these breaches were attributable to want of due diligence as to seaworthiness on

---

[58] When asking for certification that three counsel had been necessary, counsel for the owners, Stephen Chapman QC, described it 'as a very heavy case', to which Salmon J responded, 'Yes; you need say no more on that' ([1961] 1 Lloyd's Rep 159 (QBD) 175).

[59] *Hongkong Fir Shipping* [1962] 2 QB 26 (QBD) 34.

[60] *Hongkong Fir Shipping* [1961] 1 Lloyd's Rep 159 (QBD) 167 (Salmon J).

[61] *Ibid* 169.

[62] *Hongkong Fir Shipping* [1961] 1 Lloyd's Rep 159 (QBD) 169.

the part of the owners and their servants. Only on the third alleged breach of the charter, relating to the steaming capacity of the ship, did Salmon J find in the owners' favour.

However, having largely failed on the facts, the owners won on the law. Relying, inter alia, on *Havelock v Geddes*[63] and *Stanton v Richardson*[64], Salmon J concluded that neither the unseaworthiness of the vessel nor the failure to maintain her in an efficient state had in themselves entitled the charterers to terminate the charter. It followed that the charterers could not succeed in their defence unless the delay in remedying the breaches had been, or had appeared likely at the date of repudiation to be, so great as to frustrate the commercial purpose of the charter. In this connection, the learned judge pointed out that by mid-September the vessel had admittedly been in every respect seaworthy, and that she was still then available for about 17 months under the charter. The basic idea of frustration—and here Salmon J was drawing on case law relating to the doctrine of frustration in the modern sense, not 'frustration' by breach—was

> to look at the delay and the events that have occurred against the period and other terms of the charterparty and decide whether in truth the circumstances in which performance is called for would render it a thing radically different from that which was undertaken.[65]

Applying that test, the judge concluded that the charterparty had not been frustrated by the delays, and gave judgment for the owners for an agreed sum of £158,729 (well over £2 million in today's money) plus interest.[66] In a note on the decision in the *Cambridge Law Journal*, Len Sealy wrote that it laid down 'no new principle, either of maritime law or of general contract'.[67]

## E. THE DECISION OF THE COURT OF APPEAL

Since so much money was involved, it is not surprising that the charterers appealed. The appeal was heard in late October and early November 1961 by Sellers LJ, Upjohn LJ and Diplock LJ (who had been appointed to the Court of Appeal only a couple of weeks earlier, on 12 October). Counsel for the charterers was Ashton Roskill QC, who had represented the shipowners in *Universal*

---

[63] *Havelock v Geddes* (n 17 above).

[64] *Stanton v Richardson* (n 18 above).

[65] *Hongkong Fir Shipping* [1962] 2 QB 26 (QBD) 40.

[66] The charterers had, it seems, originally counter-claimed for damage suffered as a result of the delays, but this claim was later abandoned, presumably because, in the light of the off-hire clause and the fall in freight rates, the delays had actually worked to their benefit.

[67] [1961] *Cambridge Law Journal* 152, 152. Sealy thought that the main lesson of the decision concerned the use of words, in particular the term 'frustration', and regretted that Salmon J had not made it clear that, even if the yardsticks for discharge by breach and discharge by frustration were the same, the doctrines were not.

*Cargo Carriers Corp v Citati*,[68] and who was later to deliver important judgments on the scope of the *Hongkong Fir* decision in both the Court of Appeal[69] and the House of Lords.[70] Although Mr Roskill did argue (as he had below) that the seaworthiness obligation was a condition, he seems to have focused his submissions on the frustrating delay issue. Salmon J had been wrong to apply a test derived from the doctrine of frustration, he contended, since the delays had been caused by the owners' breaches of contract, and in such a case the proper yardstick to be applied in deciding whether a delay entitled the innocent party to repudiate was whether, in the light of the object of the innocent party, the delay was unreasonable. Stephen Chapman QC, who appeared for the owners, said that as far as the law was concerned, the judgment below had been 'wholly right'.[71] Seaworthiness was a warranty, he submitted, and although it would probably be right to say that even a breach of warranty might sometimes be repudiatory, this would only be where it was so serious as to destroy the commercial purpose of the contract. Similarly, the appropriate test for delay was whether it had frustrated the commercial purpose of the contract,[72] and since in the present case this test was not satisfied, the charterers had not been entitled to throw up the charter.

Fittingly enough, the final word on the Boxing Day charterparty came just before Christmas, on 20 December 1961. Both the substance and the tone of the first judgment—that of Sellers LJ—indicate that he considered the case to be a straightforward one. The first issue, his Lordship said, was whether seaworthiness was a condition. Ships had been held to be unseaworthy in a variety of ways, and it would be 'unthinkable that all the relatively trivial matters which have been held to be unseaworthiness could be regarded as conditions', which would in themselves justify cancellation by the charterer.[73] It was true that if the charterers had known of the unseaworthiness on delivery they could have refused to accept the vessel until the owners had put things right, and that if the owners had then refused or been unable to rectify the breach, or if the delay in remedying the breach would have been so long as to frustrate the commercial purpose of the charter, then the charterers would have been entitled to treat the contract as at an end. However, the issue here was the respective rights of the parties where the vessel had been accepted and used, and in these circumstances it was not open to the charterers to rely on the obligation of seaworthiness as a

---

[68] *Universal Cargo Carriers Corp v Citati* (n 43 above). He had also appeared for the plaintiff advertising company in the *Aerial Advertising* case (n 37 above).
[69] *The Hansa Nord* (n 34 above).
[70] *Bunge Corp v Tradax Export SA* (n 2 above).
[71] *Hongkong Fir Shipping* [1962] 2 QB 26 (CA) 46.
[72] Mr Chapman appears to have justified this test by reference to the doctrine of renunciation: 'What has to be determined is whether there has been conduct on the part of the shipowner which demonstrates that he will not or cannot perform his obligations under the contract. If the stage is reached that the shipowner is offering to fulfil an agreement which is in substance entirely different from that which he contracted to perform, the other party can refuse to accept it as performance of the original contract' ([1962] 2 QB 26 (CA) 48).
[73] *Hongkong Fir Shipping* [1962] 2 QB 26 (CA) 56.

condition precedent to their obligation to pay hire. His Lordship then reviewed the case law on charterparties referred to above. The authorities both reinforced his conclusion that seaworthiness was not a condition and demonstrated that a test of 'frustration' should be applied to the delay caused by the breaches. Both limbs of the charterers' argument therefore failed.

Upjohn LJ began his judgment by expressing his entire agreement with what Sellers LJ had said. As to seaworthiness, the authorities were quite clearly to the effect that it was not a condition. Why was this? The answer was straight-forward[74]:

> It is for the simple reason that the seaworthiness clause is breached by the slightest fail-ure to be fitted 'in every way' for service. Thus, to take examples from the judgments in some of the cases I have mentioned above, if a nail is missing from one of the tim-bers of a wooden vessel or if proper medical supplies or two anchors are not on board at the time of sailing, the owners are in breach of the seaworthiness stipulation. It is contrary to common sense to suppose that in such circumstances the parties contem-plated that the charterer should at once be entitled to treat the contract as at an end for such trifling breaches.

His Lordship went on to say that when it came to considering the remedies available for the breach of a contract term the classification of a term as a condition or warranty might not provide a complete answer. It was open to the parties to make it clear, either expressly or by necessary implication, that a par-ticular stipulation was to be regarded as a condition, *any* breach of which would entitle the innocent party to treat the contract as at an end. But even if this were not deemed to be the case on the true construction of the contract—so that the term was a warranty—it did not follow that damages would necessarily be a suf-ficient remedy; rather, the remedies open to the innocent party for breach of such a stipulation depended 'entirely upon the nature of the breach and its fore-seeable consequences'.[75] And in the absence of a renunciation by a shipowner of his obligations under the charter, the question was whether the breach of the stipulation went so much to the root of the contract that it made further com-mercial performance of the contract impossible—or, in other words, whether the whole contract was frustrated. If so, the innocent party could treat the con-tract as at an end; if not, he was limited to damages. And as far as the initial unseaworthiness in this case was concerned, that test had not been satisfied. On the delay issue, Upjohn LJ agreed with both Salmon J and Sellers LJ that the authorities pointed clearly to a test of frustration, and since it had not been seriously argued that the delays in the case had amounted to a frustration of the charter, the appeal must be dismissed.

Before we turn to the analysis of Diplock LJ, a couple of observations can be made about these two judgments. The most interesting aspect of the judgment of Sellers LJ is perhaps the distinction which his Lordship drew between a

---

[74] *Hongkong Fir Shipping* [1962] 2 QB 26 (CA) 62–63.
[75] *Hongkong Fir Shipping* [1962] 2 QB 26 (CA) 64.

wholly executory charter and one in which the vessel had been accepted and used, although it must also be said that this aspect of his analysis was not fully developed. Apart from this distinction, the judgment was entirely orthodox, and perfectly consistent with the 19th-century charterparty cases on which it relied. The same could be said for the judgment of Upjohn LJ, except for the fact that his Lordship made it clear that, provided its consequences were sufficiently serious, a breach of warranty might entitle the innocent party to terminate the contract.[76] This was, as we have seen, implicit in the earlier case law, but Upjohn LJ nevertheless deserves credit for making the point expressly, and for asserting (as Diplock LJ was also to do) that the late 19th century condition/warranty distinction did not provide a comprehensive answer to the vexed question of discharge for breach.

Still, there is no doubt that the most junior member of the panel stole his colleagues' thunder. In his judgment, Diplock LJ said very little about the appeal itself, preferring to make what he described as 'some general observations upon the legal questions' which it involved.[77] His starting point was that unless the parties or Parliament had expressly stated that an event would discharge one of the parties from further performance of his undertakings, it was up to the court to decide whether or not it had this effect, with the test being whether the occurrence of the event deprived that party 'of substantially the whole benefit which it was the intention of the parties as expressed in the contract that he should obtain as the consideration for performing those undertakings'.[78] His Lordship went on to say that this test applied regardless of whether or not the event came about through the other party's breach. However, he acknowledged that the consequences of the event were different in the two cases, because where the event occurred as a result of one party's breach, the principle that a man should not be allowed to take advantage of his own wrong dictated that the party in breach should not be able to rely upon it as relieving him of the further performance of his undertakings, and that the innocent party had a choice as to whether he did so or not.

The next step in his Lordship's analysis was to point out that, once it was appreciated that it was the event (and not the fact that the event was a result of a breach of contract) that relieved the innocent party of the further performance of his obligations, it became clear that the question of whether the innocent party was so relieved could not be answered

> by treating all contractual undertakings as falling into one of two separate categories: 'conditions' the breach of which gives rise to an event which relieves the party not in default of further performance of his obligations, and 'warranties' the breach of which does not give rise to such an event.[79]

---

[76] See also his judgment in the later case of *Astley Industrial Trust Ltd v Grimley* [1963] 1 WLR 584, 598–99.

[77] *Hongkong Fir Shipping* [1962] 2 QB 26 (CA) 65.

[78] *Hongkong Fir Shipping* [1962] 2 QB 26 (CA) 66.

[79] *Hongkong Fir Shipping* [1962] 2 QB 26 (CA) 69.

He went on[80]:

No doubt there are many simple contractual undertakings, sometimes express but more often because of their very simplicity ('It goes without saying') to be implied, of which it can be predicated that every breach of such an undertaking must give rise to an event which will deprive the party not in default of substantially the whole benefit which it was intended that he should obtain from the contract. And such a stipulation, unless the parties have agreed that breach of it shall not entitle the non-defaulting party to treat the contract as repudiated, is a 'condition'. So too there may be other simple contractual undertakings of which it can be predicated that no breach can give rise to an event which will deprive the party not in default of substantially the whole benefit which it was intended that he should obtain from the contract; and such a stipulation, unless the parties have agreed that breach of it shall entitle the non-defaulting party to treat the contract as repudiated, is a 'warranty'. There are, however, many contractual undertakings of a more complex character which cannot be categorised as being 'conditions' or 'warranties' if the late nineteenth-century meaning adopted in the Sale of Goods Act, 1893 . . . be given to those terms. Of such undertakings all that can be predicated is that some breaches will and others will not give rise to an event which will deprive the party not in default of substantially the whole benefit which it was intended that he should obtain from the contract; and the legal consequences of a breach of such an undertaking, unless provided for expressly in the contract, depend upon the nature of the event to which the breach gives rise and do not follow automatically from a prior classification of the undertaking as a 'condition' or a 'warranty'.

The duty of a shipowner to proceed with all reasonable dispatch was an example of such an undertaking, as was the obligation as to seaworthiness at issue in the instant appeal. It followed that what the judge had had to do in this case was

to look at the events which had occurred as a result of the breach at the time at which the charterers purported to rescind the charterparty and to decide whether the occurrence of those events deprived the charterers of substantially the whole benefit which it was the intention of the parties as expressed in the charterparty that the charterers should obtain from the further performance of their own contractual undertakings.[81]

And since the judge had asked himself this question, and had arrived at the right answer, Diplock LJ agreed that the appeal must fail.[82]

A number of points can be made. The first is that—unlike Salmon J, Sellers LJ and Upjohn LJ—Diplock LJ felt no need to separate out the breaches of the charterparty and the delays to which they gave rise, which in itself perhaps demonstrates the power and the simplicity of his analysis. The second point is that right from the start Diplock LJ made it clear that the parties could them-

---

[80] *Hongkong Fir Shipping* [1962] 2 QB 26 (CA) 69–70.

[81] *Hongkong Fir Shipping* [1962] 2 QB 26 (CA) 72.

[82] Leave to appeal was refused, and although a stay of execution was given to the charterers to enable them to apply to the House of Lords for leave, their application, if made, must have been refused—itself perhaps an indication that the case was not especially controversial.

selves elevate a term to the status of a 'condition'. It follows, therefore, that when he said that an undertaking of which it could be predicated that every breach must give rise to an event which would deprive the party not in default of substantially the whole benefit which it was intended that he should obtain from the contract was a 'condition', this was not intended to be an exhaustive definition of the concept, as has sometimes subsequently been made out.[83] (On the other hand, the later criticism that his Lordship's analysis left no scope for the courts to *imply* that the parties intended any breach of a term to entitle the innocent party to terminate the contract is more justified, since he consistently refers to the parties stating this 'expressly'.[84]) The third point is that Diplock LJ could not have asserted more clearly the consistency of the rules governing discharge by frustration and discharge for breach. It is therefore all the more remarkable that this central tenet of his analysis seems so often to be overlooked today. And the final point is that the most novel aspect of his analysis was the suggestion that there was a third category of terms—later christened 'innominate' or 'intermediate' terms—alongside conditions and warranties (at least as these had been defined in the Sale of Goods Act 1893).

At the same time, the modern tendency to cite the judgment almost exclusively in terms of its recognition of this third category of terms seems rather a simplistic way of encapsulating the very sophisticated analysis which it presents. After all, the whole point of Diplock LJ's analysis was that (in the absence of express stipulation otherwise) it is an *event* which relieves a party from the further discharge of his contractual obligations, rather than a breach by the other party of an obligation which has been the subject of an a priori classification. And, as has been pointed out,[85] this emphasis on the gravity of the breach ties in with Upjohn LJ's judgment (where the 'intermediate' term concept was not employed), albeit with the caveat that while Upjohn LJ focused on the nature of the breach and its *foreseeable* consequences, Diplock LJ referred instead to the *actual* consequences of the breach.[86]

---

[83] See eg Treitel, *Some Landmarks of Twentieth Century Contract Law* (n 4 above) 116–18. See also, but more equivocally, *Bunge Corp v Tradax Export SA* [1981] 2 All ER 513 (CA) 536–38 (Megaw LJ); Bridge, 'Discharge for Breach of the Contract of Sale of Goods' (n 6 above) 908. Cf *Bunge Corp v Tradax Export SA* (n 2 above) 715 (Lord Wilberforce) and 726 (Lord Roskill).

[84] See below, text preceding n 114.

[85] Carter, Tolhurst and Peden, 'Developing the Intermediate Term Concept' (n 4 above) 270.

[86] Though when Diplock LJ turned to the facts of the case at the end of his judgment, he referred ([1962] 2 QB 26 (CA) 72) both to 'the delay which had already occurred' by the time of the purported termination and to 'the delay which was likely to occur'. This did not prevent Lord Devlin from later criticising his approach on the grounds that the innocent party might have to make up his mind what to do at the time of the breach, and hence could not 'wait upon the event': Lord Devlin, 'The Treatment of Breach of Contract' (n 90 below) 197.

## F. DEVELOPMENTS SINCE *HONGKONG FIR*

The immediate response to the *Hongkong Fir* decision appears to have been rather muted,[87] although a case note by Michael Furmston appeared in the *Modern Law Review*,[88] in which he commented with prescience that it was 'probably premature to attempt any definite assessment of the significance' of Diplock LJ's judgment. The first real harbingers of the enormous influence which the case was to have came in two law review articles published in the 1960s. The first of these was an article by Francis Reynolds in the 1963 *Law Quarterly Review*, in which he drew heavily upon the *Hongkong Fir* decision in support of his argument that the condition/warranty dichotomy was, as part of the general theory of contract, confusing and misleading, and that in general contract law the notions of conditions and warranties should be abandoned, and attention focused instead upon the nature of the breach.[89] The second was an article in the 1966 *Cambridge Law Journal* entitled 'The Treatment of Breach of Contract',[90] in which Lord Devlin, whose reasoning in *Universal Cargo Carriers Corp v Citati*[91] had foreshadowed much of what was to follow in *Hongkong Fir*, subjected the judgments in the later case to a detailed and sophisticated analysis. Consistently with his reasoning in *Universal Cargo Carriers*, his Lordship conceptualised the *Hongkong Fir* decision as one concerned with the circumstances in which a breach of warranty could discharge a contract,[92] and said that the doctrine involved 'slips into place' alongside the 'doctrine of dissolution by frustration'.[93]

The first in-depth judicial scrutiny of the *Hongkong Fir* case came in *The Mihalis Angelos*[94] in 1971. The issue was whether a shipowner's contractual assurance of expected readiness to load, in a voyage charter, was a condition of the charterparty. The Court of Appeal held that it was, with the result that if such an assurance was false the charterer could throw up the charterparty. Since such a clause is not a promise that the ship will be ready to load on the given date, but rather an assurance by the owner that he honestly expects that it will

---

[87] In the first edition of his textbook, which was published just after *Hongkong Fir* was decided, GH Treitel simply referred to it as an illustration of a common law rule that breach of any term (condition or warranty) discharged the innocent party if it deprived him substantially of what he bargained for: *The Law of Contract* (London, Stevens & Sons, 1962) 527. GC Cheshire and CHS Fifoot were more critical in their textbook *The Law of Contract*, 6th edn (London, Butterworths, 1964), arguing (at 126) that the seaworthiness clause in the case had not created a single intermediate obligation but rather a bundle of conditions and warranties.

[88] M Furmston, 'The Classification of Contractual Terms' (1962) 25 *Modern Law Review* 584.

[89] FMB Reynolds, 'Warranty, Condition and Fundamental Term' (1963) 79 *Law Quarterly Review* 534.

[90] Lord Devlin, 'The Treatment of Breach of Contract' [1966] *Cambridge Law Journal* 192.

[91] *Universal Cargo Carriers Corp v Citati* (n 43 above).

[92] See, eg Devlin, 'The Treatment of Breach of Contract' (n 90 above) 193.

[93] Devlin, 'The Treatment of Breach of Contract' (n 90 above) 203.

[94] *Maredelanto Compania Naviera SA v Bergbau-Handel GmbH, The Mihalis Angelos* [1971] 1 QB 164 (CA).

be (and that his expectation is based on reasonable grounds), this hard-line approach was scarcely surprising. Nor was it inconsistent with the reasoning in the *Hongkong Fir* case, as Lord Denning MR was keen to demonstrate. There were many contract terms that did not fit into either the warranty or condition categories, he said, and in such cases the issue was whether or not the breach went to the root of the contract. However, there was also a considerable body of law by which certain stipulations had been classified as conditions, and in such cases any failure to perform, however slight, entitled the other party to terminate the contract. In the judgment of Megaw LJ, on the other hand, there is an undercurrent of hostility towards an approach to discharge focused on the consequences of the breach, on the grounds that it is inimical to certainty[95]:

> One of the important elements of the law is predictability. At any rate in commercial law, there are obvious and substantial advantages in having, where possible, a firm and definite rule for a particular class of legal relationships: for example, as here, the legal categorisation of a particular, definable type of contractual clause in common use. It is surely much better . . . when a contractual obligation of this nature is under consideration, and still more when [the parties] are faced with the necessity for an urgent decision as to the effects of a suspected breach of it, to be able to say categorically [whether or not the innocent party can put an end to the contract] rather than that they should be left to ponder whether or not the courts would be likely, in the particular case . . . to decide that in the particular circumstances the breach was or was not such as 'to go to the root of the contract'.

This emphasis on the importance of predictability and certainty was to come to the fore a decade later, when the House of Lords considered the scope of the *Hongkong Fir* decision in *Bunge Corp v Tradax Export SA*.[96] In the meantime, however, there was *The Hansa Nord*,[97] where the familiar pattern of the spillover of sales law into general contract law was reversed. German sellers had agreed to sell Dutch buyers 6,000 tons of citrus pulp pellets CIF Rotterdam, with each shipment to be treated as a separate contract. On the arrival of the first consignment of 3,400 tons, it was found that part of the cargo in one hold had been damaged by over-heating, and the buyers rejected the whole cargo on the basis (inter alia) that the pellets had not been shipped 'in good condition', as required by clause 7 of the contract. The goods having been sold off by order of a Dutch court, the buyers bought them through an intermediary for less than one-third of the contract price, and used the pellets, as originally intended, to make cattle food. Following arbitration proceedings, the Court of Appeal decided (inter alia) that the obligation to ship the pellets in good condition was not a condition of the contract, and that since the breach in question had not gone to the root of the contract the buyers had not been entitled to reject the consignment.

---

[95] *Maredelanto Compania Naviera SA v Bergbau-Handel GmbH (The Mihalis Angelos)* [1971] 1 QB 164 (CA) 205.
[96] *Bunge Corp v Tradax Export SA* (n 2 above).
[97] *The Hansa Nord* (n 34 above).

Lord Denning MR repeated what he had said in *The Mihalis Angelos* about the condition/warranty dichotomy not being exhaustive, citing *Hongkong Fir* in support, and held that this was true of contracts for the sale of goods as well as other contracts, notwithstanding section 11(1)(b) of the 1893 Act. It followed that in all contracts the task of a court faced with the question of whether the innocent party was discharged by the other's breach was to consider, first, whether the term was, on its true construction,

> a condition strictly so called, that is, a stipulation such that, for any breach of it, the other party is entitled to treat himself as discharged

and secondly, if it was not, to ask whether the breach that had taken place went to the root of the contract.[98]

In his judgment, Ormrod LJ enthusiastically endorsed the central tenet of Diplock LJ's analysis in *Hongkong Fir*: it was now accepted as a general principle

> that it is the events resulting from the breach, rather than the breach itself, which may destroy the consideration for the [innocent party's] promise and so enable him to treat the contract as repudiated.[99]

However, when it came to the precise mechanics by which this principle was to be given effect, his Lordship clearly preferred Upjohn LJ's approach to that of Diplock LJ—strictly speaking, he said, it was doubtful whether the 'creation of a third category of stipulations'[100] was necessary, since the same result could be achieved by the recognition of a 'back-up' rule of the common law that termination was justified where a breach of warranty went to the root of the contract.

Roskill LJ agreed that the doctrine of the *Hongkong Fir* case was 'of universal application': there was no reason why the law relating to sales contracts should differ from the law relating to the performance of other contractual obligations.[101] Moreover, he said that the courts 'should not be over ready . . . to construe a term as a condition'[102]:

> In principle, contracts are made to be performed and not to be avoided according to the whims of market fluctuation and where there is a free choice between two possible constructions, I think the court should tend to prefer that construction which will ensure performance, and not encourage avoidance of contractual obligations.

If we set this statement alongside the words of Megaw LJ in *The Mihalis Angelos*, then the central tension in this area of law—between sanctity of contract on the one hand, and commercial certainty on the other—becomes apparent. The substantive issues underlying the conceptual controversy had now been revealed.

---

[98] *The Hansa Nord* (n 34 above) 60.
[99] *The Hansa Nord* (n 34 above) 83.
[100] *The Hansa Nord* (n 34 above) 84.
[101] *The Hansa Nord* (n 34 above) 71.
[102] *The Hansa Nord* (n 34 above) 70.

It was 20 years after the judgments in *Hongkong Fir* had been handed down before the House of Lords was first called upon, in *Bunge Corp v Tradax Export SA*,[103] to consider them in any depth, though Lord Wilberforce had previously welcomed the fact that the law of contract now attended more 'to the nature and gravity of a breach', rather than accepting 'rigid categories which do or do not automatically give a right to rescind',[104] and other members of the House had acknowledged the existence of a third category of intermediate terms.[105] In any case, the existence of this category was taken as read in *Bunge*,[106] where the House held that a stipulation in an f.o.b. contract requiring the buyer to give 15 days' notice of the readiness of the vessel was not an intermediate term, but rather a condition, with the result that even the most minor breach gave the seller the right to terminate the contract. Central to that conclusion was the argument from commercial certainty which Megaw LJ had made in *The Mihalis Angelos*. Lord Wilberforce said, for example, that the adoption of the 'consequences of the breach' approach across the board would be 'commercially most undesirable',[107] while Lord Lowry spoke of the 'enormous practical advantages in certainty'.[108] Even Lord Roskill, who in *The Hansa Nord* had emphasised the need to encourage performance of contracts rather than their avoidance, now spoke of the need also to bear in mind the need for certainty:

> Parties to commercial transactions should be entitled to know their rights at once and should not, when possible, be required to wait upon events before those rights can be determined.[109]

These certainty considerations led their Lordships to hold that that in mercantile contracts two types of term could generally be assumed to be conditions, namely time clauses,[110] and terms compliance with which was a condition precedent to the ability of the other party to comply with another term (as here, where the seller's ability to perform his obligation to nominate a loading port was dependent on the buyer's having previously nominated the vessel).[111]

---

[103] *Bunge Corp v Tradax Export SA* (n 2 above).

[104] *Reardon Smith Line Ltd v Yngvar Hansen-Tangen* [1976] 1 WLR 989 (HL) 998. See also *Bremer Handelsgesellschaft mbH v Vanden Avenne-Izegem PVBA* [1978] 2 Lloyd's Rep 109 (HL) 113; and *Federal Commerce & Navigation Co Ltd v Molena Alpha Inc* [1979] AC 757 (HL) 778–79, where, in the context of anticipatory breach, his Lordship cited the judgment of Diplock LJ for the proposition that 'to amount to a repudiation a breach must go to the root of the contract'.

[105] See eg *Schuler AG v Wickman Machine Tool Sales Ltd* (n 6 above) 264 (Lord Simon). Lord Diplock reiterated the approach to discharge for breach which he had put forward in *Hongkong Fir* in *Photo Production Ltd v Securicor Transport Ltd* [1980] AC 827 (HL) 849, though without reference to the intermediate term concept.

[106] In the Court of Appeal, Megaw LJ had said that no one now doubted the existence of such a category of terms: *Bunge Corp v Tradax Export SA* [1981] 1 All ER 513, 536.

[107] *Bunge Corp v Tradax Export SA* (n 2 above) 715.

[108] *Bunge Corp v Tradax Export SA* (n 2 above) 720.

[109] *Bunge Corp v Tradax Export SA* (n 2 above) 725.

[110] *Bunge Corp v Tradax Export SA* (n 2 above) 716 (Lord Wilberforce).

[111] *Bunge Corp v Tradax Export SA* (n 2 above) 729 (Lord Roskill). See also 716 (Lord Wilberforce).

Alongside this emphasis on the need in certain contexts for the certainty provided by a priori classification, there can also be seen in *Bunge* a renewed focus on the construction of the contract as a guide to the remedies available for its breach. According to Lord Scarman, for example, the *Hongkong Fir* case had been 'concerned as much with the construction of the contract as with the consequences and effects of breach', and hence the first question was always whether, on the true construction of a term, and the contract of which it was a part, the term was a condition, an innominate term, or a warranty.[112] Similarly, Lord Lowry said that it was by construing a contract that one decided whether or not a term was a condition, and not by looking at the consequences of its breach.[113] In fact, however, Diplock LJ had downplayed the intentions of the parties in his judgment in *Hongkong Fir*, which was hardly surprising, since it was precisely this kind of focus on the construction of the contract which had given birth to the condition/warranty dichotomy in the first place. Hence, while he did make it clear that the parties could *expressly* assign a term to the conditions category, Diplock LJ at no point said that this could also happen by necessary implication. This aspect of his analysis was the subject of criticism in *Bunge*,[114] where their Lordships said—as Upjohn LJ had in his judgment in *Hongkong Fir*[115]—that such an intention could indeed be implied.[116]

A final point to note about *Bunge v Tradax* is that their Lordships' references to the *Hongkong Fir* case were almost all to the judgment of Diplock LJ,[117] and that they seem unquestioningly to have accepted that the most important legacy of the case had been the development of the 'intermediate term'. This can be contrasted with the earlier Court of Appeal cases, where reference had also been made to Upjohn LJ's judgment, and where the intermediate term concept had sometimes been either ignored or expressly rejected. Quite why this shift of

---

[112] *Bunge Corp v Tradax Export SA* (n 2 above) 717.

[113] *Bunge Corp v Tradax Export SA* (n 2 above) 719.

[114] *Bunge Corp v Tradax Export SA* (n 2 above) 726 (Lord Roskill).

[115] *Hongkong Fir Shipping* [1962] 2 QB 26 (CA) 63. See also his speech in *Suisse Atlantique Société D'Armement Maritime SA v NV Rotterdamsche Kolen Centrale* [1967] 1 AC 361 (HL) 422.

[116] *Bunge Corp v Tradax Export SA* (n 2 above) 717 (Lord Scarman), 719 (Lord Lowry), and 726 (Lord Roskill). The reliance placed in this connection on an alleged change of heart on Lord Diplock's part in *Photo Production Ltd v Securicor Transport Ltd* appears to have been based on a misinterpretation of the passage in question. In the passage (at [1980] AC 827, 849), Lord Diplock refers to a situation where the parties 'have agreed, whether by express words or *by implication of law*' that any breach of a term shall entitle the other party to terminate the contract (my emphasis). In *Bunge Corp v Tradax Export SA* (n 2 above) Lord Roskill (at 726) reads the words in italics as synonymous with 'by necessary implication', but in fact it is clear from a later passage of Lord Diplock's speech that he had in mind situations where a term is made a condition by statute, or—in the case of deviation in a contract for the carriage of goods by sea—by what he terms 'implication of the common law': see [1980] AC 827, 849–50.

[117] See *Bunge Corp v Tradax Export SA* (n 2 above) 715 (Lord Wilberforce), 717 (Lord Scarman), 718–19 (Lord Lowry), and 725–26 (Lord Roskill). The only mention of the judgments of Upjohn LJ and Sellers LJ is with reference to the importance of the construction of the contract: see 717 (Lord Scarman) and 725 (Lord Roskill).

emphasis took place is open to question, but the most likely explanation is that the House of Lords was simply reflecting a consensus which had by then emerged as to the significance of the *Hongkong Fir* decision.

Before I turn to look at that consensus in more detail, one subsequent development should be mentioned. This was the enactment of the Sale and Supply of Goods 1994, which amended the Sale of Goods Act 1979 in a number of important respects. For present purposes, the most interesting of these amendments was the new section 15A, which removed the right of a commercial buyer to reject goods for breaches of the implied conditions as to correspondence with description or sample, fitness for purpose, and satisfactory quality if the breach was 'so slight that it would be unreasonable' for him to exercise it.[118] It would be a mistake to suppose that this provision transforms the relevant implied conditions into intermediate terms in cases where it applies, since it does not follow from the fact that a breach is not so slight as to make it unreasonable to reject that it deprives the buyer of substantially the whole benefit which it was intended that he should obtain from the contract.[119] Nevertheless, the new section did create a significant inroad into the rigid condition/warranty dichotomy in the legislation relating to the sale of goods, and the policy underlying it was, as Sir Guenter Treitel has pointed out, similar to that on which the development of the intermediate term had been based, namely the prevention of opportunistic termination.[120]

## G. PERCEPTIONS OF *HONGKONG FIR*

By the time that *Bunge Corp v Tradax Export SA* was decided, at the beginning of the 1980s, a consensus appears to have emerged as to the true significance of the *Hongkong Fir* decision. This consensus is reflected in contract textbooks, and also in other writings of leading commentators, such as Sir Guenter Treitel's essay on 'Types of Contractual Terms' in his book *Some Landmarks of Twentieth Century Contract Law*.[121] The three most noticeable aspects of the consensus are, first, that the focus is almost entirely on the judgment of Diplock LJ; secondly, that the case is considered to be synonymous with a tripartite classification of contractual terms as conditions, warranties and intermediate terms;[122] and thirdly, that the connections drawn in the case between discharge for breach and discharge by frustration are downplayed or ignored.

---

[118] This rule does not apply where 'a contrary intention appears in, or is to be implied from, the contract': s 15A(2). Similar rules apply where the seller delivers the wrong quantity of goods (s 30(2A)), and in other contracts for the supply of goods: Supply of Goods (Implied Terms) Act 1973, s 11A; Supply of Goods and Services Act 1982, s 5A.

[119] E Peel, *Treitel's The Law of Contract*, 12th edn (London, Sweet & Maxwell, 2007) 895.

[120] *Ibid*, 894–95.

[121] Treitel, *Some Landmarks of Twentieth Century Contract Law* (n 4 above).

[122] See Carter, Tolhurst and Peden, 'Developing the Intermediate Term Concept' (n 4 above) 271.

The first two aspects of this consensus are of course connected, because it is only in the judgment of Diplock LJ that there can be found any evidence for the view that a third category of term is required; Upjohn LJ's analysis was clearly to the effect that a sufficiently serious breach of warranty entitled the other party to bring the contract to an end. It must be admitted, however, that this was also the most innovative aspect of the *Hongkong Fir* decision, for although there was plenty of prior authority to the effect that the seriousness of the consequences of a breach might entitle the other party to terminate, this idea had not previously been conceptualised in terms of a *tertium quid* between conditions and warranties. Whether a third category was actually required is another matter.[123] In the end, the question boils down to whether or not there is a need for a category of 'warranties', breach of which can never give rise to a right to terminate the contract. There are two reasons why such a category might be thought to be necessary. The first is that the Sale of Goods Act contains two such terms: the implied terms as to freedom from encumbrances and quiet possession.[124] And the other reason is that the parties to a contract ought to be able to stipulate, if they so wish, that no breach of a given term will entitle the other party to terminate, no matter how serious its consequences: the parties' right to make any term a 'warranty' in this sense is the logical corollary of their right to make any term a condition.[125]

The first of these justifications for the warranty category is of course grounded in an approach to discharge for breach which is antithetical to the focus on the consequences of breach apparent in *Hongkong Fir*, and to this extent the intermediate term concept can be seen as a compromise between these two competing approaches. The most innovative aspect of the *Hongkong Fir* case was, on this analysis, an attempt to integrate the consequences of the breach approach with the a priori classification approach. By contrast, the more conservative position taken by Upjohn LJ set up a direct clash between the two—a clash, it should be said, which was nothing new, but which had largely been obscured by the fact that one approach was principally associated with sales contracts and the other with charterparties. The development of *general* contractual principles for discharge by breach, however, did perhaps require the

---

[123] Australian commentators have taken the view that it was not: see eg Grieg and Davis (n 7 above) 1209–10; JW Carter, *Breach of Contract*, 2nd edn (London, Sweet & Maxwell, 1991) para 426; NC Seddon and MP Ellinghaus (eds), *Cheshire and Fifoot's Law of Contract*, 9th Australian edn (Sydney, Butterworths, 2007) para 21.11. For a judicial endorsement of the view of these commentators, see the recent judgment of Kirby J in *Koompahtoo Local Aboriginal Land Council v Sanpine Pty Ltd* [2007] HCA 61, (2007) 241 ALR 88. However, although the rest of the Court in *Koompahtoo* acknowledged (at [50]) that 'the adoption of other taxonomies for contractual stipulations' might result in outcomes similar to those arising out of the threefold classification, their Honours upheld the approach taken by Diplock LJ in *Hongkong Fir*, which they said 'had long since passed into the mainstream law of contract as understood and practised in Australia' (*ibid*).

[124] See the Sale of Goods Act 1979, s 12.

[125] See E McKendrick, *Contract Law: Text, Cases and Materials*, 2nd edn (Oxford, Oxford University Press, 2005) 958. The possibility has been adverted to by the courts: see, eg *Re Olympia & York Canary Wharf Ltd (No 2)* [1993] BCC 159 (QBD) 166 (Morritt J).

compromise which the intermediate term concept represented. This becomes evident if we consider how awkward it would have been for the Court of Appeal to have decided *The Hansa Nord* the same way without the intermediate term option. As it was, it was a big leap to hold that the condition/warranty dichotomy in section 11(1)(b) was not exhaustive, but it would have been more difficult still to have directly contradicted the definition of a warranty in that section by holding that, in the event of a sufficiently serious breach of warranty, the buyer could reject the goods.[126]

As there is precious little evidence that contract parties ever *wish* to exclude the remedy of discharge for breach,[127] the second justification for the tripartite classification does not carry a great deal of practical weight, but since they must in theory be *able* to do so, it does seem that (at least notionally) there is a need—quite apart from the Sale of Goods Act—for three types of contract term, rather than two. On the other hand, this presupposes that some kind of a priori classification of contract terms is required, in itself a questionable assumption. After all, it would be perfectly plausible to deal with the question of discharge for breach by simply asking two questions: first, whether the availability or exclusion of the remedy was in the circumstances determined by law or (expressly or by necessary implication) by the parties, and, secondly, if not, whether the breach in question had gone to the root of the contract.[128] In other words, there is not really any need to classify the term which has been broken in order to determine whether or not the remedy of discharge is available. Admittedly, the distinction between the two approaches is merely terminological, but a semantic shift might nonetheless be advantageous, since the current emphasis on the classification of terms blurs the central message of the *Hongkong Fir* case—that the primary focus should not be on the term itself, but the effects of its breach.[129] It is also worth noting that in contract textbooks, the classificatory scheme is generally not to be found alongside the discussion of discharge for breach, but

---

[126] Though this was in fact the import of Ormrod LJ's analysis in the case. See also Peel, *Treitel's The Law of Contract* (n 119 above) 898, where it is argued that the Act may not exhaustively state the effects of a breach of warranty.

[127] Carter, *Breach of Contract* (n 123 above) para 607 describes it as 'an extreme conclusion' which a court will be reluctant to reach.

[128] This is similar to the approach which Lord Diplock himself took in *Photo Production Ltd v Securicor Transport Ltd* [1980] AC 827 (HL) 849, though he there requires the parties to have stipulated for the discharge remedy expressly, and he does not avert to the possibility of their having intended that the remedy *not* be available. See also the minority judgment of Kirby J in *Koompahtoo Local Aboriginal Land Council v Sanpine Pty Ltd* (n 123 above) at [114], though again his Honour does not mention the possibility of the parties intending that discharge not be available in the case of a serious breach.

[129] A point emphasised by the earliest commentators on the case: see Reynolds, 'Warranty, Condition and Fundamental Term' (n 89 above) 545; Devlin, 'The Treatment of Breach of Contract' (n 6 above) 192. A more recent text that makes the same point is Carter, *Breach of Contract* (n 123 above) para 617 ('the basis of the *Hongkong Fir* doctrine is not so much the tripartite classification of contractual terms as the view that the remedies . . . open to a promisee on the occurrence of a breach of contract, do not depend solely on the character of the term breached').

in an earlier chapter on the terms of the contract,[130] a tendency which surely serves more to obscure than to elucidate.

Another unfortunate tendency of the contract textbooks, which reflects the modern consensus on *Hongkong Fir*, is to downplay or ignore the very strong connection between discharge for breach and discharge by frustration. This seems strange, because it was a central pillar of Diplock LJ's analysis. Since it was obviously an event which discharged the contract in a case of frustration (there being no breach), it made sense, he argued, for it also generally to be an event—the consequences of the breach—which discharged the contract in breach cases.[131] As we have seen, this linkage of the two doctrines was nothing new. An important strand of the modern frustration doctrine (exemplified by *Jackson v The Union Marine Insurance Co*[132]) had, after all, developed directly out of the concept of frustrating delay used in the 19th-century charterparty cases,[133] and the connection between the two doctrines had been commented upon many times before, not least by Devlin J in his judgment in *Universal Cargo Carriers Corp v Citati*.[134] However, this aspect of the analysis in the *Hongkong Fir* case appears largely to have disappeared from view, along with the connection between discharge for breach and discharge by frustration more generally.[135] This is unfortunate, because it serves to obscure the common thread which runs between the two doctrines, namely the idea that (in the absence of contrary agreement) a person is generally discharged from his contractual obligations only if to require continued performance would in effect be to hold him to an obligation into which he did not enter in the first place.[136] Furthermore, the connection is of practical significance, because it demonstrates

---

[130] See, eg *Anson's Law of Contract* (n 6 above); JC Smith, *The Law of Contract*, 4th edn (London, Sweet & Maxwell, 2002); E McKendrick, *Contract Law*, 6th edn (Basingstoke, Palgrave Macmillan, 2005); *Cheshire, Fifoot and Furmston's Law of Contract*, 15th edn (Oxford, Oxford University Press, 2007). Exceptions are Peel, *Treitel's The Law of Contract* (n 119 above) and R Halson, *Contract Law* (Harlow, Longman, 2001).

[131] A point previously made in AL Corbin, *Corbin on Contracts*, one vol edn (St Paul, MN, West Publishing, 1952) para 1253: 'The fact that it is not breach as a mere wrong that discharges the other party is indicated by the fact that the very same failure of performance may operate as a discharge, whether it is a wrongful failure or not'. This logical connection between the two doctrines is also emphasised by AM Shea, 'Discharge from Performance of Contracts by Failure of Condition' (1979) 42 *Modern Law Review* 623, 624, and was reiterated by Lord Diplock himself in *United Scientific Holdings Ltd v Burnley BC* [1978] AC 904 (HL) 928.

[132] *Jackson v The Union Marine Insurance Co* (n 20 above).

[133] 'The word "frustration" was originally used to describe the situation where one party caused the delay in breach of contract and it is only in more recent years that it has usually been confined to events outside the control of the parties' (Furmston, 'The Classification of Contractual Terms' (n 88 above) 585). See further on the development of the frustration doctrine, R McElroy and G Williams, *Impossibility of Performance* (Cambridge, Cambridge University Press, 1941) ch 6.

[134] *Universal Cargo Carriers Corp v Citati* (n 43 above) esp 433–35. He also emphasised the link extra-judicially: Devlin, 'The Treatment of Breach of Contract' (n 6 above) 202–203.

[135] But cf *Great Peace Shipping Ltd v Tsavliris Salvage (International) Ltd* [2002] EWCA Civ 1407, [2003] QB 679 [82] (Lord Phillips MR).

[136] See *Davis Contractors Ltd v Fareham UDC* [1956] AC 696 (HL) 729 (Lord Radcliffe): 'It was not this that I promised to do'.

that the *Hongkong Fir* test of discharge is a very difficult one to satisfy. As has recently been pointed out[137]:

> The symmetry between the breach of an intermediate term which is required to justify termination and satisfaction of the test of commercial frustration gives effect to a very specific policy. In the absence of agreement that a particular term is a condition, termination of a commercial contract is a matter of last resort. The promisee must be content with damages unless the event which results from the promisor's breach makes further performance impossible, futile or extremely onerous.

It could even be argued that once it is appreciated that in cases not involving a breach of condition, the test for discharge for breach is (at least in theory[138]) precisely the same as the test for discharge by frustration,[139] the certainty objection to the intermediate term largely falls away—after all, the criticism usually made of the frustration doctrine is that it is too narrowly drawn, precisely so as not to create uncertainty. Admittedly, this does give rise to another concern, which is that the test laid down for discharge for breach in the *Hongkong Fir* case is too severe: can it really be right that a party is only discharged on the ground of the other's breach in cases where the consequences are so serious that they would have discharged the contract automatically if they had occurred without any breach at all?[140] There is perhaps no obvious answer to this question,[141] but it is clear that the important issues raised by the connection between the two doctrines will be overlooked if attention is not drawn to it in the first place.

## CONCLUSION

At least two general conclusions can be drawn from the history of the *Hongkong Fir* decision. The first is the danger of codification in a common law

---

[137] Carter, Tolhurst and Peden, 'Developing the Intermediate Term Concept' (n 4 above) 272–73.

[138] H Beale, *Remedies for Breach of Contract* (London, Sweet & Maxwell, 1980) 45, expresses doubt as to whether the courts do in fact apply the same test.

[139] See *Universal Cargo Carriers Corp v Citati* (n 43 above) 434 (Devlin J); *Hongkong Fir Shipping Co* [1962] 2 QB 26 (CA) 69 (Diplock LJ); *Trade and Transport Inc v Iino Kaiun Kaisha Ltd* [1973] 1 WLR 210 (CA) 223 (Kerr LJ) (delay required for charterer's failure to load to discharge shipowner same as delay required to discharge both parties under frustration doctrine).

[140] See Weir, 'Contract—The Buyer's Right to Reject Defective Goods' (n 5 above) 35. See similarly Furmston, 'The Classification of Contractual Terms' (n 88 above) 585. It is also noteworthy that the test for 'fundamental breach' employed by international instruments such as the UNIDROIT Principles and the UN Convention on Contracts for the International Sale of Goods—whether the breach substantially deprives the innocent party of what he was entitled to expect under the contract—seems broader than the *Hongkong Fir* test, which refers to the substantial deprivation of the *whole* benefit which it was intended that the innocent party should obtain.

[141] A possible justification for the *Hongkong Fir* rule is that in the case of failure of performance through breach the innocent party has an alternative remedy in the form of damages, which are of course not available when the failure is not wrongful: see *Corbin on Contracts* (n 131 above) para 1013. Note also Michael Bridge's argument that the strictness of the *Hongkong Fir* test is a reaction to counterbalance to the widespread designation of express and implied terms as conditions: 'Do We Need a Sale of Goods Act?' in J Lowry and L Mistelis (eds), *Commercial Law: Perspectives and Practice* (London, LexisNexis Butterworths, 2006) 34.

system. In many ways, the villain of the story which has been presented here is the Sale of Goods Act 1893, since the condition/warranty dichotomy would surely not have taken hold in the way in which it did if it had not been enshrined in that legislation. Lord Diplock himself clearly thought that the Act had had a pernicious influence as far as general contract law was concerned. Writing extra-judicially in the 1980s, he said that the way in which the statute had been interpreted had 'stereotyped the common law at the stage of development which it had reached at the time of the passing of the Act' and that this stereotyping had prevented the law of contract from developing in response to changes in society and business practice.[142] Similarly, Michael Bridge has written, with reference to the Sale of Goods Act, that[143]

> a tightly-drafted statute which purports to be a code and yet renders necessary resort to a developing common law, a law which may have changed greatly from that body of operative law in place at the date the statute was first passed, presents the courts with an unfortunate compromise between pure common law and pure code.

The other conclusion that might be drawn is the difficulty of developing general principles of contract law which are suitable for all the different types of contract which come before the courts. It was, after all, no coincidence that the two rival approaches to discharge for breach manifested themselves most often in two very different types of contract—the sale of goods and the charterparty—since, while the high degree of presentiation (of a 'present binding of the future'[144]) inherent in the condition/warranty dichotomy was just about plausible in the context of a discrete transaction such as a sale, it was completely unsuited to the ongoing relationship between the parties to a charterparty, not least a two-year time charter of the kind involved in the *Hongkong Fir* case. In hindsight, then, the real achievement of Diplock LJ may have been to make possible a fusion of these two competing approaches into a theory which could be applied equally successfully to both discrete and relational transactions. We might therefore conclude with the uplifting thought that the intermediate term did not only come between—it also brought together.

---

[142] Diplock, 'The Law of Contract in the Eighties' (n 33 above) 373–74.
[143] Bridge, 'Discharge for Breach of the Contract of Sale of Goods' (n 6 above) 926.
[144] I Macneil, *The Relational Theory of Contract*, D Campbell (ed) (London, Sweet & Maxwell, 2001) 182.

# 10

# Suisse Atlantique Société d'Armament SA v NV Rotterdamsche Kolen Centrale (1966)

ROGER BROWNSWORD*

## A. INTRODUCTION

THE LAW LORDS delivered their speeches in *Suisse Atlantique*[1] in Spring 1966, shortly before my cohort of fellow LSE undergraduates sat their first-year Contract examinations. Bill Wedderburn gave a memorable lecture on the implications of the case. I confess that I cannot recall precisely what he said about such nice questions as the distinction between breach of a fundamental term and fundamental breach, the significance of the innocent party electing to affirm the contract rather than treating it as repudiated, and the difference between substantive rules of law and mere rules of construction. For, this was a magisterial lecture that went, in every sense, over most of our young heads, being addressed not only to the student class but also to several members of the academic staff who were in attendance at the back of the packed lecture theatre. Whatever *Suisse Atlantique* was about, the Wedderburn lecture made an enduring impression, leaving the audience in no doubt that this was a landmark case.

As is well known, the Law Lords' speeches in *Suisse Atlantique* are very short on the issues as originally pleaded (on the core ratio of the decision) and very long on the invited submission on fundamental breach. With regard to the points of law covered by the core ratio (essentially, concerning the claimant ship-owners' argument that the defendant charterers, having deliberately gone slow in loading and unloading the chartered vessel, were in breach of an implied term of co-operation), it is generally thought that the case is of little interest. For

---

* I am indebted to Bill Wedderburn who, although unable to retrieve his notes of 40 years ago, was nevertheless able to offer me a number of very helpful comments on a draft of this paper. Needless to say, the errors and omissions in 2008 are all mine, as they were back in 1966.
[1] *Suisse Atlantique Societe d'Armement SA v NV Rotterdamsche Kolen Centrale* [1965] 1 Lloyd's Rep 166 (Mocatta J); [1965] 1 Lloyd's Rep 533 (CA); [1967] 1 AC 361 (HL).

example, Professor Guenter Treitel, in a lengthy and incisive comment on the case, dismissed the argument originally relied on by the ship-owners as raising 'no issue of general interest in the law of contract'.[2] By contrast, the extended remarks on the issues raised by the amended plea are thought to be of seminal importance, reining back the cavalier (substantive rule of law) use of the doctrine of fundamental breach and restoring the classical virtues of freedom of contract and the primacy of the contractors' clearly–expressed intentions.[3] If *Suisse Atlantique* is one of the great cases of the century, the conventional wisdom is that this is not because it upheld the decision already arrived at in the lower courts (because this was a mere rubber-stamping exercise); nor is it because it exerted a major influence on the way that future courts would deal with standard form exclusion and limitation clauses (because it was destined to be overtaken by unfair contract terms legislation); but, rather, because it sought to arrest the corrosion of freedom of contract and reinstate it as the hallmark of English contract law.

In this paper, I will challenge the conventional wisdom in two ways. First, I will suggest that the issues raised by the initial formulation of the claim (the issues covered by the ratio) are of capital importance. The fact that the courts found it so easy to dismiss the claimants' argument speaks volumes about the implicit values of English contract law. In particular, it speaks to the adoption of a robust individualism as the 'default ethic'—an ethic that views it as entirely unproblematic that, on a falling freight market, the charterers delayed loading and unloading because they preferred to pay the agreed rate of damages rather than pay the contract freight rates. By contrast, in the *Hongkong Fir* case,[4] where the charter was entered into in the same month as that in *Suisse Atlantique*, and where the charterers again found themselves operating on a falling freight market, the Court of Appeal signalled serious concern about the charterers' attempt to characterise the owners' breaches as repudiatory in order to present themselves with the option of withdrawing from the charter. Given that the charterers in *Suisse Atlantique* were contract-breakers, while the charterers in *Hongkong Fir Shipping* were the wholly innocent recipients of an un-seaworthy vessel, the attitude of the Law Lords in the former case is all the more striking.

The second way in which I will challenge the orthodox view is not by claiming that their Lordships' extended secondary remarks about fundamental breach are unimportant, but by suggesting that they speak less to freedom of contract than to the sustainability of the general law of contract. While the Law

---

[2] GH Treitel, 'Fundamental Breach' (1966) 29 *Modern Law Review* 546, 547.

[3] See, eg the largely supportive reviews in B Coote, 'The Effect of Discharge by Breach on Exception Clauses' (1970) 28 *Cambridge Law Journal* 221; and PN Legh-Jones and MA Pickering, 'Harbutt's "Plasticine" Ltd v Wayne Tank and Pump Co Ltd: Fundamental Breach and Exemption Clauses, Damages and Interest' (1970) 86 *Law Quarterly Review* 513.

[4] *Hongkong Fir Shipping Co Ltd v Kawasaki Kisen Kaisha Ltd*, [1962] 2 QB 26 (CA), discussed by Donal Nolan in ch 9 of this volume.

Lords proclaim that the doctrine of fundamental breach should be treated as an aspect of the interpretation of contracts rather than as a rigid rule that prohibits certain classes of exception or limitation clauses, readers are left in no doubt that, under the guise of various rules of construction, their Lordships retained the ability (and the willingness) to observe freedom of contract in the breach. Particularly where standard form exemption clauses were used against vulnerable consumer contractors, we can be confident that the Law Lords would prove to be every bit as protective as the Denning Court of Appeal of that period. But, if the secondary remarks are not about licensing stronger bargaining parties to exploit the position of weaker parties, what is their purpose? In my view, they should be seen as an attempt to resist the fragmentation of the common law of contract, particularly the impending bifurcation of the consumer and commercial law of contract. With the enactment of the Unfair Contract Terms Act in 1977, that resistance was to prove short-lived. However, the fragmentation of the general, largely commercial, law of contract is a live issue today as we see a potential conflict between the law of contract that is thought to work well for UK plc and that which serves the home market (especially that regulating transactions between powerful business contractors and small businesses). In this sense, if we accept that *Suisse Atlantique* was one of the great contract law precedents of the 20th century, it was very much a case of that century rather than of the century that lies ahead.

The paper is in three parts. First (in part II), I make a few short remarks about the background to the dispute in *Suisse Atlantique* and the way that the claimants' argument was first presented and then transformed for the appeal to the House of Lords. Secondly (in part III), I reconsider the significance of the first version of the claim and its peremptory rejection at all levels. Thirdly (in part IV), I focus on those parts of the Law Lords' speeches for which the case is famous, re-interpreting them as an attempt to maintain the integrity of a general law of contract.

## B. THE BACKGROUND TO THE CASE

At first blush, *Suisse Atlantique* looks like a distinctly unpromising candidate for a leading case, let alone the case of the century. Indeed, as Diplock LJ remarked at the start of his short judgment in the Court of Appeal, 'I am afraid I think this is a very simple case'[5]—a view apparently shared by the other members of that court, Sellers and Harman LJJ, who joined their colleague not only in rejecting the claim but also in refusing to give leave to appeal to the House of Lords. Had the case gone no further, it surely would have left little or no footprint in the archives of the common law. So, what was it about the appeal to the House that transformed the apparent significance of the case?

---

[5] *Suisse Atlantique* (n 1 above) [1965] 1 Lloyd's Rep 533 (CA) 540.

Stated shortly, the claimants, the Swiss owners of the motor vessel, *General Guisen*, argued that they had not received the performance that they reasonably expected from the defendant charterers, a Dutch company. The charter in question, a two-year consecutive voyage charterparty, had been entered into in December 1956. It was accepted by the defendants that, in breach of contract, they had taken considerably more time than the charter permitted for loading and discharging the vessel in port. However, the charter provided that, in these circumstances, the charterers should pay damages at an agreed rate of $1,000 per day to the owners; and these demurrage payments (in total some $150,000) had been made and duly accepted by the owners. Effectively, so far as Mocatta J and the Court of Appeal judges were concerned, that was that—there were a number of breaches of the express terms of the charter, the damages agreed under the contract had been paid, and the owners had been properly compensated.

There was, however, rather more than this to the owners' claim that they had not received the performance that they reasonably expected under the charter. It was the owners' contention that the charterers had deliberately taken their time with loading and discharging the vessel because it made economic sense for them to pay demurrage at the agreed rate rather than pay the freight rates set by the contract. It was not altogether clear why the charterers found themselves in this position, but a plausible view is that this reflected the way freight rates had moved at that time, first moving up when the charter was entered into (because of the closure of the Suez canal in the previous month) and then down (once the Suez canal reopened in April 1957). At all events, the claimants argued that this strategic conduct by the charterers meant that, instead of some 14–17 voyages that might reasonably have been expected, there were only eight trans-Atlantic voyages during the period of the charter. This, they argued, was in breach of an implied term for co-operation and was worth some $580,000 (if 14 voyages)–$875,000 (if 17 voyages) in damages.

Even if the courts had been prepared to embrace the idea of an implied duty of co-operation, which would not have been unprecedented,[6] the owners actually pitched their claim for implicit co-operation very steeply in their own favour. Quite how much co-operation a commercial contractor might reasonably expect where its economic interests are in conflict with the economic interests of a co-contractor is moot. However, if the owners' objection in *Suisse Atlantique* was that the charterers had not taken account of their (the owners') legitimate interests, the charterers surely could have met this complaint without having entirely to subordinate their own economic interests to those of the owners—which, seemingly, was what the owners were arguing for by way of

---

[6] See JF Burrows, 'Contractual Co-operation and the Implied Term' (1968) 31 *Modern Law Review* 390; and, in the modern case-law, see eg *Scally v Southern Health and Social Services Board* [1992] 1 AC 294 (HL); *Philips Electronique Grand Public SA v British Sky Broadcasting Ltd* [1995] EMLR 472 (CA); *Philips International BV v British Satellite Broadcasting Ltd* [1995] EMLR 472 (CA); and *Timeload v British Telecommunications plc* [1995] EMLR 459 (CA).

co-operation. At all events, the owners' argument received no support from either Mocatta J or the Court of Appeal. Quite simply, it was ruled, the only performance that the owners could reasonably expect was the performance that they had contracted for. There was no express term in the charter setting a minimum or other number of voyages and, even allowing for some flexibility in commercial dealings, the proposed implied term could not be brought on board so long as 'business efficacy' set the standard. If the claimants were going to improve on the demurrage rates they needed to find another argument. As it proved, that other argument was along the lines that the charterers' delays amounted to more than a mere breach; the delays, it was suggested, constituted a repudiatory or 'fundamental breach'.

At the time of *Suisse Atlantique*, the notion of a fundamental breach had acquired something of an aura—as Lord Hodson put it,

> the expression 'fundamental breach' is of comparatively recent origin and has seemed to have attained some mystical meaning in the law of contract.[7]

Nevertheless, we might wonder quite how the claimants (or, for that matter, the Law Lords) thought that this particular trick might work. In the initial presentation of their argument, the claimants argued that the self-serving and wilful delays by the charterers amounted to a breach of an implied term of the contract. They did not claim that this amounted to a repudiatory breach, but they asserted that there was a breach going beyond the simple failure to load and unload the cargo within the permitted times. As Lord Upjohn cast it, the owners' claim could not get to first base unless there was

> a larger obligation upon the charterers to load and discharge the cargo within the laydays so that the owners may benefit from the profitable employment of their ship contemplated by the charterparty for the period of the charter.[8]

Yet, it was precisely the proposition that there was such a larger obligation that was emphatically rejected by the lower courts. How, then, we might wonder, could it possibly assist the owners' case if the alleged (non-repudiatory) breach of this non-existent larger obligation was characterised instead as a repudiatory or fundamental breach? If there never was a co-operative obligation of the kind presupposed by the owners' claim, it surely made no difference whether the alleged breach was repudiatory or not: the claim still did not get to first base.

In the event, the House of Lords not only permitted counsel for the owners to switch the basis of their appeal from one seemingly hopeless case to another, they allowed them to get to first base by assuming, for the sake of argument, that the charterers' delays might amount to a fundamental breach. However, they did this without spelling out precisely how we should understand the elusive larger obligation to which the breach related. And, in more than one way, this

[7] *Suisse Atlantique* (n 1 above) [1967] 1 AC 361 (HL) 409–10.
[8] *Suisse Atlantique* (n 1 above) [1967] 1 AC 361 (HL) 417.

failure incurred costs. For, when the Law Lords returned to the question of whether, as a matter of construction, the demurrage clause covered the hypothetical fundamental breach, they tended to revert to the actual matrix in which, as all courts held, there was no larger obligation. So, for instance, when towards the end of his speech, Lord Reid turns to the applicability of the demurrage clause, he starts by saying that he does not view the delays as defeating the main object of the contract, which is to say, he does not think that the delays actually amounted to the hypothesised fundamental breach. But, then, restoring the hypothesis, he adds that if the delays did amount to a fundamental breach, the owners were restricted by the demurrage clause because 'they elected that the contract should continue and they did so in the knowledge that this clause would continue'.[9] Granted, by affirming a fundamental breach, the owners remained bound by the demurrage clause, but the owners' point was that the clause by which they remained bound applied only to delays that arose in the usual course of things and not to delays artificially created by the charterers for their own economic advantage. One senses that Lord Reid is struggling to maintain the hypothesis of a fundamental breach and, without the constant reminder of the larger obligation supposedly breached by the charterers, the process of construing the contract gets dragged back to what the Law Lords see as the actual matrix.[10]

If we are seriously interested in the co-operative claim, the Law Lords' speeches seem less than adequate. Initially, they each give the straightforward version of the claim short shrift, but then, when the claim gets hypothetical support, it is not properly substantiated and the matrix for the construction of the contract is, to say the least, hazy. With this short reminder of the background, we can now take a harder look at the question that the claimants sought to put on the agenda.

## C. THE ISSUE OF NO INTEREST

The original version of the owners' claim was thought, at the time, to be of little interest: it was swiftly dispatched by the courts, and I am probably in a minority of one in recalling this aspect of the case as having some significance. Certainly, I can find no encouragement for such an idiosyncratic view in the Law Lords' speeches. Quite characteristically, Viscount Dilhorne saw the matter as entirely straightforward, saying[11]:

---

[9] *Suisse Atlantique* (n 1 above) [1967] 1 AC 361 (HL) 407.
[10] We see this, too, in Lord Hodson's speech. At [1967] 1 AC 361, 414, his Lordship said: 'On the construction of this contract I am of opinion that the parties have agreed to limit the damages payable for detention at the agreed demurrage rate and that there is no reason for not so limiting them whether or not there was an intention on the part of the respondents wilfully to limit the number of voyages'. In other words, Lord Hodson is saying that it makes no difference whether the charterers acted in a self-serving way, which is to say that they were under no co-operative obligation.
[11] *Suisse Atlantique* (n 1 above) [1967] 1 AC 361 (HL) 389.

In my opinion, no such contractual right [to a certain number of voyages or to co-operative efforts to make the maximum number of voyages] is to be implied either on the construction of the charterparty or by operation of law. The charterparty might have provided that not less than a certain number of voyages should be accomplished. It did not do so.

As represented before their Lordships, although the breach was now upgraded as possibly repudiatory and fundamental, the claim was still essentially that the self-serving conduct of the charterers breached the implicit co-operative norms of the contractual relationship. As Lord Reid remarked,[12]

> [The owners'] allegation would appear to cover a case where the charterers decided that it would pay them better to delay loading and discharge and paying the resulting demurrage at the relatively low agreed rate, rather than load and discharge more speedily and then have to buy more coal and pay the relatively high agreed freight on the additional voyages which would then be possible.

So, even though the claim was now dressed up in different doctrinal language, in substance it was the same. The Law Lords were perfectly aware of the essential nature of the complaint, and like the courts below, they did not see any merit in it. For the Law Lords in the mid-1960s it was perfectly natural to assume an ethic of self-reliance as the default position for contract law.

Surely, though, there is nothing new in this? Is it not a relatively consistent thread of English contract law—or, at any rate, the commercial law of contract—that contractors are permitted (although, of course, not required) to conduct themselves in an entirely self-interested fashion? Indeed, it is and this is so much the culture of the century that the judges at all levels in *Suisse Atlantique* do not even pause to give the matter a second thought. Nevertheless, it is important to see just how powerful this culture is.

## 1. The Culture of Self-reliance

Before the parties have entered into a contractual relationship, the classical view is that they are *permitted* to deal with their cards close to their chests. Again, it should be emphasised that nothing in the classical law *requires* parties to deal in this manner. Hence, the substantial empirical evidence that highlights a co-operative approach to contracting in many business communities does not of itself point to a defect in the classical law. To the extent that the classical law is prescriptive, it is merely in the default ethic that it assumes. Nevertheless, that default position is potentially very significant. So, for example, in *Smith v Hughes*, Lord Cockburn CJ famously says[13]:

---

[12] *Suisse Atlantique* (n 1 above) [1967] 1 AC 361 (HL) 397.
[13] *Smith v Hughes* (1871) LR 6 QB 597, 603–4.

The question is not what a man of scrupulous morality or nice honour would do under such circumstances. The case put of the purchase of an estate, in which there is a mine under the surface, but the fact is unknown to the seller, is one in which a man of tender conscience or high honour would be unwilling to take advantage of the ignorance of the seller; but there can be no doubt that the contract for the sale of the estate would be binding.

And, then, in *Walford v Miles*,[14] it is Lord Ackner's turn to emphasise that, in the negotiating stage (covered by an adversarial ethic), neither side owes anything to the other. A duty to negotiate in good faith, Lord Ackner asserts, would be 'inherently repugnant to the adversarial position of the parties'.[15] Notice, though, Lord Ackner is not saying that adversarial dealing is inherent in the very idea of contract; it is simply that this is the legal default position for the regulation of negotiations.

Once parties are in a legal relationship with one another, we might expect the default position to change somewhat; the parties, after all, are no longer 'strangers'. However, if one side is in breach, it is perhaps understandable that the extra-contractual default should be restored. At all events, the classical view is that where one party is in breach of contract, then the innocent party may legitimately take up any of the legally available options irrespective of whether this is for self-serving economic advantage—in other words, self-reliance is once again the default ethic. One of the clearest examples of this approach is *Arcos Ltd v EA Ronaasen and Son*,[16] where the Law Lords unanimously ruled that sellers who failed to deliver goods corresponding precisely to the contractual description had no cause for complaint if, on a falling market, buyers then rejected the goods purely for their own economic advantage. According to Lord Atkin,[17]

[i]f a condition is not performed the buyer has a right to reject. I do not myself think that there is any difference between business men and lawyers on this matter. No doubt, in business, men often find it unnecessary or inexpedient to insist on their strict legal rights. In a normal market if they get something substantially like the specified goods they may take them with or without grumbling and a claim for an allowance. But in a falling market I find the buyers are often as eager to insist on their legal rights as courts of law are to maintain them. No doubt at all times sellers are prepared to take a liberal view as to the rigidity of their own obligations, and possibly buyers who in turn are sellers may dislike too much precision. But buyers are not, so far as my experience goes, inclined to think that the rights defined in the code [ie the Sale of Goods Act] are in excess of business needs.

[14] *Walford v Miles* [1992] 2 AC 128 (HL).
[15] *Ibid* 138. Similarly, see eg Slade LJ in *Banque Financière de la Cité SA v Westgate Insurance Co Ltd* [1989] 2 All ER 952 (CA) 1013; and May LJ in *Bank of Nova Scotia v Hellenic Mutual War Risks Association (Bermuda) Ltd, The Good Luck* [1989] 3 All ER 628 (CA) 667.
[16] *Arcos Ltd v EA Ronaasen and Son* [1933] AC 470 (HL).
[17] *Ibid* 480.

Hence, the uncompromising view is seen (accurately or otherwise) as being congruent with business practice and expectation.

This brings us to *Suisse Atlantique* itself. Now, on the facts, this is different from the negotiation cases because the parties are in a contractual relationship; and it is different from cases like *Arcos* because the complaint is made not by the party in breach, but by the innocent party. If we think that a plea for co-operation is much less attractive when made by a party in breach (albeit a costless and trivial breach), then cases such as *Arcos* will seem to make some sense. However, where the plea comes from exactly the opposite direction, it is not so obvious that the classical default makes sense. On the face of it, what is so striking about the Law Lords' position in *Suisse Atlantique* is that, without hesitation, they default to upholding the right of a contract-breaker to act in a self-serving manner in just the way that they would resort to the same default in contractual negotiations or where it is the innocent party who exercises its remedial options. Neglecting co-operativism, the Law Lords saw no problem in the defendant charterers' playing the contract to their own economic advantage, seemingly treating the payment of agreed damages as an option on the same par as performance. So it is that their Lordships presuppose a particularly aggressive and one-sided version of efficient breach theory.[18]

Let me try to spell this out even more clearly. The Law Lords say that the owners could have contracted for co-operation by expressly stipulating that so many voyages should be made. Not having so contracted, the owners had no reasonable cause for complaint when the number of voyages fell below their reasonable expectation. Suppose, then, that the charterers pursued their own economic advantage to the point where they made no attempt to load the vessel and, instead, they simply paid demurrage. Suppose that during the charter period, only two or three voyages were made. If we treat the charterers as having a clean choice between either (a) loading up and paying freight or (b) not loading and paying demurrage, this might be taken to imply that failure to load is not actually a breach at all. In which case, the Law Lords might have rebuked the owners by saying that they could have contracted for loading by expressly stipulating that the charterers should so load and that if they failed to do so, they would be in breach. However, in *Suisse Atlantique* no one was arguing that the contractors treated delays beyond the lay days as anything other than a breach and demurrage as anything other than damages. Rather, what we have is a panel of Law Lords who proceed as though it makes not the slightest difference whether the charterers have a contractual option to buy their way out of a loading obligation or whether failure to load in time is a breach that sounds in liquidated damages. Either way, the default position is that the charterers may elect to pay the money and the owners, with their complaints about non-co-operation, are left to whistle in the wind.

---

[18] Cf the general line of critique in D Friedmann, 'The Efficient Breach Fallacy' (1989) 18 *Journal of Legal Studies* 1.

If we turn the situation around, what happens then? Let us suppose that the charter was entered into a year or so before the closure of the Suez Canal and that, once the Canal was closed, freight rates rise sharply. In such circumstances, the owners of the vessel decide that in pursuit of their own economic advantage, they will simply sail away to do business with the highest bidder. Of course, such a move will only make economic sense for the owners if they will be better off after paying whatever damages have to be paid to the charterers; and so we might take comfort in the thought that a profitable breach of this kind will be the exception rather than the rule. Even so, why should we need to take comfort? What is wrong with the *Suisse Atlantique* logic that seems to have it that parties enter into contractual obligations on the basis that they will perform rather than pay damages only so long as they find it economically advantageous to do so? True, recalling Lord Wilberforce's oft-quoted phrase, this does not quite reduce the contract to a mere declaration of intent. Even so, it is pretty close to the line, and the non-co-operative version of contract, when made explicit, radically transforms what contractors seem to be bargaining for.

In *Suisse Atlantique*, considerable attention is paid, particularly in Lord Wilberforce's speech, to the significance of a breach being deliberate.[19] In the context of the claimants' argument, the relevance of the point is to underline the fact that the charterers made a calculated choice between breach and performance. However, the Law Lords do not see a question about co-operation here. Rather, the question is one of how the deliberate nature of the breach plays in relation to the distinction between a fundamental term and fundamental breach. To which, the answer is that where the breach is of a fundamental term it matters not whether the breach is deliberate; for any breach, deliberate or otherwise, of a fundamental term gives rise to a right to withdraw. On the other hand, if the term that is breached is not a fundamental term, the question of whether there is a right to withdraw will turn on a number of considerations, including the attitude of the contract breaker; and so, where such a breach is deliberate this might assist the argument for the right to withdraw. Although this might have clarified the law at the time, it is of little interest nowadays.

What is of more interest nowadays is whether there are ever any circumstances in which the deliberate and calculating nature of the breach is viewed as significant. Arguably, *Attorney-General v Blake*[20] is just such a case. The relevant wrongdoing in this case was by George Blake, the notorious spy, whose autobiography, *No Other Choice*, contained information that was covered by the Official Secrets Act 1989 and disclosure of which was in breach of the terms of his one-time contract of employment with the Crown. The Attorney-General sought to prevent royalties, being held to Blake's account by his British publishers, from being paid to him. If ever there was a case designed to raise the heckles, this was it. Blake, having been convicted of espionage, had escaped from

---

[19] *Suisse Atlantique* (n 1 above) [1967] 1 AC 361 (HL) 434–5.
[20] *Attorney-General v Blake* [2001] 1 AC 268 (HL).

prison where he was serving a 42-year custodial sentence; and, years later, from the safe distance of his flat in Moscow, he claimed to be entitled to realise the profit from a publication the content of which was a testimony to his various wrongs. Outraged by this prospect, the majority of the House of Lords allowed that this was an exceptional case where, even if the Crown had suffered no loss to its expectation interest, justice required that an order be made to disgorge Blake's profits.

This, of course, is exceptional. In the case-law both before and after *Blake*,[21] the courts have confirmed that it is one thing for a contractor to profit from a contractual wrong, quite another for a spymaster to do so. In the ordinary course of commercial dealing, it seems that there always will be another choice—the choice of performing or not performing as it suits one's economic interests.

## 2. The Counter-Culture of Co-operation

The charter in the *Hongkong Fir Shipping* case[22] was made in the same month as that in *Suisse Atlantique*. It, too, felt the impact of the closure and re-opening of the Suez Canal; and it has long been the academic view that the Court of Appeal introduced the innominate term as a strategy for countering opportunistic withdrawals. The waters are muddied in the case because, on the facts, the owners' breach was far from trivial. Nevertheless, it is a plausible view that *Hongkong Fir Shipping* represents the beginning of a modern counter-culture of co-operation in commercial contracting.

It is in this light that we might read the majority Law Lords' speeches in *Schuler v Wickman*[23] and co-operation is unmistakably the default ethic in *The Hansa Nord*, where Roskill LJ said[24]:

> In my view, a court should not be over ready, unless required by statute or authority so to do, to construe a term in a contract as a 'condition' . . . In principle, contracts are made to be performed and not to be avoided according to the whims of market fluctuation and where there is a free choice between two possible constructions I think the court should tend to prefer that construction which will ensure performance and not encourage avoidance of contractual obligations.

---

[21] Before *Blake*, see eg *Surrey County Council v Bredero* [1993] 1 WLR 1361 (CA); after *Blake*, see, eg *AB Corporation v CD Company, The 'Sine Nomine'* [2002] 1 Lloyd's Rep 805, where the arbitrators (rejecting a *Blake*-inspired argument) emphasised the reality that it is by no means uncommon for commercial contracts to be broken because a more profitable opportunity has arisen, that international commerce is 'red in tooth and claw', that compensatory damages will usually suffice, and that commercial law should not seek to impose moral judgments, or to punish contract-breakers (eg by awarding punitive damages).

[22] *Hongkong Fir Shipping* (n 4 above).

[23] *Wickman Machine Tool Sales Ltd v L Schuler AG* [1974] AC 235 (HL).

[24] *Cehave NV v Bremer Handelsgesellschaft mbH, The Hansa Nord* [1976] QB 44 (CA) 70—71.

Similar sentiments underlie Lord Hope's comments in *Total Gas Marketing Ltd v Arco British Ltd*[25]:

> The bargain was struck against the background of a market for gas which had proved in the past to be extremely volatile. Substantial changes in the open market price of this commodity would be bound to affect the value of the investment by either party in the transaction. One of the purposes of an agreement of this kind is to eliminate the risk of having to carry the burden of such price changes. It is no secret that the reason why the buyer wishes to terminate the agreement is that the market has now turned in its favour. It can obtain gas elsewhere more cheaply than it would have been required to take gas from the Trent reservoir under the agreement. No doubt it will seek to renegotiate a fresh bargain with the seller for the supply of the Trent gas at a more favourable price. The buyer is not to be criticized if the wording of the agreement permits this course. But the Court should be slow to lend its assistance. Commercial contracts should so far as possible be upheld. This is especially so where the party who seeks to preserve the contract has incurred expenditure after it was entered into with a view to performing it in the future over a period of many years . . . It is disappointing to find that in this case it has not been possible to construe the agreement in such a way as to provide the seller with the protection which it was designed to achieve.

Again, in *Page v Combined Shipping and Trading Co Ltd*,[26] the first reported case under the Commercial Agents Directive,[27] we have a tension between (a) the supposed common law principle that where a contract-breaker has some control over (or choice about) how the contract would have been performed, the assumption is that the party in breach would have performed

> in the way most favourable to himself, that is in the way which most reduces the sum which he will have to pay as damages,[28]

and (b) that the claimant is entitled to be compensated on the basis of 'proper performance' by the contract-breaker.[29] Given that this was an appeal on a preliminary point of law, the Court of Appeal did not need to decide any more than that the plaintiff had an arguable case for damages assessed by reference to a good faith proper performance.

No doubt, many further illustrative examples—all examples, it should be said, from the commercial law of contract—could be offered. However, this proves little other than that there is a degree of support for a co-operative default. The question that invites some reflection is whether there is any reason why the law of contract *should* adopt co-operation as its default position. If a rational choice between self-reliance and co-operation is to be made, which default should be adopted?

[25] *Total Gas Marketing Ltd v Arco British Ltd.* [1998] 2 Lloyd's Rep 209 (HL) 223.

[26] *Page v Combined Shipping and Trading Co Ltd* [1997] 3 All ER 656 (CA).

[27] Directive 86/653/EEC. The Directive provides, inter alia, that the principal must act in good faith.

[28] *Page v Combined Shipping* (n 26 above) 659 (Staughton LJ).

[29] The claimant relied on Reg 17(7) of the Commercial Agent (Council Directive) Regulations 1993 (SI 1993/3053).

There is a well-known theoretical argument in support of co-operation, the gist of which is that co-operation, particularly in repeat dealings, generates gains for the parties that they would not otherwise achieve. Co-operation is the basis for win-win outcomes. However, where the market moves up and down, there is always the temptation to defect from the agreed deal.[30] If one party defects, this disrupts the win-win basis of the relationship and replaces it with a short-term win (for the defecting party)-lose (for the non-defecting party) outcome. The relationship is unlikely to be restored without some reversal and, quite possibly, it will be beyond retrieval—which means that, instead of win-win, we now have lose-lose. This is a poor result whether one views it through the eyes of game theory or moral theory,[31] whether the puzzle is located in contract law or in regulation more generally,[32] and it seems to be an opportunity missed whether we are thinking about the relationship between the particular parties or the reputation and value of the institution of contract law itself.[33]

If we accept the validity of these arguments, then such considerations point to the law of contract assuming an institutional responsibility for channelling transactors towards co-operation as their default position. This is not to say, of course, that the law of contract should not sanction breach of contract. On the contrary, contract law should be tough on defection from contracts, but it should judge defection relative to mutual co-operative benefit. Hence, unless the parties have exercised their freedom of contract to modify the co-operative default ethic, the contractors should know that defection from the co-operative approach for the sake of short-term advantage-taking simply is not tolerated.

## 3. Taking Stock

In a well-known article, Lord Goff rightly observed that the law of contract and its practitioners are responsible for oiling the wheels of commerce.[34] The law of contract is not simply there for our intellectual amusement; the idea is that it should give some added value to the economy and to society, as otherwise we might as well abolish it. We know that in some places, the law is perceived to be, at best, an irrelevance and, at worst, more of a hindrance than a help[35]; and

[30] Cf SJ Burton, 'Breach of Contract and the Common Law Duty to Perform in Good Faith' (1980–81) 94 *Harvard Law Review* 369.

[31] See D Gauthier, *Morals by Agreement* (Oxford, Oxford University Press, 1986).

[32] See, eg I Ayres and J Braithwaite, *Responsive Regulation* (Oxford, Oxford University Press, 1992) ch 3.

[33] R Brownsword, '"Good Faith in Contracts" Revisited' (1996) 49 *Current Legal Problems* 111; and R Brownsword, 'Contract Law, Co-operation, and Good Faith: The Movement from Static to Dynamic Market-Individualism' in S Deakin and J Michie (eds), *Contracts, Co-operation and Competition* (Oxford, Oxford University Press, 1997) 255.

[34] The Rt Hon Sir R Goff, 'Commercial Contracts and the Commercial Court' (1984) *Lloyd's Maritime & Commercial Law Quarterly* 382.

[35] Seminally, see S Macaulay, 'Non-Contractual Relations in Business' (1963) 28 *American Sociological Review* 55, and then a stream of writing, by Macaulay and others, that followed his lead.

so we need to try to design it in the right way. Whether the right design involves a default for self-reliance or one for co-operation is quite a complex matter.[36] In this light, what makes *Suisse Atlantique* such a surprising case is not that self-reliance was so emphatically presupposed but that no one thought that the owners' claim for co-operation merited a second thought.

## D. THE INTEGRITY OF THE COMMON LAW OF CONTRACT

At the time of *Suisse Atlantique*, it was the Law Lords' pronouncements on the doctrine of fundamental breach that seemed to be seminal. Even though counsel agreed that the doctrine was no more than a principle of construction rather than a rule of (substantive) law, it was thought to be important that this should be expressly confirmed.

In this part of the paper, I will start by rehearsing the two reasons, famously given by Lord Reid, against the view that fundamental breach might be a rule of law. My suggestion is that we should view their Lordships as making a last ditch attempt to maintain the integrity of what was still essentially the common law of contract. Prompted by this thought, I will then comment on three aspects of what I see as the disintegration of the common law of contract: first, the development of a discrete body of law to regulate consumer contracts; secondly, the imposed (tort-like) character of the obligations set by this body of consumer law; and, thirdly, the pressure to attend more precisely to the distinction between contract law for the home market and contract law for international contractors.

Although, in this part of the paper, the emphasis is on fragmentation rather than co-operation, the nature of the fragmentation again highlights the question of co-operation. For, the consumer law regime that has splintered from the general law of contract embeds the principle that suppliers will respond to the reasonable expectations of their consumer customers (in other words, consumer law is designed to channel suppliers towards a co-operative ethic); and the fundamental distinction between a competitive model of contract law that is available for international traders and a model that is more attuned to the home marketplace is precisely that the latter adopts a co-operative ethic as its default position.

### 1. Lord Reid's Two Reasons

The first reason that Lord Reid gave for rejecting the proposition that the doctrine of fundamental breach was a substantive rule of law was that there was a

---

[36] See S Deakin and J Michie (eds), *Contracts, Co-operation and Competition* (Oxford, Oxford University Press, 1997).

lack of clarity about how far such a rule might reach. If the rule provided that in the event of a fundamental breach, the contract breaker would not be permitted to rely on various kinds of exemption and limitation clauses, which kinds of clauses would be covered? If the delays in *Suisse Atlantique* amounted to a fundamental breach by the charterers, would they be denied reliance on the demurrage clause? Would fundamental breach bring an end to agreed damages clauses that were intended by the parties to set the extent of their liability for breach? If so, Lord Reid opined, that would be to go beyond the intentions of the authors of the fundamental breach doctrine.

In retrospect, the first of Lord Reid's reasons looks pretty weak. For, this is not so much an objection to fundamental breach as a rule of law but an objection to the fundamental breach doctrine being implemented as an *uncertain* rule of law. Certainty and calculability matter to commercial contractors and so, if the fundamental breach doctrine were to take effect as a rule, there would need to be clarification about its range. Indeed, there would need to be guidance of the kind that the Law Lords might well have given had they been minded to instate a rule of fundamental breach. The fact that they were not minded to do so draws on Lord Reid's second reason.

In one the best-known sections of Lord Reid's speech, his Lordship outlines the second reason for eschewing the rule of law view[37]:

> Exemption clauses differ greatly in many respects. Probably the most objectionable are found in the complex standard conditions which are now so common. In the ordinary way the customer has no time to read them, and if he did read them he would probably not understand them. And if he did understand and object to any of them, he would generally be told he could take it or leave it. And if he then went to another supplier the result would be the same. Freedom to contract must surely imply some choice or room for bargaining.
>
> At the other extreme is the case where parties are bargaining on terms of equality and a stringent exemption clause is accepted for a quid pro quo or other good reason. But this [fundamental breach] rule appears to treat all cases alike. There is no indication in the recent cases that the courts are to consider whether the exemption is fair in all the circumstances or is harsh and unconscionable or whether it was freely agreed by the customer. And it does not seem to me to be satisfactory that the decision must always go one way if, e.g. defects in a car or other goods are just sufficient to make the breach of contract a fundamental breach, but must always go the other way if the defects fall just short of that. This is a complex problem which intimately affects millions of people and it appears to me that its solution should be left to Parliament.

As a rule of construction, fundamental breach invites application in a way that is sensitive to differences of bargaining strength, and so on. Whereas exceptions in commercial contracts might be freely accepted for a price adjustment, or the like, the same exceptions in consumer contracts are likely to be unilaterally imposed. Granted, such a strategy involves a degree of uncertainty but,

---

[37] *Suisse Atlantique* (n 1 above) [1967] 1 AC 361 (HL) 406.

unlike the uncertainty associated with the proposal for a substantive rule of law, such uncertainty would be of a positive and productive kind. Moreover, this approach has the virtue of strengthening the link between legal doctrine and the contractors' intentions.

What do we make of this second reason? Without question, Lord Reid's view of the landscape of transactions is a fair reflection of what we nowadays take for granted. However, the willingness to distinguish between commercial and consumer transactions is the first step towards the reconfiguration of the general law of contract—albeit a reconfiguration that Lord Reid was trying very hard to confine within the traditional mould of English contract law.

## 2. A Separate Body of Consumer Law of Contract

Essentially, a distinction between commercial and consumer transactions might register in doctrine in one of two ways: either by way of explicit and open bifurcation or by stealth, implicitly and covertly. By arguing for a rule of construction, I suggest that Lord Reid is best interpreted as hoping to avoid the former and, thus, maintain the façade of a set of common law principles stretching across the entire range of transactions from small consumer purchases to multi-million pound commercial transactions. The common law rules on incorporation were the same; the common law rules for the interpretation of contracts were the same, there was just one common law for the common law world of contract. Although it might be an open secret that the rules would be applied differentially to consumers and to business contractors, it was not yet freely admitted by the English judiciary that the adjudication of contract disputes might be result-orientated. After all, it was still another five years before Lord Reid would publish his famous paper on judicial law-making.[38] And, it certainly was not freely admitted that a consumer law of contract was in danger of breaking free from the main body of contract law to assume a life of relative autonomy.

Before long, the myth of a 'one-size fits all' law of contract was to be exploded. Rapidly, as responsibility for the regulation of unfair terms was handed over to the legislative branch (indeed, as Lord Reid proposed),[39] it became clear that the regulation of consumer contracts was evolving as a specialised and discrete branch of the law. Before long, we had the explicit bifurcation between consumer and business contracts that runs right through the Unfair Contract Terms Act 1977, the implementation in English law of a raft of European Directives that deal specifically with the rights of consumers (notably, concerning unfair terms

---

[38] Lord Reid, 'The Judge as Law Maker' (1972) XII *Journal of the Society of Public Teachers of Law* 22.

[39] Granted, this seemingly speaks against my reading of Lord Reid's intentions. However, I take Lord Reid's concern to be with the integrity of the common law of contract, not the common law as modified by legislative intervention.

and sale of goods), the de-coupling of commercial from consumer sales in section 4 of the Sale and Supply of Goods Act 1994, and so on. Even in the common law of contract we find special rules being developed, quite explicitly, to compensate consumer (but not business) contractors for their disappointment and their displeasure.[40] The tide was, and is, unstoppable.

However, this is by no means the whole story. The Law Lords in *Suisse Atlantique* not only failed to prevent the fragmentation of the law of contract, they failed to prevent the consumer law of contract from becoming a branch of the law that is not truly a division of the law of contract at all.


## 3. Obligations Based on Consent and Imposed Obligation

In both the common law and the civilian world, it is axiomatic that contract is founded on consent, that contractual obligations are voluntarily assumed, and that the consensual basis of contract is defeated where obligations are taken on in a context coloured by fraud or coercion.[41] Indeed, we might already think that we see in the body of EU consumer contract law precisely such a harmonised regional code founded on the idea that consumer transactions should be the product of the purchaser's free and informed consent.[42]

On the face of it, the idea of contract as a consent-based transaction is an innocent one. However, the fact is that our understanding of contractual obligation as consent-based fluctuates between two rather different things. Sometimes our focus is on the contractors' consensual choice of a particular body of rules to govern their dealings; at other times (as in the European consumer code), our focus is on the parties' consent to the terms of a particular transaction and not, as such, to the rule framework that regulates the making and performance of that transaction. In other words, we look sometimes for consensual engagement of a particular body of rules, but, at other times, we are looking for a consensus ad idem in relation to a particular exchange. Whereas the former relies on consent to justify applying the body of rules so engaged, the latter relies on consent to bind a party to a particular transaction. Whereas the former is prior to, and external to, the law of contract as such, the latter is an exercise within the law of contract. My point is not simply that our understanding of the relevance of consent so fluctuates; it is that the location of consent matters greatly to what we regard as distinctively matters of *contractual* obligation. Contrary to the conventional wisdom, I suggest that it is the antecedent, or external, consent that holds the key to distinctively *contractual* obligation.

[40] See *Jarvis v Swans Tours Ltd* [1973] QB 233 (CA); *Watts v Morrow* [1991] 4 All ER 937 (CA); *Hayes v James & Charles Dodd (a firm)* [1990] 2 All ER 815 (CA); and *Farley v Skinner (No 2)* [2001] UKHL 49, [2002] AC 732.
[41] See, eg H Kötz and A Flessner, *European Contract Law: Volume One* (Oxford, Clarendon Press, 1998).
[42] For a striking case in point, compare the form and substance of Directive 2005/29/EC (the Unfair Commercial Practices Directive) [2005] OJ L/149, 11 June 2005.

If we follow this line of thinking, we will arrive not only at a re-focused understanding of the correct (consent-based) configuration of the doctrinal set associated with the law of contract but also at a radically different characterisation of the products of the emerging consumer law of contract. So far as the former is concerned, the key point is that in an ideal-typical (consent-based) legal regime, much of the doctrine that is currently viewed as internal to the law of contract would need to be transferred to a consent-clearing body of law that is external to, and antecedent to, the law of contract—indeed, to a body of doctrine that acts, as it were, as a condition precedent to be satisfied before the law of contract is treated as having been engaged. A number of doctrines would be transferred in this way but the keystone would be the doctrine of intention to create legal (or contractual) relations. As for a different characterisation of the consumer law of contract, we would see that a great deal of transactional activity, especially that in the consumer marketplace, is regulated by a body of imposed law (that is, by a background law of transactions). To be sure, on paper, there is an opt-out—consumers might declare that they do not intend to create contractual relations. However, de facto, the obligations so imposed cannot be accounted for by a consent-based theory; and, insofar as contractual obligations are taken to be consent-based, these obligations (ostensibly obligations of contract law) should not be characterised as contractual at all. Instead, these are obligations that look much more like the imposed obligations of tort or restitution. It follows that a great deal of the harmonised products of EC law are 'contractual' only in name. On the other hand, those products, such as the *Principles of European Contract Law*,[43] that (at any rate, in principle) are available for parties to engage by opt-in truly are contractual in character. It follows that, in one sense, European contract law is less harmonised than we might suppose (because what is being harmonised via the consumer protection Directives is not contract law at all), but, in another sense, the project of harmonising contract law in Europe is already complete.

Elsewhere, I have responded to the objection that it surely is not practical to restrict the application of the law of contract to those who have actively and self-consciously opted in, who have engaged the law in a way that satisfies the antecedent rule of an intention to enter into a particular regime of contractual relations.[44] I will not rehearse that response here other than to correct one possible misunderstanding.

---

[43] O Lando and H Beale (eds), *Principles of European Contract Law, Parts I and II* (Dordrecht, Kluwer Law International, 2000); and O Lando, E Clive, A Prüm and R Zimmermann (eds), *Principles of European Contract Law, Part III* (Dordrech, Kluwer Law International, 2003).

[44] R Brownsword, 'Contract, Consent, and Complexity: Re-inventing Intention to Create Legal (Contractual) Relations' in P Odell and C Willett (eds), *Civil Society* (Oxford, Hart Publishing Ltd, 2008 (forthcoming)). For some reflections on the autonomy-enhancing effects of such a re-think, see R Brownsword, 'Zum Konzept des Networks im englischen Vertragsrecht' (2006) 23 *KritV* 129 (also 'Network Contracts Re-visited' in G Teubner and M Amstutz (eds), *Networks: Legal Issues of Multilateral Contracts* (2008 (forthcoming)); and, in relation to electronic contracting, compare DR Johnson and D Post, 'Law and Borders—The Rise of Law in Cyberspace' (1996) 48 *Stanford Law Review* 1367.

Let us suppose that active (authentic) contracting appeals to some agents but not to others. Some consumers would welcome the opportunity to self-regulate; others would not. Does it follow that the latter are then excluded from the market, from supplying or procuring goods and services? Not at all: what the latter are excluded from (by their own self-conscious decision or lack of interest or inclination) is governance by a law of contract that they have consensually engaged. In the absence of self-governance—ie in the absence of authentic contractual governance by consent—such passive agents will be regulated by the background law of transactions. The justification for enforcing such background regulation will not be procedural; it will not be based on consent. Rather, as with all imposed obligations, the justification will be substantive, resting on the merits.

Finally, it should be said that my assumption is that the state has no preference for authentic contracting or for imposed background regulation of the marketplace. On this basis, it matters not whether regulation of the marketplace is modelled on contract and consent or on a background law of transactions that imposes a fair and workable regime of tort-like or restitutionary rules. It follows that we might be indifferent whether the rules enforced against contractors are justified by reference to their consent or by reference to their fair and reasonable content. What we should not tolerate is the myth that what passes in modern legal regimes for contractual obligation is based on the parties' consent. Quite simply, if we want to explode this myth, we either have to abandon the idea that we are dealing with authentic contractual obligation where consent is a fiction or we must get serious about consent—which means getting serious about the antecedent consensual engagement of the law of contract.[45]

## 4. Contract at Home and Contract Abroad

We are not quite done. Although it is accepted that much of the protection of consumer contractors will be orchestrated by European law-makers, there is considerable resistance in some English quarters to proposals for a more general European law of contract.[46] The reason for such resistance is not so much the fear that a regional code of contract would swallow up what is left of our local law but that it would present itself as a competitor to English law as the law of choice for international commercial transactions. Ironically, anxieties are heightened rather than assuaged by assurances that the European code, although reflecting much of civilian thinking, would not be so very different to English law. Irrespective of whether such fears and anxieties are justified, they

[45] See, further, R Brownsword, *Contract Law: Themes for the Twenty-First Century*, 2nd edn (Oxford, Oxford University Press, 2006) ch 12.
[46] See House of Lords European Committee, *European Contract Law—the Way Forward?* HL Paper 95 (London, TSO, 5 April 2005).

highlight the impossibility of the dual mission set for the English law of contract. On the one hand, this body of law is trying to structure and serve commercial markets at home; on the other hand, it is also offering itself as a set of rules to be engaged by the community of international commercial contractors. In other words, even if we strip consumer contracting out of the law of contract, we find that the law is seeking to serve (many different) markets both at home and abroad. Crucially, where it is supposed that the worldwide popularity of English contract law as the law of choice owes something to its classical market-individualist features, this understandably inhibits the adoption of (co-operative) doctrines, such as good faith or unconscionability, that have a degree of flexibility as well as inviting a welfarist interpretation. Where static market-individualist values are applied in the context of international commercial litigation (involving shipping, carriage, or commodities or the like), on many occasions, this might be entirely appropriate—after all, this might be just the basis on which, in cases like the *Suisse Atlantique*, the Swiss owners and the Dutch charterers contracted. However, where such values are applied to domestic commercial disputes, this might be altogether less appropriate, leaving one with the sense that domestic litigants are being short-changed in order to subsidise our export trade. At all events, one must wonder for how long the general law of commercial contracts can sustain itself when there is such a fundamental fault-line running through it.

We can gather together some of these reflections by reviewing the much-debated modern case of *Baird Textile Holdings Ltd v Marks and Spencer plc*.[47] In *Baird* there was no dispute about the conspicuously co-operative relationship between the parties. Baird had been a principal supplier to Marks and Spencer for 30 years and, in practice, there was a considerable degree of horizontal integration between the businesses. Even Marks and Spencer's director for procurement attested that the relationship with suppliers, such as Baird, was symbiotic—if not a partnership in the strict legal sense, business was most definitely conducted in a spirit of co-operation.[48] Given this background, Baird was understandably aggrieved when, without warning, Marks and Spencer notified it that, as from the end of the then current production season, all supply arrangements were to be determined. In response, Baird argued that it was entitled to a reasonable period of notice (some three years) during which time it could make the necessary adjustments to its business. Such an entitlement, Baird argued, arose either under an implicit contract or by way of an estoppel. If there had been an express framework contract governing the relationship between the parties and including a termination clause, Baird might have argued that, in the

---

[47] *Baird Textile Holdings Ltd v Marks and Spencer plc* [2001] EWCA Civ 274, [2002] 1 All ER (Comm) 737. This, it should be noted, was a case argued on preliminary points. Baird, having commenced proceedings (pleading contract and estoppel) against Marks and Spencer, the latter applied under CPR r 24.2 for summary judgment to the effect that the former had no reasonable prospect of succeeding on either ground.

[48] *Baird Textile Holdings* (n 47 above) [2001] EWCA Civ 274 [4].

light of the prevailing co-operative culture, the notice period should be extended to reflect the duration of the dealings between the parties. However, in the absence of such an express contract, Baird relied on the co-operative culture to argue for an implied contract.[49] The Court of Appeal took their bearings from individualistic thinking in order to reject this argument. As Mance LJ put it,[50]

> [i]t is evident that Baird felt, quite rightly, that it had achieved a long and very close relationship, an informal business 'partnership', with M & S, and that it could, as a practical matter, rely on this and M & S's management's general goodwill and good intentions. But managements, economic conditions and intentions may all change, and businessmen must be taken to be aware that, without specific contractual protection, their business may suffer in consequence. I do not think that the law should be ready to seek to fetter business relationships, even—and perhaps especially—those as long and as close as the present, with its own view of what might represent appropriate business conduct, when the parties have not chosen, or have not been willing or able, to do so in any identifiable legal fashion or terms themselves.

So, even in a co-operative context, individualistic doctrinal thinking can assert itself, whether (as in *Baird*) by seizing on the absence of an explicit contractual commitment or by declining to imply a contract (or a term) articulating a co-operative obligation, or (as in Lord Wilberforce's dissent in *Schuler v Wickman*[51]) by emphasising the significance of an explicit contractual reservation. Sometimes, as Stewart Macaulay would put it, the 'paper deal' trumps what one party at least has taken to be the 'real (co-operative) deal'.[52] Sometimes, the case simply bottoms out on the default ethic of self-reliance.

## E. CONCLUSION

The short verdict on *Suisse Atlantique* is that the courts failed to address a question that is about as fundamental as any question can be to the design of a contract law regime—namely, whether it is geared for co-operation and trust or for self-reliance and defensive dealing. Instead, the Law Lords, having been diverted by another question—a question that they thought was fundamental—tried to prevent the break-up of a body of law that was already too full of fault lines.

The mission of the general law of contract, as presupposed by *Suisse Atlantique*, is two-fold. First and foremost, the mission is a facilitative one:

[49] In part, Baird's implied contract argument failed because the court reasoned: (i) according to the orthodox test, terms are not to be implied into a contract unless it is strictly necessary to do so; (ii) the test for implying a contract cannot be less demanding than that for implying a term into a contract; and so (iii) the test for implying a contract must be at least as demanding as the necessity test for implied terms. Notoriously, though, the necessity test for implied terms presupposes a context of adversarial dealing; and, it only makes sense in a case such as *Baird TextileHoldings* if we suppress the co-operative context in which the parties dealt for 30 years.
[50] *Baird Textile Holdings* (n 47 above) [76].
[51] *Wickman Machine Tool Sales Ltd v L Schuler AG* (n 23 above).
[52] S Macaulay, 'The Real and the Paper Deal: Empirical Pictures of Relationships, Complexity and the Urge for Transparent Simple Rules' (2003) 66 *Modern Law Review* 44.

under the banner of freedom of contract, contractors are permitted, indeed encouraged, to develop their own model sets of terms and conditions. The fact that this freedom finds expression in many different forms of contract and that disputes are generally settled by reference to the particular forms employed in no sense detracts from the integrity of the general body of common law. Secondly, where contractors fail to make decisive express provision for some matter, the general law supplies a range of default provisions to resolve disputes. These default provisions are set on the basis of a robust individualistic ethic. In *Suisse Atlantique*, while the Law Lords direct almost all their energy at confirming the facilitative nature of the mission, because the courts at all levels are so accustomed to the individualistic default setting, they waste very little energy in engaging this position.

It is widely recognised that *Suisse Atlantique* was not able to resist the articulation of a regulatory style of consumer contract law. What this betokened was not merely some fresh limits to freedom of contract but the re-classification of consumers and their suppliers from the category of contract to that of status. However, in many ways, the more interesting issue is in relation to the default position. While self-reliance might be the appropriate ethic in some markets, it is not so clear that this is right for other markets, particularly those involving small businesses or contractors who have a long-term record of dealing with one another. If contract law is to adjust to this challenge, it either needs to become more regulatory (treating small business contractors as if they were consumers)[53] or to have a default that is more flexible and sensitive to the parties' actual or rational expectations.

[53] In this regard, we should take note of the Law Commission, *Unfair Terms in Contracts* (Law Com No 292 and Scot Law Com No 199, 2005). However, we also need to hedge against the corporate network that might be hidden behind the veil of a small business.

# 11

# *Reardon Smith Lines Ltd v Yngvar Hansen-Tangen, The Diana Prosperity (1976)*

MICHAEL BRIDGE

Ship demand, measured in ton miles of cargo, is mercurial and quick to change, sometimes by as much as 10–20 per cent in a year.[1]

## A. INTRODUCTION

THE DECISION OF the House of Lords in *Reardon Smith Lines Ltd v Yngvar Hansen-Tangen, The Diana Prosperity*[2] is an important sale of goods decision without being a sale of goods case. It is indicative of the restrictions placed in recent decades on the scope of the description obligation of the seller of goods that have served to limit the termination rights of buyers.[3] In the case of unascertained goods, it might at one time have been said that every statement constituting part of the description of the goods was the equivalent of an express 'warranty', and not a warranty in the narrow sense of a term collateral to the main purpose of the contract[4] but rather a condition that permitted the buyer to terminate the contract, regardless of the consequences, venial or grave. Those days have now passed and the forces that have diminished the prospects of an express term being classified as a condition have had the same narrowing effect on the scope of section 13 of the Sale of Goods Act 1979,[5] which is the provision dealing with contractual description.

---

[1] M Stopford, *Maritime Economics* (London, Routledge, 1997) 117.

[2] *Reardon Smith Lines Ltd v Yngvar Hansen-Tangen, The Diana Prosperity* [1976] 1 WLR 989 (HL).

[3] See *Hongkong Fir Shipping Co Ltd v Kawasaki Kisen Kaisha* [1962] 2 QB 26 (CA); *Cehave NV v Bremer Handelsgesellschaft mbH, The Hansa Nord* [1976] QB 44 (CA).

[4] Sale of Goods Act 1979 s 62(1), deriving from *Chanter v Hopkins* (1838) 4 M & W 399, 404; 150 ER 1484, 1486 (Abinger CB).

[5] Unless otherwise stated, all references are to the 1979 Act rather than its consolidated 1893 predecessor. Where a section number is referred to in relation to a pre-1979 case, it will be to a statutory provision that was not changed in any relevant respect in 1979.

It is a well-known feature of English sale of goods law that it is responsive to market conditions and readily grants rights of termination for breach, whether under the Sale of Goods Act or at common law. Despite the trend set in motion by *Hongkong Fir Shipping Co Ltd v Kawasaki Kisen Kaisha, The Hong Kong Fir*[6] to deal with express terms of quality and condition as intermediate stipulations of the contract, this trend has had no appreciable effect on documentary and time obligations, which have for the most part been treated as contractual conditions. In the latter case, this has been despite language in the Sale of Goods Act that gives no encouragement at all to their treatment as conditions.[7] The statutory initiative taken in section 15A of the Sale of Goods Act to curb abusive termination in commercial cases has not been defined in terms wide enough to trench upon time and documents.

In volatile freight and commodity markets, the justification for the grant of rights of termination in the case of breaches of time obligations that appear not to have serious consequences is that the nature of the risk changes the market for the goods. July wheat is not the same commodity as August wheat. For that reason, in *Bowes v Shand*,[8] a c.i.f. buyer of Madras rice to be shipped in March was able to reject documents showing a February shipment. The concept of description played a substantial part in the conclusion reached by the House of Lords. In the case of large items, such as ships, it might be thought that their value would not be as volatile as oil or wheat; ocean-going vessels have a commercial life of about 25 years before they are disposed of in the scrap market, often to be broken up in the Indian sub-continent.[9] Although the freights or charter hire sums that they might earn from year to year may be variable, the length of the shipping cycle[10] is such that their owners should ordinarily be able to take the rough with the smooth during the life of the ship.

The case of *The Diana Prosperity*, however, gives the lie to this simple view of goods and markets. It concerned an innovative financing scheme that involved a series of long-term charters[11] to a head charterer, fixed in advance of

---

[6] *Hongkong Fir Shipping* (n 3 above), discussed in ch 9 of this volume by Donal Nolan.

[7] The Act is silent on the subject of documentary performance. It states neutrally, in s 10, that the time of performance by the seller is a matter of contractual construction and states also that the time of payment is presumptively *not* of the essence of the contract.

[8] *Bowes v Shand* (1877) 2 App Cas 455 (HL).

[9] See www.greenpeace.org/india/campaigns, complaining that ship breaking and its environmental hazards have been exported from the affluent world to the third world, and observing that 95% of ships are made of steel and that, when scrapped, 'can make the owner a *profit* of about 1.9 million US dollars' (emphasis added), which is an unusual way to define profit.

[10] The shipping cycle may broadly be defined as the period between two dates: the first date is when there ceases to be an equilibrium of supply and demand for tonnage in conditions of stable freight rates; and the second date is when those conditions of equilibrium return. In between, there occurs a rise in newbuildings, an oversupply and a collapse of freight rates, and a shortage of tonnage and ensuing rise in freight rates when vessels are scrapped. The cycle averaged 8.2 years between 1872 and 1989: Stopford, *Maritime Economics* (n 1 above) 46. The average cycle is therefore about one-third of the life of an ocean-going vessel.

[11] Some tanker operators at that time were prepared to avoid the relatively safe option of sheltering within long-term charters by taking substantial risks on the spot market. See the profile in

a ship's construction—indeed, the ship was one of many that were being dealt with in this way—in order to underpin the construction of the ship in the first place by guaranteeing a long-term, settled income stream. The entity responsible for this scheme was Sanko and the scheme it sponsored, if it did not cause the collapse of the oil tanker market in 1975, at least aggravated the consequences of that collapse. In 1975, when the market did collapse, tankers built in the late 1960s were scrapped long before they reached the end of their natural life-cycle.

An outside observer of the various shipping markets over time might have cause to speculate on the romance of the sea whilst remaining still at a loss to explain why so many hard-headed investors become involved in it, despite its many uncertainties and its long history of boom and bust. There are so many easier ways to make money that it is difficult to find other reasons for the attractions of the shipping world.

The purpose of this chapter is, first, to place the decision in *The Diana Prosperity* in its commercial context and to tell a story about risk, commercial versatility and diversification, and the harsh realities of the shipping world. The second purpose is to make a polemical point about description in sale of goods law. Description is very much a creature of its time. It emerged before there existed any clear separation of sale of goods law from general contract law, at a time when the test for an operative mistake, the definition of a discharging breach of contract and the difference between a mere representation and a contractual warranty were in the melting pot. Had description not been codified in the Sale of Goods Act 1893, it would have been part of the lawyer's lexicon but it would not have had the significance that it enjoys from being installed by statute as an implied promissory condition. My claim is that no purpose is any longer served by the continuing existence of an implied condition in the Sale of Goods Act that the goods supplied correspond to their contractual description. Article 2 of the US Uniform Commercial Code manages perfectly well without it.[12] Description is dealt with in Article 2 but not as a matter of an implied obligation. Rather, it is just an aspect of express warranty. Article 2's predecessor, the Uniform Sales Act 1906, has both an express warranty provision capable of dealing with matters of description and an implied warranty of description.[13] In his monumental treatise on sales law, Samuel Williston, the draftsman of the Uniform Sales Act, had some difficulty

---

*Time* magazine (28 July 1975) of the Norwegian Hilmar Reksten, who sometimes chartered vessels from other firms that he might re-charter them on the spot market. He signed a contract in 1973 for the construction of four ULCCs (ultra-large crude carriers), each of 420,000 dwt (deadweight tons), in Norwegian shipyards, which he had to cancel at the cost of US$67m. 'Deadweight' tonnage is the measure of water displaced by a ship minus the 'lightweight' of the ship, which is the weight of the ship stripped to bare essentials and minus crew, stores and fuel.

[12] See Art 2-313(1)(b) of the Uniform Commercial Code (US).
[13] Sections 12 and 14.

in justifying two overlapping provisions.[14] The approach taken in Article 2 is also taken in the United Nations Convention on the International Sale of Goods 1980.[15] In both instruments, express obligation is recited as an addition to the seller's basic duty to deliver the agreed goods. Given developments in the law relating to description in modern times, exemplified by *The Diana Prosperity*, the time has come to jettison description from sale of goods law. This cannot be accomplished by judicial means alone, though such means have largely marginalised description. Instead, as part of the revision of sale of goods law that is unlikely ever to take place,[16] description should receive its legislative quietus.

## B. FACTS

A close observer of string selling in international sales will see that disputes between seller and buyer are frequently arbitrated between parties in the middle of a string, neither of which is the party whose actions triggered the breach of contract, the subject of the particular arbitration. Thus, in the leading case of *Bunge Corp v Tradax Export SA*[17] the buyer giving 11 days' notice of readiness to load instead of the required 15 days did so because of delays in passing on to it a notice originating from the end buyer and charterer of the nominated vessel. In *The Diana Prosperity* the position is not dissimilar in that the dispute between Hansen-Tangen and Reardon Smith originated in actions taken by other parties in a chain governing the building of a tanker and its subsequent chartering and sub-chartering. With any litigation in the middle of a string, a defendant is always keenly aware that the claim it is fighting is the very claim that it has adopted or will adopt in the character of claimant against the next party in the string. This is true of *The Diana Prosperity*.

The disputed contract in *The Diana Prosperity* was a time sub-charter dated 2 October 1973 on 'Shelltime 3' terms by the defendants to the plaintiffs of a tanker of some 87,600 dwt[18] for a period of five years at US$4.50 per ton per month. The defendants in turn were to have the tanker under an intermediate time charter for the same period, entered into 14 months earlier, from the third

---

[14] S Williston, *The Law Governing Sales of Goods*, revised edn (Boston, Baker Voorhis & Co Inc, 1948) §223a: 'in the United States . . . a description of the goods which form the subject-matter of a contract of sale is within the meaning of Section 12 of the Statute defining express warranty; so that whether reliance is placed on Section 12 or Section 14 [the description provision], the result inevitably should be that any descriptive statements, upon which the buyer justifiably relies, constitute a warranty'.

[15] See Art 35(1).

[16] I have argued the case for such a revision in J Lowry and L Mistelis (eds), *Commercial Law: Perspectives and Practice* (London, Butterworths LexisNexis, 2006) 15.

[17] *Bunge Corp v Tradax Export SA* [1981] 1 WLR 711 (HL).

[18] When the vessel was later owned by the Teekay Corporation, it was listed as having a deadweight of 81,279 tons.

party, Sanko, at US$3.15 per ton per month, again on Shelltime 3 terms.[19] At the time of its signing on 15 August 1972, the intermediate charter granted by Sanko was for 10 years at the rate of US$3.00 per ton per month. This amount was 50 cents less than the prevailing market figure, but a 10-year charter promised the disponent owner a continuing and long-term stream of income. The Sanko plan depended upon the entry by Sanko into intermediate charters even before the tankers were built. It ultimately involved the construction of about 50 Aframaxes,[20] to be sub-chartered eventually to European shipping interests, whose advantage in taking long-term sub-charters lay in these commitments amounting to off-balance-sheet financing arrangements.

The Sanko plan promised, however, very slim margins for Japanese yards, since the 'keen prices' extracted from the builders by Sanko enabled Sanko to charter the vessels at favourable rates.[21] The terms of the shipbuilding contracts put a strain on the builders' resources, and there was pressure to reduce the number of 'newbuildings' in consequence of the appreciation of the yen, and the dollar currency difficulties to which this gave rise, and also due to OECD allegations of Japanese dumping, with the Japanese Government reducing the number of export licences. Sanko was able to cancel (at a cost) 18 of the intermediate charters[22] but charterers of the remaining 32, including Hansen-Tangen, wished to continue, though they did consent to the lesser term of five years at the slightly higher rate of US$3.15. The market at that time had risen to US$4.50, which represented the sub-charter rate to Reardon Smith, against the background of an expectation that rates would rise higher still. The sub-charter was concluded four days before the start of the 1973 Arab-Israeli War.[23]

Sanko itself chartered the Aframax in the present case, under the terms of a 10-year head charter dated 28 March 1973, from a Liberian company called Sculptor, for whom one of the Sumitomo companies (SKK) agreed to build the tanker. The terms of the charter to Sanko are not recorded but it is likely to have been a bareboat charter, so that the vessel was crewed by Sanko personnel. Through these and similar means, Sanko was particularly successful in increasing its tonnage without incurring heavy capital expenditure. In consequence, the formal owners of the vessels it chartered, like Sculptor, behaved more like

---

[19] The intermediate charters were brokered by a firm called AALL & Co (see www.aall.co.jp), which had been founded in Japan as a trading company by a Norwegian national in 1904. After evolving its business into ship-brokering and chartering, AALL subsequently diversified into financial services, alongside real estate activities in Japan and the United States.

[20] See definition at n 34 below. There were just under 30 intermediate charterers of the 50 or so tankers.

[21] P Stokes, *Ship Finance: Credit Expansion and the Boom-Bust Cycle* (London, Lloyd's of London Press, 1992) 17.

[22] Paying about $US3 m per tanker, accepted by P&O, Ben Line, British & Commonwealth and NSU: Stokes, *Ship Finance* (n 21 above) 17.

[23] On the same day as war broke out (6 October 1973), Lloyd's List reported: 'Buoyant tanker charter markets would now appear to have stopped the bottom falling out of the highly controversial [Sanko] arrangement'.

financiers than ship operators.[24] Sanko's position in the building and chartering chain, therefore, was not unlike the position of a bank that, having granted a loan, then seeks to disintermediate itself from that loan by selling it off and thus clearing it from its balance sheet. Just as the bank makes money from the difference between the interest it charges the borrower and the interest blended into the sale price of the loan, so Sanko sought to gain from the difference between the charter rates it paid under the head charter and the charter rates it received under the intermediate charter, whilst divesting itself from the ownership risk. The case does not record the former rate, which in a sense sums up the spirit of the case and the enterprise. Sanko was the architect and driver of the scheme but it sat in the middle of the chain.

It is critical to an understanding of the Sanko plan to understand 'shipping risk',[25] which has been defined as the financial risk associated with the ownership of a major capital asset, the ship, whose value rises and falls dramatically according to supply and demand in relation to the services the ship can provide. In conditions of 'industrial shipping', cargo interests, such as oil companies, own their own ships or else charter them from independent ship-owners under pre-construction time charters. The post-1973 volatility that invaded the oil market—and prompted a movement away from spot trading in oil on the Rotterdam market—also led to increasing levels of activity on the part of oil traders, who, acting pragmatically and without seeking to enter the field of long-term planning, preferred to charter ships on voyage terms when moving oil. They did not assume shipping risk. The Sanko plan, therefore, was conceived in a stable world and was implemented just as that world was about to collapse.

The final point to note about the chain is that the nominal builder of the ship, SKK, in turn sub-contracted the building to Osaka Zosen, which in turn sub-sub-contracted it to Oshima Zosen. The legal difficulties in the present case arose out of that sub-sub-contract. The contractual structure of the various shipbuilding and chartering contracts can be arranged as follows:

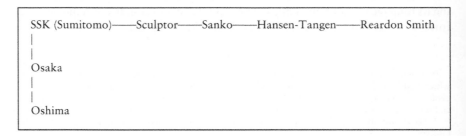

---

[24] Stokes, *Ship Finance* (n 21 above) 4, referring to the so-called Shikumi-Sen arrangement with Hong Kong ship-owners.

[25] Stopford, *Maritime Economics* (n 1 above) 38–9.

Because charter rates had fallen so far, by the time of trial, as to net the plaintiffs a likely loss of £5m over the term of the sub-charter, they had every reason to refuse tender of the tanker if able to do so. If the defendants in turn were able to resist delivery of the tanker under the charter, then Sanko stood to lose some £6m over the five-year term of the charter.[26]

Reardon Smith, the sub-charterer, rejected the tender of the tanker and, by means of a summons, sought the determination of the question whether they were entitled to do so. The grounds upon which Reardon Smith claimed to be entitled to terminate the sub-charter—and which came to be adopted by Hansen-Tangen as against the intermediate charterer, Sanko, as third party— were quite simple and ran as follows. Under an addendum to the intermediate charter, Sanko agreed to deliver to Hansen-Tangen a vessel of about 87,600 dwt 'to be built by Osaka Shipbuilding Co. Ltd. and known as Hull No. 354, until named'. The sub-charter from Hansen-Tangen to Reardon Smith was substantially on back-to-back terms and called for a 'Newbuilding motor tank vessel called Yard No. 354 at Osaka Zosen'. (Osaka Zosen meant the Osaka Shipbuilding Co. Ltd.[27]) Reardon Smith had insisted on seeing the intermediate charter before agreeing to the sub-charter. Because the Osaka yard was not large enough to construct a vessel of the agreed size, the work was carried over into the Oshima yard, 300 miles away,[28] in which Osaka Shipbuilding Co Ltd had a 50 per cent stake.[29] The intended vessel, bearing hull number 354 on Osaka's books, became, in the application to the Japanese Ministry of Transport for a licence to build the tanker, hull number 004 on Oshima's books. Work done on the tanker at Oshima was carried out under the supervision of Osaka; a number of key personnel at Osaka were also seconded or transferred to the Oshima yard. At trial, in the Court of Appeal and in the House of Lords, it was held that the tanker tendered could not be rejected by the sub-charterer, Reardon Smith, and indeed conformed to the requirements of the sub-charter.

Those are the bare facts of the case. Before turning to the reasoning in the House of Lords and the courts below, it is instructive (and interesting) to look in greater detail at some of the parties appearing in this case and the places where the events occurred. When that is done, some measure of the impact of the oil crisis precipitated by the Arab-Israeli War 1973 is in order.

---

[26] The loss figures here are those given at trial by Mocatta J: *Reardon Smith Lines Ltd v Yngvar Hansen-Tangen* [1976] 2 Lloyd's Rep 60 (QB) 61. In the Court of Appeal, Lord Denning MR speaks non-specifically of losses of £11 m 'and probably much more': *Reardon Smith Lines Ltd v Yngvar Hansen-Tangen* [1976] 2 Lloyd's Rep 60 (CA) 68.

[27] Located on the island of Honshu.

[28] On the island of Kyushu.

[29] The arrangement, together with the role of the Japanese Ministry of Transport, is set out at some length in the judgment of Mocatta J at first instance: *Reardon Smith Lines* (n 26 above) (QB).

## C. PARTIES AND EVENTS

### 1. Sanko

The Sanko Steamship company,[30] rescued in a reduced state by the Japanese equivalent of Chapter 11 proceedings in 1985[31] when it had incurred debts of 550 billion yen, did not prior to that date behave like a conventional Japanese company operating in harmony with Japanese bureaucracy, as so many other companies had done.[32] Instead, it has been described as 'a lone wolf—an anomaly in cooperation conscious Japan'.[33] It did not submit to administrative guidance nor to dependence upon Japanese banks and, on its way to becoming the world's largest shipping line by the early 1970s, it hatched the innovative Sanko plan, based originally on an order of some 100 Aframax[34] tankers, though some 51[35] were in the result actually built. The Sanko plan in effect transferred the market risk to charterers of the tankers, though Sanko remained at risk of those charterers becoming insolvent and they in turn remained at risk of sub-charterers' insolvencies. It may be that Sanko's ability to survive the 1975 tanker

---

[30] Sanko was founded in 1934 with the assistance of Toshio Komoto who, at the time of the 1985 reorganisation (see below), was a Minister without Portfolio in the Japanese Government and had previously been Deputy Prime Minister. He had not, since his political rise in 1982 to a leadership role within the ruling Liberal Democratic Party, surrendered his dominant shareholding interest in Sanko.

[31] Not surprisingly, the Sanko website (www.sankoline.co.jp) skips the events of the mid-1980s and then offers the following bland observation: 'In 1989 owing to drastic changes in the world economy Sanko Line reorganized to streamline operations and became a more efficient and modernized Company'.

[32] In the early 1960s, a Japanese law was passed (A Law Concerning Temporary Measures for Reorganization of Shipping Enterprises) to create special incentives to promote a consolidation of the then-ailing shipping industry into six core companies. Because of the close governmental supervision to which the law gave rise, Sanko declined to participate in the scheme and, despite minor harassment from the Japanese Ministry of Transport, raised its own equity finance to expand its fleet: P Tresize and Y Suzuki, 'Politics, Government and Economic Growth in Japan', in H Patrick and H Rosofsky (eds), *Asia's New Giant* (Washington, The Brookings Institute, 1976) 795 fn 80.

[33] R Seeman, 'Sanko Steamship—Japan's Largest Bankrupcy' *The Japan Lawletter* (November 1985).

[34] A conventional way of referring to mid-sized tankers in the range of 80–120,000 dwt (dead-weight tons). Aframax tankers operate mainly in the intra-regional trade of the Mediterranean, the Caribbean, the Far East and the North Sea, where the ports and canals are often too small to handle the really large vessels, VLCCs (very large crude carriers, up to 300,000 dwt in size) and ULCCs (which can reach up to about 550,000 dwt): see Wikipedia entry for 'Aframax'. Aframax tankers are larger than Panamax vessels and smaller than Suezmax vessels, which respectively are vessels capable of negotiating the locks of the Panama Canal and the Bridge of the Americas at Balboa, and the Suez Canal (which has no locks but which imposes draught restrictions, which particularly affect tankers). 'Afra' stands for 'average freight rate assessment'. Some sense of the dramatic increase in the size of tankers to take advantage of the economies of scale comes from the fact that a tanker of Aframax size, launched in 1957, was at that time the largest tanker in the world (the *TT Universe Leader* of 84,750 dwt): HL Beth, A Hader and R Kappel, *25 Years of World Shipping* (London, Fairplay Publications, 1984) 29.

[35] There is a discrepancy between the number recorded in the case, 50, and the number, 51, that appears in the broader literature.

crisis[36] was responsible for the excessive optimism that led to it launching a second major scheme in order to trade out of its financial difficulties, which involved the construction of 123 handy-sized[37] bulk carriers.[38] Various trading companies were to place orders with shipbuilders and then charter the ships for lengthy terms to Sanko. It seems to have been Sanko's corporate strategy that this order would drive up the price of ships so that competitors would end up with higher running costs than Sanko. This daring scheme culminated in the 1985 insolvency proceedings that, over a three-year period and with generous assistance from Sanko's three main bankers, produced a much-reduced shipping company.[39] At the current time, Sanko is still in business but its fleet ownership[40] of 118 vessels has remained at approximately 1985–88 levels.[41]

## 2. Reardon-Smith

The rise and fall of the house of Reardon Smith[42] is grist to the mill for those who say that family businesses rarely survive beyond two generations. The shipping company of that name went into liquidation in the mid-1980s, having started in the tramp steamer business in 1905 in Cardiff Docks on the back of the South Wales coal boom in the years preceding the First World War. The fleet grew to 39 vessels by 1922. As coal declined in the 1920s and early 1930s, the

---

[36] Referred to in *Time* magazine as one of the worst depressions ever in the tanker business (10 March 1975).

[37] In the range 28–40,000 dwt: see Wikipedia entry for 'Tonnage'.

[38] These schemes led to criticism of Sanko as being bold to the point of recklessness and as becoming a 'dangerous overreacher', producing 'highly damaging effects on the shipping industry': P Stokes, *Ship Finance* (n 21 above) 74–7.

[39] R Seeman, 'Sanko Steamship—Japan's Largest Bankrupcy' *The Japan Lawletter* (November 1985), noting in some detail the negotiations between the Japanese receiver and various chartering companies. The same author notes in critical detail the attempts made by the receiver to maintain charter payments on profitable ships while stopping payment on other charters: 'Sanko Steamship— Bankruptcy' *The Japan Lawletter* (March 1986). This is typical behaviour for receivers, administrators and (to a lesser extent because of their limited management powers) liquidators: *Re Atlantic Computers Ltd* [1991] Ch 505.

[40] It is a striking feature of the shipping world that the words 'owner' and 'ownership' are loosely used for companies that have chartered vessels.

[41] As of 1 September 2006 (see www.sankoline.co.jp). This is the approximate number recommended at the time of the 1985 rehabilitation plan, when the company then owned about 260 ships.

[42] An account of the company is given by PM Heaton, *Reardon Smith Line: The History of a South Wales Shipping Venture* (Newport, Starling Press, 1984). The company changed its name to Reardon Smith Line Ltd in 1928. There is also a Reardon Smith archive in the Glamorgan Record Office. The founder of the company, Captain William Reardon Smith, came from Appledore. He at one time captained a ship owned by WJ Tatem, another Appledore native, who gave his name to the frustration case of *WJ Tatem Ltd v Gamboa* [1939] 1 KB 132. Reardon Smith became a baronet in 1920 in recognition of his contribution to the war effort. Sir William was a benefactor of the National Museum of Wales in Cardiff and established the Reardon Smith Nautical College to train young people for the merchant navy. The College closed its doors in the 1990s and subsequently Sir William's grandsons established the Reardon Smith Nautical Trust in 2004. Sir William died in 1935 and was succeeded by his son, Sir Willie Reardon Smith. There is a bust of Sir William in the Marble Hall inside Cardiff City Hall.

company diversified into the American liner trade, which lasted until 1937, before trying its hand in the oil tanker business. The company did not long survive the collapse of the tanker market in 1975 but has continued in one form in the business of managing foreign ships. The story of Reardon Smith[43] is the modern history of English shipping on a small scale, the failure of which is the inverse of the remarkably successful Norwegian shipping trade. Reardon Smith seems to have operated over the years on very tight margins.

### 3. Yngvar Hansen-Tangen

Although referred to at first instance in the plural as the defendants, there is nothing to indicate that Yngvar Hansen-Tangen was other than an individual. The trial judgment refers to him by name as making inquiries of Sanko. Hansen-Tangen's shipping interests appear to have centred on Kristiansand. There is no reference to him by name, or to a corporation with a similar name, as a member of INTERTANKO (the organisation of independent tanker operators[44] that accounts for 75–80 per cent of the overall tonnage in the tanker market consisting of vessels larger than 10,000 dwt). Nor is there mention of a Hansen-Tangen, whether individual or corporate, as a current member of the Norwegian Shipowners' Association.[45] If Hansen-Tangen, the individual or the corporation, disappeared from the Norwegian shipping scene, as appears to be so, that disappearance cannot be put down to a continuing decline in the Norwegian shipping industry. There was nevertheless a Norwegian shipping crisis that came in the mid-1970s; it might have put paid to Hansen-Tangen as a substantial or even extant concern in the tanker business.[46]

As for the shipping business in Norway during the relevant period, in the words of the Norwegian Shipowners' Association,[47]

[a]ll curves were pointing upwards around 1970. All prognoses forecast high, stable and permanent growth in oil carriage and world trade.

It is astonishing how easy it is, even in a cyclical industry like shipping, to believe that boom and bust have been eliminated, to be replaced by continuous, organic

[43] An unflattering account of life on a Reardon Smith ship around 1950 was given in 2004 by Peter Kearon, a former seaman on the *Jersey City*, who refers to 'tight fisted owners such as Reardon Smith embedded in a pre-war scrooge mentality'. The ship itself is described as a 'rat-run, cockroach-infested utility tramp ship', laid down in 1942 in Sunderland, that was 'built to be sunk' in the Second World War: see www.nlsme.co.uk/Newsletters. The NLSME is the North London Society of Model Engineers, which states on its website that the views of its correspondents are not necessarily those of the Chairman or Council of the NLSME.
[44] It excludes the oil majors from membership.
[45] See www.rederi.no.
[46] There is, however, some evidence of Hansen-Tangen family interest in the North Sea oil drilling equipment business. According to www.v-tech.no, Tore Hansen-Tangen is the CEO of V-Tech AS, a company formed in 1998 and a leading innovator in the field of top-side offshore oil drilling equipment.
[47] NSA Annual Report 2001, available at www.rederi.no.

growth. When it came, the downturn was savage. In the words of the Association again,

> the shipping industry experienced a crisis which became longer, deeper and more painful than anyone had thought possible. Shipping companies big and small crumbled and fell . . . The fleet shrank.

The Norwegian Government had to intervene to protect national shipping companies. After weathering the crisis, the industry was well placed to rebound and take advantage of the opening up of the North Sea oil fields in the 1970s. From the end of the 1980s to about the current date, the Norwegian fleet expanded by about 100 per cent, and the increase was even greater when foreign flags were taken into account.

## 4. Oshima Shipbuilding

Oshima Shipbuilding was founded as a joint venture between Sumitomo Corporation, Sumitomo Heavy Industries and Daizo (which was formerly Osaka Zosen). It started operating in June 1974 and launched its first ship in 1975. The years to 1979 were very difficult; the workforce had to be reduced by more than half to 785 employees and sub-contractors. Oshima then abandoned the depressed tanker market and repositioned itself to become a specialist in the manufacture of Handymax[48] and Panamax bulk carriers. It became the first shipbuilding company to manufacture a double-hull bulk carrier. By the turn of the century it had become heavily engaged in the building of dry bulk carriers, avoiding any return to the tanker market in the interests of maximum productivity. In 1988, the parent company (formerly Osaka Zosen) moved all of its shipbuilding operations from Osaka to Oshima,[49] despite the vulnerability of the latter site to typhoons.[50]

## 5. *The Diana Prosperity*

The vessel survived the tanker crisis of the mid-1970s. Unlike other tankers, it was not prematurely scrapped or converted into a floating oil tank. As is customary upon the sale of a vessel, its name was changed—to the *Oshima Spirit*—when it was sold in 1988. It seems at that time to have come into the hands of

[48] Vessels in the range 35–60,000 dwt: see Wikipedia entry on 'Tonnage'.
[49] Oshima island came under the jurisdiction of a Christian feudal lord towards the end of the Tokugawa Shogunate (1603–1867). A rich vein of coal was discovered on the island in 1935 and shipbuilding proved to be the saviour of the island's economy when coal consumption fell around 1970.
[50] Oshima's corporate aim is to deliver its vessels one month before the agreed date. Apart from its dry bulk carrier business, Oshima also started a tomato farm, opened a hotel and became a producer of tinned hawthorn juice.

the Teekay Shipping Corporation,[51] which later sold it in (American) fiscal year 1996. The 1976 decision of the House of Lords was not the vessel's last encounter with the law. It featured again, posthumously, in a New York District Court decision of 2000.[52] The case involved a cargo claim based on an alleged leakage of water from the vessel's steam coils in the course of a voyage from Los Angeles to Taiwan. The claimant failed to discharge the burden of proof imposed by the federal Carriage of Goods by Sea Act that the oil was in good order and condition at the time of loading. The vessel had a number of further name changes[53] before it was broken up in Chittagong in 1999.[54]

## 6. The Arab-Israeli War 1973 and the Ensuing Oil Crisis

According to one commentator, referring to the increase in shipping activity that occurred after the 1967 Arab-Israeli War:

> From 1967 to 1973, shipping enjoyed a reputation as one of the most glamorous, exciting and rewarding sectors for medium-term finance.[55]

There was 'mass euphoria' in the tanker market in the early 1970s.[56] Inflation was seen an enhancing the value of ships. Favourable loans granted in Japan by the Japanese Development Bank[57] assisted greatly in reducing demand volatility in the shipbuilding sector. The demand for oil transportation was rising at a faster rate than the growth in the oil tanker fleet.[58] Shipowners, especially tanker owners, were prepared to pay a significant premium on the price of ships in return for early delivery, thus bringing about a 'spectacular bubble in ship prices'.[59]

The 1973 war and the ensuing formation of OPEC and the cutting-back of oil production by oil-exporting nations[60] certainly had a dramatic effect on the market price of oil.[61] The reduction in oil traffic undoubtedly had a depressing

---

[51] Teekay's records show the original Oshima yard number of 004: www.mattmar.com.au/fleet_list_teekay.htm.

[52] *Westport Petroleum Inc v M/V Oshima Spirit*, 111 F Supp (2d) 427 (2000) (SDNY).

[53] In 1995 it became *The Erissos*, in 1998 *The Erissos XL*, and in 1999 *The Skamneli*. The details are taken from http://www.miramarshipindex.org.nz (which again shows the original Oshima yard number of 004).

[54] On 16 June 1999.

[55] Stokes, *Ship Finance* (n 21 above) 3.

[56] Stokes, *Ship Finance* (n 21 above) 5.

[57] Note, however, that Sanko operated outside the formal administrative/banking structure.

[58] The latter grew by 14% in 1973: Stokes, *Ship Finance* (n 21 above) 28.

[59] Stopford, *Maritime Economics* (n 1 above) 63, citing P Hill and R Vielvoye, *Energy in Crisis* (London, Robert Yateman, 1974).

[60] See the Wikipedia Chronology or World Oil Market Events (1970–2005).

[61] For example, the six Gulf members of OPEC raised the posted price of crude oil from US$5.12 a barrel to US$11.65 with effect from 1 January 1974. On 5 November 1973, Arab oil producers declared a 25% production cut below September levels, and introduced later further cuts for non-friendly nations.

effect on freight rates and tanker values but, above all, the prime cause in the collapse of the tanker market seems to have been the oversupply of tankers.[62] Favourable loans granted by national export credit departments have been blamed for contributing to the crisis, since without them, tanker orders might otherwise have been cancelled in the face of the oversupply.[63] The fall in the value of tankers was catastrophic. Stopford cites the case of a 1972 VLCC newbuilding of 200,000 dwt that fell in value from US$52m in 1973, to US$23m in 1974, US$10m in 1975, US$9m in 1976 and US$5m in mid-1977.[64] The fall in value greatly exceeded the normal depreciation of a vessel with a projected working life of 25 years. It was only later that a modest recovery began in the tanker market. The shipping world was not designed for the faint-hearted or risk-averse.

## D. THE REASONING IN THE CASE

As stated above, the sub-charterers in *The Diana Prosperity* were unsuccessful all the way up to and including the House of Lords. At first instance, Mocatta J declined to hold that the relevant words in the sub-charter and intermediate charters were non-contractual, merely because their only purpose was identify the subject-matter. The issue that gave him the greatest difficulty was whether, because the tanker was built at Oshima instead of Osaka, this gave rise to a breach of the contractual requirement of correspondence with description. He noted that there was no statutory provision on description in the case of charters, and took account of recent intermediate stipulation developments in the Court of Appeal in general contract law.[65] There was a breach of the sub-charter but it did not go to the root of the contract and so the sub-charterer was not entitled to terminate the contract.

In the Court of Appeal, Lord Denning MR's starting point was a fundamental one: 'Is this the vessel?'[66] He concluded that it was because the tanker was to be built in Japan. This fact coloured the interpretation of the charter, since in Japan the numbering of a hull at Oshima was an acceptable way of representing a hull number in Osaka, as sub-contracting the building of an entire vessel

---

[62] The order books for newbuilding tankers amounted to 698 tankers with a cumulative deadweight tonnage of 96m dwt on 1 July 1972. This figure had risen to 939 tankers at 144m dwt on 1 July 1973. The figure one year later was 1338 tankers at 196m dwt. (Source: Beth, Hader and Kappel, *25 Years of World Shipping* (n 34 above) 35; the same authors assert that the extra 196m dwt were not needed and that the existing fleet of 233m dwt at that time was adequate.) According to Stokes, *Ship Finance* (n 21 above) 5, the events of 1973 did not precipitate the tanker crisis.

[63] Stokes, *Ship Finance* (n 20 above) 6–7.

[64] Stopford, *Maritime Economics* (n 1 above) 64.

[65] *Hongkong Fir Shipping Co Ltd v Kawasaki Kisen Kaisha* [1962] 2 QB 26 (CA); *Cehave NV v Bremer Handelsgesellschaft mbH* (n 3 above). Reliance was also placed on the decision of Devlin J in a charter case: *Cargo Ships 'El-Yam' Ltd v Invotra* [1958] 1 Lloyd's Rep 39 (QB).

[66] *Reardon Smith Lines* (n 26 above) [1976] 2 Lloyd's Rep 60 (CA) 71.

was a common trade usage in that country. If, nevertheless, there had been a breach of the sub-charter, he declined to apply to charter contracts the difference between the identity of goods and their attributes,[67] which he found too elusive. The contractual description did not amount to a promissory condition since the 'only misdescription is one of nomenclature'[68] and not of function. In agreeing with Mocatta J,[69] he therefore held that the breach, if it did occur, did not go to the root of the contract so as to permit termination of the sub-charter. Stephenson LJ's judgment was to the same effect as Lord Denning's:

> The *Diana Prosperity* is to all relevant intents and purposes Osaka no. 354 and must be accepted as the chartered vessel.[70]

Bridge LJ, finally, took the same approach to the interpretation of the contract, dismissing hull numbers and the like as 'mere labels' and scathingly criticising those

> charterers and their brokers, none of whom took the slightest interest in the background to this essentially Japanese venture until the plaintiffs, at the end of the line, saw in this technicality a possible escape from their onerous obligations under the sub-charter.[71]

In the House of Lords, the sub-charterers were again held bound to take delivery of the tanker. According to Lord Wilberforce,[72] it was impermissible to go as far in interpreting the contract as had occurred in the Court of Appeal, by introducing into the interpretation of a sub-charter the practices carried out in Japanese shipbuilding of which those parties—both European companies—were unaware. Nevertheless, contracts ought not to be interpreted in a vacuum but rather within the factual matrix surrounding their conclusion. The disputed words were only 'simple substitutes for a name', helping to identify the same subject-matter for each of the contracts in this particular contractual string. This would assist in raising finance to support each contractual arrangement. It was not appropriate to treat those words as contractual conditions, since they were a matter of unilateral declaration and not negotiation in each of the charter contracts. Moreover, the strict authorities on sale of goods, some of which were due for 'fresh examination' in the House of Lords because they were 'excessively technical', should not be extended to contracts of the present kind. These authorities, if applied in the present case, would permit termination in the case of 'any departure from the description'. The proper approach in a case of

---

67 See Lord Diplock in *Ashington Piggeries Ltd v Christopher Hill Ltd* [1972] AC 441 (HL) 503.
68 *Reardon Smith Lines* (n 26 above) [1976] 2 Lloyd's Rep 60 (CA) 73.
69 *Reardon Smith Lines* (n 26 above) [1976] 2 Lloyd's Rep 60 (CA) 73.
70 *Reardon Smith Lines* (n 26 above) [1976] 2 Lloyd's Rep 60 (CA) 75.
71 *Reardon Smith Lines* (n 26 above) [1976] 2 Lloyd's Rep 60 (CA) 77–9. Bridge LJ also noted that the descriptive language used in the sub-charter was looser than that used in the intermediate charter: *Reardon Smith Lines* (n 26 above) [1976] 2 Lloyd's Rep 60 (CA) 79.
72 With whom Lords Kilbrandon and Simon and Viscount Dilhorne (to some extent at least) agreed, the last-named adding some observations of his own.

this kind[73] was to ask if 'a particular item in a description constitutes a substantial ingredient in the "identity" of the thing sold'. If it did, then that item should be treated as a condition.

Lord Wilberforce also expressed a preference for modern authorities in general contract law that were 'more rational' than the Sale of Goods Act 1893 in 'attending to the nature and gravity of a breach'. So far, it is not completely clear what Lord Wilberforce is saying, but he does appear to be saying that a package of descriptive words should be broken down. The words that are a substantial ingredient in the identity of a thing will be treated as promissory conditions, the implication being that the number of such words will be limited. Other words will give rise to termination rights only if, in the circumstances, the breach of contract respecting them goes to the root of the contract. At this point in his speech, Lord Wilberforce had not said, as the Court of Appeal did, that Hansen-Tangen, because of the proper interpretation of the words, was not in breach of contract.

By way of an explanatory gloss, Lord Wilberforce then went on to criticise further the strict approach to description exemplified by the sale of goods authorities. He did this by drawing a difficult distinction between words that are part of the identity of a thing and words that merely identify it. The disputed words in the present case served the latter purpose in attaching the tanker to the various contracts. Had they constituted part of the identity of the goods, then the sub-charterers would have been entitled to reject the tender of delivery on the ground that that tanker was not the tanker contracted for. The disputed words, moreover, did serve in fact to identify the tanker because the tanker was capable of being described as both hull number 354 Osaka and hull number 004 Oshima, and built by Osaka

> as the company which planned, organized and directed the building . . . though it could also be said to have been built by Oshima.

Lord Wilberforce went on to say: 'No other vessel could be referred to: the reference fits the vessel in question'.[74] This adds up to an opinion that the sub-charterers were not in breach of contract at all. The conclusion reached by Lord Wilberforce is therefore the conclusion reached by the Court of Appeal, but it is difficult to see, despite Lord Wilberforce's criticism of the court below, that there exists any difference at all between the two approaches taken to the interpretation of the sub-charter.

Lord Russell added the further valuable point that, under the 'domestic contract', namely the shipbuilding sub-contract between the Sumitomo company

---

[73] Lord Wilberforce acceptance of the need for a stricter approach might be taken 'as regards the description of unexamined future goods (eg commodities)' (*Reardon Smith Lines* (n 2 above) [1976] 1 WLR 989 (HL) 998) is discussed below.

[74] Lord Russell expressed the same view: '[T]here is no difficulty in identifying the *Diana Prosperity* as the vessel subject to the sub-charter': *Reardon Smith Lines* (n 2 above) [1976] 1 WLR 989 (HL) 1001.

(SKK) and Osaka, Osaka was entitled to sub-sub-contract the whole construction of the vessel to Oshima. Whatever views might be taken of the charter contracts, a contract for the building of a ship is a personal contract that cannot be delegated to a third party to perform without the consent of the purchaser of ship. Apart from this, he agreed with the rest of the House that there had been no breach of the sub-charter.

The conclusion reached by the House of Lords and the Court of Appeal is, it is submitted, plainly right. So far as it could not be said that any other tanker might have been tendered in fulfilment of the charter contracts, no other conclusion is possible. Applying the classifications of the Sale of Goods Act to the charter contracts, their subject-matter consisted of future goods. Moreover, though this is less clear, those future goods were also specific—that is, unique—goods. Future goods are perfectly capable of being specific goods.[75] Apart from this primary basis of the decisions of the Court of Appeal and House of Lords, both courts were also justified in holding back the strict sale of goods authorities on description.

## E. EVALUATION OF THE CASE

*The Diana Prosperity* is therefore an authority on the interpretation of contracts. So far as the modern dispensation in interpreting contracts avoids the literal interpretation of contracts and even permits courts to interpret contracts in a way that contradicts the primary meaning of words used in a written contract,[76] then it does confront established, strict authorities on the sale of goods. Lord Atkin's famous observation that an inch does not mean about an inch[77] is by no means one that Lord Hoffmann would subscribe to, though Lord Hoffmann might find it rather harder to assert that peaches packed in cases of 24 tins means the same thing as peaches packed in cases of 30.[78]

A great deal has been written in recent years on the subject of contractual interpretation, which—though vital background to any study of *The Diana Prosperity*—is not the theme of this paper. The theme I wish to pursue on the present occasion is the impact that *The Diana Prosperity* might be said to have on sale of goods law. Throughout *The Diana Prosperity*, one is conscious of a judicial desire to hold back the sale of goods authorities when dealing with a dispute in a charter contract. But is an hermetic separation of the two bodies of law appropriate? Viscount Dilhorne in *The Diana Prosperity* stated:[79]

---

[75] As in the famous case of *Varley v Whipp* [1900] 1 QB 513 (Div Ct).

[76] See, in particular, *Investors Compensation Scheme v West Bromwich Building Society* [1998] 1 WLR 896 (HL).

[77] *Arcos Ltd v EA Ronaasen & Son* [1933] AC 470 (HL).

[78] *Re Moore & Co and Landauer & Co* [1921] 2 KB 119 (CA).

[79] *Reardon Smith Lines* (n 2 above) [1976] 1 WLR 989 (HL) 1000.

Strong arguments can no doubt be advanced for not altering rules which have stood for so long and for not now restricting the right of a purchaser of goods which do not answer the description of those he agreed to buy.

An appraisal of the development of description in the sale of goods and an assessment of its current role are nevertheless timely. Lord Justice Roskill once remarked that:[80]

> Sale of goods law is but one general branch of contract. It is desirable that the same principles should apply to the law of contract as a whole and that different legal principles should not apply to different branches of that law.

The first point to note about sale of goods law and description is that description is a matter of implied rather than express obligation. This is odd[81] in that description is dependent upon the very words used by the parties when contracting. This point therefore calls for a close examination of pre-statutory authorities. Before this exercise is attempted, it is instructive to consider three statements of Diplock LJ in *Hongkong Fir Shipping Co v Kawasaki Kisen Kaisha*.[82] The first statement, based on an analysis of the leading frustration case of *Jackson v Union Marine Shipping Co*,[83] is that the release of a party from a contract, whether for breach or frustration, turns upon the gravity of an event and not upon its occurrence being due to a breach of contract.[84]

The second statement of Diplock LJ is the test he lays down for a discharging event: a party should thereby be deprived of substantially the whole benefit that the parties intended he should receive under the contract in return for performing his own undertakings.[85] The difficulty with this test lies in the need to reconcile it with the autonomy given to contracting parties to decide for themselves whether a future event possesses the necessary gravity. This autonomy is famously expressed by Blackburn J in *Bettini v Gye*,[86] where he states that the parties have the power to do this even if the court itself would not have characterised the breach of contract as having the necessary gravity to give rise to discharge rights.[87] It is not so much Diplock LJ's ascription of discharge to the event that creates the problem; rather, it is the requirement in the test he lays down for discharge, that there should occur a deprivation of substantially the whole benefit of the contract. In so many cases of promissory conditions the occurrence of a deprivation to such an extent is a fiction. The fiction, moreover,

---

[80] *Cehave NV v Bremer Handelsgesellschaft mbH* (n 3 above) 71.

[81] Williston notes that the implied warranty of correspondence 'might more properly . . . be called express, since it is based on the language of the parties', but then notes the continuing hold of 'customary' language: Williston, *The Law Governing Sales of Goods* (n 14 above) §223.

[82] *Hongkong Fir Shipping* (n 3 above). See further Chapter 9 (above).

[83] *Jackson v Union Marine Shipping Co* (1874) LR 10 CP 125.

[84] *Hongkong Fir Shipping* (n 3 above) [1962] 2 QB 26 (CA) 68–9.

[85] *Hongkong Fir Shipping* (n 3 above) [1962] 2 QB 26 (CA) 70.

[86] *Bettini v Gye* (1876) 1 QBD 183, 187.

[87] The tension between parties' and the court's point of view is well expressed in the unsatisfactory judgment of the Court of Appeal in *Rice v Great Yarmouth BC* [2003] TCLR 1.

is compounded when the conclusion reached that a term is a promissory condition derives from trade practice and understanding[88] rather than the particular language used by the parties in describing the term or in stating the consequences of its breach. The introduction of party autonomy seems also to have created difficulties in understanding the meaning of warranty. When Abinger CB referred to warranty as collateral to the main purpose, or rather 'object', of the contract, he was not referring to the difference between conditions and warranties as we understand it today with the aid of the Sale of Goods Act. He was contrasting warranty with event in the character of non-performance.[89] The breach of a term designated by the parties—or even characterised by the Sale of Goods Act—as a condition does not as such amount to non-performance in fact. Express warranty was collateral having regard to the circumstances in which it was given—'separate from, or subsequent to, the seller's promise to sell'. In the modern law, however, we are left with a distinction to be drawn between warranty, as meaning contractual promise, and warranty, as meaning a lesser term of the contract whose breach sounds in damages.

The third statement of Diplock LJ concerns his reference to the former practice of separating the condition precedent, or event, giving rise to contractual discharge and the warranty associated with it. He refers to the modern practice of dispensing with the 'now unnecessary colophon'—the recitation of the discharging event as having been caused by a breach of warranty—and conflating the event and the warranty.[90] Hence the modern practice of naming as (promissory) conditions all those contractual terms whose every breach gives rise to discharge rights.[91] To understand description and the approach of Lord Wilberforce in *The Diana Prosperity*, however, it is useful to restore Lord Diplock's colophon, which is the prelude to unbundling description. An examination of the 19th century authorities is instructive, especially since a number of them concern bills of exchange payable to bearer where bills were discounted on a non-recourse basis and the discounter, not having signed the bill, did not incur liability on it. This amounted to the absence of a colophonic warranty and a clear focus in the relevant case on the nature of the event permitting release from the contract. It is quite a rare description case in this period that involves the buyer seeking damages over and above the recovery of any money paid or the pleading of a defence to payment.[92] As these and other description cases show, a clear kinship emerges from a comparison of the gravity of a discharging event under the general law of contract, the test of an operative common mistake at common law and the non-compliance with description that is of the necessary gravity to permit discharge. The retrenchment of description to the

---

[88] *Maredelanto Compania Naviera SA v Bergbau-Handel GmbH, The Mihalis Angelos* [1971] 1 QB 164 (CA).

[89] *Chanter v Hopkins* (1838) 4 M & W 399, 404; 150 ER 1484, 1486–7.

[90] *Hongkong Fir Shipping Co* (n 3 above) [1962] 2 QB 26 (CA) 71.

[91] A practice deplored by Williston, *The Law Governing Sales of Goods* (n 14 above) §180.

[92] One example, discussed below (text to n 127), is *Allan v Lake* (1852) 18 QB 560, 118 ER 212.

core identity of the goods, evident in *The Diana Prosperity*, with further words of 'description' in the broad sense being treated as intermediate stipulations—which is what Lord Wilberforce's speech in *The Diana Prosperity* leads to—has been achieved against the grain of section 13 of the Sale of Goods Act. The Act does not sanction a distinction between core description and collateral description, but that distinction was drawn in *The Diana Prosperity*. And in doing this, the House of Lords demonstrated the redundancy of section 13 as well as its propensity to obstruct a similar approach to a conventional sale of goods case.[93]

An examination of the description cases can usefully start with *Bannerman v White*,[94] which concerned statements, made by a grower of hops to a hop merchant, that sulphur had not been used in the growing of 300 acres of hops.[95] The Burton brewers had earlier stated that they would not buy hops that had been treated with sulphur, in response to which hop merchants, before the contract date, had sent a circular to hop growers that they would not in future buy any hops without a guarantee that sulphur had not been used. Although *Bannerman v White* has often been used as an authority on express warranty,[96] the case centred on the buyer's defence to an action by the seller for the half of the agreed price that had fallen due under the contract. The central question in the case for present purposes was whether these words gave rise to a condition releasing the buyer from having to comply with the contract. The buyer's plea of *non assumpsit* was that the goods delivered were not the goods that he had ordered. The jury found that the seller's representation that sulphur had not been used in growing the crops[97] was a part of the contract and a warranty to that effect, and the court ruled that the defendant buyer was not bound to pay the price, on the basis that the seller's undertaking 'was the condition upon which the defendants contracted'. As Erle CJ expressed it:[98]

> If the parties so intend, the sale may be absolute, with a warranty superadded; or the sale may be conditional, to be null if the warranty is broken. And upon this statement of facts, we think that the intention was that the sale should be null if sulphur had been used.

The hops were plainly useless to the buyer, given the implacability of the Burton brewers. This point, together with the gravity of the event in supporting cases, confirmed that what the buyer received was altogether different from what the buyer ordered. The condition found in *Bannerman v White* was, though not stated to be such by the court, an implied condition, which is the source of the seller's description obligation in section 13 of the Sale of Goods Act being rooted in an implied condition of the contract. The warranty itself given by the seller of

[93] In this connection, it is interesting to consider the Uniform Sales Act 1906 and the thoughts of its draftsman, Samuel Williston, quoted in n 14 above (*The Law Governing Sales of Goods*).
[94] *Bannerman v White* (1861) 10 CB (NS) 844, 142 ER 685.
[95] This was a very large quantity indeed. The agreed price of the hops was £16,701 10s.
[96] See old editions of Smith and Thomas's *Casebook on Contract*.
[97] It had been used in five out of the 300 acres, but there was no way of separating the two quantities of hops.
[98] *Bannerman v White* (n 94 above) CB (NS) 844, 860; 142 ER 685, 692.

the hops was only an incidental matter because the buyer was not counter-claiming damages for breach of warranty.[99] Had the buyer been seeking the recovery of moneys paid, the necessary gravity of the event would have been expressed in the total failure of consideration that the buyer would have had to establish when substantiating the money claim.

Description is treated as a matter of implied condition also in *Wieler v Schilizzi*,[100] where the buyer succeeded in an action to recover an advance payment made for a quantity of 'Calcutta linseed, tale quale'.[101] The significance of *'tale quale'* is that the seller was not giving a warranty,[102] so the buyer, in order to succeed, had to show that the goods delivered were not the goods bargained for. The buyer succeeded because linseed adulterated with 15 per cent of rape and mustard seed did not pass the market test of linseed, which allowed a maximum adulteration of two to three per cent.[103]

The cases on negotiable instruments and bonds emphasise the gravity of the event that is necessary for a discharge preceding an action to recover money paid, and indeed do so in a particularly pure way because commercial paper when compromised is truly worthless and does not possess even scrap value. In *Young v Cole*,[104] a number of bonds that had not been officially stamped were sold as Guatemala bonds. Since the absence of a stamp rendered the bonds worthless, they did not conform to the Stock Exchange understanding of Guatemala bonds. It was a buyer's action for the return of money paid on a total failure of consideration and the court held that there had been a total failure. In the words of Tindal CJ:[105]

> It seems, therefore, that the consideration on which the Plaintiff paid his money has failed as completely as if the Defendant had contracted to sell foreign gold coin and had handed over counters instead.

Neither the buyer nor the seller of the bonds was aware of the need for a stamp, so the case may be understood in contemporary language as an authority on common mistake. Tindal CJ was quite clear that no warranty had in this case been given by the seller that the bonds were Guatemala bonds. This feature of

---

[99] For Abinger CB's insistence that it is the contract itself, rather than any warranty, that imposes the obligation to deliver the goods contracted for, so as to give rise to a contractual non-performance if the goods as described are not delivered, see *Chanter v Hopkins* (1838) 4 M & W 399, 404; 150 ER 1484, 1486–7.

[100] *Wieler v Schilizzi* (1856) 17 CB 619, 139 ER 1219.

[101] The delivery terms were not entirely clear. It looks like a c.i.f. contract, but the statement in the case of the buyer's duty to pay suggests that the goods were sold on a 'to arrive' basis, in which case the risk of loss in transit would remain on the seller and the contract could not truly be classified as a c.i.f. contract.

[102] This is also a significant feature of *Nichol v Godts* (1854) 10 Ex 191, 156 ER 410, where a contract for foreign refined rape oil 'warranted only equal to samples' did not prevent the buyer in a non-acceptance action successfully pleading that the seller was not ready and willing to deliver the contract goods.

[103] As claimed by the buyer, with no rebuttal in the report.

[104] *Young v Cole* (1837) 3 Bing (NC) 724, 132 ER 589.

[105] *Ibid* 731. See also Bosanquet J at 731 ('worthless paper').

the case was well understood by Williams J in *Dawson v Collis*,[106] where he said: 'The distinction between a warranty and a condition is taken in *Young v Cole*'. He was not of course referring to a promissory condition in the Sale of Goods Act sense. The condition identified in *Young v Cole* as a discharging event was not connected to the intention of the parties.

*Jones v Ryde*[107] was a case concerning a discounted bill that had been forged but had not been signed by the seller. The seller's refusal to indorse the bill did

> not rid him of the responsibility which attaches on him for putting off an instrument of a certain derscription (*sic*), which turns out not to be such as he represents it,

but again it was a case of a buyer seeking the return of his money on a total failure of consideration. A forged bill being worthless, the discounting buyer was successful. Similarly, in the well-known case of *Gompertz v Bartlett*,[108] a bill payable to bearer was sold without recourse. Besides not indorsing the bill, the seller stipulated that it was being sold without a warranty. The bill was sold under the description of a foreign bill and was unstamped. Both seller and buyer believed it to be a foreign bill, in which case a stamp was not required by law. In fact, the bill had been drawn in England, which meant that, since it was unstamped, it could not be enforced against any of the parties to it. The buyer was entitled to recover the price he paid for the bill, since it did not match the description under which it was sold. According to Lord Campbell CJ: 'The case is precisely as if a bar was sold as gold, but was in fact brass'.[109] And reference was also made to Abinger CB's famous dictum in *Chanter v Hopkins*[110] that the delivery of beans under a contract for the sale of peas was a 'non-compliance with the contract'. Lord Campbell went on to say that

> this is not a case in which an article answering the description by which it was sold has a secret defect, but one in which the article is not of the kind which was sold.[111]

The money paid by the buyer was recoverable as money paid under a mistake of fact, though on the facts, since the bill was worthless without a stamp, the requirement of a total failure of consideration would have been met.

These core cases on description were all about the recovery of the buyer's money.[112] The existence, or not, of a warranty was an incidental matter. Despite superficial appearances, this is also true of *Barr v Gibson*,[113] which

---

[106] *Dawson v Collis* (1851) 10 CB 523, 530; 138 ER 208, 210.

[107] *Jones v Ryde* (1814) 5 Taunt 488, 128 ER 779.

[108] *Gompertz v Bartlett* (1853) 2 E & B 849, 118 ER 985. See also *Gurney v Womersley* (1854) 4 E & B 132, 119 ER 51, where all signatures on a bill sold without a warranty had been forged, with the exception of the forger's own signature. The money paid was recoverable as on a total failure of consideration.

[109] *Gompertz v Bartlett* (n 108 above) 2 E & B 849, 853.

[110] *Chanter v Hopkins* (1838) 4 M & W 399, 150 ER 1484.

[111] *Gompertz v Bartlett* (n 108 above) 2 E & B 849, 854.

[112] Similar to a recovery of money case for present purposes is an action of the seller for non-acceptance by the buyer, where the buyer, as a defence to the duty to pay, pleads that the seller was not ready and willing to deliver the agreed goods: *Nichol v Godts* (1854) 10 Ex 191, 156 ER 410.

[113] *Barr v Gibson* (1838) 3 M & W 391, 150 ER 1196.

concerned the sale of a ship that, unknown to the parties at the time of the contract, had run aground on an island in the Gulf of St Lawrence. The buyer's action for damages, on the ground that the seller had undertaken that he had the power to sell a ship when in fact he had not, was an action for breach of a covenant in the deed poll by which the ship was sold. The central question in the case was whether, given its parlous situation, the vessel could still be described as a ship, on which point the court sent the case back for a retrial. At trial, the buyer had been successful but the damages recovered precisely matched the price that the buyer had paid. So it was an action for the recovery of money paid under another name. The case is also of significance for Parke B's statement that

> the bargain and sale of a chattel, as being of a particular description, does imply a contract that the article sold is of that description.[114]

This 'contract' is the implied condition of correspondence with description. Parke B also made it clear that seaworthiness and serviceability were not part of description.[115]

The treatment of description as a matter of implied agreement opened the door to the parties to expand the range of circumstances in which the rights of discharge from the contract might arise. In *Gompertz v Denton*, for example, the court in the case of an unsound horse refers to the absence of any right to return the horse in the absence of fraud, or a post-contractual agreement to rescind the contract or 'a condition in the original contract authorizing the return'.[116] The use of implied agreement also permitted the parol evidence rule to be avoided at a time when the rule possessed real power. The demise or disappearance of the parol evidence rule,[117] with its replacement by broad rules of contractual interpretation that examine the full factual matrix of a contract, has done much to undermine the case for a distinct concept of compliance with description. It has done this by taking the fetters off express warranty. In recent times, the rediscovery of the intermediate stipulation highlighted the potential mischievous effects of description, especially when—as at times it had been in the past—it was given too broad a scope.

Despite its particular treatment in the Sale of Goods Act, description is nowhere defined in the Act. Moreover, on close examination, it is apparent that there are two related concepts at work: first, the question whether a sale takes place by description, and secondly, the question of what constitutes words of description in the technical sense under section 13 of the Sale of Goods Act.[118]

---

[114] *Ibid* 3 M & W 399.

[115] *Barr v Gibson* (n 113 above) 3 M & W 399.

[116] *Gompertz v Denton* (1832) 1 C & M 207, 149 ER 376, after referring to *Street v Blay* (1831) 2 B & Ad 456, 109 ER 1212. See also the discussion of the latter case in *Kennedy v Panama, New Zealand and Australian Royal Mail Co Ltd* (1867) LR 2 QB 580, 587 (Blackburn J).

[117] Law Commission, *Law of Contract: Parol Evidence Rule* (WP No 70, 1976); Law Commission, *Law of Contract: Parol Evidence Rule* (Law Com No 154, 1986).

[118] This distinction is elided in one of the leading modern cases, *Harlingdon and Leinster Enterprises Ltd v Christopher Hull Fine Art Ltd* [1991] 1 QB 564 (CA).

Over the years, the courts, starting from a position that drew a substantial distinction between specific and unascertained goods, or more particularly between seen and unseen goods, when defining the scope of description, have substantially aligned the two categories so that the scope of description is the same for both.

Turning first to the earlier 19th century authorities, technical words of description were differentiated, at least in analytical terms, from mere warranties. In the former case, as seen above, the supply of non-complying goods was a matter of contractual non-performance rather than the breach of something collateral to the main object of a contract, like a warranty.[119] This carries echoes of a distinction inherited by civilians from Roman law, where a distinction is drawn for practical purposes, affecting limitation periods for example, between the supply of something inferior (a *peius*) and the supply of something different (an *aliud*).[120] The description obligations of the seller were thus infringed in a case where the seller delivered the inferior 'Western Madras' cotton instead of the 'Long-staple Salem' cotton required by the contract and 'a different species of cotton altogether'.[121] In other cases, it has to be conceded that the supposed difference in kind necessary to establish the implied agreement for the discharge of the contract comes close to masking a mere difference in quality, as where Epsom salts were contaminated by oxalic acid,[122] 'Calcutta linseed, *tale quale*' was heavily adulterated with rape and mustard seed,[123] and 'foreign refined rape oil' was adulterated with hemp oil.[124] Although description was supposed to go to the heart of performance, these decisions[125] do appear to stretch the notion of performance. In at least some of these cases, description played the part of protecting a buyer who might otherwise have had no recourse in the absence of an express warranty of quality given by the seller.[126] There is certainly one case from the same period when description went so far as even to take over from warranty the function of awarding damages in excess of the contract price. That case was *Allan v Lake*,[127] where seeds sold as 'Skirving's Seeds' were in fact an inferior seed whose lower yield became evident only when the

---

[119] *Chanter v Hopkins* (n 110 above).

[120] On the distinction between the seller's delivery obligation and the guarantee against latent defects, see, eg J Huet, *Les principaux contrats spéciaux*, 2nd edn (Paris, LGDJ, 2001) §§11238 *et seq*. Thirty years is common as the general limitations rule, eg, French Code civil, Art 2262. But in French law an action to have the contract set aside because goods are defective must be brought within a short period ('*bref delai*'), which does not apply to the case where the goods delivered were not the goods ordered.

[121] *Azémar v Casella* (1867) LR 2 CP 677, 680–81 (Martin B). Had there been a mere difference in quality, the buyer would have been restricted to a price allowance clause in the contract.

[122] *Josling v Kingsford* (1863) 13 CB (NS) 447, 143 ER 177.

[123] *Wieler v Schilizzi* (n 100 above).

[124] *Nichol v Godts* (1854) 10 Ex 191, 156 ER 410.

[125] See the commentary on them by S Stoljar, 'Conditions, Warranty and Descriptions of Quality—I' (1952) 15 *Modern Law Review* 425, 440.

[126] See also *Barr v Gibson* (n 113 above), as discussed by Stoljar, 'Conditions, Warranty and Descriptions of Quality—I' (n 125 above) 432.

[127] *Allan v Lake* (1852) 18 QB 560, 118 ER 212.

farmer planting them had gathered in the crop. What prevents these decisions from being seen as 'quality' cases under another name is the reference to the market understanding of the way that goods not even warranted may properly be described to a buyer who has not seen them.[128] In all of these cases, the buyer received goods that he could not dispose of in the market.

The extension of description so as to include adulterated or contaminated goods seems to have had the consequence of conflating a warranty (whose existence was previously disputed) that the goods accord with their description, to the implied condition that they correspond to that description.[129] So far as description in this way took on the role of protecting the buyer from defects of quality, it added little if anything to merchantable quality as perceived around the same time, apart from providing a way around the rule in *Street v Blay*.[130] Indeed, in *Wieler v Schilizzi*, Lord Ellenborough's judgment in the early merchantable quality case of *Gardiner v Gray*[131] is recited at length in the arguments. *Wieler v Schilizzi*, like *Nichol v Godts* and *Josling v Kingsford*, seems more aptly to be treated as a case on merchantable quality than as a case on description. According to Lord Ellenborough, a buyer of waste-silk, having had no chance to inspect the goods before the contract, has even in the absence of warranty the benefit of an 'implied term' that he receive 'a saleable article answering the description in the contract'. Hence, the answer to the jury question, whether the buyer got the goods he bargained for, depended upon

> whether the commodity purchased . . . be of such a quality as can reasonably be brought into the market to be sold as waste-silk.

From a guarantee of minimum quality in a world of natural commodities that are inherently imperfect and always adulterated to a degree, the implied condition of merchantable (now 'satisfactory') quality later evolved in a world of attainable manufacturing perfection to provide as much protection as any express warranty of quality that could be bargained for. The modern development and scope of the implied terms of satisfactory quality and reasonable fitness for purpose, together with the readiness with which express warranties will be inferred, have to all practical intents obviated any need for such a protective role to be played by description at the margins of quality. The American Uniform Sales Act 1906 provides in this respect an interesting picture of a body of law that has not quite reached its mature state of development. In section 14, there is a warranty that the goods shall correspond to their contractual

---

[128] See *Nichol v Godts* (1854) 10 Ex 191, 156 ER 410 (no custom found that the adulterated goods could be sold in the market as foreign refined rape oil); *Wieler v Schilizzi* (n 100 above) ('passing in the trade by the commercial name of linseed oil'); *Josling v Kingsford* (1863) 13 CB (NS) 447, 143 ER 177 ('the oxalic acid of commerce').

[129] Williston, *The Law Governing Sales of Goods* (n 14 above) §225, noting the law settling in favour of the conclusion that descriptive statements amount to a warranty.

[130] *Street v Blay* (1831) 2 B & Ad 456, 109 ER 1212, discussed below.

[131] *Gardiner v Gray* (1815) 4 Camp 144, 171 ER 46.

description,[132] but there is also an express warranty provision in section 12,[133] which is just as much applicable to matters of description as section 14 itself.[134] When the Uniform Sales Act was superseded by Article 2 of the Uniform Commercial Code, section 12 was succeeded by Article 2-313 and section 14 disappeared.

Later cases in the 19th century stretched the scope of description for unascertained and unseen goods so that it came to embrace all attributes of the goods,[135] culminating in Salmond J's dictum that:[136]

> The statutory implied condition of correspondence with the description means in the case of unascertained goods that a buyer is not bound to accept in performance of the contract a delivery of goods different in any respect whatever from this which the vendor promised to supply him.

Treating this dictum as the high-water point of description, it is plain that it involves treating every statement constituting part of the contractual description as though it were a promissory condition in its own right. It is also plain that such an attitude cannot stand with the modern movement towards intermediate stipulations in the case of express undertakings regarding condition and quality. Although Lord Wilberforce in *The Diana Prosperity* had the delicacy not to cite the decision of the House of Lords in *Arcos Ltd v Ronaasen & Sons*[137] as a description case that was ripe for reconsideration in modern times, it plainly is, not just because of the strict way that the words were interpreted but rather because the particular exact dimensions of the wooden staves in question hardly seems to be a matter of non-performance, especially where those same staves were suitable for the purpose for which the buyer required the goods.

One factor that in the past favoured an expansive treatment of description was that it gave the court an opportunity to break away from the rule in *Street v Blay*.[138] According to this rule, in the case of specific goods, the effect of the passing of property was to confine the buyer to an action for damages for breach of warranty.[139] This rule was preserved in the old section 18 *Rule 1* of the Sale

---

[132] 'Where there is a contract to sell or a sale by description, there is an implied warranty that the goods shall correspond with their description'.

[133] 'Any affirmation of fact or any promise by the seller relating to the goods is an express warranty if the natural tendency of such affirmation or promise is to induce the buyer to purchase the goods, and if the buyer purchases the goods relying thereon. No affirmation of the value of the goods, nor any statement purporting to be a statement of the seller's opinion only shall be construed as a warranty'.

[134] Williston, *The Law Governing Sales of Goods* (n 14 above) §223a. But Williston goes on to say that s 14 is confined to identity: §225.

[135] *Bowes v Shand* (1877) 2 App Cas 455 (HL); *Varley v Whipp* (n 75 above).

[136] *Taylor v Combined Buyers Ltd* [1924] 2 NZLR 627.

[137] *Arcos Ltd v EA Ronaasen & Son* (n 77 above).

[138] *Street v Blay* (n 130 above).

[139] See the summary of this case by S Stoljar, 'Conditions, Warranty and Descriptions of Quality—II' (1953) 16 *Modern Law Review* 174, 184: 'What the common law had done was to call the seller's descriptive statement as to the quality of goods a "condition" where the sale was by description and to call it a "warranty" where the sale was for specific goods'.

of Goods Act 1893, repealed by the Misrepresentation Act 1967. Since section 18 *Rule 1* applied only to unconditional contracts, and since a contract where the seller had breached section 13 was not to be regarded as an unconditional contract for present purposes,[140] the treatment of description in an expansive way for goods that the buyer had not had the opportunity to examine[141] preserved the buyer's right to reject the goods despite the execution of the contract. Somewhat fictitiously, the buyer could claim a total failure of consideration that the passing of property would otherwise have countervailed according to the rule in *Street v Blay*. Since 1967, the passing of property in specific goods has been no bar to their rejection, and description therefore need not be pressed into fictitious service in aid of preserving the buyer's right of rejection.

In modern times, the expansive character of description, apparent in cases of unascertained goods, has been restricted so that all goods, unascertained and specific, have acquired a descriptive scope that embraces the identity of the goods sold and not their incidental attributes. An early move in this direction was made by Bailhache J in *T&J Harrison v Knowles & Foster*,[142] where in a case of specific goods the judge drew upon the distinction between conditions and warranties when deciding if statements made about the deadweight capacity of certain ships entailed a breach of section 13 of the Sale of Goods Act. The words were a matter of warranty since they did not make the ships delivered different in kind from the ships sold. More recently, in *Ashington Piggeries Ltd v Christopher Hill Ltd*,[143] the presence of a poisonous additive in connected contracts involving the sale of herring-meal and mink feed containing herring-meal did not give rise to a breach of section 13. Lord Wilberforce drew a distinction between description and quality, the former being understood in a commercial sense when answering the question whether the goods supplied are the agreed goods possessed of an additional quality or an aggregate of goods.[144] The analysis is not perspicuously clear, but the intent is to confine description to the essence or identity of goods.[145] Lord Guest, similarly, concluded that the presence of the poisonous additive did not give rise to a different substance: 'There was no loss of identity'. In concluding also that the words 'f.a.q.' (fair average quality) were not words of description, he reasoned that they did not serve to identify the goods that the seller had to tender in fulfillment of the contract.[146]

---

[140] *Varley v Whipp* (n 75 above).

[141] *Varley v Whipp* (n 75 above).

[142] *T&J Harrison v Knowles & Foster* [1917] 2 KB 606, affd on other grounds [1918] 1 KB 608.

[143] *Ashington Piggeries Ltd v Christopher Hill Ltd* [1972] AC 441 (HL).

[144] *Ibid* 489. Viscount Dilhorne, similarly, distinguishes between kind and quality (*ibid* 485) (but dissents in his conclusion that the contaminated goods did amount to a difference in kind); Lord Diplock distinguishes between quality and identity (*ibid* 503).

[145] See also *Couchman v Hill* [1947] KB 554 (CA) 559 (Scott LJ): 'I think every item of description which constitutes a substantial ingredient in the "identity" of the thing sold is a condition'.

[146] *Ashington Piggeries* (n 143 above)[1972] AC 441 (HL) 475. Lord Hodson, similarly, thought the function of section 13 was to identify the goods and that words could not be words of description if they did not identify the goods: 466 and 470.

In *The Diana Prosperity* itself, Lord Wilberforce, as seen above, was keen nevertheless to stress that the function of words in identifying goods did not thereby make them words of description if they did not also go to the identity of the goods.

The confinement of description to the identity of the goods means that description in section 13 adds nothing to the seller's duty of delivery in section 27 of the Sale of Goods Act. Both cases, to revert to the language of Abinger CB,[147] amount to non-performance of the contract. Yet, things are not quite so simple. Lord Wilberforce in *The Diana Prosperity* retreats somewhat from the position he took in *Ashington Piggeries* when remarking that

> a strict and technical view must be taken as regards the description of unascertained future goods (e.g., commodities) as to which every detail of the description must be assumed to be vital.[148]

The sale of unascertained future goods is a very wide category indeed and was certainly present in *Ashington Piggeries*. It is difficult to see the reasons for Lord Wilberforce's change of position—which appears to confuse the lay and technical meanings of description—unless it is inspired by the desire not to excite the commodities markets. In *Ashington Piggeries*, Lord Diplock had something to say that might assist a resolution of the matter: 'It is open to the parties to use a description as broad or as narrow as they choose'.[149] That same confusion of the two meanings of description is apparent here too, but Lord Diplock's words, drawing as they do on party intention, suggest that the contractual force of express words going beyond identity should depend upon whether the contracting parties regarded them as giving rise to express terms of the contract, either promissory conditions or intermediate stipulations. That is not a matter for section 13. The work of an expansive section 13 can therefore be divided between the seller's delivery duty and the express terms of the contract. The continued existence of section 13 only serves to obscure that important line. Where words in the broadly descriptive sense are used, it is better to turn to express warranty than to distort description, which should instead be seen as pertaining to the seller's basic duty of delivery. If descriptive words have a particular force in the commodities markets, then, instead of stretching section 13, it would be preferable to treat such words as go beyond the identity of the goods as the subject-matter of express warranty—with the question whether that warranty amounts to a promissory condition or remains as an intermediate stipulation to be determined by all the circumstances of the case, including implied intention and the understanding of the market.

---

[147] *Chanter v Hopkins* (n 110 above) 4 M & W 399, 404; 150 ER 1484, 1487. A modern example of non-performance, the delivery of Suffolk Punch horses instead of the tractor ordered by the buyer, is given by Lord Reid in *Suisse Atlantique Société d'Armement Maritime SA v NV Rotterdamsche Kolen Centrale* [1967] 1 AC 361 (HL) 404.
[148] *Reardon Smith Lines* (n 2 above) [1976] 1 WLR 989 (HL) 998.
[149] *Ashington Piggeries* (n 143 above) [1972] AC 441 (HL) 503.

If Lord Wilberforce did not let the description genie out of the bottle, the case for repealing section 13 is that it has no role to perform. If he did release the genie, so that words going beyond identity were automatically to be treated as promissory conditions, then this is hard to reconcile with the development of intermediate stipulation analysis.[150] It would be better for those additional words to be assessed in the same way that express words are assessed in a contract for the supply of services or the chartering of a vessel. The way forward in this respect would be to repeal section 13.

## F. CONCLUSION

All told, the world in which description operates today is a different world from the one in which it was conceived. Modern authorities, including *The Diana Prosperity*, have largely drawn the fangs from a potentially expansive concept of description so as to prevent it from too readily being used to overturn a bargain and agreed allocation of risk. Nevertheless, it is not easy for a modern observer to detect any description case that could not be resolved adequately with the tools of modern contract law. The sale of a welded wreck of a car could have been perfectly well settled by a finding that the seller had warranted the car as being of a stated engine capacity and year of manufacture.[151] The sale of a painting as the work of a German expressionist could likewise be treated as going to express warranty.[152] Indeed, that decision, whether one agrees with its invocation of reliance or not, can be said to have been made according to modern notions of express warranty[153] under the cover of an application of section 13 of the Sale of Goods Act.

Assuming now the breach of an express undertaking, the next question concerns the remedy: termination or damages. The merit of the general contractual approach is its flexibility and the fact that it dispenses with the uncertainty of the timid statutory power introduced on the recommendation to prevent strategic contractual termination.[154] Intermediate stipulation analysis (subject to one important point) may be employed to determine whether the buyer of goods is entitled to terminate the contract. The reserved point concerns the unnecessary strictness of the test used for determining the existence of termination rights in such cases. So long as implied contractual terms are so intensively characterised as conditions and cover such extensive ground, it is tempting to consider express contractual obligations as being of lesser importance. But, if the scope of statu-

---

[150] See *Cehave NV v Bremer Handelsgesellschaft mbH* (n 3 above).

[151] *Beale v Taylor* [1967] 1 WLR 1193 (CA).

[152] *Harlingdon and Leinster Enterprises Ltd v Christopher Hull Fine Art Ltd* (n 117 above).

[153] Williston was clear that reliance was an essential element of warranty, looking both to its roots in assumpsit and in the action on the case for deceit: Williston, *The Law Governing Sales of Goods* (n 14 above) §§195, 206.

[154] Sale of Goods Act s15A, as added by the Sale and Supply of Goods Act 1994.

tory obligations is reined in[155] this ought to open for examination the question whether the test for a discharging breach of contract—that it deprive the promisee of substantially the whole benefit of the contract—is too strict. The United Nations Convention on the International Sale of Goods 1980 does not have anything corresponding to promissory conditions. The fundamental breach test for avoidance,[156] perhaps not surprisingly, is therefore defined so as to make it easier to 'avoid' (that is, terminate) the contract than the test for a discharging breach of an intermediate stipulation in English law.

Modern approaches to contractual interpretation and the development of modern contract law both demonstrate that there is no longer any need for section 13 of the Sale of Goods Act. It is not needed, as formerly it was, to serve as a control on entry into the implied condition of merchantable quality.[157] As stated earlier, there is no section 13 in the United Nations Convention or in Article 2 of the US Uniform Commercial Code. That same message flows, albeit directly, from *The Diana Prosperity*. Description may no longer be the destroyer of bargains but it is a concept that now either lacks a purpose or has the capacity to work mischief. The real significance of *The Diana Prosperity*, not itself a sale of goods case, was that it showed just how dispensable is section 13 of the Sale of Goods Act.

[155] As was done covertly with the implied term of merchantable quality in *Cehave NV v Bremer Handelsgesellschaft mbH* (n 3 above).

[156] Article 25 of the Convention calls for a substantial deprivation of the benefit that a contracting party is entitled to expect. This is not the same as a deprivation of substantially the whole benefit.

[157] See the Sale of Goods Act 1893 s 14(2).

# 12

# *Johnson v Agnew* (1979)

## CHARLES MITCHELL

## A. INTRODUCTION

*J*OHNSON *v AGNEW*[1] is a significant decision in the recent history of English contract law for several reasons. First, the case contains a clear and often-cited statement of the rule which now governs termination for breach of contract, that acceptance of a repudiatory breach discharges both parties from future performance of their contractual obligations, but leaves their accrued rights and obligations intact. Secondly, the case overrules earlier authorities which held that a claimant who initiates proceedings for specific performance (or who wins a decree of specific performance) forfeits his right to terminate the contract by accepting the defendant's repudiatory breach. Thirdly, the case holds that when a decree of specific performance is made, the contract continues under the court's control, so that a further order is needed to dissolve the decree before either party can terminate the contract for breach and ask for damages. Fourthly, the case confirms that common law damages for breach are normally assessed at the date of breach, but it also holds that this is not an absolute rule, and that the court can fix some other date if justice so requires. Fifthly, the case says that the principles of assessment that govern common law damages also govern equitable damages awarded under section 2 of the Chancery Amendment Act 1858 (Lord Cairns' Act), which has since been re-enacted as the Supreme Court Act 1981, section 50.[2] Each of these findings will be discussed in turn, after an account has been given of the facts and reasoning of the case.

---

[1] Megarry J's decision in the Chancery Division on 25 February 1977 is unreported. The Court of Appeal's decision on 13 December 1977 is reported at: [1978] Ch 176; [1978] 2 WLR 806; [1978] 3 All ER 314; (1979) 38 P & CR 107. The House of Lords' decision on 8 March 1979 is reported at: [1980] AC 367; [1979] 2 WLR 487; [1979] 1 All ER 883; (1979) 38 P & CR 424; (1979) 251 EG 1167. References hereafter are to the appellate decisions in the Law Reports, ie [1978] Ch 176 and [1980] AC 367 respectively.

[2] Section 2 of the 1858 Act provided that '[i]n all cases in which the Court of Chancery has jurisdiction to entertain an application for an injunction against a breach of any covenant, contract, or agreement, or against the commission or continuance of any wrongful act, or for the specific performance of any covenant, contract, or agreement, it shall be lawful for the same court, if it shall think fit, to award damages to the party injured, either in addition to or in substitution for such

## B. THE FACTS

As Lord Wilberforce said at the time, the facts of *Johnson v Agnew* were 'commonplace, indeed routine'.[3] Michael and Renee Johnson owned a farm named Sheepcote Grange, in Woodburn Common, Buckinghamshire. The property consisted of the grange itself and some grazing land, both of which were mortgaged to various lending institutions. On 1 November 1973 the Johnsons entered a contract with Adeline Agnew, under which she agreed to buy the property for £117,000. The Johnsons had got into arrears with their mortgage repayments, but completion of the sale agreement would have placed ample funds at their disposal to pay off the mortgagees and buy a new property. Hence, they also entered a contract to buy another property from a third party for £34,000, taking out a bridging loan for the entire sum from their bank to finance this purchase. Agnew accepted the Johnsons' title (which disclosed the existence of the mortgages) and agreed a form of conveyance, but when the agreed date for completion arrived in December 1973, she failed to complete, and although the parties negotiated a new completion date in January 1974, she then failed to complete again.

In March 1974, the Johnsons issued a writ claiming specific performance or equitable damages under Lord Cairns' Act, or else a declaration that they were no longer bound to perform the contract, along with further relief. They won summary judgment for specific performance in June 1974, but the order was not drawn up and entered until November 1974, and they subsequently took no steps to enforce it. The mortgagees had won orders for possession and sale of the property in the meantime, and the Johnsons' lawyer advised them that there was no point in trying to enforce the court order against Agnew, because they would be unable to perform their own contractual obligations once the property was sold to satisfy the mortgagees. In the event, performance of the contract became impossible for the Johnsons on 3 April 1975, when the grazing land was sold; the grange was subsequently sold on 20 June 1975.

---

injunction or specific performance, and such damages may be assessed in such manner as the court shall direct'. The section was repealed by the Statute Law Revision and Civil Procedure Act 1883 because it was believed to be no more than a procedural section which had enabled the Chancery courts to award common law damages, and which had therefore been superseded by the Supreme Court of Judicature Act 1873: *Chapman, Morsons & Co v Guardians of Auckland Union* (1889) 23 QBD 294 (CA) 299 (Lord Esher MR). However, the House of Lords held in *Leeds Industrial Co-operative Society Ltd v Slack* [1924] AC 851 that the courts' jurisdiction to award damages under the 1858 Act had survived repeal of the statute, and many cases were subsequently decided on this basis until the Supreme Court Act 1981 s 50 unequivocally placed the court's jurisdiction to award equitable damages onto a statutory footing. For discussion, see JA Jolowicz, 'Damages in Equity— A Study of Lord Cairns' Act' [1975] *Cambridge Law Journal* 224, 227–30; PM McDermott, *Equitable Damages* (Sydney, Butterworths, 1994) ch 3; and for judicial statements that the courts' former jurisdiction under Lord Cairns' Act is now embodied by s 50, see eg *Jaggard v Sawyer* [1995] 1 WLR 269 (CA) 284 (Millett LJ); *Regan v Paul Properties DPF No 1 Ltd* [2006] EWCA Civ 1319, [2007] Ch 135 [24] (Mummery LJ).

    [3] *Johnson v Agnew* (HL) (n 1 above) 390.

The mortgagees realised about £48,000 when selling the properties. This was much less than the purchase price agreed by the parties, and in fact was not even enough to discharge the Johnsons' mortgage debts. The Johnsons were therefore faced with insolvency, and on 25 September 1974 a bankruptcy petition was presented by their creditors. However this was adjourned sine die, while the Johnsons sought to recover their situation by suing Agnew. On 5 November 1975, they issued proceedings against her seeking (1) an order that she should pay them the purchase price (less an amount which she had paid as a deposit, and giving credit for the amounts realised by the mortgagees' sales), and also an inquiry as to equitable damages, or alternatively (2) a declaration that they were entitled to treat the contract as having been repudiated, to keep the amount paid as a deposit, and to have an inquiry taken as to common law damages.

When the case came on for trial, the Johnsons were represented by Peter Millett QC, whose subsequent career as a distinguished judicial exponent of equitable doctrine needs no rehearsal here,[4] and Dirik Jackson. Counsel for Agnew were JH Hames QC and James Denniston. The case was heard at first instance by Megarry V-C, before whom the only remedy sought was the first part of the first head of relief described above. The Vice-Chancellor was not asked for equitable damages, nor was he asked to grant the second head of relief, although counsel reserved the right to ask for it on appeal. This was understood by both sides to be precluded by *Capital and Suburban Properties Ltd v Swycher*,[5] where the Court of Appeal had previously held that a claimant's decision to seek specific performance binds him to an irrevocable election—either when proceedings are initiated, or at the latest when the order is made—which subsequently prevents him from accepting the defendant's repudiation and asking for damages. Megarry V-C refused to grant the first head of relief because there was no mutuality between the parties: ie he would not order Agnew to perform her contractual obligations when the Johnsons could not provide her with counter-performance. Hence the Johnsons were left with nothing at all.

The Johnsons appealed, and the Court of Appeal upheld the Vice-Chancellor's refusal to order Agnew to pay them the balance of the purchase price. The court also declined to award common law damages, holding that this was precluded by *Swycher*. Buckley LJ had been a member of the court that had decided *Swycher* and he saw no reason to depart from his earlier view. However, he and the other members of the Court of Appeal in *Johnson* also held that the Johnsons were entitled to equitable damages under Lord Cairns' Act. Hence they discharged the order for specific performance which had been entered in November 1974, and ordered an inquiry as to equitable damages as at that date.

---

[4] In his judicial capacity he subsequently considered *Johnson* on several occasions: see *Hillel v Christoforides* (1991) 63 P & CR 301 (ChD) (discussed in the text to n 53 below); *Jaggard v Sawyer* [1995] 1 WLR 269 (CA) (discussed in the text to n 103 below); *Hurst v Bryk* [2000] UKHL 19, [2002] 1 AC 185, 193–4.

[5] *Capital and Suburban Properties Ltd v Swycher* [1976] 1 Ch 319.

Agnew appealed to the House of Lords, where the only speech of substance was given by Lord Wilberforce. Their Lordships overruled *Swycher* and held that where an order for specific performance has not been complied with, the claimant can come back into court with a view to having the order dissolved and a new order made, granting him permission to terminate the contract for breach and to claim common law damages. Hence the Johnsons were entitled to recover common law damages, and so the questions arose, (a) whether these are assessed on a different basis from equitable damages under Lord Cairns' Act, and (b) what is the date at which each type of damages should be assessed? Lord Wilberforce held that common law and equitable damages are assessed on the same basis, and that where the contract is one of sale, the principle that compensatory damages should place the claimant in the same position as if the contract had been performed normally leads to assessment of damages as at the date of breach. However the court has the power to fix some other date where this would be appropriate, and where the innocent party has reasonably continued to press for completion, but the contract has been lost for a reason other than his own fault, damages should be assessed as at the date when the contract is lost.

The appropriate date for assessing damages was therefore 3 April 1975, this having been the date when the Johnsons' remedy of specific performance had been aborted, for a reason that was not their fault—namely, the mortgagees' exercise of their power of sale. Responsibility for this lay with Agnew, since it would have been averted if she had paid the Johnsons and so enabled them to pay the mortgagees.[6] The upshot was that Agnew would have had to pay the Johnsons the difference between the contract price and the price realised by the mortgagees (subject to a set off for her deposit), since the Johnsons had been under no duty to mitigate their loss by seeking another purchaser prior to the date when the grazing land was sold, and afterwards they could not reasonably have been expected to find a purchaser for the grange before that was sold too, since this would have taken at least three months.[7]

## C. RETROSPECTIVE AND PROSPECTIVE DISCHARGE

In the course of finding for the Johnsons, the House of Lords overruled a line of cases, deriving from Sir George Jessel MR's dictum in *Henty v Schröder*, that a vendor of land

---

[6] The House of Lords seems to have agreed with the Court of Appeal's factual findings on this point, for which see *Johnson v Agnew* (CA) (n 1 above) 192–3 (Buckley LJ) and 199 (Goff LJ).

[7] Lord Wilberforce does not spell this out in his speech, but the significance of the date for assessment emerges from counsels' arguments: *Johnson v Agnew* (HL) (n 1 above) 387–8.

could not at the same time obtain an order to have the agreement rescinded and claim damages against the claimant for breach of the agreement.[8]

This statement had been followed several times, most notably by Romer J in *Barber v Wolfe*[9] and Megarry J in *Horsler v Zorro*,[10] both of whom had taken it to mean that acceptance of a repudiatory breach 'rescinds' the contract ab initio, so that the injured party can have a restitutionary claim to recover benefits he has transferred to the other party, but cannot claim damages for breach of contract because the contract is retrospectively deemed never to have existed. Both judges cited Cyprian Williams' influential practitioner texts on the sale of land, where *Henty* was given as authority for this proposition.[11] However, Williams' analysis was subsequently attacked in the *Law Quarterly Review* by Michael Albery QC,[12] whose criticisms were then found persuasive by Goff LJ in *Buckland v Farmer & Moody (a firm)*.[13] In that case the claimants were ordered to pay damages when they failed to complete a contract for the sale of land, and the vendor accepted their repudiation and 'rescinded' the contract. The claimants sued their solicitors in negligence for failing to advise them that the vendor could not recover damages following such a 'rescission', and their claim was rejected, both Buckley and Goff LJJ holding that damages were available in cases of this kind.[14]

In *Johnson*, Albery's article and Goff LJ's comments in *Buckland* were both drawn to the attention of the House of Lords by counsel for the Johnsons, who invited their Lordships to give Williams' 'heresy' the coup de grace.[15] Lord Wilberforce duly obliged, overruling *Henty*, *Barber*, and *Horsler*,[16] and making some tart remarks about 'the dangers . . . of placing reliance on textbook authority for an analysis of judicial decisions'.[17] Lord Wilberforce also held that

> whatever contrary indications might be disinterred from old authorities, it is now quite clear, under the general law of contract, that acceptance of a repudiatory breach does not bring about 'rescission ab initio'[18]

and this rule applied to contracts for the sale of land just as it did to every other contract. Hence, when the Johnsons had eventually accepted Agnew's repudiation, the contract had been prospectively discharged, and so there was no conceptual obstacle to their recovering common law damages.

---

[8] *Henty v Schröder* (1879) 12 Ch D 666 (ChD) 667.

[9] *Barber v Wolfe* [1945] Ch 187 (ChD), esp 189.

[10] *Horsler v Zorro* [1975] Ch 302 (ChD), esp 309 and 311.

[11] TC Williams, *The Contract of Sale of Land* (London, Sweet & Maxwell, 1930) 119; TC Williams, *Treatise on the Law of Vendor and Purchaser*, 4th edn, JM Lightwood (ed) (London, Sweet & Maxwell, 1936) vol II 993, 1004, and 1006. Williams cited other authorities, but only one was on point, namely *Hutchings v Humphreys* (1885) 54 LJ Ch 650 (ChD), where North J simply followed *Henty*.

[12] M Albery, 'Mr Cyprian Williams' Great Heresy' (1975) 91 *Law Quarterly Review* 337.

[13] *Buckland v Farmer & Moody (a firm)* [1979] 1 WLR 221 (CA) 237.

[14] *Ibid* 231–2 and 237–8.

[15] *Johnson v Agnew* (HL) (n 1 above) 385–6.

[16] *Johnson v Agnew* (HL) (n 1 above) 398.

[17] *Johnson v Agnew* (HL) (n 1 above) 395.

[18] *Johnson v Agnew* (HL) (n 1 above) 393.

Disinterring some of the old authorities pre-dating *Henty*, one finds that the idea of retrospective discharge dates back at least to *Dutch v Warren*,[19] a case decided in the Court of Common Pleas in 1720, where it was said that a plaintiff who paid money under a contract which was breached by the other party could rescind the contract ab initio and recover his money via an action for money had and received. Later cases extending well into the second half of the 19th century took the same line, requiring contracts to be set aside retrospectively before an action for money had and received or a quantum meruit action would lie. So, for example, in *Hochster v de la Tour*, Crompton J observed in the course of argument[20]:

> When a party announces his intention not to fulfil the contract, the other side may take him at his word and rescind the contract. The word 'rescind' implies that both parties have agreed that the contract shall be at an end as if it had never been.

However, this was not the aggrieved party's only option, for Crompton J thought that[21]

> the party may also say: 'Since you have announced that you will not go on with the contract, I will consent that it shall be at an end from this time; but I will hold you liable for the damage you have sustained; and I will proceed to make that damage as little as possible by making the best use I can of my liberty'.

Retrospective and prospective discharge were therefore seen as alternatives. Where a repudiatory breach was committed, a plaintiff might decide to ask for rescission of the contract ab initio if, for example, he could recover more by bringing an action for money had and received than he could by bringing an action for compensatory damages. But if he chose this option, then he would put it beyond his power to ask for damages, since these could only be awarded for a breach of contract, and no breach could have occurred if there had never been a contract. In other situations, the plaintiff's better option was to ask for the contract to be prospectively discharged, and many authorities make it clear that plaintiffs were entitled to do this in the 18th and 19th centuries.[22] For example, the fact that a vendor had accepted a purchaser's repudiatory breach was no bar to the enforcement of a resale condition that was commonly inserted into contracts for the sale of land—something which would have been impossible if the

---

[19] *Dutch v Warren* (1720) 1 Stra 406, 93 ER 598. For a more accurate report, the editor directs the reader to Lord Mansfield's discussion in *Moses v Macferlan* (1760) 2 Burr 1005, 1010–11; 97 ER 676, 680.

[20] *Hochster v De la Tour* (1853) 2 E & B 678, 685; 118 ER 922, 924–5. See also *Bartholomew v Markwick* (1864) 15 CBNS 711, 716; 143 ER 964, 966 (Erle CJ); and for additional cases and secondary sources, see C Mitchell and C Mitchell '*Planché v Colburn*' in C Mitchell and P Mitchell (eds), *Landmark Cases in the Law of Restitution* (Oxford, Hart Publishing, 2006) 65, 89–91.

[21] *Ibid*.

[22] TA Baloch, 'Legal History: The Beginning But Not Necessarily the End' (2007) 18 *King's College Law Journal* 187, 193–5, gives several examples.

clause had been retrospectively wiped away with the rest of the contract.[23] Still more pertinently for present purposes, in both *Sweet v Meredith*[24] and *Watson v Cox*,[25] a decree was made for specific performance of a contract for the sale of land, the defendant failed to comply with the order, and the plaintiff was then given a further order discharging the contract and ordering an enquiry into the assessment of damages.

Returning to *Henty*, we find that the facts of the case were essentially identical with those in *Sweet* and *Watson*, but although they were cited to him, Sir George Jessel MR declined to follow these authorities, and said that the plaintiff could not win an order to have the agreement rescinded and simultaneously claim damages. The report of *Henty* is very brief, and the judge's comments are not explained, but it is difficult to believe that he intended to make new law by holding that rescission ab initio was the only possible consequence of accepting a repudiatory breach, leaving the plaintiff with no means of recovering damages. Possibly he confused 'rescission' for breach of contract and 'rescission' for inherent invalidity by reason of misrepresentation or undue influence[26]—although in *Johnson* Lord Wilberforce thought this a 'desperate hypothesis'.[27] Alternatively, it may be that Jessel MR's comments were directed towards a pleading point. One possibility, canvassed in *Johnson*,[28] is that the plaintiff in *Henty* had failed to file a new bill, contrary to the finding in *Hythe Corporation v East*[29] that the Chancery courts could not make a damages award by way of supplementary decree on motion to a plaintiff who had previously won a decree of specific performance: in other words, plaintiffs in this position were required to bring a fresh set of proceedings to recover damages.[30]

Whatever the true explanation of *Henty*, it was definitively overruled in *Johnson*, and it is now beyond doubt not merely that prospective discharge can follow acceptance of a defendant's repudiatory breach of contract, but also that this is its *only* possible effect, rescission ab initio having fallen by the

---

[23] *Ibid* 193–4, citing *Hagedorn v Laing* (1815) 6 Taunt 163, 128 ER 996; *Maclean v Dunn* (1828) 4 Bing 722, 130 ER 947; *Icely v Grew* (1836) 6 Nev & Man 467, 469; *Lamond v Davell* (1847) 9 QB 1030, 115 ER 1569; and earlier cases in E Sugden, *Practical Treatise of the Law of Vendors and Purchasers of Estates* (London, Brook and Clark and Butterworth, 1805) 25.

[24] *Sweet v Meredith* (1863) 4 Giff 207, 66 ER 680. See also *Clark v Wallis* (1866) 35 Beav 460, 55 ER 974.

[25] *Watson v Cox* (1873) LR 15 Eq 219; also reported at (1873) 42 LJ Ch 279.

[26] As argued in Albery, 'Mr Cyprian Williams' Great Heresy' (n 12 above) 342.

[27] *Johnson v Agnew* (HL) (n 1 above) 394.

[28] *Johnson v Agnew* (HL) (n 1 above) 384. See also Lord Wilberforce's comments at 394–5.

[29] *Hythe Corporation v East* (1866) LR 1 Eq 620.

[30] It would have been characteristic of Sir George Jessel to spring a point of this kind on counsel without warning. Compare his deployment of the Common Law Procedure Act 1854 s 79 and the Judicature Act 1873 s 25(8) to grant injunctions in *Beddow v Beddow* (1878) 9 Ch D 89, *Anglo-Italian Bank v Davies* (1878) 9 Ch D 275, and *Aslatt v Southampton Corp* (1880) 16 Ch D 143; all discussed in P Mitchell, *The Making of the Modern Law of Defamation* (Oxford, Hart Publishing, 2005) 87–8.

wayside.[31] However, this prompts a further question. Given that retrospective discharge was formerly thought to be a necessary preliminary to quantum meruit actions and actions for money had and received, can such claims now lie in cases where a repudiatory breach has been accepted, and a contract has been prospectively discharged? Much of the reasoning in the old cases depended on a theory of 'quasi-contractual' claims which has now been discredited.[32] The courts thought that claims of this kind rested on an implied contract between the parties, which bound the defendant to make restitution to the claimant. This led them to hold that no restitutionary claim would lie while the parties' relationship was governed by an express contract that remained 'open' because it had not been rescinded ab initio—the problem being that the terms of the express contract entitling the defendant to keep the benefit would contradict the terms of an implied contract requiring restitution. This implied contract reasoning would no longer be thought correct. However, concerns remain that allowing a claim in unjust enrichment while an inconsistent promise subsists between the parties would subvert their contractual allocation of risk, suggesting that restitutionary recovery should be denied where a contract has been prospectively terminated, to the extent that this would contradict accrued rights under the contract.[33] Where a claim in unjust enrichment would not contradict accrued rights, however, there can be no objection in principle to restitutionary recovery merely by dint of the fact that other aspects of the parties' relationship are still governed by their agreement. Hence, as Lord Atkin held in *Fibrosa Spolka Akcyjna v Fairbairn Lawson Combe Barbour Ltd*, the right to recover money paid under a contract for a consideration that has subsequently failed does 'not depend on the contract being void ab initio'.[34]

---

[31] Besides Lord Wilberforce's comments in *Johnson*, notable dicta to this effect include: *Boston Deep Sea Fishing and Ice Co v Ansell* (1888) 39 Ch D 339 (CA) 365 (Bowen LJ); *Macdonald v Dennys Lascelles Ltd* (1933) 48 CLR 457, 476–7 (Dixon J); *Heyman v Darwins Ltd* [1942] AC 356 (HL) 399 (Lord Porter); *Fibrosa Spolka Akcyjna v Fairbairn Lawson Coombe Barbour Ltd* [1943] AC 32 (HL) 52–3 (Lord Atkin) and 65 (Lord Wright); *Moschi v Lep Air Services Ltd* [1973] AC 331 (HL) 349–50 (Lord Diplock) (though cf Lord Simon's comments at 356); *Photo Production Ltd v Securicor Ltd* [1980] 1 AC 827 (HL) 844–5 (Lord Wilberforce); *Bank of Boston Connecticut v European Grain and Shipping Ltd, The Dominique* [1989] AC 1056 (HL) 1098–9 (Lord Brandon); *Manifest Shipping Co Ltd v Uni-Polaris Insurance Co Ltd, The Star Sea* [2001] UKHL 1, [2003] 1 AC 469 [50] (Lord Hobhouse).

[32] *Fibrosa Spolka Akcyjna v Fairbairn Lawson Combe Barbour Ltd* [1943] AC 32 (HL) 63–4 (Lord Wright); *Pavey & Matthews Pty Ltd v Paul* (1987) 162 CLR 221, 227 and 254–7; *Baltic Shipping Co v Dillon* (1993) 176 CLR 344, 356–7; *Westdeutsche Landesbank Girozentrale v Islington LBC* [1996] AC 669 (HL) 710 (Lord Browne-Wilkinson).

[33] See, eg *Taylor v Motability Finance Ltd* [2004] EWHC 2619 (Comm) [24]–[25] (Cooke J). See also G McMeel, 'Unjust Enrichment, Discharge for Breach, and the Primacy of Contract' in A Burrows and Lord Rodger (eds), *Mapping the Law* (Oxford, Oxford University Press, 2006) 223.

[34] *Fibrosa Spolka Akcyjna v Fairbairn Lawson Combe Barbour Ltd* [1943] AC 32 (HL) 57, instancing *Wright v Newton* (1835) 2 C M & R 124 by way of example—a case in which money paid as deposit in a contract of sale was recoverable where the contract was defeated by the fulfillment of a condition subsequent. See also *Roxborough v Rothmans Pall Mall Australia Ltd* (2001) 208 CLR 516, where the court was even willing to countenance recovery of benefits under a contract which was neither unenforceable, void, voidable, nor discharged for breach or frustration, but where the basis upon which the defendant had been paid had ceased to be capable of performance.

Where a benefit has been transferred under a contract that is prospectively discharged, a sensitive exercise in construction may have to be undertaken to determine the basis of the transfer and whether it failed. The court must attend to the difference between the right to receive a benefit, retention of which is conditional upon the happening of a future event, and the right to receive a benefit, retention of which is not conditional upon anything. The court must also bear in mind that the basis of the transfer may not have failed, even though the claimant seems not to have obtained what he wanted in return. For example, the basis of a payment will not have failed if it was intended to be a deposit to bind the payer to perform,[35] or to be payment for work actually done in the performance of the contract,[36] or to be recoverable only within a contractual regime for repayment.[37] It is also worth remembering that in some cases, even if the basis has not failed, the claimant may still have some hope of restitution under the courts' jurisdiction to relieve from penalties and forfeitures.[38]

Some of the possibilities are illustrated by *Mayson v Clouet*.[39] There a purchaser of land paid a deposit and instalments towards the purchase price, but then failed to pay the balance. The vendor terminated the contract for breach and the question arose whether the purchaser could recover his payments. The Privy Council held that the extent of his restitutionary entitlement must depend on the terms of the contract. This provided that the deposit was non-refundable and so the vendor could keep it, as he had an accrued contractual right to do so. However, the instalments could be recovered, as it was clear from the contract that they would not be forfeited in the event of the purchaser's breach.

## D. ELECTION

In *Capital and Suburban Properties Ltd v Swycher*,[40] the Court of Appeal held that a claimant who seeks specific performance makes an irrevocable election that prevents him from subsequently claiming damages from the other party. This decision was partly motivated by a desire to rationalise *Henty*, although their Lordships went further than Jessel MR because the logic of their analysis

---

[35] *Howe v Smith* (1884) 27 Ch D 89; *Monnickendam v Leanse* (1923) 39 TLR 445.

[36] *Hyundai Heavy Industries Co Ltd v Papadopoulos* [1980] 1 WLR 1129 (HL); *Stocznia Gdanska SA v Latvian Shipping Co* [1988] 1 WLR 574 (HL).

[37] *Pan Ocean Shipping Corporation v Creditcorp Ltd, The Trident Beauty* [1994] 1 WLR 161 (HL).

[38] But NB the majority judgments in *Stockloser v Johnson* [1954] 1 QB 476 (CA) must now be read in the restrictive light of *Shiloh Spinners Ltd v Harding* [1973] AC 691 (HL) and *Union Eagle Ltd v Golden Achievement Ltd* [1997] AC 514 (PC); and cf *On Demand Information plc v Michael Gerson (Finance) plc* [2001] 1 WLR 155 (CA).

[39] *Mayson v Clouet* [1924] 1 AC 980 (PC), followed in: *Macdonald v Denis Lascelles Ltd* (1933) 48 CLR 457; *Dies v British International Mining and Finance Corp Ltd* [1939] 1 KB 724 (KBD); *Gallagher v Shilcock* [1949] 2 KB 765 (KBD); *Rover International Ltd v Cannon Film Sales Ltd (No 3)* [1989] 1 WLR 912 (CA).

[40] *Capital and Suburban Properties Ltd v Swycher* (n 5 above).

led them to conclude that *Sweet* and *Watson* had been wrongly decided. Buckley LJ gave two reasons for the election rule. The first was that damages and specific performance are mutually inconsistent, because a claimant vendor cannot ask for damages for breach 'and at the same time compel the purchaser to remedy the breach by performing the contract',[41] and so a claimant's decision to ask for specific performance necessarily entails a decision to forfeit his right to claim damages. The second reason was that allowing the claimant to recover damages would be pointless because it would not improve his position once he had won a decree of specific performance. This followed from the fact that a vendor who won an order for specific performance could 'work out' the decree by recovering the price due from the purchaser, if necessary by exercising his vendor's lien, and the amount recoverable by this means would never be less than the amount of damages which might be awarded.[42]

In *Johnson* Lord Wilberforce held that this reasoning was unsound, and overruled *Swycher*.[43] He accepted that it would be inconsistent for a claimant who has terminated the contract and won damages to come back into court and ask for specific performance, because the parties' relationship has come to an end. But he held that the converse proposition does not hold true, because an order for specific performance does not prolong the parties' relationship eternally and unconditionally. Instead the contract is kept provisionally alive while the claimant tries to enforce it, and if these efforts prove unsuccessful, then there is no inconsistency in allowing him subsequently to terminate the contract and recover damages. Buckley LJ's second reason was equally flawed. As the facts of *Johnson* showed, situations can arise where a claimant simply cannot 'work out' a decree of specific performance by performing his own obligations in exchange for the defendant's counter-performance, for example because the intervention of third party rights renders the claimant's performance impossible. In such cases the claimant's only remedy must be a damages award. The whole of Buckley LJ's reasoning also proved too much, since it suggested not only that the claimant should be denied damages, but also that he should be denied the right to rescind the contract (something to which Buckley LJ thought he should be entitled, in line with *Henty*[44]).

## E. JUDICIAL DISCRETION TO DISSOLVE ORDERS FOR SPECIFIC PERFORMANCE

Lord Wilberforce's reasons for rejecting *Swycher* are compelling. Less happily, though, he also held that when a decree of specific performance is made, the

---

41  *Capital and Suburban Properties Ltd v Swycher* (n 5 above) 327.
42  *Capital and Suburban Properties Ltd v Swycher* (n 5 above) 328.
43  *Johnson v Agnew* (HL) (n 1 above) 398–9.
44  *Johnson v Agnew* (CA) (n 1 above) 188.

contract continues 'under control of the court',[45] so that a further court order is needed to dissolve the decree before either party can terminate the contract for breach and ask for damages. Furthermore, he held that the court can decline to dissolve the decree 'if to do so would be unjust'.[46] The advantage of this is that it enables the court to prevent a claimant who has won an order for specific performance from changing his mind and asserting a right to damages after the defendant has detrimentally relied on the court's original order. However, it means that whenever an order for specific performance is made, the parties' original rights under the contract are replaced by a set of new equitable rights which replicate the parties' original rights—including the right to terminate the contract for breach—but which are subject to equitable principles that would not have affected the parties' original rights at common law. This model of the law is complex, and it is inconsistent with Lord Wilberforce's own statement that

> if an order for specific performance is sought and is made, the contract remains in effect and is not merged in the judgment for specific performance.[47]

It is also inconsistent with Clawson LJ's previous statement in *John Barker & Co Ltd v Littman* that the court has no 'dispensing power' to dissolve an order for specific performance and order the forfeiture of a purchaser's deposit, because a vendor has the right to these things *ex debito justitiae*.[48] Hence there is much to be said for the different view that even after an order for specific performance has been made, both parties' common law rights under the contract subsist, including the right to terminate for breach and sue for damages, and that either party can exercise these rights without complying with equitable requirements such as the rule that a claimant must come into court with clean hands.[49]

Lord Wilberforce's rule was applied in *GKN Distributors Ltd v Tyne Tees Fabrication Ltd*,[50] where Nourse J held that it was 'no mere formality', and that it prevented a vendor of land who had won an order for specific performance from reselling the land to a third party without obtaining the consent of the purchaser or first applying to the court to dissolve the order and asking it to put an

---

[45] *Johnson v Agnew* (HL) (n 1 above) 398. See also Megarry V-C's comments in *Singh (Sudagar) v Nazeer* [1979] Ch 474 (ChD) 480–1: 'By applying to the court for an order of specific performance, and obtaining it, I think that the applicant has put it into the hands of the court how the contract is to be carried out. As the court has become seised of the matter, and has made an order, it seems to me that subject to anything that the parties may then agree, the working out, variation or cancellation of that order is essentially a matter for the court'.

[46] *Johnson v Agnew* (HL) (n 1 above) 399.

[47] *Johnson v Agnew* (HL) (n 1 above) 393, citing *Austins of East Ham Ltd v Macey* [1941] Ch 338 (CA) 341, where Sir Wilfrid Greene MR stressed that after an order for specific performance has been made 'the contract is still there'.

[48] *John Barker & Co Ltd v Littman* [1941] Ch 405 (CA) 412.

[49] M Hetherington, 'Keeping the Plaintiff out of his Contractual Remedies: The Heresies that Survive *Johnson v Agnew*' (1980) 96 *Law Quarterly Review* 403; RP Meagher, JD Heydon and MJ Leeming (eds), *Meagher, Gummow and Lehane's Equity: Doctrines and Remedies*, 4th edn (Sydney, Butterworths, 2002) para 20-265.

[50] *GKN Distributors Ltd v Tyne Tees Fabrication Ltd* [1985] 2 EGLR 181 (ChD).

end to the contract. The rule was also reviewed in *Gill v Tsang*[51] by Geoffrey Vos QC, sitting as a deputy High Court judge, who held that when exercising its discretion the court is not limited to a stark choice between dissolving or continuing the order, as it can also vary the terms of the original order, at least to the extent that this does not entail substantially rewriting the terms of the parties' bargain.[52]

For the most considered judicial examination of the court's discretion, however, we must go to Millett J's decision in *Hillel v Christoforides*.[53] There the claimant vendor agreed to sell his flat to the defendant purchaser for £240,000. The purchaser paid £200,000, which he had borrowed from Nationwide. The vendor used this money to pay off a first charge over the property, and to repay part of a debt to Barclays that was secured by a second charge. The purchaser went into possession, but he never paid the balance of the purchase price and completion never took place. After a year the vendor obtained an order for specific performance, with which the purchaser did not comply. After another year the vendor obtained a four-day peremptory order directing the purchaser to pay. The purchaser also failed to comply with this order. Finally, the vendor issued proceedings, seeking dissolution of the decree of specific performance, permission to treat the contract as terminated, and an inquiry into damages. By this time the purchaser owed him around £55,000.

Before these proceedings came on for hearing, Barclays obtained an order for possession and sale of the property, and said that it would not permit redemption of its charge until the vendor repaid the whole of his debt: a sum of around £180,000. This led the purchaser to argue at trial that the vendor had never been able to give good title, because Barclays would never have released its charge over the flat without receiving full payment. It followed that the contract had gone off by reason of the vendor's own default, and according to *Johnson*, this meant that the court should not grant the vendor an order dissolving the decree of specific performance. Millett J rejected this argument on the facts because the (exiguous) evidence suggested that the vendor could have cleared the charge off the title at the time when he won the four-day order. The purchaser also argued that the decree should not be dissolved because the vendor could not return the £200,000 which had been paid on to the mortgagees. Millett J rejected this, too, holding that although the vendor would undoubtedly have a cross-claim to restitution of the money following discharge of the contract for breach,

> the vendor's right to bring the contract to an end by the purchaser's breach [was] not in any way conditional upon his ability to return the money,

and the position was the same as regards the vendor's ability to secure the court's permission to dissolve the decree of specific performance.[54]

[51] *Gill v Tsang* (Ch D) 10 July 2003.
[52] *Ibid* [35]–[36] and [43]–[54].
[53] *Hillel v Christoforides* (1991) 63 P & CR 301 (ChD).
[54] *Ibid* 306.

Reviewing the relevant passage of Lord Wilberforce's speech in *Johnson* in an effort to discern the principles which should guide the exercise of his discretion, Millett J made the following observations[55]:

> It is not easy to discern the basis of the supposed discretion to grant or withhold an order dissolving the decree of specific performance and permitting the innocent party to treat the other's breach as repudiatory. As a result, it is not easy to discern principles upon which the discretion falls to be exercised. However, Lord Wilberforce referred to the application of ordinary equitable principles, and since the right to treat a repudiatory breach of contract as discharging the contract is a common law right, inherent in the contract itself, I take the relevant equitable principle to be the fundamental principle of equity which will not permit a party unconscionably to insist upon his legal rights. That is consistent with the decision in *Johnson v Agnew* itself. Once the innocent party, having obtained a decree of specific performance, gives notice that he proposes to ask the court to permit him to rescind the contract, the other party is on notice. He should complete at once, for he can no longer rely upon the subsistence of the decree of specific performance to give him further time in which to fulfil his contractual obligations.
>
> The essential question which the court must ask itself is whether, in the circumstances as they obtained at the date when that notice was given, it would be unconscionable for the innocent party to exercise his legal right to treat himself as discharged by the other's breach. Accordingly, I do not accept that the court has an unfettered discretion to consider what in all the circumstances of the case might be the fairest thing to do at the date of the hearing. The fundamental consideration must be that on a past date the applicant has given notice of his intention to treat the other party's repudiatory breach of contract as discharging him from all further performance of the contract.

Exercising his discretion with these principles in mind, Millett J concluded that the decree of specific performance should be dissolved as requested by the vendor, and that the contract should be treated as discharged by reason of the purchaser's breach[56]:

> The fundamental fact is that for a very long period after the date of completion had passed and until the vendor served his motion of notice electing, so far as lay within his power, to bring the contract to an end, the purchaser had the opportunity to perform his contractual obligations, pay the balance of the purchase price and obtain title. He did not do so and it is too late now. The contract has gone off by the default of the purchaser. In my judgment, by failing to complete before the vendor served the notice of motion, and thus obtaining the full benefit of his payment of the instalments

[55] *Hillel v Christoforides* (n 53 above) 304.

[56] *Hillel v Christoforides* (n 53 above) 307. Cf *Ahmed v Wingrove* [2007] EWHC 1777 (Ch) where an order for specific performance was made against the vendors of property but the purchaser failed to complete because (a) the vendors asserted a right of way over an access strip to their retained land (a claim they later abandoned), and (b) the purchaser was not satisfied that the vendors had placed a boundary fence in the right place and they would not let him onto the property to check. Since time was not of the essence of the contract, the judge refused the vendors' application for dissolution of the order, and instead issued a new timetable for completion.

of the purchase price, the purchaser took the risk not only that the vendor would not complete but that the vendor would be unable to return the whole of the purchase money.

## F.  COMMON LAW DAMAGES: DATE OF ASSESSMENT

There is a striking contrast between Millett J's finding that the court should not exercise its discretion to dissolve a decree of specific performance with an eye to all the circumstances as they are known at the date of the hearing, and Lord Wilberforce's view in *Johnson*, that the date for assessing common law damages need not always be the date of breach, but can be some other date if justice so requires, for example the date when the contract was lost.[57] On Millett J's view, developments subsequent to an injured party's decision to accept the other party's repudiation should be ignored when deciding whether to set aside a decree of specific performance; on Lord Wilberforce's view, developments subsequent to this date may be taken into account when assessing common law damages. Equity thus appears to be less flexible than the common law.

Lord Wilberforce cited various authorities supporting his principle,[58] and it has been followed in various contract cases where it has worked to the claimant's advantage to assess damages as at a later date than the date of breach.[59] Where a contract for the sale of land has been breached, the usual measure of damages is the claimant's loss of profit.[60] Hence disappointed vendors are usually awarded the amount by which the contract price exceeds the market price,[61] along with any consequential losses, such as the expenses of

---

[57]  *Johnson v Agnew* (HL) (n 1 above) 400–401.

[58]  *Ogle v Earl Vane* (1867) LR 2 QB 275 (QB); aff'd (1868) LR 3 QB 272 (Exch); *Hickman v Haynes* (1875) LR 10 CP 598; *Radford v De Froberville* [1977] 1 WLR 1262 (ChD).

[59]  Eg *Johnson Matthey Bankers Ltd v State Trading Corp of India* [1984] 1 Lloyd's Rep 127 (QBD (Comm Ct)); *Carbopego-Abastecimento de Combustiveis SA v AMCI Export Corp*, [2006] EWHC 72 (Comm), [2006] 1 Lloyd's Rep 736; *Bear Stearns Bank plc v Forum Global Equity Ltd* [2007] EWHC 1576 (Comm).

The principle is by no means confined to breach of contract cases, but also extends to the law of tort: *Suleman v Shahsavari* [1988] 1 WLR 1181(ChD) (breach of warranty of authority); *Smith New Court Securities Ltd v Srimgeour Vickers (Asset Management) Ltd* [1997] AC 254 (HL) (deceit); *Alcoa Minerals of Jamaica Inc v Broderick* [2002] 1 AC 371 (PC) (nuisance).

[60]  It was formerly the case that where a vendor breached a contract for the sale of land, the purchaser might be limited to damages for wasted expenditure by the rule in *Bain v Fothergill* (1874) LR 7 HL 158, which applied where the reason for the vendor's breach was his inability to show a good title for a reason other than his own fault. This anomalous rule—which ultimately derived from *Flureau v Thornhill* (1776) 2 W Bl 1078, 96 ER 635—was abrogated by the Law of Property (Miscellaneous Provisions) Act 1989 s 3. Obviously, a purchaser might still prefer to claim wasted expenditure in a case where this outstrips his loss of profit (if any): see, eg *Lloyd v Stanbury* [1971] 1 WLR 535 (ChD).

[61]  *Laird v Pim* (1841) 7 M & W 474, 478; 151 ER 852, 854 (Parke B). Where the property is resold soon after the purchaser's breach, the resale price will often be taken as strong evidence of the market value, depending on the circumstances of the resale: *Noble v Edwardes* (1877) 5 Ch D 378; *York Glass Co Ltd v Jubb* (1925) 134 LT 36; *Keck v Faber* (1926) 134 LT 36.

the abortive sale[62]; conversely, disappointed purchasers are usually awarded the amount by which the market price exceeds the contract price,[63] along with any additional profits that they may have hoped to make from dealing with or developing the property,[64] provided that these were reasonably within the contemplation of the parties at the time when the contract was entered.[65] In modern conditions, the market value of real property tends to increase with the passing of time, so that it lies in the interests of a purchaser, rather than a vendor, to argue for a later date for the assessment of damages. That purchasers can do this is strongly suggested by *Wroth v Tyler*,[66] a case on equitable damages under Lord Cairns' Act which is considered in the next section.

First, though, another question arises in connection with the date for assessment of common law damages, namely whether the courts have a discretion to set a date later than the date of breach not only where this would work to the advantage of the claimant, but also where it would work to the advantage of the defendant? This issue was not addressed by Lord Wilberforce in *Johnson*, but as Andrew Burrows has written,[67]

> logical symmetry, avoidance of overcompensation, and adherence to the duty to mitigate dictate that the same flexibility should be adopted as where assessment at a later date is to the claimant's advantage.

Support for this view can now be derived from *Golden Strait Corp v Nippon Yusen Kubishika Kaisha, The Golden Victory*,[68] which concerned a time-charter for seven years that was wrongfully repudiated by the charterers when they re-delivered the vessel four years early, in December 2001. The owners accepted the repudiation and terminated the contract. The question then arose whether the damages payable by the charterers should be assessed in relation to the whole of the outstanding term of the contract, or only between the date of termination and March 2003, when the second Gulf War broke out. The charterparty contained a war clause, and the charterers argued that they would have invoked this clause to repudiate the contract, so that it would now be inappropriate for the court to award damages for the owners' loss between March 2003 and December 2005. The Court of Appeal found for the charterers,

---

[62] *Essex v Daniell* (1875) LR 10 CP 538 (Div Ct of CP) 553 (Brett LJ).

[63] *Engell v Fitch* (1869) LR 4 QB 659; *Diamond v Campbell-Jones* [1961] Ch 22 (ChD). Again, where the property is resold soon after the vendor's breach, for example because the vendor has broken his contract in order to sell at a higher price to another party, the resale price may be taken as evidence of the market value: *Godwin v Francis* (1870) LR 5 CP 295; *Goffin v Houlder* (1921) 90 LJ Ch 488; *Ridley v De Geerts* [1945] 2 All ER 654 (CA).

[64] *Cottrill v Steyning & Littlehampton BS* [1966] 1 WLR 753 (QBD); *Malhotra v Choudhury* [1980] Ch 52 (CA) 80 (Cumming-Bruce LJ).

[65] Under the rule in *Hadley v Baxendale* (1854) 9 Exch 341, 156 ER 145.

[66] *Wroth v Tyler* [1974] Ch 30 (ChD).

[67] AS Burrows, *Remedies for Torts and Breach of Contract*, 3rd edn (Oxford, Oxford University Press, 2004) 192–3.

[68] *Golden Strait Corp v Nippon Yusen Kubishika Kaisha, The Golden Victory* [2007] UKHL 12, [2007] 2 AC 353.

holding that the paramount consideration should be to achieve an assessment which most accurately reflects

> the actual loss which the owners can, at whatever is the date of assessment, now be seen to have suffered.[69]

This decision was upheld by a majority of the House of Lords, who held that the need to avoid over-compensation outweighed the need for commercial certainty.

The dissenting minority held precisely the opposite, and there can be no doubt that the effect of the majority's decision is to open up a wide field for litigation. As was observed by Sir Guenter Treitel,[70] supervening events which follow termination for breach can come in many forms, making it difficult to predict when the courts will say that they should be taken into account when assessing damages. One knotty issue is whether a defendant should escape liability for damages by pointing to a cancellation clause in the contract, and arguing that he would have invoked the clause at some time after the date of breach, in order to escape from a bad bargain? Another is whether it should make a difference that the defendant has made a profit through his wrongdoing? Outside the law of contract, we find *Solloway v McLaughlin*[71] and *BBMB Finance (Hong Kong) Ltd v Eda Holdings Ltd*,[72] which hold that where goods are irreversibly converted and not recovered, but are later replaced by the defendant with substitute goods bought for lower price, then the court should assess damages as at the date of conversion, so that the claimant can recover the difference between the market price at the date of conversion and the market price at the date of replacement. However, it requires a stretch to say that these cases are concerned with compensating the claimant, and in *Kuwait Airways v Iraqi Airways (Nos 4 and 5)* Lord Nicholls preferred to view them as examples of cases where damages were assessed 'by reference to the benefit obtained by the wrongdoer'.[73]

## G. EQUITABLE DAMAGES UNDER LORD CAIRNS'S ACT: PRINCIPLES OF QUANTIFICATION

In *Wroth v Tyler*[74] the defendant vendor lived with his wife and (adult) daughter in a bungalow. He entered a contract with the claimants to sell the bungalow

---

[69] *Golden Strait Corp v Nippon Yusen Kubishika Kaisha, The Golden Victory* [2006] EWCA Civ 1190, [2006] 1 WLR 533 [26] (Lord Mance). Cf *Findlay v Howard* (1919) 58 SCR 516, 544 (Mignault J): 'Where future damages are claimed, future conditions must necessarily be considered, and what better evidence of conditions, which were in the future at the date of breach, can be made than by shewing, at the date of trial, what has actually occurred since the breach of contract?'.

[70] Sir GH Treitel, 'Assessment of Damages for Wrongful Repudiation' (2007) 123 *Law Quarterly Review* 9, 16.

[71] *Solloway v McLaughlin* [1938] AC 247 (PC).

[72] *BBMB Finance (Hong Kong) Ltd v Eda Holdings Ltd* [1990] 1 WLR 409 (PC).

[73] *Kuwait Airways v Iraqi Airways (Nos 4 and 5)* [2002] UKHL 19, [2002] 2 AC 883 [87]–[89].

[74] *Wroth v Tyler* (n 66 above).

with vacant possession for £6,000. After contracts had been exchanged, the defendant's wife entered a notice onto the Land Register of her rights of occupation under the Matrimonial Homes Act 1967. She did not want to move, and she hit on this device as a means of preventing the sale from going ahead. The defendant failed to persuade her to remove this notice, and so he had to tell the claimant purchasers that he could not complete. He offered to pay damages, but the claimants issued a writ seeking specific performance, equitable damages under Lord Cairns' Act, and other relief. Megarry J refused to order specific performance, as this would effectively force the defendant to bring proceedings against his wife and might split up their family. However, he considered that the claimants were entitled to equitable damages, and so the question arose whether the date at which these should be assessed was the date of breach, which was taken to be the date fixed for completion (when the bungalow had been worth £7,500), or the date of trial (by which time the value of the bungalow had risen to £11,500).[75] Megarry J fixed on the latter date, and awarded equitable damages of £5,500, rejecting the argument that the defendant should not pay so much because the scale of the increase in house prices was not in the contemplation of the parties, albeit that some rise in prices had been contemplated.[76]

Arguing in favour of this outcome, counsel for the purchasers had cited cases holding that the date for assessment of common law damages need not always be the date of breach, and had invited Megarry J to follow these, on the basis that the principles governing the assessment of common law and equitable damages were the same.[77] However, Megarry J found it unnecessary to refer to these authorities because he thought that different principles govern the assessment of common law and equitable damages.[78] He gave two reasons for this. First, it was clear that damages are available under Lord Cairns' Act in situations where they cannot be awarded at common law, as in *Eastwood v Lever*,[79] where the right infringed was a purely equitable right under a restrictive covenant to which the defendant was not a party, and *Leeds Industrial Co-operative Society Ltd v Slack*,[80] where the House of Lords awarded equitable damages in lieu of a *quia timet* injunction.[81] In Megarry J's view,

---

[75] Megarry J also heard argument on the question whether damages under Lord Cairns' Act were affected by the rule in *Bain v Fothergill* (n 60 above), but he did not have to decide this point, as he considered that the facts did not fall within the scope of the rule because there had been no defect of title at the date of contract, and a subsequent or supervening defect could not bring the rule in into operation: *Wroth v Tyler* (n 66 above) 53–6.

[76] This aspect of Megarry J's decision was subsequently affirmed in *Johnson v Gore Wood & Co (No 2)* [2003] EWCA Civ 1728 [93]. See also *H Parsons (Livestock) Ltd v Uttley Ingham & Co Ltd* [1978] QB 791 (CA) 813; *Brown v KMR Services Ltd* [1995] 2 Lloyd's Rep 513 (CA) 557.

[77] *Wroth v Tyler* (n 66 above) 36.

[78] *Wroth v Tyler* (n 66 above) 57–60.

[79] *Eastwood v Lever* (1863) 4 De G J & S 114, 128; 46 ER 859, 865 (Turner LJ).

[80] *Leeds Industrial Co-operative Society Ltd v Slack* [1924] AC 851 (HL).

[81] Consistently with this, Goff LJ subsequently held in *Price v Strange* [1978] Ch 337 (CA) 358, that in a case where the doctrine of part performance applied, equitable damages could be awarded in substitution for specific performance even though an action for damages at common law was precluded by the Statute of Frauds (see *Massey v Johnson* (1847) 1 Ex 241, 154 ER 102).

the contention that there is jurisdiction to award damages on a scale different from that applicable at law is a fortiori the established jurisdiction to award damages when no claim at all lies at law.[82]

Secondly, Megarry J observed that section 2 of the Chancery Amendment Act 1858 gave the courts a power 'to award damages to the party injured . . . in substitution for such . . . specific performance', and he thought that this 'at least envisages that the damages awarded will in fact constitute a true substitute for specific performance',[83] so that they should be quantified with a view to giving the claimant 'as nearly as may be what specific performance would have given'.[84] In support of this proposition, he cited *Leeds* and other cases which held that the statute empowered the courts to award damages in lieu of an injunction, the purpose of which is to compensate the claimant for future wrongs, and which (unlike common law damages[85]) are not limited to compensation for wrongs which have already happened.[86] Applying this principle to the facts of *Wroth* produced the conclusion that equitable damages should be assessed at the date of judgment, to reflect the fact that specific performance was a 'continuing remedy' to which the claimants would still have been entitled at the date of judgment, had it not been inappropriate to make such an order for the reasons described above.[87]

Writing shortly after Megarry J's decision in *Wroth*, JA Jolowicz thought it 'no more than a straightforward and . . . obviously correct award of damages in equity',[88] but in *Johnson*, Lord Wilberforce found that he 'could not agree with it', to the extent that it 'establishes a different basis [for the assessment of equitable damages] from that applicable at common law'[89] he could find 'no warrant [in Lord Cairns' Act] for the court awarding damages differently from common law damages'.[90] These comments were made without the benefit of argument, since neither party in *Johnson* had contended that the measure of damages under Lord Cairns' Act differs from the measure of common law damages.[91] They were also obiter, since the result in *Wroth* was consistent with Lord Wilberforce's further finding that if justice so requires, common law damages can be assessed as

---

[82] *Wroth v Tyler* (n 66 above) 58.
[83] *Wroth v Tyler* (n 66 above) 58.
[84] *Wroth v Tyler* (n 66 above) 59.
[85] *Backhouse v Bonomi* (1861) 9 HLC 503, 11 ER 825; *Darley Main Colliery v Mitchell* (1886) 11 App Cas 127; *West Leigh Colliery Co Ltd v Tuncliffe & Hampson Ltd* [1908] AC 27 (HL); *Midland Bank plc v Bardgrove Property Services Ltd* (1992) 65 P & CR 153 (CA).
[86] *Leeds Industrial Co-operative Society Ltd v Slack* (n 80 above) 859 (Viscount Finlay) and 865 (Lord Dunedin). See also *Fritz v Hobson* (1880) 14 Ch D 542, 556 (Fry J); *Chapman, Morsons & Co v Guardians of Auckland Union* (1889) 23 QBD 294 (CA) 298 (Lord Esher MR); *Dreyfus v Peruvian Guano Co* (1889) 43 Ch D 316 (CA) 342 (Fry LJ).
[87] *Wroth v Tyler* (n 66 above) 60.
[88] Jolowicz, 'Damages in Equity—A Study of Lord Cairns' Act' (n 2 above) 233–4.
[89] *Johnson v Agnew* (HL) (n 1 above) 400.
[90] *Johnson v Agnew* (HL) (n 1 above) 400.
[91] *Johnson v Agnew* (HL) (n 1 above) 379 and 387.

at some date other than the date of breach.[92] He also accepted that the Act 'created a power to award damages which did not exist before at common law', because it empowered the courts to award equitable damages where 'damages could not be claimed at all at common law',[93] yet as Peter McDermott has pointed out, this was inconsistent with his Lordship's view that the statute merely empowered the Chancery court to award common law damages[94]:

> Either a statute is or is not a procedural statute. It is submitted that there is some difficulty in Lord Cairns' Act being a procedural statute in the case of a breach of contract, but not being a procedural statute in the case of a quia timet injunction, a restrictive covenant to which a plaintiff was not a party, or part performance.

As McDermott explains,[95] Parliament's intention when enacting Lord Cairns' Act was to undo the consequences of Lord Eldon's decision in *Todd v Gee*,[96] which required suitors whose claims for equitable relief were declined by the Court of Chancery to start new actions for damages in the common law courts. As a result of bad drafting,[97] however, the statute conferred a more extensive jurisdiction on the Court of Chancery than was possessed by the common law courts, because it empowered the court to make damages awards in cases where common law damages were not available. In such cases the assessment of equitable damages was necessarily governed by different principles from those which govern the assessment of common law damages—and once one accepts this, it then becomes hard to resist the further conclusion drawn by Megarry J in *Wroth*, that the courts need not assess damages in lieu of an injunction or specific performance on the same basis as common law damages, albeit that situations may often arise where this is appropriate because it produces the most equitable outcome.[98]

Later English courts have tended to treat Lord Wilberforce's comments on *Wroth* as correct but to limit their application. For example,[99] in *Gur v Bruton*, Dillon LJ stated that although the court in *Johnson* had 'laid down the general principle that the purpose of Lord Cairns' Act was merely procedural', it had also 'recognised that the jurisdiction to award [equitable damages] might arise in some cases in which damages could not be recovered at common law'.[100] Hence he considered that *Johnson* had not affected the authority of *Hooper v*

---

[92] Cf *Domb v Isoz* [1980] Ch 548, where the CA analogised from Lord Wilberforce's findings to hold that equitable damages should be assessed as at the date when the claimants elected to abandon their appeal from the trial judge's refusal to grant them specific performance, and to claim equitable damages in lieu.

[93] *Johnson v Agnew* (HL) (n 1 above) 400.

[94] McDermott, *Equitable Damages* (n 2 above) 108–9.

[95] McDermott, *Equitable Damages* (n 2 above) ch 2.

[96] *Todd v Gee* (1810) 17 Ves Jun 273, 34 ER 106.

[97] McDermott, *Equitable Damages* (n 2 above) 34. Cf Jolowicz, 'Damages in Equity—A Study of Lord Cairns' Act' (n 2 above) 227 and 251: 'unwittingly'.

[98] Cf *JG Collins Insurance Agencies Ltd v Elsley* [1978] 2 SCR 916, 935 (Dickson J).

[99] See also Stuart Smith LJ's comments in *Dyer v Barnard* (CA) 16 April 1991.

[100] *Gur v Bruton* (CA) 29 July 1993.

*Reynolds*[101]—a case in which the Court of Appeal had awarded equitable damages in lieu of an injunction for the cost of remedial work to the claimant's property, to circumvent the difficulty that common law damages could not be recovered for depreciation in the market value of the claimant's property attributable to the risk or even certainty of a future nuisance by the defendant.[102]

Similarly, in *Jaggard v Sawyer*[103] the Court of Appeal awarded damages in lieu of an injunction to prevent the defendants from trespassing on the claimant's property, and assessed these with a view to compensating the claimant for future infringements of his property right. Reviewing Lord Wilberforce's comments Millett LJ said that these[104]

> must not be taken out of context. Earlier in his speech Lord Wilberforce had clearly recognised that damages could be awarded under Lord Cairns' Act where there was no cause of action at law, and he cannot have been insensible to the fact that, when the court awards damages in substitution for an injunction, it seeks to compensate the plaintiff for loss arising from future wrongs, that is to say, loss for which the common law does not provide a remedy. Neither *Wroth v Tyler* nor *Johnson v Agnew* was a case of this kind. In each of those cases the plaintiff claimed damages for loss occasioned by a single, once and for all, past breach of contract on the part of the defendant. In neither case was the breach a continuing one capable of generating further losses. In my view Lord Wilberforce's statement that the measure of damages is the same whether damages are recoverable at common law or under the Act must be taken to be limited to the case where they are recoverable in respect of the same cause of action. It cannot sensibly have any application where the claim at common law is in respect of a past trespass or breach of covenant and that under the Act is in respect of future trespasses or continuing breaches of covenant.

Various Commonwealth cases have gone further than this, however, adopting Megarry J's reasoning in *Wroth* to develop special principles of assessment for equitable damages in cases where common law damages could alternatively have

---

[101] *Hooper v Reynolds* [1975] Ch 43 (CA). *Hooper* is irreconcilable with Lord Upjohn's statement in *Redland Bricks Ltd v Morris* [1970] AC 652 (HL) 665, that Lord Cairns' Act had 'nothing whatever to do with the principles of law applicable to this case', but in principle *Hooper* should be preferred to *Redland* for the reasons set out in Jolowicz, 'Damages in Equity—A Study of Lord Cairns' Act' (n 2 above) 242–5 and Burrows, *Remedies for Torts and Breach of Contract* (n 67 above) 366.

[102] *West Leigh Colliery Co Ltd v Tunnicliffe & Hampson Ltd* [1908] AC 27 (HL).

[103] *Jaggard v Sawyer* [1995] 1 WLR 269 (CA). See also *Bracewell v Appleby* [1975] Ch 408 (ChD); *Marcic v Thames Water Utilities Ltd (No 2)* [2001] EWHC 394 (Tech), [2002] 2 WLR 1000. Cf *A-G v Blake* [2001] 1 AC 268 (HL) 281 (Lord Nicholls): although Lord Cairns' Act 'had the effect of enabling the court . . . to award damages in respect of the future as well as the past, the Act did not alter the measure to be employed in assessing damages' and so 'in the same way as damages at common law for violations of a property right may be measured by reference to the benefits wrongfully obtained by a defendant, so under Lord Cairns' Act damages may include damages measured by reference to the benefits likely to be obtained in future by the defendant'.

[104] *Jaggard* above n 103, 290–91.

been awarded. The most significant of these is *Semelhago v Paramadevan*.[105] There the parties entered a contract for the sale of a house for $205,000 with a closing date at the end of October 1986. The purchaser had $75,000 in cash, and he planned to mortgage his existing house to secure a loan for the remaining $130,000. To this end he negotiated a six-month open mortgage, intending to sell his existing house over the next six months and repay the loan with the proceeds. However, the vendor reneged on the deal and transferred title to a third party in December 1986. The purchaser therefore issued a writ for specific performance or damages in lieu, and stayed in his existing house. This was worth $190,000 in the autumn of 1986, but had risen in value to $300,000 by the time of trial. By then the new house which he had planned to buy from the vendor had also risen in value, to $325,000.

At trial the purchaser elected to take damages rather than specific perform-ance, and in line with *Wroth* the trial judge assessed these at $120,000, repre-senting the difference between the purchase price and the value of the new house at the time of trial. The Ontario Court of Appeal reduced this to $81,000, accepting the vendor's argument that certain items should be deducted, namely the interest which the purchaser had avoided paying on the $130,000 loan which would have been needed to finance the purchase, the interest earned on the $75,000 that he would have used for the down payment, and the legal fees which he would have incurred. The vendor appealed, arguing that a deduction should also be made to reflect the fact that the purchaser's existing house had risen in value, a gain which he would not have made if he had sold it as planned. The Supreme Court of Canada rejected this argument, Sopinka J stating that[106]

> If the respondent had received a decree of specific performance, he would have had the property contracted for and retained the amount of the rise in value of his own prop-erty. Damages are to be substituted for the decree of specific performance. I see no basis for deductions that are not related to the value of the property which was the subject of the contract. To make such deductions would depart from the principle that damages are to be a true equivalent of specific performance.

---

[105] *Semelhago v Paramadevan* [1996] 2 SCR 415. See also *Souster v Epsom Plumbing Contractors Ltd* [1974] 2 NZLR 515 (NZ High Ct); *Metropolitan Trust Co of Canada v Pressure Concrete Services Ltd* (1975) 60 DLR (3d) 431 (Ont CA); *306793 Ontario Ltd in Trust v Rimes* (1979) 25 OR (2d) 79 (Ont CA); *Kopec v Pyret* (1987) 36 DLR (4th) 1 (Sask CA); *Rosser v Maritime Services Board (No 2)* NSW Sup Ct (Eq Div) 17 September 1996; *Mills v Ruthol Pty Ltd* NSW Sup Ct (Eq Div) 24 June 2004. *Semelhago* also holds that contracts for the sale of land are not routinely specifically enforceable, and requires claimants to produce evidence that the property is 'unique to the extent that its substitute is not readily available': [1996] 2 SCR 415 [22] (Sopinka J). This aspect of the case lies beyond the scope of the present discussion, but for critical comment see R Chambers, 'The Importance of Specific Performance' in S Degeling and J Edelman (eds), *Equity in Commercial Law* (Sydney, Lawbook Co, 2005) 431.

[106] *Semelhago v Paramadevan* [1996] 2 SCR 415 [19], followed in: *Payne v Carr* (Ontario High Ct) 19 December 1996 [70]; *Munn v Worden* (New Brunswick QB) 17 April 1997 [44]–[51]; *Inmet Mining Corp v Homestake Canada Inc* 2002 BCSC 61 [394]–[417]; *Shapiro v 1086891 Ontario Inc* (Ontario High Ct) 20 March 2006 [152]–[153].

This result seems to over-compensate the claimant by overriding the normal rule that a claimant must mitigate his loss between the date of breach and the date of judgment. However, *Semelhago* is a perfectly logical extension of the *Wroth* principle that equitable damages under Lord Cairns' Act are a monetary substitute for specific performance. As Lionel Smith has observed[107] the purpose of an order for specific performance is not to compensate the claimant for the loss of his performance interest under the contract, but to vindicate his performance right by compelling the defendant to perform his promise. If equitable damages in lieu of specific performance are awarded with the same goal in mind, then the duty to mitigate has no application for the same reasons that it has no application to a claim for specific performance:[108] since neither remedy is designed to compensate the claimant for his loss, complaints that the claimant has been 'over-compensated' miss the point.[109]

Of course, equity is not the only body of law that is capable of manufacturing remedies which are designed to vindicate a claimant's contractual performance rights. Common law remedies are also awarded with this end in mind—awards of an agreed sum are an obvious example—and there is no reason in principle why damages awards should not also be made at common law with a view to achieving this goal.[110] This might then lead us to speculate whether the damages award in *Johnson* should itself be seen as an award of this kind? This understanding of the case would dovetail with Lord Wilberforce's finding that damages should be assessed as at the date when the contract was lost and with it the Johnsons' continued ability to press for performance. It would also explain why no question arose of reducing these damages to reflect the fact that the Johnsons had made no attempt to mitigate their loss. This was not because it was 'reasonable' for them to defer taking steps in this direction, as Oliver J had previously suggested in *Radford v De Froberville*,[111] but because they had the right not to do any such thing for as long as they could legitimately

[107] LD Smith, 'Understanding Specific Performance' in N Cohen and E McKendrick (eds), *Comparative Remedies for Breach of Contract'* (Oxford, Hart Publishing, 2005) 221. This argument is also made in C Webb, 'Performance and Compensation: An Analysis of Contract Damages and Contractual Obligation' (2006) 26 *Oxford Journal of Legal Studies* 41, developing ideas in D Friedmann, 'The Performance Interest in Contract Damages' (1995) 111 *Law Quarterly Review* 628.

[108] For the proposition that a claimant seeking specific performance owes no duty to mitigate his loss, provided that he has a legitimate interest in continuing to insist upon performance, see eg *Asamera Oil Corp Ltd v Sea Oil and General Corp* [1979] 1 SCR 633, 666–7 (Estey J).

[109] As discussed in Webb, 'Performance and Compensation' (n 107 above) 65–7, the fact that performance interest claims are not concerned with compensation for loss is not the only reason for thinking that the doctrine of mitigation has no relevance to claims of this kind. Different views can be taken of the principles and policies underlying the doctrine, and depending on the view one takes, additional arguments may also be needed to explain why the doctrine does not apply to claims of this kind.

[110] The argument that 'cost of cure' damages can be explained as an award to vindicate the claimant's performance interest is reviewed in Webb, 'Performance and Compensation' (n 107 above) 57–61.

[111] *Radford v De Froberville* [1977] 1 WLR 1262, 1286 (Oliver J), approved in *Johnson v Agnew* (HL) (n 1 above) 401.

insist on the defendant's performance. The varying dates set for the assessment of both common law and equitable damages in analogous cases concerning contracts for the sale of land can be explained in line with this theory on the basis that a claimant's right to specific performance is not absolute, but is subject to equitable principles, so that it can be lost by delay.[112]


## H. CONCLUSION

In *Johnson v Agnew* Lord Wilberforce rightly took pleasure in sweeping away an 'accumulated debris of decisions and textbook pronouncements which [had] brought semantic confusion and misunderstandings' into the law governing contracts for the sale of land.[113] By rejecting theories of retrospective discharge for breach and election which had forced injured parties to choose between specific performance and damages, he made the law clearer and fairer. His findings with regard to the principles governing the date of assessment for common law damages were flexible and just. His belief that common law and equitable damages should be assessed by reference to a set of common principles opens up the possibility that in suitable cases both types of damages might be awarded with a view to vindicating a claimant's contractual performance right. It also suggests that the day may not be far off when damages for anticipated wrongs are available at common law.[114]


---

[112] *Hickey v Bruhns* [1977] 2 NZLR 71 (NZ High Court); *Malhotra v Choudhury* [1980] 1 Ch 52 (CA); *New Zealand Land Development Co Ltd v Porter* [1992] 2 NZLR 462 (NZ High Court; *Domowicz v Orsa Investments Ltd* (1994) 20 OR (3d) 722 (Ont High ct); *Garbens v Khayami* (1994) 17 OR (3d) 722 (Ont High Ct).

[113] *Johnson v Agnew* (HL) (n 1 above) 391.

[114] A Burrows 'We Do This at Common Law but That in Equity' (2002) 22 OJLS 1, 12. Cf *Dennis v Ministry of Defence* [2003] EWHC 793 (QB), where Buckley J awarded common law damages for nuisance which apparently included the loss of capital value that would be sustained by the claimant in the event that he sold his house at a future date during the currency of the defendant's continuing nuisance; and *Transco plc v Stockport MBC* Technology & Construction Ct 7 May 1999, where His Honour Judge Howarth awarded common law damages for negligence, and under the rule in *Rylands v Fletcher* (1868) LR 3 HL 330, to compensate the claimant for the cost of remedial works undertaken to prevent damage from occurring (reversed on liability: [2001] EWCA Civ 212, [2001] Env LR 44; [2003] UKHL 61; [2004] 2 AC 1).